THE AGE OF REFORM
1250–1550

The Age of Reform 1250–1550

AN INTELLECTUAL AND
RELIGIOUS HISTORY OF
LATE MEDIEVAL AND
REFORMATION EUROPE

STEVEN OZMENT

NEW HAVEN AND LONDON
YALE UNIVERSITY PRESS
1980

Designed by Sally Harris
and set in VIP Baskerville type.
Printed in the United States of America by
Murray Printing Company, Westford, Mass.

Library of Congress Cataloging in Publication Data

Ozment, Steven E
  The age of reform (1250–1550).

  Includes index.
  1. Church history—Middle Ages, 600–1500.
2. Reformation. 3. Theology, Doctrinal—History—
Middle Ages, 600–1500. 4. Theology, Doctrinal—
History—16th century. 5. Civilization, Medieval.
BR270.09   274   79-24162
0-300-02477-0

1   2   3   4   5   6   7   8   9   10

For Heiko and Toetie

Contents

Illustrations

ix

Preface

Scholarship on Reformation Europe has entered a new period of experimentation in both method and subject matter, and coming decades may witness a transformation of the field. In recent years urban social history, witchcraft and witch-hunts, prosopography, and popular culture have become new areas of study in their own right. So varied is Reformation historiography becoming that future generations of scholars and students may find themselves able to glimpse the whole only through highly specialized parts.

The present book is an interpretation of the intellectual and religious history of the period. It too is a partial perspective on the whole, but, I believe, the most telling one if we search the period for the issues that made it historically unique, generated institutional change, and have most influenced subsequent generations.

My presentation follows a traditional format, from which I have, however, departed by devoting a large portion of the book to the Middle Ages, a point of view I hope the reader will find illuminating. This effort to view the Reformation from the perspective of the Middle Ages reflects the conviction that it was both a culmination and a transcendence of medieval intellectual and religious history.

The book has evolved from lectures to Yale students between 1968 and 1978. It is fitting that I publish it at this time, when I depart Yale for another university and turn to new historical interests. Since my own student days I have been fascinated by the interplay of ideas and their extraordinary social force, especially in the Age of Reformation. Throughout the book I have been concerned to make complex patterns of thought intelligible and show how closely intertwined with reality seemingly abstract ideas and beliefs in fact were. I have been particularly concerned to convey the important role individuals played in the formation of the laws and institutions of sixteenth-century society. I have also wanted to make the people and movements here treated memorable to the reader; the modern Western world, for good or ill, remains in ways both direct and indirect very much under their influence.

Like all events in organized human society, the Reformation was embedded in the social reality of people's lives. Scholars who are today delineating the social structures and conflicts that made the sixteenth century susceptible to religious and other ideological change are bound to provide much data for speculation on the relationship between class, wealth, occupation, and religious choice. The basic religious options themselves, however, were not the simple result of collective modes of thought and action. Communities elected to turn Protestant, remain Catholic, strike compromises, or ignore both, but they did not create the basic alternatives. The religious beliefs and practices that reshaped sixteenth-century towns and territories were the work of generations of intellectuals and reformers, trained theologians and educated laymen, who drew on ancient traditions and competed for the loyalty of a laity acutely sensitive to the societal consequences of religious issues. The present study concentrates especially on the evolution of these options and the individuals and movements who shaped them most decisively.

Portions of the work have been previously published. The section "Luther and Scholasticism" in chapter 6 is a shortened version of "Luther and the Later Middle Ages: The Formation of Reformation Thought," in *Transition and Revolution: Problems and Issues of European Renaissance and Reformation History,* edited by Robert M. Kingdon (Minneapolis: Burgess Publishing Co., 1974), pp. 109–29. The sections "Protestant Reformers: Biblical Humanists or New Scholastics?" and "Protestantism and Humanist Educational Reforms" in chapter 8 are condensed from "Humanism, Scholasticism, and the Intellectual Origins of the Reformation," in *Continuity and Discontinuity in Church History: Essays Presented to George Huntston Williams on the Occasion of His 65th Birthday,* edited by F. Forrester Church and Timothy George (Leiden: E. J. Brill, 1979), pp. 133–49. And chapter 12 revises an essay of the same title that appeared in *Concilium* 8 (1972):39–56. I am grateful to the editors and publishers for permission to reproduce this material.

The John Simon Guggenheim Foundation assisted the work by providing a fellowship for research and writing in 1978, and the A. Whitney Griswold Fund of Yale University paid the services of a typist.

I received helpful criticism and/or advice from Abigail Freedman, Frank M. Turner, Michael Stoff, Walter Cahn, and especially Andrea Ozment, whose patience with the work was very great. I also owe a special debt of gratitude to Edward Tripp, without whose enterprise the book would have been a far lesser undertaking.

S. O.
Timothy Dwight College
Yale University
June 1979

CHAPTER 1

The Interpretation of Medieval Intellectual History

MANY scholars feel that the intellectual history of the Middle Ages reflects the peaks and valleys of its political and social history. There is nothing particularly artificial about this view; rises and declines in thought and culture *are* often directly connected with larger historical fortunes. The close relationship between prosperity, patronage, education, and the arts, for example, is a well-known feature of the Renaissance. But sometimes the relationship between the intellectual history of a period and its larger political and social history is more subtle, and reading the former in light of the latter can be misleading.

The relationship seems most straightforward in the early Middle Ages (476–ca. 1000). Medieval history began with the political collapse of a civilization: the fall of the Roman Empire after a century of military factions, recurring disease and famine, and sheer impoverishment, all of which left western Europe powerless before invading barbarian tribes. In 476, the traditional date for the fall of the empire, Romulus Augustulus, the last western emperor, was deposed, and a barbarian chieftain assumed his place. Thereafter Western civilization entered a period of steep cultural decline, described by Renaissance thinkers, with some exaggeration, as the "dark middle age" between classical antiquity and the "reborn" civilization of the fourteenth and fifteenth centuries.

During the early Middle Ages, Goths, Vandals, Burgundians, and Franks dominated western Europe, while the Arabs controlled the Mediterranean. Although the Mediterranean did not become the "Moslem lake" Henri Pirenne once depicted, Western trade and commerce with the Levant fell off significantly, much to the material and cultural detriment of the West. The great cities of the old Roman Empire declined as populations migrated to interior regions. Western people were effectively cut off from both ancient and contemporary sources of learning and science and forced to fall back on native resources. Experimentation with new political and social forms began.

Sheer physical survival preoccupied most people in the early Middle Ages. As large numbers populated the countryside, there evolved that peculiar fusion of Germanic, Roman, and Christian practices that we speak of today as "feudal society." To an unusual degree, the most important figures in the early Middle Ages were farmers and soldiers. The task of preserving basic social structures was paramount, and little time and treasure could be given over to the higher goals of civilization; supplying the basic physical needs of life allowed little beyond a rudimentary development of education and culture. Between 875 and 950, Western society seemed on the verge of total collapse when the Carolingian empire, already weakened by physical partition among Charlemagne's contending grandchildren, was assailed by new invasions of Vikings, Magyars, and Saracens. If the characterization "dark age" may be justifiably applied to any time in the Middle Ages, it would be this seventy-five-year period in the late ninth and tenth centuries.

What of the intellectual history of the period? Like the larger political and social history, it too was characterized by experimentation and preservation. In the century of Rome's fall lived the single most influential thinker in the Western intellectual tradition—Saint Augustine (354–430). Augustine was to the intellectual history of the Middle Ages what classical civilization was to its political and cultural history: a creative source, whose recovery and study spurred new directions of thought and controversy down through the Reformation of the sixteenth century. After Augustine there were no "giants" of Western intellectual history until Anselm of Canterbury in the eleventh century. During this intervening intellectual "dark age" only a few significant thinkers were active, and their importance lay primarily in their role as translators and commentators, that is, as men who preserved and transmitted a few of the writings and teachings of ancient masters.

One of the most important of these custodians of antiquity was Boethius (ca. 480–525), an eminent member of the Roman senatorial aristocracy and chief minister to the Ostrogoth king Theodoric. Although best known for his *Consolation of Philosophy*, a Stoic work written in prison while he awaited execution on charges of treason, Boethius is far more important as the major source before the thirteenth century of Western knowledge of Aristotle. He made Latin translations of Aristotle's basic works on logic, the *Categories* and *On Interpretation*, and wrote commentaries on them; in addition, he translated Porphyry's *Isagoge*, an introduction to Aristotle's *Categories*, and his commentaries on Aristotle. These became the only works by and about Aristotle known in the West until the full recovery of his logical, physical, and metaphysical writings in the twelfth and thirteenth century. An admittedly modest collection, Boethius's translations and commentaries were still sufficient to give birth to scholastic method in the twelfth century. He also translated works of Euclid and Ptolemy into Latin, together with other classical tracts on arithmetic and music that became mainstays of the monastic and urban cathedral schools, the first formal Western educational institutions.

What Boethius was to the Aristotelian tradition, Dionysius the Areopagite and John Scotus Erigena, together with Augustine, were to the Platonic and Neoplatonic traditions. To enhance the importance of his work Dionysius pretended to be the biblical disciple of St. Paul possessed of a secret knowledge of God. He was actually an early sixth-century figure. He is most famous for his mystical theology, which contrasts affirmative and negative ways to God and found a wide audience among scholastics in the high and later Middle Ages. Erigena (ca. 810–77) directed the waning Carolingian palace school in the mid-ninth century. An authority on the Greek church fathers, he translated the writings of Dionysius from Greek into Latin, making them available to scholastic philosophers and theologians, and was in addition an original thinker in his own right.

The Carolingian renaissance of the late eighth and early ninth centuries was a true shaft of light within the relative cultural darkness of the early Middle Ages. Charlemagne accumulated a great deal of wealth from the tribes he conquered, and a substantial portion was used to attract Europe's best clerical scholars to the imperial palace at Aachen. While Charlemagne appreciated learning for its own sake, he created the palace school in order to upgrade the administrative skills of the clerics and noblemen who staffed the fledgling royal bureaucracy. The school was under the direction of the Anglo-Saxon master Alcuin of York (ca. 735–804), an imported scholar attracted by promises of land and power. The palace school in Aachen provided basic instruction in the seven liberal arts, with special concentration on grammar, logic, and mathematics, that is, on training in reading, writing, speaking, and sound reasoning, the basic tools of government. By preparing the sons of noblemen to run the religious and secular offices of the realm, court scholarship directly served Carolingian kingdom building.[1] Here we see how Western intellectual and religious history developed in tandem with Western political expansion.

If experimentation and preservation characterized the early Middle

1. Cf. Henri Pirenne, *A History of Europe*, trans. B. Miall (Garden City, N.Y., 1956), 1:70–71.

Ages, self-discovery and definition marked the high Middle Ages (1000–1300). In this period Western people began to assert their identity as they came to know and impose themselves on others. Two larger developments made this possible. The first was the revival of trade and towns in the eleventh century, which provided new resources for the higher tasks of civilization. The second was the emperor Otto I's defeat of the Hungarians at Lechfeld in 955, a victory that secured Western borders against foreign invasion from the East and made possible a long-absent internal political stability.

A new self-awareness gripped both the church and the "state" during the high Middle Ages. In the tenth century a monastic reform movement swept the church, and the clergy determined to make themselves sole masters within the spiritual realm. Emerging from a monastery in Cluny in south-central France, this movement reached its peak in the pontificate of Pope Gregory VII (1073–85), the pope who brought the emperor Henry IV to his knees in the snows of Canossa. The Investiture Struggle, which persisted through the last quarter of the eleventh and into the twelfth century, saw popes and kings alternately humiliate each other. It also gave rise to the distinctive Western separation of church and state when the emperor signed the Concordat of Worms in 1122, forfeiting any right to invest bishops with the ring and staff symbolic of spiritual authority. The spheres of ecclesiastical and secular jurisdiction were firmly demarcated, although emperors continued to aspire to be popes and popes to be emperors. The Cluny reform and Gregorian papacy brought a new religious discipline and sense of purpose to the western church at the papal, episcopal, and parochial levels. In 1215 the Fourth Lateran Council gave the church both a lasting doctrinal definition and an administrative organization reaching from pope to parish. This council promulgated the dogma of transubstantiation, placed limits on the number of religious orders, and made annual confession and communion mandatory for all laity.

Parallel developments occurred in secular politics and society. It was during the high Middle Ages that national dynasties and distinctive parliamentary institutions formed in France and England. In this period a new sense of regional loyalty and lay administrative competence appeared, and secular values began to displace those of the clergy. This gave rise over the centuries to a view of the king and the nation-state, rather than the pope and the church, as the community commanding highest allegiance. On the foundations of the new political stability, urbanization, and religious reform, a true cultural renaissance occurred in the twelfth and thirteenth centuries. It was marked by the rise of universities and scholasticism and the recovery of the full corpus of Aristotle's work. Professional elites of physi-

cians, lawyers, and theologians appeared for the first time, and trade associ-
ations and guilds were formed to protect the interests of merchants and
skilled artisans. At every level people discovered and defined themselves by
making new boundaries, alliances, dogmas, laws, and organizations.

The new strength of Western people also affected their character. Previously fearful and preyed upon by foreign invaders, they now became
themselves the known world's aggressor and missionary with the launching
of a long series of crusades to the Holy Land in 1095. These initially religious ventures dramatized the new Western cultural and religious unity and
also, especially after the Fourth Crusade conquered Constantinople in
1204, opened new routes of Western commerce.

For such reasons the twelfth and thirteenth centuries have been described as "the fullest development of all the potentialities of medieval
civilization."[2] Many medieval scholars even argue that these centuries were
of greater significance for the formation of Western ideas and institutions
than the later Italian Renaissance and Protestant Reformation.

The intellectual history of the high Middle Ages, like its larger political
and social history, is also marked by self-discovery and definition. Many of
the most important medieval thinkers were active in the twelfth century.
There was Anselm of Canterbury (1033–1109), "the summit of the early
scholastic genius and ripest fruit of the monastic schools,"[3] famous for his
logical proofs of the existence of God and the necessity of the Incarnation.
There was Bernard of Clairvaux (1091–1153), writer of odes to the Virgin,
preacher of crusades, organizer of both the Cistercian Order and the
Knights Templar, and the magisterial ecclesiastical figure of his day. There
was Hugh of St. Victor (d. 1142), author of *The Sacraments of the Christian
Faith,* the first large summary of medieval theology. There was Peter Abelard
(1079–1142), the most controversial of the first generation of scholastic
theologians, whose *Sic et non* (1122), a work that juxtaposed seemingly
contradictory statements on the same topic by traditional authorities,
proved a major step in the maturation of scholastic method. There was
Peter Lombard (ca. 1100–1160), author of the *Four Books of the Sentences*
(1150–52), the basic textbook for advanced theological study in the high
and later Middle Ages. There was Irnerius (ca. 1050–1130), a Bolognese
lawyer who directed the recovery of Roman law, a major event also in the
political history of the Middle Ages, for Roman law, by its strong defense of
the sovereignty of rulers, helped kings and emperors to consolidate their
realms under one supreme authority, overturn tribal and customary laws,

2. Joseph R. Strayer, *Western Europe in Middle Ages: A Short History* (New York, 1955),
pp. 9, 127.
3. David Knowles, *The Evolution of Medieval Thought* (New York, 1962), p. 98.

and maintain independence from the pope. There was Gratian (d. 1159?), Irnerius's ecclesiastical counterpart, the author of the *Concordance of Discordant Canons,* or *Decretum* (1140), the authoritative text of canon law, without the aid of which popes would have remained the pawns of kings and church councils. And finally, there was John of Salisbury (ca. 1115–80), one-time secretary of Thomas à Becket and author of two major works: the *Policraticus,* an influential dissertation on statecraft, and the *Metalogicon,* an important historical source of our knowledge of the century's scholastic debates.

The new intellectual discipline came to be known as "dialectic." In its fully developed form it proceeded from questions (*quaestio*), to the views pro (*videtur quod*) and con (*sed contra*) of traditional authorities on a particular subject, to the author's own conclusion (*responsio*). Because they subjected the articles of faith to tight logical analysis, the exponents of the new rational methods of study became highly suspect in the eyes of church authorities. They may be compared with the new class of money-rich merchants who emerged at this time and also upset tradition because as men of wealth who did not own land, they did not fit into the accustomed social divisions of clergy, nobility, and peasantry. Scholastics equipped with dialectic were to the intellectual history of the Middle Ages what merchants equipped with new business methods were to its social and political history—a seemingly alien body, intruders within traditional medieval society, who both fascinated their conservative critics and challenged previous perceptions and ways of doing things.

In the mid-eleventh century a powerful ecclesiast, Peter Damian (1007–72), warned that theology was on the verge of becoming the handmaiden of philosophy. The proper relationship between philosophy and theology, between reason and faith, became a major problem for thinkers of the high and later Middle Ages. Already in the eleventh century a dialectician, Berengar of Tours (ca. 1010–88), had questioned theological arguments made in defense of the evolving church, teaching that the bread and wine of the Eucharist were truly converted into the body and blood of Christ by the priest's consecration of the sacramental elements (eventually the dogma of transubstantiation). Lanfranc of Bec (1010–89), an ecclesiast in the mould of Peter Damian, who also feared the new rationalism in theology, forced Berengar into a humiliating recantation of his doubts about transubstantiation. Abelard was both the boldest and most skillful of the new dialecticians; it is probably true, as he himself boasted, that he never met his intellectual equal during his lifetime. He became also the most assailed for alleged misuse of the new techniques of logical argument. He was censured for a defective view of the Trinity (tritheism); for denying that Christ's Atone-

ment had an objective significance beyond its subjective effect on the believer (instead of satisfying the devil's right over fallen man, as tradition
argued, Christ's Incarnation and Crucifixion were seen by Abelard to be
moral acts intended to move people to love of God); for minimizing the
moral consequences of original sin (Abelard recognized more free will and
natural goodness in fallen man than the church allowed); and for overstres-
sing the subjective intention of an act rather than its objective nature and
consequences in the determination of goodness and evil (for Abelard, only
conscious consent·made an evil act sinful; and deeds done under compulsion or in ignorance, no matter how heinous, were not sinful).[4] Later
scholastics also reacted against the subjective strain in Abelard's teaching on
sacramental confession. A contritionist, Abelard taught that the subjective
attitude of the penitent contributed more to the reception of divine forgiveness than did the priest's words of absolution. Thomas Aquinas and
Duns Scotus opposed such a point of view as detracting from the jurisdictional and sacramental powers of the church.

As the case of Abelard demonstrates, to be rigorously logical was not
necessarily to be orthodox. On the other hand, unquestioned orthodoxy did
not necessarily add logical force to one's arguments. If dialecticians like
Abelard seemed overly curious and critical, stolidly orthodox thinkers who
employed the new dialectical method could also be carried away. The chief
example here is Anselm of Canterbury, who believed he had proven the
existence of God by purely logical argument and demonstrated the Incarnation by "necessary reasons." Such presumption, like the heterodoxy of
Abelard, should be seen, however, as a sign of the vitality of twelfth-century
intellectual life, when medieval thinkers first discovered the pains and
pleasures of truly critical thought.

All roads in Western medieval intellectual history lead finally to the full
recovery of Aristotle's writings in the thirteenth century. Obtained in large
part by the visits of Western scholars to Moslem Spain, the Aristotelian
corpus arrived laden with controversy, for it came with extensive commentaries by Arab philosophers, most notably, Avicenna and Averroës. This
body of material spurred the development of all the potentialities of medieval thought, as scholasticism now reached its maturity. The interpretation
of Aristotle and his Islamic commentators stimulated the formation of rival
Franciscan and Dominican schools, the former associated with the names of
Alexander of Hales, Bonaventura, and Duns Scotus, the latter with Albert
the Great and Thomas Aquinas. The thirteenth century became peculiarly

4. The best treatment of Abelard is Leif Grane, *Peter Abelard: Philosophy and Christianity
in the Middle Ages* (New York, 1970).

the age of the great *summa;* then, as never before or after, the effort was made to bring together within the space of a single work the whole of human knowledge and divine truth.

If the early Middle Ages were a time of preservation and the high Middle Ages a period of self-discovery and definition, the later Middle Ages (1300–1500) must be seen as a period of unprecedented challenge. Basic social structures and values were put to a terrible test. As never before, not even during the century of the Roman Empire's collapse, Western people walked through the valley of the shadow of death. The greatest famine of the Middle Ages struck in the second decade of the fourteenth century, and an estimated two-fifths of the overall population of Europe died when bubonic plague, or the Black Death, following the trade routes, erupted in midcentury. The Hundred Years' War between England and France not only spanned the fourteenth and fifteenth centuries, but also introduced the weaponry of modern warfare, in the form of gunpowder and heavy artillery, during its later stages. Great agrarian and urban revolts by the poor rent the social fabric in both town and countryside. Religious and moral foundations were shaken by a schism in the church that produced no less than three competing popes and colleges of cardinals by 1409. Little wonder that one of the most popular modern books on the later Middle Ages bears the title *The Waning of the Middle Ages.*

The response to challenge was creative and successful. By the mid-fifteenth century a recovery from the demographic crisis, the great population loss of the fourteenth century, was well under way. The fifteenth century saw a true renaissance of culture and learning in Italian and north European cities as the doors to antiquity opened wide. New monarchies formed under Louis XI in France, Ferdinand and Isabella in Spain, and Henry Tudor in England brought a new political stability. The independent nation-states of Europe progressively superseded the universal church as the community of highest allegiance, and the great conflicts between papal and royal power that had preoccupied so many minds and consumed so much talent during the Middle Ages became a thing of the past. By the end of the Middle Ages the nations of Europe transcended themselves not by sending delegations to Rome, but by undertaking competitive voyages to the Far East and the Americas.

Like its larger political and social history, Western thought during the fourteenth century has traditionally been interpreted as a steep decline from greatness. Noting that the fourteenth century was the great age of mysticism and also witnessed the formation of factional theological schools, scholars have characterized the age generally as a retreat into subjective experience and dogmatism. One modern authority describes the intellectual options of the period as either "practical skepticism" or "blind fideism."[5] Even the great Renaissance philosophers have been seen as only imitators of the ancients, paling before the great scholastics of the thirteenth century. Most criticized as responsible for the "fall" of Western thought is the dominant philosophical and theological school of the late Middle Ages, Ockhamism. To many scholars, Ockham and his followers stand to the intellectual history of the Middle Ages as the Black Death to its social history, the Hundred Years' War to its political history, and the great Schism to its ecclesiastical history, that is, as its most severe crisis. Here, however, the reading of intellectual history as a mirror of the political and social history of an age runs the danger of gross misjudgment, as present-day Ockham research is pointing out. Even so strong a modern critic of Ockhamism as Gordon Leff has recently confessed to having "misrepresented" Ockham in earlier studies.[6]

The scholar who has contributed most to the view of late medieval intellectual history as a decline from greatness is the late Etienne Gilson, the modern authority on medieval scholasticism. Gilson's conclusions are set forth in his magisterial *History of Christian Philosophy in the Middle Ages* (1955), and his main theses have been popularized in a little work entitled *Reason and Revelation in the Middle Ages* (1938). Gilson measured the whole of medieval thought by the work of Thomas Aquinas. Few thinkers in Western thought have received so enthusiastic and uncritical an endorsement from a historian as that accorded Aquinas by Gilson. The historical achievement considered to be justification for such praise was Aquinas's peculiar synthesis of reason and revelation, his union of philosophy and theology, Aristotle and Augustine—what the thirteenth century considered the highest human knowledge and divine truth. Aquinas is said to have related the two so that "they can neither contradict each other, nor ignore each other, nor be confused with each other."[7] In the Aquinas Lecture at Marquette University in 1951, Gilson put the case for Aquinas:

> Some disciples of Augustine have accused Aquinas of being too much a philosopher, while at the same time some disciples of Aristotle were accusing him of being too much a theologian; but Aquinas knew Augustine no less well than did the Augustinians, and he knew Aristotle better than most of the Aristotelians. Where what Augustine had said

5. David Knowles, "A Characteristic of the Mental Climate of the Fourteenth Century," in *Mélanges offerts à Etienne Gilson* (Toronto, 1959), p. 323; see also Gordon Leff, "The Fourteenth Century and the Decline of Scholasticism," *Past and Present* 9 (1956):30–39.

6. *William of Ockham: The Metamorphosis of Scholastic Discourse* (Manchester, 1975), p. xiii.

7. *The Christian Philosophy of St. Thomas Aquinas* (New York, 1956), p. 23.

An allegorical image of St. Thomas Aquinas, enthroned, teaching and overcoming heresy. Attributed to the School of Messina (fifteenth century). During his stay with the Cologne Dominicans (1248–52) under the tutelage of Albert the Great, Thomas's brothers reportedly dubbed him "the dumb ox" (*bovem mutum*), a reference to his unusually large physique and personal reserve, the latter reflective of his profound contemplation. His two major works were the *Summa Contra Gentiles,* written between 1259 and 1265 for use against Jews and Moslems by Christian missionaries in Spain, and the *Summa Theologiae,* written between 1266 and 1273 as a textbook for beginners in theology. In 1879 the pope declared Thomas's teaching, as here set forth, the touchstone of Catholic theology, a declaration that made official what had been standing practice for centuries.

was right, Thomas would say that Augustine was right; and where Aristotle had been right, Thomas would agree with Aristotle. But in those instances when neither Augustine nor Aristotle had been quite right, Thomas would simply make them say what was true, that is, what they themselves should have said in order to be perfectly right.... Very few among us can imagine such a pure love of truth, that is, a genius both capable of improving upon Aristotle and Augustine, and yet disinterested enough to credit them with his own discoveries.[8]

Like every other medieval theologian, Thomas Aquinas was aware of fundamental differences between theology and philosophy.[9] The first principles of theology came from God through a special biblical revelation and were not the result of rational reflection on worldly experience. Theology was a science based on revealed, not natural, data. There was no empirical evidence for such things as the existence of God as a Holy Trinity, the creation of the world in time, an original sin staining all mankind, the Incarnation of God in Jesus Christ, the power of church sacraments to convey grace, the existence of purgatory, the resurrection of the human body, and the Last Judgment of mankind. All medieval thinkers knew that these were *credenda,* things believed on the authority of the Christian church.

It was the peculiar genius of Thomas Aquinas, according to Gilson, to carry these matters beyond the traditional statement of basic differences. Aquinas called attention to areas in which the data accessible to reason and those provided by revelation, despite their different sources, actually overlapped and mutually supported one another, that is, to areas in which people had both natural, rational knowledge and divinely revealed knowledge of one and the same thing. For example, that a wise, omnipotent, and omniscient God exists and that man's soul is immortal were not only data of revelation, but also conclusions to which normal rational activity might lead. Could one study a flower without coming finally to ask about the reality of God? Could one look into one's own soul without discovering its origin and destiny in eternity? Aquinas believed that finite effects naturally attest their maker, and reason inexorably seeks the first principles of things.

That reason and revelation could bear witness to the same truths within a limited sphere indicated for Aquinas their essential unity. Ultimately reason and revelation, philosophy and theology, nature and grace, the state and

8. *Wisdom and Love in St. Thomas Aquinas* (Milwaukee, 1951), pp. 27–28.
9. See the collection of texts on this topic in *St. Thomas Aquinas: Theological Texts,* ed. Thomas Gilby (London, 1955), pp. 1–33; and *The Pocket Aquinas,* ed. Vernon J. Bourke (New York, 1973), pp. 283–315.

the church, secular life and religious life were neither strangers nor an-
tagonists, but close relations. Reality is one; truth is one—no conviction was
more medieval than that. This was the belief behind the Thomist maxim
that grace does not destroy nature, but perfects it, a subtle formula that
both enhanced the secular world and justified ecclesiastical paternalism
and self-aggrandizement.

Gilson believed that Aquinas perceived the unity of reality more clearly
than any other medieval thinker. Other philosophers and theologians erred
either in the direction of "theologism," a point of view which assumes the
self-sufficiency of revelation, or of "rationalism," the declaration of the
sufficiency of unaided reason.[10] Gilson pointed to the extreme fideism of
Tertullian, who said he believed because it was absurd, and saw Bernard of
Clairvaux, Peter Damian, and the Spiritual Franciscans as kindred spirits.
He found an even larger group of so-called moderate fideists, thinkers who
made faith and transrational experience primary but were not necessarily
aloof from or hostile to reason. Augustine, Anselm, and Bonaventura
are cited here, together with the majority of the Franciscans, who followed St. Francis in making will and love primary in all religious matters.
At the other extreme were the pure Aristotelians, led by the Islamic
philosopher Averroës (1126–98), who considered rational knowledge far
superior to any and all information derived from faith. Averroës wrote of
Aristotle: "His teaching is the highest truth, since his thought was the end of
human understanding. . . . Aristotle was created and given to us by divine
providence so that we could know all that it is possible to know."[11]

Gilson's views have had an especially strong influence on the assessment
of late medieval thought. After Aquinas and the so-called golden age of
scholasticism, Gilson saw a steady decline into confusion in the intellectual
history of the fourteenth and fifteenth centuries. He believed that the Parisian condemnations of Aristotelianism in the late thirteenth century initiated the fateful descent. In 1270 the bishop of Paris, Stephan Tempier,
condemned thirteen philosophical propositions without identifying their
exact sources. Seven years later, with the encouragement of Pope John XXI
(1276–77), Tempier condemned 219 propositions, which he now ascribed
to philosophers enamored of Aristotle and his Islamic commentators: Siger
of Brabant (ca. 1240–84), an Aristotelian philosopher and member of the
arts faculty at Paris, Boethius of Sweden, a colleague of Siger, and un-
specified "others." A few of the condemned propositions touched certain
teachings of Thomas Aquinas, and it has been argued that the condemna-

10. Gilson elaborates on these categories in *Reason and Revelation in the Middle Ages*.
11. Text in *Friedrich Ueberwegs Grundriss der Geschichte der Philosophie*, ed. Bernhard
Geyer (Basel, 1967), 2:316.

tions were "as much a victory over Thomism as over so-called Latin Averroism," that is, as critical of a moderate theological use of Aristotle as of Averroistic extremes.[12]

What were these dangerous teachings? The propositions condemned in 1270 taught such things as panpsychism ("that there is one and the same intellect for every man"); astrology ("that all things that happen on earth are determined by the necessary movements of celestial bodies"); the uncreated nature of the world ("that the world is eternal"); and the utter perishability of created things ("that God cannot convey immortality and incorruptibility on mortal corruptible beings").[13] Among the propositions condemned in 1277 were overt attacks on the data and methods of theology.

Medieval ecclesiasts did not believe in the neutrality of speculation; the medieval university was not a marketplace for the free exchange of ideas. Throughout the Middle Ages and into early modern times, the ideational was also "ideological"; authorities viewed ideas in terms of their implications and practical consequences. The late Middle Ages became a period of great "intellectual" heretics, men like Meister Eckhart and John Wyclif, who neither identified with nor led dissenting movements, yet whose ideas seemed to inspire and justify them.[14] The medieval church stubbornly resisted all forms of true secular autonomy, whether the independent study of philosophy apart from theology or the independent operation of secular political power apart from church oversight and freedom to interfere. The

12. Gordon Leff, *Paris and Oxford Universities in the Thirteenth and Fourteenth Centuries* (New York, 1968), p. 229. I agree with F. van Steenberghen that the Aristotelianism condemned in 1270 and 1277 was less directly Averroistic than pure Aristotle. Siger's and Boethius's main source was Aristotle himself, not his Islamic commentators; they were radical Aristotelians rather than Averroists. *Aristotle and the West*, trans. L. Johnston (Louvain, 1955), pp. 219–29. However, it should also be appreciated that Averroës too was a radical Aristotelian.

13. The thirteen condemned propositions were: "1) Quod intellectus omnium hominum est unus et idem numero; 2) Quod ista est falsa vel impropria: homo intelligit; 3) Quod voluntas hominis ex necessitate vult vel eligit; 4) Quod omnia, que hic in inferioribus aguntur, subsunt necessitati corporum celestium; 5) Quod mundus est eternus; 6) Quod nunquam fuit primus homo; 7) Quod anima, que est forma hominis secundum quod homo, corrumpitur corrupto corpore; 8) Quod anima post mortem separata non patitur ab igne corporeo; 9) Quod liberum arbitrium est potentia passiva, non activa; et quod necessitate movetur ab appetibili; 10) Quod Deus non cognoscit singularia; 11) Quod Deus non cognoscit alia a se; 12) Quod humani actus non reguntur providentia Dei; 13) Quod Deus non potest dare immortalitatem vel incorruptionem rei corruptibili vel mortali" (*Chartularium universitatis Parisiensis*, ed. H. Denifle and E. Chatelain [Paris, 1889], 1:486–87). Both condemnations (1270 and 1277) are discussed by Gilson, *History of Christian Philosophy*, pp. 402–10.

14. Cf. Herbert Grundmann, "Hérésies savantes et hérésies populaires au Moyen Age" in Jacques Le Goff, ed., *Hérésies et sociétés dans l'Europe pré-industrielle 11e–18e siècles* (Paris, 1968), pp. 209–18.

theology of Thomas Aquinas is a commentary on the repugnance of such independence to the medieval Christian mind.

The Parisian condemnations of Aristotelianism demonstrated the church's self-defense as much as its aggression. There is no question that many of the propositions condemned by Tempier represented a wholesale assault on medieval Christian teaching. To argue that they were "less an attack on the foundations of faith than the assertion of independently formed philosophical opinions"[15] overlooks medieval disbelief in the neutrality of ideas and the logical consequences for Christian doctrine of many of these philosophical opinions. If there is but one eternal mind or intellect of which all created minds are transient epiphenomena, how can there be personal merit or immortality? What need is there for individuals to confer with priests? If all earthly events occur necessarily, then neither God nor man is free, and fate, not providence, reigns supreme. To teach that the world is eternal is to deny the Book of Genesis. If God cannot convey immortality on mortal souls, then to what purpose does the church distribute sacraments and healing graces, and how shall bodies be raised on the last day? The medieval ecclesiast could not look on the speculations of Parisian Aristotelians as harmless philosophical opinions.

One might think that the condemnation of such teachings would have gladdened the heart of a Catholic historian like Gilson. Yet he found these condemnations to be the key negative turning point in the history of Western thought; they were, in his opinion, a purely defensive act on the part of the church, prophetic of the future course of Western intellectual and religious history. In the place of a careful rational refutation of error, like those earlier attempted by Albert the Great and Thomas Aquinas, Bishop Tempier and Pope John XXI simply issued a blanket condemnation. The church did not challenge bad logic with good logic or meet bad reasoning with sound; it simply pronounced *Anathema sit*. Theological speculation, and with it the medieval church itself, henceforth increasingly confined itself to the incontestable sphere of revelation and faith. Gilson believed that in subsequent centuries rational demonstration and argument in theology became progressively unimportant to religious people, while faith and revelation held increasingly little insight into reality for secular people. "Theologism" on the part of the church and "rationalism" on the part of its critics became the norm. In the Gilsonian vision, reason and revelation, nature and grace, philosophy and theology, secular man and religious man,

---

15. Leff, *Paris and Oxford Universities*, p. 237; *The Dissolution of the Medieval Outlook: An Essay on Intellectual and Spiritual Change in the Fourteenth Century* (New York, 1976), p. 24. Leff also sees the condemnations as "marking the beginning of philosophy's circumscription" (ibid., p. 25).

the state and the church—all progressively lost their common ground and went their separate ways after 1277. The Parisian condemnations were the starting point of a development that ended with a theologian's description of reason as the "devil's whore" and with Luther's declaration that Aristotle was to theology as darkness to light.

After the Parisian condemnations, Gilson argued further, the work of the Franciscans Duns Scotus (ca. 1265–1308) and William of Ockham (ca. 1285–1347) further undermined the Thomist synthesis. Scotus was seen to narrow the range of scholastic speculation by finding far fewer theological truths philosophically arguable than had Aquinas and other thirteenth-century theologians.[16] The hallmark of Scotist theology was its appreciation of God's distance and otherness. The vast differences between God and man moved Scotus far more than areas where reason and revelation overlapped and seemed to suggest a unity of things human and divine. Will, not intellect became the central theological category in Scotist theology; what God and man did was more basic than what they were in themselves. The primary object of faith ceased to be God as pure being (*actus purus*) and became God as he revealed himself to man in Scripture. And the latter required trusting acceptance from man, not rational understanding.

Gilson found in Ockham the extreme conclusion of Scotist voluntarism and covenant theology: the confinement of theology to the sphere of faith and revelation and the denial of any rationally convincing knowledge of God. "Ockham is perfectly safe in what he believes; only he does not *know* what he believes, nor does he need to know it."[17] Here, for Gilson, the divorce between reason and revelation became final and the golden age of scholasticism effectively came to an end. Faith that was content simply to believe had supplanted faith that sought full understanding.

Other scholars, sharing Gilson's perspective, believe a natural alliance existed between Ockhamist philosophy, which denied direct rational knowledge of God, and Neoplatonic mysticism, popular in the fourteenth and fifteenth centuries, which sought God in transrational and even arational experience.[18] They also believe that it was not coincidental that the leader of the Protestant Reformation was a careful student of both Ockham and the German mystics.

---

16. *History of Christian Philosophy*, pp. 454–65.

17. Ibid., p. 498.

18. See especially Walter Dress, *Die Theologie Gersons: Eine Untersuchung zur Verbindung von Nominalismus und Mystik im Spätmittelalter* (Gütersloh, 1931); and Gilson, *History of Christian Philosophy*, pp. 528–34. Cf. S. Ozment, "Mysticism, Nominalism, and Dissent," in *The Pursuit of Holiness in Late Medieval and Renaissance Religion*, ed. Charles Trinkaus and Heiko A. Oberman (Leiden, 1974), p. 92.

For Gilson, the fourteenth century stands as a sad essay in "speculative lassitude."[19] That Duns Scotus was known as the "subtle doctor" (*Doctor subtilis*) and Ockham as the "doctor who is more than subtle" (*Doctor plusquam subtilis*) might have caused him to pause before making such an assessment, but he did not have all the facts at hand, and he was enamored of Thomas Aquinas. His critics have accused him of confusing the history of Western thought with the narrow problem of the relationship between reason and revelation. Such criticism underestimates what Gilson perceived to be at stake in the dissolution of the Thomist synthesis. At issue for him was the modern division of Western society into its distinctive secular and religious elements. Medieval belief in the harmony of reason and revelation had borne the possibility of uniquely uniting Western society, and the loss of such belief entailed also the loss of this possibility. From such a perspective far more was at stake in the golden age of scholasticism than simply a few theological questions.

Not all, not even most, scholars would agree, however, that the fourteenth and fifteenth centuries marked the waning of Western speculation. Indeed, much recent scholarship has been specifically devoted to overturning this particular point of view. Much of it has understandably come from Franciscan, Augustinian, and Protestant scholars, who do not immediately associate the Dominican Thomas Aquinas with the final word in philosophy and theology. That rare genius also existed after the thirteenth century is now fully appreciated, and new candidates for the title "summit of medieval thought" have been located in the fourteenth, fifteenth, and even sixteenth centuries. Duns Scotus, for example, has been praised over Aquinas and even to the detriment of later Franciscan thinkers.[20] Ockham has been presented as a defender of the old ways against innovating Thomists and Scotists, and the traditional charges against him of skepticism, Erastianism, and Pelagianism have been vigorously challenged.[21] Rich harvests of me-

---

19. *History of Christian Philosophy*, pp. 470–71. The phrase is used in reference to Peter of Candia, who spent the last year of his life as the Pisan pope Alexander V (1409–10).

20. See the studies of Werner Dettloff, O.F.M., *Die Lehre von der Acceptatio Divina bei Johannes Duns Skotus mit besonderer Berücksichtigung der Rechtfertigungslehre* (Werl/Westf., 1954); *Die Entwicklung der Akzeptations- und Verdienstlehre von Duns Skotus bis Luther* (Münster i.W., 1963).

21. Among Ockham's modern defenders are E. A. Moody, *The Logic of William of Ockham* (New York, 1935); Gerhard Ritter, *Marsilius von Inghen und die okkamistische Schule in Deutschland* (Heidelberg, 1921); *Via antiqua und Via moderna auf den deutschen Universitäten des xv. Jahrhunderts* (Heidelberg 1922/Darmstadt, 1963); Paul Vignaux, *Justification et prédestination au XIVe siècle* (Paris, 1934); *Nominalisme au XIVe siècle* (Montreal, 1948); Philotheus Boehner, *Collected Articles on Ockham* (St. Bonaventure, New York, 1958); Arthur S. McGrade, *The Political Thought of William of Ockham: Personal and Institutional Principles* (Cambridge, 1974); Leff, *William of Ockham*, pp. 398, 495. For a summary and interpretation of revisionist work

dieval thought have been found in Meister Eckhart,[22] Jean Gerson,[23] Nicholas of Cusa,[24] and Gabriel Biel.[25]

Movements too have their advocates. One study has found the origins of all the reform movements of the sixteenth century—humanist, Catholic, and Protestant—in the fifteenth-century *Devotio Moderna,* a lay religious movement.[26] Deep religious currents and continuing scholastic traditions have been shown to exist within the Italian Renaissance, correcting Jacob Burckhardt's one-sided picture of Renaissance culture as secular and presenting Italian humanists as a watershed in medieval religious history.[27] In the wake of the Second Vatican Council, both Catholic and Protestant ecumenists have gone so far as to suggest that Martin Luther and Thomas Aquinas actually taught much the same thing, only from different philosophical points of view, an argument that, if true, would not only place Martin Luther at the summit of medieval thought, but would also take the arguments of Gilson full circle.[28]

One of the more interesting defenses of fourteenth-century thought, suggestive of a point of view this work will develop, is tucked away in the somewhat obscure writings of a modern Augustinian scholar, Damasus Trapp. Trapp describes the fourteenth century as the most intellectually fertile period of the Middle Ages and believes it became such because of the difficulties created by the great system builders of the thirteenth century. In

---

on Ockham, see William J. Courtenay, "Nominalism and Late Medieval Religion," in *The Pursuit of Holiness,* pp. 26–58, and "Nominalism and Late Medieval Thought: A Bibliographical Essay," *Theological Studies* 33 (1972): 716–34; Helmar Junghans, *Ockham im Lichte der neueren Forschung* (Berlin, 1968).

22. See below, p. 127.

23. André Combes, *Essai sur la critique de Ruysbroeck par Gerson,* vols. 1–3 (Paris, 1945–59), and *La théologie mystique de Gerson,* vols. 1–2 (Rome, 1963).

24. F. Edward Cranz, "Cusanus, Luther, and the Mystical Tradition" in *The Pursuit of Holiness,* pp. 93–102; Gilson, *History of Christian Philosophy,* pp. 534–40. For a treatment of Cusa as a modern thinker, see Ernst Cassirer, *The Individual and the Cosmos in Renaissance Philosophy* (New York, 1963).

25. Heiko A. Oberman, *The Harvest of Medieval Theology: Gabriel Biel and Late Medieval Nominalism* (Cambridge, Mass., 1963).

26. Albert Hyma, *The Christian Renaissance: A History of the Devotio Moderna* (New York, 1925; Hamden, Conn., 1965); *The Brethren of the Common Life* (Grand Rapids, 1950). See also below.

27. Giuseppe Toffanin, *Storia dell'unamesimo,* vols. 1–3 (Bologna, 1952); Charles Trinkaus, *"In Our Image and Likeness:" Humanity and Divinity in Italian Humanist Thought,* vols. 1–2 (Chicago, 1970).

28. Hans Küng, *Rechtfertigung: Die Lehre Karl Barths und eine katholische Besinnung* (Einsiedeln, 1957); Stephen Pfürtner, *Luther and Aquinas on Salvation* (New York, 1964); and especially Otto Pesch, *Die Theologie der Rechtfertigung bei Martin Luther und Thomas von Aquin* (Mainz, 1967). See also the recent effort to relate Luther positively to the late medieval mystical traditions: Bengt R. Hofmann, *Luther and the Mystics* (Minneapolis, 1976).

the thirteenth century, which Trapp calls "the great century of speculation," Albertus, Aquinas, Bonaventura, and Scotus actually generated as much confusion as understanding for their scholastic successors. Confronted by contradictions within and between these great theological systems, the thinkers of the fourteenth century were forced to reexamine the historical sources and theoretical cogency of their arguments. In this way the fourteenth century developed what Trapp describes as new "historico-critical" and "logico-critical" attitudes that made it "the great century of criticism."[29] The highest importance was placed on historical accuracy and consistent argument. Far from logic chopping and destructive criticism, the intense source analysis and logical investigations for which the early fourteenth century is so well known were initially the result of efforts to understand and harmonize the theological systems of the thirteenth century.

Trapp singles out the fourteenth-century Augustinian Gregory of Rimini (d. 1358) as the model of the new criticism. Gregory's concern for historical accuracy (he was reputed to be the best Augustine scholar of the Middle Ages) and his opposition to philosophical subtlety (he became a major critic of Ockham's theology) anticipated the work of Italian humanists. Only recently have scholars begun to appreciate fully the degree to which the historical scholarship of the Augustinian order was a "cradle of humanism."[30] Before scholarly preoccupation with the past and concern for

29. "Augustinian Theology of the Fourteenth Century: Notes on Editions Marginalia, Opinions, and Book-Lore," *Augustiniana* 6 (1956): 146–274. Gordon Leff's revised view of Ockham approaches Trapp's assessment of the fourteenth century. Leff sees the "inauguration of the displacement of the medieval world view" in the fourteenth century's attempt to explain the world in natural terms, both fundamental traits of Ockham's philosophy (*The Dissolution of the Medieval Outlook*, pp. 6–7). Leff summarizes: "The paradox, in the light of the received view of the fourteenth century, is that the change denotes an almost naive confidence in the intelligibility of the world and the capacity of reason to discern it. It inaugurated a new path of inquiry which, greatly modified, was ultimately to be vindicated in subsequent developments, both scientific and logical. But in the context of the fourteenth century it could only be destructive of the existing modes without being comprehensive enough to substitute a new outlook" (ibid., pp. 15–16). The Gilsonian strain, so prominent in Leff's earlier works, still remains evident, however, in the revision. "The new windows opened by Ockham also opened the way to the sterile cavilling that exclusive concern with formal meaning for its own sake must always bring to philosophy and in this case to theology as well. Compared with the thirteenth century, the result was disequilibrium" (ibid., p. 19). Like Gilson, Leff sees a "widespread loss of speculative nerve" in the fourteenth century.

30. "The Augustinian Order can be said to have provided if not the cradle of Italian humanism then certainly the first allies, eagerly exploiting the new scholarly vistas for the study of St. Augustine" (H. A. Oberman, "Headwaters of the Reformation: Initia Lutheri— Initia Reformationis," in *Luther and the Dawn of the Modern Era: Papers for the Fourth International Congress for Luther Research*, ed. H. A. Oberman [Leiden, 1974], p. 70). See also Rudolf Arbesmann, *Der Augustiner-Eremitenorden und der Beginn der humanistischen Bewegung* (Würzburg, 1965).

accurate texts were associated so exclusively with Italian humanists, they were major traits of Augustinian scholars. In Italy Dionigi da Borgo S. Sepulcro O.E.S.A. (d. 1342) influenced Petrarch, and Bartholomeo da Urbino O.E.S.A. (d. 1350) collected the works of St. Augustine and prepared a gross concordance. In Germany the Italian-trained Osnabrück Augustinian Gottschalk Hollen (d. 1481) cited classical authors in his sermons and conveyed Italian learning to German Augustinian convents. Humanist skills and interests were prominent among Erfurt Augustinians on the eve of the Reformation, thanks to the work of Johann Lang (1488–1548), an accomplished Hebraist and Graecist and friend of Luther, and Johannes Altensteig, the author of a major dictionary of late medieval philosophy and theology, the *Vocabularium theologiae*.[31]

Trapp finds a lapse in intellectual rigor not among the Augustinians and Franciscans of the fourteenth century, but among the philosophers and theologians of the fifteenth, who, weary with the involved scholastic debates of the fourteenth century, simply retreated to the great masters of the thirteenth century. If one follows Trapp's interpretation, it is in the fifteenth century, when scholars began to repeat Albertus, Aquinas, Bonaventura, and Scotus uncritically, that one finds "speculative lassitude." Trapp attributes the intellectual decline of this century to two sources, the "mistrust [of] the freedom-loving theologians of the fourteenth century" by the orthodox, and the indolence of "easy-going scholars," who found it "so much more convenient to study one author rather than ten or twenty."[32] Like war-weary Europeans who surrendered to strong-arm rule in the late fifteenth century, many argument-weary scholars appear to have given their minds passively to the intellectual giants of the past on the eve of the Reformation.

What Trapp and others have done for the rehabilitation of the fourteenth century, Heiko A. Oberman has attempted for the fifteenth century. His *Harvest of Medieval Theology*, published in 1963, was a major defense of the basically orthodox and reform character of late medieval nominalism, especially in the work of Gabriel Biel (ca. 1420–95). The nominalists are depicted as representing a broad spectrum of scholars, including Cistercians, Franciscans, Augustinians, Dominicans, and seculars, who searched for a "catholic via media" between the contending schools and traditions of the thirteenth century.[33] Acknowledging the basically synthetic rather than

31. Junghans, "Der Einfluss des Humanismus auf Luthers Entwickung, bis 1518," *Luther Jahrbuch 1970*, ed. Franz Lau (Hamburg, 1970), pp. 53–55.

32. Trapp, "Augustinian Theology of the Fourteenth Century," p. 215.

33. *The Harvest of Medieval Theology*, pp. 423–28. Leff finds Oberman's efforts to define a uniform school of nominalists in the fourteenth and fifteenth centuries fundamentally dis-

critical character of Biel's mind, Oberman still stresses the constructive side of fifteenth-century speculation and strongly rejects any suggestion of a "disintegration" of late medieval thought; Biel attests a "harvest," not the "waning," of medieval theology. In a later work, *Forerunners of the Reformation* (1966), Oberman has urged scholars to drop altogether the idea of pervasive intellectual decline as a proper perspective from which to approach the period and to appreciate lines of continuity and discontinuity at their face value.[34]

It will be an argument of subsequent chapters that rather than being a perfect norm from which later medieval thought strayed, the scholastic synthesis of reason and revelation in the thirteenth century was a chief source of both the intellectual and ecclesiopolitical conflicts of the later Middle Ages; not the rejection of Thomism, but its persistence and embrace by church authority created new and serious problems for both church and society. How did this come about? It was an axiom of Thomist theology that nature found its perfection in grace, that religion completed natural virtue.[35] Aquinas brought reason and revelation together, but strictly as unequals; he joined the profane with the sacred, but only on a continuum. In this union reason, philosophy, nature, secular man, and the state ultimately had value only in subservience to the higher goals of revelation, theology, grace, religious man, and the church. Such a vision inspired the papal bull *Unam sanctam* (1302), wherein Pope Boniface VIII boldly asserted the church's temporal powers against the kings of France and England and triggered the most serious confrontation between church and state in the Middle Ages,[36] one from which the medieval church never fully recovered. Among its sources, this famous bull directly paraphrased Aquinas. It did so because Thomist theology was the most sophisticated statement of the medieval belief in the secondary significance of the lay and secular world, a congenial ideology for a church besieged by independent and aggressive secular political powers. The conflict that more than

torting. "The label of nominalism . . . lies like a pall—recently renewed [an apparent reference to Oberman's *Harvest of Medieval Theology*]—across the philosophy and theology of the fourteenth century. It overrides the heterogeneity which is its most notable aspect and is expressed in the very eclecticism of the period" (*The Dissolution of the Medieval Outlook*, pp. 12–13).

34. *Forerunners of the Reformation: The Shape of Late Medieval Thought* (New York, 1966), pp. 32–43.

35. *Summa theologiae* (Marretti ed.), Ia, Q. 1, art. 8, ad. 2: "Cum enim gratia non tollat naturam, sed perficiat, oportet quod naturalis ratio subserviat fidei." This statement is made in defense of theology as a rational science.

36. See Brian Tierney, *The Crisis of Church and State 1050–1300* (Englewood Cliffs, N.J., 1976), pp. 182–83, and the discussion below, p. 145.

any other may be said to have sent religious man and secular man in opposite directions in the later Middle Ages was one in which a pope attempted to enforce upon the world a vision of politics and society that Thomas Aquinas articulated more eloquently than any other medieval thinker. The central problem of late medieval intellectual and religious history was the mentality that had given birth to the synthesis of reason and revelation, the presumptuous, seductive vision of high medieval theology.

CHAPTER 2

The Scholastic
Traditions

How Man is Saved:
Theories of Salvation
from Augustine to Gabriel Biel

THE Middle Ages were an age of faith, perhaps more erratically and with greater aberration than we previously believed, but an age of faith nonetheless. They were also an age of clergy and theologians. Clergy influenced the affairs of both kings and common folk, and theology reigned supreme—if not always uncontested—as queen of the sciences. The church was a major landowner, and church courts administered both laws and taxes. Church-sponsored sacramental and pilgrimage piety provided the major forms of popular entertainment and also became a very big business. Religious figures and issues had the social impact that political figures and issues have today.

For both religious and secular reasons, medieval men and women took sin, death, and the devil seriously. Medieval ecclesiastical institutions were built on the credulity of the educated as well as the uneducated, the politically powerful as well as the masses. Manifold devotional practices nurtured religious belief. These practices were in turn justified by a pervasive concept of man's religious nature and destiny, which secular and regular clergy communicated by sermon, symbol, and personal example. The precise definition of man's religious nature and destiny was the peculiar responsibility of the theologians in the schools and universities. Behind the many ecclesiastical laws and ordinances that governed daily life and the popular devotional practices that consumed religious energies were the reflections of the theologians.

Among these learned men none influenced medieval theology and religion more than St. Augustine. What Plato and Aristotle were to medieval philosophy, Augustine was to medieval theology. The fundamentals of Western religious thinking about sin and grace, providence and predestination, the church, and political power and the state received classic expression in Augustine's *Confessions* and *City of God*. Augustinianism provided arguments for both sides in the major theological debates of the Middle Ages.

How did Augustine understand man's religious nature and destiny? In book 1 of the *Confessions* he wrote of himself: "In this was my sin, that not in God but in his creatures, in myself and others, did I seek pleasure, honors, and truth."[1] The *Confessions* detailed, with much psychological insight, human sinfulness in various stages and vocations of man's life: the totalitarian demands of infants, the idle pranks and cruel delinquencies of youth, the day-to-day conflicts of marriage, the pride of academicians. Augustinianism is especially characterized by the belief that man, by every present measure, is a fallen, sinful creature. As a Christian, Augustine also believed that such selfishness and egoism had not always characterized man and need not continue to dominate him. Because of his extremely lofty view of what man once had been and might once again, in part, become, Augustine held the present life in low esteem. All thinkers tend to use limiting concepts, ideal constructs by which they measure and judge the present. For medieval Christian thinkers, the biblical description of Adam before the Fall was the test for the present life. Adam was for Augustine what Camelot became for medieval troubadours, the state of nature for Hobbes and Rousseau, and the presidency of Lincoln for American politicians.

According to Augustine, Adam's unique mark had been an "ability not to sin" (*posse non peccare*).[2] As a free agent, his uniqueness lay in his ability to be exactly as he chose—sinless or sinful. Specifically, Adam had the power to subject his desires to his will and his will to his knowledge of what was good, that is, to God, and to live a perfectly "ordered" life, alienated not from himself, the world, or God. Augustine writes of man in Paradise:

In Paradise man lived as he desired, so long as he desired what God commanded. He lived in the enjoyment of God, and was good by God's goodness; he lived without any want and had it in his power so to live eternally. He had food that he might not hunger, drink that he might not thirst, the tree of life that old age might not waste him. There was in his body no corruption . . . which could produce in him any unpleasant sensation. He feared no inward disease, no outward accident. Soundest health blessed his body, absolute tranquillity his soul. As there was no excessive heat or cold in Paradise, its inhabitants were exempt from the vicissitudes of fear and desire. No sadness of any kind was there, nor any foolish joy; true gladness flowed ceaselessly from the presence of God, who was loved "out of a pure heart. . . ." The honest love of husband and wife made a sure harmony between them. Body

1. *The Confessions of Saint Augustine*, trans. John K. Ryan (Garden City, N.Y., 1960), bk. 1, ch. 20, p. 63.

2. See Reinhold Seeberg, *Text-Book of the History of Doctrines*, trans. C. E. Hay (Grand Rapids, Mich., 1964), 1:341–45.

An image of St. Augustine, bishop of Hippo.
Attributed to Lorenzo d'Alessandro.

The Fall into Sin. Lucas Cranach the Elder. Before they ate the fruit of the forbidden tree, Adam and Eve were completely at peace with themselves, their maker, and nature. Through the calm beauty of Eden Cranach conveys to the viewer a sense of impending doom as Adam and Eve proceed to transgress God's commandment.

Aristotle and Phyllis. Urs Graf. The subordination of man's will and desires to his reason—the hierarchical ordering of the soul's faculties—was both a classical and a Christian ideal. From Augustine to the Reformation, Christians believed that the Fall left man's will and reason easy prey to his lower nature. Here the philosopher Aristotle, the summit of human reason in the estimation of medieval intellectuals, is depicted as utterly powerless before the sensuous charms of the beautiful Phyllis. (In Greek mythology, Phyllis was a princess in Thrace who drove her estranged husband mad and arranged his death by a secret charm.) Medieval Christians believed that their sacraments and virtues made possible the reordering of the soul's faculties so that desire remained within the will's control and the will under the sure guidance of a reason ordered to God. The subjection of Aristotle to Phyllis first appeared as a sermon topic in the thirteenth century and became popular in drawings and woodcuts during the later Middle Ages.

and spirit worked harmoniously together, and the commandment was kept without labor. No languor made their leisure wearisome; no sleepiness interrupted their desire to work.[3]

In Paradise, man was a model of willed self-control. Augustine suggested that even sexual intercourse occurred without lust, the organs of reproduction activated by calm rational volition, not by uncontrollable passion.[4] The classical ideal of man and the Christian view of his original perfection were here joined: habitual order reigned over prelapsarian man, who had reasoned control of his faculties. He obeyed and enjoyed God and used the world for his creaturely comforts, not as an object to be worshiped in God's place.

The Fall reversed everything; thereafter fallen man lost his self-control and became a "slave to lust." He now obeyed and enjoyed the world, his desires having become the rider and his will the horse, and God was to all intents and purposes forgotten. Henceforth, according to Augustine, man was "not able not to sin" (*non posse non peccare*). Augustine's predilection for describing the power of sin by reference to sexual desire may have been intended to illustrate the bondage of man's will to his passions in the most forceful way. For Augustine, pleasure in anything other than God was sinful, and one in the grip of sexual passion not only found pleasure in a creature, but did so to such a degree that the creaturely satisfaction of desire became an all-consuming obsession that overrode all moral and religious considerations. For his late Roman readers, who were familiar with both sexual passion and the classical ideal of a life ordered by reason, this was a most convincing example of the domination of man's higher by his lower faculties.

Such a view of man's fallen nature and present life remained basic to medieval theology. "We commit a sinful act," wrote Thomas Aquinas, "by turning to a temporal attraction without being duly directed to our last end [i.e., God]."[5] Exactly why man fell from his original state of righteousness remained something of a mystery for both Augustine and the theologians of the Middle Ages, but all agreed that something very basic was thereafter missing from human nature. The scholastics of the twelfth and thirteenth centuries spoke of the loss of a special grace (*donum superadditum*), which God had given Adam in addition to the other gifts of creation and which

---

3. *City of God*, trans. Marcus Dods, in *A Select Library of the Nicene and Post-Nicene Fathers of the Christian Church*, vol. 2, ed. Philip Schaff (Grand Rapids, Mich., 1956), bk. 14, ch. 26, p. 281.

4. *City of God*, bk. 14, chs. 15–16, pp. 274–76.

5. *St. Thomas Aquinas: Theological Texts*, ed. Thomas Gilby (London, 1955), p. 124.

made it possible for him to gain special insight into himself, his maker, and the world.[6] This special grace had assisted him, so long as he willed in accordance with it, to live an ordered life. Its forfeiture by the Fall left man unable to conform his mind and will to God even when he wanted to do so and hence "unable not to sin."

When Augustine wrote the *Confessions* he was bishop of Hippo, a prominent ecclesiastic convinced of the healing power of the church's sacraments. He recounted how he came to take pity on the Manichaeans after his conversion, because "they did not know of these sacraments, these medicines, and raged madly against the antidote by which they could become sane."[7] This was also the advantage of Christianity over Platonism. Christians did not contemplate truth at a distance, Augustine argued, but grasped it directly by faith; nor did they look for strength to a deity who remained beyond this world, but found it in one who had become flesh and dwelt among men.[8] The power to heal the will and restore man to self-control was tangibly present in the Incarnation of Christ and the sacraments of the Christian church. Here, for Augustine, lay the superiority of Christian faith and revelation over all the ancient philosophies. He commented on this superiority in the following statement, which gives a Christian resolution to the problem of man as classical philosophy had defined it.

> In all our actions and movements, in every activity of the creatures, I find two times, the past and the future. I seek the present, nothing stands still: what I have said is no longer present; what I am going to say is not yet come; what I have done is no longer present; what I am going to do is not yet come; the life I have lived is no longer present; the life I have still to live is not yet come. Past and future I find in every creature-movement: in truth, which is abiding, past and future I find not, but the present alone, and that unchangeably, which has no place in the creature. Sift the mutations of things, you will find *was* and *will be;* think of God, you will find the *is* [*est*], where was and will be cannot exist. To be so then thyself, rise beyond the boundaries of time. But who can transcend the powers of his being? May he raise us there who said to the Father: "I will that they also be with me where I am." And so, in making this promise, that we should not die in our sins, the Lord Jesus Christ, I think, said nothing else by these words than, "If you

6. See Seeberg, *Text-Book of the History of Doctrines,* 2:114–15, 153, 197.

7. *Confessions,* bk. 9, ch. 4, p. 210; see also bk. 5, ch. 9, p. 125. On the Manichaeans, see below, p. 44.

8. Ibid., bk. 6, chs. 4–5, pp. 138–39; bk. 7, ch. 9, pp. 168–69; bk. 7, chs. 18–19, pp. 176–77; bk. 7, ch. 21, p. 180.

believe not that I am" God, "you shall die in your sins." God be thanked
that he said, "If you *believe* not" and did not say, "If you comprehend
not." For who can comprehend this?[9]

The power to be constant amid the flux and disorder of life was available
to all in Catholic Christianity. What Adam lost when he fell and the
philosophers of antiquity had sought in vain by their speculations Augustine believed he had found in the Christian church. As the continuation of
the power of the Incarnation, the church had the authority to forgive sin; its
revelation enlightened man's mind; its sacraments, "the medicine of immortality," healed his will. Later scholastic theologians described the grace
conveyed by the sacraments as a *gratia gratum faciens,* a power that really
changed life. Sacramental grace became the equivalent in the present life of
the lost supernatural aid that had specially assisted Adam in living a life
ordered to God in Paradise.

A high doctrine of church authority has remained an Augustinian legacy.
"I would not have believed the gospel," Augustine wrote in the *Confessions,*
"had the Catholic church not moved me to it." This statement echoed
throughout the Middle Ages whenever the authority of the church required
a defense, whether in the determination of the truth of Scripture or in the
coercion of heterodox belief.[10] Against the Donatists, who taught that baptism and ordination administered by morally unworthy persons—
specifically, priests who had lapsed into paganism during the Diocletian
persecution—had no validity, Augustine insisted, and the medieval church
always agreed, that gross immorality on the part of a priest did not
minimize the efficacy of the church's sacraments; to believe otherwise was
to permit human weakness to impede the work of God.[11] Later scholastics
described the sacraments as working *ex opere operato,* that is, simply by virtue
of their sheer objective performance, not *ex opere operantis,* because of the
personal character or contribution of the agent who performed them.

Another significant and controversial legacy of Augustine to the scholastic traditions of the Middle Ages was his strong doctrine of predestination.
After his conversion, Augustine saw the hand of God shaping his destiny
from infancy.[12] In the *City of God* he elaborated a doctrine of supralapsarian

9. *Lectures or Tractates on the Gospel According to St. John,* trans. J. Innes (Edinburgh,
1874), vol. 2, lect. 38/10, pp. 8–9.
10. Seeberg, *Text-Book of the History of Doctrines,* 1:312; Heiko A. Oberman, *The Harvest of
Medieval Theology: Gabriel Biel and Late Medieval Nominalism* (Cambridge, Mass., 1963), p. 370.
11. Seeberg, *Text-Book of the History of Doctrines,* 1:313–28; Peter Brown, *Augustine of
Hippo: A Biography* (Berkeley, 1969), pp. 212–25.
12. Cf. *Confessions,* bk. 1, ch. 6, pp. 46–47.

predestination, according to which God had determined the fate of every individual in eternity even before the world was created and Adam had fallen. Augustine postulated two communities of angels, one upright and good, another wicked and evil, from which derived human communities of the elect and the reprobate, both communities determined in and persisting throughout eternity.[13] Stern as this doctrine might appear to the modern reader, it was not originally intended to demean man, but to praise God and console the despairing. To Augustine, it meant that even though all external evidence suggested that blind fate or fortune controlled the world, God was actually present and guiding it to a sure end appointed in eternity.[14] Predestinarians have traditionally found comfort, not insult, in such belief.

Between the years 412 and 421, Augustine clashed with the Pelagians over the degree to which people might control their spiritual destiny, and these confrontations hardened his views on original sin and predestination. Pelagius (fl. 400–418) was not a bishop at the top of society, but a monk at the bottom, who preached among dock workers and other urban poor. Their different social positions doubtlessly influenced their respective beliefs and ideals.[15] Unlike Augustine, Pelagius believed that each person had a clear responsibility for his own salvation, that the race went to those who ran it well, and all who chose to run well could do so. To Pelagius, Augustine's teaching on original sin and predestination exaggerated human weakness and divine sovereignty and invited apathy and immorality. Where Augustine seemed to damn man and praise God, Pelagius exhorted people to work out their own salvation in fear and trembling. The church of the fifth and sixth centuries agreed with Augustine and condemned Pelagianism at the councils of Carthage (418), Ephesus (431), and Orange (529), although the last did not adopt Augustine's extreme views on the irresistibility of grace for the elect and the damnation of the reprobate already in eternity. The debate between adherents of Augustine and Pelagius did not end there, however, but persisted down through the Middle Ages and into the Reformation. Indeed, no topic was more hotly argued among scholastic theologians and Protestant reformers than the nature of religious justification and predestination.

According to the orthodox teaching of the medieval church, three things were required to make fallen man righteous again: an infusion of healing grace, and this meant direct reliance on the church and its sacraments,

---

13. *City of God*, bk. 11, ch. 33, p. 224; bk. 12, ch. 27, p. 244.

14. This against classical views of human history. See Charles N. Cochrane, *Christianity and Classical Culture: A Study of Thought and Action from Augustus to Augustine* (New York, 1957), pp. 456–515.

15. Brown, *Augustine of Hippo*, pp. 340–75.

which formed the narrow gate to salvation; the free turning of the will to God and away from sin, or ethical cooperation with grace; and the remission of the guilt incurred by sin by priestly absolution.[16]

The sacraments of baptism and penance were basic to this process of religious restoration. The grace of baptism was believed to neutralize the individual's responsibility for original sin ("washes away the whole guilt of punishment belonging to the past"), while the grace of penance gave aid against persisting actual sins ("a sacramental cure which purges us from sin after baptism").[17] The church baptized infants to remove the guilt and penalty they automatically incurred as offspring of Adam. Baptism and last rites were the two sacraments medieval men and women did not neglect, even those who in most other respects appear to have been religiously indifferent.[18]

Baptism was believed not only to remove original sin, but also to destroy any actual sins present at the time and to weaken the inclination to sin that remained in the baptized. The latter, known as the *fomes peccati,* or "tinderbox" of sin, was an inherent weakness of all people after the Fall.[19] In time everyone, including the baptized, succumbed to the human inclination to sin. Hence, all needed recourse to what medieval theologians called the "second plank after shipwreck," the sacrament of penance.

No more than baptism, however, was penance a definitive resolution of man's sinful state. Through the sacrament of penance one again received healing grace, which destroyed the sin immediately present and weakened, but again did not remove, the inclination to sin in the future. The penitent, like the baptized, soon succumbed to the temptation to sin and found himself, if earnest, returning to the sacrament of penance in what became a recurring cycle of sin and absolution. In practice, a sense of steady moral improvement and a gradual approximation of that ordered obedience to God that marked the life of Adam before the Fall should result from such religious activity. But in theological doctrine the medieval Christian was always sinning, always beginning anew, always returning to the sacraments for short-lived strength and assurance. This well-developed medieval belief appeared among the judgments of the faculty of the University of Paris that led to the execution of Joan of Arc in 1431: "This woman sins," pronounced

16. "Quatuor ... requiruntur ad iustificationem impii: sc. gratiae infusio; motus liberi arbitrii in Deum per fidem; et motus liberi arbitrii in peccatum; et remissio culpae" (Thomas Aquinas, *Summa Theologiae,* I–II, Q. 113, art. 6, Resp.).

17. Aquinas in Gilby, *Theological Texts,* no. 606, p. 361; no. 629, p. 378.

18. See Jacques Toussaert, *Le sentiment religieux en Flandre à la fin du moyen-âge* (Paris, 1963), p. 489.

19. See Oberman, *Harvest of Medieval Theology,* p. 127.

her judges, "when she says she is as certain of being received into Paradise as if she were already a partaker of... glory, seeing that on this earthly journey no pilgrim knows if he is worthy of glory or of punishment, which the sovereign judge alone can tell."[20] In medieval theology people were always *viatores,* pilgrims unworthy and uncertain of their fatherland.

Before the Ockhamists made Pelagianism a major issue in medieval theology, the scholastic debate over religious justification focused on the question of how grace could be present in man's soul. How can something divine be within human nature? If medieval philosophers had problems conceiving the existence of a universal within a particular, there were even greater difficulties for theologians who tried to imagine godly purity within a finite sinful creature. Peter Lombard determined the direction of this prolonged debate. In book 1, distinction 17 of his famed *Sentences,* Lombard, discussing religious justification, asked: "Is the love by which we are saved a created habit of our soul, or is it the very person of the Holy Spirit dwelling within us?" Is that which heals and saves a person part of his own nature, something he himself has developed as his own possession, or is it the indwelling spirit of God, a divine power in but not of him? Lombard opted for the latter solution, maintaining that the love by which people love God and their fellow man so as to merit salvation was the spirit of God working internally, without their aid or volition.[21] Man is saved by an uncreated, not a created habit, by uncreated, not created, love, by the Holy Spirit within, not by an acquired talent he can call his very own. When the young Luther wrote his commentary on the *Sentences* in 1509/10, he strongly agreed, against the majority of scholastics, with this interpretation by Lombard.[22]

Thomas Aquinas opposed Lombard on this issue, arguing that saving charity must be a voluntary act arising from a disposition man *could* call his own. He wrote in pointed summary:

Peter Lombard held that charity was not a created reality, but the Holy Spirit dwelling in the soul. He did not mean that the Holy Spirit was identified with our movement of love, but that charity, unlike the other virtues, such as faith and hope, was not elicited from a habit which was really our own. [In this] he was trying to enhance charity.... This

---

20. *The Trial of Jeanne d'Arc,* trans. W. P. Barrett (New York, 1932), 320–21.

21. "Spiritus sanctus est amor sive charitas, qua nos diligimus Deum et proximum; quae charitas cum ita est in nobis, ut nos faciat diligere Deum et proximum, tunc Spiritus sanctus dicitur mitti vel dari nobis; et qui diligit ipsam dilectionem qua diligit proximum, in eo ipso Deum diligit, quia ipsa dilectio Deus est, id est, spiritus sanctus" (I *Sent.* d. 17, art. 2, p. 54).

22. See Paul Vignaux, *Luther, Commenteur des Sentences* (Paris, 1935).

opinion [however] tends rather to discredit charity. It would mean that
active charity rises from the Holy Spirit so moving the mind that we are
merely passive, and not responsible for our loving or otherwise. This
militates against the character of a voluntary act. Charity would not
then be a voluntary act. There is a problem here, for our loving is very
much our own.[23]

According to Aquinas, grace is in the soul as a reality connatural to man;
otherwise, saving acts of charity would be done involuntarily and, as it were,
by another. Although its ultimate origin is divine, the love by which people
love God and their fellow man in a saving way is a created love, a truly
human habit.

Aquinas found a solution in Aristotelian philosophy. Grace, he argued, is
in the soul not as a substantial form, but as an accidental form (*forma
accidentalis*).[24] In Aristotelian philosophy a substantial form denotes the
essence of a thing, that which makes it what it is or in terms of which it is
defined. Man's substantial form, for example, is his reason; reason makes
man a unique creature and defines his nature. An accidental form, by
contrast, while very much a part of an individual, remains nonessential to its
definition as the particular thing that it is. A man's color, height, and such
acquired abilities as running and singing, for example, are accidental forms,
nonessential to his being a rational creature.

The ingenuity of Aquinas's solution can be elucidated by a modern
example. I am man simply by virtue of the fact that I have the power of
reason. If, however, I want to be a "tennis-playing man," then I must acquire, through an infusion of instruction and my own exercise and practice
on the basis of this instruction, the habit of playing tennis. I remain man in
the fullest sense of the word whether or not I can play tennis, for the ability
to play tennis is essential only to my becoming a tennis-playing man, not to
my being man. For Aquinas, grace exists in the soul in the same way that the
habit of playing tennis exists in a person. With the infusion of supernatural
grace an individual receives the essential foundation, an initial disposition,
basic instruction, as it were, in how to order his life in obedience to God. He
must still exercise the grace he has received in order to become "expert" in
the art of loving God and man. For Aquinas, the infused habit of grace is
that without which one could never become a Christian and enter heaven;

23. Gilby, *Theological Texts*, no. 407, p. 214.
24. *Summa theologiae*, Q. 110, art. 2, Resp. ad 2: "Et quia gratia est supra naturam
humanam, non potest esse quod sit substantia aut forma substantialis; sed est forma accidentalis ipsius animae. Id enim quod substantialiter est in Deo, accidentaliter fit in anima partic-
ipante divinam bonitatem."

one may be man without grace, but not a "Christian man." Aquinas further believed that once the habit of grace had been inculcated it could never be completely lost, even though it might for long periods go unexercised. Here we see Aquinas once again working out an ingenious middle way: grace is not in the soul as its substance; neither is it there so as to be absolutely no part of it; it is *really,* but *accidentally,* there.

Duns Scotus (ca. 1265–1308) led a critical Franciscan reaction to Aquinas's views on the infused habit of grace. Strongly influenced by Augustine's teaching on predestination, Scotus looked with suspicion on the definition of Christians in terms of something they could be said to possess as their own within their souls. Did this mean that God, who is omnipotent and free over creation, was in some way bound to accidental forms within the souls of mere creatures, obliged to save any and all who tried to love him habitually? Was not God free to be where and with whom he pleased, regardless of the qualifying circumstances? For Scotus, only God's will could be primary in the definition of the Christian. What God decreed in man's regard was far more important to his salvation than any quality of soul he might come to possess; people were saved only because God first willed it, never because they were intrinsically worthy of it.

Before Ockham turned his razor against Scotist and Thomist epistemology,[25] Scotus applied a razor of his own to Thomist soteriology on this particular issue. Scotus stated his principle of theological economy in the axiom "Nothing created must, for reasons intrinsic to it, be accepted by God" *(nihil creatum formaliter est a deo acceptandum).*[26] This meant that what was created and finite could in no way determine what was uncreated and infinite. Every relationship God had outside himself was, by definition, absolutely free, contingent, unconditioned, in no way obligatory. From Scotus's perspective, Aquinas bound God too closely to the church's system of grace and tended to lose sight of the great distance that obtained between God's eternal will and its execution in time through created orders and finite agents.[27] Thomist theology seemed to run the danger of entangling the divine will in the secondary causation of the church, priests, sacraments, and accidental forms of grace. While Aquinas believed with every medieval theologian that God could never properly be called a debtor to man, he did argue that God was a debtor to himself, to what he, as First Cause, had established. In this sense God remained obligated to himself to carry

25. See below, p. 56.
26. Werner Dettloff, *Die Entwicklung der Akzeptations- und Verdienstlehre von Duns Skotus bis Luther* (Münster i. W., 1963), p. 39 and passim.
27. Wolfhart Pannenberg, *Die Prädestinationslehre des Duns Skotus* (Göttingen, 1954), pp. 39–42.

through to a salutary conclusion what he had freely set in motion, a debtor to his chosen system of salvation.[28]

Scotus certainly had no desire to place God's ordinations in doubt, but he did look on them as utterly contingent and playing only a secondary role in the economy of salvation. Severe qualifications were theoretically placed on the media of salvation—churches, priests, sacraments, and infused grace— lest they presume upon God's sovereignty over his creation and the primacy of his will in salvation. Scotus sharply distinguished between what God had chosen to do in eternity (God's will) and the means by which he actually implemented his decisions in time (the execution of his will). The former was primary and crucial. *Necessary* divine relations existed only within the Godhead, there, in eternity, where Father, Son, and Holy Spirit, taking counsel with themselves, decided to create and save a portion of mankind.[29] In eternity God had determined within himself everything that would be, including who would and who would not be saved; having so determined, he then, freely and wisely, but also secondarily, elected agents to execute his will in time. Means other than churches, priests, sacraments, and infused grace *could* have been chosen, for in eternity an infinite number of possibilities lay before him. Indeed, he was free to save people directly without any intervening agents. The choice of particular means to execute the divine will had nothing to do with any intrinsic value they possessed, and their importance continued to lie only in their having been chosen by God. For Scotus, the means of salvation were like the crown of a king or the flag of a nation; their value lay not in themselves but in God's decision to identify with them, to make them symbols and instruments of divine presence and will. Scotus wrote of the grace-induced habit of love: "Love [*caritas*] is a true reason for divine acceptance, but it is the second, not the first reason, and it is contingent, not necessary."[30] Beyond any intrinsic goodness such acts of love may possess, they merit salvation only because God has gratuitously promised to accept them as such.[31]

What counted first, for Scotus, was God's pleasure: if God willed in eternity to save a person, it would be done; how it was accomplished remained secondary. To put the issue another way, for Scotus, in distinction from

28. Cf. *Summa theologiae*, Ia IIae, Q. 114, art. 1, ad tert.: "Quia actio nostra non habet rationem meriti nisi ex praesuppositione divinae ordinationis, non sequitur quod Deus efficiatur simpliciter debitor nobis, sed sibi ipsi: inquantum debitum est ut sua ordinatio impleatur." See also Ia, Q. 19 (Utrum voluntas Dei semper impleatur), art. 6, ad tert.

29. Paul Vignaux, *Justification et Prédestination au 14ᵉ siècle* (Paris, 1934), pp. 17, 27–28.

30. "Caritas est ratio acceptandi objectiva: non prima, sed secunda; non necessaria, sed contingens." Cited by Vignaux, *Justification et Prédestination*, p. 20.

31. "Ille actus sit condignum meritum, hoc est ultra naturam et bonitatem actus intrinsecam, ex mera gratuita acceptatione divina" (I *Sent.* [Vives ed.], Q. 3, d. 17, art. 26, p. 85).

Aquinas and other contemporaries, people were beautiful to God because God first loved them; God did not first love them because they were intrinsically beautiful. Confessed and graced to the fullest possible measure, one was still worthy of salvation only because God had willed one to be such. Scotus wanted to communicate this point above all others, and it became one on which Ockham also would dwell.

This subtle but important difference between Scotus and Aquinas on the nature and role of secondary causes in salvation found expression also in their understanding of the way sacraments work. For Aquinas, sacraments were instrumental causes of grace and salvation. They really contained and communicated grace; that was why they were so indispensable to salvation. A parallel may here be drawn with Thomist epistemology:[32] as Aquinas believed that universals were really in things and, as so-called intelligible species, also really in the mind, so he believed that grace was really in sacramental rituals and elements and, as an accidental form, also really in the soul. Scotus, by contrast, identified with a tradition that explained the efficacy of the sacraments in terms of a covenant made by God. Sacraments work not because they intrinsically contain and convey grace, as a cause intrinsically contains and conveys its effects (Aquinas),[33] but because God has agreed to be present with his grace when the sacraments are performed; they are *conditiones sine quibus non* for the reception of grace.[34] Where Aquinas placed the secondary cause, the sacrament itself, in the foreground, Scotus placed the will of God. Sacraments were efficacious media of grace for both, but for Scotus they were emphatically subordinate to the divine will. Aquinas left a succinct, critical summary of the alternatives:

> Not all theologians are agreed on how sacraments work. Some contend that no power resides in them, but that when they are received grace is granted by God then specially present; their causality is like that of a *conditio sine qua non*, as, for instance, when by commercial convention the bearer receives so much money on presentation of an equivalent token. So God has convenanted that whoever takes a genuine sacrament will receive grace, not from the outward sign [i.e., not from the sacramental ritual and elements themselves], but from God. This opinion, which appears to have been held by the Master of the Sentences, does not sufficiently bring out the greater dignity of the Christian

32. See below, p. 49.
33. Gilby, *St. Thomas Aquinas: Theological Texts*, no. 599, p. 357.
34. On sine qua non causality, see W. J. Courtenay, "Covenant and Causality in Pierre d'Ailly," *Speculum* 46 (1971): 99–119; Oberman, *Harvest of Medieval Theology*, p. 189.

sacraments. . . . We should go farther and affirm that the sacraments of the New Law really contribute to the reception of grace.[35]

For Scotus and his followers, there was nothing necessary and absolute this side of eternity. That is the upshot of these discussions about secondary causes. All medieval theologians, of course, subscribed to this in principle, but after the presumptuous syntheses of the thirteenth century, a systematic restatement seemed required. Scotus's intention had been not to denigrate created things, but to define their nature more accurately in the light of eternity. To some, however, Scotist "divine psychology" seemed a very unnatural perspective with mischievous consequences for the church and its media of salvation. Most people, both simple and learned, found priests and sacraments primary in the actual course of salvation; the church was the point at which believers consciously dealt with God—there, where he revealed and executed his will in time, not while he was formulating it in eternity.

A strong critical reaction to Scotus's views came from Peter Auriole, O.F.M. (ca. 1280–1322). Although philosophically in agreement with Ockham on epistemological questions, Auriole was not prepared to entertain the new departures of Scotist covenant theology. Beginning with a basic Thomist position on the importance of the created habit of grace, he drew the extreme conclusion Scotus had warned against. Auriole rebutted Scotus by literally standing his argument on its head. Where Scotus had exalted the divine will as the primary and crucial cause of salvation, Auriole insisted that the reason for divine acceptance lay "in re," in the very nature of the one accepted and saved. Against the Scotist axiom "Nothing created must, for reasons intrinsic to it, be accepted by God," Auriole argued that God could only be present where grace and love were present: "Love is the cause of divine acceptance by its very nature and of necessity" (*Caritas est ratio acceptationis ex natura rei et de necessitate*).[36] As iniquity was intrinsically despicable to God and repelled him, love was intrinsically agreeable and attracted him. By nature God inclined to all who possessed and evidenced his grace; he loved people only as they were themselves beautiful. If man could be justified without a habit of love, Auriole concluded, then it would never have been given to him, for neither God nor nature "multiplies entities uselessly or beyond necessity."[37] Salvation was a matter of like attracting

---

35. Gilby, *St. Thomas Aquinas: Theological Texts,* no. 596, p. 355. On the reference to the commercial conventions of the time, which are obviously influencing theological thinking, see W. J. Courtenay, "The King and the Leaden Coin: The Economic Background of 'sine qua non' Causality," *Traditio* 28 (1972): 185–209.

36. Vignaux, *Justification et prédestination,* pp. 43, 52; Dettloff, *Die Entwicklung der Akzeptations- und Verdienstlehre von Duns Skotus bis Luther,* pp. 39, 47, 76.

37. Vignaux, *Justification et prédestination,* p. 57.

like, not of covenants and willed agreements. Auriole believed that such a point of view ensured equity in salvation: to deal with people according to their intrinsic nature and value is to deal with them justly; to consider what they are and do as secondary is arbitrary and unjust.[38]

It is not fanciful to draw a parallel between Auriole's defense of the created habit of grace on the theological level and the proclamations of the church's temporal importance that were occurring during his lifetime in the ecclesiopolitical sphere. Auriole wrote at a time when the medieval church was fighting a losing battle to retain its legal and economic power in France and England. In this period the king of France hounded Pope Boniface VIII to his death and exercised inordinate influence over a new papacy removed from Rome to Avignon. Auriole's theory of grace and salvation was a kind of soteriological *Unam sanctam,* a declaration of the irresistible power of the church's proscriptions, sacraments, and grace against a point of view that reduced them to the limited status of contingent means for the execution of the divine will.

Auriole believed that acts of love intrinsically won divine acceptance whether they were considered in terms of God's absolute or his ordained power,[39] that is, whether one dealt with God in eternity or with the execution of his will in time. If such a point of view exaggerated the Thomist view of grace, the response of William of Ockham was an extreme restatement of the Scotist alternative. Wielding what may be described as a theological version of his more famous philosophical razor,[40] Ockham exalted what he called a "famous proposition of theologians" that acknowledged the absolute power of God: "Whatever God can produce by means of secondary causes, he can directly produce and preserve without them" (*Quidquid Deus producit mediantibus causis secundis potest immediate sine illis producere et conservare*).[41] As, by his absolute power, God could produce in the mind intuitive knowledge of something nonexistent, so could he save people without infused habits of grace: "It is possible for someone to be accepted and loved by God without any inherent supernatural form in his soul; it is even possible for someone who has a supernatural form [of grace] in his soul not to be accepted by God."[42] Unlike Auriole, Ockham saw no necessary relationship between salvation and grace-induced habits of love.

---

38. Ibid., p. 73.
39. Dettloff, *Die Entwicklung der Akzeptations- und Verdienstlehre,* p. 47.
40. See below, p. 56.
41. *Ockham: Philosophical Writings,* ed. Philotheus Boehner, O.F.M. (New York, 1962), p. 25.
42. Cited by Dettloff, *Die Entwicklung der Akzeptations- und Verdienstlehre,* p. 264. See also Gordon Leff, *William of Ockham: The Metamorphosis of Scholastic Discourse* (Manchester, 1975), pp. 470–75.

Ockham's reputation as a revolutionary theological thinker has resulted from the extremes to which he went to establish the contingent character of churches, priests, sacraments, and habits of grace. He drew on two traditional sources. The first was Augustine's teaching that the church on earth was *permixta,* that is, that some who appear to be saints may not be, and some who appear not to be saints may in fact be so, for what is primary and crucial in salvation is never *present* grace and righteousness, but the gift of perseverance, which God gives only the elect known to him.[43] Ockham's second source was the distinction between the absolute and ordained powers of God, the most basic of Ockham's theological tools. Ockham understood this critical distinction as follows:

> Sometimes we mean by God's power those things which he does according to laws he himself has ordained and instituted. These things he is said to do by ordained power [*de potentia ordinata*]. But sometimes God's power is taken to mean his ability to do anything that does not involve a contradiction, regardless of whether or not he has ordained that he would do it. For God can do many things that he does not choose to do. . . . These things he is said to be able to do by his absolute power [*de potentia absoluta*].[44]

Ockham seemed to delight in demonstrating the contingency of God's ordained power—what God had actually chosen to do in time—by contrasting it with his absolute power, the infinite possibilities open to him in eternity. According to his absolute power, God could have chosen to save people in ways that seem absurd and even blasphemous.[45] For example, he could have incarnated himself in a stone or an ass rather than in a man,[46] or he could have required that he be hated rather than loved as the condition of salvation.[47] Such statements have been interpreted as sheer, destructive

43. *City of God,* bk. 1, ch. 35, p. 21.

44. *Quodlibeta* VI, q. 1, cited by Dettloff, *Die Entwicklung der Akzeptations- und Verdienstlehre,* p. 282 and Courtenay, "Nominalism and Late Medieval Religion," p. 40.

45. Later thinkers apparently looked on God's absolute power as *presently* active, that is, they believed that God could and did on occasion override his ordinations by his absolute power—as when miracles interrupted the ordained laws of nature or when he converted St. Paul directly from heaven. Ockham saw such things as being within the scope of God's *ordained* power and stressed the normative character of present divine action, that is, God's fidelity to what he had in fact chosen to do, secondary and contingent though it was. See Oberman, *Harvest of Medieval Theology,* pp. 45–46; William J. Courtenay, "Nominalism and Late Medieval Religion," in *The Pursuit of Holiness in Late Medieval and Renaissance Religion,* ed. Charles Trinkaus and Heiko A. Oberman (Leiden, 1974), pp. 37–43; Ozment, "Mysticism, Nominalism, and Dissent," in ibid., pp. 70–71.

46. Oberman, *Harvest of Medieval Theology,* pp. 255–58.

47. Leff, *William of Ockham,* pp. 497–98.

mischief on Ockham's part, and they largely account for his reputation as a skeptic. What other purpose can speculation on what God could have done and is theoretically still free to do serve than to make people doubt the laws of nature and the authority of the church? One critic has labeled Ockham's theology an "as if theology," a theology of possibilities that belittles the actual teaching of Scripture and tradition.[48] Another has accused him of emptying the concept of infused grace of any meaning, putting the church on the defensive against its secular critics, and crippling forever the enterprise of scholastic theology.[49] If God's will is everything, grace and love seem unnecessary for salvation. If churches, priests, and sacraments make up only one of an infinite number of ways in which God could save people, how essential are they in the final analysis? Who, after Ockham, would aspire to write a *Summa theologiae?* Contingency seems so to fill the earth in Ockham's theology that his critics have even found in it the beginning of modern relativism.

Others argue that Ockham's theology was a wholesome defense of God's freedom over his creation, very much within the Augustinian theological tradition. His speculation on God's absolute power is seen to be a sound, if occasionally shocking, reminder of the finitude of creatures—and at a point in history when popes and canon lawyers seemed to forget that the church, too, was a creature in time. In the most recent scholarship, Ockham has emerged as a conservative reformer, not a revolutionary. Rather than believing that God actually suspended the laws of nature and ignored the priestly sacramental system of salvation, despite his theoretical ability to do so, Ockham too taught that God normally saved people by grace-induced habits of love. Where he drew the line more indelibly than most, however, was at the suggestion that people were *necessarily* saved by such habits. That, he believed, was an insult to both human and divine freedom.

It is the essence of the Ockhamist theology that developed from Scotist principles that salvation could never finally be dependent upon qualities within individuals or upon assumed real connections between God, grace, and the soul, even though God had elected to save people by infused habits of grace. In matters of salvation, beauty, in the final analysis, lay always and only in the eye of the divine beholder. Man's salvation depended ultimately on the trustworthiness of the divine will, on God's fidelity to his ordinations, on whether God would keep his word. Here was the unique emphasis of both Ockhamist theology and philosophy. Covenants—words and promises—linked the soul with God in matters of salvation just as verbal conventions

48. Erwin Iserloh, *Gnade und Eucharistie in der philosophischen Theologie des Wilhelm von Ockham: Ihre Bedeutung für die Ursachen der Reformation* (Wiesbaden, 1956), pp. 77, 179–80. See also Gordon Leff, *Bradwardine and the Pelagians* (Cambridge, 1957), p. 132.

49. Dettloff, *Die Entwicklung der Akzeptations- und Verdienstlehre,* pp. 363–65.

linked the mind with reality in matters of true knowledge.[50] People came to grips with the world around them through signs and terms voluntarily instituted; and they worked out their salvation on the basis of laws voluntarily established by God.

Far from issuing in a destructive fideism, this point of view was at least as conducive to the conservation of a vibrant ecclesiastical institution and spiritual life as a more generous view of the theological reach of reason and the metaphysical concept of the working of grace. If, as Ockham argued, revelation was the exclusive access to God, then much hinged on the example and credibility of its custodian; in the very contingency of the Christian church lay an urgent mandate to reform it, not to oppose it, and certainly not to seek alternatives to it. Secondary though they were to the divine will, biblical revelation and sacraments were all people had, or could expect to have, of God in this life, and as such, their guardian must be immaculate. It was out of such considerations that Ockham, alone among the great scholastic theologians, distinguished himself by daring to challenge the legitimacy of a pope (John XXII) whom he believed to be heretical in his theological teaching and outrageously presumptuous in his claims to temporal power. From this perspective Ockham's theology contained a profound ethical mandate.[51]

In arguing against Peter Auriole, Ockham, contrary to his stated intention, left himself open to the charge of Pelagianism. In opposition to Auriole's making salvation conditional upon the presence of a supernatural habit of grace, Ockham argued that one could perform works acceptable to God simply by doing the best one could with one's natural moral ability *(ex puris naturalibus)*.[52] Not only did Ockham believe it possible for those lacking such a habit to love God above all things and detest sin, but he argued further that God found it "fitting" to reward with an infusion of grace those who did so. Whereas Aquinas and Auriole had required the presence of such grace before any positive relationship with God could exist, Ockham made the reception of grace a reward for prior moral effort.

Ockham's intention, again in the spirit of Scotist covenant theology, had been to exalt God's will as the decisive agent in salvation: will freely responding to will brought God and man together and initiated the process of salvation without the need for any intervening, infused supernatural habit. In so arguing, Ockham appeared to free divine acceptance from absolute

---

50. See below, pp. 60, 244.

51. See Arthur S. McGrade, *The Political Thought of William of Ockham: Personal and Institutional Principles* (Cambridge, 1974), pp. 47–74, 185–96.

52. Vignaux, *Justification et prédestination*, pp. 120–24; Leff, *William of Ockham*, pp. 293–95.

dependence on infused habits of grace only to make God's will dependent on the good works man could do in his natural moral state. Unassisted ethical cooperation now preceded, as a condition, the infusion of grace, which, with subsequent ethical cooperation, won man salvation. To the traditional mind such an argument was Pelagianism.

Ockham anticipated such a charge and attempted to rebut it. He argued that Pelagius had taught that man in his natural state, without divine grace, was able to avoid all actual and original sin and perform good works worthy, not just of the reward of grace, but of eternal life itself. That, Ockham maintained, was something he himself could allow only as a theoretical possibility within God's absolute power.[53] From Ockham's point of view, the basic difference between himself and Pelagius was that Pelagius believed that people could earn salvation by doing their natural moral best, while he taught that they could only receive the *grace necessary to salvation* by such effort. Critics have insisted that Ockham's teaching was, at the very least, "semi-Pelagian."[54] Ockham, however, remained convinced that the rewarding of moral effort with an infusion of grace was a set part of God's chosen way of salvation. If that was Pelagianism, it was such by God's own design.

The great Augustine scholar Gregory of Rimini (d. 1358) agreed fully with Ockham's criticism of Auriole; only by God's having freely chosen to create it (*ex mera ordinatione et voluntate divina*) did there exist any necessary connection between salvation and works of grace. However, Gregory was less interested in Auriole's errors than in Ockham's. He pounced on Ockham's statement that man could naturally do good works and love God above all things without the special aid of grace. Despite Ockham's own protests, Gregory interpreted this to mean that a person could actually become worthy of eternal life by the exercise of his natural moral ability—sheer Pelagianism, even by Ockham's definition.[55] Gregory shared Augustine's deep pessimism about human nature and believed that without the special assistance of grace man was not only completely incapable of morally

53. "Et si dicis quod prima conclusio continet errorem Pelagii, respondeo quod non: quia Pelagius posuit quod de facto non requiritur gratia ad vitam aeternam habendam, sed quo actus ex puris naturalibus elicitus est meritorius vitae aeternae de condigno. Ego autem pono quod solum est meritorius per potentiam Dei absolutam acceptantem" (*Quodlibeta* VI, Q. 1, cited by Vignaux, *Justification et prédestination*, p. 127); "Ad errorem Pelagii dico quod ipse posuit quod aliquis ex puris naturalibus potest vitare omne peccatum actuale et originale et mereri vitam eternam de condigno. Et in hoc errat" (*Dubitationes addititie* AA–BB; cited by Leff, *William of Ockham*, p. 494, n. 208; see also Iserloh, *Gnade und Eucharistie*, p. 127).

54. Oberman, *The Harvest of Medieval Theology*, pp. 209–11, against Vignaux, who does not believe Ockham was Pelagian. See also Leff, *William of Ockham*, p. 495, who agrees with Vignaux.

55. Vignaux, *Justification et prédestination*, pp. 149–52; Dettloff, *Die Entwicklung der Akzeptations- und Verdienstlehre*, pp. 317–22.

good acts, but his every deed was deficient. Even Adam in Paradise required God's special assistance to do anything good.[56] If Adam in paradise needed special divine aid to know and do what was good, how much more so fallen man? Gregory's final word to Ockham was an uncompromising Augustinian-Scotist doctrine of supralapsarian predestination as extreme as any in the Middle Ages. According to Gregory, God saved no one because of his foreknowledge of the good he would do, nor did he damn anyone because of his foreknowledge of the evil he would commit; he predestined and reprobated in eternity purely as he pleased, without any consideration of merit or demerit.[57]

Although no new arguments appeared, the debate did not end with Gregory of Rimini. On the eve of the Reformation, Gabriel Biel (ca. 1420–1495), an Ockhamist theologian whom Luther studied closely, defended Ockham against Rimini's attack. Luther, in turn, took up Rimini's banner against both Ockham and Biel and accused the whole of late medieval theology, with the exception of Gregory of Rimini, of being tainted with Pelagianism.[58] Less than a decade later, in 1524, Erasmus defended a position very close to that of Ockham and Biel against Luther in a famous debate over whether the will was bound or free in salvation.[59] The basic controversy persisted into the confessional age of the late sixteenth and seventeenth centuries, when Socinians and Arminians opposed Calvinist doctrines of original sin and predestination on the Protestant side and Jesuits battled the Augustinian strains in Jansenism on the Catholic. In religious controversy nothing is so new as what is old.

How Man Truly Knows:
Theories of Knowledge
from Augustine to Ockham

THE major philosophical problem of the Middle Ages was the nature of human knowledge. What did it mean to know something and to know it truly? How did knowing occur? What were its presuppositions and its limits? How these questions were answered depended very much on how one conceived man and reality. Medieval epistemology was a long essay on medieval man's concept of himself and his world. To the question "How does man know truly?" three distinct answers were given, one by Augustine, another by Thomas Aquinas,

56. "Bene vivere sine adjutorio Dei etiam in Paradisio non erat in potestate; erat autem in potestate male vivere" (cited by Vignaux, *Justification et prédestination,* p. 159).

57. Ibid., pp. 165–72.

58. See below, p. 232.

59. See below, p. 294.

Theology, the Queen of the Sciences. Gregor Reisch. A woodcut depicting the levels of scholastic learning, from Gregor Reisch's *Margarita philosophica* (1503). The figure opening the door to the house of knowledge is Nicostrata. A daughter of the river god Ladon in Greek legend, she came to be credited with introducing the alphabet into Italy and adapting it for use by the Latins. At the lower levels the students study the grammars of Donatus and Priscian, then move up to logic (Aristotle), rhetoric and poetry (Cicero), and arithmetic. Thereafter they study music (Pythagoras), geometry (Euclid), astronomy (Ptolemy) and, going still higher, physics and ethics (Seneca). Finally, they reach the summit of knowledge, theology and metaphysics (Peter Lombard).

and the third by William of Ockham, and each had its peculiar consequences for the shape of theology and religious institutions.

Augustine

Augustine was heir to both Platonic and Christian traditions of thought and is commonly viewed as their most perfect union. As Thomism is regarded as the exemplary synthesis of Aristotelian philosophy and Christianity, Augustinianism is viewed as an exemplary synthesis of Platonism, especially in its Plotinian or Neoplatonic form, and Christianity. In the *Confessions*, Augustine actually recounted three major stages of personal conviction—Manichaeism, Platonism, and Christianity—and elements of all three remained prominent in his mature thought.

The philosophical system with which he identified in his youth was Manichaeism, a philosophy in many ways ideally suited to a young intellectual. Its origins were Eastern and its name derived from Mani (215–73), who taught that the world was divided into spheres of light and goodness and of darkness and evil, both real and substantial.[60] Manichaeans further believed that a peculiar deity reigned over each of these spheres. Christians influenced by Manichaeism associated the wrathful God of the Old Testament with the world of darkness and evil and the loving God of the New Testament with that of light and goodness. Manichaeans saw the human soul as a member of the sphere of light, but imprisoned in a body and a physical world that were essentially evil. Their belief that evil was a substance in its own right and not merely an accident of being, as Christianity taught, made Manichaeism a heresy in the eyes of the church. Christians also considered the extreme disparagement of the body and the physical world heretical, although Christianity, too, disparaged the physical creation when it considered its fallenness.

To understand the attractiveness of Manichaeism it must be remembered that the ancient and medieval world, accustomed to regular famine, plague, and war, knew firsthand the cruelty and impermanence of physical existence. Augustine and his contemporaries witnessed the slow collapse of the Roman Empire. Manichaeism became for many an intellectually satisfying explanation of this painful experience. But the Manichaeans also inspired their adherents. They taught that the soul, as a particle of light entrapped in darkness, must struggle throughout life to lift itself through the tiers of darkness that enshroud the physical world into the sphere of light. The return of the soul to its eternal origin began already in this life. The truly

60. See Steven Runciman, *The Medieval Manichee* (Cambridge, 1947).

elect, the special group of perfect ones, made their way out of the darkness and into the light by the solitary and ascetic route of severe self-denial in food, association, and sex. Ordinary devotees were permitted, however, to take a more circuitous route; they might, with voluntary restraint, marry and work in the world. Their final salvation, however, was seen to come more slowly, for they had to pass through many purifying reincarnations before they could return to the light from whence they came. Christians, too, practiced severe self-denial and believed in a purgatorial period after death, but unlike the Manichaeans, they derived such practice and belief from the conviction that man had fallen from an original perfection, not from a belief that his created nature was essentially corrupt.

Because evil was considered substantial and the god of darkness a real being, Manichaean philosophy understood moral lapsing. It recognized the presence of a real enemy in life and the need for near superhuman effort to resist him. Augustine later criticized the Manichaeans for relieving him of all sense of guilt, so he felt no compulsion to confess his sin.[61] On the other hand, precisely because opposition to evil required such heroic effort, Manichaean philosophy could also make the highest moral demands on its adherents. Tolerance of moral lapsing combined with high moral challenge must have appealed to the weak but idealistic young Augustine. A philosophy of life that urges one to take the highest ground, yet makes failure and defeat understandable, is most congenial for young people. Manichaean philosophy was also demanding intellectually. It taught a complex cosmology with many theological abstractions, a near incomprehensible view of the world that may also have attracted the bright young rhetorician Augustine.

Augustine finally despaired of his Manichaean teacher, Faustus, and rejected Manichaean philosophy because of what he described as two basic errors: its depiction of God as a divisible, corporeal substance and its conception of evil as an independent reality.[62] He praised the Platonists for delivering him from these errors and setting him on the path to Christianity by their teaching that God was a fully spiritual, transcendent, and inconceivable being and evil only a privation of goodness without independent substance. So highly did Augustine think of the Platonists that he imagined Plato becoming a Christian "with the change of a few words and sentiments."[63]

In the Platonic tradition Augustine also encountered a strong dualism,

61. Brown, *Augustine of Hippo*, p. 176.

62. *The Confessions of St. Augustine*, bk. 4, ch. 15, pp. 108–09; bk. 5, ch. 10, p. 127; bk. 7, ch. 1–2, pp. 158–59.

63. *Of True Religion* in *Augustine: Earlier Writings*, trans. J. H. S. Burleigh (Philadelphia, n.d.), ch. 4/6, p. 229.

which remained basic to his own philosophy and theology. The Platonists postulated a world of being, composed of eternal ideas or forms, which they believed to be immaterial, invisible, and intelligible in nature: a world on the order of mind. Juxtaposed with this world was one of becoming and flux, composed of transient, particular physical things. This cosmological dualism directly influenced the Platonist view of human nature and knowledge. To the imperishable world of forms corresponded the mind of man, which had true and sure knowledge; to the perishable world of becoming corresponded man's physical and mortal body, whose sensations and phantasms made possible only unsure faith and opinion.

For the Platonists, knowledge was always and only of the universal, never of a particular thing; when one knew something, one knew it as a universal truth. This was the fundamental epistemological axiom of the Middle Ages, not seriously challenged until William of Ockham. Platonists reasoned that knowledge belonged to the permanent world of being, while particular things were members of the transient world of becoming. Hence, it was only because individual things approximated their universal archetypes, that is, the eternal models from which they derived, and in this way continued to participate in the world of being, that they could be surely known. One knew a particular chair before one, for example, because one had direct access in one's mind to the universal concept or form, "the Chair," which a particular chair approximated and reflected. Particulars were in this way known *indirectly* through universals; the mind's *direct* contact with individual things produced only phantasms and unsure opinion.

The important presupposition behind this theory of knowledge was that only like could know like, another basic medieval axiom. Only the immaterial could affect the immaterial; an invisible, eternal soul or mind could only be moved by invisible, eternal universals. The parallel to this philosophical teaching in the sphere of theology and religion was the belief that only a soul that had been purified and "likened" to God could truly know and be one with him. This presupposition lay behind the sacraments of the church, which, by infusing grace into the soul, likened it to God so that it could truly know him. Such a view of salvation dominated medieval theology until Martin Luther challenged it by arguing that people who remained sinful in themselves and unlike God could nonetheless be one with him by faith.

Augustine shared much of the Platonic cosmological and epistemological scheme, but he transformed it in fundamental ways by integrating his Christian beliefs into it, particularly the belief in a Trinitarian God who was incarnate in Jesus Christ. According to Augustine, to have true knowledge, one must not concentrate on the sensory world outside oneself, but retreat into the eternal world within oneself, through which one can rise above oneself to truth. "Do not go abroad. Return within yourself. In the inward man dwells truth."[64] Here, in very literal form, we find the movement of Platonist epistemology from outside (the world of the senses) to within (the world of the mind) to above oneself (the world of eternal forms). The Christian modification of this scheme occurred in Augustine's identification of Christ as in the indwelling eternal Word, who teaches man the truth.

> Concerning universals of which we can have knowledge, we do not listen to anyone speaking and making sounds outside ourselves. We rather listen to Truth which presides over our minds within us. . . . Our real teacher is he who is so listened to and is said to dwell in the inner man, namely Christ, the unchangeable power and eternal wisdom of God.[65]

For the Platonists, knowledge of eternal norms and standards came by way of memory, the great "belly of the mind" (*abditum mentis*).[66] This was the doctrine of recollection, or anamnesis, according to which the mind, in a precreated state, once beheld the eternal forms of things, which have remained implanted in its memory and can again be known when memory is awakened. Plato depicted Socrates as a midwife eliciting the eternal truths of geometry from uneducated slaves and youths by simply asking them questions. The Socratic method of teaching assumed that truth was already within the student, who needed only to be awakened to it. Truth could be known by all who would simply pause in the world of flux and remember their origin in eternity.

Augustine replaced the Platonic doctrine of recollection with his own distinctive doctrine of "divine illumination," one of his most influential teachings. This doctrine placed the eternal forms of the Platonists within the mind of the triune Christian God, thereby making them truly *divine* ideas. Hence, when one plumbed the depths of one's mind in search of truth, one found there, not an innate ability to recollect eternity, as the Platonists had taught, but Christ, the eternal wisdom of God, the second person of the Trinity, whose very name was Truth. Through the illumination of Christ, indwelling truth, the mind received divine light by which it could know truly. Whether pagan or Christian, people understood and functioned within the world around them, thanks to this special grace of God. Without such divine illumination, all they would know was a chaos of phantasms. According to Augustine, just as God frees the will so that people

64. Ibid., ch. 19/72, p. 262.
65. *The Teacher*, ch. 11/38, p. 95; Cf. *Confessions*, bk. 10, chs. 5 and 8.
66. See *Confessions*, bk. 10, ch. 14, pp. 242–43.

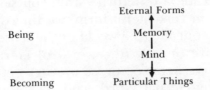

Platonic Recollection

When one enters into oneself, one finds
Christ, the eternal son of God, who mediates
the world of eternal ideas, that is, the mind
of God, which illuminates the human mind
so that it can truly know the particular things
of the world.

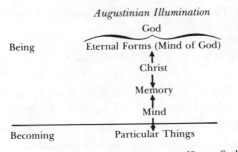

Stimulated by particular things, the mind
remembers eternal forms, which the
particular things of the world imperfectly
reflect, and in the light of this memory, that
is, through remembered forms, the mind
truly knows particular things in the world.

Augustinian Illumination

can truly do good things, so he enlightens their minds so that they can surely know. (See diagram.)

It has been argued that Augustine demeaned the body and physical life to the point that sensation played little part in his theory of knowledge.[67] He spoke of the soul's "sensing through the body," but it is not clear exactly what role sensation played for him in the knowing process. His Platonic bias against the physical world and his own Christian aversion to "the flesh" were probably influential here. The strong impression remains that he believed that all one needed for true knowledge was God and the soul.

It is at this point that the teaching of Thomas Aquinas contrasts strikingly with that of Augustine. Largely because Aristotle replaced Plato as the philosophical component of Christian theology for Aquinas, his theology contained a heightened appreciation of the physical world and the role of the senses in the knowing process.

67. See M. C. D'Arcy, S. J., "The Philosophy of St. Augustine," in M. C. D'Arcy, S. J., et al., *St. Augustine* (Cleveland, 1961), pp. 171–80.

Aquinas

In his *Metaphysics*, Aristotle puzzled over Plato's disembodied world of universals and rejected it. Such entities, he concluded, must either exist within particular things, and hence be truly related to them, or remain the products of wishful thinking, the projection of the world of perishable particulars into an imperishable world of eternal ideas.[68] Aquinas shared this Aristotelian sentiment to a large degree. He was well informed about the points at issue between Plato and Aristotle[69] and in the *Summa contra Gentiles* agreed with Aristotle that "universals are not subsistent things, but have their being only in singulars."[70] For Aquinas, as for Aristotle, the first principles of things are within things themselves.

Moving from Augustine to Aquinas, the reader is struck by Aquinas's sense of the connectedness of reality. In place of gross dualism comes detailed integration: being is in act; form is in matter; the soul is in the body; universals are in particulars. The emphasis shifts from spiritual transcendence to spiritual immanence. No longer are the world of things and the processes of sensation short-circuited. Knowledge begins with sensory experience of the visible, physical world. According to Aquinas's epistemological maxim: "There is nothing in the mind that was not first in the senses" (*Nihil in intellectu quod prius non fuerit in sensu*),[71] a most difficult axiom for Plato and Augustine and all who believe in the utterly transcendental character of ultimate reality and true knowledge.

In the Platonic-Augustinian tradition, where knowledge was possible apart from sensory experience, there was belief in innate, a priori ideas and truths. Prior to any experience of particular things, one had a true general knowledge of the world and of God. A lot could be known with one's eyes closed, so-called necessary truths of reason and even some basic data of divine revelation. The most celebrated case in point is probably Anselm of Canterbury (1033–1109), an extreme representative of this tradition, although he did not develop a formal epistemology. Anselm maintained that man had in his mind the idea of that than which nothing greater could be conceived; he insisted further that this idea must be none other than the Christian God; and he concluded still further that this idea must also exist in reality apart from the mind. In so arguing, Anselm never left his own

---

68. See D. J. Allan, *The Philosophy of Aristotle* (London, 1963), pp. 16–20; W. D. Ross, *Aristotle: A Complete Exposition of His Works and Thought* (Cleveland, 1962), pp. 155–56.

69. Thomas Gilby has nicely excerpted the meatier passages: *St. Thomas Aquinas: Philosophical Texts* (New York, 1962), pp. 239–45.

70. *Summa Contra Gentiles* I, 1, c. 65, cited in *Friedrich Ueberwegs Grundriss der Geschichte der Philosophie,* ed. Bernhard Geyer (Basel, 1967), 2:432; henceforth: Ueberweg-Geyer.

71. See Frederick Copleston, *A History of Philosophy* (Westminster, Md., 1960), 2:392–93.

mind, although some, especially his contemporary critic Guanilo, believed him to have been out of his mind. Here is the most succinct statement of Anselm's classic proof of God's existence:

> Even the fool ... must be convinced that a being than which none greater can be thought exists at least in his understanding, since when he hears this he understands it, and whatever is understood is in the understanding. But clearly that than which a greater cannot be thought cannot exist in the understanding alone. For if it is actually in understanding alone, it can be thought of as existing also in reality, and this is greater. Therefore, if that than which a greater cannot be thought is in the understanding alone, this same thing than which a greater cannot be thought is that than which a greater can be thought. But obviously this is impossible. Without doubt, therefore, there exists both in the understanding and in reality, something than which a greater cannot be thought.[72]

In his treatise *Why God Became Man (Cur Deus homo)*, Anselm attempted "to prove by necessary reasons (Christ being put out of sight, as if nothing had ever been known of him) that it is impossible for any man to be saved without him."[73] Having no recourse to revelation, remaining within the limits of reason alone, Anselm believed it possible to demonstrate the necessity of the Incarnation for man's salvation.[74] Some have argued that he was only explicating a logic peculiar to faith, not presenting himself as a skeptic who trusted reason alone.[75] Such an explanation modernizes Anselm, however, as if he were a post-Kantian theologian. The *Proslogion* and *Why God Became Man* were an eleventh-century scholar's extrapolation on the presuppositions of Platonic epistemology.

In the teaching of Thomas Aquinas the reader finds no innate, a priori ideas leading necessarily to the demonstration of eternal truths. If, as

---

72. *Proslogion*, in *A Scholastic Miscellany: Anselm to Ockham*, ed. and trans. Eugene R. Fairweather (Philadelphia, 1956), p. 74.

73. In *A Scholastic Miscellany*, p. 100.

74. William J. Courtenay points out how different Anselm's method was from that of later nominalists, concluding that they might best be seen as "opposite points of view." He summarizes: "Anselm's entire theological method depends on the fact that there is one best way of doing things—the way God did them, consistent with his nature and wisdom—*therefore*, one should be able to establish that the way God did act was the only valid way, otherwise God would not have done it that way.... The very reluctance of Anselm to engage in 'potentia absoluta discussions' [like those of the nominalists] follows from his refusal to differentiate divine nature and will or to differentiate between revealed will and the possibilities open to God before he acted" ("Necessity and Freedom in Anselm's Conception of God," in *Die Wirkungsgeschichte Anselms von Canterbury: Akten der ersten Internationalen Anselm-Tagung Bad Wimpfen—13. September bis 16 September 1970*, pp. 60–62).

75. John McIntyre, *St. Anselm and His Critics* (Edinburgh, 1954), pp. 26–29.

Aquinas argued, nothing is in the mind that was not first in the senses, then any knowledge man has, whether of eternal or temporal truths, must begin with the finite effects of the world around him. Sensation and reflection on the data of sensory experience suffice in themselves for all true knowledge. Divine illumination, as Augustine understood it, becomes unnecessary and knowing a very natural process.

When Aquinas demonstrated the existence of God and his essential attributes, he proceeded a posteriori, not a priori, that is, he argued from particular things actually experienced to a general statement of truth. His point of departure was the natural world around him, what his eyes had seen and his ears had heard, not an idea in his mind. Beginning with particular effects, Aquinas inquired after their ultimate source. The experience of change and motion raised the question of a first mover; the order of efficient causes, a first cause; contingent beings, a necessary being; degrees of perfection, the most perfect, a "pure act"; and evidence of design and purpose, a planner who organized it all.[76] The presupposition behind each of these arguments was that everything had an ultimate ontological explanation, a final reason for being, which Aquinas believed to be God.

Whereas for Augustine, the discarnate Christ mediated all true knowledge, for Aquinas, man's natural powers of sensation and reason sufficed. On this question there was no "ghost" in Aquinas's system. For Augustine, to speak of reason was to speak of the mind of man illumined by the mind of God. For Aquinas, to speak of reason was to speak of the mind of man naturally exercising its own innate talents.

Aquinas here anticipated future developments in Western thought, which, long before the Enlightenment, began to endow human reason with attributes previously accorded the Holy Trinity. In the sixteenth century Sebastian Castellio described the Holy Spirit as the "reason of [human] reason" (*ratio rationis*). He believed that reason intrinsically contained divine illumination, the light that the Augustinian tradition had ascribed to the discarnate Christ. Castellio argued against the Calvinists, who stood in the Augustinian tradition, that the conclusions of commonsense judgment, based on the normal exercise of one's reason, formed the highest court of appeal in religious disputes; he believed such judgments to be sovereign over the contradictions of Scripture, tradition, and the arguments of theologians. For Castellio, reason was a living prophet within every person and pronounced through him the very truth of God.[77]

76. See the exerpts in Gilby, *Philosophical Texts*, pp. 48–66.
77. *De arte dubitandi et confidendi, ignorandi et sciendi,* ed. Elizabeth Feist, in *Per la storia degli Eretici Italiani del Secolo XVI in Europa,* ed. D. Cantimori and E. Feist (Rome, 1937), pp. 307–14. Relevant texts are translated and discussed in my *Mysticism and Dissent* (New Haven, 1973), pp. 189–202.

Aquinas would strongly have disavowed such pretentious claims, yet his "secularization" of the knowing process was an important step in this direction. Rather than the alleged skepticism of William of Ockham, it may have been an epistemological revolution traceable to Aquinas's criticism of Augustinian epistemology that prepared the way for the modern belief that there are no truths beyond the truths of reason. Certainly no such claims could properly have evolved from the philosophical views of Augustine, for whom all knowledge remained a special gift of God, conveyed from without. Aquinas himself may have unwittingly sown the seeds for the dissolution of his own synthesis of reason and revelation and prepared the way for the rationalism of the modern world.

Turning to the mechanics of human knowledge, Aquinas defined three basic steps in the knowing process. The first was sensation, the indiscriminate collection and presentation of data to the "passive intellect," that is, the mind in a passive, receptive mood. This data entered the mind as a collection of phantasms, a confused picture of individual things, fuzzy particulars, which, however, did have certain identifiable, universal features. Aquinas, like Aristotle, believed that universality was an intrinsic quality of individual things. That individual things shared common features made possible the second step in the knowing process: the *abstraction* of the universal. The "active intellect," the mind in its active mode, isolated and abstracted the universal aspects that it found in particular things of the same species. In the third and final step of the knowing process, the abstracted universal, which Aquinas called an "intelligible species," that is, the species in an intellectual rather than an objective mode of being (*in mente* rather than *in re*), served as the medium through which the mind knew individual things.

For Aquinas, universals had both a natural being in particular things and an intellectual being, as intelligible species, in the mind. These were major points of difference with the Platonic/Augustinian tradition. There remained nonetheless more continuity between the views of Aquinas and Augustine than may at first glance appear. First, the universal, not the particular, was still the immediate object of knowledge for both. For Aquinas as much as for Augustine, the particular could be known only mediately, through the universal.[78] Neither believed that direct knowledge

---

78. As Aquinas summarizes:

Rational knowledge lights primarily on the form of natural things, and secondarily on their matter as related to form. Form as such is universal, so the mind's bent to form does not enable it to know matter except in general terms. . . . Obviously then, the reason cannot know singulars directly. . . . Nevertheless, the mind is indirectly involved with singulars facts inasmuch as it merges into the sense-powers, which are engaged with

of singulars was possible. Aquinas placed universals within things, took them out again as intelligible species in the mind, and only then, by way of these abstracted universals, did he know individual things. Save for the process of abstraction, which displaced the Augustinian doctrine of illumination, Augustine's basic epistemological conviction—that knowledge could only be of the universal—remained intact. The medieval bias in favor of spiritual or intellectual reality remained as prominent in Aquinas's epistemology as in Augustine's.

A second line of continuity between Augustine and Aquinas was the persisting belief that like could know only like. It was the generic kinship of the universal in the thing and the universal in the mind that made knowledge possible for Aquinas.[79]

There is a final commonplace. Despite his Aristotelian belief that universals were in things, Aquinas, as a theologian, also believed that they existed outside of and prior to individuals in the mind of God. Disassociating himself from the Platonists' belief in independently self-subsistent and effective forms (*per se subsistentes et causantes immediate formas sensibilium*), Aquinas still acknowledged a basic point of agreement with the Platonists: "Forms which are in matter come from forms which are without matter, and to that extent the saying of Plato is true: that separate forms are the principles of forms which are in matter."[80] Hence, Aquinas found the universal in the mind of God (*ante rem*), in the individual thing (*in re*), and, through abstraction, in the human mind (*in mente*).

As I pointed out at the outset of this chapter, epistemology is a window onto metaphysics; a theory of knowledge is a commentary on one's under-

---

particular things. The process works both ways. First in the direction from things to mind, corresponding to the movement of the sensitive part into the mind to reach its climax there. Thus the mind knows the singular by a sort of reflection, for from knowing its own object, namely some general type, it can bend back and be aware of its own activity and then continue to the concept which is a principle of the activity, and thence to the image from which the concept is drawn; in this way the mind comes by some knowledge of the singular. The second direction is from soul into things, starting from mind and leading into the sensitive parts. Because the mind governs the lower powers and the particular reason, which is the faculty of individual situations, it comes to entertain the knowledge of singular things (*De veritate*, 5, cited by Gilby, *Philosophical Texts*, pp. 247-48).

79. M. H. Carré comments: "Material things, so far as they are known, must exist in the knower, not indeed materially, but immaterially. . . . The realm of objects is a mode of the same reality which is found in consciousness; there is an essential kinship, a correspondence, between mind and things" (*Realists and Nominalists* [Oxford, 1946], p. 70).

80. *Contra Gentiles*, I, iii, c. 24, cited by Ueberweg-Geyer, p. 432. Aquinas, as a Christian thinker, believed, like Augustine, that the forms of things existed within and had their effect in the world only through the divine mind.

standing of reality. In contrast to the strong dualism of the Platonic/
Augustinian tradition, a striking feature of Thomist philosophy is its appreciation of the interconnectedness of reality. The underlying metaphysical presupposition of Thomist epistemology was a belief that real relations
held between God, the mind of man, and the world of finite things. The
universal in the individual thing was believed to be really related to that
which preexisted in the mind of God as an archetype of creation, and to that
which came to exist in the mind of man as an abstracted intelligible species.
For Aquinas, God, man, and the world were connected to one another not
by verbal or artificial relations, but by the structure of reality itself. They
related to one another like tendons to bones and muscles, not like a bride to
a bridegroom or a friend to a friend; the relationship was organic, not
covenantal. Gilson offered the following summation of Aquinas's metaphysical vision and the "spirit of Thomism":

> That knowing being, man, is bound to God by his deepest ontological
> root, and has to look no further [than to himself and to his experience
> in the world] for the entrance to the paths which will lead him to the
> knowledge of his cause. If he pursues its metaphysical analysis far
> enough, any being whatsoever will place man in the presence of God.
> God is in everything as its cause. His action affects everything in its very
> act of being. . . : *Oportet quod Deus sit in omnibus rebus, et intime.*[81]

The assumption that real relations existed between God, man, and the
world made possible Aquinas's confidence in a posteriori proofs of God's
existence; finite effects led necessarily to their origin, because they were
really connected with it. The same assumption underlay Aquinas's distinctive views on the "analogical" character of human knowledge and discourse
about God.[82] According to Aquinas, one could speak meaningfully of one's
relationship to God by analogy with one's relationship with one's fellow man
because a real relationship existed between the values people shared and
those God had prescribed. Such discourse was not univocal, that is, a perfect
one-to-one correspondence, because in relation to God people remained
imperfect. If, for example, I say that God is good, having derived my
concept of goodness from experience with my fellow man, I can only mean
by this a goodness of a much higher order than that which pertains among
men. On the other hand, Aquinas believed there was a definite similarity

81. *The Christian Philosophy of St. Thomas Aquinas*, trans. L. K. Shook, C.S.B. (New York,
1956), p. 372.
82. See the texts excerpted by Gilby, *Philosophical Texts*, pp. 93–94; Copleston, *A History
of Philosophy*, 2:352–58.

between human and divine goodness and such statements about God were not sheer conjecture. If they were not univocal, neither were they equivocal. For Aquinas, human experience was a positive basis for understanding religious relations, because God and man shared a common reality. Aquinas, who had a genius for finding the middle way, used the term *analogical* to describe discourse about God that derived from human experience and which neither fully corresponded nor yet completely missed the mark. People knew and spoke of God by analogy with human experience because a real, albeit imperfect, relation existed between God, man, and the world of human discourse.

Ockham

William of Ockham has the reputation of a revolutionary within the scholastic, spiritual, and ecclesiopolitical traditions of the later Middle Ages: within scholasticism because of his teaching on universal concepts and the absolute power of God; within spirituality because of his close identification with the cause of Franciscan poverty; and within church and state because of his call for the removal of Pope John XXII (1316–34) from office and his support of the pope's political adversary, Louis IV of Bavaria. In 1324, Pope John summoned Ockham from England to the papal court in Avignon to defend alleged errors in his philosophy and theology. While there, Ockham concluded that Pope John, the most powerful of the Avignon popes, was himself manifestly heretical. This was not because the pope had interrupted Ockham's studies, although this seems to have put Ockham, who had an unusually high sense of the scholar's calling, in a critical frame of mind. The pope's error lay rather in his condemnation of the views on apostolic poverty held by the left wing of the Franciscan order.[83] After leaving Avignon, Ockham joined the outlawed Franciscan superior general, Michael of Cesena, in refuge at the court of Louis IV, from where he wrote tracts against Pope John and in defense of both the Franciscans and the emperor.

We are here, however, concerned with Ockham's break with the traditional epistemologies of the Middle Ages. Ockham opposed theories of knowledge espoused by Augustine, Henry of Ghent, Thomas Aquinas, and especially Duns Scotus, although Scotus had helped point the way for Ock-

83. These events are chronicled by McGrade in *The Political Thought of William of Ockham*, pp. 1–78. Ockham later charged the pope with holding heretical views on the beatific vision, since John had taught that the souls of the faithful did not fly immediately upon their death to their final resting place in heaven, there to await reunion with their resurrected bodies at the end of time, but rather lay dormant with their dead bodies, pending the latter's resurrection. On the poverty dispute, see below, p. 109.

ham in both his philosophical and theological teaching.[84] In each case
Ockham challenged the assumption that universals or some similar self-
subsisting common nature played the essential role in the knowing process.[85] Ockham did not believe that a distinct and independent universal
could be in an individual thing. If such a universal were in a thing in the
normal way in which one thing is said to be "in" another, then it was either a
part of the thing itself, like a heart within a body, and therefore not a
universal but a particular, or it was identical with the thing in which it was,
and hence also not a universal but the individual itself. Nor could Ockham
grasp the concept of an abstracted "intelligible species." If such an undem-
onstrable phantom was the key agent of human knowledge, then knowledge was surely in a precarious state; dependence on such an obscure
explanation seemed to invite skepticism.[86] It was in order to *secure* the
foundations of human knowledge, not to undermine them, that Ockham
wielded his famous razor against his predecessors.

Ockham's razor was a principle of economy in explanation. "Plurality is
not to be posited without necessity" (*Nunquam ponenda est pluritas sine necessitate*); "What can be explained by assuming fewer terms is vainly explained
by assuming more" (*Frustra fit per plura quod potest fieri per pauciora*).[87] Of
what use, Ockham asked, beyond confusing the mind, was talk about universals in things, or a formally distinct common nature in things (Scotus), or
intelligible species in the mind? According to Ockham's razor, the simpler
explanation is always the better; the fewer moving parts in an argument, the
less wear and tear on the mind. This principle was not original with Ockham. Peter of Spain, later Pope John XXI (1276–77), stated it in his com-
pendium of logic, the *Summulae logicales*. But Ockham was the first to make
a virtue of it, to become, as Reinhold Seeberg put it, "fanatical about
logic."[88]

Ockham's epistemological revolution came through his insistence that

84. Gordon Leff has a nice summary of the points of contact and divergence between
Scotism and Ockhamism. See *The Dissolution of the Medieval Outlook: An Essay on Intellectual
and Spiritual Change in the Fourteenth Century* (New York, 1976), p. 56.

85. For Duns Scotus, "being qua being," not an intelligible species (as for Aquinas) or God
(as for Augustine and Henry of Ghent), was the primary natural object of the intellect. See
Effrem Bettoni, *Duns Scotus: The Basic Principles of His Philosophy* (Washington, 1961), p. 32.

86. Ockham was hardly alone in this sentiment. Peter Auriole, Durandus of St. Pourçain,
and Henry of Harclay also denied the need for intelligible species in order to have true
knowledge of individual things.

87. I *Sent.* d. 27, q. 2 K; *Summa totius logicae*, I, 12 (Venice, 1522), fol. 6 r. A; cited by
Ueberweg-Geyer, p. 576.

88. *Lehrbuch der Dogmengeschichte* (Erlangen, 1898), 2:170.

individual things could be known as individual things, that direct, un-
mediated knowledge of particulars was possible.[89] He reached this conclusion by reducing all human knowledge to two basic categories: intuitive and
abstractive. Intuitive knowledge was that which formed the basis for all
"existential judgments," that is, all statements that an individual thing presently exists and can be confirmed by eyewitnesses;[90] to intuit means to
behold and gaze on something attentively. Ockham believed it natural to
man to know individual things directly in an intuitive way. If one sees
something and others attest it, then it is known; that was the simplest and
most credible account of how man knows. Knowledge of reality was therefore not dependent on mediated contact with it through assumed self-
subsisting universals in things, or common natures, or abstracted universals
in the mind. People had a direct, evident, conscious experience of individual things, and this intuitive contact with reality sufficed, in and of itself,
to certify human knowledge. For Ockham, the mind naturally had a
proper, simple, unconfused, and fully dependable cognition of singular
things. No more need be said; nothing else need be postulated; no further
terms need be assumed.

Ockham described the second basic type of knowledge as abstractive and
here offered his account of the universal aspect of knowledge. Unlike intuitive knowledge, abstractive knowledge did not concern itself with existential
judgments; it was knowledge people had regardless of whether or not what
they knew presently existed outside the mind.[91] Abstractive knowledge was

89. Leff summarizes:

In the course of establishing [the primacy of the individual], Ockham makes knowledge
of the material individual at once directly accessible to the intellect and more perfect
than that of a universal concept or image itself derived from knowledge of individuals.
He thereby reverses both the traditional Augustinian belief in the independent non-
sensory origin of intelligible knowledge, as coming exclusively from the intellect, and the
Christian Aristotelian—predominantly Thomist—view of universal knowledge as primary and the proper object of the intellect. In each of these he was preceded by Duns
Scotus; but he surpassed Duns in making the individual alone real and always the first
object known, regardless of whether or not distinctly known, and denying any role to
species in its attainment (*William of Ockham*, pp. 76–77).

90. "Intuitive cognition of a thing is cognition that enables us to know whether the thing
exists or does not exist, in such a way that, if the thing exists, then the intellect immediately
judges that it exists and evidently knows that it exists, unless the judgment happens to be
impeded through the imperfection of this cognition" (*Ockham: Philosophical Writings*, p. 23).
See the discussion by Paul Vignaux, *Nominalisme au XIVe siècle* (Montreal, 1948), pp. 11–45;
Philotheus Boehner, "The Notitia Intuitiva of Non-existents According to William of
Ockham," in *Collected Articles on Ockham*, ed. E. M. Buytaert (St. Bonaventure, N.Y., 1958),
pp. 268–91; and Leff, *William of Ockham*, pp. 6–14.

91. "Abstractive cognition . . . is that knowledge by which it cannot be evidently known

founded on intuitive knowledge, however, and Ockham assured his reader that the two were closely connected; all intellectual abstractions ultimately derived from and were based upon actual experience of a world outside the mind.

Ockham described one's memory of what was once empirically verified as *simple* abstractive knowledge. Here were all the objects and events of past experience, things that one once beheld and now retained and could retrieve in memory, whether or not they presently existed outside the mind. The mind, however, could also construct new objects and relationships, truly "mental beings," which never had nor ever would exist literally outside the mind. Such constructive mental activity formed *complex* abstractive knowledge. Here, according to Ockham, were all the imaginative fictions and formulas of purely abstract thought, and along with them universal concepts. By the same process by which the mind created a unicorn by imaginatively grafting a spirelike horn onto the forehead of a horse, it legislated universals. From its intuitive and simple abstractive knowledge of many individuals of the same species, the mind generalized a universal concept and term that stood for all members of that species. For example, from my intuitive knowledge (or past experience) of many individual trees, which now exist in my memory as simple abstractive knowledge, I naturally form in my mind, as a sign of the many, a singular concept, "the Tree," which stands for all the individual trees I have and will ever know. This concept also becomes a term I can use to designate this species in conversation with others who have had the same experience of individual trees.

Ockham argued emphatically that such universals had no independent existence in individual things outside the mind: "No universal really exists outside the mind in individual substances, nor is any universal a part of the substance or being of individual things."[92] "The universal is not in the thing any more than the word 'man' is in Socrates or in others it denotes."[93] For Ockham, universals really existed in only two modes and places: naturally in the mind and conventionally in words.

> There are two kinds of universal. There is one which is naturally universal [*universale naturaliter*], that is, it is a sign naturally predicable of many things in the same way that smoke naturally signifies fire, a groan

whether a contingent fact exists or does not exist. In this way abstractive cognition abstracts from existence and non-existence; because, in opposition to intuitive cognition, it does not enable us to know the existence of what does exist or the non-existence of what does not exist" (*Ockham: Philosophical Writings*, pp. 23–24).

92. From the introduction to the *Expositio aurea*, cited by Ueberweg-Geyer, p. 576.

93. Cited by Paul Vignaux, *Philosophy in the Middle Ages: An Introduction* (Cleveland, 1962), p. 169.

the pain of a sick man, and laughter an inner joy. Such a universal is nothing other than a content of the mind [*intentio animae*]; therefore no substance or accident outside the mind is such a universal. . . . The other kind of universal is so by convention [*universale per voluntariam institutionem*]. In this way an uttered word, which is really a single quality, is universal; for it is a conventional sign meant to signify many things [*signum voluntarie institutum ad significandum plura*]. Therefore, just as the word is said to be common so it can be said to be universal. But it is not so by nature, only by convention [*non habet ex natura rei, sed ex placito instituentium tantum*].[94]

This should not be taken to mean, however, that there is no foundation in extramental or extraverbal reality for the existence of universals. For Ockham, universals were not arbitrary, subjective concepts; they came into existence only after the mind had actually experienced many individuals with common features which really did exist outside the mind.[95] We should not suspect Ockham of solipsism or skepticism when he asserts: "Universals have only subjective being; their being is their being known" (*universalia tantum habent esse obiectivum ita quod eorum esse est eorum cognosci*),[96] as if our minds were prisoners of themselves. Universal concepts do have roots in extramental reality, although they do not exist "out there," independently, as both Augustine and Aquinas in their different ways believed.

Assuming there is continuity between the way things were yesterday and the way they will be tomorrow, universal concepts and terms are trustworthy representations of reality, according to Ockham. Ockhamists have traditionally been recognized as helping prepare the way for experimental and observational science by their firm insistence on the primacy of intuition and immediate experience in the acquisition of knowledge. On such a basis they rejected Aristotle's explanation of motion as either a natural attraction of objects to their developed forms or the consequence of a present violent force and substituted the scientific theory that motion resulted from the "impetus" imparted to an object by an outside force.[97]

94. From the *Summa logicae*, ch. 14, in *Ockham: Philosophical Writings*, p. 34.
95. Boehner describes Ockham's epistemology as "realistic conceptualism" (concepts are derived from reality), not subjective idealism. "Since conceptualism is characterized by the affirmation of universals in the mind and by the denial of any universality outside the mind, Ockham's theory is conceptualism. Since, however, realism can be characterized by the affirmation of a correspondence or similarity between concepts and reality, or by the intentionality of concepts as regards reality . . . Ockham's conceptualism has to be qualified as realistic conceptualism, and not as idealistic conceptualism" ("The Realistic Conceptualism of William of Ockham," in *Collected Articles on Ockham*, p. 163).
96. I *Sent.* d. 2, q. 8, cited by Ueberweg-Geyer, p. 577.
97. "Ockhamism . . . helped to create an intellectual climate which facilitated and tended

Ockhamist epistemology had larger consequences for both theology and ecclesiastical institutions. At the base of Aquinas's theory of knowledge lay a hierarchically ordered world in which real relations were believed to exist between God, man, and created things. In Ockham's philosophy, "artificial" relations replaced assumed real relations between God, man, and the world. For Ockham, the world was contingent, not necessary, and only concepts, words, and promises bound man to God and to the world. In eternity God could have chosen to create a totally different world. Man too is presently free to organize the world in concepts and terms of his own choosing. One might still believe that God had created the best of all possible worlds, arbitrary though the world's origin and laws appeared to be from the perspective of eternity. And people might still believe that their language and concepts truly reflected the world around them, conventional though both were now seen to be. More, however, could not be said.

Ockham thoroughly rejected the metaphysic of essences and the metacategories so popular among thirteenth-century scholastics, which he believed had entangled God, man, and the world in a great chain of presumed ontological links and forces.[98] He described "divine ideas" as merely the knowledge God could be said to have of the particular things he had created; just as man's ideas or concepts reflected his encounter with and ordering of the world he intuited, so God "knew" the world he created. There was no grand system of divine ideas interlocking divine, human, and physical reality as with Augustine, Aquinas, and even Scotus. "Ideas," Ockham wrote, "are not in God really, as part of his very nature [*subiective et realiter*], but only as objects [*in ipso objective*]—as the individual things he knows."[99] Universals as eternal archetypes really in the mind of God and in

---

to promote scientific research. For by directing men's minds to the facts or empirical data in the acquisition of knowledge it at the same time directed them away from passive acceptance of the opinions of illustrious thinkers of the past" (Copleston, *A History of Philosophy*, 3:166). See also Anneliese Maier, *Die Impetustheorie der Scholastik* (Vienna, 1940). Eric Cochrane's recent rejection of late medieval nominalism in favor of humanism as the movement that "facilitated the birth of Galilean science" is exaggerated on both counts: "Science and Humanism in the Italian Renaissance," *AHR* 81 (1976): 1039–57, esp. pp. 1044, 1050–57. Although Ockhamists may not have been as progressive as some later, technologically inclined humanists, *both* movements contributed to the formation of a climate of thought congenial to the rise of Galilean science.

98. See H. A. Oberman, "Headwaters of the Reformation: Initia Lutheri—Initia Reformationis," in *Luther and the Dawn of the Modern Era: Papers for the Fourth International Congress for Luther Research*, ed. H. A. Oberman (Leiden, 1974), p. 57; Copleston, *A History of Philosophy*, 3:61.

99. I *Sent.* d. 35, q. 5 G, cited by Ueberweg-Geyer, p. 579. On Ockham's differences with Aquinas, Henry of Ghent, and Duns Scotus on the way creatures exist in the mind of God, see A. B. Wolter O.F.M., "Ockham and the Textbooks: On the Origin of Possibility," *Franziskanische Studien* 32 (1950): 82.

individual things as principles of their being and intelligibility fell away. Universals were distinctly human phenomena confined to the ordinary processes of a finite mind interacting with its perceived environment. The "secularization" of the knowing process begun by Aquinas here reached a true completion.

For Ockham, traditional philosophical and theological problems no longer opened onto such vast horizons as they had done with his predecessors; Ockham forced speculation to become more modest. Theological conclusions that came easily for Aquinas became impossible in the new Ockhamist world. If one cannot believe that the particular things of the world are essentially connected with their ultimate cause, then it becomes difficult to argue confidently from finite effects to the existence of God. For Ockham, there was no more rational basis for belief in God's existence or the immortality of the soul than there was for the existence of intelligible species and common natures. All such things become genuine matters of faith.

Does this mean that Ockham was, after all, the skeptic so many textbooks have accused him of being? Paul Vignaux declared that Ockham effectively ended speculative theology and the medieval quest to raise faith to rationality (*fides quaerens intellectum*).[100] That is surely an extreme judgment. It is true that after Ockham theology became more self-consciously a reflection *on revelation,* confined to a peculiar realm of belief, and progressively dropped the claim to be a truly rational science. Within the *via moderna,* the school of the Ockhamists, the sphere of faith widened, while that of "rational" religion shrank. The new nonscientific character of theology did not, however, hamper efforts to elucidate the faith, nor did it inhibit theological speculation.

A second consequence of the Ockhamist worldview is more subtle. It involved an alteration of the boundary situation of medieval Christians, a change that may also reflect the physical insecurity of the fourteenth century. By comparison, there was far more security within the Augustinian and Thomist worldviews than in the Ockhamist, given initial belief in a triune God. Augustine and Aquinas had seen all reality as grounded in the being of God and extrapolated their theologies from such belief. From their point of view, the greatest trauma for the believer was the possible nonexistence of God, for if God was not, then nothing could truly be or be known. By dwelling so intently on God's will rather than his being, Ockham created the conditions for a new spiritual anxiety—not the possible nonexistence of

---

100. *History of Medieval Philosophy: An Introduction,* p. 176. Leff speaks of "a virtual abandonment of a systematic attempt at a natural theology in the thirteenth-century sense of finding natural reasons for revealed truths." In this sense, Ockham's was "a system to end system" (*The Dissolution of the Medieval Outlook,* pp. 16, 91).

God, but the suspicion that he might not keep his word; that he could not be depended upon to do as he had promised; that the power behind all things might ultimately prove to be untrustworthy and unfriendly; that God, in a word, might be a liar. Not God's existence, but his goodness; not the rationality of faith, but the ability to trust God—these became major spiritual problems.

It was not accidental that a form of philosophical realism rather than the nominalism of Ockham became the preferred philosophy of ecclesiastical authority. The medieval church had a definite theological and political stake in moderate realist epistemology. Such a point of view was more congenial to a high theological frame of mind than nominalism. It far better served the desire to make church doctrine rationally respectable and universally acceptable. It also avoided the apparent skepticism into which two fourteenth-century nominalists, Nicholas of Autrecourt and John of Mirecourt, had fallen. A realist could understand how a universal could be in many places at one and the same time and better appreciate the doctrine of the Trinity—how three could be one and one could be three. Trinitarian speculation with nominalist presuppositions, on the other hand, ran the apparent danger of tritheism, which some found in Abelard's theology.[101] A realist who assumed universality to be in individual things could better appreciate the way "humanity" was incarnate, crucified, and resurrected in the one man Jesus. Nominalist presuppositions, by contrast, left one to view the universal significance of Christ's life, death, and resurrection as simply the result of God's decision to value it so highly.

The medieval church had an even more profound political stake in realism. Fourteenth-century church authority perceived in Ockham's thought a threat to the exclusive mediatorial role of the church. In a world where real relations existed between God and man, the church, as intermediary, held a dominant position. If nature and supernature were bound together in such a way that nature's end was necessarily a supernatural end, and if the church's sacraments and revelation were the indispensable links between nature and supernature, then the medieval church, standing between man and God, nature and nature's end, had a very basic claim on people and the temporal world. It was precisely such an assumption that underlay papal claims to temporal power.[102]

Ockham also believed that the church held a unique position in the world as mediator between man and God; however, it held such a position as the result of a special covenant, by an artificial arrangement, not because it was

101. Cf. Denzinger (Errors of Peter Abelard According to the Council of Sens), pp. 235–37.
102. See below, p. 147.

the most essential link in a grand metaphysical hierarchy of being. From this point of view, the church lost any claim it might presume to hold over people by virtue of its and their nature—and it did so at a time when royal apologists argued persuasively that the pope held no legitimate political sovereignty over people.[103] Ockham's theology transformed the church into a strictly historical reality, a creature in time and an object of faith that could no longer present itself as the passageway through which all life necessarily passed en route to a preordained supernatural end. Ockhamism was not a philosophy congenial to a church struggling, as the fourteenth-century church was, to maintain its political and economic power against the rising nation-states of Europe and to resist new secular challenges to its cultural, educational, and religious leadership.

What Scripture Means: The Interpretation of the Bible in the Middle Ages

IT is a truism that every age interprets the past in light of its present experience. Historical studies often say as much about the age in which they are written as they do about the age they describe. Witness, for example, the popularity of psychohistory and quantitative studies in introspective and computerized modern American society. Because we tend so strongly to peer into the past like Narcissus into his pool, historical dialogue ever threatens to become a contemporary monologue, merely a searching for the present in the past. Also, in historical study like wants to know like.

The art of making the past relevant to the present was perfected by ancient and medieval Christians, who found their own religious past to be an often unpalatable Old Testament. Christians believed that they lived under a New Covenant, which had fulfilled the promises of the Old. From this perspective they looked on the Jewish past as a preparation for the Christian present; the meaning of the Old Testament lay not directly in itself, but in the Christian future it prophesied.

The issue became urgent for the early church, for so many passages from the Old Testament and Jewish traditions had found their way into the New Testament and Christian teaching. Borrowing heavily from these sources, the New Testament writers had closely identified the new church with them. This, however, presented problems for a new religion in competition with the sophisticated philosophies of the ancient world.[104] The Old Testament's

---

103. See below, p. 148.

104. The shaping of early Christian thought on biblical and classical anvils is lucidly dealt with in Hans von Campenhausen, *The Fathers of the Greek Church*, trans. Stanley Godman (New York, 1959); and *Men Who Shaped the Western Church*, trans. Manfred Hoffmann

anthropomorphic descriptions of God and the many reports of his routinely harsh treatment of his own and other peoples seemed to contradict both classical reason and Christian charity. Christian thinkers concerned to make the new religion intellectually respectable to pagan intellectuals confronted in the Old Testament a God who strolled about the Garden of Eden, chatted with women about pregnancy, commanded a father to sacrifice his own son, demanded that enemies be punished rather than forgiven, and inspired prophets to preach holy wars. Shadow had clearly to be distinguished from promise, figure from substance. The biblical past had to be brought more directly into line with present Christian teaching and practice.

One early Christian thinker, a second-century figure named Marcion, proposed the most extreme solution. Influenced by the ascetic and dualist philosophy of Gnosticism, he concluded that the Old Testament was no book for Christians, that it had been written at a time when there was no knowledge of the true God, and that its God was actually a wrathful creator, responsible for the fallenness of the world, who had nothing in common with the loving God of the New Testament. Marcion not only denied that the Old Testament revelation had any connection with Christianity, but even created his own canon from Luke's gospel and congenial Pauline epistles.[105]

The early church fathers, especially Irenaeus and Tertullian, were strongly anti-Gnostic and opposed Marcionite efforts to dismiss the Old Testament. There was simply too much of the Old in the New to adopt so radical a solution, and the church condemned Marcionism as heresy. Shadow and reality were to be distinguished, but in such a way that the continuity of the two Testaments and the Christian witness of the Old were recognized and preserved.

Allegorical interpretation of Scripture became the accepted solution.[106] This method of reading Scripture permitted one to look beyond the literal meaning of a text and concentrate on its alleged hidden and true meaning. The Old Testament did not need to be set aside, only understood according to its true importance as prophecy of Christianity.

Once again it was Augustine who prepared the way for the work of medieval theologians. Allegorical interpretation of Scripture had been instrumental in his own conversion from classical philosophy to Christianity,

---

(New York, 1964); and Cochrane, *Christianity and Classical Culture*, which deals exclusively with Augustine.

105. On the basic teaching of Marcion, as reported by Tertullian, see Seeberg, *Text-Book of the History of Doctrines*, 1:102–04.

106. See Gerhard Ebeling, *Evangelische Evangelienauslegung* (Munich, 1942), pp. 110–11.

largely through the influence of Ambrose, bishop of Milan. Augustine wrote in the *Confessions* of the joy he found in Ambrose's sermons, which were ruled by the principle "The letter kills, but the spirit quickens": Ambrose would "draw aside the veil of mystery and spiritually lay open things that interpreted literally seemed to teach unsound doctrine; he would say nothing that caused me difficulty."[107]

Augustine believed that everything in the Bible was there for man's edification. For the most part, this was self-evident and the intention of biblical verses clear. On the other hand, one frequently came upon statements that seemed neither to edify nor to support basic Christian teaching. According to Augustine, the Christian exegete should not abandon such passages as aberrations, but rather make them useful to the faith by figurative or allegorical interpretation.[108] That, for Augustine, became the great merit of allegory: it let one raise to an edifying metaphorical meaning what was offensive or irrelevant when interpreted literally, so nothing in the Bible need be superfluous to the Christian.

Theologians like Origen and Augustine, who were famed for allegorical interpretation, acted neither unreasonably nor with malice when they tried to make the Old Testament appropriate reading for Christians. They sincerely believed that Christianity was the truth to which all truth necessarily led; to their minds, it was a high compliment to recognize the Hebrew Scriptures as God's prophecy of Christ, however offensive the label "Old Testament" might be to Jews.

The danger arose, however, that allegorical interpretation, blessed by church tradition, would strip the Old Testament of any intrinsic historical meaning; allegory threatened to become an instrument of "aggression" by which Christian writers might lay claim to any non-Christian material they desired to appropriate. Was the whole of the past to have value only as it prefigured Christianity? In the Middle Ages this threat materialized when Christian exegetes effectively transformed the Old Testament into a Christian book and made classical philosophy the handmaiden of Christian theology.

As the art of biblical interpretation matured, medieval Christian scholars came to view Scripture in four possible categories of meaning, summarized in the following hermeneutical rhyme, which originated with John Cassian (ca. 360–435) and remained popular into the sixteenth century.

---

107. *Confessions*, bk. 6, ch. 4, p. 138.

108. Augustine's hermeneutical principles were formulated in his *On Christian Doctrine* and *On the Spirit and the Letter*. See the discussion by James S. Preus, *From Shadow to Promise: Old Testament Interpretation from Augustine to the Young Luther* (Cambridge, Mass., 1969), pp. 9–23; and Ebeling, *Evangelische Evangelienauslegung*, pp. 121–26.

Littera gesta docet,
Quid credas allegoria,
Moralis quid agas,
Quo tendas anagogia.

The letter shows us what God and our fathers did;
The allegory shows us where our faith is hid;
The moral meaning gives us rules of daily life;
The anagogy shows us where we end our strife.[109]

A passage of Scripture has four possible meanings; the letter, the allegory, the moral teaching, and the anagogy. The letter is simply the obvious historical or literal sense, what the text immediately states and directly means. The allegory, the moral teaching, and the anagogy are three possible spiritual meanings of the letter. The allegory is the import of the text for the church and Christ, the ecclesiastical or christological doctrine that the text supports. The moral teaching, or tropological sense, is the import of the text for the individual believer—the soteriological meaning, or what it says about the individual's salvation. The anagogy is the text's meaning as far as transcendent reality and future events are concerned, that is, the mystical, metaphysical, and eschatological secrets hidden in the text. Medieval exegetes interrogated the Bible systematically in terms of its teaching about the church, Jesus Christ, the individual believer, and the life to come.

To take an example, in Psalm 76 it is written: "In Judah God is known, his name is great in Israel." Literally, this verse refers to the southern and northern kingdoms of the Hebrew people in biblical times, a subject not particularly pertinent to medieval Christians. Allegorically, however, it can be applied to the church and Jesus, where God is known through his revelation and saving act of redemption. In terms of its moral teaching, it can be referred to the soul, heart, or mind of the individual believer, where God is known in prayer and meditation. Anagogically, it can direct the Christian to heaven and the Last Judgment, where God's greatness and will shall be known in the fullest sense. The four meanings of Scripture transformed the Song of Songs into an extended Christian parable. No longer the lyric picture of a king's frolicking with his mistresses, Solomon's song was seen to describe God's love of Christ and the church (the allegory), the soul's love of God (the moral lesson), and the joy of heaven (the anagogy).

Spiritual interpretation made the Psalms the most popular *Christian* book of the Middle Ages. Spiritual interpretation also served to keep many bril-

109. Cited by Robert M. Grant, *A Short History of the Interpretation of the Bible* (New York, 1963), p. 119; cf. Gerhard Ebeling, "Hermeneutik," *Die Religion in Geschichte und Gegenwart* (1959), 3:249–50.

liant and curious clerical minds from the brink of boredom and possible heresy. Although they may strike the modern reader as sheer fantasy, the three spiritual senses of Scripture seem actually to have *limited* and *disciplined* speculation on the Bible.[110] By designating three permitted spiritual meanings of Scripture in correlation with the three basic spheres of church life and doctrine (ecclesiology and Christology, soteriology, and eschatology), the medieval church gave its "phi beta kappas" their heads, yet also turned them in directions beneficial to it.

As allegorical interpretation became ascendant, Christian scholars, influenced by Jewish exegetes like Rashi (1040-1105), came to the defense of historically minded exegesis—at least to a point. Four standout as proponents of biblical interpretation respectful of the literal meaning of a text: Hugh and Andrew of St. Victor,[111] Thomas Aquinas, and Nicholas of Lyra. These four revived a distinctive Christian tradition appreciative of the letter of Scripture that dated from the third-century school of Diodorus of Tarsus (d. 392) and his student Theodore of Mopsuestia (ca. 350-428), which was located in Antioch. These Antiochenes had opposed the allegorical methods of Clement of Alexandria (ca. 150-ca. 220) and his more famous pupil, Origen (ca. 185-ca. 254), whom they looked on as depriving biblical history of its reality by abstract figurative interpretation.[112]

None of these Christian defenders of the letter of Scripture, however, wanted to end spiritual interpretation of the Bible. They stressed the literal meaning of a text, whether in the Old or the New Testament, as the essential "foundation" of all subsequent spiritual meanings and opposed spiritual interpretation that lacked or ignored such a foundation. They did not raise historical meaning over theological meaning—no medieval Christian was capable of that—but they did help prevent a total eclipse of appreciation for the historicity of texts. When the literal meaning of a text was taken seriously, even if only as a sine qua non for spiritual interpretation, Christian scholars found themselves involved in grammatical and historical investiga-

110. "An effort to stop, through regulation by church dogma, the danger of an allegorical fantasy, which would digress into the heretical" (Gerhard Ebeling, "The New Hermeneutics and the Young Luther," *Theology Today* 21 [1964]: 39).

111. Beryl Smalley writes of the Victorines and their influence: "Belonging to their century, they had a strong sacramental sense, which gave them a new devotion to the 'letter' of Scripture. They still thought in metaphors which subordinated the literal sense to the spiritual; but they conceived it as something essentially laborious and creative; it was 'digging the foundation,' not 'stripping off the veil' or 'breaking down the prison.' Andrew realized what a delightful occupation digging could be" (*The Study of the Bible in the Middle Ages* [Notre Dame, Ind., 1964], p. 196). Smalley sees a serious waning of interest in such "digging"— devotion to the letter of Scripture—in the fourteenth and fifteenth centuries (ibid., p. 357).

112. See a brief contrast in Grant, *A Short History of the Interpretation of the Bible*, pp. 75-101.

tions that would otherwise have been ignored altogether. Such "Judaizing," as their critics called it, discouraged unfounded speculation and promoted a more critical biblical scholarship.

Thomas Aquinas's hermeneutics mirrored his epistemology. Having embraced sensory experience in place of Augustinian illumination as the basis of human knowledge, he was philosophically predisposed to begin with the "literal" meaning of things. For Aquinas, the literal sense of Scripture was the first and most basic meaning of Scripture, and he insisted that the exegete dwell on this before passing on to possible spiritual meanings.

> God, who is the author of Holy Scripture, possesses the power not only to adapt words to meanings, which we [too] can do, but also to adapt things to meanings. What is peculiar to Holy Scripture is this: the things there signified by words may also in their turn signify other things. The first signification, whereby words signify facts, is called the historical and literal sense; the second signification, whereby the facts signified by the words also signify other facts, is called the spiritual sense. Note that the spiritual sense is based on and presupposes the literal sense.[113]

According to Aquinas, the literal sense of Scripture is the direct signification of the words; the spiritual sense is that which the things signified, in their turn, further signify. For example, Psalm 22 begins with the words: "My God, my God, why hast thou forsaken me," words familiar to medieval Christians as those that Jesus spoke on the cross. Literally, these words refer to David, the assumed speaker in the Psalms, who here recounts his own suffering. In a spiritual sense, however, David himself signifies another who suffered, Jesus Christ. This second, spiritual meaning of the passage can also be described as a "prophetic" or "prophetic-spiritual" sense, when David is seen to speak as a prophet, filled with the Spirit, who foretells the crucifixion of Jesus.

Aquinas as usual struck a middle course, avoiding both extreme literal and extreme spiritual interpretation. On the one hand, he stressed the importance of the historical sense of Scripture as the foundation for *all* other possible meanings: there could be no spirit without the letter, and the exegete had a responsibility to investigate and understand the letter before he sought any spiritual meanings. On the other hand, Aquinas remained a medieval Christian who could not look on the literal sense of a text, especially that of the Old Testament, as anything more than a point of depar-

---

113. *Summa theologiae*, Ia, Q. 1, art. 10 in Gilby, *St. Thomas Aquinas: Theological Texts*, no. 27, p. 17.

ture; no medieval Christian could be expected to derive a primary satisfaction from David's having cried out: "My God, my God, why hast thou forsaken me." The true meaning of this text for the Christian was that which it had as a prophecy of Jesus—what the Holy Spirit intended to say through David about the Christian future. What was primary in the exegetical sequence proved of secondary importance in the life of the Christian.

After Aquinas two thinkers represented the extremes of medieval Christian exegesis of the Bible: Nicholas of Lyra and Jacques Lefèvre d'Etaples. Lyra (ca. 1270-1340) was a Franciscan and Aristotelian deeply influenced by rabbinical scholars. He commented extensively on both Testaments and has gained the reputation of being the strongest Christian defender of the literal sense of Scripture in the Middle Ages. His aversion to extreme allegorical interpretation was reflected in his preference for speaking, not of literal and spiritual senses of Scripture, but of a "double literal sense." Commenting on 1 Chronicles 17:13, where God says to Solomon, "I will be a father to him and he will be like a son to me," Lyra, taking note that St. Paul had applied this statement to Jesus in Hebrews 1:5, maintained that the passage was spoken not literally of Solomon and spiritually of Jesus, but *literally of both,* Solomon being God's son by grace and Jesus his son by nature.[114] This meant for the biblical exegete that the words of Scripture should always be taken literally so far as possible; prophecies of Jesus Christ were literally such, not hidden meanings in texts conveyed by the Holy Spirit through persons who, at the time they spoke or wrote, remained dumb to the meaning of their words. Lyra preferred to speak of a "literal-prophetic" rather than a prophetic-spiritual sense of Scripture. The effect of his work was to give a new importance to the literal sense of Scripture and to make historical study of the Old Testament more compatible with Christian faith and more respectable among Christian scholars.

If Lyra was the strongest Christian defender of the literal sense of Scripture, Jacques Lefèvre d'Etaples (ca. 1455-1536) represents an extreme development of Christian spiritual exegesis. A humanist, Christian Neoplatonist, and religious reformer whose commentaries on the Psalms impressed the young Luther, Lefèvre reacted strongly against the exegetical tradition Lyra had helped form, criticizing Lyra as a dangerous "Judaizer" who agreed more with the rabbis than with Jesus. Lefèvre too wanted to have only one sense of Scripture, but the applied Christian or spiritual sense, a "literal-spiritual" sense, not the literal-historical sense of Lyra. He argued that the only meaning of Scripture relevant to Christians was that intended by the Holy Spirit. Whatever did not directly promote

114. Preus, *From Shadow to Promise,* pp. 68–69.

Christian doctrine and spiritual life remained a killing letter; only harm lay in the purely historical investigations pursued by Lyra, for they diverted the reader from a direct Christian application of texts. For Lefèvre, the Psalmist was nothing more than a passive mouthpiece of the Holy Spirit who praised Jesus Christ. Lefèvre summarized his views in the introduction to his commentary on the Psalms (1508):

> I often asked the few monks who tried to find nourishment in Scripture what sweetness they experienced.... Most... answered that as often as they fell into... the literal sense, especially when they tried to understand the... Psalms, they became utterly sad and downcast.... I began to consider that perhaps this had not been the true literal sense but rather... a pseudo sense.... I went for advice to... the Apostles, the Gospel writers, and the prophets who first... opened the door of understanding of the letter of Scripture, and I seemed to see another sense of Scripture: the intention of the prophet and of the Holy Spirit speaking in him. This I call "literal" sense. No other letter has the Spirit conveyed to the prophets or to those who have open eyes.... Those who do not have open eyes... have another letter... which... kills and opposes the Spirit.... This they call the literal sense—not the literal sense of the prophets, but rather of certain rabbis. They interpret the divine hymns of David for the most part as applying to David himself, to his anxieties during the persecution by Saul and the other wars he fought. They do not regard David in these Psalms as a prophet but rather as a chronicler of what he has seen and done, as if he were writing his own history. But David himself says... "The Spirit of the Lord spoke through me...." And divine Scripture calls him *the* man in all of Israel to whom it was given to sing about the Christ of the God of Jacob and the true Messiah.[115]

Lyra and Lefèvre represent the poles of late medieval Christian exegesis. The long-term future lay more with Lyra than with Lefèvre, in large part because of the influence of the textual studies of humanism, which appreciated both original texts and historical context, although both humanists and the Protestants who adopted their educational reforms retained an interest in allegorical interpretation of the Old Testament. Historical exegesis also won support from the biblical and historical studies of late medieval monastic schools, especially the scholarship of the Augustinian order.[116] English friars of the fourteenth century became very fond of

115. In Heiko A. Oberman, *Forerunners of the Reformation: The Shape of Late Medieval Thought* (New York, 1966), p. 298.
116. See above, p. 18.

classical literature, history, and myth, and such studies, while falling short of critical humanist scholarship, and even providing new "spiritual detours" around the letter of Scripture, still enriched biblical exegesis and sermons.[117]

Lyra and Lefèvre appear to have played a role in the formation of Reformation theology, which also began as an effort to explain what Scripture means. At the outset of his first lectures on the Psalms (1513–15), Martin Luther wrote under the influence of Lefèvre and in opposition to Lyra. He dismissed the literal-historical sense of Scripture as "carnal and Jewish"[118] and followed Lefèvre in seeking a direct Christian relevance at every level of Scripture. Luther wrote as if the Psalms referred to Jesus both literally and spiritually, as if, indeed, Jesus were the literal sense of the *whole* of Scripture. Some scholars have seen the origins of Reformation theology in this radical christological interpretation of the Psalms, arguing that justification by faith originated in Luther's reduction of the traditional four senses of Scripture to two: Christ as the literal sense and faith in Christ as the moral sense, so faith became Jesus Christ tropologically understood, or what Jesus means *for me*.[119]

Another, more controversial thesis argues that Luther increasingly favored Lyra and attempted to relate the theological meaning of the Psalms to their historical reality as his lectures progressed.[120] Impressed by the historicity of God's promises to mankind, Luther came to speak more often about the concrete trials and joys of believing God's word and less about a transcendental conformity with Jesus Christ by faith. Rather than reading the Psalms exclusively as if Jesus were speaking directly to him and soliciting personal faith, he began to appreciate them as the witness of a historical person, David, who, like himself and other Christians, had to sustain his life by faith in God's word and promise.[121] In this interpretation it was the correlation of existential faith with God's biblical promise rather than with Jesus Christ as a hidden speaker in the Psalms that gave birth to Reformation theology.

117. See Beryl Smalley, *English Friars and Antiquity in the Early Fourteenth Century* (New York, 1960).

118. Preus, *From Shadow to Promise,* p. 145. In a tabletalk of 1531, Luther says, "Lyram contemnebam, quanquam post viderem eum valere ad historiam." See WATr 1 no. 116 (between 9. and 30. Nov., 1531), in Otto Scheel, *Dokumente zu Luthers Entwicklung (bis 1519),* no. 190 (Tübingen, 1929), p. 73.

119. Ebeling, "The New Hermeneutics and the Young Luther." pp. 41–44; "Die Anfänge von Luthers Hermeneutik," *ZThK* 48 (1951): 172–230; "Hermeneutik," col. 251. Cf. Erich Vogelsang, *Die Anfänge von Luthers Christologie* (Berlin, 1929), pp. 50–75.

120. Preus, *From Shadow to Promise,* pp. 182, 189n.

121. This is the thesis of Preus, which my *Homo Spiritualis* supports: *From Shadow to Promise,* pp. 226–27, 268; *Homo Spiritualis* (Leiden, 1969).

Since in Luther's mature theology Jesus Christ was seen to be God's word and promise in an exclusive, all-sufficient sense, these two interpretations need not be necessarily opposed; faith's conformity with Christ was, for Luther, quite simply its grasping God's biblical word and promise. The very competition of these two points of view, however, highlights the way the Reformation attempted both to resolve and to transcend the exegetical problems of the Middle Ages.

If the well-known rhyme *Si Lyra non Lyrasset, Lutherus non saltasset,* ("Had Lyra not lyred, Luther would not have danced") overstates Luther's debt to Lyra, it is still true that the historical exegesis exemplified by Lyra played a role in the formation of Reformation theology, and the latter stood in direct continuity with medieval exegesis.[122] This is as true for the English as for the German Reformation. Lyra's works were embraced by English humanists and reformers in the early sixteenth century, most notably by John Colet, who came to share Lyra's criticism of spiritual interpretation and appreciation of the literal sense of Scripture.[123]

---

122. See Smalley, *The Interpretation of the Bible in the Middle Ages,* pp. xvi–xvii.
123. A. G. Dickens, *The English Reformation* (London, 1964), pp. 64–65.

CHAPTER 3

The Spiritual
Traditions

Critics of Scholasticism

BY the end of the fourteenth century, when scholasticism had run its course as a creative movement and its excesses and limitations had become all too evident, critics returned to patristic and monastic ideals in an effort to revive traditional religious life both within and beyond the universities. Two of the most effective late medieval spiritual reformers were trained scholastics themselves: Jean Gerson and Nicholas of Clémanges. In bringing together traditional spiritual complaints against the schoolmen, they set forth independently many of the substantive criticisms and reforms of the humanists. So effective were these native critics of scholasticism that modern scholars have occasionally treated them as humanists.[1] Gerson and Nicholas are another reminder, however, that humanism was itself a movement within the larger scholastic and spiritual traditions of the Middle Ages and neither the first nor necessarily the most profound critical alternative to scholasticism.

In his magisterial study, *On Mystical Theology*, Gerson (1363–1429), chancellor of the University of Paris and an accomplished spiritual writer, contrasted the different approaches to God and religion in scholastic and mystical theology. The work was both a summary of the temperamental differences that historically divided the scholastic and spiritual traditions and an eloquent statement of the latter's superiority. Scholastic and mystical theologians were seen to differ, first of all, in their basic sources. Scholastics

---

1. See E. F. Jacobs, "Christian Humanism," in *Europe in the Late Middle Ages,* ed. John Hale et al. (London, 1965), pp. 238–39. A. L. Gabriel better recognizes their independence: "Such Navarrists as Gerson and Pierre d'Ailly knew the classics better than some of their humanist successors; and Nicholas Clémanges felt more aversion for the old scholasticism than did the Renaissance" ("The College System in the Fourteenth Century Universities," in *The Forward Movement of the Fourteenth Century,* ed. F. L. Utley [Columbus, 1961], p. 97). On Nicholas's humanist contacts, see Ezio Ornato, *Jean Muret et ses amis Nicholas de Clémanges et Jean de Montreux* (Geneva, 1969).

derived their information about God and religion from God's "outward effects"; they studied the Bible and church history and read theological commentaries. Mystical theologians, by contrast, found their basic sources in records of God's "internal effects," that is, in evidence of divine presence in the recorded history and tradition of the heart. A second difference cited by Gerson was that scholastics relied on reason and distrusted the emotions, while mystical theologians trusted the affections—provided they had been disciplined by true doctrine—and believed that the reasons of the heart were closer to God than the speculations of the mind. Third, while scholastics strove to behold God as the highest truth, mystical theologians sought to embrace him as the highest good. A fourth difference lay in the mystical theologian's belief that love could reach farther than reason and help the mind transcend its natural limitations; following the *pes amoris*, the *pes cognitionis* was able to enter regions otherwise inaccessible to it. Gerson compared this to the way fire caused water to boil over; heated by love, the mind bounded to new heights.[2]

Gerson drew two further contrasts between scholastic and mystical theology. He described the mystical way to God as the more democratic: "even young girls and simple people [*idiotae*]" could become experts in mystical theology, where love and personal experience, not formal university training, were the essential requirements. Finally, Gerson presented the mystical way as intrinsically more self-fulfilling, since love gave both the heart and the mind a satisfaction beyond any that the mere technical knowledge of scholastic theologians could provide.[3]

As chancellor of the University of Paris, Gerson was a lightning rod for the conflicts within and between the various faculties. Within his own theological faculty, warring Scotist, Ockhamist, and Thomist factions proved so frustrating to him that he threatened to resign in March 1400.[4] The threat won him new political power within the university, which made possible a positive effort to reform Parisian education by recapturing the unity of theology and spirituality that Gerson believed existed in the days of the church fathers and, more recently, in the life and work of the two

2. *Ioannis Carlerii de Gerson de mystica theologia*, ed. André Combes (Lugano, 1958), cons. 2, p. 8, 1. 4; *cons.* 29, p. 73, 1. 7, pp. 75–76, 1. 51.

3. *De myst. theol. spec., cons.* 30, p. 78, 1. 33; p. 79, 1. 45. Gerson also saw a certain neutrality in scholastic theology that let it be deceived and abused, while mystical theology held to its objective so firmly that only external coercion could distract it from its true end (ibid., cons. 32, p. 82, 1. 4; cons. 33, pp. 86–87, 1. 17).

4. *Oeuvres complètes*, ed. Palémon Glorieux (Paris, 1960), 1:113; John Connolly, *John Gerson: Reformer and Mystic* (Louvain, 1928), p. 79.

medieval theologians who became his personal models: Bernard of Clair-vaux and Bonaventura.[5]

In his first reform proposals, Gerson traced the problems of the theologi-cal faculty to what he called "useless, unedifying, and insubstantial teach-ings," by which he meant primarily the extreme speculations of Scotist theologians on such impossible topics as the generation of the Holy Trin-ity.[6] Gerson believed that such probings beyond the mind's ken gave laymen a false picture of Christianity and led other scholars in the university to suspect that the theologians preferred utterly incredible and absurd things (*incredibilia et absurdissima*) to the Bible and moral theology. These speculations divided the theological faculty itself, one side accusing the other of being bumpkins (*rudes*), while the other charged their critics with pure fantasy (*curiosi et phantastici*). Gerson found that scholastics generally had transmuted traditional theological vocabulary, in use since patristic times, into a language only experts understood. He described a favorite of the Parisian scholastics, Raymond Lull (1235–1316), a Franciscan tertiary, as a theologian who used terms even the theologians had not heard before.[7]

Gerson proposed two basic remedies: first, he would require students to read less of book 1 of Lombard's *Sentences,* where the nature of God is dealt with, and to give more attention to books 2 through 4, where they would learn about Jesus, the church, the sacraments, and the life to come—topics assumed less likely to occasion flights of fancy and bitter argument; second, he would forbid the discussion of sophistical questions (*sophismata*) and all topics declared suspect and scandalous by the church.[8]

5. Gerson is a witness to the thesis of François Vandenbroucke, O.S.B., who sees a divorce of theology and piety after the twelfth century with the rise of scholasticism. See part II: "New Milieux, New Problems: From the Twelfth to the Sixteenth century," in Jean LeClercq, François Vandenbroucke, Louis Bouyer, *The Spirituality of the Middle Ages* (London, 1968). Vandenbroucke cites Dante as the last to maintain their unity effectively (ibid., 364–72). On Gerson's concept of reform, see Louis B. Pascoe, S.J., *Jean Gerson: Principles of Church Reform* (Leiden, 1973).

6. Among the debated questions: "That God has the absolute power not to bring forth the Holy Spirit. That in God the generation of the Son, as such, is nothing. That the production of the Spirit precedes the Spirit's absolute perfection. That the Father and the Holy Spirit are not knowledge, and the Father and the Son are not love. That the eternal Son can generate another Son because He has equal power with the Father" (*Oeuvres complètes,* 2:27). Gerson singles out John of Ripa and other Scotists who go beyond Duns Scotus (ibid., 3:242–43).

7. *Oeuvres complètes,* 2:26–27; see P. Glorieux, "Le chancelier Gerson et la réforme de l'enseignement," *Mélanges offerts à Etienne Gilson* (Toronto, 1959), 285–98.

8. *Oeuvres complètes,* 2:28.

In a series of letters to the masters of the college of Navarre, written between April and September 1400, Gerson elaborated his educational ideals. Convinced that the old teachers and truths were far superior to the new, he scolded professorial permissiveness and the arrogance, especially of younger scholars, which had caused the old masters to be neglected and almost completely forgotten.[9] He cited the confession of an old rector of the University of Paris, Jean Buridan (ca. 1300–ca. 1359), who said he had often been deceived by the newer theologies, but never by that of the ancients. What was old should guide and temper the new, not, as was presently the case, be subverted by it.[10]

As a guideline in the selection of a curriculum for the young, Gerson proposed that study have as its goal *sapida scientia*, knowledge that could be felt and applied, knowledge that touched the heart and made one charitable as well as enlightened the mind. This required a curriculum that gave as much attention to moral theology and preaching as to the study of doctrine. It meant concentration on those scholastic doctors who had written "in a purer and more wholesome manner," among whom Gerson listed Bonaventura, Aquinas, Durandus of St. Pourçain, and Henry of Ghent. "Recent authors," ostensibly extreme Scotists and Ockhamists, whose commentaries, Gerson was ashamed to confess, confused purely logical questions with the true subject matter of theology, should be avoided altogether.[11]

Gerson combed both ancient and medieval history for edifying sources. In the area of the sacred history he recommended the *Dialogues* of Gregory the Great, the historical works of Eusebius and Cassiodorus, the lives of the church fathers, Augustine's *Confessions*, and the legends of saints. Under the category of "mystical expositions of sacred Scripture," he proposed Gregory's *Moralia in Job* and *Pastoral Rules*, Bernard's sermons on the Song of Songs, Richard of St. Victor's writings on contemplation, and the works of

---

9. Ibid., 2:37–38. Gerson comments on the neglect of the old and the arrogance of contemporary scholars: "Video tot et tanta volumina ab egregiis et summi ingenii atque sapientiae viris conscripta, neglecta tamen a plurimis ita ut vix nudo nomine cognoscantur. Video inquam et gemebundus detestor vel ignaviam vel arrogantiam nostram. . . . Sunt qui nescio quibus nugis ineptissimisque novitatibus membranas et auditorum, praesertim expertorum, mentes occupant" (ibid., p. 31). "Bene actum esset cum humana natura quae cognitionis avida est si seposita curiositate vel audiendi vel afferendi semper aliquid novi, ipsa jam bene inventis sobria humilitate prius uteretur. . . . Attamen hoc non potest aut vix potest persuaderi scolasticis, praesertim junioribus. Delectat quippe eos nescio quomodo citius vel transcribere vel studere recentius compilata quam vetera, more puerorum qui novos fructus licet acerbiores, edunt avidius quam maturos, digestos et sanos" (ibid., p. 42).

10. *Oeuvres complètes*, 2:32.

11. Ibid., pp. 33–34.

William of Paris. Other recommendations were Augustine's *City of God* and the works of Paulus Orosius, Jerome, and Lactantius.[12]

Gerson's model curriculum retained the scholastic disputation, but only as it remained modest and genial, "as is fitting in the quest for truth." The goal of such disputation was to stabilize the truth within the mind of the student and nurture the skills needed to transmit it effectively, that is, to inculcate a degree of eloquence,[13] another "humanist" ideal prominent within this scholastic reform program. To help revive preaching within the university, Gerson arranged for the return in 1403 of the Dominicans, the Friars Preachers, who had been expelled in 1387 following a controversy over the Immaculate Conception with the then dominant Franciscans.

Gerson found in the great Franciscan Bonaventura the perfect model for students. Bonaventura had the rare ability to balance the intellective and affective life and keep metaphysical speculation within the bounds of logic and common sense, talents Gerson found sadly lacking in the scholastics of the later Middle Ages. In a letter written toward the end of his life (7 December 1426), Gerson described Bonaventura's work:

> Bonaventura inflames the affections, while at the same time instructing the mind. Where so many others only confuse the mind and burden it with [scholastic] "qualifications," "prior and posterior arguments," "signs," and "contingencies," Bonaventura unites one with God in ecstatic love.[14]

If men like Bonaventura, Bernard, and Alexander of Hales were again made subjects of study and personal models for students, Gerson concluded, illogical and unedifying theological speculation would quickly and properly terminate.

Gerson saw the schoolmen he criticized as scholars who failed to subject their speculation to common sense and their study to love. To correct the first fault he urged them to set aside their new logic and terms, which had only led them to speculate beyond the bounds of their competence, and begin afresh with the basic logical writings of Aristotle.[15] To bring specula-

---

12. Ibid., p. 34.

13. Ibid., pp. 34–35.

14. Ibid., p. 280. See Giles Constable, "The Popularity of 12th Century Spiritual Writers in the Late Middle Ages," in *Renaissance Studies in Honor of Hans Baron*, ed. A. Molho and J. A. Tedeschi (Dekalb, Ill., 1971), pp. 3–28.

15. In the following passages it is clear that Gerson has in mind extreme metaphysical speculation, like that of the Scotists earlier criticized (see above). The Ockhamists (Terministas) would seem to be his firm allies in ending such speculation. "Conquisitores veritatis nostri temporis in Theologia, sub specie subtilitatis et titulo Metaphysicae, magnam nimis induxerunt confusionem, dum, omissa communi Logica, quam Aristoteles et alii consequen-

tion under the aegis of love, Gerson recommended the study of traditional mystical theology and provided his own magisterial treatise on the subject. His ideal was speculation chastened by logic, inflamed by affection, and put into practice.[16] In a memorable analogy, he once pointed out that just as honey required a honeycomb, devotion needed to be structured by an erudite and orthodox mind.[17] Conversely, the honeycomb needed to be filled: the ideas of the mind must also warm the heart and lead to activity in the world.

Nicholas of Clémanges (ca. 1363–1437), a student of d'Ailly and Gerson and a Parisian scholar in his own right, served for many years as secretary to the Avignon pope Benedict XIII (1394–1423), while continuing to teach intermittently in Paris. A member of a factious theological faculty and a close observer of the comings and goings at a papal court in a time of schism, Nicholas came to place exceedingly high value on simplicity and good deeds. Whereas Gerson had sought to unify the speculative and the active life, while at the same time preserving the integrity of each, Nicholas magnified practice as the only goal of theological study. His critique of scholasticism approached that of extreme humanist critics like Hermolao Barbaro and Ulrich von Hutten. "Theological study," he wrote, "is nothing but the workshop of the pastor and preacher."[18]

> The first task of a theologian or preacher—I take the two to be the same—is to live according to God's command [*bene secundum Deum vivere*] and thereby imitate Christ who "[first] began to work and [then] to teach" (Acts 1:1), that is, he did not start with doctrine, but with

ter tradiderant et servabant, ipsi novos sibi terminos assumpserunt; aut forte per ignorantiam Logicae, aut per negligentiam et contemptum; aut quia voluerunt sibi facere nomen ex inventione novitatum, dum repugnantes eis vocant rudes et Terministas, nec reales in Metaphysica, quasi sine terminis loqui possint" (*De modis significandi*, in *Joannis Gersonni opera omnia*, ed. L. E. Du Pin [Antwerp, 1706], 4:819). He censured the subtlety of metaphysicians in his *De concordia metaphysicae cum logica:* "Subtilitas metaphysicantium si quaerit reperire in rebus ipsis secundum suum esse reale, tale esse quale habent in suo esse objectali, jam non est subtilitas, sed stoliditas et vera insania. Quid enim est insania, nisi judicare res prout sunt in sola phantasia, quod ita sint ad extra, qualiter est in furiosis, phantasticis atque reverisantibus; qui sc. somniant vigilando; dum similitudines rerum pro rebus accipiunt" (ibid., p. 824).

16. Two axioms from the *De concordia metaphysicae cum logica* summarize it: "Metaphysicalis inquisitio quaeritur inepte fieri de ente et suis passionibus, si non praecesserit sufficiens notitia de ente logicali seu de Logica, qualem tradit Aristoteles studiose." "Theologica perscrutatio sistere non debet in sola intelligentia vel illuminatione intellectus, sed labi debet et liquefieri ad inflammationem affectus" (Du Pin, 4:828).

17. "Bonum est mel cum favo, sapor scilicet devotionis cum lumine eruditionis" (*Epistola prima ad fratrem Bartholomaeum*, in André Combes, *Essai sur la critique de Ruysbroeck par Gerson* [Paris, 1945], 1:634, 1. 6).

18. *De studio theologico* (ca. 1410) in Luc d'Archery, *Spicilegium; sive, Collectio veterum aliquot scriptorum qui in Galliae bibliothecis delituerant* (Paris, 1723), p. 479b.

deeds. Lest he teach rightly but act wrongly and thereby render his preaching ineffectual, he first embodied his teaching in deeds, which have greater force than words.[19]

Nicholas scorned the schoolmen not only for their involved syllogisms and philosophical abstractions, but also for what he considered their practical irresponsibility. He accused scholars of living in an ivory tower (*quieta otio agente*), of being listless and effete (*inertes homines otio in studiis marcentes*), and preferring the subtleties of their own imagination (*subtilia*) to the useful works (*utilia*) of the church fathers. Made "frigid, torpid, and arid" by their narrow scholarly interests, they were invariably slow to preach. Their scholarly degrees and honors only made them politically ambitious, not desirous to impart knowledge to others. They pandered to prelates and popes in the hope of gaining ecclesiastical benefices, thereby causing great harm to local parishes, which had to fund these nonresident clerical scholars. Nicholas compared the schoolmen to physicians who, having learned their trade, sit around and talk about it while people die of plague.[20]

Gerson had been careful not to magnify the importance of religious practice to the detriment of the scholarly life, nor to sanction an erudition that ignored the world. In Nicholas we find strong anti-intellectual tendencies, which became typical of much late medieval and Reformation criticism of scholasticism. Actually, Nicholas only expanded on a religious anti-intellectualism that was bone and fiber of the medieval spiritual traditions and had fostered dissent and reform throughout the Middle Ages. For Nicholas, preaching excelled study, the parish the university, practice the life of the mind, as love excelled knowledge. He strongly suspected that impractical genius and unapplied knowledge, common marks of the pure scholastic, were refined iniquity.[21] One can hear in him the advice of conscience to the friars in *Piers Plowman:* "Give up studying logic and learn to love."[22] He also reflects the fifteenth-century piety associated with the Modern Devotion, a movement that exalted devout and moral exercises (*studium devotum et morale*) over purely intellectual pursuits and rejected as useless any endeavor that did not immediately serve inner devotion and ethical practice.[23] Indeed, Nicholas is a mirror of the criticism of scholasti-

19. Ibid., p. 475a.
20. Ibid., pp. 476b–479b.
21. Ibid., p. 478b.
22. William Langland, *Piers the Ploughman*, trans. J. F. Goodridge (Baltimore, 1966), p. 252.
23. See R. R. Post, *The Modern Devotion* (Leiden, 1968), p. 320; G. Gieraths, "Johannes Tauler und die Frömmigkeitshaltung des 15. Jahrhunderts," in *Johannes Tauler: Ein deutscher Mystiker. Gedenkschrift zum 600. Todestag*, ed. E. M. Filthaut (Essen, 1961), pp. 422–34.

cism at both popular and clerical levels by both humanists and scholastics.

Nicholas may also be seen as anticipating the Reformation's ideal of a practiced ministry. Despite their important theological differences, one can still hear in Nicholas the later protest of the young Luther against the abstractions of Dionysius the Areopagite: "One becomes a theologian by living, indeed, by dying and being damned, not by understanding, reading, and speculating."[24]

If it is a measure of the vulnerability of scholasticism on the eve of the Reformation that its self-criticism could be as uncompromising as that directed against it from the outside by humanists, it is a sign both of the complexity of medieval intellectual history and the ability of the scholastic traditions to survive that a major humanist thinker, Pico della Mirandola (1463–94), became the most eloquent champion of scholasticism at the close of the fifteenth century. Pico's famous defense came in response to Hermolao Barbaro, a humanist and rhetorician, who had ridiculed scholastics as "men extinct even during their lifetimes" and scolded Pico for wasting his time with their works. Perceiving more clearly than Barbaro the limits of rhetoric and eloquence as tools of reform, Pico praised the work of Aquinas,[25] Duns Scotus, Albertus Magnus, and Averroës. These were not men, he pointed out, to be found in the company of mere grammarians and pedagogues, but philosophers, companions of the truly wise, who studied the first principles of things human and divine. Their minds, not their tongues, were filled with mercury. If scholastics appeared overly subtle and sharp, scrupulous and curious, anxious and morose, it was because they were involved in a most serious quest for truth.[26] Pico considered the real danger to be not that men would go too far in the investigation of first principles, as the critics of scholasticism charged, but that they might lose interest in first principles altogether. He saw the ideal of the ancients to lie in wisdom, not oratory, *ratio* not *oratio*, *doctrina* not *dictio*. He noted that Plato had excluded the poets from his republic, and Cicero had preferred ineloquent prudence to uninformed loquacity.[27]

Pico summarized his case by contrasting Lucretius's *De rerum natura* with John Scotus Erigena's *De divisione naturae*. Lucretius wrote about God and

24. See below, p. 120.

25. Pico was especially fascinated and inspired by Aquinas's effort to harmonize theology and philosophy, faith and knowledge. See Gerd Schulten, "Giovanni Picos Brief über das humanistisch-christliche Lebensideal und seine europäische Rezeption," in *Kontinuität und Umbruch: Theologie und Frömmigkeit in Flugschriften und Kleinliteratur an der Wende vom 15. zum 16. Jahrhundert*, ed Josef Nolte et al. (Stuttgart, 1978), p. 7.

26. *Corpus reformatorum*, 9:678–80. See Quirinus Breen, "Giovanni Pico della Mirandola on the Conflict of Philosophy and Rhetoric," *JHI* 13 (1952): 384–412.

27. *Corpus reformatorum*, 9:683, 686.

nature in elegant poetic Latin much admired by humanists, yet he taught that providence took no account of human events and everything that happened was the result of a fortuitous collision of atoms. Erigena, by contrast, wrote awkwardly, using inept Greek phrases, yet he taught that God was a separate mind, who knew and directed all things to their proper end; what he lacked in style, he made up for in truth.

> Who can doubt that Erigena philosophizes more truly than the eloquent Lucretius? See how Erigena speaks with a clumsy tongue, but Lucretius with a foolish mind; Erigena is unaware of the rules of the grammarians and poets, but Lucretius does not know the decrees of God and nature; Erigena speaks with the most childish of tongues, yet he understands things that cannot be praised too highly; Lucretius, on the other hand, preaches the most eloquent impieties.[28]

It was a cardinal principle of scholasticism that error is more to be feared than impracticality, shallowness more than ineloquence. This was the principle Pico defended against the critics of scholasticism.[29]

> They sin who tear asunder eloquence and wisdom, but what is all eloquence without understanding, save, as Cato says, vocabularies of the dead? We can live without language, although not well, but we cannot live at all without the mind. He who is untouched by good letters may not be humane, but he who is destitute of philosophy is no longer a man.[30]

It was a cardinal principle of medieval spirituality that impractical wisdom—ideas and doctrines that do not edify individuals and society—is useless and properly spurned. This, too, was a principle formed over many centuries. The Bible and monasticism blessed it, and the weight of tradition came heavily to favor love and deeds over reason and reflection.

The modern Western world seems to have resolved this old conflict in

28. Ibid., p. 686.

29. On this point he and Gerson are allied, even though Pico understood wisdom and truth more broadly than Gerson. Compare Gerson's strictures against overly curious scholars: "Contemnere claras et solidas doctrinas, quia leves videntur, et ad obscuriores se transferre, signum est curiositatis et originalis corruptelae poenitentiae et credulitati adversae.... Notat haec consideratio eos theologos, qui vel grammaticis auctoribus, vel historiis secularibus, vel poetis, vel eloquentiae priscorum oratorum, vel mathematicis inquisitionibus principalius insistunt, quam theologicis materiis, facientes de accessorio principale" (*Contra curiositatem studentium, Oeuvres complètes,* 3:298).

30. "Peccant qui dissidium cordis et linquae faciunt, sed quid excordes tota sunt lingua, nonne sunt mera (ut ait Cato) mortuaria glossaria? Vivere sine lingua possumus, forte non commode, sed sine corde nullo modo possumus. Non est humanus qui sit insolens politioris literaturae, Non est homo qui sit expers Philosophiae" (*Corpus reformatorum,* 9:686).

favor of the spiritual traditions: it does not admire and encourage impractical genius. "The best ideas are ideas that help people," the motto of one
of the largest modern corporations, could have been written by any late
medieval critic of scholasticism. The conflict, however, remained very much
alive in the age of Reformation and was made all the more interesting and
complex by the fact that monks, scholastic theologians, and humanists alike
turned Protestant and undertook from this new vantage point new educational reforms.[31]

Monastic Piety

THE values of the medieval
spiritual traditions evolved from
patristic and monastic culture.
There the *Lebemeister,* the masters of living well to God, always excelled the
Lesemeister, the masters of reading and teaching correctly about God.
"There are some who do more praying than reading," wrote the Parisian
chancellor and church historian Peter Comester (d. 1179/80); "they are the
cloister dwellers; there are others who spend all their time reading and
rarely pray; they are the schoolmen."[32] Whereas the scholastic program of
study proceeded from question to argument, the monastic program moved
from reading to meditative prayer and contemplation. Universities trained
scholars to form questions from their reading and argue the unresolved
issues by citing authorities pro and con. Such a regimen encouraged pedan-
try, scholarly factions, and verbal battles over where truth lay. In the cloisters monks and nuns read to prepare themselves for meditation, which gave
way not to disputation, but to prayerful reflection, a training program
described by Jean LeClercq as "the love of learning and the desire for
God."[33]

The monastic *lectio* had its dangers, however. Contemplation could lead
to idleness, the neglect of both God's truth and one's moral duty to others.
As Augustine warned:

> No man has a right to lead such a life of contemplation as to forget in
> his own ease the service due to his neighbor; nor has any man a right to
> be so immersed in active life as to neglect the contemplation of God.

31. See below, p. 309.
32. Cited by Jean LeClercq, *The Love of Learning and the Desire for God,* trans. Catherine
Misrahi (New York, 1962), p. 198. A helpful aid is Giles Constable, *Medieval Monasticism: A
Select Bibliography* (Toronto, 1976).
33. *The Love of Learning and the Desire for God,* pp. 91, 198–99.

The charm of leisure must not be indolent vacancy of mind, but the investigation or discovery of truth.[34]

What was required was a life in which contemplation and activity complemented one another; quiet, scholarly devotion should lead to both inward peace of mind and humble ethical practice within a community of like-minded believers. That was the goal of the cloistered life and an ideal that inspired the medieval spiritual traditions both within and outside the monastery.

Monasticism originated, however, in a much less sophisticated form of Christian asceticism. In New Testament times Christians denied and punished themselves in imitation of Christ, who had instructed those who would follow him to "take up a cross." They believed that to suffer as Christ had suffered was to approximate his relationship with God. Not only the severely ascetic desert monks, but also early Christian leaders—Jerome, for example—felt obliged to go into the wilderness, fast, and meditate in imitation of Christ's forty days in the desert. An early monastic motto held that those visited by men cannot be visited by angels. The reformer and organizer of Western monasticism, Benedict of Nursia (ca. 480–ca. 543), is reported by his biographer, Pope Gregory the Great, to have lived for three years in a cave at Subiaco, avoiding all human contact and subsisting on bread and water lowered to him by rope, all in obedience to Christ's counsel of self-denial.[35] Still, Benedict's Rule, which set the basic pattern for all Western monastic orders and remained the exclusive guide to monastic life until the eleventh century, actually lessened the severe asceticism of earlier centuries. It regularized the monk's life within a structured community and arranged his activities so that a reasonable amount of time was given over each day to sleep (eight and a half hours), religious offices (three and a half hours), reading and meditation (four and a half hours), manual labor (six and a half hours), and eating (one hour—each monk received two cooked meals and a pound of bread daily).[36]

The solitary life of withdrawal from the world was also believed to be the most perfect form of Christian confession, second only to actual martyrdom. The early church celebrated the martyrs as the most perfect Christians, who had given their lives in witness to the faith, the fullest possible self-denial. When Roman persecution of Christians waned in the fourth century, the monastic life replaced martyrdom as the badge of Christian

34. *City of God,* bk. 19, ch. 19, p. 413.
35. *Life and Miracles of St. Benedict,* trans. O. J. Zimmermann, O.S.B., and B. R. Avery, O.S.B. (Collegeville, Minn., 1949), pp. 4–5.
36. Owen Chadwick, *Western Asceticism* (Philadelphia, 1958), p. 28.

St. Benedict. The Master of Messkirch (ca. 1538).

perfection. Both as an institution and as a frame of mind, monasticism became the spiritual successor to Christian martyrdom. If one could not die literally in confession of the faith, one might "die" to oneself by ascetic self-denial in the midst of life. The goal of the mystical contemplation practiced by the cloistered became complete self-forgetfulness, a spiritual death of one's natural self and a transformation into a godlike self.

A final motive behind the growth of monasticism was a desire on the part of many devotees to set themselves apart from a Christianity that had become the established religion. In the Edict of Milan (313) Constantine the Great confirmed the legal status of Christianity and made it the favored religion within the Roman Empire. In the mid-fourth century the emperor Theodosius I (ca. 346–95) raised Christianity to the official religion. As being a Christian seemed increasingly routine, the flight to the desert became a way to preserve the primitive Christian spirit.

Medieval tradition richly blessed the monastic life. Augustine described it as the fullest possible realization of the kingdom of God this side of eternity.[37] Gregory the Great, the Doctor of Contemplation, divided Christians into three ascending orders: laity, (secular) clergy, and monks and nuns.[38] From Jerome to Bernard of Clairvaux, the monastic life was praised as a "second baptism." According to Bernard, becoming a monk so reformed the divine image in man and conformed him to Christ that he was more like an angel than like other men.[39] Needless to say, their greater obedience and self-sacrifice in imitation of Christ and self-awareness as successors to the church's martyrs and preservers of original Christian ideals gave the monks a sense of religious superiority over ordinary lay Christians and the secular clergy.

A basic monastic discipline developed in the West around John Cassian's *De institutis coenobiorum* and *24 Collationes* and the Rule of Benedict. Desert retreats, fasting, manual labor, long watches, and pilgrimages became standard monastic practices. Corporal punishment was not spared those to whom such discipline came hard. Sexual purity was enforced by means ranging from special prayers to repeated immersions in cold water.

During the first Christian millennium, a lay or "worldly" asceticism developed in western Christianity on the model of the ascetic practices of the cloistered. From the penitential practices of monks, especially those in Ireland and England, evolved the church's sacrament of penance for the laity. Monks were required to confess their every sin privately to their abbot, who lived in close proximity to his charges.[40] According to the Rule of Benedict, the monk's willingness to tell all to his abbot was a high degree of humility: "[He holds back] none of the evil thoughts that enter his heart, nor the sins committed in secret, but humbly confesses them."[41] Monks who so opened their hearts to their abbots could expect both absolution and indulgence. The abbot also imposed special works of satisfaction as a meet penance for the more serious sins, what came to be known as "mortal," in distinction from "venial," sins. Among such penances were the recitation of prayers,

---

37. Gerhart B. Ladner, *The Idea of Reform: Its Impact on Christian Thought and Action in the Age of the Fathers* (New York, 1967), p. 364.

38. LeClercq et al., *The Spirituality of the Middle Ages*, pp. 7–10.

39. "Praeeminens universis vitae humanae generibus huiuscemodi conversatio professores et amatores suos angelis similes, dissimiles hominibus facit; imo divinam in homine reformat imaginem, configurans nos Christo instar baptismi. Et quasi denique secundo baptizamur" (*De praecepto et dispensatione*, 17 [54] PL CLXXXII, 889B, cited by Ladner, *The Idea of Reform*, p. 4).

40. This changed in the later Middle Ages when higher clergy became aloof from the socially inferior lower clergy.

41. *St. Benedict's Rule for Monasteries*, trans. L. J. Doyle (Collegeville, Minn., 1947), p. 26.

fasting, and pilgrimages. The abbot excommunicated recalcitrant monks from fellowship.

Like monks in their community, laity too came to be expected to confess their sins frequently, receive absolution, and perform works of satisfaction imposed by their local priest. The church provided special indulgences to lighten the earnest penitent's burden and applied the discipline of excommunication to repeated offenders.[42] Not surprisingly, the lay religious movements of the Middle Ages often assumed a semimonastic character; until the Protestant Reformation, lay religious practice remained an imitation of clerical religious practice.

The foundation of the Benedictine monastery of Cluny in 910 began a reform movement in western monasticism that dominated religious life for almost three centuries. The Cluny reform came in response to several crises within the church. Clerical education and morality, especially the discipline of celibacy, had lapsed in the post-Carolingian church, and Cluny spirituality resolved to improve both. More serious still was the political domination of the church symbolized by the emperor's customary investment of bishops in their offices by presenting them the ring and staff of episcopal authority. During the Carolingian and Ottonian dynasties emperors routinely used the church as an instrument of political and social control. So intertwined had the ecclesiastical and secular realms become that the clergy seemed more like servile royal bureaucrats than divinely commissioned shepherds of souls.[43] The Cluny reform was the clergy's declaration of independence from ignorance, concubines, and kings. Cluny reformers sought to subject secular as well as regular clergy to celibacy and to distinguish clearly the jurisdiction of secular rulers from that of popes and bishops. After the victories of Pope Gregory VII (1073–85) and his successors, the Concordat of Worms (1122) declared the investment of bishops in their offices to be the strict right of ecclesiastical authority.

The religious zeal unleashed by the Cluny reform gave birth to crusades to the Holy Land and new religious orders, both of which showed clear marks of their inspiration. Crusaders were promised a plenary indulgence for their sins, and many apparently looked on their venture as an imitation of the self-sacrifice of the religious, even as an approximation of their higher spiritual perfection. The new religious orders of Canons Regular (fd. 1050–1100), Carthusians (fd. 1084), Cistercians (fd. 1098), and Praemonstratensians (fd. 1121) attempted to recapture the religious purity

42. See Reinhold Seeberg, *Text-Book of the History of Doctrines*, trans. C. E. Hay (Grand Rapids, Mich., 1964), 2:42–47; Thomas N. Tentler, *Sin and Confession on the Eve of the Reformation* (Princeton, 1977), pp. 302–04, 328–30.

43. See Heinrich Fichtenau, *The Carolingian Empire: The Age of Charlemagne*, trans. Peter Munz (New York, 1964), pp. 130–31.

of the church fathers. Communities of Canons Regular sprang up through-out the second half of the eleventh century. These were independent groups of clergy and lay penitents who were united by their common adoption of the Rule of St. Augustine, a short monastic guide dating in its oldest version from around 500. The Carthusians attached special importance to silence, manual labor, and the strict suppression of sexual desire. They continued to practice self-flagellation after Pope Clement VI forbade flagellant processions in 1349 because of the hysteria they created among laity. The Cistercians, who were also exceptionally puritanical, came to be known as the White Monks because of their immaculate white robes and barren, whitewashed buildings. The Praemonstratensians, who took their name from the monastery at Prémontré, were among several religious communities that adopted the Rule of St. Augustine. (The Victorines were another.) Their all-white attire, symbolic of the quest for apostolic purity, made them known as the White Order. (Cistercians wore black hoods with their white robes.)

The Cistercians have been described as the "fullest development of medieval monasticism."[44] An observant wing of the Benedictine order in protest against Cluny's alleged compromise of the monastic ideal, Cistercians were a reform of the reform. Bernard of Clairvaux, who brought Cistercian spirituality and theology to maturity, and Peter the Venerable, the abbot of Cluny, sharply debated the respective merits of the austere Cistercian approach and the more tolerant Benedictine view of the religious life.[45] The modern authority on Cistercian spirituality, Jean LeClercq, believes that the order was a true "school of spirituality," a perfect union of theology and piety. He describes Bernard as the "last of the Church Fathers" and Cistercian spirituality as the final successful expression of the patristic ideal before the rise of scholasticism rent theology and piety asunder.[46] Bernard himself, however, remained torn between the active and the contemplative life and never balanced to his own satisfaction the worldly business of the order and his political activity as a churchman with the work of God in prayer, study, contemplation.[47]

Bernard's treatise *On Loving God (De diligendo Deo)* presents a perfect

44. LeClercq et al., *The Spirituality of the Middle Ages,* p. 187.

45. See *The Letters of Peter the Venerable,* ed. by Giles Constable, vols. 1–2 (Cambridge, Mass., 1967).

46. LeClercq et al., *The Spirituality of the Middle Ages,* pp. 191–200.

47. Bernard's letters are the best commentary: *Bernard of Clairvaux Letters,* vols. 1–2, trans. Bruno S. James (London, 1953). See also the biographical records by contemporaries: *St. Bernard of Clairvaux: The Story of His Life as Recorded in the Vita Prima Bernardi by Certain of his Contemporaries, William of St. Thierry, Arnold of Bonnevaux, Geoffrey and Philip of Clairvaux, and Odo of Deuil,* trans. G. Webb and A. Walker (London, 1960).

summary of the monastic ideal of the higher Middle Ages, an unblinking monk's-eye view of human nature and destiny. What the modern reader finds here appears so utterly alien to modern values that a special effort is required to appreciate Bernard's point of view. In searching for an aid to elucidate the treatise in the most sympathetic way, I was reminded of a play from the early 1960s, Paddy Chayefsky's *Gideon,* a strikingly appropriate modern counterpart.

The theme of Chayefsky's play is the progressive rebellion or liberation of Gideon from dependence on God. At the play's start God inspires Gideon, who is absolutely obedient to him, to win battles over Israel's enemies "for God's sake." As the play progresses, Gideon begins to win battles, "for God and Gideon," then, "for Gideon and God," and, finally, by the play's end, "for Gideon" alone. As the play closes, Gideon declares his full independence from God, whom he finds too difficult a concept for man. One may interpret the play to be a commentary on modern man's seeming abandonment of traditional religion.

The monastic world of Bernard was the antitype of this modern morality play. Bernard began with man in complete independence from God, and very much to man's detriment, and traced progressive stages of reliance on God, finally to the point of complete identification of his own with God's will. The journey people should undertake was one from utter freedom and self-sufficiency to a dependence on God so abject that all sense of self vanished.

> At first, (1) man loves only himself and for his own sake . . . knowing nothing beyond his own desires. But when he discovers that he cannot stand by himself alone, he begins to seek and love God by faith. In this second stage, (2) he loves God, not for God's sake, but for his own sake. Having been forced by his need to grasp something more permanent than himself, man begins to love and worship God . . . and gradually attain an experiential knowledge of God. Consequently, God becomes sweet to him . . . and (3) he now loves God not for his own sake only, but also for God's sake. Truly man remains a long time in this stage; in fact, I doubt that anyone perfectly reaches beyond it in this life to the point where (4) God is loved only for God's sake. Let those who have come so far assert it; for my part, I must say that it seems to me to be impossible [in this life].[48]

Bernard here describes four stages of religious progression, which he would interpret as spheres of life.

48. *PL,* 182, col. 998C.

1. There is man alone, who knows and loves only himself, and this is the state of the world outside the church.

2. There is man who loves God, but solely for what he can get out of it. This is a love of God based on fear and the hope of gaining an eternal reward and characterizes most lay Christians.

3. There is man who loves God also for God's sake, because he knows that God is good and worthy of love in and of himself without regard to any rewards that might result. Here the cloistered people are found.

4. Finally, there are those who love God simply and solely for God's sake and conform their will so perfectly to his that they have become oblivious to themselves. Here are the truly perfect, those rare individuals with whom Bernard dared not identify himself, who receive already in this life a true foretaste of the life to come.

In Bernard's scheme, monks and nuns live between the third and fourth stages, trying to love God for God's sake and aspiring to love him even to the point of complete self-forgetfulness. Through prayer, fasting, study, manual labor, spiritual exercises, and enforced conformity in dress and manners—the complete regulation of both external and internal life—the religious strove to eradicate their own wills. According to Bernard, they must overcome that "leprosy of the heart" which causes them to give credence to their own desires and counsel (*propria voluntas et proprium consilium*) rather than to God's, and replace it with a selfless self, who can pray, "not as I will, but as you will."[49] A fourteenth-century German mystical treatise, the *German Theology*, later made famous by Martin Luther, characterized the goal of the contemplative life as the falling away of man's every sense of self—his *selbheit, ichheit,* and *eigen:* "The created will must flow into the eternal will, there dissolve itself and come to nought, so that only the eternal will remains to will, to want, and to be."[50] Of such notions were born both saintly reformers and heretical fanatics.

For the new monastic orders of the twelfth century, theology was immediate practical wisdom, not abstract dogmatic knowledge; it was a way of living, not a body of doctrine, something to be realized in love and contemplation, not by dialectical reasoning. Hugh and Richard of St. Victor, like Bernard, believed that the end of theology was affective union with God, not a creedal statement or great theological *summa*. They drew freely on themes from Dionysian mysticism, which placed God so far beyond the reach of reason that "ignorance" was said to be the surest route to him.[51]

49. Ibid., 183, col. 289D.
50. *Theologia Deutsch,* ed. Hermann Mandel (Leipzig, 1908), ch. 25, p. 53.
51. See below, p. 118.

The Victorines did not thereby forsake intellectual activity of a rational nature any more than Bernard, but they did subordinate it totally to a larger experiential end.

The spiritual life of the laity was also affected by these movements and ideals.[52] A growing lay fascination with the religious life developed in close proximity to the piety of the new monastic orders. This is the period in which the custom of elevating the host, that is, raising high the bread and wine of the Eucharist and shouting out the name of Jesus, became the high moment in the celebration of the Lord's Supper. The twelfth century also saw the beginning of lay confraternities devoted to the Eucharist.[53] Such practices reflected the popular side of the evolving doctrine of transubstantiation, which Pope Innocent III declared official dogma at the Fourth Lateran Council in 1215 and according to which the bread and wine of the Eucharist were transformed into the body and blood of Christ by the priest's consecration. The age that believed that universals were really in particulars also believed that Jesus's risen body was really in bread and wine. In the new Eucharistic piety we find a convergence of popular religion, scholasticism, and the ecclesiastical history of the Middle Ages.

Devotion to the Virgin, vigorously promoted by such church leaders as Anselm of Canterbury and Bernard, also peaked in the twelfth century. Marial piety found expression in art, architecture, and statuary, as well as in the growth of legends and miracles ascribed to the Virgin.[54] The Ave Maria and other popular prayers to the Virgin date from the twelfth century, as does the Rosary, the so-called Psalter of Mary. Patron saints became exceedingly popular and their shrines sites of great pilgrimages.[55] With the popularity of the saints came a new fascination with relics. Traffic in relics, both legitimate and spurious,[56] became an international business facilitated by the Crusades, and grew in size throughout the later Middle Ages down to the Reformation. Luther's patron and protector, Frederick the Wise, main-

52. For surveys with excellent bibliographies, see LcClercq et al., *The Spirituality of the Middle Ages*, pp. 243–82; Gabriel La Bras, *Institutions ecclésiastiques de la chrétienté médiévale*, (Paris, 1964), vol. 2.

53. See Peter Browe, *Die Verehrung der Eucharistie im Mittelalter* (Munich, 1933); *Die eucharistische Wunder des Mittelalters* (Breslau, 1938); Jean Deschamps, *Les confréries au Moyen Age* (Bordeaux, 1958).

54. See Stephen Beissel, *Geschichte der Verehrung Marias in Deutschland während des Mittelalters* (Freiburg im Breisgau, 1909).

55. See Stephan Beissel, *Die Verehrung der Heiligen und ihrer Reliquien im Deutschland bis zum Beginne des 13. Jahrhunderts* (Freiburg im Breisgau, 1892); H. Siebert, *Beiträge zur vorreformatorischen Heiligen- und Reliquienverehrung* (Freiburg, 1907); Ronald C. Finucane, *Miracles and Pilgrims: Popular Beliefs in Medieval England* (London, 1977).

56. See the recent study of Patrick J. Geary, *Furta Sacra: Thefts of Relics in the Central Middle Ages* (Princeton, 1978).

tained and displayed in Wittenberg as late as 1520 one of the largest relic collections ever assembled.[57]

Two important forms of communal ascetic piety emerged among the laity in the later Middle Ages, the Beguines and the Modern Devotion. Beguines were at first pious laywomen who wore a habit and practiced poverty and chastity, while living with their families, or alone, and working in the world. Their male counterparts, far fewer in number, were known as Beghards. Beguines and Beghards exemplify several of the spiritual movements of the later Middle Ages. They fall under monastic piety, since they formed their own cells and cloisters, most of which were eventually integrated into the established orders of Cistercians, Dominicans, and Franciscans. Beguines can also be studied under mysticism, since some of the more famous "bridal mystics" were Beguines (Hadewich and Mechthilde of Magdeburg, for example). They can be treated among the varieties of heterodox spirituality and heresy, since some beguinages, or houses for these lay sisterhoods, succumbed to the teachings of Waldensians and Cathars ("pure ones") and were condemned and persecuted by the church as "Free Spirit" heretics. The term *beguine* appears to have derived from "Albigensian," a description of Cathars congregated around the French town of Albi in south-central France, who became the object of a papal crusade.[58]

In the late twelfth and early thirteenth century beguinages sprang up in the towns of the Netherlands, the Rhineland, and France. The "religious women's movement," as it is today called, reflected the population explosion of the high Middle Ages as well as its heightened religiosity. There were increased numbers of women seeking to employ their talents in rewarding ways. The movement also reveals the plight of unmarried women, who had few vocational options in medieval society, yet tremendous energy and time on their hands. Large numbers of unmarried, unoccupied, and spiritually idealistic women, predominantly from the higher and middle social strata—that is, widows, spinsters, and daughters of noblemen and merchants—found in beguinages an outlet for both their emotional and social needs. In addition to regular participation in a variety of religious activities, these women also worked as seamstresses, baby-sitters, and nurses to the sick and needy. As the example of the city of Cologne attests, unattached women from the lower social classes also found their way into city-

---

57. Julius Köstlin, *Friedrich der Weise und die Schlosskirche zu Wittenberg* (Wittenberg, 1892), p. 17.

58. The literature on the etymology of the term is discussed fully by Frederick M. Stein, in *The Religious Women of Cologne 1120–1320* (Dissertation, Yale University, 1977), pp. 6–7, 69. See also the large study of E. W. McDonnell, *The Beguines and Beghards in Medieval Culture* (New Brunswick, 1954).

sponsored beguinages, over one hundred of which, consisting of ten to twelve members each, were established in Cologne between 1250 and 1350.[59]

In the mid-thirteenth century the church began to suppress convents that had fallen under the influence of heresy. The established religious orders strictly supervised the beguinages and conformed them to accepted doctrines and practices. Many Beguines were directly integrated into established orders. Heterodox convents persisted, however, especially in southern France.

The appeal of heterodox convents to medieval women, especially of the lower and middle social strata, and both social and religious. On one level the attraction seems to have been simply an available religious vocation, a need the established orders were not equipped to meet on the large scale required when the Beguine movement exploded. The need for community with one's social peers was more important to most Beguines than the degree of a convent's theological orthodoxy. Heterodox convents, however, appear also to have emancipated medieval women from their accustomed inferior status to a degree unknown in the orthodox convents, or anywhere else in medieval society for that matter. The dualist heresy to which some beguinages succumbed taught that women were the spiritual equals of men and permitted them to share religious authority and responsibility.[60] The dogmatic basis for this enhancement of woman's religious role was the belief that men and women differed essentially only in terms of their physical bodies, which held no importance in the larger scheme of things. Before God and in heaven, men and women were divine souls and their sexual differences and attendant inequalities nonexistent.

Such beliefs worked to give women a greater role in the religious cult; Cathars permitted women to perform priestly rites. These beliefs also recast sexual ethics as the medieval church conceived them. Rejecting the body as totally evil, Cathars urged their adherents not to procreate the species and apparently denied their sacrament, the *consolamentum,* a laying on of hands, to pregnant women. Their practices of contraception and abortion influenced the church's strictures against both.[61] On the other hand, if the records of church inquisitors can be believed, Cathars, convinced that what

59. See Stein, *The Religious Women of Cologne,* pp. 87, 172. Stein estimates that there were 1,200 Beguines in Cologne by 1320. See also Johannes Asen, "Die Beginen in Köln," *Annalen des Historischen Vereins für den Niederrhein* (1927–29), 111:81–180; 112:71–148; 113:13–96.

60. Gottfried Koch, *Frauenfrage und Ketzertum im Mittelalter: Die Frauenbewegung im Rahmen des Katharismus und des Waldensertums und ihre sozialen Wurzeln (12.–14. Jahrhundert)* (Berlin, 1962), pp. 181–85.

61. John T. Noonan, Jr., *Contraception: A History of Its Treatment by the Catholic Theologians and Canonists* (New York, 1967), pp. 221–44. Cf. Christopher Brooke, "Heresy and Religious Sentiment, 1000–1250," in *Medieval Church and Society* (London, 1971), pp. 139–61.

counted religiously was the attitude of one's mind and soul, also permitted ordinary devotees to do as they pleased with their bodies, short of procreative marriage. Some medieval women might have found the prospect of guilt-less fornication, a rare notion in medieval religious history, at the very least intriguing. A parallel may be drawn here with the celebration of unmarried erotic love in the court literature of southern France in the twelfth century, the promotion of which was another way some medieval women rebelled against masculine domination of their lives.[62]

Catharist Beguines and Beghards were condemned by the Council of Vienne in 1312 for allegedly teaching such things as:

1. That man in this life can attain so great a degree of perfection that he is rendered completely sinless and need progress no further in grace.
2. That it is not necessary to fast or pray after one has attained such perfection, since he is now able to subject his sensual nature completely to his rational and spiritual nature, even to the point of permitting his body to do as it pleases.
3. That those who reach the aforesaid degree of perfection and spirit of freedom are no longer subject to human obedience, nor obligated to fulfil the commandments and precepts of the church. As they [the heretics] say, "Where the spirit of the Lord is, there is liberty" (2 Cor. 3:17).
4. That man can attain in this life every degree of beatitude he will know in the future life.[63]

A Beguine, Marguerite of Porête, was burned at the stake in Paris in 1310 for allegedly teaching that the perfect are "beyond virtue." The vast majority of Beguines, however, remained quite docile and orthodox; they supported the Crusades enthusiastically and became leaders of the church's new eucharistic devotion. A recent study has portrayed Beguines and Beghards accused of the Free Spirit heresy as being for the greater part medieval equivalents of modern day "hippies," idealists who were trying, in their own somewhat eccentric way, to "quicken the life of the inner man."[64]

---

62. See Friedrich Heer, *The Medieval World: Europe 1100–1350*, trans. Janet Sondheimer (New York, 1962), p. 172.

63. Denzinger, nos. 891–899, p. 282. Catharist teaching is reported, quite uncritically, by Emmanuel Le Roy Ladurie in *Montaillou, village occitan de 1294 à 1324* (Paris, 1975).

64. Robert E. Lerner, *The Heresy of the Free Spirit in the Later Middle Ages* (Berkeley, 1972), pp. 62, 233, 240. Lerner does find that those accused of Free Spirit heresy practiced "autotheism" (that is, they believed they became totally identical with God) and intentionally circumvented the sacraments.

Little evidence is found to substantiate charges of organized antinomianism, and reports of gross sexual immorality are dismissed as rhetorical, even conspiratorial, efforts by church authorities to discredit an alternative lifestyle that offended contemporary tastes. Beguines and Beghards, it is concluded, were "free spirits" in the sense in which the humanist philosopher Pico della Mirandola was a free spirit, as people open to new ideas, experiences, and sources of authority, not in the depraved moral sense alleged by inquisitorial depositions.

In the medieval spiritual traditions the line between heresy and orthodoxy could be exceedingly fine, especially at the inception of a heresy. As Gordon Leff has put it, "The road to heresy was paved with piety," and the ultimate test of heresy a very practical one: whether an individual or a group obediently submitted to the doctrinal authority of the church.[65] The condemned had usually begun with an accepted teaching or practice— poverty, self-denial in imitation of Christ, a heartfelt experience of God— and progressively made it the exclusive touchstone of a true religious life. When a traditional teaching or practice was exaggerated in this way, spirituality tended to become heterodox, and persistence in it, often in the name of fidelity to a higher truth, brought open dissent and criticism, which church authority refused to abide.

Heterodox spirituality bridged all social classes, and this made it a particularly serious matter for church authority. As the Beguines illustrate, the lay religious movements of the Middle Ages were not simply "poor man's religion," but a piety for all whose religious ideals were unusually high, whether educated or uneducated, rich or poor. The late German historian Herbert Grundmann argued this point at length against Marxist and other interpretations of medieval heresy as ideologies for the economically impoverished and socially estranged.[66] Grundmann demonstrated that inquisitorial descriptions of heretics as "coarse," "simple," and "unlettered" (*rustici, idiotae, illiterati*) established primarily that the accused were not trained clergy and scholars with authority in spiritual matters. He argued further that their self-description as weavers (*texerants*) often referred to a vocation they had freely *chosen* rather than to their true social origins. Grundmann believed that the religious movements of the high and later Middle Ages were filled with people who *willed* to live a simple life and practice a humble trade in imitation of Jesus, a carpenter, St. Paul, a tentmaker, and St. Peter, a fisherman. The leaders of such movements, often from affluent and educated families, were attracted to the religious

65. Gordon Leff, *Heresy in the Later Middle Ages* (Manchester, 1967), 1:1–4, 12.
66. See Martin Erbstösser and Ernst Werner, *Ideologische Probleme des mittelalterlichen Plebejertums: Die freigeistige Häresie und ihre sozialen Wurzeln, Forschungen zur mittelalterlichen Geschichte*, 7, (Berlin, 1960), which is critical of Grundmann.

life not to make a purely political protest against economic exploitation and social alienation, but to take a spiritual stand against the gross materialism of the age. Franciscan and Dominican friars came initially in disproportionate numbers from the ranks of ministerials and patricians, both groups experiencing new political and economic freedoms in the thirteenth century and devoted to the principle that virtue and deeds, not birth, determined a person's worth.[67] Among those who forsook wealth and rank to lead a life of poverty in imitation of Jesus and the Apostles were Peter Waldo, the founder of the Waldensians, Francis of Assisi, the founder of the Franciscans, and Clare, the organizer of the early Franciscan women. Discontent and ideological "mobility" resulting from socioeconomic grievances and resentments were important preconditions of medieval reform movements, especially when it came to the mobilization of popular support, but the leadership of such movements belies a purely materialistic interpretation of the motives and goals of the participants.

The medieval church did not choose to reason with heterodox religious movements. It responded instead with fire and sword, the Inquisition and the crusade. During the pontificate of Pope Alexander III (1159–81), the Inquisition appeared as an instrument of coercive episcopal authority to ensure diocesan discipline. Pope Innocent III (1198–1216) centralized it in the papacy, and it became henceforth a judicial proceeding carried out by papal legates chosen from the established monastic or mendicant orders. Pope Innocent also launched the Albigensian Crusade in 1209, a twenty-year effort to eradicate heresy in southern France. This was a fateful event within the spiritual traditions that may be compared with the Parisian condemnations of Aristotelianism in 1270 and 1277 within the scholastic traditions. Church authority did not reason with heterodox spirituality any more than it would with heterodox theology and philosophy. By the time of the pontificate of Gregory IX (1227–41) a vast network of courts and procedures had evolved to check heresy.

When it regularized the repressive measures of the Inquisition the papacy acknowledged its inability to direct the new religious movements of the twelfth and thirteenth centuries peacefully into channels that served medieval church and society. Gordon Leff, who does not sympathize with heterodox piety, cites as the "special failure of the later medieval church"—one greater, he believes, than its simony, pluralism, immorality, greed, or injustice—"the absence of a countervailing spirituality."[68] That

---

67. *Religiöse Bewegungen des Mittelalters* (Darmstadt, 1961), pp. 19–38, 168–69; John B. Freed, *The Friars and German Society in the Thirteenth Century* (Cambridge, Mass., 1977), pp. 118, 122, 129–31, 134.

68. *Heresy in the Later Middle Ages*, 1:29–30; *The Dissolution of the Medieval Outlook: An Essay on Intellectual and Spiritual Change in the Fourteenth Century* (New York, 1976). p. 120.

conclusion may appear exaggerated in light of the Dominican and Franciscan expansion of lay participation in the religious life. It must also be recognized that some groups demanded a religious purity far beyond any human capacity, and the church could tolerate such idealism only at its peril. Still, the high degree of religious experimentation by both heterodox and orthodox groups in the later Middle Ages attests a failure of the medieval church to meet the original aims of the lay ascetic movements of the high Middle Ages.

A second great ascetic movement that drew large numbers of laity was the Modern Devotion of the late fourteenth and fifteenth century. With the exception of the observantine Windesheim congregation, which adopted the Rule of St. Augustine in 1387 and became an influential regular order of strictest discipline, the Brothers and Sisters of the Common Life, like the Beguines and Beghards, avoided formal vows, while nonetheless living freely together in a common life with a serious commitment to poverty, chastity, and obedience. Unlike the Beguines and Beghards, however, they remained uniformly orthodox in doctrine and absolutely loyal to the church, a reflection perhaps of the Inquisition's success over the preceding centuries.

The founder of the Modern Devotion, Gerard Groote (1340–84), a lay preacher and deacon who reportedly declined the priesthood out of humility, gathered like-minded laity and clergy into a common life. Groote was a wealthy, well-traveled man who had studied in Paris, Cologne, and Prague. The Carthusians, the order that perhaps best preserved the religious priorities of early Christian culture during the later Middle Ages, strongly influenced him. Although a student of the German and Netherlands mystics, especially Meister Eckhart and Jan van Ruysbroeck, Groote turned away from speculative mysticism. He was basically a pious and practical man opposed to intellectual pursuits that did not immediately serve the needs of piety. His aim was to keep religion simple, devout, and charitable. His successor, Florence Radewijns (1350–1400) further organized and expanded the movement on these principles after Groote's death. As the fifteenth century began, the movement was well established, and by mid-century brother-houses and sister-houses dotted the Netherlands, central Germany, and the Rhineland.

In both theology and religious practice, the Modern Devotion seems to have been almost totally unoriginal. Because it revived the ideals of the Canons Regular and the mendicant orders at a time when the established orders of the church were in disrepair, the movement became a force within the religious life of the laity and in the monasteries, which adopted its reforms.

Devotionalists wrote large numbers of popular spiritual tracts.[69] The book that best summarized and popularized their ideals was Thomas à Kempis's *Imitation of Christ,* a work that consisted of four parts, three of which dealt with the inner life and one with the Eucharist. Kempis admonished both clergy and laity to live simply, deny themselves and the world, and humbly obey their superiors—the basic monastic virtues.

Scholars are divided over how the movement should be assessed. Some stress the anti-intellectual strains in Devotionalist piety and view the movement as a logical result of a separation of theology and spirituality brought about by the dominance of scholasticism in the thirteenth and fourteenth centuries. Others damn the movement as a narrow, subjective form of piety that undermined church doctrine and institutions for the sake of individual ethical concerns. On the other hand, the movement has been praised as the source of all the significant reforms of the sixteenth century, whether humanist, Protestant, or Catholic.[70] Major humanists and reformers, both Protestant and Catholic, came under the influence of the Brothers during their student years; Rudolf Agricola, Erasmus, and Luther are three prominent examples. The late R. R. Post, author of what many consider a near definitive study of the movement, sharply rejected this view. He pointed out that the Brothers did not formally educate anyone, but mainly ran boarding schools and looked after the religious needs of resident students. Their scholarly interests remained rudimentary and subservient to practical piety. In addition, they promoted the *contemptus mundi* of traditional monasticism, which most humanists and Protestants rejected. All things considered, Post believed that the Modern Devotion stood more in contrast than in continuity with the reform movements of the sixteenth century.[71]

Post's views have recently been challenged, however, as too harsh, and the Brothers' positive points of contact with humanism and Protestant reform have been reemphasized. Although not themselves educators, the Brothers did encourage humanistic work when they came in contact with it, mainly because of their own desire to ensure uniform liturgical texts. Like humanists, they recognized that transmission corrupted texts and saw profit in measuring their own liturgies, the Vulgate, and works of the church fathers against the originals. Like Protestants, they believed that Scripture held the central place in the spiritual life. They also weakened scholasticism by their complete immunity to it.[72]

69. See LeClercq et al., *The Spirituality of the Middle Ages,* pp. 428–39.

70. This is the thesis of Albert Hyma, cited above, p. 17.

71. R. R. Post, *The Modern Devotion: Confrontation with Reformation and Humanism* (Leiden, 1968), esp. pp. 675–80.

72. Helmar Junghans, "Der Einfluss des Humanismus auf Luthers Entwicklung bis

While the Modern Devotion may in some ways be said to have anticipated and aided the reform movements of the sixteenth century, its main achievement lay in the revival of traditional monasticism on the eve of the Reformation. It demonstrated that the desire to live a simple communal life of self-denial in imitation of Christ and the Apostles was as much alive at the end of the Middle Ages as it had been in the primitive church.

The Franciscan Movement

IN the high and late Middle Ages large numbers of laity and clergy were gripped by the biblical ideal of apostolic poverty. This was an ominous development in spirituality for the authority of the church and rapidly produced a widespread counter-religious culture.[73] The ideal of poverty gave birth to the twelfth-century and thirteenth-century heresies of the Arnoldi, Humiliati, Waldensians, and Cathars, inspired the comparatively docile Beguines and Beghards, and became the most prominent feature of late medieval heresy and reform. The main task of the new mendicant orders of Franciscans and Dominicans, which the pope confirmed in the first quarter of the thirteenth century, was to contain the poverty ideal and turn it to constructive use within the church. They preached against heresy and heterodoxy, developed so-called third orders for pious laity, and assisted the secular clergy as confessors and preachers. Inspired by the example of their founder, however, the Franciscans produced their own heterodox interpretation of the poverty ideal and became as serious a problem for church authority as the heresies they were commissioned to combat.

Francis of Assisi was born in 1181 or 1182, the son of a wealthy cloth merchant, and grew up in the climate of intense religious piety created by the new monastic orders of the eleventh and twelfth centuries. During his lifetime the materialism of urban society, which the growth of trade had markedly increased, and the secular ambition of the papacy, which political success had made all too manifest, became popular objects of criticism. This was the period in which popes Alexander III (1159–81) and Innocent III (1198–1216) transformed the papacy into the political and commercial

---

1518," *Luther-Jahrbuch 1970*, ed. Franz Lau (Hamburg, 1970), pp. 57–61; Heiko A. Oberman, *Werden und Wertung der Reformation. Vom Wegestreit zum Glaubenskampf* (Tübingen, 1977), pp. 56–71.

73. Leff sees the poverty ideal as producing a new historical criticism of the church based on the perceived discontinuity between the (pure) apostolic church and the (flawed or fallen) post- or non-apostolic church (*The Dissolution of the Medieval Outlook*, p. 130). See also Norman Cohn, *The Pursuit of the Millennium* (New York, 1961), pp. 163–68.

power attacked by reformers down to the Reformation. In this period the distinction between the church as the papacy, or "Rome," and the church as the "body of the faithful," a distinction that became commonplace in the later Middle Ages, first gained currency. The Waldensians, who anticipated the spiritual ideals of the Franciscans, translated and circulated passages of the New Testament which depicted the simple life of Jesus and his disciples as the one for all true Christians to follow.[74] Jesus's mission to the twelve apostles (Matt. 10:8-11) seized Francis and inspired the Franciscan ideal of poverty:

> Heal the sick, raise the dead, cleanse lepers, and cast out demons. You received without pay, give without pay. Take no gold, nor silver, nor copper, in your belts, no bag for your journey, nor two tunics, nor sandals, nor a staff; for the laborer deserves his food. And whatever town or village you enter, find out who is worthy in it, and stay with him until you depart.

Basing it on similar injunctions by Jesus, Francis formulated the first Franciscan Rule in 1209. Around this Rule Francis gathered his followers, each of whom took Lady Poverty to bride. After some hesitation, Pope Innocent III approved the Rule. Although adverse to the creation of new orders—he formally prohibited such at the Fourth Lateran Council (1215)—the pope needed obedient allies who led exemplary, apostolic lives, and Francis and his followers promised to be such.[75] The previous half century had seen heterodox spirituality escalate to dangerous levels, together with the church's repressive countermeasures. The Council of Verona had condemned such groups as the Cathars, Patarines, and Humiliati in 1184 for heresies stemming from the poverty ideal.[76] It is revealing of both the historical situation and papal motivation that Innocent recognized the small band of Franciscans in the same year that he launched the Albigensian Crusade.

Francis composed the second, definitive Rule of the order in 1221, and Pope Honorius III approved it in 1223 (hence, the so-called *Regula bullata*). Francis cited three distinguishing marks of the Friars Minor: poverty, itinerant preaching, and manual labor, of which poverty was the most impor-

74. For a summary of Waldensian tenets, see the excerpts, in Jeffrey B. Russell, *Religious Dissent in the Middle Ages* (New York, 1971), pp. 41-53.

75. See John Moorman, *A History of the Franciscan Order* (Oxford, 1968), pp. 10-19. See also Cajetan Esser, O.F.M., *Origins of the Franciscan Order* (Chicago, 1970); Malcolm D. Lambert, *Franciscan Poverty: The Doctrine of the Absolute Poverty of Christ and the Apostles in the Franciscan Order 1210-1323* (London, 1961).

76. Denzinger, nos. 760-61, p. 242.

tant. The Rule forbade members even to touch money, save when the care of a sick brother or sister (the Poor Clares were the women's wing of the movement)[77] required it, and members were honor-bound to live proudly as beggars. According to the Rule:

> The brothers should consider it a privilege to live with the outcasts of the world: the sick, the weak, the poor lepers, and the beggars of the road. When the need arises, they are to beg without any sense of shame.... Jesus, like Mary and the disciples, was a poor man and a wanderer; he was not above accepting charity.... Alms are the hereditary right of the poor, guaranteed for them by our Lord Jesus Christ.[78]

On September 14, 1224, while at the hermitage of the order on Mount La Verna, Francis, climaxing a long prayerful vigil, miraculously received stigmata, that is, wounds in his hands and feet like those of one who had been crucified. These bleeding wounds were hidden from all save his closest friends, and Francis suffered from them for the rest of his life. The stigmata became the key event in his life for Franciscan spiritual writers. To those around him they were a special sign of the degree to which he had imitated and conformed his life to Christ. Others, learning of these wounds, concluded that Francis was himself a Christ-like person of more than human significance, even the messiah of a new age.[79] As we shall see below, spiritual stigmatization became the peculiar goal of Franciscan mysticism.[80]

Francis lent support to those who wanted to see him and his movement as unprecedented since apostolic times. In April 1226, six months before his death, he composed his *Testament,* a controversial farewell to his followers. He had long sensed the papacy's fear of the Franciscan ideal, especially the order's denial to the religious of the right to own fixed properties and hold worldly power. Popes did not want such a point of view applied to other orders, much less to themselves, by critical clergy and laity. They determined to domesticate the primitive Franciscan ideal. In his *Testament,* Francis, perceiving this threat to the original Franciscan spirit, refused every compromise and bound his true followers to strict observance of poverty:

> [In the beginning] we were simple and subject to all. I did manual labor and wished to do it. I hope that all the brothers will do honest work

77. Moorman, *A History of the Franciscan Order,* pp. 32–39.

78. In *Brother Francis: An Anthology of Writings by and about St. Francis of Assisi,* ed. Lawrence Cunningham (New York, 1972), pp. 102–104.

79. See below, p. 112.

80. See below, p. 121.

The Stigmatization of St. Francis. Giotto.

with their hands. Those who are not skilled in work should learn a trade, not in order to gain a good wage for their effort, but in order to give a good example and avoid idleness. When the reward of work is not forthcoming, let us return to the table of the Lord in begging door to door. . . . Let the brothers beware of accepting churches, poor inhabitations, or other [fixed] constructions made for them, unless they conform to the demands of holy poverty, as we have promised in the Rule to live always as wayfarers and pilgrims. I make it an imperative demand of obedience that no brother dare accept any privilege from the Roman curia, either by himself or through an intermediary, for a church or any other place using the pretext of the needs of preaching or a refuge from persecution.[81]

Francis died on October 3, 1226. From one point of view he had bequeathed his order and the church an impossible ideal, one that would have destroyed both as viable historical institutions had it been enforced on the scale desired by his observant followers. From another point of view his legacy was a devotion to purity without which a religious institution becomes indistinguishable from the world around it.

Francis was hardly in his grave when a struggle began to define the character of the Friars Minor. Pope Gregory IX canonized Francis less than two years after his death. It does not detract from Francis's saintliness to recognize as a motive behind this early canonization the pope's desire to bring Francis and his order under the firm authority of the church; saints are distinguished by nothing so much as their fidelity to the church.

The Franciscan order was early divided between observant and conventual wings, between those who wished to live in strictest fidelity to Francis's *Testament* and those who desired a more settled and traditional order. The battle over the order's character was fought even in the biographies of Francis.[82] Thomas of Celano (ca. 1190–1260), a close friend and original disciple, spoke for the observants when he wrote the first account of Francis (*Vita prima*) in 1228, which depicted Francis and his work as larger than life and dwelt on the unique and the miraculous. Celano wrote a second biography in 1247 portraying a more human and heroic Francis. This was followed by still a third biographical work, a collection of miracle stories that circulated around 1253.

The counterpoint to Celano's work was Bonaventura's *Legenda maior* (1263). Bonaventura drew freely from Celano's biographies to construct his own account, but in such a way as to alter significantly the meaning of

81. In *Brother Francis,* pp. 51–52.
82. See Moorman, *A History of the Franciscan Order,* pp. 151–54, 281–87.

Francis's life and teaching. In 1266 the Paris chapter of Franciscans declared Bonaventura's biography the official life of Francis and ordered all previous efforts rescinded.

As general of the order from 1257 to 1274, Bonaventura earned the reputation of being its "second founder" because of his brilliant organizational work. His goal was to unify the observant and conventual wings— mostly, however, on the latter's terms. He wrote an authoritative exposition of the Rule, which spiritualized some of its harsher points and attempted to adjust the primitive ideals of poverty and itinerancy to a fixed institutional framework. Bonaventura did not believe that a life of poverty meant going without good food, clothing, and shelter, nor did he find it amiss if some Friars Minor, like himself, chose to substitute mental and spiritual work— that is, scholarship and meditation—for manual labor. In arguing thus, Bonaventura did not see himself as compromising original Franciscan ideals, but as making it possible for the order to thrive historically. His work had the effect, however, of lessening original Franciscan rigor. Poverty became more a spiritual ideal than a literal one, an attitude of heart and mind, not an actual physical state. John Moorman has described the turning point in the history of the order marked by Bonaventura's generalate:

> There was [henceforth] to be greater security and stability, greater privilege and prestige. The typical friar was to be no longer the wandering evangelist who worked in the fields, tended the sick, slept in barns and churches, a simple, devout, homely soul content to take the lowest place and be *idiota et subditus omnibus,* but a member of a religious house, well educated and well trained, a preacher and director of souls, a man whom the community could respect and whose services would be valued.[83]

Throughout Bonaventura's lifetime a significant body of Franciscans opposed all efforts to conventualize the order. For them, poverty was a literal state and all ownership of property and possessions a manifest contradiction of the order's original charter. This observant ideal was volatile dissent in its own right, but it became all the more explosive when Franciscans integrated it with a revolutionary philosophy of history set forth by an equally idealistic contemporary of St. Francis, the Calabrian monk Joachim of Fiore (ca. 1132–1202). Joachim had joined the Cistercian abbey of Sambucina at age fifteen and was ordained priest in 1168. By 1177 he had risen to the position of abbot in the monastery in Corazzo. Disillusioned by what he considered laxness and indiscipline among the White Monks, he

83. Ibid., p. 154.

departed the order in 1192. After a brief period in the wilderness he founded the Abbey of San Giovanni of Fiore, henceforth the home of the Florensians, a new order approved by Pope Celestine III in 1196. The Florensians continued independently until 1633, after which time they were reabsorbed into the Cistercian order.[84]

Like St. Francis, Joachim too found inspiration in certain passages of the New Testament, especially several that seemed to promise a unique new age for mankind. Ephesians 4:11–13 spoke of a time of maturity and the fullness of the knowledge of God: "God's gifts were that some should be apostles, some prophets, some evangelists, some pastors and some teachers, for the work of the ministry, for the building up of the body of Christ, until we all attain to the unity of the faith and the knowledge of the Son of God, to mature manhood, to the measure of the stature of the fulness of Christ." According to 1 Corinthians 13:9–10: "Our knowledge is imperfect and our prophecy is imperfect, but when the perfect comes, the imperfect will pass away." Revelation 14:6 seemed to speak even of a new gospel: "Then I saw an angel flying in mid-Heaven with an eternal gospel to proclaim to those who dwell on earth, to every nation and tribe and tongue and people." Joachim perceived a prophetic-spiritual meaning in each of these passages. Here was the promise of full and complete knowledge of God, a time when the church's pastors and teachers would be superseded by an eternal gospel addressed to a mankind come of age. Joachim believed this new age to be something beyond the fulfilment of prophecy in Jesus Christ—the promise of a *new* and *better* world order. Beyond Judaism and Christianity lay still a third, superior religious age and culture.

Joachim elaborated his beliefs in three principal works, written while he was still with the Cistercians: the *Liber concordiae novi et veteris testamenti*, the *Expositio in Apocalypsim*, and the *Psalterium decem chordarum*. His originality lay especially in the ingenious way he historicized the doctrine of the Trinity.[85] In Joachim's vision, the unfolding of secular history, the history of salvation, and the trinitarian nature of God were one process. There is a period in history which can be said to be "of the Father," another "of

84. On Joachim's biography, see Morton Bloomfield, "Joachim of Flora: A Critical Survey of his Canon, Teachings, Sources, Biography, and Influence," *Traditio* 13 (1957): 249–311, reprinted in *Joachim of Fiore in Christian Thought: Essays on the Influence of the Calabrian Prophet*, ed. Delno C. West (New York, 1975), 1:29–92. See also G. La Piana, "Joachim of Flora: A Critical Survey," in ibid., pp. 3–28; and Johannes Huck, *Joachim von Floris und die joachitische Literatur: Ein Beitrag zur Geistesgeschichte des hohenstaufischen Zeitalters* (Freiburg, 1938).

85. Marjorie Reeves, *The Influence of Prophecy in the Later Middle Ages: A Study in Joachimism* (Oxford, 1969), pp. 20, 31. Ernst Benz, *Ecclesia Spiritualis: Kirchenidee und Geschichtstheologie der franziskanischen Reformation* (Stuttgart, 1934), p. 6.

the Son," and still a third "of the Holy Spirit," and each has its peculiar religious ideals and supporting institutions. As the Son is begotten by the Father, the Age of the Son follows the Age of the Father, and as the Holy Spirit proceeds from Father and Son, the new Age of the Spirit succeeds that of the Son. The time from Adam to the birth of Christ, the historical period recorded in the Old Testament, is the Age of the Father. The time of the New Testament and the Christian church down to Joachim's lifetime, or what Joachim calls "these times," is the Age of the Son. Since Joachim appears to have calculated each age to consist of forty-two generations, signs of the transition to the new Age of the Spirit might be expected to appear around the mid-thirteenth century. Joachim himself described the first two generations after 1200 as crucial in this regard, but he did not venture an actual date or designate a shorter span of time.

As each age has its historical span, so each has its peculiar culture, prototype, and precursor.[86] The culture of the Age of the Father is patriarchal; Joachim described it as an *ordo conjugatorum*. Here the father-dominated family, in which hierarchical authority reigns supreme, is the model. The culture of the Age of the Son is priestly-clerical, with many independent units of authority, reflective of the autonomous monasteries and fiefdoms of the Middle Ages. Joachim described it as an *ordo clericorum*. The culture of the dawning Age of the Spirit is to be communitarian, as monastic values penetrate society at large. Joachim described it as an *ordo monachorum*. Here authority and status are democratized within communities of men and women who consider themselves equals.

The Age of the Father has two prototypes: Abraham, the father of the Jews, and Moses, the stern lawgiver. The prototype of the Age of the Son is the apostle Peter, the busy, disciplined ecclesiast, and that of the Age of the Spirit, the apostle John, the mystic and contemplator.

Joachim believed that each age was already latent and evolving within the preceding age. In the Old Testament, the reign of King Hezekiah, when Isaiah and Hosea, the prophets of mercy and compassion, were active, anticipated the Age of the Son. Joachim apparently considered another ruler contemporary with Isaiah and Hosea, King Uzziah, who had been stricken with leprosy for profaning holy things, to be a negative precursor of the Age of the Son, foreshadowing perhaps the Investiture Struggle, when the church wrested its offices from secular domination. Joachim cited Benedict of Nursia, the effectual founder of Western monasticism, as the precursor of the Age of the Spirit already within the Age of the Son.

Joachim borrowed various metaphors and analogies to convey the qual-

86. Benz, *Ecclesia spiritualis,* pp. 9–16; Reeves, *The Influence of Prophecy,* pp. 16–27.

itative differences between the three ages. For example, the Age of the Father is characterized by fear of the stern patriarch; the Age of the Son, by faith and trust—monastic vows and feudal oaths may have been Joachim's model; and the Age of the Spirit, by a sense of equality and love. In the Age of the Father men are servants; in that of the Son, freemen; in that of the Spirit, friends. The Age of the Father is one of slavery; that of the Son, the "bondage" of sons; that of the Spirit, genuine freedom. Law reigns supreme in the Age of the Father; mercy, in the Age of the Son; and the "fulness of mercy," in the Age of the Spirit. The Age of the Father is starlight; that of the Son, dawn; that of the Spirit, the full light of day. The Age of the Father is winter; that of the Son, spring; that of the Spirit, summer. The Age of the Father is the root; the Age of the Son, the stalk; and the Age of the Spirit, the harvested grain.[87]

Despite his own good intentions, Joachim's philosophy of history proved hostile to the medieval church at several points. In Joachim's vision present religious institutions, which included a papacy successfully pretending to great power status, were in the process of transformation into communities modeled on the virtues of observant monasticism. This transformation was believed to be a matter of revelation and prophecy; God had ordained the evolution of a spirit-guided church and culture from the papal church and culture. Joachim did not thereby intend to oppose the papacy. To him it was the legitimate and rightful institution for the Age of the Son and had by no means fully run its course during his lifetime. He did, however, believe that the new age was dawning and saw clear signs of it in the growing numbers of monastic orders and the burgeoning lay piety of the twelfth century. His own order of Florensians testified to the transformation of priestly-clerical culture into monastic culture. This incipient transformation did not, however, justify revolutionary activity or even mild disobedience to help the new age along. Joachim expected the new to displace the old peacefully by a gradual evolution.

Although theologians later challenged his philosophy of history and the church condemned it when Spiritual Franciscans demonstrated its revolutionary possibilities, Joachim himself was censured only for seemingly heretical views on the Trinity—and that posthumously. Joachim had written a tract critical of Peter Lombard's teaching on the Trinity, and the Fourth Lateran Council condemned his alternative views in 1215. The Council accused him of stressing God's triune nature to the detriment of his unity, teaching that "three are one" rather than the traditional "three-in-one."[88] Joachim had objected especially to Lombard's description of God as

---

87. Benz, *Ecclesia spiritualis*, pp. 9–10.
88. Reeves, *The Influence of Prophecy*, pp. 31–32; Denzinger, nos. 803–808, pp. 261–63.

a "summa res non generans," the highest being, absolutely complete in himself. To Joachim this must have sounded as if God were some kind of Aristotelian Unmoved Mover, aloof from the historical process. Joachim's most basic tenet was God's active involvement in three stages of history. Unfortunately, as the historical stages were distinct, so also seemed to be the deity who acted in each. To the degree to which his speculation on the historical process led him to speak as a tritheist, his philosophy of history can also be said to have been very much at issue in the condemnation of 1215.

Another feature of Joachim's view of history that proved hostile to the medieval church was his belief in the penultimate character of the past; a more perfect future, not the restoration of an ideal past, obsessed Joachim. In this Joachim differed not only with the church authorities, but also with the poverty movements of his day. What was authoritative in the past was not necessarily to be taken as authoritative in the present and the future. As good and profound as Jewish culture had been, it proved only a shadow to Christian culture; and as good and profound as the New Testament and medieval Christianity were, they too would give way to a still more perfect form of human community. For Joachim, the best was always still to be.

By such reasoning Joachim's prophecy of a new age sanctioned innovation against tradition and implied that authority need not be based on precedent. More so than Ockhamist philosophy, Joachim's prophecy stressed to contemporaries the contingency of the world as presently known. It did this, however, not by pointing to an infinite number of possibilities open to God in eternity, but by directing people to a new, superior form of life still in the future. For Joachim, each age bore its own peculiar divine authorization. As the past had its unique standards and practices, so too would the future. As the standards of the Age of the Father ("an eye for an eye, a tooth for a tooth") gave way to those of the Age of the Son ("turn the other cheek"), so must those of the Age of the Son give way to those of the dawning new age—the egalitarian, communal life of mutual love.[89]

Joachim's philosophy of history strongly appealed to some of the followers of St. Francis. Francis had had no messianic illusions about himself and certainly no revolutionary intentions. This is clear from his *Testament,* where, despite a stubborn defense of apostolic poverty, he still declared his wish "firmly to obey the minister general [of the Order] and whatever guardian it pleases him to place over me."[90] The stigmata, which

89. Benz summarizes the extreme logical conclusion of such reasoning: "Joachim's promise of a coming time of the Spirit that would dissolve and absorb the papal church and culture . . . was no longer a form of the Catholic church. At its root it was nothing less than a new religion with a new order of life; a free community of the church of the Spirit, without a pope, without sacraments, without a sacred book, without theological education, and without a clergy" (*Ecclesia spiritualis*, p. 47).

90. In *Brother Francis,* p. 52.

might have occasioned spiritual pride in another, led Francis only to greater self-effacement. Certain of his followers, however, were always less modest in his behalf and attributed to him a more than human significance. The question was now posed: Could St. Francis be the messiah of the third age prophesied by Joachim? Could Francis's *Testament* even be the "eternal gospel" sent to guide the Age of the Spirit as the New Testament had guided the Age of the Son?

The biographies and legends of Francis written by observant Franciscans and later Spirituals created the conditions for just such an intertwining of Franciscan poverty and Joachite prophecy. Thomas of Celano presented Francis as one sent by God to introduce a new era of reform and his work as a special outpouring of God's spirit. The *Legend of Three Companions,* an anonymous work apparently derived from unused material collected by Celano for his first biography, contained many stories that dwelt on the special and miraculous character of Francis. One of these stories is a parable derived from a dream Francis allegedly recounted to Pope Innocent III prior to the pope's approval of the Rule. It tells of a king who secretly married a poor woman and had many beautiful children by her. One day these children appeared at the gate of the king's castle and asked to see their father. Thinking them street urchins, the guards proceeded to drive them away. The king, drawn by the commotion, recognized his children and welcomed them into his castle as his own.[91] When the king is seen to be God (or God's vicar), Francis the woman in the forest, and their children the observant members of the Franciscan order, a powerful declaration of the uniqueness of the Franciscans is here made.

The popular stories collected and circulated by Franciscan Spirituals in the late thirteenth century and published in the fourteenth under the title *Fioretti,* or *The Little Flowers of St. Francis*—a Tuscan translation from a collection known as the *Actus beati Francisci* (1322–28)—compared Francis and his followers directly with Christ and his Apostles. One story draws the parallel:

> St. Francis in all the acts of his life was like Christ, our blessed Lord. Even as Christ when he began to preach chose twelve apostles whom he taught to renounce all worldly things and follow him in poverty and other virtuous deeds, so St. Francis also chose in the beginning of the foundation of his order twelve companions, who vowed to live in abject poverty. As one of the twelve apostles of Christ was reproved by God and went out and hanged himself by the neck, so one of the twelve companions of St. Francis, the same who was called Brother John, did

91. Benz, *Ecclesia spiritualis,* pp. 78–79; Moorman, *A History of the Franciscan Order,* p. 19.

turn apostate and hang himself by the neck.... And as those holy apostles were a wonder to all men because of their sanctity and humility ... so too was the sanctity of the most holy companions of St. Francis. From the days of the apostles down to the present time the world has known no such wonderful and holy men. Indeed, as St. Paul was snatched up into the third heaven, so too was a certain follower of St. Francis, Brother Guy.[92]

The medieval church recognized the dangers latent in such glorifications of Francis and his order. An early defensive measure had been to canonize Francis, by which act Pope Gregory IX acknowledged his uniqueness, but strictly as an obedient son of the church, not as a new messiah or revolutionary reformer. Pope Gregory had also taken immediate steps to restrict the Franciscan ideal of poverty. In 1229 he issued the bull *Quo elongati*, which declared Francis's *Testament* unratified and hence an invalid, nonbinding guideline for the order. This action confined the order to the Rule as approved in 1223 and made it clear that the pope, not St. Francis, had the final word on the constitution and theology of the order.

The pope's views on apostolic poverty were of course considerably more flexible than those of St. Francis. According to the strict interpretation championed by observant Franciscans and later Spirituals, the vow of poverty meant that one actually lived as a pauper, owning nothing and using only what was absolutely necessary for bare subsistence; poverty was actual poor use (*usus pauper*), literal physical sacrifice. Over against this high ideal stood the need for a church order to have stable institutions if its material needs were to be met, the respect of its friends and enemies maintained, and the spirits of its members kept high. To survive historically, the order required property, clothing, entertainment, and a few luxuries. Under Gregory, absolute poverty became almost a legal fiction. According to *Quo elongati*, Franciscans had a *usus rerum*, a "use" of things without "possession" of them. The order held the fixed properties and worldly goods of a traditional monastic order, but "as though not"—as mere users, in moderation, not as those who actually possessed and "dominated" them. In many places, Franciscan houses became a peculiar kind of public property, serving the local community also as fortresses, city halls, auditoriums, and even hotels.[93]

John of Parma, the general of the order from 1247 to 1257, feared that papal subtlety would completely subvert the Franciscan ideal and fought to

---

92. *The Little Flowers of St. Francis of Assisi,* trans. Abby L. Alger (Mt. Vernon, n.d.), pp. 7–8. On the sources, see Moorman, *A History of the Franciscan Order,* pp. 288–89.

93. Leff, *Heresy in the Later Middle Ages,* 1:66–67; Moorman, *A History of the Franciscan Order,* p. 180. Freed, *The Friars and German Society in the Thirteenth Century,* p. 51.

preserve the primitive principles of St. Francis. His efforts were undermined, however, by the extreme actions of the Spirituals and by Bonaventura, who succeeded him as general of the order in 1257. Bonaventura
agreed with Pope Gregory that the vow of poverty should be carried out
"within a conventual framework harnessed to learning, buildings, papal
privileges, and stability."[94] Bonaventura looked on St. Francis as a truly
exceptional person, not, however, as a model every Franciscan, much less
every Christian believer, need try to imitate literally. The Spirituals considered such an attitude a betrayal of their founder's legacy. Had Francis lived
to see the comparatively benign poverty of the conventuals, he might well
have joined them in the ensuing battle with church authority.[95]

Two Spirituals brought the conflict over poverty to a head in the mid-
thirteenth century by explicitly wedding Franciscan poverty to Joachite
prophecy. The first was a Pisan Franciscan, Gerard of Borgo San Donnino,
a reader in theology at the Franciscan convent in Paris. Gerard published
without authorization his *Introduction to the Eternal Gospel,* a commentary on
Joachim's major writings in which he praised Joachim as a true prophet.
Pope Alexander IV condemned this work in 1255, and in 1263 a provincial
council in Arles condemned Joachim himself; the latter action, however,
remained local and never reached the level of a formal papal proscription.
The furor caused by Gerard's work forced John of Parma, a strong supporter of the Spirituals' cause, to resign his position in favor of Bonaventura.[96]

No less serious was the work of Peter John Olivi (1248–98), the leader of
the second generation of Spirituals and a kind of patron saint to Provençal
Beguines. Like John of Parma, Olivi too feared papal vitiation of the original Franciscan ideal. His sensitivity to laxness within the order did not,
however, lead him to demand an impossible perfection of Franciscans. He
believed that only flagrant and repeated self-indulgence in material goods
should be treated as a mortal transgression of the vow of poverty. Olivi
wanted a Rule that upheld the perfection taught and embodied by St.
Francis, yet also allowed for greater and lesser degrees of realization.[97] He
served as a member of the committee that drafted Pope Nicholas III's
commentary on the Rule, the bull *Exiit qui seminat*(1279), an important
theoretical defense of the Franciscans against their local clerical critics.
Nicholas declared Franciscan poverty to be a moderate *usus facti;* Francis-

94. Leff, *Heresy in the Later Middle Ages,* 1:84, 95.

95. I think Leff's judgment is correct: "The Spirituals, for all their excesses, were St.
Francis's true heirs; their very extremism was an extension of his" (ibid., 1:63).

96. See Rosalind B. Brooke, *Early Franciscan Government: Elias to Bonaventura* (Cambridge, 1959).

97. David Burr, *The Persecution of Peter Olivi* (Philadelphia, 1976), pp. 16–17.

The coming of Antichrist in the seventh age of the world. From Hartmann Schedel's *Liber Chronicarum* (Augsburg, 1497). Belief in the approaching end of the world was widespread in the later Middle Ages. Schedel here depicts the appearance of true and false preaching, as prophesied in Scripture, and the persecution of the righteous by Antichrist and his legions. Schedel believed that the righteous, who are here defended by the archangel Michael, would remain locked in battle with Antichrist for four and one-half years before the millennium began. The reform movements and councils of the fourteenth and fifteenth centuries heightened expectations of an imminent, decisive confrontation between good and evil, thus encouraging such apocalyptic beliefs. Scholars have also related the social conservatism of the Lutheran Reformation to its founder's belief that the world's end was near.

cans truly had the "use of [material] things in fact," although not "in right," that is, as their owner, who remained the pope, or, often, the towns in which the mendicants dwelt. Olivi argued, against later attempts to eradicate the Spirituals' interpretation of poverty, that *Exiit qui seminat* and other papal rulings favorable to Franciscan poor use were, as papal decrees, inerrant and incontrovertible—an argument that has led a modern scholar to the conclusion that Olivi actually originated the doctrine of papal infallibility.[98]

Around 1297, shortly before his death, Olivi published his *Commentary on the Apocalypse*, in which he appropriated Joachim's historical periodization. He adopted both Joachim's *sevenfold pattern*—that is, the seven ages of the Old Testament, which comprised the first five ages of the so-called world-week and included the Age of the Father, when the laws of nature and Scripture governed the world; and the seven ages of the Christian Church, which comprised the sixth age of the world-week (from the birth of Christ to the Last Judgment) and included the Ages of the Son and the Spirit, when grace and love rule the world—and his *threefold pattern*, that is, the three Ages of Father, Son, and Holy Spirit. Olivi depicted his own time as the period of transition from priestly-clerical culture to "that chaste and sweet contemplation typical of monks and the religious."[99] He also depicted St. Francis as a messianic and apocalyptic figure, the very angel of Revelation 7:2, who bore the seal of the living God. In Olivi's scheme the controversy between the pope and the Spirituals over poverty became the climax of a cosmic struggle between good and evil that foreshadowed the last days of the world.[100]

The yoking of observant Franciscanism and Joachite prophecy in the work of Gerard and Olivi presented a clear and present danger to hierarchical church authority. Thomas Aquinas was among the theologians to challenge Joachim's philosophy of history. He raised the question "Whether the New Law [the New Testament] will endure until the end of the world," and responded that "no state of earthly life can be more perfect than that of the New Law," that is, papal church and culture, and "one ought not expect a future state in which the grace of the Holy Spirit will be received in more perfect form than it has been received until now."[101] The

---

98. See Brian Tierney, *Origins of Papal Infallibility 1150–1350: A Study on the Concepts of Infallibility, Sovereignty, and Tradition in the Middle Ages* (Leiden, 1972), pp. 115–130.

99. Burr, *The Persecution of Peter Olivi*, p. 19.

100. Ibid.; Leff, *Heresy in the Later Middle Ages*, 1: 138–39. Even in his role as inaugurator of the Age of the Spirit, Francis remained for Olivi subordinate to Christ and basically a "renovator," not one who broke radically with the past. Burr stresses this point in distinguishing Olivi from Joachim (*The Persecution of Peter Olivi*, p. 19).

101. *Summa theologiae*, I^{a}II^{ae} Q. 106, art. 4, Resp.

third age envisioned by Joachim was eschatological, beyond history, not within it.

Papal decree firmly established this point of orthodox doctrine during the fourteenth century. At the Council of Vienne (1311–12) Pope Clement V (1305–14) condemned the errors of Olivi and the Provençal Beguines and Beghards together with the Spirituals' strict interpretation of the vow of poverty.[102] Pope John XXII (1316–34), who seemed the Antichrist to the Spirituals, settled the quarrel in a series of bulls that ended Franciscan poverty as St. Francis and the Spirituals had conceived and practiced it. The bull *Quorundam exigit* (October 1317) set the tone for all subsequent papal action. "Poverty is great," John declared against Spirituals and Beguines in Provence, "but integrity is greater, and obedience is the greatest good"— this because poverty is alleged to be a physical matter, involving only worldly goods, whereas obedience is a matter of the heart and mind and deals with spiritual goods.[103] The bull *Gloriosam ecclesiam* (January 1318) accused the Spirituals of the Donatist heresy, charging that they confused their allegedly superior state of personal sanctity with sacramental power and ecclesiastical authority.[104] Two further bulls, issued in 1322 (*Quia non-nunquam* and *Ad conditorem canonum*), struck down the major theological basis for the strict interpretation of the vow of poverty by denying the distinction between use and ownership that popes Gregory IX and Nicholas III had previously recognized. In John's view, what one ate, wore, and lived in, one also possessed and exercised dominion over; there was simply no such thing as pure *usus pauper* or simple *usus facti*. The final blow to strict Franciscan poverty came the following year in the bull *Cum inter nonnullos* (November 1323). Here John declared that Jesus and the Apostles had possessed goods both privately and in common and were not themselves practitioners of the abject poverty urged by observant Franciscans and Spirituals.[105]

These and subsequent bulls on the subject received strong protests from the Franciscan general, Michael of Cesena (1316–1342), and from William of Ockham, who had become alienated from the pope at this time

---

102. Denzinger, nos. 891–908, pp. 282–85.

103. Leff, *Heresy in the Later Middle Ages,* 1: 208.

104. "Secundus error, quo praedictorum insolentium conscientia maculatur, venerabiles Ecclesiae sacerdotes aliosque ministros sic iurisdictionis et ordinis clamitat auctoritate desertos, ut nec sententias ferre, nec sacramenta conficere, nec subiectum populum instruere valeant vel docere, illos fingentes omni ecclesiastica potestate privatos, quos a sua perfidia viderint alienos: quia apud ipsos solos (ut ipsi somniant) sicut spiritualis vitae sanctitas, sic auctoritas perseverat, in qua re Donatistarum sequuntur errorem" (Denzinger, no. 912, p. 286).

105. Ibid., nos. 930–31, pp. 288–89.

on other grounds.[106] Michael initially joined the pope in opposition to the extremes of the Spirituals, but as it became clear that the pope intended to remove every basis for living a life of poverty as St. Francis had taught it, Michael found his differences with the pope greater than those with the Spirituals. He reiterated, to little avail, the Franciscan belief that property resulted from the Fall and that "new men," that is, observant Franciscans, were capable of using material things, even consumables, without exercising dominion over them. Michael finally took refuge with the emperor Louis of Bavaria, an enemy of the pope, who found many allies among the Spirituals and even personally paraphrased Olivi's *Commentary on the Apocalypse* in criticism of the pope's stand on poverty.[107]

Pope John responded to these developments with still another bull, *Quia vir reprobus* (November 1329), which condemned poor use and asserted what henceforth became the definitive position of the church: evangelical perfection is strictly a matter of *spiritual* abnegation, not the literal renunciation of physical possessions. Even before the Fall, John declared, God had given man lordship and dominion over the earth.[108] Ownership of property was not a mark of *fallen* man, but a divine dispensation already at man's creation, hence, something neither Franciscans nor any other religious need forswear.

By the late 1320s, the poverty issue was virtually decided. In February 1326, the pope condemned Olivi's *Commentary*. Leading Spirituals fled to other orders; Ubertino de Casale became a Benedictine; Angelo Clareno, a Celestinian. The poverty ideal henceforth acquired a more traditional and subtle expression.

The papacy's response to the Spirituals was realistic, in that it cautioned them against thinking that perfection was normative, and self-serving, in that it urged the followers of Francis to be loyal to their founder's example as an obedient son of the church. To the papacy, Peter's church was the only possible church this side of eternity; there was no fuller knowledge of God or communication of his spirit beyond that which it provided. The modern historian Vandenbroucke faithfully records the papal reading of this episode in church history, when he concludes that the poverty crisis "led thinking men to discover the decisive norm in obedience."[109]

Is there, then, to be no penetration beyond history in time, no foretaste of eternity in this life? The medieval church did acknowledge that a few could

106. See above, p. 55.

107. Burr, *The Persecution of Peter Olivi*, pp. 88, 92.

108. Leff, *Heresy in the Later Middle Ages*, 1: 247; Burr, *The Persecution of Peter Olivi*, pp. 82–83.

109. LeClercq et al., *The Spirituality of the Middle Ages*, p. 300.

rise beyond the bounds of time and experience a genuine "third age" in the present life. This was not, however, by Joachite prophecy but by rare mystical experience. Mysticism made it possible for individuals to pass momentarily beyond the limitations of the present age and touch eternity. In the fourteenth century, mysticism became to the poverty movement of the twelfth and thirteenth centuries what monasticism had been to martyrdom in the early Christian centuries: the continuation in a new form of an ideal that had ceased to be practicable. Those who could not be impoverished in fact would become so in mind and in spirit.

Varieties of Mystical Experience

MEDIEVAL mystical writings range from sermonettes to magisterial philosophical tracts and bridge the barriers of sex, age, social class, education, and heresy. They are the most universal literature of the Middle Ages. We find both "mysticism" and "mystical theology." The former describes the experience of true mystics, those who claim to have experienced God intimately. Mystical theology, on the other hand, describes the learned study of mysticism by university scholars and the pursuit of mystical experience by clergy and laity who never actually achieve it. Modern scholars, noting the pervasive lay interest in the religious life and the egalitarianism that pervaded both orthodox and heterodox movements, speak of a "democratization" and "laicization" of mystical experience in the later Middle Ages. True mystics however, were always considered rare. Seekers after the mystical way were many; but the number of experienced mystics quite small. Mysticism was democratized only in principle; while *anyone* could receive the special grace of mystical union, official church teaching and majority opinion, understandably fearing the social consequences of large numbers of people who believed they had known God by direct experience, recognized very few genuine mystics. Mysticism nonetheless became a recognized feature of medieval intellectual and religious life. All agreed that the mystic had reached the summit of piety, the highest possible religious goal of earthly life.

Modern scholars contrast two basic types of mysticism in the later Middle Ages. One is a Latin tradition that tends to be Cistercian or Franciscan in religious order and eclectic in theological orientation, drawing heavily on traditional monastic piety and the writings of Dionysius the Areopagite. It is prejudiced in favor of the will, love, and practical piety and Christocentric and volitional as regards the mystical union (one embraces Christ, or conforms one's will to God in Christ, in mystical union). Such Christocentric and volitional mysticism had a reputation for orthodoxy, and Bernard of Clairvaux and Bonaventura are its outstanding examples.

On the other hand, there is a predominantly Germanic mystical tradition that tends to be Dominican in religious order and Albertist, Thomist, and Neoplatonist in theology. It is concerned more with intellect than with will or practiced piety and stresses contemplation and an intellectual vision of God. Theocentric and essentialist as regards mystical union, it seeks a merger with a divine abyss rather than conformity with Christ (one is said to lose one's being in God like a drop of water in a vat of wine). Such theocentric and essentialist mysticism was considered heterodox by the church, and Meister Eckhart became its outstanding representative.[110]

Beyond this gross contrast, mysticism may be seen as a spiritualizing or internalizing of the ideal of absolute poverty, the ideal that had originally inspired the monastic reform movements of the high Middle Ages and gripped large numbers of pious laity. The Waldensian, Beguine, and Franciscan movements were born of the desire "naked to follow the naked Christ," each movement taking Christ's call to self-denial in a literal sense. When the poverty ideal was transposed from the world to the cloister and there "domesticated," it evolved from such literal physical deprivation to more subtle forms of interior self-sacrifice. The regimen of monastic piety became one not only of material self-denial, but also of prolonged prayer and contemplation designed to "impoverish" one's conscious, sinful self by flooding the heart and mind with feelings and thoughts of Christ and God. When the Dominicans and Franciscans regularized German beguinages in the thirteenth century, they found such mystical practices far advanced among their new charges and also encountered the first poetry celebrating high mystical experience. The philosophical and theological mysticism of Meister Eckhart and other fourteenth-century German Dominicans emerged from this encounter of traditional Dominican theology and spirituality with the new piety and religious language of cloistered groups like the Beguines.[111]

---

110. This summary is informed by Joseph Bernhart, *Bernhardische und Eckhartische Mystik in ihren Beziehungen und Gegensätzen* (Kempton, 1912), p. 156; Erich Vogelsang, "Luther und die Mystik," *Luther Jahrbuch* (1937): 32, distinguishing Dionysian, Latin (Bernard, Bonaventura, Hugo of St. Victor) and German (Tauler, Wessel Gansfort, Johannes Goch, and the *Theologia Deutsch*) mysticism; Kurt Ruh, "Zur Grundlegung einer Geschichte der franziskanischen Mystik," in *Altdeutsche und altniederländische Mystik*, ed. Kurt Ruh (Darmstadt, 1964), pp. 240–74, esp. 264–65; Herbert Grundmann, "Die geschichtlichen Grundlagen der deutschen Mystik," in ibid., pp. 72–99; and David Knowles, *The English Mystical Tradition* (New York, 1961), pp. 2–3.

111. Grundmann, "Die geschichtliche Grundlagen der deutschen Mystik," pp. 84–89.

A second basic trait of medieval mysticism is the belief that the religious realities confessed in faith can actually be experienced. The mystic ventures into a realm inaccessible to the normal processes of sensation and reasoning and well beyond the grasp of faith itself; hence, the superiority of the mystically experienced over ordinary believers. Medieval authorities on the subject, like Bonaventura and Gerson, contrasted mystical theology with symbolic and dogmatic theology. Whereas the latter discoursed about God and religious life by analogy with worldly experience (symbolic theology) or on the basis of Scripture and church tradition (dogmatic theology), mystical theology found its knowledge of God in experiences beyond the reach of man's ordinary cognitive and volitional powers. Hence, the concern among mystical writers to designate a special faculty of the soul more profound than reason and will, what Evelyn Underhill once described as a "homing instinct," something deep within the human soul that constantly reminds it of its eternal origin in God.[112] Some medieval authorities described this inner inclination as a "spark of the soul" (*scintilla animae* or *synteresis*) and, depending on the writer's bias, it was interpreted as a depth dimension of reason, will, or both. Mystical writers influenced by Neoplatonism tended to describe this inclination as the operation of a unique ground of the soul (*Seelengrund*), a concept closely related to memory, which, in the Neo-platonic-Augustinian tradition, was seen to be the deepest part of the soul, a vanishing point that drops off into eternity.[113]

A final basic characteristic of mysticism is its extreme attachment to what I earlier described as the principle of likeness.[114] No group exalted this most medieval of beliefs more than the mystical writers. Being "like" God (*similitudo, conformitas*) was, for all, the essential condition of union with God—and with good reason. Mystical experience was considered a foretaste of the future when God will again be, as he was before the Creation, "all in all." Man's eternal origin and goal—perfect oneness with God—gave content to the mystical way. Hence, the repeated stress by all mystical writers on withdrawal from the world, transcending reason, and retreating into the depths of one's being where one is most "like God." Wherever he is found,

---

112. *Mysticism: A Study in the Nature and Development of Man's Spiritual Consciousness* (New York, 1961), p. 23.

113. See Heinrich Appel, "Die Syntheresis in der mittelalterlichen Mystik," *ZKG* 13 (1892): 535; H. Kunisch, *Das Wort 'Grund' in der Sprache der deutschen Mystik des 14. und 15. Jahrhundert* (Osnabrück, 1929); H. Hof, *Scintilla animae* (Lund, 1952), 161; W. Frei, "Was ist das Seelenfünklein beim Meister Eckhart?" *Theologische Zeitschrift* 14 (1958): 89–100; Paul Wyser, O.P., "Taulers Terminologie vom Seelengrund" in *Altdeutsche und altniederländische Mystik*, pp. 324–52.

114. See above, p. 46.

the mystic aspires to abolish his finite and sinful individuality, to think and will as God thinks and wills, to reach the point where God is both subject and object of his mind, to be, in short, where all that is and is known is God.

Dionysian Mysticism

There are three distinct major medieval mystical traditions: the Dionysian, the Franciscan, and the Eckhartian. The first derives its name from Dionysius the Areopagite, an enterprising late-fifth-century theologian who purported to be the biblical Athenian convert of St. Paul writing in the first century. The Neoplatonism that fills his work has put the lie to that claim, although this was not appreciated until the Renaissance, when Lorenzo Valla and Erasmus effectively questioned his identity. While the author's true identity remains ùnknown—he is referred to today as the "Pseudo-Dionysius"—he was probably a Syrian ecclesiast. His writings, all in Greek, became well known among Eastern Christian scholars in the sixth century, and after John Scotus Erigena translated them into Latin in the ninth century, they became popular in the West. These writings were much respected and often commented on by scholastics, who found in them both a mine of information and a new intellectual challenge. The Dionysian universe, with divinity cascading down from above, also attracted late medieval popes, who used its imagery to depict the church as the unfolding of Peter and to place secular power beneath spiritual power in the hierarchy of being.

Dionysian mysticism is especially distinguished by its emphasis on God's transcendence of reason. No other medieval theologian stressed the hiddenness of God, even as revealed in Scripture, more than Dionysius. He made a famous distinction between affirmative and negative ways to God, the *via affirmativa* and the *via negativa*. According to the former, positive things could be said of God on the basis of Scripture, where it is revealed that God is one, a trinity, a universal cause, wise and fair, a benevolent being, and the like.[115] But Dionysius was struck by the irony of Scripture's revelation: it concealed far more about God than it revealed. Indeed, the main thing conveyed about God by the Bible seemed to be his unfathomable nature and unapproachable majesty. Scripture names and describes one whom Scripture itself says cannot be named and described. According to Dionysius, we learn from Scripture that God is "a Mind beyond the reach of mind and a Word beyond utterance, eluding discourse, intuition, name, and every kind of being."[116] In a certain sense, then, the affirmative way of

115. *On the Divine Names*, in *Dionysius the Areopagite: On the Divine Names and The Mystical Theology*, trans. C. E. Rolt (London/New York, 1966), pp. 55-56.
116. Ibid., p. 53.

Scripture is more titillation than revelation, an approach to God that prepares and entices one onto a still higher way. Dionysius writes:

> At present we employ (so far as in us lies) appropriate symbols for things divine; and, then, from these, we press on upwards according to our powers to behold in simple unity the Truth perceived by spiritual contemplations, and leaving behind us all human notions of godlike things, we still the activities of our minds and reach (so far as this may be) into the Super-Essential Ray.[117]

The affirmative way thus opens onto the negative way, which is the mystical way, so that the reality of God can be reached beyond his names.[118] Dionysius urged man to "go beyond all mind and reason," denying every name and description of God, becoming "totally dumb," so that, in such ignorance and unknowing, he might know him who is unutterable and nameless.[119] In summary:

> The divinest knowledge of God, that which is received through *unknowing,* is obtained in that communion which transcends the mind, when the mind, turning away from all things and leaving even itself behind, is united to the dazzling rays, being from them and in them illumined by the unsearchable depth of Wisdom.[120]

> [In this experience man is] plunged ... into the darkness of unknowing ... and through the passive stillness of all his reasoning powers [is] united by his highest faculty to him who is wholly unknowable, of whom thus, by a rejection of all knowledge, he possesses a knowledge that exceeds his understanding.[121]

Such speculations fed anti-intellectual sentiment, especially in circles opposed to scholasticism, but they also inspired reform-minded scholastics like Gerson, the author of his own magisterial mystical treatise, and Nicholas of Cusa, whose *On Learned Ignorance* was strongly Dionysian. In the mid-fifteenth century a Carthusian monk, Vincent of Aggsbach (d. ca. 1460), a self-styled expert on the mystical teaching of Dionysius, became embroiled in a quarrel with Cusa over whether antecedent or concomitant knowledge

117. Ibid., p. 58.
118. "We have given our preference to the Negative way, because this lifts the soul above all things cognate with its finite nature, and, guiding it onward through all the conceptions of God's Being which are transcended by that Being exceeding all Name, Reason, and Knowledge, reaches beyond the farthest limits of the world and there joins us unto God himself, in so far as the power of union with him is possessed even by us men" (ibid., p. 189).
119. Ibid., p. 188; *The Mystical Theology,* in ibid., p. 198.
120. *On the Divine Names,* p. 152.
121. *The Mystical Theology,* p. 194.

of God occurred in the affective union with him attained by the negative way. Vincent, denying the possibility of such knowledge, attacked Gerson for affirming its existence. According to Vincent, Gerson had confused contemplation with mysticism and improperly injected the cognitive content of contemplation into mystical union when he defined the latter as an "experiential knowledge of God" received through affective embrace.[122] For Vincent and the so-called spiritual Dionysians who followed him, mystical union with God occurred only in and through "ignorance and unknowing."[123]

Love without knowledge of the object of one's love was an absurd concept to scholastics. Cusa accused Vincent of misunderstanding Dionysius, who, Cusa argued, had never taught that one could love something one did not also know. For Cusa, as for Gerson, an intuitive vision and knowledge of God—an "experiential knowledge," a "learned ignorance," a "knowing unknowing"—remained a prominent feature of mystical union.[124]

Vincent has been seen to represent an extreme anti-intellectualism on the eve of the Reformation and even to anticipate Martin Luther's attack on reason and scholasticism in the name of faith alone. Luther, however, cannot be so neatly placed within the Dionysian mystical tradition. While initially attracted to the negative way because of its recognition of God's transcendence and hiddenness, Luther came to believe that Dionysius actually committed the very fault that he had sought to correct in others. For one who praised ignorance and unknowing, Dionysius knew and wrote all too much about God, speculating on his nature far beyond the competence of reason and completely apart from the only true "access" to God, his revelation in Jesus Christ.[125] Hence, Luther's famous outburst against Dionysius's treatise *On the Divine Names:* "One becomes a theologian by living, indeed, by dying and being damned, not by understanding, reading, and speculating."[126]

122. Gerson, *De myst. theol. spec.*, cons. 28, p. 72, 1. 34; *De Myst. theol. pract.*, cons. 12, p. 208, 1. 5ff; p. 210, 1. 44–p. 211, 1. 55. See E. Vansteenberghe, *Autour de la docte ignorance: une controverse sur la théologie mystique au XVe siècle* (Münster, 1915), pp. 25–31.

123. "Ignote vel inscium consurgere oportet, id est sine cogitacione concomitante" (Vincent d'Aggsbach, *Traité contre Gerson* [1453], ed. Vansteenberghe, *Autour de la docte ignorance*, p. 190).

124. Vansteenberghe, *Autour de la docte ignorance*, pp. 19–21, 35–36. See also Uberweg-Geyer, pp. 634–36.

125. See H. A. Oberman, "Simul Gemitus et Raptus: Luther and Mysticism" in *The Reformation in Medieval Perspective*, ed. S. E. Ozment (Chicago, 1971), pp. 219–51. On the incarnate Christ, not mystical raptus, as the only "accessus" to God (stressed in criticism of Dionysian mysticism), see *Lectures on Romans, WA* 56, p. 299, 1. 27. For possible influence of Cusa (via Jacques Lefèvre d'Etaples) on Luther's theology—and by this route the larger Dionysian tradition—see Reinhold Weier, *Das Thema vom verborgenen Gott von Nikolaus von Kues zu Martin Luther* (Münster/Westf., 1967).

126. WA 5, p. 163.

Bonaventura and Franciscan Mysticism

No mystical treatise says so much in so short a space as Bonaventura's *Journey of the Mind to God (Itinerarium mentis in Deum),* a small summa of Franciscan spirituality and mysticism. Bonaventura, who, for reasons shortly to be explained, came to be known as the Seraphic Doctor, entered the Franciscan order in Paris in 1243, where he studied with Alexander of Hales (ca. 1186–1245), the founder of the original Franciscan school. In 1257, Bonaventura succeeded John of Parma as general of the Franciscan order. A most effective leader, he gave the order its distinctive philosophy and theology, developed its organizational structure, and laid down lasting rules and regulations. If Francis was the heart of the order, Bonaventura can be called its muscles and sinews. Canonized in 1482, he was declared an authoritative teacher of the church—a *doctor ecclesiae*—in the sixteenth century.

The Franciscans had something that no other religious order or movement in the Middle Ages could claim: a founder who had conformed his life to Christ to the point of receiving the wounds of Christ in his own body. On Mount La Verna a seraph in the likeness of Christ crucified had appeared to Francis and, embracing him, left stigmata in his hands, feet, and side. We have seen how this event led Francis's radical followers to proclaim him a messiah sent to usher in a new Age of the Spirit. This famous episode also directly informed Franciscan mysticism. The goal of mystical practice, according to Bonaventura, is the peace that comes from being crucified with Christ as St. Francis was. The mystical union itself is a *transitus,* a dying with Christ and passing over with him into God the Father. Unlike Dionysian mysticism, the union is Christ-centered rather than God-centered; but unlike Cistercian bridal mysticism, which is also Christocentric, the experience is one of painful ecstasy, not the sweet embracing described by Bernard of Clairvaux. Bonaventura claims to have had a mystical vision of the stigmatization of St. Francis on Mount La Verna, and the image of Francis stigmatized defined not only the goal of Bonaventura's mysticism, but also gave the *Journey of the Mind to God* its very literary structure.

Bonaventura began his little classic with a description of the world as a ladder to God, by which man ascends through three distinct spheres of reality in pursuit of his goal.

> Relative to our life on earth, the world is a ladder by which we ascend to God. We find here certain traces or images of God. Some are corporeal, some spiritual, some temporal, and some eternal. Some are outside us and some are within us. To reach an understanding of the First Principle, God, who is most spiritual and eternal and above us, we should journey through the traces of God which are corporeal and

St. Bonaventura, the Doctor Seraphicus.
Bonfigli (1472).

temporal and *outside* ourselves. Here we enter onto the path to God. We should then enter into our own minds, where the eternal and spiritual image of God is present *within* us. Here we enter into the truth of God. Finally, we should pass over into that which is eternal, most spiritual and *above* us. . . . Such passing over is to rejoice in the knowledge of God.[127]

For Bonaventura, man is a microcosm of the universe at large and naturally disposed in his own being to make this journey. His soul has powers which respond to the outside world (*animalitas, sensus, imaginatio*), reach into the internal, intelligible world (*spiritus, ratio, intellectus*), and can transcend both the corporeal and the intelligible world and touch that which is divine and supramental (*mens, intelligentia, apex mentis*).[128] The journey to God cannot, however, be made solely by the aid of man's natural powers, well-endowed though he may be, because man is also a fallen creature. He cannot even see God's traces in the outer world without prayer and "a cleansing illumination." The higher one ascends, the greater becomes one's dependence on grace and special divine assistance; the journey is only for the earnest believer.

Bonaventura complicated the journey by duplicating the three main stages so that they became six: there is a *twofold* ascent to God outside, within, and beyond oneself. The duplication of the stages of the journey is accomplished by the application of a transcendence-immanence formula to each of the three main stages. According to Bonaventura, one journeys to God by seeing him both *through (per)* and *in* his traces, that is, as one who is both beyond the marks he has left and yet also still present in them. Thus, God is seen through the world as its creator—the mark of the craftsman being on his work—and also in the world as its providential guide and principle of life. These are the first two stages of the mind's journey, its discovery and appreciation of God's traces "outside" itself.

God is seen also to be "within" man in two ways, and these form the third and fourth stages of the journey. He is seen through the soul, his natural image, which points away from itself to its origin, and as a vivifying presence in the soul reformed by grace. In the fifth and six stages of the journey, God is found "above" man as unity, that is, as One beyond time in whom the world has both its beginning and its end, and as a Holy Trinity, that is, as self-giving goodness in the world, as one incarnate, crucified, and resurrected in the Son and an abiding, life-giving Spirit.

127. Translation based on Saint Bonaventura; *The Mind's Road to God,* trans. George Boas (New York, 1953), ch. 1, sect. 2, p. 8; Latin: *S. Bonaventurae opera omnia V: Opuscula varia theologia* (Quaracchi, 1891), pp. 295–313.

128. *Mind's Road to God,* 1, 5–6, p. 9.

One of the reasons cited by Bonaventura for duplicating the stages of the mind's journey is that such duplication reflects the six symmetrical wings of the seraph who appeared to St. Francis at the time of his stigmatization. The duplication is said also to reflect the six days God worked to create the world, before resting on the seventh. The mind, too, must undergo a six-day labor before it can know the seventh day of mystical peace.[129]

THE WORLD OUTSIDE

In the first stage of the journey the mind beholds God through his traces in the world at large (*speculatio Dei per vestigia eius in universo*). It is a peculiarity of Franciscan mysticism and spirituality to view the world as a sacrament, that is, as a sign of God's power and glory. According to Bonaventura, apprehension of the things of the world by the senses ought to lead directly to reflection on their origin, magnitude, multitude, beauty, plentitude, functions, and order. This may occur by simple contemplation, by a reverent reflection peculiar to faith, or by careful rational analysis. However they are approached, the things of the world should be seen to reflect divine power, wisdom, and goodness. Bonaventura believed that a healthy mind saw God when it looked upon the world; one that did not was blinded by the scales of sin.[130]

When this first stage is duplicated, God is seen to be *within* as well as beyond the world (*speculatio Dei in vestigiis suis in hoc sensibili mundo*); the world both points away from itself to God and manifests him as a living presence. Bonaventura explained divine presence in the world in strongly Neoplatonic-Augustinian terms.[131] To know the things of the world entails far more than mere sensation and cognition; it is also a matter of delight—an affective response—and of judgment—the exercise of moral and religious sentiment—for feeling and evaluating are also intrinsic to knowing. According to Bonaventura, the more closely acquainted the mind becomes with something, the more it penetrates its individuality and knows it on the higher level of its exemplary being in the mind of God; in this way the wisdom of God is perceived to be within things. Study of the world opens the mind to that storehouse of memory in which lie the infallible laws by which things are judged and valued, and as the mind appreciates their beauty and proportion according to these laws, it judges them to be living pictures of God's wisdom. "Every creature is by nature a sort of picture and likeness of eternal wisdom."[132]

129. Ibid., prologue, sects. 2–3, pp. 3–4; 1, 5, p. 9.
130. Ibid., 1, 10–13, p. 11; 15, p. 13.
131. Ibid., ch. 2, sects. 4–7, pp. 16–18.
132. Ibid., 2, 9–12, pp. 18–21.

Some believe that this Franciscan appreciation of nature encouraged a more scientific stance toward the world; "observational science becomes . . . the fulfilment of a religious obligation."[133] The sacramental view of the world encouraged meditation on its patterns, symmetry, and regularity, which were seen to be manifestations of divine presence, and such meditation, although religiously motivated, led in turn to that detailed examination of nature on which empirical science thrives. Roger Bacon (ca. 1214–92), inventor of a rudimentary telescope, thermometer, and gunpowder, was a Franciscan, and Franciscans, especially Ockham and his students, have their place in the scientific movement of the later Middle Ages.[134] By contrast, both Dionysian and Eckhartian mysticism viewed preoccupation with the external world as a deadly pitfall on the mind's journey to God and confined the pilgrim to the inner world of the soul.

THE WORLD WITHIN

Having found God in the world, the mind is directed to look deep within itself and behold him through his image imprinted on its natural powers of memory, intellect, and will (*speculatio Dei per suam imaginem naturalibus potentiis insignitam*). Like the external world, man himself is a sacrament of God's power and glory. Already in the duplication of the first stage of the journey he had turned inward, as his experience of the outer world awakened his memory of the eternal rules and laws of things. In the present stage the mind appreciates its godlike ability to span time, remembering the distant past and reaching back into eternity. Finding the "undying light" of the eternal forms of things in itself, it begins to look beyond itself to the very mind of God. Intellect and will also drive the mind beyond itself. Memory reaches for eternity, the intellect for the truth, and will for the highest good—ultimately for the eternity, truth, and goodness which only God is.[135] Like the Holy Trinity, in whose image they are made, the three powers of the soul are said to be "consubstantial, coequal, coeval, and mutually immanent"; as the Father begot the Son and Father and Son the Holy Spirit, memory is said to beget intelligence, and memory and intelligence together to "breath forth love" or will,[136] so striking becomes the reflection of God in the nature and activity of his image.

The mind can behold God not only through its own nature and activity as his image, but also as one present *within* it. Such is not true of the fallen and

---

133. Boas's introduction to ibid., p. xix.
134. See Copleston, *A History of Philosophy,* 3: 165–79.
135. "Memory in its operations leads to eternity, intelligence to truth, and the power of choice to the highest goodness" (*Mind's Road to God,* 3, 4, p. 26).
136. Ibid., 3, 5, p. 26.

corrupted soul, only of the soul healed by grace. A ladder higher than that
of man's natural powers is thus required to reach this stage. Hence, in the
duplication of this second stage, the saving work of Christ becomes prominent. God is beheld in his created image only insofar as it is reformed by
grace (*speculatio Dei in sua imagine donis gratuitis reformata*); such a reformed
and illumined mind becomes a "house of God."[137]

THE WORLD ABOVE

Having followed God's traces in the outer world and the soul, the mind
enters the penultimate stage of its journey by rising above itself. Divinely
reformed, it is able to transcend itself and approach God as he is in himself.
The mind now receives a vision of divine unity through its primary name,
which is Being (*speculatio divinae unitatis per eius nomen primarium quod est
Esse*); it comes to know God as the beginning and the end, the one from
whom all things have come and to whom all things must return.[138]

The duplication of this final stage brings a vision of the divine Trinity in
its name, which is Goodness (*speculatio beatissimae trinitatis in eius nomine quod
est Bonum*). Here God is seen to be not only the perfect unity of being,
before and after time, but also generous, self-giving being.[139] Reciprocal
love reigns among the members of the Trinity, and each goes out of himself
for the sake of humankind: the Father creates; the Son takes flesh, dwells
among men, and dies for their sins; and the Spirit remains an abiding
source of illumination and sustenance. To behold God as Trinity is to contemplate in the "stupor of wonder." This is the end of the mind's journey to
God, the "perfection of the mind's illumination."[140]

What is left for the mind to do? Absolutely nothing; it has gone as far as
its own nature and God's grace can take it. Now, on the seventh day of its
journey, the mind must rest. In darkness and silence it embraces the
crucified Christ and experiences what Bonaventura describes as a "mystical
self-transcendence, through which peace is given to the understanding, as
affection passes over into God through ecstasy."[141] At this point Bonaventura's mysticism becomes strictly Dionysian. "In this transition," he writes,
"all intellectual operations must be halted and discarded, while the highest
peak of affection is transferred and transformed totally into God."[142] The
mind is not permitted to enter the promised land; having expended itself

137. Ibid., 4, 2, p. 28; 8, p. 32.
138. Ibid., 5, 7–8, pp. 37–38.
139. Ibid., 6, 2–3, pp. 39–40.
140. Ibid., 6, 3, p. 40; 7, p. 42.
141. Ibid., 7, p. 43.
142. Ibid., 8, 4, p. 44.

during the six days of the journey, it falls by the side, and the soul is carried, unknowingly, over into God by ecstatic love and affection. Like St. Francis at the time of his stigmatization, the mystic dies with Christ and returns with him to the Father.

Meister Eckhart

Germany and England were home to the great mystics and mystical movements of the fourteenth century. In England this was the active period of Richard Rolle, Walter Hilton, and Julian of Norwich, and it also saw the appearance of the anonymous Dionysian tract *The Cloud of Unknowing*.[143] Especially in Germany, mysticism, both on popular and intellectual levels, reached extremes that the church deemed heretical. In this regard the name of Meister Eckhart (ca. 1260–ca. 1327), who was both a profound scholar and a popular vernacular preacher, commands our attention. Eckhart continues to be a controversial subject, although in recent times a major revision of the traditional interpretation of his work has made him a much more sympathetic figure.[144] His friends see him as he saw himself—a badly misunderstood and falsely condemned loyal son of the church. His critics, on the other hand, believe that he was at the very least an unwitting theorist for revolutionary religious movements. Some praise him as a brilliant Neoplatonist and Thomist, a genius within the spiritual traditions comparable to his contemporary, William of Ockham. Others, however, spurn him as a second-rank scholastic and purveyor of heresy.[145]

Eckhart, the son of a nobleman, was educated by the Dominicans of Cologne and held major administrative and academic posts within the order. He was prior of the Erfurt order from 1294 to 1298. He studied and taught in Paris between 1302 and 1303. From 1303 to 1307 he served as father superior of the order in Saxony and from 1307 to 1311 as its vicar-general in Bohemia. Thereafter he was administrator, teacher, and preacher in Paris (1311–13), Strasbourg (1313–23), and Cologne (1323–27). In Strasbourg and Cologne he regularly preached to and advised nuns of the Dominican, Benedictine, and Cistercian orders, as well as Beguines both

143. See Knowles, *The English Mystical Tradition;* Phyllis Hodgson, "Walter Hilton and *The Cloud of Unknowing,*" *Modern Language Review* 50 (1955): 395–406; Paul Molinari, S.J., *Julian of Norwich: The Teaching of a 14th Century English Mystic* (New York, 1958). A *Fourteenth Century English Mystic Newsletter,* ed. R. Bradley and V. Lagorio, was created in 1976.

144. See C. F. Kelley, *Meister Eckhart: On Divine Knowledge* (New Haven, 1977) and the recent collection of articles under the title "Meister Eckhart of Hochheim: 1227/28–1978" in *The Thomist* 42 (1978), esp. the selections by John Caputo and Roger Schürmann.

145. Assessments of Eckhart from the fourteenth century to the present are traced by Ingeborg Degenhardt, *Studien zum Wandel des Eckhartbildes* (Leiden, 1967).

attached and unattached to these orders. These women recorded and preserved many of his controversial vernacular sermons.

Eckhart requires the reader who would understand his teaching to attempt to think as he thought: "principially," from the point of view of the First Principle, *sub specie aeternitatis*.[146] One must begin quite literally "in the beginning." Asked to trace his lineage, a modern reader would probably cite his parents and grandparents and think two generations of forebears a sufficient identification. When Eckhart pondered his origins, however, he reached all the way back to eternity, to a life he had in God before the creation of the world and time. Eckhart's conception of man's eternal birth and preexistence in God is the key to his mystical teaching, as it is also to that of his influential and orthodox disciple, Johannes Tauler (ca. 1300–61). So it is here that we too must begin.

Eckhart described his origin thus:

> When I first was, I had no God and was merely myself [that is, in eternity God, as an object distinct from knowing subjects, did not exist; all was undifferentiated godhead]. I neither willed nor desired anything, for I was then pure being [*ein ledic sin*] and knew myself by divine truth. I wanted only myself and nothing else; what I wanted I was and what I was I wanted. Here I was free of God and all things. . . . I am my own first cause, both of my eternal being and of my temporal being. I was born to and for eternity and because of my eternal birth, I shall never die. By virtue of this eternal birth I have been ̇eternally, I am now, and I shall be forevermore. What I am as a creature in time will die and come to nought, for what comes with time must pass away with time. [However] in my birth everything was begotten; I was the cause of myself and everything else. Had I willed it, neither I nor the world would have come to pass; had I not been, there would have been no God [that is, all would have remained undifferentiated godhead].[147]

For Eckhart, this precreated state was also the final end of life—all things return to the undifferentiated godhead—and mystical union a present foretaste of it. While other mystical writers, both before and after Eckhart, also derived from John's Gospel (1:3–4) a belief that created life was once

146. See Kelley, *Meister Eckhart*, pp. 24–26.
147. *Deutsche Mystiker des 14. Jahrhunderts: Meister Eckhart*, ed. Franz Pfeiffer (Leipzig, 1857), 2: 281, 1. 20–25; 284, 1. 1–10. Compare Tauler, *Die Predigten Taulers*, ed. Ferdinand Vetter (Berlin, 1910), pp. 331, 1. 32–332, 1. 4. The sixteenth-century Lutheran Spiritualist Valentin Weigel, who embraced German mystical teaching in opposition to established Lutheran theology, appealed to this passage in Eckhart. *V. Weigels sämtliche Schriften* (Stuttgart-Bad Cannstatt, 1966), 3: 66–67.

"life in God," they did not extrapolate so boldly. Gerson, for example, writing almost a century after Eckhart's posthumous condemnation in 1329, expressed the orthodox interpretation when he warned against the pantheistic dangers that lay in speculation on man's preexistence in God. He accused the Netherlands mystic Jan van Ruysbroeck, whose early writings were deeply influenced by Eckhart, of falling prey to such dangers. According to Gerson, life was not in God in the sense that all things were "really and essentially identified" with his very being, but in the sense in which we say that a plan preexists in the mind and will of an artist or an idea is one with the mind and intention of an inventor, that is, truly in him, but also quite distinct from him.[148]

No other mystical thinker stressed more than Eckhart the belief that man was truly "of God's race and kin" (*gotes geslehte und gottes sippe*), a kinship resulting from man's precreated oneness in God.[149] This belief came to expression in his anthropology, another controversial area of his teaching. According to Eckhart, there is something in the soul that fully transcends its created nature, has nothing in common with temporal reality, and is completely self-sufficient.[150] He described it variously as a "spark of the soul" (*fünklein*),[151] a "virginal power," and the "ground" (*grunt*) of the soul; were the whole soul such, he declared, it would be "uncreated and uncreatable."[152] This power was further said to know only God and to receive him directly in his full, naked majesty: "By nature the ground of man's soul is receptive to nothing but the divine Being, directly and without mediation. Here God enters the soul totally, not with a part [of himself] ... and he alone touches the ground of the soul."[153]

Other mystical thinkers also believed that the soul was endowed with an irrepressible orientation toward God. But apart from the tradition shaped by Eckhart, this spark was normally understood to be a part of the created structure of the soul, a "spark of reason" or a "spark of the will." It was a residue of ethical goodness in man that had survived the Fall to give him a reliable natural inclination to truth and goodness, not a special structure

148. See Gerson's sermon *A Deo exivit* (March 1402), *Oeuvres complètes*, 5: 13-14; translated in *Jean Gerson: Selections*, trans. S. Ozment (Leiden, 1969). Cf. André Combes, *Essai sur la critique de Ruysbroeck par Gerson* (Paris, 1959), 3: 220-23, 269-70.

149. *Deutsche Mystiker des 14. Jahrhunderts*, 2: 420, 1. 31-40.

150. *Meister Eckehart: Deutsche Predigten und Traktate*, ed. Josef Quint (Munich, 1955), p. 294, 1. 7-14.

151. *Meister Eckhart: Die deutschen und lateinischen Werke: Die deutschen Werke: Meister Eckharts Predigten*, ed. Josef Quint (Stuttgart-Berlin, 1936), 1: 506-08.

152. Ibid., p. 482.

153. *Meister Eckehart: Deutsche Predigten und Traktate*, p. 417, 1. 7-11. Elsewhere Eckhart writes that "dise Kraft [the Fünklein] nimmt Gott ganz entblösst in seinem wesenhaften Sein; sie ist eins in der Einheit, nicht gleich in der Gleichheit" (*Die deutschen Werke* 1: 482).

beyond his ordinary spiritual powers that hearkened him back to preexistence in eternity.

Eckhart also diverged sharply from traditional teaching about mystical union. Here man's preexistent oneness in the godhead clearly provided the model. Eckhart saw mystical union as something more than simply becoming like God by perfectly conforming one's mind and will to his; it was rather a matter of being God again, of returning to the undifferentiated godhead. He described the progress to mystical union:

> The more one thing is like another, the more it seeks after it . . . and leaves behind its former self, departing from all that its object is not. The more unlike its old self it becomes, the more it remakes itself in the image of the object it so passionately pursues. . . . But there can be neither rest nor satisfaction . . . until the two are at last united in One. Therefore, our Lord spoke through the prophet Isaiah . . . "Neither height, nor depth, nor likeness, nor love's peace shall satisfy me. . . ." Our Lord Jesus Christ besought his Father that we should be made One—not merely united, but joined together in him and with him in the one single One.[154]

Mystical union is still more explicitly related to preexistence in eternity in the following description:

> A great master says that his [unitive] breakthrough [*durchbrechen*] to God is more excellent than his emanation from God. When [he says] I flowed from God, all things recognized God [that is, as an object distinct from themselves]. But there was no happiness for me in this, for I was then only a creature among creatures. In the breakthrough to God, however, I will be free in God and free from his will, that is, from God's works and from God himself [that is, from God as a reality standing over against me]. For then I am [again] above all creatures, and neither God nor a creature [for such distinctions do not exist in the undifferentiated godhead]. Rather now and forevermore I am what I was [before my creation]. . . . In the breakthrough to God I discover that God and I are one.[155]

The reader senses both the profundity and the heterodoxy of Eckhart's teaching when it is contrasted with the bridal mysticism of Bernard of

---

154. "Niht alleine vereinet, mer: ein einic ein" (*Daz Buoch der götlichen Troestunge*, in *Deutsche Mystiker des 14. Jahrhunderts*, 2: 431, 1. 1–17). See Tauler's account of man's evolution from formless fetus to "the uncreated, eternal Word of the heavenly Father" (*Die Predigten Taulers*, p. 136, 1. 29).

155. *Deutsche Mystiker des 14. Jahrhunderts*, 2: 284, 1. 11–22.

Clairvaux and Jean Gerson, both of whom carefully acknowledged distance between the soul and God even at the moment of their most intimate embrace. According to Bernard, in mystical union

> God and man remain distinct from one another. Each retains his own will and substance. They do not mingle their substances, but rather consent in will. This union is for them a communion of wills and an agreement in love [*communio voluntatum et consensus in charitate*].[156]

Gerson, more elaborately, stated:

> When the heart and mind, purified and intimately aware of God, have progressed so far that they now give no thought to carnal joy or to any servile or mercenary act, know nothing of God that is harsh, unfriendly, upsetting or confusing and no longer look on God as an avenger who makes retribution but know him only as the completely desirable, "sweet and gentle" [Ps. 86:5], totally to be loved "even if he slay me" [Job 13:15], so set only upon the business of love, then fly secure into the arms of the Bridegroom, clasp that divine Friend with the purest embrace, plant upon him the most chaste kiss of peace, surpassing all understanding [Phil. 4:7], so that you can say with joyful, amorous devotion: "My beloved is mine, and I am his" [Song of Sol. 2:16].[157]

Modern defenders of Eckhart argue that his description of unitive life in God did not intend to remove all distinction between God and the soul, and they dismiss the charge of "pantheism" as a misunderstanding of his teaching. Appeal is made to analogies Eckhart used in his descriptions of mystical union. For example, he likened the union of the soul with God to the way a drop of water poured into the ocean becomes the ocean, yet not the ocean it, concluding: "So the soul becomes divine, but not God the soul; the soul loses its characteristics [*Namen*] and virtue, but not its will and being. [In its union with God] the soul is in God as God is in himself."[158] Eckhart's most

---

156. *Sermones in Cantica Canticorum*, no. 70, in *PL* 183, p. 1126. Etienne Gilson comments: "The mystical union integrally respects this real distinction between the Divine substance and the human substance, between the will of God and the will of man. It is neither a confusion of the two substances in general, nor a confusion of the substances of the two wills in particular; it is their perfect accord, the coincidence of two willings. Two distinct spiritual substances—two substances even infinitely distinct—two wills no less distinct as far as concerns the existential order, but in which intention and object coincide to such an extent that the one is a perfect image of the other. There we have the mystical union and unity as St. Bernard conceived them" (*The Mystical Theology of St. Bernard*, trans. A. H. C. Downe [London, 1940], p. 123).

157. *De myst. theol. pract.*, cons. 12, p. 216, 1. 122–35.

158. *Meister Eckehart: Deutsche Predigten und Traktate* (1955), no. 55, p. 410, 1. 5–11.

famous analogy was that of a mirror's reflection of the sun's rays back into the sun. As the sun is in the mirror and the reflected rays of the mirror in the sun, and yet the sun loses nothing of itself and both sun and mirror remain absolutely distinct from one another, "so God is in the soul with his nature, being, and divinity, yet he is not the soul; and the soul's reflection in God is God, yet the soul remains itself."[159]

The point of Eckhart's work, however, and certainly its effects on others beyond his control, was not to exalt the distance creation had placed between God and man, but to overcome it. For every subtle description of mystical union that can be found in his writings, there exist several provocative ones.[160] In the final analysis, Eckhart begrudged all reality beyond the eternal birth; for him, man was meant to be in God, not to live as a creature in the world.

Eckhart's considerable subtlety was lost on his contemporaries, most of whom saw such matters in far more practical terms. He has a long and impressive list of opponents, who feared the theological and social implications of having large numbers of people believe they were one with the very being of God. Among the critics of Eckhartian mysticism were the general chapter of the Dominicans of Toulouse; the spiritual writer Gerhard Zerbolt of Zutphen; Jan van Ruysbroeck, an early admirer, who later discovered the error of his ways under church criticism; Gerard Groote, founder of the Brothers of the Common Life and a careful student of Eckhart, who forbade the Brothers to teach any of his condemned articles or even to own the books in which they were contained;[161] William of Ockham, who found the Eckhartian mixed liquids metaphor of mystical union "fantastical";[162] and Johannes Wenck, Nicholas of Cusa's critic, who found pantheism in both Eckhart and Cusa, whom Eckhart greatly influenced.[163] Both the Col-

---

159. Ibid., no. 26, p. 273, 1. 1–9.

160. Here one might instructively compare again Bernard of Clairvaux, who also used analogies to describe the union with God. Bernard likened the union of the saints with God to a drop of water mingled in wine, to molten iron become like fire itself, and to air so flooded with sunlight that it appeared to be itself sunlight. Bernard, however, proceeded directly from such analogies to conclude: "So it must be [that the saints lose all their human affections and are transferred totally into the will of God], for how will God be all in all, if something of man still remains? Yet human substance *will* remain, although in another form, glory, and power" (*De diligendo Deo,* ch. 10, *PL,* 182, 991 A–B).

161. See Maria A. Lücker, *Meister Eckhart und die Devotio moderna* (Leiden, 1950).

162. See the discussion by Robert E. Lerner, "The Image of Mixed Liquids in Late Medieval Mystical Thought," *Church History* 40 (1971): 397–411.

163. On the influence of Eckhart on Cusa, see Herbert Wackerzapp, *Der Einfluss Meister Eckharts auf die ersten philosophischen Schriften des Nikolaus von Kues* (1440–1450) (Münster, 1962). Late-medieval opinion pro and con on Eckhart is traced by Degenhardt, *Studien zum Wandel des Eckhartbildes,* pp. 33–50.

ogne and later papal condemnation of Eckhart's teaching called attention especially to its feared impact on the "hearts of simple people."[164]

The papal condemnation of twenty-eight errors in Eckhart's teaching on March 27, 1329, has nonetheless remained controversial.[165] Some believe that its origins were completely political, a patent conspiracy by rival Cologne Franciscans, who initiated the process against Eckhart in 1326. One view even holds that Eckhart's condemnation was a papal effort to appease Franciscans angered by the canonization of Thomas Aquinas (1323) and other favors bestowed on the Dominicans.[166] Others believe that the fault lay in the ambiguous and incautious phrasing of Eckhart's vernacular sermons, which lacked the precision of his scholarly Latin writings. The credibility of this thesis is lessened somewhat by the fact that Latin formulations were also among the propositions censured in Eckhart's works; for example, the statement: "Just as in the sacrament [of the Eucharist] bread is converted into the body of Christ, so I am converted into God; for God is present to effect his very being in me, not simply a similar being."[167] Almost all of Eckhart's defenders see him as a thinker ahead of his time, who was taken too literally by contemporaries incapable of penetrating his thought.

The times in which Eckhart lived played a major role in his condemnation, but probably not because his contemporaries were less precocious than he. Similar mystical themes, albeit in less sophisticated formulations, had been set forth earlier by Beguines, for example, in Mechthilde of Magdeburg's *Flowing Light of the Godhead* (composed 1250–65). After a near decade of persecution, the Beguines were condemned in 1312 by the Council of Vienne for claiming, among other things, a temporal perfection as great as that of the afterlife.[168] In 1296, Pope Boniface VIII condemned as Free Spirit heretics laity who "dogmatized that they could bind and loose, hear confessions, absolve sins, and preach, while denying such power to the church (which they said was not as perfect as they)."[169] Pope John XXII,

---

164. Josef Koch, "Meister Eckharts Weiterwirken im Deutsch-Niederländischen Raum im 14. und 15. Jahrhundert," *La mystique Rhénane: Colloque de Strasbourg 16–19 Mai 1961* (Paris, 1963), 133–56; Denzinger, no. 979, p. 294.

165. Of the twenty-eight posthumously condemned articles, seventeen (nos. 1–15, 27, and 28) were pronounced heretical in word and content and eleven (nos. 16–26) as overly bold and suspect of heresy, although capable of being interpreted in a Catholic or orthodox sense ("nimis male sonare et multum esse temerarios de haeresiqui suspectos, licet cum multis expositionibus et suppletionibus sensus catholicum formare valeant vel habere"). Denzinger, no. 979, p. 294.

166. See Otto Karrer, *Meister Eckharts Rechtfertingungsschrift vom Jahre 1326* (Erfurt, 1927), p. 19.

167. Denzinger, no. 960, p. 292.

168. See above, p. 93.

169. Denzinger, no. 866 ("Saepe sanctam Ecclesiam"), p. 278.

who would later censure Eckhart, condemned the Spiritual Franciscans in 1318 for similar pretensions to supreme holiness of life and religious authority.[170] On the eve of Eckhart's condemnation, in 1327, John condemned Marsilius of Padua for teaching, among other things, that it was within the province of the emperor "to correct, raise up, put down, and punish" the pope.[171]

Eckhart lived and preached at a time when popular religious movements and royal aggression had successfully challenged the authority of the papacy. His teaching was condemned in 1329 because, fairly or unfairly, it was perceived to be of one piece with this challenge, at the very least to provide theoretical support for those who made it. The historical context in which something is said or done also becomes a part of its meaning. In a more peaceful period of the church's history, Eckhart might have been more charitably treated, if not any better understood, but not in the first quarter of the fourteenth century.

From another angle, Eckhart emerges as the prototypical medieval man, a perspective from which his condemnation becomes most ironic. Where can one find a bolder assertion of the stock medieval belief that man's origin and destiny are supernatural? Where in the Middle Ages is it taught more forcibly that "to be" is to be in God?[172] Who more than Eckhart believed that "my truest I is God?"[173] In condemning Eckhart's teaching, the medieval church may also have condemned the logical conclusion of some of its most cherished beliefs.

170. See above, p. 113.
171. See below, p. 154.
172. See *Die deutschen Werke* 1:69–70.
173. Kelley, *Meister Eckhart,* pp. 61–69.

CHAPTER 4

The Ecclesiopolitical
Traditions

Secular and Theocratic
Concepts of Government

ANY effort to interpret medieval political and ecclesiopolitical thought must come to grips at the outset with the work of Walter Ullmann, professor of medieval ecclesiastical history at the University of Cambridge. Ullmann is to the political traditions of the Middle Ages what Etienne Gilson is to the scholastic— the author of a synthesis both authoritative and highly controversial. It is Ullmann's view that diametrically opposed concepts of government and law competed in the Middle Ages and that their conflict gave the political history of the period its dynamic. One he describes as an "ascending" view of power, according to which power originates in the community at large and ascends from below, that is, from the many to the one, from "the people" to the sovereign. The other concept of government and law Ullmann describes as a "descending" view of power, according to which power rests in a supreme sovereign and descends to subordinate members within a great hierarchy of being.[1]

Ullmann has characterized the ascending theme as populist and representative of the secular mind and finds its main sources in the pagan classics, especially Aristotle, and in medieval Germanic laws and customs. By contrast, the descending theme is seen to be theocratic and representative of the clerical mind, having its roots in Christian sources, especially the writings of Dionysius the Areopagite and such biblical sanctions of government as Romans 13:1: "Let every person be subject to the governing authorities; for there is no authority except from God, and those that exist have been instituted by God." Within the medieval church, Ullmann identifies the descending view of government with the canon lawyers, while he

---

1. *A History of Political Thought: The Middle Ages* (Baltimore, 1970), pp. 12–13; *Principles of Government and Politics in the Middle Ages* (London, 1966), pp. 20–23. See further Francis Oakley, "Celestial Hierarchies Revisited: Walter Ullmann's Vision of Medieval Politics," *Past and Present* 60 (1973): 6–10.

associates the ascending view with the conciliarists, proponents of the authority of church councils over popes.

Ullmann's critics have accused him of making the political events and thought of the Middle Ages far simpler than they actually were. In a recent critique, Francis Oakley carefully documented the case built up against Ullmann over the years and leveled his own charge of oversimplification.[2] It is argued against Ullmann that Christian tradition not only sponsored a theocratic view of political authority, but also became a source of political egalitarianism and ascending themes of government. Nor can the pagan classics be taken as exclusively populist in political theory; they also depicted the emperor as divine and sanctioned a descending view of power. Further, medieval kings were not exclusively proponents of an ascending view of power any more than medieval popes were exclusively supporters of a descending view; actual historical practice reveals greater variation and complexity in governmental form and theory than Ullmann seems to allow. Again, canon lawyers, strong proponents of the descending view, were also a major source of the conciliar theory of church government,[3] while major conciliar theorists (the fathers of the Council of Constance, for example), who strongly defended the ascending view, also supported a strong papal role in church government. Royal apologists like John of Paris actually drew on the writings of canon lawyers to support ascending views of political power and the king's case against the pope.[4] Even the authority of Aristotle was not exclusively on the side of the proponents of the ascending concept; Aristotelian entelechy, his teaching on the evolutionary development of potentiality to perfect actuality, served both descending and ascending views of power. Finally, there is the case of Thomas Aquinas, whom Ullmann found particularly important for the success of the ascending view of government, yet who was among the sources paraphrased by Boniface VIII in that most theocratic of papal bulls, *Unam sanctam*.

Ullmann may well have seen the forest more clearly than the trees; certainly his critics have successfully demonstrated that he is more suggestive at the point of synthesis than he is convincing in the task of analysis. However, the whole is always more than the sum of its parts. Although Ullmann's synthesis does tend to lack subtlety and nuance (perhaps not as much, however, as his critics allege), he nonetheless has magnified what are uncon-

2. Oakley, "Celestial Hierarchies Revisited," pp. 3–48.

3. The magisterial work on the subject is Brian Tierney's *Foundations of the Conciliar Theory: The Contribution of the Medieval Canonists from Gratian to the Great Schism* (Cambridge, 1955). Directly critical of Ullmann's views is A. M. Stickler, "Concerning the Political Theories of the Medieval Canonists," *Traditio* 8 (1949–51): 450–63.

4. See especially Tierney, *Foundations of the Conciliar Theory*, pp. 161–78.

testably competing tendencies in late medieval life and society. John Morrall alludes to a similar contrast when he defines the theme of medieval political history and theory as "the rise, development, and collapse of the ideal of a Christian commonwealth and its replacement by a return to a more purely political conception of the state."[5]

Finding it revealing that some historians can describe the Sicily of Frederick II and the England of Edward I as "already modern," while other historians look on the empire of Charles V and the England of Henry VII two centuries later as "still medieval," Bernard Guenée has warned against too hastily describing a period as complex as the later Middle Ages as one of clear transition from "feudal" to "modern" concepts of government and law.[6] This also applies to the developments we have traced within the scholastic and spiritual traditions, where the "old" and the "new" also coexisted with one another. On the other hand, in each tradition we can discern a strong movement favoring the lay and the secular world against the official clerical and religious world and encouraging innovation beyond tradition as the eve of the Reformation approaches. The integrity of secondary causes, that is, things finite, secular, and natural, was successfully contested in this period. Against an ecclesiastical institution that, invariably in theory and where possible in practice, sanctioned the secular world and natural goals only as they subserved a larger religious world and so-called supernatural ends, temporal reality came increasingly to be appreciated in its own right. Within the scholastic traditions, this contest seems most visible in Ockham's philosophy and theology, with its many-layered defense of individuals (also a major feature of Ockham's political thought)[7] and its personalizing of religious relationships in covenantal terms. In the spiritual traditions, the contest is apparent in the mystic's insistence on the authority of his own individual experience; in lay contentment with the simplest ethical religious practice—or even with none at all; in the laity's demonstrated disinclination to have their personal habits examined and weighed *sub specie aeternitatis* by priests in confession; in humanist preoccupation with the past on its own terms, study of ancient languages for their own sake, and support of purely civic virtues, and, finally, in the emergence of national religious movements with a social and political conscience, like the Hussites.

The contest for this-worldly goals and values found its most literal expression, however, in the political struggle between kings and popes in the later Middle Ages. The rising nation-states of Europe, in quest of full secu-

5. *Political Thought in Medieval Times* (New York, 1962), p. 11.
6. *L'Occident aux XIVe et XVe siècles: Les états* (Paris, 1971), pp. 78–82.
7. Arthur S. McGrade, *The Political Thought of William of Ockham: Personal and Institutional Principles* (Cambridge, 1974), pp. 116–17, passim.

lar independence and autonomy, acted decisively to curtail the traditional pre-eminence of Peter and, so far as possible, to transform the medieval church into a docile department of the inchoate sovereign state.

The Pre-eminence of Peter

HOW did the papacy become so politically powerful in the first place? Until the fourteenth century medieval Europe had been a peculiarly "Christian commonwealth"; where a genuine sense of transregional unity and cooperation existed, it resulted more from religious bonds than from any clear political or "national" identity. This is the basic reason why ecclesiopolitical conflicts and the papacy loom so large in the political history and thought of the Middle Ages; the church was always there as a higher, alternative authority. The presence of the sacred is as inescapable in the political history of the Middle Ages as it is in its intellectual and social history.

In the major controversies between temporal and spiritual power during the Middle Ages the church protested its spiritual autonomy and temporal power against secular aggression and outright political control of rights, functions, and territories it deemed uniquely its own. The papacy's extremely high view of its own authority in the world and comparatively low estimate of temporal power was partially simple self-defense. And when forced to defend itself, no other medieval institution had richer intellectual resources for convincing an age open to religious argument of its authority. It based its self-defense on claims to spiritual and temporal authority over the laity, including kings and emperors, and on alleged divine and secular rights to great temporal power and property, the justification of which was seen to lie in the Bible, church tradition, and manifest historical precedent.

There was, first of all, that most subversive of books, the Bible. Certain passages, it was argued, granted the pope, as Christ's vicar, power on earth. The most important of these was Matthew 16:19, a key statement that helped extend the sovereignty of the bishop of Rome over the church at large.

> You are Peter and on this rock I will build my church, and the powers of death shall not prevail against it. I will give you the keys of the kingdom of heaven, and whatever you bind on earth shall be bound in heaven and whatever you loose on earth shall be loosed in heaven.

In the matter of the pope's temporal power, however, the Bible proved ambiguous. Romans 13, for example, exhorted the faithful to obey all worldly authority as divinely instituted, and Luke 20:25 commanded, "Render to Caesar the things that are Caesar's." However, the biblical conception of authority as dual—as both temporal and spiritual—did not lessen the church's assertion of Peter's pre-eminence within the secular world. This is true also of perhaps the most balanced statement of the relationship between secular and ecclesiastical power, the famous letter of Pope Gelasius I (492–96) to Emperor Anastasius in 494. Gelasius declared that Peter, who administers the higher end of divine salvation and will speak at the Last Judgment for the kings of men, had a far greater responsibility on earth than Caesar, whose mission was to provide only short-term, temporal well-being.[8]

Papal claims to worldly pre-eminence were also assisted by the patristic and Augustinian characterization of the political community as secondary and artificial, a providential adjustment to man's fallen, fratricidal nature. In this interpretation, God originally intended people to be subject neither to sin nor to one another, and brought the political community into existence only after the Fall to punish fallen people and preserve them from self-destruction.[9] Augustine praised the Christian church over the Roman political community as the "only republic" in which one could find "true justice" and recognized Roman government as only an aid to the greater peace of heaven.[10] As long as it could be effectively argued that man's true end was supernatural and his true home a heavenly community, those who administered directly to that higher end and community were in a position to assert their superiority over those who merely tended man's penultimate temporal needs.

In addition to theological arguments in favor of Peter's worldly pre-

8. "Two there are . . . by which this world is chiefly ruled, the sacred authority [*auctoritas*] of the priesthood and the royal power [*potestas*]. Of these the responsibility of the priests is more weighty in so far as they will answer for the kings of men themselves at the divine judgment. Know . . . that, although you [Emperor Anastasius] take precedence over all mankind in dignity, nevertheless you must piously bow the neck to those who have charge of divine affairs and seek from them the means of your salvation. . . . For if the bishops . . . recognizing that the imperial office was conferred on you by divine disposition, obey your laws so far as the sphere of public order is concerned . . . with what zeal ought you to obey those who have been charged with the administration of the sacred mysteries?" Cited in Brian Tierney, *The Crisis of Church and State 1050–1300* (Englewood Cliffs, N.J., 1964), pp. 13–14.

9. Augustine, *The City of God*, trans. Marcus Dods, in *A Select Library of the Nicene and Post-Nicene Fathers of the Christian Church*, ed. Philip Schaff (Grand Rapids, Mich., 1956), bk. 19, ch. 15, p. 411.

10. Ibid., bk. 2, ch. 21, p. 36. "The heavenly city . . . while in its state of pilgrimage [on earth], avails itself of the peace of earth, and, so far as it can without injuring faith and godliness, desires and maintains a common agreement among men regarding the acquisition of the necessities of life and makes this earthly peace bear upon the peace of heaven" (ibid., bk. 19, ch. 17, p. 412).

eminence, there were important historical precedents. Bishops and popes had effectively excommunicated emperors and lesser political figures; on occasion they even had brought them to public penance for manifest sins and crimes. Ambrose, bishop of Milan, so dealt with Emperor Theodosius in 390, demonstrating, as Ambrose put it, that the emperor is "within and not above the church." Frankish bishops had anointed Carolingian rulers even before Christmas Day, 800, when Charlemagne set an important precedent by receiving the imperial crown directly from Pope Leo III (795–816). After Pope John XII (955–64) crowned Otto I emperor in 962, papal coronation of the Holy Roman Emperor remained a tradition until the sixteenth century.

Like biblical arguments, however, historical precedents also served both sides. A pope who crowned an emperor recognized the emperor's divinely ordained authority to rule, and an emperor who was within the church might, as the most powerful lay member of the body of the faithful, claim a special responsibility for the church's welfare and direction. In the early Middle Ages, Merovingian and Carolingian kings, like earlier western and eastern emperors, had little difficulty subjecting the church to their will. Indeed, Carolingian bishops appear at times to have been hardly more than royal bureaucrats and agents of state,[11] and Carolingian kings appropriated church lands at will to provide fiefs for their royal vassals.

In reaction to such secular domination, the church produced ingenious defenses like the "Donation of Constantine" (750–800). This contrived document reported that the Emperor Constantine had given the contemporary Pope Sylvester the emperor's palace, as preferment, "and likewise all provinces, palaces, and districts of the city of Rome and Italy and of the regions of the West," when the imperial capitol was transferred to Constantinople.[12] On this basis popes claimed to possess broad temporal powers as well as the keys to the kingdom of heaven. Even when popes conceded secular dominion to the emperor, as political realism deemed they must, the "Donation" continued to serve their purposes. It was argued in the twelfth century, for example, that secular power, in the person of Constantine, had given the material sword or secular authority, that is, coercive temporal jurisdiction, to the church and that the church, in response, had graciously returned such authority to the emperor to be used under the church's supervision—the dirty work of corporeal and capital punishment being unfit for clerical hands. What else was Pope Leo's coronation of Charlemagne in 800 than papal magnanimity?[13]

11. See above, p. 86.
12. Henry Bettenson, *Documents of the Christian Church* (New York, 1961), pp. 141–42.
13. Cf. Morrall, *Political Thought in Medieval Times*, pp. 55–56.

With such historical practices as papal coronation of emperors in mind, theologians and canonists spoke of the church's right to "institute" and "judge" royal power. Like philosophy in the schools and the liberal arts in the monasteries, secular power also was to be a handmaiden to those entrusted with the higher responsibility of guiding man to his final end.

The Cluny reform movement of the late tenth and eleventh centuries, named after an observant Benedictine monastery in east-central France, precipitated the first great contest between royal and papal power. The Cluny reformers absolutely rejected the subservience of clergy to royal authority and especially resented the easy compliance of German bishops with the wishes of Ottonian rulers. These reformers also attacked the confusion of the sacred with the profane represented by clerical concubinage, surrogate marriages that assimilated clergy to their secular surroundings and made them less distinct from the laity. Clergy who became fathers desired a secure inheritance for their children, and this made them easy prey to secular manipulation.[14] For the Cluny reformers, the pope was the only sovereign of clergy and the church their only spouse.

In the eleventh century both kings and popes assumed the unity of Christendom, while at the same time recognizing distinctive spheres of secular and ecclesiastical life. At issue between them was which side would hold the upper hand in the ecclesiastical sphere: imperial power, with its toadying bishops or a papacy inflamed by the monastic ideal of strict religious separation from the world. Popes devoted to Cluny's reforms came to power in the mid-eleventh century and asserted their independence. Pope Leo IX (1048-54) sponsored measures against both simony, the sin of selling spiritual things—in this instance, church offices by permitting kings to install their chosen clergy in them—and concubinage. Leo also appointed Cluniacs to key administrative posts in Rome. Pope Stephen IX (1057-58) reigned without imperial ratification, contrary to an edict of Otto I that required such royal approval. Pope Nicholas II (1059-61) took the unprecedented step of establishing a special college of cardinals in 1059, a body appointed by and answerable to the pope that henceforth elected the new pope when the papal office fell vacant. By the creation of the college, the church attempted to reduce extraneous political influence on the election of popes.

Pope Gregory VII (1073-85) extended the church's declaration of independence from secular rulers to the episcopacy. In 1075, he condemned under penalty of excommunication lay investiture of clergy at any level. He struck primarily at the emperor's established custom of investing bishops in

14. Christopher Brooke, "Gregorian Reform in Action: Clerical Marriage in England, 1050-1200," in *Medieval Church and Society* (London, 1971), pp. 69-99, esp. 72-73.

their offices by presenting them with the symbols of episcopal authority. Gregory's prohibition came as a jolt to Emperor Henry IV (1056–1106), who suddenly found himself under papal order to "secularize" his empire, as it were, by drawing a distinct boundary between royal and ecclesiastical spheres of authority and jurisdiction. Battle lines quickly formed: on the one side, the emperor with his loyal German bishops and a feudal nobility as intent on controlling their local clergy as the emperor his bishops; on the other side, the pope with his Italian cardinals, reform-minded monasteries, and factious German princes, who sided with Gregory because his ruling weakened imperial power in Germany.

After Henry denounced Gregory, his loyal German bishops declared their independence from the pope in a special assembly in Worms in January 1076. Gregory responded by excommunicating Henry in February and absolving his subjects from loyalty to him. On the eve of these events Gregory had admonished the emperor with the major biblical and traditional supports for the worldly supremacy of Peter:

> It would have been becoming to you, since you confess yourself to be a son of the Church, to give more respectful attention to the master of the Church, that is, to Peter, prince of the Apostles. To him, if you are of the Lord's flock, you have been committed for your pasture, since Christ said to him: "Peter, feed my sheep" [John 21:17], and again: "To thee are given the keys of Heaven. . . ." [Matthew 16:19]. Now, while we, unworthy sinner that we are, stand in [St. Peter's] place of power, still whatever you send to us, whether in writing or by word of mouth, he himself receives, and while we read what is written or hear the voice of those who speak, he discerns with subtle insight from what spirit the message comes. Wherefore Your Highness should beware lest any defect of will toward the Apostolic See be found in your words or in your messages and should pay due reverence, not to us but to Almighty God, in all matters touching the welfare of the Christian faith and the status of the Church.[15]

In brief, to deal with Peter's successors was to deal with Almighty God.

After his excommunication, the emperor faced the prospect of a widespread revolt under the leadership of the duchy of Saxony; he had no recourse but to come to terms with the pope. This he did in a famous scene outside Gregory's castle retreat at Canossa in late January 1077, where he begged for three days before receiving absolution. Although Gregory's victory over the emperor was not soon forgotten by Gregory's successors, it

15. In Tierney, *The Crisis of Church and State,* p. 58.

was in fact quite short-lived. Absolved by the pope, Henry regrouped his forces, regained power within the empire, and continued to treat the affairs of the church as if they were his own. Gregory excommunicated him a second time in March 1080, but repeated excommunication of the same individual had a greatly diminished effect. A settlement of the conflict came finally in 1122 with the signing of the Concordat of Worms, by which Henry V (1106–25) renounced any power to invest bishops with ring and staff, while Pope Calixtus II (1119–24) acknowledged the emperor's right to be present at the election of German prelates, judge disputed elections, and receive homage from newly elected bishops and abbots who served lands the emperor had bestowed on the church. The emperor continued to have a considerable political role in church affairs.

The high-water mark of papal power and influence was reached during the pontificate of Innocent III (1198–1216), who proclaimed and practiced a papal near theocracy. Innocent wrote of his office:

> To [the pope] is said in the person of the prophet: "I have set you over nations and over kingdoms, to root up and to pull down and to waste and to destroy and to build and to plant." [Jer. 1:10] To me also is said in the person of the apostle: "I will give to you the keys of the kingdom of heaven. . . ." Thus, others were called to a part of the care, but Peter alone assumed the plenitude of power.[16] You see then who is this servant set over the household, truly the vicar of Jesus Christ, successor of Peter, anointed of the Lord, a God of Pharaoh, set between God and man, *lower than God but higher than man,* who judges all and is judged by no one.[17]

Innocent, who likened the relationship of popes and kings to that of the sun and the moon,[18] destroyed and planted at will. He intervened in the

---

16. In canon law "plenitude of power" (*plenitudo potestatis*) was something the head of a corporation derived from the corporation members and exercised only in conjunction with them, not an all-embracing authority conferred on the pope directly by God. See Tierney, *Foundations of the Conciliar Theory,* pp. 141–53. Alexander III appears to have been the first pope to have employed the term in opposition to the corporation theory, which permitted the members of a body to share power with the head. This is a distinctly *papal* source of "infallibility" and should be distinguished from that notion of papal infallibility developed, for other reasons, by Peter Olivi and the Spiritual Franciscans. See Brian Tierney, *Origins of Papal Infallibility: 1150–1350* (Leiden, 1972), p. 32. Whereas Alexander III interpreted his "plenitude of power" to mean that he held exclusive jurisdictional and administrative authority within the church, Innocent attempted to extend such jurisdiction throughout the secular world as well.

17. Tierney, *The Crisis of Church and State,* pp. 131–32. Emphasis mine.

18. "The Creator of the Universe set up two great luminaries in the firmament of heaven; the greater light to rule the day, the lesser light to rule the night. In the same way for

imperial election of 1202. After a dispute with King John of England over the appointment of a new archbishop of Canterbury, he excommunicated the king in 1209 and forced from him a humiliating oath of fealty in 1213. He made the Inquisition and crusade effective weapons against internal religious dissent. He recognized and enlisted the mendicant orders of Franciscans and Dominicans in the church's campaign against heterodox spirituality. He established minimal standards for lay religious belief and practice. He and his successors, Gregory IX (1227–41) and Innocent IV (1243–54), waged so effective a campaign against the Hohenstaufen emperors, who unwisely attempted to dominate southern Italy and Sicily, that Germany was left politically fragmented until the nineteenth century.[19]

Innocent left behind an example of Peter's pre-eminence which his successors could neither forget nor repeat. Many of the papacy's problems in the late Middle Ages stemmed directly from the pope's continuing conception of himself as more politically powerful than he could be in the new world of ascendant secular nation-states.

Royal and Papal Apologists

AS popes had their canon lawyers and apologists, kings and emperors had their jurists and publicists, both secular and clerical. Royal pamphleteers found their defense of royal prerogative greatly aided by the revival of Roman law in the twelfth century. Because it exalted the rule of a single political sovereign, Roman law contained resources for the argument that the pope and the church held a subordinate role within a larger political commonwealth over which the emperor alone ruled supreme. Royal apologists were further aided by the thirteenth-century recovery of Aristotle's works, especially the *Politics,* which appeared in Latin around 1260, one of the last of the philosopher's works to become known in the West. Aristotle viewed man as being by nature a social creature; the political community was rooted in the very nature of things, not in man's caprice.[20] Here was an effective counterar-

---

the firmament of the universal Church, which is spoken of as heaven, he appointed two great dignities; the greater to bear rule over souls (these being, as it were, days), the lesser to bear rule over bodies (these being, as it were, nights). These dignities are the pontifical authority and the royal power. Furthermore, the moon derives her light from the sun, and is in truth inferior to the sun in both size and quality, in position as well as effect. In the same way the royal power derives its dignity from the pontifical authority" (Bettenson, *Documents of the Christian Church,* pp. 157–58).

19. See Geoffrey Barraclough, *The Origins of Modern Germany* (New York, 1963), pp. 207–13, 231–33.

20. W. D. Ross, *Aristotle* (Cleveland, 1962), p. 232.

gument to the traditional Augustinian demeaning of the state as a providential adjustment to man's corrupt and fallen nature. No less an authority than Thomas Aquinas sided with Aristotle, although not because
Aquinas believed, as did Aristotle, that the secular community was completely autonomous and an end in itself.[21]

Arguments from both Roman law and Aristotle came into play during the
conflict between Pope Boniface VIII (1294–1303) and Philip IV of France
(1285–1314) at the turn of the fourteenth century. This confrontation
ended forevermore a dominant papal role in international politics and
sparked the most sophisticated and fateful discussion of political sovereignty in the Middle Ages.

France and England were on the brink of war when Boniface became
pope. As both countries mobilized, they used the pretext of preparing for a
crusade to tax the clergy, a legal ground for taxing clergy in earlier times.
The Fourth Lateran Council had decreed in 1215, however, that clergy
could be taxed only with prior papal consent. Boniface viewed such unilat-
eral taxation of the clergy as a brazen assault on traditional clerical rights.
Remembering the way earlier popes had successfully subdued hostile kings
and emperors, he issued the bull *Clericis laicos* on February 5, 1296,
threatening with excommunication rulers who continued to tax clergy in
defiance of the pope.

French retaliation was swift and most effective. Philip IV forbade the
exportation of bullion from France, depriving the papacy of essential
revenues. In February 1297, Boniface privately conceded Philip the right to
tax French clergy "in an emergency" and left to the king's discretion the
definition of emergency. This private agreement became formal in July in
the bull *Etsi de statu,* after which Philip increasingly controlled the French
church. In 1301 the French king, seemingly spoiling for another fight with
the pope, imprisoned and successfully tried for treason Boniface's legate to
Paris, Bernard Saisset. Boniface could not sidestep so direct a challenge to
his authority. Demanding the unconditional release of his legate, he re-
voked all previous agreements on the matter of clerical taxation and issued
a new bull, *Ausculta fili* (December 1301), which pointedly informed Philip,
"God has set popes over kings and kingdoms" and demanded Philip's immediate subjection to the head of the ecclesiastical hierarchy. Approximately a year later, on November 18, 1302, Boniface made a last-ditch stand
against state control of national churches by issuing the bull *Unam sanctam,*
which declared temporal power "subject" to the spiritual power of the

21. Aquinas praised political community and natural virtue because he saw them as
necessary *conditions* for the realization of man's religious or supernatural end; he always
believed them to be inferior and subservient to the latter.

A memorial statue of Pope Boniface VIII. Arnolfo di Cambio and assistants. Perhaps to bolster psychologically his falling power, Boniface ordered many sculptures of himself. He was not as imposing a world figure as he appears here.

church, which was further said to "institute" and to "judge" it if it has not been good.[22]

Like legal beavers, papal apologists labored methodically to construct a protective dam against the surging tide of secular power. They based papal claims on the long-standing belief, enshrined in church law, that things temporal and secular were essentially inferior to things spiritual and religious. The ghost writer of *Unam sanctam*, Giles of Rome (ca. 1245–1316),[23] after 1292 general of the Augustinian order, drew especially on Augustine and Pseudo-Dionysius in his *De potestate ecclesiastica* (1301) to exalt the ecclesiastical over the political community as the sole community of true righteousness and dominion. Giles argued matter-of-factly that as the soul excelled and ruled over the body, so the pope and spiritual power excelled and rightfully ruled over kings and temporal power.

> All temporal things are placed under the dominion and power of the church.... The power of the supreme pontiff governs souls. Souls ought rightly to govern bodies.... But temporal things serve our bodies. It follows then that the priestly power which governs souls also rules over bodies and temporal things.[24]

James of Viterbo (ca. 1255–1308), like Giles an Augustinian monk, described the church as the only perfect "kingship or royal authority" (*regnum*) on earth. As fallen man needs grace to reach perfection, so secular kingship needs the perfect kingship of the church to complete itself. "All human power is imperfect and unformed unless it be formed and perfected by the spiritual power."[25] This is not only a restatement of St. Augustine's low opinion of the state apart from the church, but also an ecclesiopolitical formulation of Thomas Aquinas's principle that "grace perfects nature."

22. *Clericis laicos* in Bettenson, *Documents of the Christian Church*, pp. 159–161; *Etsi de statu* and *Unam sanctam* are excerpted in Tierney, *The Crisis of Church and State*, pp. 178–79, 188–89.

23. See Aegridius Romanus, *De ecclesiastica potestate*, ed. Richard Scholz (Weimar, 1929), pp. x–xi.

24. Tierney, *The Crisis of Church and State*, p. 199. Another summary: "The temporal sword, as being inferior, is led by the spiritual sword, as being superior, and the one is set below the other as inferior to a superior" (ibid., p. 198). On the application of the soul-body metaphor to the relationship of church and state, see Walter Ullmann, *Medieval Papalism* (London, 1949), p. 82. Alan Gewirth points out that pre-Marsilian writers like John of Paris and Dante, who insisted on a duality of spheres of power, especially opposed the "indiscriminate argument from one kind of order to another, for example, from the superiority of grace over nature, or of spiritual ends over temporal ends, to the political jurisdiction of the spiritual over the temporal power" (*Marsilius of Padua: The Defender of Peace*, vol. 1, *Marsilius of Padua and Medieval Political Philosophy* [New York, 1951], p. 17).

25. Cited by Morrall, *Political Thought in Medieval Times*, p. 89.

Aquinas himself had argued that the temporal power is to be obeyed rather than the spiritual in those things that pertain to civil government (according to Matthew 22:21: "Render to Caesar the things that are Caesar's"), "*unless* perhaps the secular power is joined to the spiritual, as in the pope, who holds the apex of both authorities, the spiritual and the secular."[26] The medieval theological belief in the ordering of all the parts of the universe to God in a great chain of being (*ordinatio ad unam*) expressed itself in papal political theory by the pope's insistence on the subordination of all people to the papacy.[27]

Among the royal apologists who refuted this view of papal power in defense of the claims of kings, two of the most effective were John of Paris (d. 1306) and Marsilius of Padua. As the first step in overturning traditional arguments in defense of papal supremacy, John, a French Dominican and a careful student of Aristotle's *Ethics* and *Politics*, rejected the application of the soul-body metaphor to the relation of church and state. The state no less than the church dealt with matters of virtue, administered to souls as well as to bodies, and had a spiritual end or purpose to its work.

> As for the argument that corporeal beings are ruled by spiritual beings and depend on them as on a cause, I answer that an argument so constructed fails . . . because it assumes that royal power is corporeal and not also spiritual and that it has charge of bodies and not also of souls, which is false. . . . [Royal power] is ordained, not for any common good of the citizens whatsoever, but for that which consists in living according to virtue. Accordingly, the Philosopher says in the *Ethics* that the intention of a legislator is to make men good and to lead them to virtue, and in the *Politics* that a legislator is more to be esteemed than a physician, since the legislator has charge of souls, the physician only of bodies.[28]

John gave natural virtues and civic goodness an independent spiritual significance: in the high art of making good citizens, the state is absolutely

26. The passage is in Tierney, *The Crisis of Church and State*, p. 171. Tierney gives it a minimal interpretation, arguing that Aquinas had in mind the pope's dual powers within central Italy (ibid., p. 167). A similar interpretation is made by Thomas Gilby, *St. Thomas Aquinas: Theological Texts* (London, 1955), p. 399, n. 4. Morrall, however, concludes that "Aquinas seems here to be upholding direct papal temporal power in the widest sense" (*Political Thought in Medieval Times*, p. 83). See the similar point of view of F. Aveling, "St. Thomas Aquinas and the Papal Monarchy," in *The Social and Political Ideas of Some Great Medieval Thinkers*, ed. F. J. C. Hearnshaw (New York, 1932), pp. 102–103.

27. See Gewirth, *Marsilius of Padua and Medieval Political Philosophy*, p. 16.

28. In Tierney, *The Crisis of Church and State*, p. 210. There are two English translations of John's *On Royal and Papal Power*: by J. A. Watt (Toronto, 1971) and Arthur P. Monahan (New York, 1974).

supreme. "Even without Christ as ruler," he argued in his treatise *On Royal and Papal Power* (1302–03), "there is the true and perfect justice which is required for the state, since the state is ordered to living in accordance with acquired moral virtue, to which it is accidental that it be perfected by any further virtues [i.e., those of the church]."[29] As what is beyond the natural end of something is accidental to it, the state can only be said to be inferior to the church if the state seeks to acquire the type of community made possible by the church, that is, to become itself what the church is. The church then becomes superior to the state in the way in which a scholar may be said to be superior to a physician who wants to become a cultivated person.[30] Should the scholar seek to become a physician, then the roles of superiority would be reversed. In other words, there is no *essential* subordination of the one to the other. Church and state relate to one another not as superior to inferior in a unitary hierarchy of being, but as two fully autonomous powers, each sovereign within its respective sphere. John taught a dualism of worldly power, acknowledging the divine origin and mandate of both church and state.[31]

Such "parallelism" went far toward dispelling the monolithic spiritual hierarchy defended by Giles of Rome and other extreme papal apologists. It was the political philosopher and imperial publicist Marsilius of Padua (ca. 1290–1343), however, who brought the royalist critique of papal claims to temporal power to its fullest expression. He has been seen as the secular counterpart to the extreme papalists, for he exalted the secular ruler and the state over the church as unequivocally as they exalted the pope and the church over the state.[32] Truly, the political designation "Erastian" could as easily be "Marsilian"; as the Heidelberg physician Thomas Erastus later defended the right of civil authority to control moral discipline against Calvinist efforts to gain unrestricted power of excommunication within the Palatinate, so Marsilius two centuries earlier argued for the removal of all coercive jurisdiction from the pope and its confinement exclusively to reigning imperial or temporal authority.

29. Cited in the introduction to Marsilius of Padua, *The Defender of Peace: The Defensor Pacis,* trans. Alan Gewirth (New York, 1967), p. xlviii.

30. Ibid., p. L.

31. John also argued for the independence of secular power on historical grounds, pointing out that "royal power both existed and was exercised before papal, and there were kings in France before there were Christians" (Tierney, *The Crisis of Church and State,* p. 208).

32. "Where the extreme papalists [Giles of Rome, James of Viterbo, Henry of Cremona, Augustinus Triumphus, and Alexander of St. Elpidius] asserted a thorough-going control of the spiritual power over the temporal and where the moderates on both sides [John of Paris, Thomas Aquinas, and Dante] argued for a parallelism of the two powers, Marsilius set up a thorough-going control of the temporal over the spiritual" (Gewirth, *Marsilius of Padua and Medieval Political Philosophy,* p. 9).

Like Erastus, Marsilius's training was in medicine, not in theology. In 1313 he became rector of the University of Paris and there completed in 1324 what many believe to be the most important medieval treatise on politics, the *Defender of Peace*. Three church-state conflicts were in Marsilius's mind when he wrote this work. The first was the decades-long struggle by the city councils of Padua to bring local clergy under the civic code and restrict papal interference in the city's life. Such efforts brought papal interdiction of the city in 1283, but the Paduans persisted and eventually succeeded in subjecting their clergy to civil control. The *Defender of Peace* may be seen as an effort to apply the successful Paduan solution to Europe as a whole.[33] The two other conflicts Marsilius had in mind when he wrote the *Defender of Peace* were the recent confrontation between Boniface VIII and Philip the Fair and the ongoing contemporary challenge of the emperor-elect Louis of Bavaria (1314-46) by Pope John XXII, who had supported Louis's Hapsburg rival for the imperial crown. Marsilius and his assistant John of Jandun (ca. 1275-1328) took refuge at Louis's court in 1326.

Marsilius wrote the *Defender of Peace* in search of what he called "tranquility.... the highest temporal good.... the truth which leads to the salvation of civil life, and which is also of no little help for eternal salvation."[34] On neither local, national, nor imperial levels could Marsilius find such tranquility in Europe, and he believed the fault lay squarely with the clergy, who, falsely claiming broad temporal powers, boldly intruded themselves into purely secular affairs. Civil life, Marsilius concluded, could be "saved" only if the church were confined to its proper spiritual functions and assisted rulers in promoting the larger goals of the political community.

Unlike his contemporary William of Ockham, who also opposed John XXII and defended Louis of Bavaria, Marsilius wrote out of deep philosophical conviction. Ockham's peculiar philosophical and theological views played far less a role in his stance than his personal experience; he simply became convinced that the pope had transgressed the limits of his rightful authority when he condemned Franciscan poverty and challenged the legitimacy of a duly elected emperor. As he drew his arguments from

33. Nicholai Rubenstein, "Marsilius of Padua and Italian Political Thought of his Time," in *Europe in the late Middle Ages*, ed. John Hale et al. (London, 1970), pp. 44-75; Gewirth, *Marsilius of Padua and Medieval Political Philosophy*, pp. 23-27. Padua abolished the privileged clerical status that gave clergy civic benefits without their also having to meet civic obligations and exempted them from the judgments of civil courts. Civil jurisdiction was extended over the clergy in all civil and criminal cases. On the influence of Aquinas's actual political experience on his political ideas, see Jeremy Catto, "Ideas and Experience in the Political Thought of Aquinas," *Past and Present* 71 (1976): 3-21.

34. *Defender of Peace*, bk. 1, ch. 1, sect. 5, p. 6; ch. 2, sect. 3, p. 9.

traditional church law, Ockham posed far less a threat to the doctrine of nonerring papal authority than Marsilius did.[35]

Marsilius's fundamental notion was that all coercive power on earth lay with "the people"; the people, as "human legislator," were the source of all worldly authority. It was not the "head-bishop" in Rome, but the people who were judged by none save God; the people were lower than God but greater than man. Through the will and consent of the people, both legitimate political and ecclesiastical power came into existence. In both church and state, authority flowed from the members to the head. The secular ruler received his mandate from the *universitas civium,* the citizenry as a whole, who traditionally expressed their will through representative assemblies or councils; the pope received his power from the *universitas fidelium,* the whole body of the faithful, who traditionally expressed their will through church councils. With this basic argument—the sovereignty of the people and their representative bodies—Marsilius set out to remove every vestige of coercive judgment and power from Pope John XXII and his successors.

Marsilius was nothing if not shrewd. Finding that the pope identified the "church" with Rome and looked on his temporal power and immunity from civil law as "spiritual" rights, Marsilius appealed to the apostolic understanding of "spiritual" realities.[36] The clear message of Holy Scripture, he argued, was that "neither the Roman bishop called pope, nor any other bishop or priest, or deacon, has or ought to have any rulership or coercive judgment or jurisdiction over any priest or non-priest, ruler, community, group, or individual of whatever condition."[37] The church was strictly a sacramental institution with one essential and legitimate business: otherworldly salvation. It had "absolute sovereignty," but over a kingdom not of this world. It had divine laws, but the rewards and punishments they meted out belonged to a future life, not to the present;[38] coercive punishment of those who transgressed divine laws awaited the Last Judgment.

The authority of popes, bishops, and priests was thus seen by Marsilius to be strictly moral and pedagogical; they might teach about salvation, threaten eternal punishment, and promise eternal rewards for certain types of behavior, but clergy had no right whatsoever to coerce others. In this life only temporal power could proscribe and punish heretics and only as they

35. See the discussion in McGrade, *The Political Thought of William of Ockham,* pp. 28–43.

36. *Defender of Peace,* bk. 2, ch. 2, sect. 3, p. 103; sect. 5, pp. 105–6.

37. *Defender of Peace,* bk. 2, ch. 4, sect. 1, p. 113. Ockham too insisted that an errant ruler's lay subjects, not the pope, must be the source of any corrective action against him. McGrade, *The Political Thought of William of Ockham,* pp. 95–97.

38. *Defender of Peace,* bk. 2, ch. 8, p. 158.

transgressed human, not divine, laws against such beliefs and conduct.[39] If the church wanted to assert itself in the temporal world, it might do so by attempting to "moderate human acts"[40] and, in this way, assist the realization of tranquility.

Marsilius saw in papal power of excommunication and interdict, and in claims to a "plentitude of power" even over temporal things, the "fall" of the church from its original spiritual mission. He believed this fall had occurred already in the fifth and sixth centuries during the pontificates of Simplicius (468–83) and Pelagius I (556–61).[41] He summarized his case against the pope in this matter:

> Only the general council [i.e. the people as the *universitas fidelium*], and no bishop or priest or particular group of them, has the authority to excommunicate any ruler, province, or other civil community, or to forbid them the use of divine offices. For if a priest or bishop or some particular group of them, moved by ignorance or malice, excommunicates or lays under interdict a ruler or a province, there results great scandal to the peace and quiet of all the faithful. This was very recently shown . . . when Boniface VIII . . . tried to excommunicate Philip the Fair of bright memory . . . and to lay his kingdom and adherents under interdict, because this king protested against a written document [*Unam sanctam*] . . . published by Boniface . . . which . . . concluded that all rulers, communities, and individuals in the world are subject in coercive jurisdiction to the Roman pope. . . . Boniface's intention was to stir up against Philip as many of the other Christian rulers and peoples as he could. . . . Such [actions by popes] . . . must be checked forthwith; and the procedure whereby such interdicts and excommunications are inflicted must be controlled and left only to the general council of Christians, whose judgment, under the guidance of the Holy Spirit, cannot be perverted by ignorance or malice.[42]

Marsilius described the corruption of the papacy in terms of an illicit evolution of papal power. In the beginning the apostles freely elected Peter to the honorary position of their spokesman. However, what began as voluntary obedience to one freely chosen soon became an established custom. Then the popes themselves presumed that they could command such obedience. From thence came the proclamation of a papal plenitude of power. Thereafter followed threats of papal anathema, excommunication,

39. Ibid., bk. 2, ch. 10, sect. 1–9, pp. 173–79.
40. Ibid., bk. 1, ch. 6, sect. 1, p. 21.
41. Ibid., bk. 2, ch. 25, sect. 7, pp. 335–36; sect. 17, p. 342.
42. Ibid., bk. 2, ch. 21, sect. 9, pp. 293–94.

and interdict and declarations of clerical exemption from civil law.[43] One originally intended to serve as a kind of executive secretary of "the general council of the faithful legislator" and execute the will of the "people" as expressed in their representative assembly[44] had instead transformed himself by stages into a veritable tyrant.

The *Defender of Peace* stood the medieval "chain of being" on its head. Whereas in the traditional clerical view authority flowed from God to the pope and to temporal rulers, Marsilius saw authority invested by God in "the people," who expressed their will in two ways: as the human legislator or citizenry, empowering the king to rule their temporal lives, and as the body of the faithful, empowering the pope to direct their spiritual lives. The king and the state, whose goal was civic virtue and tranquility, took priority in the present life over the pope and the church, whose goal was religious virtue and eternal bliss. Marsilius interpreted the "Donation of Constantine" as proof of the emperor's authority "to institute, empower, and judge" the pope. As the "Donation" made clear to Marsilius, it was the emperor Constantine who first raised the Roman bishop and the Roman church to worldly power by giving them property, rights, and privileges,[45] and what the emperor had freely brought into being he could also regulate. The opposed views of the flow of authority can be summarized by the following diagrams:

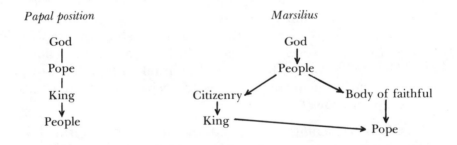

Marsilius subjected all the clergy, including the pope, to the example of Jesus and the apostles. As the latter had renounced all worldly possessions and submitted themselves to reigning political authority, so too should contemporary clergy. Marsilius defended the bull *Exiit qui seminat,* which had initially recognized Franciscan poor use, or use without ownership, and condemned *Cum inter nonnullos,* which denied that Christ and his apostles had practiced absolute poverty. Marsilius directly defended the "meritori-

43. Ibid., bk. 2, ch. 22, sects. 14-20, pp. 308-313; ch. 23, sects. 1-13, pp. 313-20.
44. Ibid., bk. 2, ch. 22, sects. 5-6, pp. 301-02.
45. Ibid., bk. 2, ch. 22, sects. 9-10, pp. 305-06.

ous or supreme poverty" of the Franciscans as an ideal not just for one order of the church, but for *all* clergy,[46] and he drew from this ideal conclusions the church would hear again (and condemn) in John Wyclif:

> The legislators or rulers can lawfully, in accordance with divine law, seize and use on their own authority all goods which remain over and above the needs of the gospel ministers. . . . For with food and raiment the priests should be content.[47]

Here was the feared political application to the church at large of Waldensian and Franciscan notions about clerical poverty. On October 27, 1327, Pope John XXII condemned Marsilius and John of Jandun for teaching the following heresies:

1. That when his disciples found a silver coin in the mouth of a fish and Jesus told them to give it to Caesar [Matt. 17:26], Jesus did this not in a condescending way, freely and out of piety, but because such homage was due to Caesar. That all the temporal things of the church are subservient to the emperor, and he can take them as his own.
2. That the blessed apostle Peter had no more authority than the other apostles, nor was he the head of the other apostles. For Christ left no head of the church, nor did he make any one [apostle] his vicar.
3. That it is within the province of the emperor to correct, institute, destroy, and punish the pope.
4. That all clergy, whether the pope, archbishop, or simple priest, are by Christ's institution of equal authority and jurisdiction.
5. That the pope or the whole church taken together can punish no man, however sinful he may be, coercively, unless the emperor concede this power to them.[48]

Marsilius's teaching challenged the traditional spiritual hierarchy of being that had been taught by both Augustine and Thomas Aquinas. The *Defender of Peace* has justifiably been described as a "subversion" of the papal monarchy.[49] Although theoretical parallels are far clearer than any direct

---

46. Ibid., bk. 2, ch. 13, sects. 6-38, pp. 199-215. Georges de Lagarde discusses the peculiarity of Marsilius's universal clerical vow of poverty and sees a basic Waldensian motif in it. *La Naissance de l'esprit laïque au declin du moyen âge: Le Defensor pacis* (Louvain/Paris, 1970) 3: 335, 343-44, 348-51.

47. *Defender of Peace*, bk. 2, ch. 21, sect. 14, p. 297.

48. Denzinger, nos. 941-946, pp. 289-90.

49. Gewirth, *Marsilius of Padua and Medieval Political Philosophy*, pp. 271-77. Gewirth comments on the revolutionary aspect of Marsilius's teaching:

> In a few scattered contexts . . . Marsilius affirms the superior value of the future life; but at no point does he indicate that the goods of the present life must be ordered to or

historical connections, Marsilius's political philosophy has been closely associated with the Protestant Reformation. One scholar suspects that a 1522
Basel edition of the *Defender of Peace* influenced Zwingli's argument that
elected rulers could be deposed by the common action of those who chose
them.[50] Other scholars associate Marsilius with the state-church of
Lutheranism and the *cuius regio, eius religio* formula of the Peace of Augsburg (1555).[51] Thomas Cromwell enlisted English humanists in the service of King Henry VIII after the king's break with Rome, and among their
many publications in defense of the royal supremacy was William Marshall's
abridged English translation of the *Defender of Peace,* published in 1535.[52]
Even if it did not directly influence them, Marsilius's teaching clearly anticipated and assisted major developments in sixteenth-century political
thought that were favorable to the Reformation.

*The Schism and the Rise
of the Conciliar Theory
of Church Government*

IN the Swiss city of Constance a
great council of the church met
during the years 1414–17. At its
height it consisted of twenty-nine cardinals, three patriarchs, thirty-three
archbishops, and a hundred doctors of theology.[53] The council convened
because a schism had existed in the church for thirty-six years, since 1378.
When the council fathers assembled in Constance in November 1414, there

---

perfected by other-worldly goods. His usual procedure, rather, is to set temporal and
eternal happiness side by side as two kinds of "sufficient life" or "ends desired by man,"
as if they were of equal value deriving from the same kind of natural desire. Indeed, he
does not hesitate to say, in opposition to Augustine, that men should "enjoy (*frui*) civil
happiness, which seems the best object of desire possible to man in this world, and the
ultimate aim of human acts" (ibid., p. 78).

Cf., however, Alexander Passerin D'Entreves, who holds the opposite point of view, in *The
Medieval Contribution to Political Thought: Thomas Aquinas, Marsilius of Padua, Richard Hooker*
(New York, 1939?), p. 75.

50. Ernst Staehelin, "L'édition de 1522 du 'Defensor Pacis' de Marsile de Padoue," *Revue
d'histoire et de philosophie religieuses* 24 (1954): 209; G. R. Potter, *Zwingli* (Cambridge, 1976), p.
120, n. 5. Luther appears to have had no direct contact with this edition.

51. See D'Entreves, *The Medieval Contribution to Political Thought,* p. 82; Johannes Heckel
strongly disassociates Marsilius's political philosophy from Luther's theology, although he
observes parallel ideas in the Lutheran princes. "Marsilius von Padua und Martin Luther:
Ein Vergleich ihrer Rechts- und Soziallehre," *Zeitschrift der Savigny-Stiftung für Rechtsgeschichte* 75 (1958): 268–336, esp. 271, 328–29, 331–35. Flacius numbered Marsilius among
Protestant forerunners in the *Catalogus testium veritatis.* Cf. below, p. 239.

52. James K. McConica, *English Humanists and Reformation Politics Under Henry VIII and
Edward VI* (Oxford, 1965), pp. 133–37. See also A. G. Dickens, *The English Reformation*
(London, 1964), p. 110.

53. For both secondary narrative and contemporary accounts of the council, see *The
Council of Constance: The Unification of the Church,* trans. Louise R. Loomis, ed. John H.
Mundy and Kennerly M. Woody (New York, 1969).

were no less than three duly elected popes—one in Rome, another in Avignon, and a third in Pisa—each with a supporting college of cardinals and political allies and each claiming to be the true Peter. After months of internal confusion and bickering, the council, stabilized, passed legislation declaring itself the supreme authority within the church. This occurred in the decree *Sacrosancta* (April 15, 1415), which asserted:

> This holy Council of Constance . . . declares, first, that it is lawfully assembled in the Holy Spirit, that it constitutes a General Council, representing the Catholic Church, and that therefore it has its authority immediately from Christ; and that all men, of every rank and condition, including the pope himself, are bound to obey it in matters concerning the Faith, the abolition of the schism, and the reformation of the Church of God in its head and its members. Secondly, it declares that anyone, of any rank and condition, who shall contumaciously refuse to obey the orders, decrees, statutes or instructions, made or to be made by this holy Council, or by any other lawfully assembled general council . . . shall, unless he comes to a right frame of mind, be subjected to fitting penance and punished appropriately.[54]

Although the conciliar era proved a short-lived experiment in representative church government, scholars of Western political thought have attached the greatest importance to this decree. The late English political historian John Neville Figgis praised *Sacrosancta* for anticipating the future course of Western civilization in both the secular and the ecclesiastical spheres. "Probably the most revolutionary official document in the history of the world," he declared in a much-quoted statement, "is the decree of the Council of Constance asserting its superiority to the pope, and striving to turn into a tepid constitutionalism the divine authority of a thousand years."[55]

The Council of Constance was far more conservative than scholars of Figgis's generation recognized. The council fathers were neither students of Marsilius of Padua nor forerunners of Martin Luther. Still, Constance did inaugurate a conciliar movement that survived for almost half a century and continued to influence both secular advocates of representative government and religious reformers long after the revived papal monarchy crushed the conciliar movement in the mid-fifteenth century. Later Calvinist advocates of resistance to tyrants appealed directly to Constance and its more radical successor, the Council of Basel, as models of the people's

---

54. Bettenson, *Documents of the Christian Church*, pp. 192–93.
55. *Studies of Political Thought from Gerson to Grotius* (Cambridge, 1931), p. 32.

right to enforce standards of conduct on both religious and political leaders.[56] A political lesson was drawn from Constance's reaction to ecclesiastical crisis: as a church council, led by the Holy Spirit in obedience to Christ and speaking for the whole body of the faithful, had deposed competing popes who endangered the well-being of the church, so lower magistrates and parliaments, mindful of the welfare of the larger political community, should resist rulers whose tyranny posed a danger to the body politic. Like Magna Carta in the political sphere, *Sacrosancta* in the religious sphere became a classic defense of the rights of the privileged many against the claims of the one.

We are, however, running well ahead of our story. Why was such a radical departure from traditional papal government of the church necessary in the first place? How did not only two, but eventually three duly elected popes come to reign simultaneously in the church?

As an aftereffect of the humiliation of Pope Boniface VIII by Philip the Fair, the papacy had moved from Rome to Avignon during the pontificate of Clement V (1305–14), where it came under strong French influence. This unprecedented circumstance of the papacy's residence on the borders of France after 1309 became known as the Babylonian Captivity of the church and resulted in an approximately seventy-year exile of the papacy from Rome. Throughout this period the great majority of the cardinals held French episcopal sees and to the outside world it often appeared that the papacy was under outright French control.

The exile from Rome ended in January 1377, when Pope Gregory XI (1370–78) returned to Rome. Following Gregory's death in March 1378, the cardinals met in Rome, and on April 8 elected an Italian, Bartholomew Prignani, the archbishop of Bari, to succeed Gregory as Pope Urban VI. Joy was brief, however, as a disaster worse than the Babylonian Captivity now befell the church.

Urban was crowned pope on April 18, and all sixteen cardinals, eleven of whom were French, attended and supported his coronation. Four months later, on August 2, 1378, the eleven French cardinals assembled in Anagni and declared that they had voted for Urban under coercion by the Roman populace and that his election was therefore invalid. They were joined by a Spanish cardinal, Peter of Luna, who would later become the Avignon pope Benedict XIII. Having declared Urban's election null and void, these twelve cardinals proceeded on September 20, 1378 to elect in his place Robert of

---

56. See *Vindiciae contra tyrannos* (1579), attributed to Philippe du Plessis-Mornay in *Constitutionalism and Resistance in the 16th Century: Three Treatises by Hotman, Beza, and Mornay*, trans. and ed. Julian H. Franklin (New York, 1969), p. 150.

Geneva, bishop of Cambrai and cousin of the French king Charles V, who assumed the title Pope Clement VII (1378–94) and took residence in Avignon. Upon Clement's election the church found itself with two popes, neither of whom was absolutely valid or invalid, since both had been elected by a majority of the same college of cardinals.[57]

Allegiance to the two courts divided along political lines. England and its allies (the Empire, Hungary, Bohemia, and Poland) acknowledged Urban VI, while France and its orbit (Naples, Scotland, Castile, and Aragon) supported Clement VII.

When the cardinals voted for Urban VI, they did so amidst great popular excitement over the return of the papacy to Rome. Crowds surrounded the conclave during its deliberations and demanded the election of a Roman successor to Gregory. It is not inconceivable that some of the cardinals had themselves been caught up in this emotion and later regretted it. Some may, as they claimed, honestly have believed that they could not elect a non-Italian without endangering their lives. There is, however, another explanation of the cardinals' action. Considerable patronage and political power were at stake in the location of the pope's residence. After his election, Urban had declared his intention to enact reforms within the Curia that would reflect the new Italian base of the papacy and diminish the power of the French cardinals. That alone made these cardinals easy prey for the pressures of the French king, who strongly opposed the papacy's removal from the sphere of direct French influence.

In earlier times the healing of schisms had been helped by the intervention of universally respected figures. After the same conclave of cardinals had elected both Innocent II (1130–43) and Anacletus II (1130–38) in 1130, for example, Bernard of Clairvaux had spoken for an alleged *sensus communis* within the church at large in favor of Innocent, who had received a minority of the votes. In the schism of 1378, however, the saints were as divided as the popes. St. Catherine of Siena (1347–80) supported Urban and condemned Clement in the most unsaintly terms, while Clement VII and his successor Benedict XIII received the strong endorsement of the popular penitential preacher St. Vincent Ferrer (1350–1419). Since God seemed to be on both sides, there remained but one solution: the intellectuals would have to decide.

In a writing of 1394, which expressed the viewpoint of scholars in the University of Paris, Nicholas of Clémanges, a student of the later masterminds of the Council of Constance, Jean Gerson and Pierre d'Ailly, cited

---

57. The events leading to the schism are summarized by August Franzen, "The Council of Constance: Present State of the Problem," *Concilium* 7 (1965): 29–68. For more detailed treatment, see Walter Ullmann, *Origins of the Great Schism* (Hamden, Conn., 1967).

three possible procedures for terminating the schism: the *via cessionis,* the *via compromissi,* and the *via concilii.*[58] The "way of mutual cession" was simplest and most direct: both popes would resign their powers and clear the way for a new election. That failing, the "way of compromise" begged the free recognition by both sides of an impartial board of respected men who would judge the matter. Both these solutions fell short of convening a general council of the church and depended for their success on the good-will of the contending popes. Gerson, who supported such solutions until 1408, described them as the "way of personal penance" (*via poenitentiae*).[59] While those around them spoke of penitence and self-sacrifice, however, the two popes protested that they had been duly elected to their office(s); as they had not been raised up on the basis of goodwill, neither should they be expected to remove themselves simply on moral grounds. After the Roman pope Gregory XII (1406–15) and the last Avignon pope, Benedict XIII (1394–1417),[60] failed to meet in Savona in 1408 and negotiate a settlement, as both had declared they would do, coercive conciliar action became the only alternative and the "way of a council" quickly won wide endorsement.

The deposition or forced resignation of a duly elected pope by the action of a general council of the church was the most difficult course to take, both legally and psychologically. It was difficult psychologically because medieval people attached great importance to orderly succession in both ecclesiastical and political office; the deposition of a duly elected pope seemed as un-thinkable as the execution of a duly crowned king. It was difficult legally because according to canon law only the pope could convene a legitimate council of the church, and neither pope was disposed to convene a council for his own deposition. Further, immunity from judgment by any save God was a traditional part of Peter's pre-eminence. As Innocent III had earlier reminded the rulers of Europe, the pope, while lower than God, was higher than man, even collective man.

The leaders of the conciliar movement—Conrad of Gelnhausen (ca. 1320–90), Henry of Langenstein (1324–97), Matthew of Cracow (ca. 1335–1410), Dietrich of Niem (ca. 1340–1418), Pierre d'Ailly (1350–1420), Ger-

58. "Epistola quam Universitas Parisiensis misit domino nostro regi Francorum de tribus viis per ipsam repertis ad extirpationem presentis Schismatis necessariis" (1394) in *Chartularium Universitatis Parisiensis,* ed. H. Denifle and A. Chatelain (Paris, 1894), 3: 618–20.

59. Sermon "Poenitemini et credite evangelio," in *Jean Gerson: Oeuvres complètes,* ed. Palémon Glorieux (Paris, 1960–), 5:465.

60. The popes of the Roman line, the recognized line of popes during the schism, were: Urban VI (d. 1389); Boniface IX (d. 1404); Innocent VII (d. 1406); and Gregory XII (resigned, 1415, d. 1417). The popes of Avignon were Clement VII (d. 1394) and Benedict XIII (deposed, 1417, d. 1423). The popes of Pisa were Alexander V (d. 1410) and John XXIII (deposed, 1415, d. 1419).

son, and Franciscus Zabarella (1360–1417)—were not firebrands, but men devoted to the rule of law and tradition. They recognized the need for a strong papal office. If they disagreed with Ockham, who believed that councils could err as easily as bishops and popes in their judgments,[61] they also disassociated themselves from Marsilius of Padua, who exalted councils over popes in principle, not just when emergencies arose, and considered every bishop a pope within his own diocese.[62] It was not only papal opposition that delayed a conciliar solution to the schism for almost thirty years; the conservatism and caution of the conciliarists themselves played a role. Before they enacted the *via concilii,* these men drew on every available canonistic tradition to justify their action, using the pope's own self-defense against him.[63]

Canon law, the bulwark of the papal office, also anticipated its abuse. It set limits to papal power and defined conditions under which an errant pope might be corrected by the judgment of others. Such theoretical safeguards also existed in the revived Roman law; even when its republican side seemed to be more conceptual than actual, Roman law too never lost sight of the principle that "the people" were the ultimate source of a ruler's "absolute" power and hence theoretically capable of regulating it.[64]

Exceptions to the pope's "plenitude of power" found a justification in the so-called heresy clause of canon law, which the canonists Ivo of Chartres (ca. 1040–1115) and Gratian (twelfth century) gave a firm place in church law. It had a historical precedent in the posthumous condemnation of Pope

61. Brian Tierney, *Ockham, the Conciliar Theory and the Canonists* (Philadelphia, 1971), pp. 26–27, 38 (= reprint from *JHI* 15 (1954): 40–70); John B. Morrall, *Gerson and the Great Schism* (Manchester, 1960), p. 119.

62. See Gerson, *De auferibilitate sponsi ab Ecclesia, Oeuvres complètes,* 3, cons. 8, pp. 298–99; G. H. M. Posthumus Meyjes, *Jean Gerson: zijn Kerkpolitiek en Ecclesiologie* (The Hague, 1963), pp. 292–93.

63. Brian Tierney has commented on this important fact:

> The widespread assumption that there was one single canonistic theory of church government which was adequately reflected in the works of such [extreme papal] publicists as Giles of Rome or Augustinus Triumphus does scant justice to the richness and diversity of canonistic speculation in this field. The theories of the more extreme papal publicists do indeed reflect one trend of canonistic thought, but the conciliar arguments in favour of a limitation of papal authority by Council and cardinals reflect another: both parties alike drew their weapons from the canonists' armoury (*Foundations of the Conciliar Theory,* p. 13).

64. Cf. Francis Oakley, *The Medieval Experience: Foundations of Western Cultural Singularity* (New York, 1974), pp. 128–29. As Myron P. Gilmore pointed out, "Although there are undoubtedly important examples of the use of Roman texts to support an argument for the existence of an absolute power [appeals to the *lex regia* and the *princeps legibus solutus*], there [are] equally important examples of the use of Roman texts to construct a theory in restraint of absolute power" (*Argument from Roman Law in Political Thought* [Cambridge, 1941], p. 131).

Honorius I (625–638) by the Council of Constantinople (681) for alleged heresy. Gratian maintained grudgingly but unequivocally that there existed a condition under which a pope could be judged by others.

> If the pope, neglectful of his own and his brethren's salvation, is proved useless and remiss in his duties and moreover drags innumerable people down with him horde-like, away from the good, he will suffer many afflictions in the slavery of hell for all eternity. [Still] let no mortal presume to argue his guilt since, though he judges all, he is not to be judged by anyone, *unless he deviates from the faith.*[65]

The twelfth-century canonist Huguccio (d. 1210), the teacher of Innocent III, went beyond Gratian to argue that a pope could be deposed for notorious fornication, robbery, and sacrilege as well as for willful heresy, for, like heresy, such crimes posed a clear and present danger to the welfare of the church. He further maintained that inferiors did not "rise up" against a superior when they took action against a pope guilty of such crimes, because a heretical or notoriously criminal pope fell beneath the simplest believer and was no Christian's superior. Exceedingly cautious, like other canonists, on so high a matter, Huguccio added the qualification that such a pope must be his *own* accuser before a process against him could be legal.[66]

For the conciliarists, the heresy and criminal clauses in canon law, no matter how guardedly stated, were proof positive that popes had no absolute immunity from criticism and coercive action. In certain exceptional situations the body of the faithful could act legally both apart from and against its head. Given the canonical "loopholes" to papal plenitude of power, the conciliarists multiplied possible exceptional situations in which independent conciliar action might occur. One of the earliest conciliar tracts, Henry of Langenstein's *Letter on Behalf of a Council of Peace* (1381), cited four such cases:[67] if a manifestly heretical pope persisted in his office and refused to summon a council; if all the cardinals were suddenly killed after the death of the pope; if the pope and the cardinals presented a doubtful decision in a matter of faith and held to it pertinaciously; and,

---

65. *Decretum Gratiani, dist.* 40, c. 6, cited by Franzen, "The Council of Constance," p. 40, n. 5 (emphasis mine). See also Tierney, *Foundations of the Conciliar Theory,* pp. 57–58.

66. Brian Tierney, "Collegiality in the Middle Ages," *Concilium* 7 (1965): 5–14, esp. p. 10; *Foundations of the Conciliar Theory,* pp. 58–65. These were essentially the same arguments used later by Ockham in his effort to have John XXII deposed for allegedly heretical views on apostolic poverty and the beatific vision. See Tierney, *Ockham, the Conciliar Theory, and the Canonists,* pp. 13–14.

67. *Letter on Behalf of a Council of Peace,* ed. and trans. James K. Cameron in *Advocates of Reform: From Wyclif to Erasmus,* ed. Matthew Spinka (Philadelphia, 1963), p. 129.

finally, if the cardinals, for whatever reason, were unable or refused to assemble and elect the pope.

The conciliarists extended such reasoning to the schism itself. What if there were two, or even three, lawfully elected popes, none of whom possessed the goodwill to cede power to the other and each of whom by their obstinacy threatened the well-being of the whole body of the faithful? Would not such a state of affairs constitute an emergency that required conciliar action apart from and against the pope? D'Ailly spoke for the other conciliarists when in 1402 he expressed his conviction that canon law also justified independent action by a council when, during a state of emergency in the church, a living pope occupying the papal chair failed to call a council of the church after being reasonably requested to do so.[68] Beyond papal heresy and notorious crimes, papal persistence in a schism that endangered the welfare of the church became itself a circumstance that justified action by the body of the faithful apart from and against its head(s).

Two fundamental distinctions underlay the conciliar theory of church government: that between the "Roman church," led by the pope, and the "Universal Church," whose head could always and only be Christ; and that between the letter of church law and its "spirit" or "true intention," which was that the law serve good and not ill. Both distinctions were prominent in the first full scholarly defense of church councils that appeared after the schism began: Conrad of Gelnhausen's *Epistola concordiae* (May 1380). Conrad argued that the church could no more be identified with the pope than a kingdom with its king, and he condemned the observance of the letter of the law to the point of transgressing its spirit. No more than the citizens of Paris need await the permission of the king before taking up arms against invaders who surprise their city, must the body of the faithful await the permission of the pope before taking measures to preserve the church from mortal danger.[69]

Appeal to the spirit of the law, or "equity" (*epikeia*), became a legal basis of conciliar action. This notion derived from Aristotle and had long been incorporated into medieval law. Equity meant the adjustment of a universal

---

68. "Ex quibus patet:... potest enim in duplici casu, ut videtur, concilium fieri sine auctoritate papae: primus sede vacante, si occurreret urgens necessitas vel evidens utilitas; secundus, si vivente papa ipse recusaret concilium facere rationabiliter requisitus." From *Tractatus de materia concilii generalis* (1402), ed. B. Meller, *Studien zur Erkenntnislehre Peter von Ailly* (Freiburg, 1954), p. 301, cited by August Franzen, "Zur Vorgeschichte des Konstanzer Konzils: Vom Ausbruch des Schismas bis zum Pisanum," in *Das Konzil von Konstanz. Beiträge zu seiner Geschichte und Theologie* (Freiburg, 1964), p. 23. D'Ailly's political thought is treated by Francis Oakley, *The Political Thought of Pierre d'Ailly: The Voluntarist Tradition* (New Haven, 1964).

69. *Epistola concordiae*, in *Wegbereiter der Reformation*, ed. Gustav A. Benrath (Bremen, 1967), pp. 143–48.

law to the particular circumstances under which the law was actually enforced. Its function was to ensure that a law preserved the original intention of the lawgiver, remaining as fair and just in its concrete application as it appeared to be in abstract theory or statute.[70]

"The pope is to be judged by no one save God" is a universal statement or law. If, however, not to sit in judgment on the pope means the continuance of a schism that threatens the body of the faithful, then the law must be adjusted to fit these new circumstances so that it serves the good it was intended to serve. Gerson summarized the conviction of all the conciliarists on this matter:

> The pope can be removed by a general council celebrated without his consent and against his will. Normally a council is not legally . . . celebrated without papal calling and approval. . . . But, as in grammar and in morals, general rules have exceptions—and especially when the infinite number of special circumstances surrounding a particular case are taken into account. Because of these exceptions a superior law has been ordained to interpret the law. This is what Aristotle called equity.[71]

Peter was commissioned by God to "feed my sheep," not to run them over a cliff. "God has given no status, no degree of dignity, no ministry of any kind," Gerson wrote, "except in order to serve the common benefit of all."[72] That is the "spirit" in which all laws, offices, and authority must be interpreted. Conciliar theorists also argued that the power of applying the principle of equity to a law lay principally with the church's doctors of theology and only secondarily with canon and civil lawyers.[73] Ockham and Marsilius of Padua probably influenced this argument by their exaltation of scholars

---

70. Aristotle described equity so:

When the law speaks universally . . . and a case arises . . . which is not covered by the universal statement, then it is right, where the legislator fails us and has erred by oversimplicity, to correct the omission [and] say what the legislator himself would have said had he been present and would have [wanted to] put into his law had he known [the particular circumstances surrounding its enforcement]. . . . This is the nature of the equitable, a correction of law where it is defective owing to its universality. (*Ethics* [McKeon, ed.], bk. 5, ch. 10, p. 1137).

71. *De auferibilitate sponsi ad Ecclesia*, p. 300. On equity, see also Conrad of Gelnhausen, *Epistola concordiae* in Benrath, *Wegbereiter der Reformation*, p. 148; and Henry of Langenstein, *Letter on Behalf of a Council of Peace*, in Spinka, *Advocates of Reform*, p. 130. Ullmann discusses the views of Conrad and Henry in *Origins of the Great Schism*, pp. 180–83.

72. *De auferibilitate sponsi ab Ecclesia*, p. 300.

73. Gerson summarizes: "Auctoritas vero doctrinaliter utendi epikeia residet principaliter apud peritos in theologia, quae est architectoria respectu aliarum, et consequenter apud peritos in scientia juris canonici et civilis prout ex principiis juris divini et naturalis habet accipere fundamenta" (*De unitate ecclesiastica*, in Glorieux, *Oeuvres complètes*, 6, cons. 5, p. 138).

trained in Bible and theology over canon lawyers as the true experts in spiritual matters.[74] As a general council excelled a schismatic pope and the spirit of the law its letter, so the theologians who served the council and the spirit of the law excelled the canon lawyers who served the pope and the letter.

The Council of Constance

IN 1409 the Council of Pisa, composed of cardinals who had defected from the Roman pope Gregory XII and the Avignon pope Benedict XIII, declared both popes heretical, deposed them, and elected in their stead a new pope, Alexander V. However, on the ground that only the pope could summon a legitimate council, the deposed popes pronounced the decrees of Pisa illegal and refused to acknowledge their deposition. With the spectacle of three popes, each with a supporting body of cardinals, reigning over Christendom and the Hussite revolution brewing in Bohemia, resistance to decisive conciliar action on the church's behalf, even among the three Curias, rapidly dissolved.

At the firm insistence of Emperor Sigismund, the second Pisan pope, John XXIII, summoned the Council of Constance in November 1414. Empowered by its own decree *Sacrosancta* (April 1415), the council proceeded to deal with three pressing matters: heresy, the schism, and the reform of the church in head and members—*causa fidei, unionis et reformationis*. It deposed John XXIII for scandalous behavior on May 29. Recognizing the council's power and determination, the Roman pope Gregory XII abdicated to it on July 4, but only after formally reconvening it on his own authority, since he did not recognize the legitimacy of its convocation by John XXIII and, presumably, the legality of the legislation it has passed in the intervening months. Gregory's action left *Sacrosancta* a dubious document in the eyes of Roman church authority, even though it made possible the healing of the schism and reestablishment of the Roman line of popes. The council later (July 26, 1417) deposed the Avignon pope Benedict XIII, who had refused to recognize any of its proceedings, before electing the cardinal-deacon Oddo Colonna as Pope Martin V on November 11, 1417.

The *translatio imperii* from pope to council is especially highlighted by the

74. Ockham argued that a theologian (like himself) had greater authority than the pope if the theologian were manifestly on the side of truth and the pope manifestly not, as Ockham believed Pope John XXII to be. See McGrade, *The Political Thought of William of Ockham*, pp. 61–63, 66. Marsilius argued that popes should be doctors of Scripture rather than "shyster [canon] lawyers" (*Defender of Peace*, bk. 2, ch. 24, sect. 9, p. 324).

execution of John Huss in July 1415. Prior to the Protestant Reformation, no religious movement had advanced more successfully against the late medieval church than the Hussites of Bohemia. The new Czech heresy, underway in Prague by 1403 with Huss as its leader, gathered the forces of Czech political and social discontent around it. What had begun as an independent native religious reform movement[75] coalesced with emergent Czech nationalism and came increasingly under the influence of the teaching of the English reformer John Wyclif. To foreign observers, this was a fearsome combination in a country that was a formidable military power.

The influence of Wyclif's writings gave the Hussite movement both an international dimension and a distinctly heretical association.[76] After the marriage of Anne of Bohemia and King Richard II in 1381, regular traffic existed between England and Bohemia. Huss's formative years as a theologian had also been a period of frequent student exchange between the universities of Oxford and Prague. Huss early read the philosophical works of Wyclif, which were strongly realist in their treatment of ideas and universals.[77] Czech students studying at Oxford, among them Jerome of Prague, returned with Wyclif's controversial theological writings on the Eucharist, simony, and the nature of earthly dominion. By 1407 the bulk of Wyclif's work was in circulation in Prague and avidly read by Huss's circle. As early as 1403 the separate German faculty within the university had led efforts to curtail Wyclif's growing popularity. Forty-five allegedly heretical teachings were excerpted from his writings and declared forbidden topics. Twenty-four of these articles were copied from a London condemnation of Wyclif's teaching in 1382 that had followed the English Peasant's Revolt of 1381.

Wyclif's views on dominion, set forth in his treatises *On Divine Lordship* (1375) and *On Civil Lordship* (1376), had earlier been condemned by Pope Gregory XI in May 1377, when the pope censured eighteen propositions drawn from the latter tract. Although Wyclif strongly criticized the church's material possessions in light of the ideal of apostolic poverty, he seems to have believed that he was only formulating scholastic theses and stating theological ideals, not providing political directives for English rulers.[78] He

75. See Matthew Spinka, *John Huss and the Czech Reform* (Hamden, Conn., 1966).

76. On the political and religious reasons behind the Czechs' adoption of Wyclifism, see Howard Kaminsky, "The University of Prague in the Hussite Revolution: The Role of the Masters," in *Universities in Politics: Case Studies from the Late Middle Ages and Early Modern Period,* ed. John W. Baldwin and Richard A. Goldthwaite (Baltimore, 1972), pp. 92–97.

77. See S. Harrison Thomson, "The Philosophical Basis of Wyclif's Theology," *Journal of Religion* 11 (1931): 86–116.

78. On Wyclif's political instincts, or rather apparent lack thereof, see T. J. Hanrahan, C.S.B., "John Wyclif's Political Activity," *Medieval Studies* 20 (1958): 154–66; Joseph H. Dahmus, "John Wyclif and the English Government," *Speculum* 35 (1960): 51–68.

stressed two basic points. First, all dominion on earth, whether secular or ecclesiastical, was a gift from God, the true owner of all things, and not an inherent right of the human owners. Property and possessions belonged to men secondarily and accidentally, not primarily and necessarily. Wyclif's second point followed logically from the first: as dominion is an intrinsic right of no man, *rightful* lordship on earth must depend on an owner's personal worthiness and merit, that is, his agreement with a divine standard of conduct. Those who abuse God's gift of dominion by living unworthy lives forfeit all rightful claim to their property and possessions in the eyes of God, even though human law and tradition may permit them to keep them. Driven to its extreme conclusion and practically applied, Wyclif's argument justified not only a ruler's confiscation of the property and possessions of "unworthy" clergy, but also a "righteous" people's confiscation of the property and possessions of unworthy rulers.[79]

Efforts to proscribe Wyclif's teaching in Prague were like attempts to ban a book in Boston: demand soared. Huss, who was rector of the university after 1403, came into prominence as Wyclif's chief defender. The Hussites, or Prague Wyclifites, called for vernacular translations of the Bible and lay communion with both cup and bread. Both demands reflected the common egalitarian strain of the dissenting spiritual movements of the late Middle Ages. Insistence on communion in both kinds gave the Hussites their name of Utraquists (*sub utraque specie*—in *both* kinds) or Calixtines (*calix*, Latin for chalice). The Hussites insisted upon punishing clergy who had sinned mortally and further questioned the power of such clergy to bind the faithful in disciplinary matters (the priest's so-called *potestas jurisdictionis*).[80] Dispute over these issues became so intense within the university that the German and other foreign masters departed Prague, leaving the university in near Hussite control and, in the eyes of Catholic Europe, a center of heresy.

Between 1403 and 1407 the Hussite party survived both papal and archiepiscopal opposition. The first direct action against Huss came in 1408, when Archbishop Zbynek of Prague suspended him from his preaching office. The following year Zbynek charged Huss with teaching that priests in mortal sin could not efficaciously administer the sacrament (the Donatist heresy) and rejecting the validity of papal excommunication.

After the Council of Pisa political events began to play a significant role in

79. See Howard Kaminsky, "Wyclifism as Ideology of Revolution," *Church History* 32 (1963): 57–74.

80. Cf. Heiko Oberman's discussion of Huss's "semi-Donatism" in distinction from Wyclif's full Donatism. Wyclif denied the sinful priest both *potestas ordinis* (power to administer the sacraments) and *potestas jurisdictionis*. *Forerunners of the Reformation* (New York, 1966), pp. 208-11.

the Hussite movement. In a delayed reaction to the Roman pope Gregory XII's support of his political rivals, King Wenceslas of Bohemia shifted his support from Gregory to the new Pisan pope, Alexander V. When Archbishop Zbynek followed the king's example, Pope Alexander gave him his leave to persecute the Wyclifites in the university.

In June 1410, church authorities publicly burned seventeen of Wyclif's writings in Prague, and Alexander's successor, John XXIII, excommunicated Huss. Huss remained defiantly outspoken. In 1411 he preached against the sale of indulgences. In 1412 he publicly defended several condemned articles of Wyclif, insisting that they could be interpreted in an orthodox way, among them: that those who cease to preach or to hear the gospel because they have been excommunicated by the pope will be treated as traitors to Christ at the Last Judgment—a challenge of the pope's coercive power; that any deacon or priest may preach God's word without special papal or episcopal authorization—so-called free preaching of the gospel, which remained a basic Hussite demand; that rulers may appropriate the temporal possessions of clergy living in mortal sin; that tithes are pure alms, not obligatory payments; and that those who are in mortal sin do not *properly* hold either civil or spiritual dominion.[81]

After 1412 the excommunicated Huss secluded himself in southern Bohemia, where he remained until his summons to appear before the Council of Constance. During this period he wrote a major treatise, *On the Church* (1413), the chief source for his condemnation at Constance. Huss set out for Constance in October 1414, bearing a safe-conduct from the Emperor Sigismund and a letter from the archbishop of Prague that attested his orthodoxy on one doctrinal issue where Wyclif was clearly heretical—the dogma of transubstantiation. Huss naïvely believed that, given a hearing before the council, he could convince his strongest critics of the truth of his views. Within weeks of his arrival in early November the council formally charged him with heresy and ordered his arrest. In the summer of 1415, following months of house arrest, he addressed the council and defended condemned teachings of Wyclif. Such eager identification with Wyclif ended any chance he might have had for a fair and impartial hearing.

Stephen Palec, once Huss's friend and ally in the early Czech reform movement, gleaned and presented to the council forty-two allegedly heretical articles from the new treatise *On the Church*. The council reduced these to thirty in the final condemnation.[82] As Huss realized his defeat, he seems

81. Gordon Leff, *Heresy in the Later Middle Ages: The Relation of Heterodoxy to Dissent c. 1250-c. 1450* (Manchester, 1967), 2: 637–38.
82. Denzinger, nos. 1201–30, pp. 322–25. The forty-five condemned articles of Wyclif (July 10, 1412) are presented with the thirty condemned articles of Huss, together with Huss's replies to each, in Matthew Spinka, *John Hus' Concept of the Church* (Princeton, 1966),

to have concluded that the Council of Constance itself was the truly guilty party deserving punishment as a revolutionary and a heretic. He argued that whereas he had criticized the pope, the council fathers had actually *revolted* against him.[83] Shortly before his execution he wrote of the council to his friends:

> These spiritual men [the fathers of Constance], who declare themselves to be the holy church and the council thrice holy and infallible . . . after adoring John XXIII on their knees and kissing his feet and calling him most holy, condemned him as a dissolute murderer, sodomite, simoniac, and heretic. [John was deposed by the council.] They have therefore cut off the church's head, torn out its heart. . . . Where . . . is the opinion of master Stanislas [Znoyma] . . . and Palec [both former allies of Huss and now his accusers] . . . who affirmed that the pope is head of the church and its perfectly sufficient governor, the heart of the church and its principle of life, the inexhaustible fount of its authority, the source from which flow the powers of his [the pope's] inferiors, the haven at once indestructible and sufficient for every Christian?[84]

Huss died at the stake on July 6, 1415. Nine months later, on March 30, 1416, his colleague Jerome followed him there. Gerson, who had urged their execution, praised the council's action against such dangerous heresy. Like Wyclif, Huss believed that reprobate men could hold no proper au-

---

pp. 397–409. The latter are translated by Spinka in his edition of Peter of Mladonvice, *John Hus at the Council of Constance* (New York, 1966), pp. 260–64.

83. Leff comments: "The council of Constance condemned Hus to death largely for saying what it had done. . . . While Hus followed Wyclif in making the pope's position depend upon election by Christ, d'Ailly and the conciliarists made it come from a general council. Both therefore denied him to be the direct successor of St. Peter. Yet it was Hus who was inculpated for a view which was not so startlingly different in its conclusions from that of his accusers" (*Heresy in the Later Middle Age,* 2: 650–52). Paul de Vooght, who holds a very similar point of view, writes of Constance's conception of its power as formulated by Gerson:

> Il serait difficile d'imaginer un pouvoir doctrinal plus considérable, plus absolu, plus tyrannique et plus arbitraire. La terre entière est justifiable devant lui. Le pape lui est soumis. Le concile trance souverainement, sans devoir rendre compte á personne puisque, s'il le veut, sans aucune forme de procès. Il décide du sort des articles qu'il juge de leur sens, même lorsqu'il est entendu qu'un autre sens est possible, conformément à la logique, la grammaire et la vérite. Peut-on s'étonner encore, après cela, des protestations de Huss qui, jusque sur le bucher, maintiendra que le concile a donné à certains de ses propos un sens que lui n'y avait pas mis? ("Jean Huss et ses juges," in Franzen, *Das Konzil von Konstanz,* p. 169).

84. Cited by Leff, *Heresy in the Later Middle Ages,* 2: 684–85. Huss wrote separate tracts against Palec and Znoyma while at Constance. In *Magistri Johannes Hus Opera Omnia* 22: *Polemica,* ed. Jaroslav Eršil (Prague, 1966), pp. 235–367.

The burning of John Huss at the Council of Constance. From Ulrich Richenthal's *Das Concilium:So zu Constantz gehalten ist worden, des jars MCCCCXIII* (Augsburg, 1536), a "modernization" of the original edition of 1483. This is a contemporary portrayal of the event which, occurring in 1415, attested the new conciliar authority within the church.

thority over others.[85] As the reprobate and the elect could be known in the present life only by the presumptive evidence of their moral conduct, no group or institution could claim a special sanctity or authority simply by virtue of historical precedent, tradition, or present office and title. Gerson singled out the denial of authority to presumed wicked and reprobate men as the most pernicious of all Huss's errors, one as fatal to kingdoms as to churches. "The government of the world," he warned, "cannot be based on predestination or love, things which remain uncertain and insecure in this life, but must rest on established ecclesiastical and civil laws."[86] The seeming

85. See *On the Church*, in Oberman, *Forerunners of the Reformation*, pp. 226–29.

86. "Error inter alios perniciosissimus quo ad omnem civitatis politicae conservationem et quietem, et quem dogmatizantes habent vitare velut radicem pestiferam, jam variis sententiarum securibus per summos pontifices et aliunde recisam videtur esse mihi ille: quod praescitus aut malus existens in peccato mortali nullam habet dominationem vel jurisdic-

anarchism latent in Wyclifite and Hussite teaching on dominion and authority justified its condemnation and Huss's execution.[87]

The Bohemian reaction to the execution of their national heroes was revolution within and aggression beyond their borders. The Hussite movement divided into moderate Utraquists, who remained loyal to Huss's original religious reforms, and uncompromising, chiliastic Taborites, who aspired to transform Bohemia into a religious and social utopia.[88] By the late 1420s Hussite armies, under the leadership of John Ziska, threatened both eastern and western Europe.

The Council of Constance executed the Czech reformers both as a demonstration of its new authority and in an effort to snip heresy in the bud. When its successors, the councils of Pavia/Siena (1423–24) and Basel (1431–49), convened, their first order of business was winning peace with the militant Hussites unleashed by Constance's action. The ultimate result of Basel's negotiations was conciliar concession of major demands and the creation of a strong national church in Bohemia, precisely what the execution of Huss and Jerome sixteen years earlier had intended to prevent.

Gerson also defended the correctness of Constance's second and more successful coercive act, the deposition of rival popes and the election of Martin V (1417–31). After the council's adjournment, Gerson reflected on its settlement of the schism in a special tract, *On Ecclesiastical Power*. Here he depicted the pope as a limited, constitutional monarch and declared that Constance had put an end to a papal teaching no less fatal than the heresy of Wyclif and Huss—the papal presumption that the head of an institution remained immune to external regulation by its members. Peter, Gerson pointed out, had originally been given pre-eminence over all others in the church for the sole purpose of avoiding schism; the power to bind and loose was given exclusively to one apostle, rather than directly and equally to all

tionem vel potestatem super alios de populo christiano. Videtur autem parvitati meae quod contra hunc errorem exsurgere deberet omnis dominatio, tam spiritualis quam temporalis, ad exterminationem magis igne et gladio quam curiosa ratiocinatione" (Letter to Conrad de Vechte, Archbishop of Prague [Paris, 24 September 1414], in *Oeuvres complètes* [Paris, 1960], 2: 162).

87. "It was a doctrine to unmake popes, trample the bishops underfoot, cripple monasticism, and provoke political and social revolution" (R. R. Betts, "Some Political Ideas of the Early Czech Reformers," *Slavonic Review* 31 [1952/53]: 32.)

88. The Taborites derived their name from the biblical Mt. Tabor, a title given to a hill near Bechyně Castle in southern Bohemia around which they gathered their congregations. See Ernst Werner, "Popular Ideologies in Late Medieval Europe: Taborite Chiliasm and its Antecedents," *Comparative Studies in Society and History* 2 (1960): 344–63; Howard Kaminsky, "Chiliasm and the Hussite Revolution." *Church History* 26 (1957): 43–71. Especially informative is Kaminsky, "Peter Chelciky: Treatises on Christianity and the Social Order," *Studies in Medieval and Renaissance History* 1 (1964): 107–79.

The consecration of Pope Martin V. From Richenthal's chronicle, *Das Concilium.* This ceremony at the Council of Constance in 1417 ended the Great Schism.

twelve, for the sake of unity and order. In doing this, Jesus and the apostles had acted as the first general council of the church. What they freely gave for the specific end of church unity and order a present-day council, standing in their place, might freely "moderate and regulate" to preserve this end. Far from having "decapitated" the church, Gerson concluded, the Council of Constance had restored its unity and brought Peter again to his rightful place and function.[89]

Although the implications of their arguments and actions proved much broader, the conciliar theorists did from within the church what kings and royal apologists had already done from outside it: they circumscribed the authority of the pope and subjected his office to the welfare and interests of a larger community.

*The Conciliar Movement
After Constance*

CONSTANCE defended the faith by executing heretics and ended the schism by electing Martin V. The third part of its program, the reform of the church in head and members, had awaited the election of the new pope. The fathers of Constance concluded that the only guarantee of reform was constant vigilance and frequent communication within the church. After Martin's election they attempted to create the machinery for such communication by passing the decree *Frequens* on October 9, 1417. *Frequens* provided for regular meetings of a general council of the church, thereby establishing the council as a permanent feature of church governance. The decree enjoined that a council be called within five years of Constance's adjournment, another within seven years of its adjournment, and thereafter "regularly" at least every ten years.[90] How did this plan fare?

In accordance with *Frequens,* Martin V convened a council in Pavia in 1423, which, however, plague forced to move almost immediately to Siena. Between natural calamity and papal intrigue, this first council after Constance accomplished little before its dissolution in March 1424. The pope understandably resented conciliar power and desired its decrease and demise. Both Martin V and his successor, Eugenius IV (1431–49), fought to

89. *Oeuvres complètes* 6, cons. 9, p. 226; cons. 10, p. 229. See also Gerson's *Propositio facta coram Anglicis, Oeuvres complètes* 6, cons. 9, p. 133. Further discussion and documentation in my "The University and the Church: Patterns of Reform in Jean Gerson," *Medievalia et Humanistica N.S.* 1 (1970): 111–26.

90. August Franzen, "Das Konzil der Einheit: Einigungsbemühungen und konziliare Gedanken auf dem Konstanzer Konzil. Die Dekrete 'Haec Sancta' und 'Frequens,'" in Franzen, *Das Konzil von Konstanz,* pp. 108–11.

restore papal supremacy within the church by frustrating the operation of councils whenever the opportunity arose.

Again in accordance with *Frequens,* Martin ordered a council to meet in Basel in July 1431. The pope died before the council convened, and his successor, Eugenius IV, fell out with the council over issues of authority. In a move to bring the council under close papal supervision, Eugenius, promising forthcoming negotiations for reunion with the eastern church, adjourned the council by fiat in December 1431, and ordered its members to reassemble at a later date in Bologna. Stung by this bold interference in its work, the council refused to adjourn and reasserted the principles of conciliar supremacy. In doing so Basel now challenged a pope who was duly elected, universally acknowledged, and ruled at a time when no threat of schism or other dire emergency threatened the church. This changed circumstance became increasingly important in the prolonged confrontation between Eugenius and the council.

The turning at this time of secular political tides away from representative government also boded well for the pope. Europe's rulers had recently learned to consolidate political and economic power and to act independently of legislative assemblies.[91] Although such forces worked in Eugenius's favor in the long run, for the moment the pope had to acquiesce and recognize Basel's declaration of conciliar rights, extreme though he felt the council's restatement to be. The decree of dissolution was withdrawn and Eugenius declared Basel to be in legitimate session.

In late 1432 the council began negotiations with the Hussites. By this date Taborite armies were a major military threat to Bavaria, Saxony, Austria, and Brandenburg. The moderate Hussites, or Utraquists, who opposed such aggression and desired peace with the Roman church, were invited by the council to send a delegation to Basel. They came with four basic demands known since their formulation in 1420 as the Four Articles of Prague: communion in both kinds; secular punishment of clergy living in manifest mortal sin; free preaching of the gospel; and clerical surrender of secular political power and property. In November 1433 the council recognized the Hussites' right under certain conditions to communion with both cup and bread and left the door open for further negotiations. Pope Eugenius watched with understandable dismay as the council negotiated points of church doctrine with heretics.

The council approached its task of reform by first restricting traditional papal privileges.[92] It limited appeals to Rome in disputed ecclesiastical

91. See below, p. 182.
92. Hubert Jedin, *A History of the Council of Trent,* trans. Dom Ernest Graf, O.S.B. (Edinburgh, 1963), 1: 18–19.

judgments, a measure that enhanced local ecclesiastical jurisdiction and discipline. It fixed the college of cardinals at twenty-four and declared that no more than one-third of the members could be from one nation, a move designed to end compliant Italian cardinalates. In June 1435 the council, which had many French members, removed papal rights to annates of benefices. This reform found quick adoption in France and Germany and significantly reduced papal revenues in both countries. By the Pragmatic Sanction of Bourges in 1438, France adopted Basel's reforms restricting papal power, and they became a lasting feature of the Gallican church. In 1439 the Germans ratified similar legislation (the Acceptation of Mainz) with widespread university and clerical support for reforms that strengthened local control of the religious life.[93] The plight of popes in the conciliar age is illustrated by the fact that between 1427 and 1436 papal revenues declined by almost two-thirds.[94]

The international Council of Basel progressively reduced the power of the papacy to a narrow Italian base. In agreements reached in 1436 and 1437 with King Sigismund and the moderate Hussites, who had subdued the Taborites in 1434, the council conceded the first three articles of Prague to the Bohemians. The council not only negotiated points of doctrine with heretics; it also granted indulgences and dispensations from impediments to marriage and absolved sins whose remission traditionally had been reserved to the pope. By 1437 it seemed that the council, to all intents and purposes, had itself become the pope.

Eugenius struck back at the council on September 18, 1437 by again dissolving it and ordering its removal to Ferrara. Although a majority of the council members opposed the transfer, Eugenius now had very enticing bait: the real possibility of a conciliar settlement of the centuries-old schism with the eastern church. Assailed again by the Turks, the eastern emperor, John VIII Palaeologus, looked to the restoration of communion with Rome as the key to obtaining western military assistance, a strategy also encouraged by the pope. The Greeks conferred with both the Council of Basel and Eugenius to determine the site of a meeting to negotiate ecclesiastical differences. A majority of the council refused to enter the orbit of papal strength and demanded that the talks take place in either Basel or Avignon. The Greeks, however, were sensitive to the pope's traditional power within the western church and insisted upon his prominent presence. They finally

93. See Joachim W. Stieber, *Pope Eugenius IV, the Council of Basel, and the Secular and Ecclesiastical Authorities in the Empire: The Conflict Over Supreme Authority and Power in the Church* (Leiden, 1978), pp. 163–65.

94. Paul E. Sigmund, *Nicholas of Cusa and Medieval Political Thought* (Cambridge, Mass., 1963), pp. 220–21.

agreed to meet in Ferrara, the site chosen by Pope Eugenius. A minority of the Council of Basel, among them Nicholas of Cusa and the powerful Cardinal Cesarini, for a term president of the council, became convinced that Basel had no right to resist the pope in this matter and journeyed obediently to Ferrara. While the immediate reason given for their departure was the importance of reunion with the eastern church, those who joined the pope had also come to believe that Basel had exceeded its rightful mandate as defined by the Council of Constance.

Those who remained in Basel proceeded to burn all their bridges to the pope. Annulling Eugenius's bull of dissolution, the Council of Basel declared itself still in legitimate session and became a schismatic council. Meanwhile, the Council of Ferrara set to work in April 1438 amid great pomp and ceremony. On June 25, 1439, the Council of Basel took the final desperate step of deposing Eugenius and electing in his stead five months later the wealthy and respected Duke Amadeus of Savoy, who became the antipope Felix V (1439–49).

A few decades earlier there had been schismatic popes; now there were schismatic councils. When schismatic popes reigned, a council of the church proved supreme; now, when there were schismatic councils, the pope would prove supreme.

The threat of plague and financial trouble occasioned the transfer of the Council of Ferrara to Florence in January 1439, where negotiations with the eastern church continued.[95] The western church attempted to be flexible on the issues of Greek liturgical practice and priestly marriage; both sides forbade the marriage of high clergy, but the eastern church had always permitted parish priests to marry. The Greeks in their turn attempted to adjust to two western peculiarities: the addition of the *filioque* clause to the Nicean-Constantinopolitan Creed, according to which the Holy Spirit proceeded from the Father "and from the Son," in the view of eastern theologians, a detraction from the Father's singular glory; and, more difficult still for the Greeks, the Roman insistence, never before recognized by the eastern church, that the pope held "primacy" in the church.

On July 5, 1439 a bull, *Laetentur coeli*, proclaimed the reunion of the eastern and western churches. The concessions by the leaders of the two sides were, however, half-hearted and quite unrealistic in light of their respective histories. Once again joy proved short-lived in Christendom. Not only did the brief reunion not issue in a permanent union, but it also failed to bring the east protection from the Turks; Constantinople fell in 1453.

95. On the Council of Florence, see Joseph Gill, *The Council of Florence* (Cambridge, 1959).

Despite the failure to reunite eastern and western Christians, the Council of Ferrara/Florence attested on an international scale to the revival of papal power after three decades of conciliar supremacy. By 1447 the Council of Basel, since transferred to Lausanne, the residence of its antipope, concurred in the election of Eugenius's successor, Nicholas V (1447–55), and encouraged Felix, whom it had created, to abdicate, which he eventually did in 1449. By 1450 the conciliar theory had effectively been beaten. Pius II (1458–64) delivered a final, if not totally fatal, blow in 1460, when his bull *Execrabilis* condemned appeals beyond the pope to councils as "erroneous and abominable."

An intriguing case study in the failure of the Council of Basel and the restoration of papal supremacy in the church is the philosopher and canon lawyer Nicholas of Cusa (1401–64). Cusa enthusiastically supported Basel until May 1437, at which time he broke with the council and joined the pope in Ferrara. He was actually a major theorist, successively, for *both* sides in the dispute. He wrote a major conciliar tract, *De concordantia catholica* (1432–33), which, presented to the Council of Basel in late 1433, formed part of its self-understanding. He also proposed a program for papal reform of the church, which he submitted to Pius II in 1459 on the eve of *Execrabilis*.[96]

Why did Cusa shift from what seems to have been one extreme to the other? Some have argued that he first became disillusioned with the council after it decided against bishop-elect Ulrich von Manderscheid, Cusa's client in a lawsuit involving the archbishopric of Trier.[97] Others have suspected that he was simply opportunistic and perceived that the route to high ecclesiastical office lay through Rome, not through a controversial council. (He did obtain both a bishopric and the cardinalate.) Still others believe that Cusa remained faithful to basic principles he had held from the start and acted differently only as he applied them to changed historical circumstances.[98] From this point of view, Basel's resistance to joining the pope in reunion talks with the Greeks led Cusa to conclude that the council no longer represented the constructive forces within the church.

As set forth in *De concordantia catholica*, Cusa's conciliar theory respected

96. "Der Reformentwurf des Kardinals Nikolaus Cusanus," ed. Stephan Ehses, *Historisches Jahrbuch der Görres-Gesellschaft* 32 (1911): 275–97.

97. For this dispute, see Erich Meuthen, *Das Trierer Schisma von 1430 auf dem Basler Konzil* (Münster, 1964).

98. The historiography of the issue is discussed by Sigmund in *Nicholas of Cusa and Medieval Political Thought*, pp. 226–28; Erich Meuthen, "Nikolaus von Kues in der Entscheidung zwischen Konzil und Papst," in *Nikolaus von Kues als Promoter der Oekumene: Mitteilungen und Forschungsbeiträge der Cusanus Gesellschaft* 9 (1971): 19–33; and James E. Biechler, "Nicholas of Cusa and the End of the Conciliar Movement: A Humanist Crisis of Identity," *Church History* 44 (1975): 5–21.

both the abiding rights of the pope and the emergency powers of councils.[99] Cusa praised the pope as the supreme head of the militant church, deemed his consent necessary for the constitution of articles of faith, and affirmed that a council normally had legitimacy only when convened by the pope. Cusa further acknowledged the pope's right to apply equity to church laws. Side by side with these statements, however, we find familiar conciliar arguments: Peter received no more power than did the other apostles; the pope remained one member within and subordinate to the universal church; the body of the faithful, represented by a council, could depose a pope who espoused manifestly heretical teachings and failed to serve the welfare of the church at large; although Peter's chair might be said to be infallible, the occupant of that chair was as capable as any other of heresy and schism. Cusa described the pope as "highest in administration" and as holding a "primacy of honor" within a general council of the church—the chief executive of a more authoritative corporation.

For Cusa, the key condition of all legitimate authority was "consent." Harmony and agreement among the various parts of the whole indicated a true council or authoritative representative body. At the base of all true government, whether secular or ecclesiastical, lay concord and consent—an underlying unity amid diversity, a coincidence of opposites, the many speaking and acting as one.

When Cusa shifted allegiance from Basel to Ferrara/Florence, he did so because he believed that Basel had ceased to be a council "in concordia et consensu." Severed from the rightful head of the church and even lacking the consent of all its own members, it no longer represented the whole body of the faithful. Such a council, Cusa believed, could draw no support from the decrees of Constance.

As a papal advocate, Cusa argued that those members of a divided council who remained in harmony with the pope more truly represented the whole body of the faithful than those who separated from him. Hence, the minority who departed Basel to join Eugenius attended the truer council, a conclusion Cusa also found evident in the fruits of the two councils.

In the 1440s Cusa became the conservative advocate of papal authority. He denied the right of the emperor to convene church councils and strictly confined the executive and legislative power of the church to the pope and the college of cardinals. The church became the "explicatio Petri," the unfolding of the power of Peter through hierarchical ranks.

99. See Sigmund, *Nicholas of Cusa and Medieval Political Thought*, p. 131. The subsequent discussion draws on Sigmund; Heinz Hürten, "Die Konstanzer Dekrete 'Haec Sancta' und 'Frequens' in ihrer Bedeutung für Ekklesiologie und Kirchenpolitik des Nikolaus von Kues," in Franzen, *Das Konzil von Konstanz*, pp. 381–96; and Morimichi Watanabe, *The Political Ideas of Nicholas of Cusa with Special Reference to his De Concordantia Catholica* (Geneva, 1963).

There is nothing in the church which is not first in Peter or his successor, and through the medium of the pope in all others. . . . All power
flows from the head of the church, where there is a plenitude of power,
and is particularized [*contracta*] in the church. . . . All power which is so
unfolded [*explicata*] in the church is contained in the pope as in a causal
principle.[100]

Such a view of papal power diminished the egalitarian strains in Cusa's
earlier theory of consent. *Where* one stood in the hierarchy of church power
became more important than sheer numbers; there was a "more weighty
part" (*pars valentior*) of the whole, and the pope and his college of cardinals
represented it. At the Council of Basel representatives of the lower clergy,
the chapters, and the universities voted along with the higher clergy, and
the doctors of theology rivaled bishops in influence. Such broadening of
authority annoyed Cusa, who complained that the council proceeded too
much along mere "mathematical" or "arithmetical" lines, without regard to
the office or position of those who voted.[101] After leaving Basel he worked
to rehabilitate a *pre*conciliar concept of the papacy, which both harked back
to the papal monarchy of the twelfth and thirteenth centuries and
foreshadowed the claims to papal infallibility set forth by Vatican Council I
in 1870.[102]

   Three points of view on the relationship between church and state competed in the later Middle Ages. One strictly subordinated secular to
ecclesiastical power and found advocates among popes and their apologists.
A second was championed by extreme royal publicists, who reversed the
papal arguments and subordinated ecclesiastical to secular power and
treated the church as a department of state. The third saw church and state
as parallel powers and attempted to acknowledge the autonomy of each
within its respective sphere. It is questionable whether this last view was ever
more than abstract theory. Its two allegedly strongest advocates, John of
Paris and Thomas Aquinas, actually tilted when pressed to one or the other
side, John favoring royal power, Aquinas papal and ecclesiastical. The
ecclesiopolitical history of the Middle Ages was never marked by true equilib-
rium; temporal and spiritual power struggled for dominance within Christian Europe in a contest secular rulers won decisively both in theory and
in fact by the eve of the Reformation.
   The conciliar movement posed many of the same issues of authority

---

100. Cited by Sigmund, *Cusa and Medieval Political Thought,* p. 266.
101. See Biechler, "Nicholas of Cusa and the End of the Conciliar Movement," p. 17;
Jedin, *A History of the Council of Trent,* 1: 19.
102. On the latter, see Sigmund, *Nicholas of Cusa and Medieval Political Thought,* p. 273.

within the medieval church that the emergent nation-states of Europe had earlier posed from without. In the debate over internal church authority, four different conceptions of the relationship between pope and council found advocates. The first called for the complete subordination of a council to the pope, a point of view exemplified by the papal monarchy of Innocent III and by the Fourth Lateran Council (1215). Here the pope was lower than God but higher than man; he might judge all, but could be judged by none. Holding a plenitude of power within the church, he remained supreme over all representative bodies; councils were extensions of his will.

The second possible relationship between pope and council envisioned a genuine sharing of authority, but with the pope clearly holding the upper hand. In this relationship Peter was the fount from whom all ecclesiastical power flowed. This was Nicholas of Cusa's point of view after leaving Basel, and it became embodied in the "papal" Council of Ferrara/Florence.

The third relationship between pope and council also envisioned a sharing of power, but with the council, not the pope, dominant. Here the church was seen to preexist its head; Peter derived from the church, not the church from Peter. As there were peoples before there were kings, so there was a body of the faithful before there was a pope. This point of view conceived the pope as a corporation executive or spokesman, an essential but by no means highest authority within the church. Gerson and d'Ailly formulated such a view, and the councils of Constance and preschismatic Basel acted on it.

Finally, there was the theory that the pope should be subject absolutely to a general council of the church representing the body of the faithful, the immediate source of all papal power. Here the pope became hardly more than a figurehead within a larger ecclesiopolitical community, subject to removal at any time by conciliar fiat. Such was Marsilius of Padua's understanding of the relationship between pope and council. The schismatic Council of Basel adopted this point of view when, in its later stages, it assumed total power within the church, deposed Eugenius IV, and elected its own antipope.

Summary   NO generalization about late medieval intellectual and religious history can be ventured without caution. Historical periods and cultures are invariably many-sided and diverse, and nuance and detail, not gross generalization, are the historian's proper subject. But the historian is also called to the task of synthesis, and his final responsibility, the goal of his craft, is to order the many and shed light on the whole.

The Middle Ages were anything but a period of conformist religion and church domination. Europe was a factious family of nation-states, not a harmonious *corpus Christianum.* Save for brief historical periods and within limited geographical areas, the medieval church was an institution very much on the defensive. The papacies of Gregory VII and Innocent III and the scholastic synthesis of Thomas Aquinas were exceptions, not the rule. Within the scholastic traditions the church as early as the eleventh century confronted new and unorthodox theological teachings inspired by the pagan Aristotle. Within the spiritual traditions the church found itself opposing a seemingly endless variety of heterodox movements inspired by the ideal of apostolic poverty and convinced that personal morality or experience, not tradition or office, gave spiritual authority. Within the political traditions kings attempted to reduce the church to purely sacramental functions and make it a compliant agent of state, while an internal conciliar movement successfully challenged papal supremacy.

The medieval church won battles, but lost wars. The papal monarchy of the twelfth and thirteenth centuries, whose ideals died hard, was no match for the new political monarchies of the fourteenth and fifteenth centuries. Papal excommunication and interdict ceased to be effective ways to implement the church's will; indeed, their exercise encouraged a new kind of spiritual identity: nationalism. The use of crusade and Inquisition against heterodox piety created permanent religious divisions within and between regions. The critical historical temper of Augustinianism and Ockhamism, popular religious movements like the Lollards and the Hussites, and royal pamphleteers who demanded national control of churches continued in sixteenth-century humanism and Protestantism. The condemned decrees of Constance found supporters among humanists, canonists (Panormitanus, for example), and Protestant reformers alike. Protestants rehabilitated condemned heretics from Marsilius of Padua to John Huss and praised them as "forerunners" of the Reformation. In northern Europe by 1500, experimentation with new religious ideas and practices, usually in the name of greater fidelity to old truths and examples, had either undermined or discredited much of what traditional church authority had considered normative spiritual practice.

It has been argued that a central aspect of late medieval thought, one under which other trends might be subsumed, is an alleged "closing of the gap between the sacred and the profane."[103] The reverse conclusion is the

103. Heiko A. Oberman, "The Shape of Late Medieval Thought: The Birthpangs of the Modern Era," *ARG* 64 (1973): 16.

far more accurate generalization: in the late Middle Ages the traditional mixing of the sacred and the profane, largely from the side of ecclesiastical power, but when possible by secular power as well, was finally overcome. Whether medieval theologians dealt with the relationship between reason and revelation, nature and grace, laity and clergy, or royal and ecclesiastical power, they had invariably envisioned a secular-religious continuum. Medieval popes aspired to enforce such a hierarchy both politically and socially. They did not think in terms of two fundamentally different and independent spheres, but of higher and lower levels of reality within a great chain of being: the church and religious values at the higher levels; the state and secular values at the lower. In the later Middle Ages the integrity and autonomy of the secular world was firmly established; the spiritual became truly spiritual, and the profane ceased to be merely profane. Nature came to mean something positive apart from its perfection by grace, and the natural world was no longer obliged to realize itself in the supernatural.

In their different ways the theologies of Ockham and Luther expressed the experience of these centuries. Both carefully confined religion within the realm of faith and recognized the utter sovereignty of temporal power within the world. And both came to terms positively with man's indomitable finitude and secularity this side of eternity. Luther, who stood at the end of this development, summarized it most radically when he argued that the man of faith remained throughout his life *simultaneously* righteous and sinful—totally righteous by his faith in Christ, yet totally sinful within himself—no longer the medieval *viator*, who was saved by a gradual spiritual transformation that made him progressively like God.

The late Middle Ages attest the final division of the sacred and the profane.[104] Late medieval thinkers justified in theory and doctrine the gap that had always existed in fact between the two. If there had ever been a chance of harmonizing the realities represented by reason and revelation, it was gone by the sixteenth century. As new religious wars engulfed Reformation Europe, religion became itself the key agent of political division and social change, no longer a means for trans-European unity and harmony.

104. I realize that in this assessment I am something of a Gilsonian.

CHAPTER 5

On the Eve of
the Reformation

The Growth of Monarchy

BY the second half of the fifteenth century, European rulers had begun to solve two major problems, and the resolution of each proved important to the success of the Protestant Reformation. First, they gained military supremacy over internal rivals and learned to govern their realms through agents whose outlook and loyalty were "national" or "territorial" rather than merely local or regional. In France, England, Spain, the city-states of Italy, and the larger German principalities, lands were politically unified and administratively organized to a degree unknown during the Middle Ages. Second, rulers secured their realms from foreign aggression and influence, especially that of the pope and the church. In the later Middle Ages the church waned as a significant international political power, and lay administrators, who put the nation-state and the monarch above the church universal and the pope, progressively replaced the clergy in royal bureaucracies.

In France the transition from feudal to monarchical state actually began with the Capetian kings and reached a decisive stage during the reign of Philip IV the Fair (1285–1314). Philip successfully contested the pope for the right to tax French clergy and make high ecclesiastical appointments. As a partial solution to his financial problems, he crushed the religious-military order of Knights Templars in a series of trials and confiscated much of their wealth and property. Using the occasion of impending war with England to muster growing national feeling around the crown, he created an efficient administrative bureaucracy and system of taxation and staffed royal offices with ruthless agents like Guillaume de Nogaret, who did not shrink from the near assassination of a pope for his king. A network of trustworthy baliffs monitored the regional courts of the land and greatly enhanced royal power and authority in the popular mind.

The Hundred Years' War (1337–1453) between France and England accelerated these developments. During this period a standing royal army formed and the king secured the right to levy, solely on his own authority, basic taxes on salt (*gabelle*), merchandise (*aides*), and property (*taille*), which brought a degree of royal fiscal independence. Persisting regional aspirations to political autonomy prevented the development of a strong national representative assembly that could function as a counterweight to the growth of monarchy, despite the Estates-General's resemblance to such a body. Capetian and Valois kings shrewdly divided and managed the constituent parts of their realm so that local loyalties and regional divisions always weakened their rivals more than the monarchy. On the other hand, the continuation of these regional identities created within France permanent bases for dissent from "national" policy. In the sixteenth century Calvinists won a sizable following among French nobles who opposed royal political consolidation at least as much as the king's Catholicism.

In England the period of the Hundred Years' War assisted governmental centralization by forcing increased cooperation between king and Parliament. By appointing landholding families as royal justices of the peace and giving them responsibility for the administration of justice in their respective regions, the king cleverly transformed local magnates into royal agents. The self-interests of nobility, clergy, and townsmen had long been protected by Magna Carta (1215), which limited by law the authority of the monarch, especially royal prerogative in taxation. Throughout the later Middle Ages, English Kings chafed at this parliamentary rein on the growth of their power, and while never removing it, they did manage by the late fifteenth century to force the nation as represented by Parliament to run in tandem with the monarchy.

Beginning with Edward I (1272–1307) English kings both centralized their power and expanded the representation of Parliament. Harmony between king and Parliament meant greater regional support for royal programs and policies. The peculiar English system of parliamentary government made possible a strong monarchy, yet also prevented the type of prolonged strong-man rule that characterized France under Louis XI (1460–83), although some have found Henry Tudor (1485–1509) a close approximation to the French model of authoritarian rule. Henry ended the internal division that had plagued England after the Hundred Years' War by subjecting factious noblemen to the decisions of a special royal privy council, the Court of Star Chamber, and by adroitly manipulating English law to the crown's advantage. The king's court relied more heavily upon Roman law, which exalted the sovereignty of the ruler as the embodiment of the people's will, than upon the common law, whose respect for tradition and custom gave greater protection to regional interests. It was another sign of the strength of the new Tudor monarchy that Henry, having secured his hereditary claim to the throne by marrying Elizabeth of York, the daughter of his rival, entered a foreign alliance with Spain by the marriage of his fifteen-year-old son, Arthur, to Catherine of Aragon. This latter marriage not only thrust England into the center of European politics, but also contributed in time to the success of the English Reformation. After Catherine's subsequent marriage to Arthur's brother, King Henry VIII, her previous marriage became the basis of a celebrated legal dispute in the 1520s between Henry, who had by then determined to divorce Catherine because of her inability to produce a male heir, and the pope, who refused to grant the desired annulment.[1]

The marriage of Isabella of Castile and Ferdinand of Aragon in 1469 created the modern state of Spain, the base of sixteenth-century Hapsburg power during the long reigns of Charles I, from 1519 to 1556 Emperor Charles V, and his son, Philip II, king of Spain (1556–98). Although the two kingdoms remained constitutionally separated, the dynastic union gave each the military strength to subdue internal rivals, secure borders against French and Moslem aggressors, and venture abroad militarily as an international power. As elsewhere on the continent when rulers consolidated their kingdoms, the cities joined the monarchy against the landed nobility, and townsmen and merchants progressively replaced noblemen and clergy as royal agents and administrators. An elaborate organization of specialized royal councils governed the realm. Ferdinand and Isabella integrated the church and the higher clergy into their government by making the Inquisition an instrument of political repression after 1479. The forced exile of the Jews in 1492 and of nonconverting Moors in 1502 further contributed to the religious uniformity that kept Spain politically and religiously one throughout the upheavals of the sixteenth century. Spain became the base of the Catholic offensive against Protestantism, the birthplace of the Society of Jesus and the home of the mystics Teresa of Avila and John of the Cross, whose methodical discipline and enthusiastic individual piety revitalized the traditional faith and won many Protestants back to the Catholic fold.

Neither Italy nor Germany achieved the national unity of France, England, or Spain during the later Middle Ages, although increased governmental control and administrative centralization occurred in both lands at regional and local levels. The great cities of Italy absorbed their surrounding countrysides and evolved into genuine territorial states, in most instances ruled by hereditary princes. The Treaty of Lodi, in effect from 1454 to 1494, maintained a balance of power among the major city-states of

1. The entire issue in all its theological, legal, and political complexity is analyzed with new information and insight by J. J. Scarisbrick, *Henry VIII* (Berkeley, 1968), esp. chapters 7 and 8.

Milan, Florence, Venice, the Papal States, and Naples and made it possible for them to act in unison against foreign aggression. The breaking of this wise treaty in 1494 by the Milanese despot Ludovico il Moro gave rise to the major European political conflicts of the first half of the sixteenth century. Fearing an attack by Milan's traditional enemy, Naples, Ludovico appealed to the French, who had ruled Naples from 1266 to 1435, to act on their dynastic claims to Naples and invade Italy. The French king Charles VIII responded greedily and transformed Italy into a stage of international warfare between France and Spain and their respective European and Italian allies. The Hapsburg-Valois conflict over Italian territories kept much of western Europe at war until 1559.

In Germany, as in Italy, administrative centralization was achieved only regionally, not on a national or imperial level; territorial princes and regional magnates, not the emperor, gained control over the country. The roots of German division trace back at least to the reign of Emperor Frederick II (1215-50), who in pursuit of imperial claims to southern Italy touched off a decades-long papal offensive against his dynasty that effectively ended it by the mid-thirteenth century. The absent and besieged emperor gave the German princes a free hand in shaping German political life, and their petty interests became supreme.[2] In 1356 the imperial Golden Bull officially recognized their autonomy. This agreement, issued by Emperor Charles IV (1347-78), repudiated direct papal involvement in imperial elections and restricted the election of the emperor to seven electoral states: four secular—the Palatinate, Saxony, Brandenburg, and Bohemia—which were recognized as autonomous political dynasties; and three ecclesiastical—the archbishoprics of Mainz, Trier, and Cologne.

Emperor Maximilian I (1493-1519) further strengthened the German princes by concessions made at a meeting of representatives of the three main political bodies of the empire—the seven electors, the numerous nonelectoral princes, and the approximately seventy-five imperial "free cities"—in Worms in 1495. Desiring peace within the empire in order to secure German soldiers for his own armies, the emperor granted German requests for a ban on interregional feuding and the establishment of an imperial Supreme Court (*Reichskammergericht*), a judicial body chosen for the greater part by the Germans themselves. Maximilian also recognized an

2. Describing Frederick's reign as "abdication pure and simple," Geoffrey Barraclough comments: "Between 1212 and 1250, sacrificed by Frederick to the exigencies of Italy, Germany took a road which differentiated its history for centuries to come . . . from that of England and France; its destinies passed out of the hands of the monarchy into the control of a princely aristocracy, whose horizons rarely extended beyond the boundaries of their own territories, and whose policy showed scant respect for the common interests and traditions of the German people" (*The Origins of Modern Germany* [New York, 1963], pp. 237, 240).

Imperial Council of Regency (*Reichsregiment*), an internal governing body with significant legislative power and executive privileges in the emperor's absence. Although the council proved short-lived—Charles V later restored it as a condition of his election as emperor—its brief existence was further testimony to the strength of the territorial states in the empire at the end of the Middle Ages.

Although the larger German states held representative assemblies, so-called *Landtage,* the territorial princes of Germany dominated their respective lands and cities. Only the imperial knights and the peasants offered violent resistance, and that proved brief and ineffectual. The tradition of regional independence and princely sovereignty became truly invincible in Germany. In 1547 the armies of Charles V defeated the Protestant princes of Saxony and Hesse, but this victory proved only a prelude to the emperor's own defeat four years later by the vanquished under the leadership of the rulers he had appointed to control them. Maximilian I summarized with wit and sad truth the dilemma of the Holy Roman Emperor throughout much of the later Middle Ages. The king of Spain, he remarked, was a king over men, because his subjects reacted to him as men may be expected to react, sometimes obeying and sometimes disobeying; the king of France, on the other hand, was a king over dumb animals, because his subjects always docilely obeyed his every command; the emperor, however, was a "king of kings," because no man did his bidding.[3]

In addition to achieving considerable political and administrative unity within their realms, Europe's rulers also succeeded in checking papal power. In the later Middle Ages church and religion acquired a marked territorial or national character. There is a long and somewhat cyclical history behind this development, which greatly aided the Reformation. After the third century, when the Emperor Constantine made Christianity the favored religion of the Roman Empire, the western church had struggled to establish its independence from secular authority. Rulers had always been inclined to look upon the church as a royal servant and department of state. So-called Erastianism, or state control of the church, which derives its name from Thomas Erastus (1524–83), physician to the Elector Palatine and opponent of Calvinist theocratic ambitions, was the original church-state relation. The papacy and episcopacy gained their first significant political independence from imperial authority only in the tenth and eleventh centuries, when the Cluny reform and Gregorian papacy laid a foundation for the peculiar western separation of church and state by defining basic spheres of secular and ecclesiastical jurisdiction. Although religion and society con-

---

3. Cited by Helmut G. Koenigsberger and George L. Mosse, *Europe in the Sixteenth Century* (New York, 1968), p. 230.

tinued to be thoroughly integrated, a lasting barrier was erected between pope and emperor, and popes thereafter enjoyed a new political power. During the pontificates of Innocent III and Innocent IV in the thirteenth century, the papacy even got the upper hand in the temporal sphere, as its successful interdiction of England and campaign against the Hohenstaufen dynasty attest.

But papal pretensions to a plentitude of power that reached even into the secular world foundered on the new political realities of the later Middle Ages. Royal pamphleteers successfully championed the rights of the political community, which also received indirect support from major religious reformers like John Wyclif in England and John Huss in Bohemia. Against the medieval theological belief that the spiritual life excelled the secular, it was argued that secular society had a moral perfection and destiny of its own apart from religion.

The reality of royal political autonomy and the force of royal argument gradually were translated into law during the fourteenth and fifteenth centuries. In England the pope's right to provide ecclesiastical benefices was struck down by statutes of Provisors in 1351 and 1390. These parliamentary acts gave the English king, not the pope, control over high English ecclesiastical appointments. When disputes over church offices arose, appeals beyond the king's court to the pope in Rome (or in Avignon from 1309 to 1377) were forbidden by statutes of Praemunire in 1353 and 1393. Traditional rights of sanctuary in religious buildings and clerical immunity from civil prosecution (benefit of clergy) were challenged during the reign of Henry VII. Two centuries of such "Erastianism" culminated in the Reformation Parliament of the 1530s, which having begun in November 1529 with measures curtailing ecclesiastical privileges and regulating mortuary and other spiritual fees, proceeded over the following decade to subject the English church to thorough royal control. It ended the independence of ecclesiastical courts;[4] withheld annates, or the first year's income of new benefices, from the pope, while recognizing in the king the power of episcopal appointment; declared the king judicially supreme in *all* legal matters within England; empowered the archbishop of Canterbury, in place of the pope, to dispense from canon law and to interdict all monetary payments to Rome; forced Convocation to recognize the king's sovereign headship of the English church, even to the point of permitting the king to declare

---

4. Among the specific grievances stated against church courts and the clergy were inordinate delays, prosecution over trivialities, inordinate fees, nepotism, payments to priests for administration of the sacraments, and the excessive number of holy days (A. G. Dickens, *The English Reformation* [London, 1964], p. 114). Compare pre-Reformation Strasbourg, Miriam U. Chrisman, *Strasbourg and the Reform: A Study in the Process of Change* (New Haven, 1967), pp. 102, 148–49.

orthodox church doctrine, which Henry VIII did in the *Ten Articles* of 1536 and the *Six Articles* of 1539;[5] annexed annates to the crown and established an annual 10 percent tax on all spiritual benefices; and, finally, dissolved English monasteries and redistributed their lands and endowments.

In fifteenth-century France the clergy adopted a set of conciliar reforms known as the Pragmatic Sanction of Bourges (1438). These reforms, which had been passed by the Council of Basel, deprived the pope of traditional rights of appointment, jurisdiction, and taxation in France and recognized the supremacy of general church councils over popes. Declaring them fundamental "Gallican Liberties,"[6] the French clergy insisted on the right of the French church to elect its own clergy, deny annates to the pope, and restrict appeals from French courts to the Curia in Rome. Such independence became a permanent feature of the French church.

In 1439, the year after the Pragmatic Sanction of Bourges, a German Diet drew up a similar agreement for the empire known as the Acceptation of Mainz. This agreement was overridden in 1448 by the Concordat of Vienna, but only at the sacrifice of papal power to the emperor. The pope, eager to overturn the legislation of Basel, conceded the emperor power to nominate all high ecclesiastical appointments in Hapsburg lands in exchange for imperial recognition of papal sovereignty within the church. Despite this concession, the pope retained greater authority in Germany than in any other major European country outside of Italy, an important factor in the political background of the Reformation.

The pope later recovered some of his lost power in France by an agreement with the French king known as the Concordat of Bologna (1516), but again only by paying a high price. In exchange for the French king's recognition of papal supremacy over church councils and of the pope's right to collect certain annates in France, Pope Leo X conceded Francis I the right to nominate candidates to all vacant archbishoprics, bishoprics, and abbacies—the concession of virtual power of appointment to almost six hundred major church offices.

Nowhere did the church come more under outright secular political domination than in Spain, in many ways the most Catholic of European

5. Parliament, however, successfully resisted a Caesaropapist interpretation of the king's headship of the church by treating it as "another facet of kingship, subject to and controlled by the same limitations as applied to secular rule." Despite this distinction, important to *both* church and Parliament, the Henrician Reformation remained one of the most striking examples of "the triumph of the laity in the realm of religion" (G. R. Elton, *Reform and the Reformation: England, 1509–1558* [Cambridge, Mass., 1977], pp. 198–99).

6. "Gallicanism" became a conscious concept in the early fifteenth century, but had actually existed as a reality for a much longer time, as the claims of French kings against popes since Capetian times indicate. See Victor Martin, *Les origines du gallicanisme*, vols. 1–2 (Paris, 1939).

countries. In 1486, Pope Innocent VIII, requiring Spanish military aid to implement papal policy in Italy, granted Ferdinand and Isabella rights of patronage to all major ecclesiastical appointments in conquered Granada. They also nominated Spanish bishops, and after 1508, Fredinand presented candidates for the major ecclesiastical posts in the New World as well. Charles V later won the right to appoint all Spanish bishops.

Jealous of their newly acquired political power over the church, Ferdinand and Isabella prevented appeals from Spanish courts to Rome in contested ecclesiastical cases and imposed new taxes on the Spanish clergy. In Sicily, Naples, and Milan, the pope's very backyard, the Spanish king could at will prevent the publication of papal bulls. It is a measure of Spanish determination to preserve this carefully constructed political control over the church that sixteenth-century Spanish rulers, whose loyalty to traditional church teaching was always unquestioned, resisted the reforms of the Counter Reformation until reassured that no revival of papal political power was intended by their implementation. For similar reasons, sixteenth-century French rulers also resisted the Tridentine reform legislation.[7]

A similar extension of civilian control over church and religion occurred in German cities and towns during the fifteenth century. Impelled by the corruption, inefficiency, and bold interference of local church authority, magistrates and city councils progressively whittled away at traditional clerical privileges and immunities. Urban governments successfully limited the traditional market regulations, right to grant amnesty and asylum, control over parish priests, and acquisition of city properties held by powerful cloisters. The treatment of all clergy as citizens rather than as a privileged elite became a pervasive feature of sixteenth-century Protestant cities and towns, at least in the early years of the Reformation.[8] This integration of religion into the civic life reflected on the urban level the same process of political consolidation and extension of secular control over religion that had long been occurring in the major monarchies.

While secular rulers succeeded in sharply curtailing Peter's temporal power, their success against representative government within their own lands actually favored the pope's recovery of his jurisdictional supremacy within the church. In the second half of the fifteenth century, Pope

7. See Victor Martin, *Le Gallicanisme et la réforme catholique: Essai historique sur l'introduction en France des décrets du concile de Trente* (1563–1615) (Geneva, 1975; reprint of original 1919 ed.).

8. See Dieter Demandt and Hans-Christoph Rublack, *Stadt and Kirche in Kitzingen* (Stuttgart, 1978), pp. 15–24; Steven Ozment, *The Reformation in the Cities The Appeal of Protestantism to Sixteenth-Century Germany and Switzerland* (New Haven, 1975), pp. 32–38, 84–89; Bernd Moeller, "Kleriker als Bürger," in *Festschrift für Hermann Heimpel zu 70. Geburtstag* (Göttingen, 1972), 2: 217; "Pfarrer als Bürger," *Göttinger Universitätsreden* 56 (1971): 5–26.

Eugenius IV and his successors overcame the forces of conciliar government that had ruled the church throughout the first half of the century and restored the papal monarchy.

It would be a mistake, however, to interpret the widespread political consolidation in the fifteenth century to mean that the political divisions of the Middle Ages came to an end as the sixteenth century began. The political unity that made a land internally strong also made it possible to venture abroad militarily, and such foreign adventures predictably recreated the conditions of internal political division and weakness. The very success of rulers in imposing their will on their subjects also heightened internal tension; political unification itself generated new forms of dissent. Despite the growth of common languages, effective central administrations, omnipresent royal agents, and official propaganda stressing the oneness of ruler and people, the locality or region continued to be far more important to the majority of people living within it than did "the empire," "the nation," or "the realm at large."[9] In this sense, feudal society persisted. As princely law displaced local custom and the king's agents local authorities, and as rulers decreasingly relied on representative bodies—the Spanish Cortes, the English Parliament, the French Estates-General, and regional diets—both new and traditional groups opposed to political centralization and inspired by revolutionary social and religious ideologies formed at both ends of the social spectrum. The stage was thereby set for militant political and social dissent and religious reform and warfare.

Population, Money, and Books

IN 1500 Europe was growing both in population and in the pursuits that enhance the quality of life—in exploration and trade, bureaucracy and technology, education and the

---

9. J. R. Hale, *Renaissance Europe: The Individual and Society 1480–1520* (New York, 1971), p. 112. J. H. Franklin comments on this complex situation: "The new monarchy of the later Middle Ages and the Renaissance presents a double aspect. One side of it was the gradual formation of a centralized administration which registered the triumph of the royal government over its older, feudal opposition. But the other side was the institutionalization, within that same administration, of the medieval principle that the king must govern with consent" (*Jean Bodin and the Rise of Absolutist Theory* [Cambridge, 1973], pp. 5–6). See also Bernard Guenée, who describes the late Middle Ages as a period of growing bureaucratization, limited monarchy, and democratization of privileges, in *L'Occident aux XIVe et XVe siècles: Les états* (Paris, 1971), pp. 80–81, 285; and Gordon Griffiths, "The State: Absolute or Limited?" in *Transition and Revolution: Problems and Issues of European Renaissance and Reformation History*, ed. by R. M. Kingdon (Minneapolis, 1974), pp. 13–52. The "continuing vitality of a feudal political outlook" is particularly stressed for the empire by Joachim Stieber, *Pope Eugenius IV, The Council of Basel, and the Secular and Ecclesiastical Authorities in the Empire* (Leiden, 1978), p. 4 and passim.

arts. Its fertility is reflected by an estimated population of 60 million. That figure may seem small by modern comparison—West Germany alone today exceeds 60 million—but it was an impressive recovery from the unprecedented population losses caused by the famines and plagues of the fourteenth century. Europeans suffered the worst famine of the Middle Ages between 1315 and 1317, and recurring poor harvests kept resistance to disease low when bubonic plague, following the trade routes from the east into and throughout western Europe, struck in midcentury. Many areas lost half of their population, and the overall decrease has been estimated at two-fifths of the previous total.[10] By 1500 these losses had been fully recovered, and the sixteenth century became a period of steady, almost universal population growth. By gross estimate the Empire, France, and Italy were the largest countries, with 12 million people in the Empire, and 10 million in both France and Italy. There were 7.5 million in Spain and 3.5 million in England. By 1600 the population in the Empire had risen to 20 million, in Franch to 15 million, in Italy to 13 million, in Spain to 10 million, and in England to 5.5 million. Europe's overall population grew to an estimated 85 million by 1600 and stabilized in the seventeenth century at about 100 million.[11]

Cities and towns contained only a small fraction of the total population; an estimated nine out of ten Europeans lived in rural areas. This generalization is somewhat deceptive, however, for urban density could be greater in some areas (Germany, the Netherlands, and Italy) than in others (Spain). In Saxony, where the Reformation began, one in five was a townsman by 1550. Reflecting the general population growth, many cities and towns doubled in size during the sixteenth century, among them Naples (possibly Europe's largest city, with 200,000 in 1500), Seville, London, Milan, Cologne, and the three major Reformation centers, Augsburg, Nuremberg, and Strasbourg. Even areas like France, where religious and civil warfare took the lives of thousands, still registered population increases in the sixteenth century. Whereas only five cities could boast more than 100,000 people in 1500 (London, Paris, Florence, Venice, and Naples), at least a dozen could do so by 1600.

Germany especially teemed with small towns. Of some 3,000 German

---

10. Harry A. Miskimin, *The Economy of Early Renaissance Europe 1300–1460* (Englewood Cliffs, N.J., 1969), pp. 25–32.

11. See L. W. Cowie, *Sixteenth Century Europe* (Edinburgh, 1977), pp. 25–29; J. R. Hale, *Renaissance Europe*, pp. 33–34; Roger Mols, S. J., "Population in Europe 1500–1700," in *The Fontana Economic History of Europe: The 16th and 17th Centuries*, ed. Carlo M. Cipolla (Glasgow, 1974), pp. 15–82; Richard S. Dunn, *The Age of Religious Wars 1559–1689* (New York, 1970), pp. 90–92; and Bernd Moeller, *Deutschland im Zeitalter der Reformation* (Göttingen, 1977), p. 29, who estimates sixteenth-century German population growth at .6 per year.

towns at the turn of the century, 2,800 had populations under 1,000 and only fifteen could boast more than 10,000. Augsburg and Cologne, with populations between 25,000 and 30,000, were the largest. Wittenberg, the birthplace of the Reformation, was by comparison a small town of only 2,500. Zurich, the home of Zwinglian Protestantism, had a population of 6,000, and Geneva, where Calvinism began, held about 15,000 people within its walls when John Calvin arrived in 1536.

While the urban centers contained only a small part of the total population, they were then, as they have always been in Western history, the sites of creative change. In the cities lived the merchants, bankers, skilled craftsmen, and scholars who possessed the power and ingenuity for innovation, and there one also found the social conflicts on which change thrives. Although the Protestant Reformation appealed to educated and uneducated alike, it presupposed for its success a literate urban culture and seems particularly to have attracted rising urban groups who had either experienced or were determined to come into a new political and economic importance. Protestant theology, especially in its Zwinglian and Calvinist forms, has been characterized by Bernd Moeller as a peculiar "urban theology" (*städtisch geprägte Theologie*), that is, as both a reflection and a defense of the social and political values of townsmen in free cities, especially their egalitarianism and strong sense of communal solidarity.[12] The Reformation expanded with great difficulty from cities and towns into the surrounding countrysides, where people clung more naively to traditional religious practices and to much pagan folklore and magic. In the 1520s and 1530s, Protestant councils would pass ordinances forbidding their citizens to worship in village churches in unreformed areas.

The later Middle Ages also saw the development of a money economy. Together with the general population increase, the new economy was a basic source of the period's social and ideological conflicts. The division between capital and labor that characterizes modern capitalism established itself at this time. This type of capitalism actually had its origins in late-eleventh-century and twelfth-century Italy, a product of the rebirth of trade and towns. So-called merchant bankers, men made rich by often monopolistic trade, progressively replaced small landholders and shopkeepers as the key economic unit in society. Whereas the latter had traditionally furnished their own capital, skill, and labor and done their own marketing, the new merchant bankers remained aloof from the "assembly lines" of their busi-

12. Bernd Moeller, *Reichsstadt und Reformation* (Gütersloh, 1962), p. 67; English translation by H. C. Erik Midelfort and Mark U. Edwards, *Imperial Cities and the Reformation* (Philadelphia, 1972).

nesses; they provided the capital for plants and the raw materials and hired skilled laborers to work them.[13]

Trade with the Near East and a vibrant urban culture had never completely died out in the great seaport towns of Italy. Italian merchants profited from the Crusades, especially the enterprising Fourth Crusade, whose capture of Constantinople in 1204 established new maritime rights for western cities throughout Byzantium. In the fourteenth century the Venetians and Genoese opened an Atlantic trade route with major centers in Bruges and London. About the same time, Baltic and North Sea traders organized the Hanseatic League, an alliance that came to include over seventy north European cities. From these commercial beginnings the Atlantic seaboard progressively displaced the increasingly Ottoman-dominated Mediterranean in economic power and importance.

The ancestors of the merchant bankers were landless men who had much to gain from the risks of foreign trade. These adventurers braved shipwreck at sea and banditry on land to buy goods as cheaply as possible at their source and sell them at the highest possible profit in western markets. As they accumulated great wealth and became respectable businessmen, they added moneylending to their activities. From successful commerce evolved banking; the merchant adventurer became a sedentary investor, relying on the mail and foreign agents to transact his business abroad. The ability to lend large sums of money to the politically powerful placed these men in a position to win favorable trade policies, even monopolies, as securities or repayments on their loans. In exchange for loans, for example, the Hapsburg rulers gave the Fuggers contracts on silver and copper mines in central Europe. The merchant bankers also acquired and expanded the industries their trade created, adding still another theater of operation; having become bankers by successful commerce, they became industrialists by successful banking.

As the acquisition of liquid assets became important, the new money economy affected the character of traditional groups and institutions. Kings and princes required ever greater revenues to maintain mercenary armies and develop loyal administrations, and they resorted to socially disruptive measures to obtain them. In the fourteenth century they revived lapsed feudal dues on noble landowners and levied new taxes on the peasantry. The political and economic decline of the nobility after the Black Death made them dependent on royal patronage. In the wake of the plague their labor costs had increased, as there were now fewer hands to till the soil,

13. Eugene F. Rice, Jr., *The Foundations of Early Modern Europe, 1460–1559* (New York, 1970), pp. 38–54.

while their agricultural produce brought a lower return, as there were fewer mouths to feed. By decreasing the number of skilled artisans, the plague also encouraged peasant flight from the land to better-paying jobs in urban industries. Forced to abandon demesne farming and commute the labor services of peasants to money payments, lords found the manorial economy engulfed by a new system of rents and wages favorable to greater peasant independence. At the same time the nobility's military usefulness had declined with the successful use of infantry and heavy artillery during the Hundred Years' War.

The nobility met its new subjection to royalty by learning to "pay court." During the later Middle Ages and into early modern times, kings used their patronage to domesticate the nobility, while at the same time helping to create a less competitive new aristocracy out of the lesser gentry and new rich townsmen. Some noblemen resisted violently their new subjection to royalty, especially in politically fragmented Germany, where no sophisticated court culture had developed to "tame" them. The unsuccessful German Knights' Revolt of 1523, led by Franz von Sickengen and supported by the humanist Ulrich von Hutten,[14] was a prominent example. In France and the Netherlands noble resistance to royal political centralization merged with the Calvinist struggle for religious freedom in the second half of the century, as many powerful noblemen aspired to impose the same regional autonomy over religious allegiance that the Diet of Augsburg made possible within the empire after 1555.

Efforts by rulers to increase revenues by raising taxes on the peasantry also triggered new social violence. In addition to levying higher taxes, rulers also issued new laws designed to bind peasants to the land and close off the economic opportunities opened by the demographic crisis. Increased taxation and such restrictive legislation provoked peasant revolts in fourteenth-century Flanders, France (1358), England (1381), and in Germany during the fifteenth and first quarter of the sixteenth century. Since such restrictive measures were normally enacted by representative assemblies, they tended to be counterproductive to royal political centralization, as rulers found themselves forced to strengthen the power of the nobility, townsmen, and clergy represented by these assemblies in exchange for desired laws. This became less of a problem in the second half of the fifteenth century, when kings learned to raise new revenues and impose their will independently of such groups.

14. See the recent work of Volker Press, *Kaiser Karl V, König Ferdinand und die Entstehung der Reichsritterschaft* (Wiesbaden, 1976); "Ulrich von Hutten, Reichsritter und Humanist 1488–1523," *Nassauische Annalen* 85 (1974): 71–86.

Several devices freed rulers from abject dependence on legislative assemblies. Kings multiplied and sold royal offices, borrowed prodigiously from Europe's great banking houses, and placed new taxes on church offices and property. In the new Protestant lands, rulers confiscated church offices and property outright and turned their endowments over to secular use. Already by the late fifteenth century the national church had become an economic asset to royalty in England, France, and especially Spain. After Henry VIII became head of the English church in 1534, he received in excess of £40,000 annually from his spiritual subjects, ten times what they had previously paid to Rome in annates and church fees.[15] In Spain Ferdinand and Isabella gained tight fiscal control over the church by taxing all clerical rents and income and appropriating one-third of all tithes collected by the church in Castile. The *cruzada*, a tax on clergy and laity originally levied to support the campaign against the Moors in Granada, continued after the conquest as a triennial tax that brought the crown almost as much revenue as it received from its new American imports.[16] The magistrates and city councils of late medieval German towns also profitably placed their clergy under local tax codes.

Like secular rulers, popes also adjusted to the new money economy and found themselves internally transformed by it. During the thirteenth and fourteenth centuries, the papacy attempted to centralize its administration and maximize revenues.[17] To fund a growing network of diplomatic agents and maintain mercenary armies, popes systematically taxed their clerical and lay "subjects." Reservation of clerical appointments to vacant offices became a key fiscal device. This practice, first begun by Pope Innocent III, reached its height in the fourteenth century under the Avignon popes, who reserved to themselves the right to fill all vacant archbishoprics, bishoprics, and abbacies as well as many lesser offices. A reserved office was filled on payment by the new incumbent of a fee known as an annate. This could be all or a sizable portion of the first year's income of the benefice in question. Until a candidate was installed, the pope collected the full income of the vacant office. While profitable to the papacy in the short run, this practice had the long-term consequence of alienating both rulers and ordinary laity from the church. From the ruler's point of view it drained away revenues that, if not going directly to the crown, at least had remained within the country and not strengthened a foreign power. After the Hundred Years'

15. Elton, *Reform and Reformation*, p. 190; Dickens, *The English Reformation*, p. 41.

16. Cowie, *Sixteenth Century Europe*, p. 115.

17. Catholic church historian Joseph Lortz speaks of an "Ineinander von kirchlich und weltlich, von kirchlich und wirtschaftlich, von kirchlich und politisch" ("Zur Problematik der kirchlichen Missstände im Spätmittelalter," *Trierer Theologische Zeitschrift* 58 [1949]: 15).

War began, the pope, then resident in Avignon, seemed too much under French influence for English kings to tolerate direct papal control over English benefices. The first Statute of Provisors, which cancelled the pope's right to "provide" English ecclesiastical offices and gave the king the income of vacant high church offices, was passed in 1351 during the pontificate of the most French and profligate of the Avignon popes, Clement VI (1342–52). In France the Pragmatic Sanction of Bourges (1438) also stopped the payment of annates, leaving the pope only a fraction of the income he had previously collected from French church offices.

From the point of view of the laity, the reservation of church offices worked to make local churches ineffectual. Church appointments often went to outsiders unaware of or indifferent to local religious needs and problems. Many, not desiring to live in obscure places, hired even less qualified substitutes to perform their offices, while they resided in Rome or other, more pleasant spots. Absenteeism from church office became a major grievance of laity against the medieval church, and it remained uncorrected until the Council of Trent took stern measures against it in the mid-sixteenth century.

As there were reserved church offices that only the pope could fill, so there were reserved sins that only papal penitentiaries could absolve. These were particular crimes against the person of clergy or the property and authority of the church.[18] Absolution from such sins, like providing for reserved benefices, became an important source of papal revenue.

Among other sources of papal income, which popes enforced by threat of excommunication, were a direct income tax of 10 percent on all clergy; fees for dispensing the laity, especially the politically powerful, from canonical prohibitions of marriage within certain forbidden degrees of kinship; fees for removing canonical barriers to the acquisition of benefices for which a cleric was not qualified or for the accumulation of more than the canonically permitted number (it was in an effort to repay loans for just such fees that Archbishop Albrecht of Mainz promoted the famous indulgence against which Luther protested); and, finally, fees for absolution from the sin of usury.[19] The pope reserved all such cases to himself and issued dispensations or absolutions on the authority of his claimed plenitude of power.

While the new money economy forced socially disruptive actions upon both kings and popes, these actions also proved religiously self-defeating for the pope. Forced by historical circumstance to act as a nation among

18. Examples are provided by Thomas N. Tentler, *Sin and Confession on the Eve of the Reformation* (Princeton, 1977), p. 306.

19. Wallace K. Ferguson, *Europe in Transition 1300–1520* (Boston, 1962), pp. 224–25.

nations, the papacy suffered outright political defeat in England and France in the fourteenth century and lost the respect of large numbers of clergy and laity throughout Europe.

The new economy also raised social tensions to new levels within urban centers. Commercial and industrial expansion created new rich classes like the *populi grassi* of the Italian cities and the merchant patriciates of northern Europe, while at the same time giving birth to a true urban proletariat. Capitalism and political centralization threatened the traditional urban ideal of society as a sacred corporation. During the Middle Ages cities had viewed themselves as special communities in which each person played an essential role irrespective of social status and was ethically responsible to all other members of the body politic. The ability of individuals and small groups to attain great wealth and political power at their own initiative changed this by giving rise to new political factions among both the successful and the oppressed.[20]

On the eve of the Reformation, city governments found themselves pressured both from without and from within. From Spain to Poland they fought a losing battle against royal and princely overlords who subjected them to higher national or territorial policy. City councils that adjusted successfully to the larger movement of political consolidation still had to face new merchant and craft guilds that demanded a direct role in local government. As soon as these guilds attained power, they proved anything but a democratic force. They became instead another conservative element within city government, using their new position to ensure monopolies and thwart competition. In this way, urban government came under the control of small oligarchies of rich merchants, guild masters, and property owners, while the majority of city dwellers, many of whom lived as paupers (as many as one in three in Florence and Nuremberg), found themselves excluded from the active political rights of citizenship. Sumptuary and other legislation attempted to keep social mobility at a minimum, but conflict continued nonetheless between the new rich merchants and the old aristocracy. Efforts by master craftsmen to restrict the admission of journeymen into their ranks and to reserve lucrative high positions for their own children and relatives predictably broke down guild solidarity, as growing numbers of journeymen found themselves denied advancement in their craft. The result was often violent social protest.

20. The disunity and factiousness of Reformation cities is especially stressed by Thomas A. Brady, Jr., against an alleged "romantic view" on the part of other scholars. *Ruling Class, Regime and Reformation at Strasbourg 1520–1555* (Leiden, 1978). See also the selections illustrating urban discontent and unrest in Gerald Strauss, *Manifestations of Discontent in Germany on the Eve of the Reformation* (Bloomington, 1971), pp. 130–43.

Did these developments create conditions favorable to Protestantism? The German sociologist Max Weber thought so. In a still controversial thesis, he argued over a half-century ago that the "Protestant ethic" of thrift and self-discipline helped propel the new money economy wherever the two met.[21] More recent studies have suggested that members of the new rising guilds, who tended to be literate and possessed a keen sense of their own individual worth, inclined more strongly than other urban groups to Protestantism, attracted by its vernacular Bible and liturgy, congregational participation, and recognition of individual religious experience.[22] Social and economic mobility, whether in the form of militant protest, as among poor journeymen and workers, or vaulting ambition, as among the more affluent artisan elites, seems to have made people susceptible to the propaganda of Protestants. By contrast, the old urban aristocracy, whose social position and economic self-interest lay in preserving the status quo, tended to remain Catholic, as did people like fishmongers and lawyers, who had an obvious stake in preserving traditional religious ritual, feasts, and laws. However, aristocrats could also support the Reformation when doing so enabled them to maintain their traditional social position and political power.[23]

A steady inflation of between 2 and 3 percent a year stalked the sixteenth century, and its cumulative effect began to be felt by midcentury. In Wittenberg the prices of basic food and clothing climbed 100 percent between 1519 and 1540.[24] By the end of the century the price of wool and grain had quadrupled in Spain, whose rulers defaulted on huge debts to the Fuggers in 1575 and 1596. Contemporaries attributed this "price revolution" to the minting of American gold and silver, which decreased the value of coinage by increasing the number of coins in circulation. Most scholars today, however, believe that the increased circulation of specie only aggravated a problem whose roots lay elsewhere, namely, in the new population growth of the century. The basic problem was not too much money, but too few goods

---

21. *The Protestant Ethic and the Spirit of Capitalism,* trans. Talcott Parsons (New York, 1958), pp. 45, 91. See below, pp. 261, 372.

22. For France, see Natalie Z. Davis, "Rites of Violence: Religious Riot in Sixteenth Century France," *Past and Present* 59 (1973): 80–81; "Strikes and Salvation in Lyons," *ARG* 56 (1965): 54; and "City Women and Religious Change in Sixteenth Century France," in *A Sampler of Women's Studies,* ed. D. G. McGuigan (Ann Arbor, 1973), p. 28. For Switzerland, see Norman Birnbaum, "The Zwinglian Reformation in Zurich," *Past and Present* 15 (1959): 39. For Germany, see Ozment, *The Reformation in the Cities,* pp. 212–31. On the relationship of literacy and Protestantism, see below, pp. 202–04.

23. A point especially stressed by Brady, *Ruling Class.*

24. Edith Eschenhagen, "Beiträge zur Sozial- und Wirtschaftsgeschichte der Stadt Wittenberg in der Reformationszeit," *Luther Jahrbuch* 9 (1927): 80–85.

and too many people—a population whose demand progressively exceeded the available supply.

In addition to new population growth, the development of capitalism, and inflation, the social landscape of the age of Reformation was also dramatically affected by the advent of printing with movable type. Luther, a theologian, was fond of describing the Reformation as the work of God's Word. However true that may have been, it was certainly the deed of the printed word. As Luther also recognized, the printing press made it possible for a little mouse like Wittenberg to roar like a lion across the length and breadth of Europe.

By the end of the fifteenth century printing presses existed in over two hundred cities and towns. An estimated six million books had been printed and half of the thirty thousand titles were on religious subjects. More books were printed in the forty years between 1460 and 1500 than had been produced by scribes and monks throughout the entire Middle Ages. Religious books continued to dominate the presses through the first decade of the Reformation, but the number of books devoted to purely secular interests steadily rose after 1530.[25] Between 1518 and 1524, the crucial years of the Reformation's development, the publication of books in Germany alone increased sevenfold. Presses existed in sixty-two German and Swiss cities by 1520, with Cologne, Nuremberg, Strasbourg, Basel, Wittenberg, and Augsburg the leading centers.[26] Between 1517 and 1520, Luther wrote approximately thirty tracts, which were distributed in 300,000 printed copies. The famous Reformation pamphlets of 1520, the *Address to the German Nobility* and the *Freedom of a Christian*, reached sixteen and nineteen editions respectively within the space of a year.[27] In 1519 the printer Froban sold the first edition of Luther's "collected works" to buyers in France, Spain, England, and Brabant.

During the Middle Ages scribes and monks had copied books on sheets of parchment, which was made from split sheepskin or calfskin (Vellum), an expensive and time-consuming process; a Bible, for example required 170 calfskins or 300 sheepskins.[28] Block-type printing had existed since the high Middle Ages, but was slow and incapable of mass production. Printing with

25. See Rudolf Hirsch, *Printing, Selling and Reading 1450–1550* (Wiesbaden, 1967), pp. 128–29. Miriam Chrisman is presently documenting the decline of religious publications in Strasbourg.

26. See Josef Benzing, *Die Buchdrucker des 16. und 17. Jahrhunderts in Deutschen Sprachgebiet* (Wiesbaden, 1963).

27. See Josef Benzing, *Lutherbibliographie: Verzeichnis der gedruckten Schriften Martin Luthers bis zu dessem Tod* (Baden-Baden, 1965–66), pp. 82–83, 87–89.

28. Rice, *The Foundations of Early Modern Europe* p. 3. Hirsch *Printing, Selling and Reading*, pp. 2–6.

Der Buchdrücker.

Ich bin geschicket mit der preß
So ich aufftrag den Firniß reß/
So bald mein dienr den bengel zuckt/
So ist ein bogn papyrs gedruckt.
Da durch kombt manche Kunst an tag/
Die man leichtlich bekommen mag.
Vor zeiten hat man die bücher gschribn/
Zu Meintz die Kunst ward erstlich triebn.

The Printer. Jost Amman. From *Das Ständebuch,* woodcuts by Jost Amman with rhymed verses by Hans Sachs (Frankfurt, 1568). Amman depicted 114 vocations, both spiritual and worldly, which he claimed encompassed "all arts and crafts, laborers, and trades, etc. from the highest to the lowest."

> I run the press.
> I turn the freshly printed page.
> As soon as my helper pounds his mallet,
> A printed sheet is made.
> Many skills are here required,
> But one can learn them easily.
> Since olden times books have been written,
> But it was first in Mainz that the art of printing was practiced.

movable metal type, which Johannes Gutenberg introduced in the city of Mainz around 1450, made it possible to reproduce multiple identical copies of a single text rapidly and economically. Accompanying this "divine art" was another technological achievement of the fifteenth century, the perfection of a process of cheap paper manufacture. Together, movable type and cheap paper released a flood of books and pamphlets upon Western Europe.

A growing, literate audience awaited them. Amidst the famines, plagues, and wars of the later Middle Ages, it is easy to forget that this was also a period of expanding lay education. During the fourteenth and fifteenth centuries, monarchs, princes, and wealthy merchants created new universities and colleges. Between 1300 and 1500 the number of European universities rose from twenty to seventy, and the same period saw a boom in the construction of new residential colleges: sixty-six were built in France, twenty-one in England, fifteen in Italy, and sixteen in Germany.[29] It has been estimated that 3 to 4 percent of Germany's population, about 400,000 people, could read by 1500.[30]

Like television in the modern world, the book and pamphlet became powerful tools of social and political change in the sixteenth century. Publishers found themselves in a very profitable business, which brought them not only fortunes, but also international fame and influence. They responded directly to demand, publishing popular works and authors clandestinely when the circumstances required it. By helping develop distinct literary cultures, these publishers contributed directly to the formation of national and regional identities. Luther's vernacular writings played a major role in shaping the modern German language, and Calvin's works did the same for French.

Printing served the designs of kings as readily as those of religious reformers. In England in the 1530s, for example, Thomas Cromwell mobilized an impressive army of English humanists to write and translate tracts favorable to King Henry VIII's assertion of royal supremacy over the English church. Among the works available were Edward Foxe's *De vera differentia regiae potestatis et ecclesiasticae*, which defined scriptural, patristic, and historical supports for royal supremacy; Lorenzo Valla's exposé of the "Donation of Constantine"; sections of Marsilius of Padua's *Defender of Peace*; Erasmus's *Julius Excluded from Heaven*, a satire on the secular pretensions of Pope Julius II, and *Creed of the Apostles*, which contained a non-

29. A. L. Gabriel, "The College System of the Fourteenth Century Universities," in *The Forward Movement of the Fourteenth Century*, ed. F. L. Utley (Columbus, 1961), pp. 82–83.

30. Moeller, *Deutschland im Zeitalter der Reformation*, p. 36.

Roman definition of the church.[31] Printing multiplied greatly the possibilities for mischief and polemic.

The ability to read nurtured the self-esteem and critical temper of the laity. The universal availability of common texts also made it possible for the first time to speak meaningfully of the "authoritative version." When the text in question was the Bible, both laymen and scholars could now appeal to the "true account," demand fidelity to the "original," and argue "from Scripture" against centuries of tradition. What the ability to criticize the "Donation of Constantine" on the basis of knowledge of the ninth century or to raise questions about the Vulgate Bible on the basis of knowledge of the original Greek or Hebrew texts did for humanist self-esteem, the ability of ordinary laity to read the Bible in the vernacular and instruct their children in it did for lay self-esteem. Direct access to sources gave laymen a sense of competence in matters previously reserved exclusively to high church authority.

The medieval church, fearing the social consequences of religious egalitarianism, had always forbidden the circulation of vernacular Bibles among the laity and vigorously suppressed the gospel translations of groups like the Waldensians and the Wyclif Bible of Lollards. With the appearance of the printing press such tight control ceased to be possible. A tool of censorship that had seen only limited use during the Middle Ages was now increasingly relied upon: the "Index of Forbidden Books," which gained prominence by the mid-sixteenth century. Pico della Mirandola's famous 900 theses and the literature of the Reuchlin affair occasioned papal censureship decrees already on the eve of the Reformation. Protestants eagerly multiplied vernacular Bibles and urged that all boys and girls be educated to vernacular literacy so that they could read the Bible directly and model their lives on it. Protestant reformers envisioned a laity knowledgeable in Scripture as the backbone of free Christian commonwealths. Nowhere was this truer than in England, where, unlike other major European countries, vernacular Bibles had not circulated freely during the fifteenth century. In 1408 the archbishop of Canterbury made the translation, dissemination, and reading of English Bibles dependent upon a prior official sanction that was in fact never given. Not until William Tyndale's translation of the New

31. Among the authors and translators were Richard Travener, Robert Wakefield, Stephen Vaughn, William Marshall, Thomas Paynell, Leonard Cox, Thomas Swinnerton, and John Rastell. James K. McConica, *English Humanists and Reformation Politics Under Henry VIII and Edward VI* (Oxford, 1965), pp. 133-42, 311-13. See also Elton, *Reform and Reformation,* pp. 195-98. For a list of English publications printed abroad in the early period of the English Reformation, among them the notorious *Supplication for the Beggars,* see Anthea Hume, "English Protestant Books Printed Abroad 1525-1535: An Annotated Bibliography," in *The Complete Works of Thomas More* 8/2 (New Haven, 1973), pp. 1063-91.

Testament, published in Cologne and Worms, became available after 1525 did the English have a printed vernacular Bible, which they avidly read. By 1538, English parsons were required to make English Bibles available in their parishes "for every man that will look and read thereon."[32] The ideal of universal vernacular literacy in the Bible persisted among Protestants even after its success forced Protestant clergy to join their Catholic counterparts in coercively censoring dissident laity who challenged the new Protestant leadership and doctrine in the name of Scripture alone.

Was the medium more important than the message? It has been argued that the printing press was less the instrument of Protestant success than the Reformation the creation of the printing press. By making it possible to define divisive theological issues precisely and disseminate them widely, printing made it impossible to contain and ignore these matters any longer. Magnified publicly in books and pamphlets, the issues of religious reform had now to be settled in direct confrontation and debate.[33]

The affinity between literacy, printing, and Protestantism in the early years of the Reformation is documented by the urban origins of the Reformation and the support given it by humanists and printers.[34] It is clear that the latter were moved as much by intellectual and economic considerations as by religious belief; humanists initially perceived Luther to be a champion of free academic debate, and printers profited from a controversy that increased demand for their publications. There is a sense in which it can be said that without humanism and printing there would have been no Reformation. On the other hand, scholarly support of religious reform and the technological capability of mass production cannot be said to have been

32. Dickens, *The English Reformation*, pp. 131–32, 135. On the circulation of vernacular Bibles in other lands, see Hirsch, *Printing, Selling and Reading*, pp. 92–93.

33. Elizabeth L. Eisenstein, "The Advent of Printing and the Protestant Revolt: A New Approach to the Disruption of Western Christendom," in Kingdon, ed., *Transition and Revolution*, pp. 244, 250, 264. Eisenstein's thesis is elaborated in *The Printing Press as an Agent of Change*, 2 vols. (Cambridge, 1978).

34. Emmanuel Le Roy Ladurie found the appeal of Protestantism in Montpellier to be greater in areas where people had the ability to sign their name, a test of at least rudimentary education (*Les paysans de Languedoc* 1 [Paris, 1966], pp. 333–56). Natalie Davis found literacy and Protestantism even more strongly correlated among the printers of Lyons ("Strikes and Salvation at Lyons," *ARG* 56 [1965]: 48–61; "The Rites of Violence," *Past and Present* 59 [1973], p. 80, n. 94). A. N. Galpern argues the same for Champagne in *The Religions of the People in Sixteenth Century Champagne* (Cambridge, Mass., 1976) p. 123. The recent dissertation of David Rosenberg, however, criticizes a too quick correlation of literacy and Protestantism on the basis of findings in Amiens, where literacy had very little to do with religious affiliation. Rosenberg demonstrates a *reverse* correlation: the parish with the highest literacy quotient had the fewest Protestant suspects and that with the highest percentage of suspects the lowest number of persons capable of signing their names. See "Social Experience and Religious Choice: A Case Study, the Protestant Weavers and Woolcombers of Amiens in the Sixteenth Century" (Dissertation, Yale University, 1978), pp. 32–49.

more important than the message itself in bringing the Reformation about. The message depended on humanists and the printing press to reach a wide audience, but it also transcended their agency. The essential condition of the Reformation's success was aggrieved hearts and minds; a perceived need for reform and determination to grasp it are the only things without which it can be said categorically there would have been no Reformation.

It is important to remember that the first half of the sixteenth century remained very much an oral age, and Protestant converts were not limited to the literate and the educated. In 1518, Luther described the "ears alone" as the organs of the Christian.[35] Protestant pamphlets and sermons, published in the thousands, were intended to be read to the nonliterate as well as by the literate. Many publications were illustrated, some virtually picture books. In France Protestants successfully proselytized among the nonliterate with hymns and songs, and everywhere cartoons and symbols conveyed the new theology.[36] What the printing press *did* accomplish was to make the sixteenth century the most theologically informed and curious in Western history so that laity, whether literate or not, saw more clearly than ever before how seemingly abstract theological issues directly affected their lives. For the first time on a mass scale people discovered how presuppositions and ideas about human nature and destiny, embodied in law and institutions, influenced the way they lived from day to day.

Religious Culture

O N the eve of the Reformation the papacy had long since ceased to be a monarchy capable of imposing its will throughout Europe as in the days of Innocent III. The political and administrative unity attained by rulers during the later Middle Ages had transformed Europe into a cluster of discrete, inward-looking sovereign nation-states and territories, each capable of doing far more harm to the pope than the pope to any one of them. By the sixteenth century the dream of a pan-European political and cultural unity, if ever such had been capable of realization, was pure fantasy, although the new emperor, Charles V, and after him his son Philip II would pursue it

35. "If you ask a Christian what the work is by which he is made worthy of the name of Christian, he can give no other answer than hearing the word of God, which is faith. Thus the ears alone are the organs of a Christian man, because not by the works of any other member but by faith is he justified and judged a Christian" (*Lectures on the Epistle to the Hebrews 1517–18*, in *Luther: Early Theological Works*, ed. and trans. James Atkinson [Philadelphia, 1962], pp. 194–95).

36. See Natalie Davis, "The Protestant Printing Workers of Lyons in 1551," in G. Berthaud et al., *Aspects de la propagande religieuse* (Geneva, 1957), pp. 247–57.

vigorously. With political "nationalism" had come also the national or territorial church, something attained in large measure in England and France
as early as the fourteenth century, when the power of the pope within these
countries was severely curtailed. Regardless of whether national and religious consciousness coalesced in support of the traditional faith, as in Spain,
or against it, as in Hussite Bohemia, by the fifteenth century rulers
everywhere resented papal claims to temporal power and Italian meddling
in their internal affairs. This feeling lay behind the strong secular political
support given the forces of decentralization within the church during the
conciliar era.[37]

Magistrates and city councils also weakened local church authority by
restricting or eliminating altogether traditional ecclesiastical and clerical
privileges and assuming direct responsibility for education, welfare, and
morals. They taxed local clergy and church property, carefully regulated
the church's acquisition of new properties within city walls, and restricted
the right of criminal asylum in urban churches and monasteries.

If, in terms of its political activity, the medieval church had ceased to be a
dominant institution on the eve of the Reformation, so too religiously, as a
system of piety, it found its efficacy questioned by laity and clergy. On the
surface there is evidence of religious vitality in the years before the Reformation.[38] New church foundations—churches, chapels, chantries—were on
the increase. Saints, pilgrimages, and masses for the dead remained popular. Henry VII of England, for example, ordered ten thousand masses for
his soul at sixpence each, and Henry VIII joined the pilgrims to Walsingham in 1517 after consumption claimed the lives of some of his pages.[39] In
large numbers both rich and poor participated in traditional religious confraternities and carnival processions. Laymen endowed special preacherships to ensure regular sermons by qualified preachers. Interest in magic
and witchcraft became so keen that official countermeasures were taken in
the 1480s, a foreshadowing of later *maleficia* trials and mass witch-hunts.
Ironically, such interest in the occult had itself long been stimulated by the
church's own demonological beliefs and Inquisitorial depictions of heretics

37. Heinrich Finke, "Die Nation in den spätmittelalterlichen allgemeinen Konzilien,"
Historisches Jahrbuch 57 (1937): 323–38, esp. 328. Finke deals especially with the organization
of the Council of Constance by national groups and their role in the council. On the Council
of Basel and secular political power within the empire, see Steiber, *Pope Eugenius IV, the
Council of Basel, and the Secular and Ecclesiastical Authorities of the Empire.*
38. See E. F. Jacob, "Founders and Foundations in the Later Middle Ages," *Bulletin of the
Institute of Historical Research* (1962): 29–46; and Lawrence G. Duggan, "The Unresponsive-
ness of the Late Medieval Church: A Reconsideration," *Sixteenth Century Journal* 9 (1978):
3–26. See also above, ch. 3.
39. Dickens, *The English Reformation,* p. 12; Scarisbrick, *Henry VIII,* p. 68.

A Pilgrimage to the Church of the Blessed Virgin in Regensburg. Michael Ostendorfer. Ordinary people were strongly attracted to ritualized pilgrimage piety with its cult of the saints, relics, special indulgences, and promise of miraculous cures. Already in the fifteenth century such reformers as Wyclif, Gerson, and Ailly protested the multiplication of shrines and new saints. Protestants condemned pilgrim shrines as hoaxes designed to fleece the credulous, and with the outbreak of the Reformation, many shrines fell victim to iconoclastic riots.

A Witches' Sabbat. Hans Baldung Grien (1514). While it is highly doubtful that witches ever actually existed, many people believed they did and were prepared to make accusations. The church assisted. Christian authorities early associated witchcraft with pagan magic, a consorting with demons and an attempt to control supernatural forces that perverted traditional devotion and set its practitioners in competition with the church's priests. By the fourteenth century ritual magic was considered *maleficium* (doing harm to others by occult means) and was condemned as heresy and apostasy. This laid the legal foundation for inquisitorial proceedings against witches. Misogyny also played a large role.

The rise in witch-hunts during the sixteenth and seventeenth centuries has been related to a surplus of poor, old, single, unproductive women (H. C. Erik Midelfort and E. William Monter); conflict between emerging individualism and the traditional communal ethic based on Christian charity (Alan MacFarlane); Protestant success in exposing traditional sacramental magic and rendering it ineffectual (Keith Thomas); and even repressed hostility to the seemingly impossible moral ideals of Christianity itself (Norman Cohn and Jeffrey B. Russell).

as members of satanic cults.[40] Still another external sign of religious vitality can be seen in the criticism of clerical abuses by reformers and humanists.

Since the thirteenth century, popular religious movements had experimented with simpler, "apostolic" life-styles. In doing so they found themselves at cross-purposes with a papacy whose pastoral role had become increasingly confused with its political and economic ambitions. Such groups as the Waldensians, Albigensians (Cathars), Spiritual Franciscans (Fraticelli), Lollards, and Hussites actually intensified biblical and monastic counsels of perfection, as they demanded from laity and clergy a far greater moral excellence than traditional church piety had done. Church authorities, viewing the goals of these movements as utopian and revolutionary, responded with condemnation and persecution.

In the century before Luther, traditional religious culture seemed no longer able to deal effectively with the religious anxiety and idealism of many people; to many it had become itself more the source than the cure of such anxiety. The failure of the late medieval church to provide a theology and spirituality that could satisfy and discipline religious hearts and minds was the most important religious precondition of the Reformation. As Lucien Febvre long ago pointed out, the essential feature of Protestantism was its ability to provide

> a remedy for the disturbed consciences of a good number of Christians . . . to propose to men, who seemed to have been waiting for it for years and who adopted it with a sort of haste and greed that is very revealing, a solution that really took account of their [religious] needs and spiritual condition. It offered the masses what they had anxiously been searching for: a simple, clear, and fully effective religion.[41]

The reigning interpretation of the Reformation's origins connects Protestantism especially with a growing *individualistic* piety that opposed, or was at

40. On the connections between witch-hunts and previous heresy proceedings, see Herbert Grundmann, "Der Typus des Ketzers in mittelalterlicher Anschauung," in *Kultur- und Universalgeschichte: Walter Goetz zu seinem 60. Geburtstag* (Leipzig, 1927), pp. 91–107, esp. 104; Hugh R. Trevor-Roper, "The European Witch-Craze of the Sixteenth and Seventeenth Centuries," in *Religion, the Reformation and Social Change* (London, 1967), pp. 100–103; Jeffrey B. Russell, *Witchcraft in the Middle Ages* (Ithaca, 1972), p. 200; and most recently, Norman Cohn, *Europe's Inner Demons: An Enquiry Inspired by the Great Witch-Hunt* (London, 1975), esp. chapters 9 and 10.

41. "The Origins of the French Reformation: A Badly-Put Question?" in *A New Kind of History and Other Essays,* ed. Peter Burke (New York, 1973), p. 60. Hubert Jedin, writing on the Reformation in Germany, concluded: "The Protestant Reformation owed its success to the fact that the attempts at reform which sprouted from the soil of the church did not come to maturity" (*A History of the Council of Trent,* trans. Dom E. Graf [St. Louis, 1957], 1: 165; see also p. 152).

least indifferent to, the many external religious observances and "magical" ritual of official church practice.[42] According to this interpretation, the medieval church had primarily itself to blame for its vulnerability to such subjective piety. Because its lower clergy were poorly trained and its higher clergy preoccupied with secular gain, traditional religious practice became, for all save a devout elite, an external "religion of observances and works," a mere "religion of habits."[43] Many laity nonetheless sincerely believed in the objective efficacy of such rituals, however mechanical they may have seemed; the possibility cannot be excluded that many may have preferred such a religion to one that demanded intense subjective involvement. A recent study of late medieval pilgrimage piety has concluded that "ritual purgation of sin was exactly what most uneducated people wanted."[44] There is evidence of far greater lay "participation" in the purely ritual sacraments of baptism and the last rites than in the personally demanding sacrament of penance, which subjected the faithful to direct priestly interrogation and required a detailed confession of all sinful thoughts and deeds.[45]

On the other hand, many laity found their inner anguish only increased by bare external religious observance; instead of giving comfort, mechanical religious ritual could also intensify and redirect the search for it.[46] Side by side with the piety of official devotion we find prophetic warnings of an imminent chastisement of corrupt clergy and the forced introduction of

42. See Joseph Lortz, *Die Reformation in Deutschland*, vols. 1–2 (Freiburg, 1962); Jacques Toussaert, *Le sentiment religieux en Flandre à la fin du Moyen Age* (Paris, 1963); Etienne Delaruelle et al., *L'église au temps du Grand Schisme et de la crise conciliare* (Paris, 1964). Felicity Heal describes late medieval English religion as "ritual centered" in distinction from the humanist (and later Protestant) emphasis on a life patterned after the Gospels, which "demanded a more positive individual commitment and understanding" (*Church and Society in England: Henry VIII to James I* (Hamden, Conn., 1977), p. 5). Keith Thomas portrays the sacramental system of the medieval church as "a vast reservoir of magical power" and sees Protestantism as especially opposed to "the magic of the opus operatum" (*Religion and the Decline of Magic* (London, 1971), pp. 45, 52). Further bibliography on these issues is in Jean Delaumeau, *Naissance et affirmation de la Réforme* (Paris, 1965), pp. 257–80, and Francis Rapp, *L'église et la vie religieuse en Occident à la fin du Moyen Age* (Paris, 1971), pp. 328–31.

43. Delaruelle, *L'église au temps du Grand Schisme*, p. 872; Toussaert, *Le sentiment religieux en Flandre*, p. 223.

44. Jonathan Sumption, *Pilgrimage: An Image of Medieval Religion* (London, 1975), pp. 268, 295. Delaruelle calls this "the religion of the priest" since the priest, not the laity, is active in it. (*L'église au temps du Grand Schisme*, p. 875).

45. Toussaert, *Le sentiment religieux en Flandre*, p. 122; L. A. Viet, *Volksrommes Brauchtum und Kirche im deutschen Mittelalter* (Freiburg i.B., 1936), pp. 88–90; Tentler, *Sin and confession on the Eve of the Reformation*, pp. 104–30.

46. Bernd Moeller, "Piety in Germany Around 1500," in *The Reformation in Medieval Perspective*, ed. S. Ozment (Chicago, 1971), pp. 50–75; Ozment, *The Reformation in the Cities*, pp. 20–21; Johan Huizinga, *The Waning of the Middle Ages*, trans. F. Hopman (Garden City, N.Y., 1954), esp. ch. 2.

religious reforms.[47] To such anguish, yearning, and criticism, late medieval preachers and Protestant reformers successfully directed their messages.

Many scholars believe that the secret of Protestant success lay in its throwing open wide the doors to direct personal involvement in religion, even to the point of replacing the traditional sacramental community and authority of the church with the narrow, subjective feelings of individuals. Some scholars actually see the appeal of the Reformation in a perverse popular perception of justification by faith as approving religious indifference, moral indiscipline, and rebelliousness.[48]

The options in late medieval religion were not, however, "subjective" religious emotion and "objective" church ritual and authority. Traditional Catholic piety never wanted for subjectivity and introspection, nor was there any lack of sacramental ritual and clerical authority in Protestantism, even though esteem for the papal hierarchy was an abiding mark of the good Catholic and liturgical simplification and lay participation in church ritual and governance constant features of Protestantism. It was not primarily magic and ritual that Protestants wanted removed from late medieval religion; their religion also had its irrational, magical, and purely ritualistic side. What Protestants set out to overcome was a perceived oppressive superstition—teachings and practices that burdened the consciences and pocketbooks of the faithful. From the point of view of the reformers, the issue in late medieval religion was not the challenge of venerable tradition and authority by disrespectful individuals bent on novelty, but a religious institution that had become ineffectual in its devotional and liturgical practice and barely credible in its doctrinal teaching.

Pre-Reformation criticism of the medieval church dwelt on institutional and doctrinal reforms as well as on unmet subjective needs; the reform movements of the late Middle Ages were not purely "moral" in nature.[49] One of the most developed criticisms of the medieval church came from the English Lollards. Reflecting both patriotic anticlericalism and the influence of John Wyclif's teaching, Lollards,[50] who were for the greater part ordinary people, mainly craftsmen, opposed the subjection of the English church to Rome, the temporal rule of the clergy, the doctrine of transubstantiation, clerical celibacy, the consecration of physical objects, masses for the dead, pilgrimages, and the veneration of images. On the positive

---

47. Robert E. Lerner, "Medieval Prophecy and Religious Dissent," *Past and Present* 72 (1976): 20; Moeller, *Deutschland im Zeitalter der Reformation,* pp. 36–47.

48. See Joseph Lortz, *Wie kam es zur Reformation?* (Einsiedeln, 1955); Toussaert, *Le sentiment religieux en Flandre,* p. 605; Galpern, *The Religions of the People in Sixteenth Century Champagne,* pp. 122–23, 157. On Lortz's influential views, see the discussion in my *Reformation in Medieval Perspective,* pp. 3–11.

49. Rapp, *L'église et la vie religieuse,* pp. 209–11, 304, 320.

50. See John A. F. Thomson, *The Later Lollards,* 1414–1520 (Oxford, 1965).

side, they demanded that clergy be devoted to their pastoral duties and that vernacular Bibles be placed in the hands of the laity.[51] Such proposals, which were also typical of reforms on the continent, survived down to the English Reformation, when Protestants revived and published them widely in support of their cause.[52]

No one has documented the physical and spiritual vulnerability of the late medieval church more thoroughly than Catholic church historian Joseph Lortz, who nonetheless denies that a church so weakened by abuses was incapable of providing earnest laity with a viable piety. By contrast, Lucien Febvre scoffed at the very notion that church abuses, regardless of their magnitude, could explain a religious revolution. The medieval church failed, he believed, precisely in those matters that touched the heart.

To understand the reform movements of the sixteenth century, it is necessary to take into account *both* ecclesiastical abuses and religious emotions, for both institutions and feelings were at stake. The seemingly opposed viewpoints of Lortz and Febvre are complementary rather than exclusive explanations of the Reformation's origins: the road to the Reformation was paved both by unprecedented abuse and a long-unsatisfied popular religious yearning.

Abuses of church power divided the higher and lower clergy, spurred competition between secular and regular clergy, and alienated many laity from both. Bishoprics became the special refuges of the nobility, the great majority of whom were appointed to these offices on the basis of economic or political considerations, not for any special religious preparation or aptitude. The leadership of many was "pervaded with legalism and denuded of missionary spirit."[53] On the eve of the Reformation, laity protested pervasive clerical fiscalism, absenteeism, maladministration, and concubinage, even the excessive numbers of clergy, which ran as high as 10 percent of the population in cities with universities and cathedral chapters.[54]

Bishops possessed broad powers of discipline over both lower clergy and the laity, which they exercised by imposing fines. They also collected payments for permitting certain activities to occur within their dioceses. In

---

51. Dickens, *The English Reformation,* pp. 23–27; Imogen Luxton, "The Reformation and Popular Culture," in Heal and O'Day, *Church and Society in England: Henry VIII to James I,* p. 67.

52. On Lollard revivals, see especially Margaret Aston, "Lollardy and the Reformation: Survival or Revival," *History* 49 (1964): 149–70; Dickens, *The English Reformation,* p. 35. Keith Thomas connects Lollard attacks on the "sacramental magic" of the medieval church with the successful Protestant rejection of such magic during the reign of Henry VIII (*Religion and the Decline of Magic,* p. 52).

53. Dickens, *The English Reformation,* p. 43. This seems peculiarly true of English bishops, who were for the greater part trained civil lawyers.

54. See Denys Hay, *Europe in the Fourteenth and Fifteenth Centuries* (New York, 1966), pp. 58–59.

central Germany, for example, bishops regularly fined or exacted fees from clergy who came late to their appointments or were absent from their pastoral duties; from all substitute clergy; from mass priests absent from their duties; from clergy performing services in offices unsanctioned by the bishop; from religious orders collecting alms for the sick; from clergy consecrated outside the bishopric who wanted to perform pastoral functions within it; and from clergy desiring to celebrate the sacraments on portable altars—apparently a tax on mendicants who assisted the secular clergy during peak religious seasons. The bishop further received payments for permitting the use of candles in weddings that occurred during proscribed seasons; for handling the bequests and making legitimate the last wills and testaments of clergy; for the installation of clergy in their offices; for issuing letters of indulgence; and for sanctioning new benefices.[55]

Like popes, bishops too had the right to absolve clergy and laity from certain reserved sins, and episcopal penitentiaries, like papal penitentiaries, received fees for doing so. Among the sins reserved to bishops were a variety of crimes against ecclesiastical authority, holy objects, and holy persons; such sexual sins as carnal relations with a monk or nun, deflowering a virgin, sodomy, and incest; such offenses against marriage vows as entering the religious life without the consent of one's spouse, treating an adulterous offspring as legitimate, and marrying someone after having been betrothed to another; such crimes of violence as homicide, infanticide, and plotting the death of one's spouse; and such various other things as public usury, notorious slander and blasphemy, perjury, and sorcery.[56]

Bishops also burdened lower clergy with concubinage fees. These were fines for cohabitation and parenthood (the so-called cradle tax) and for baptizing the children of priests and making them legitimate. The right of clergy to marry was among the prominent demands of the *Reformatio Sigismundi* (1438–39), a popular tract urging ecclesiastical and political reforms within the empire, probably written by a secular priest under the influence of the Council of Basel.[57] Clerical marriage became the most successful and lasting Protestant reform.

If the seemingly endless fiscal sanctions of bishops alienated the lower from the higher clergy, priests in their turn also subjected laity to numerous fees. Parish clergy had two basic sources of income: a portion of the tithes regularly collected from parishioners and the modest fees for performing

---

55. Werner Zeissner, *Altkirchliche Kräfte im Bamberg unter Bischof Weigand von Redwitz (1522–1556)* (Bamberg, 1975), pp. 24–27.

56. Tentler, *Sin and Confession on the Eve of the Reformation*, p. 307.

57. See the excerpts in Strauss, *Manifestations of Discontent in Germany on the Eve of the Reformation*, pp. 14–15.

the sacraments of penance, marriage, baptism, and the last rites, together
with such other pastoral duties as burials, vigils, and masses for the dead. In
the year Luther posted his ninety-five theses, priests in Bamberg charged
one wax candle and "small change" for blessing a woman in childbirth; nine
Denarii or *Pfennige* for declaring a marriage; forty-eight "and dinner" for a
wedding mass; nine for the last rites; two *Pfunde* for a burial; one *Pfund* for
vigils with readings; one *Pfennig* for a confession during Lent; and twelve
for a baptism.[58] Since an unskilled day laborer in this region earned between ten and twelve *Pfennige* per day, these fees were hardly extravagant,
taken as a whole. However, a burial at two *Pfunde*—figuring 120 *Pfennige* to
the *Pfund* after the new currency decrees of the fourteenth century—was a
near month's work for a very poor man.

In England an outstanding pre-Reformation example of church presumption, the Hunne affair, also involved the petty fiscal burdening of laity
by clergy, in this case by the charging of mortuary fees. In 1511, Richard
Hunne, a London merchant with Lollard sympathies, refused to pay for the
burial of a deceased infant. The officiating priest, apparently beset by many
examples of such lay resistance to clerical authority, determined to make an
example of Hunne and summoned him before a church court. Hunne
countersued the priest, arguing on grounds of common law that a church
court had no proper jurisdiction over a layman. By 1514 the affair had
reached the bishop of London, who brought full heresy proceedings against
Hunne. Charged, among other things, with possessing a Lollard Bible,
Hunne was sent to bishop's prison, where two days later he was found
hanged in his cell. Church officials insisted that his death was a suicide, but
all save the most naïve knew that his guards had executed him. Two weeks
later, to the outrage of many, the church burned his corpse for heresy. This
display of episcopal arrogance received only an indirect civil censure in
1515, when royal judges charged the bishop with invading the king's regality in the related Standish affair.[59] The damage to lay respect for church
authority had been great, however, and for many irreversible.[60] The later

58. Zeissner, *Altkirchliche Kräfte im Bamberg,* p. 29.

59. G. R. Elton, *Reform and Reformation,* pp. 51–55. Elton summarizes the Hunne/
Standish affair by commenting: "The lesson of 1515 is not that the church was already fully
subjected to the King's regality and supremacy, but that it had the highest opinion of its
independence, was incapable of reforming itself, and altogether failed to read the signs
aright" (p. 58).

60. The problem was not confined to secular priests and the high clergy. Laity also
resented the extensive property holdings and power of the religious houses (about 12,000
monks in England in 1500). To their neighbors the monks appeared in everyday life as
"landlords, receivers of rents and tithes, rival traders, unsatisfactory proprietors of
churches" (Dickens, *The English Reformation,* p. 55).

The Difference Between the True Religion of Christ and the False, Idolatrous Teaching of Antichrist. Lucas Cranach the Younger. In this pro-Protestant depiction, Luther, standing in his pulpit (center left) and radiated by the light of the Holy Spirit, points to the Lamb of God. Written in the spaces that extend from his hand to God (left-hand corner) are the words: "There is only one mediator; I am the way; behold, this is the Lamb of God." Jesus, in prayer, says to God: "Father, I sanctify you, I sanctify and sacrifice myself for you." On Luther's pulpit are inscribed the words "All the prophets witness to this one—that there is no other name under the heaven [by which we can be saved]" (Acts 4:10–12). In the foreground John of Saxony stands with a cross over his shoulder. The Eucharist is served in the left foreground, demonstrably with bread and cup, and a baby is baptized in the center.

On the right side stands a Catholic priest, into whose ear a mitred rat (a demonic symbol of the pope) pumps hot air. Says the priest from his pulpit: "Behold, before you lie many Roman Catholic, not heretical, ways to salvation; you can come easily into glory." In the background a bannered pilgrimage sets forth; a dead man is given a cowl and holy water; a bell is blessed; and Mass is celebrated. Before the pulpit stand clerics and laity with a candle held high and burning bright. In the right foreground indulgences are sold; over the collection plate are the words "As soon as the groschen clinks, the soul flies to heaven." Alms are stored in a large chest and sack by the table. On the sack is written: "Shame and burdens are overcome by alms." Above in the heavens, St. Francis and God look down in consternation.

anticlerical tract of Simon Fish, *The Supplication of the Beggars* (1529), depicted what had by then become a common theme of Protestant propaganda: a clergy so greedy that fees or fines accompanied its every service,
while the truly needy went hungry and destitute. Fish's work became a
favorite of Henry VIII and also circulated widely on the continent in Sebastian Franck's 1529/30 German translation.

In assessing late medieval religious culture it is necessary to take into
account its psychological effects as well as its administrative and fiscal en-
tanglements. Here the sacrament of penance, the centerpiece of late medieval church piety, is of special importance. Belief in purgatory, relics, pilgrimages, and indulgences—the greater part of popular piety—were closely
tied to this key sacrament.

There is a pervasive misconception that late medieval religion had become lax and the medieval church tolerant to a fault of human weakness, a
conclusion often drawn in contrast to Protestantism.[61] Only the religiously
indifferent, unbelieving, and/or reclusive could have found them to be
such. When religiously earnest people sought forgiveness for immoral behavior, they encountered a very demanding penitential system, one that
provided only temporary relief, and even that with conditions attached and
the threat of purgatorial suffering for unrepented sins. Full, unconditional
forgiveness of sin and assurance of salvation were utterly foreign concepts
to medieval theology and religious practice. Effective removal of religious
guilt and anxiety this side of eternity would have meant the end of medieval
religious institutions, and advocates of this-worldly perfection were roundly
condemned during the Middle Ages.[62]

The penitent who partook of the sacrament of penance was expected to be
truly attrite of heart, confess all conscious sins, receive absolution, and bear
obediently the works of satisfaction imposed by the priest as a just punishment. According to medieval theologians, confession overcame the subjective guilt one personally felt for sinning, while priestly absolution made one
fully contrite and guiltless in the eyes of God. Beyond the overcoming of
guilt, however, there remained a punishment for sinning, which had to be
borne in eternity so that the injured parties, among them God himself,
could receive full and just satisfaction. In the final stage of the traditional
sacrament, priestly absolution transformed this eternal penalty, justly imposed by God on the sinner, into a manageable temporal penalty, that is,
something the penitent could do already in this life to lessen his future
punishment; for example, special prayers, fasts, almsgiving, retreats, and

61. See Max Weber, *The Protestant Ethic and the Spirit of Capitalism*, trans. Talcott Parsons
(New York, 1958), p. 36.
62. See above, pp. 113, 133.

pilgrimages. If such works of satisfaction were neglected, the penitent could expect to burn for his laxness after death in purgatory.

It was at this point—the works of satisfaction—that indulgences became popular. The penitent could buy an indulgence and by this "good work of almsgiving" be credited with having satisfied the punishment(s) imposed by the priest. In the late Middle Ages such satisfactions, known as "letters of indulgence," came to be regularly dispensed by the pope on the basis of a declared "treasury of merit," an assumed infinite reservoir of good works at the pope's disposal. Pope Clement VI (1342–52), who proclaimed the existence of this treasury in the bull *Unigenitus* in 1343, reasoned that whereas Christ had redeemed mankind with a "copious flood" of his blood, even though a single drop would have sufficed, in order that this superabundant effusion not be rendered idle and useless, the pope might apply it to sins at his discretion. By extending indulgences to purgatory in 1476, Pope Sixtus IV (1471–84) permitted the living to buy and apply indulgences to deceased loved ones assumed to be suffering in purgatory for unrepented sins.[63] When, in Luther's time, John Tetzel preached the famous St. Peter's indulgence, he took full advantage of the emotional potential of this extension, graphically depicting the voices of wailing dead parents in purgatory, who pleaded with their children for the release that a few alms could readily purchase.[64]

The papal decree *Omnis utriusque sexus,* issued by the Fourth Lateran Council in 1215, had required annual confession of sins by all adult Christians. Throughout the later Middle Ages the church expected people to confess all conscious sins to their parish priest at least once each year and without fail during Lent. A confessional manual of 1504 obligated the penitent not only to confess all sins committed directly by deed and indirectly by counsel or inaction—so-called sins of commission and omission—but also to narrate the exact circumstances of each: with what persons and where they were committed (if clergy or church property were involved, they were "reserved sins," and absolution had to be sought from higher episcopal or papal penitentiaries); at what time they were committed (if on a Sunday or a religious holiday, they increased in seriousness); how often they were committed; why they were committed (if done out of depravity, they were more serious than if done in ignorance or fear); in what manner they were committed (a brazen public sin was worse than one done in an uncontrollable fit

63. Denzinger, nos. 1025–27, p. 1398.
64. See *Die Reformation in Augenzeugen berichten,* ed. Helmar Junghans (Düsseldorf, 1967), p. 44. Such abuses as those of Tetzel were reproved before Luther's time. The Council of Vienne in 1312 condemned pardoners for conveying the impression that indulgences could release souls from purgatory, and the Council of Constance attempted to restrict the issuance of indulgences (Sumption, *Pilgrimage,* p. 294).

of anger); and, finally the consequences to others of one's sinful acts.[65] Other manuals depicted a good confession as simple, humble, voluntary, shameful, and bitter; undertaken with the resolve not to sin again and with faith in the church's power of forgiveness; and performed promptly after the sinful act, without excuses, and in an attitude of submissiveness to the priest's judgment. Priests instructed laity that incomplete or dissembling confessions caused all their sins to remain unforgiven.[66]

How effectively did such penitential piety deal with religious needs and ideals? Setting aside the question of ecclesiastical abuses, can we estimate how satisfying late medieval religion was when it functioned as the church's theologians designed it to function? Despite evidence of poor lay attendance at confession during the later Middle Ages and fierce Protestant criticism of the sacrament as mischievous and tyrannous, a recent study has portrayed the sacrament of penance as the source of a wholesome lay piety. Thomas N. Tentler supports this thesis by drawing on the instructional manuals used by priests in their confessional practice. He finds these sources sensitive to the complexity of human motivation and the dangers of overly detailed interrogations and the inculcation of scrupulosity in the penitent. Taken as a whole, the sacrament of penance is said to have been guided by "a set of high and perhaps unrealistic ideals tempered by a more sober sense of what one can reasonably expect from penitents and clergy," so consolation and the cure of anxiety remained as prominent to the penitent as discipline and the creation of guilt.[67]

This argument seems deficient, however, when one deals with actual cases. Priests and laity were often completely frustrated when they attempted to determine degrees of consent to sin and culpability. We discover a "penchant for grading sins," especially sexual sins, and interrogating laity about their sex life. One manual, for example, alerts the priest to sixteen degrees of sexual transgression, ranging from unchaste kisses to bestiality. Among these masturbation, ranked twelfth, is presented as a more deadly sin than incest, ranked eleventh, for, it is reasoned, masturbation wastes semen altogether, while incest at least directs it toward its proper end of propagating the species.[68] We also confront the extreme Augustinian view of sexuality in these manuals; taking any pleasure in sexual intercourse is strongly condemned, and confessors are encouraged to ask married peni-

65. *Beichtbüchlein* (Augsburg, 1504), in *Drei Beichtbüchlein nach den zehn Geboten aus der Frühzeit der Buchdruckerkünst,* ed. Franz Falk (Münster i.W., 1907), pp. 84–85.

66. Ozment, *The Reformation in the Cities,* pp. 26–27; Tentler, *Sin and Confession on the Eve of the Reformation,* pp. 104–33.

67. Tentler, *Sin and Confession on the Eve of the Reformation,* pp. 103, 131, 148, 349.

68. Ibid., p. 140.

tents whether they had ends in mind other than the begetting of children and the avoidance of fornication when they engaged in sex. The more lenient works of Sylvester Prierias, Anthony of Florence, and Jean Gerson mitigated such penitential probing only by degree when they instructed the priest to scold only those penitents who confessed to having thought of someone other than their spouse during sexual intercourse.[69] Is such interrogation really designed to cure anxiety? There is, indeed, a "dark side" to the confessional literature on sex,[70] which, by any measure, was far from consoling.[71]

In the sacrament of penance, the point at which the medieval church touched the lives of laity most intimately, one finds the main failing of official church piety. That failing is the absence of a distinctive concept of lay religious life and the consequent imposition upon the laity of traditional clerical ideals. One cannot find in the literature on confession and penitential practice even a notion that religiously earnest laity may require a distinctive piety of their own, or that a moderated clerical regimen may not be the most satisfying spirituality for laity. The domination of lay piety by clerical ideals is attested not only by the preoccupation of this literature with the sexual sins of laity, but also by the penances these manuals prescribed for confessed sins. In addition to the common penances of prayer, fasting, almsgiving, and pilgrimages, one authority suggested the imposition on laity of martyrdom, religious vows, vigils, hair shirts, and flagellation.[72]

The patterning of lay piety on clerical piety was a logical consequence of traditional belief in the superiority of the clergy over the laity, a belief whose origins lay in the monastic vows of poverty, chastity, and obedience, which had exalted monks above all other believers during the first Christian centuries. The evolution of the sharp distinction between the clergy and the laity did not lead to the formation of a distinctive piety for laity, but to their being exhorted to imitate clerical piety.

That laity who desired a full spiritual life should live as nearly like clergy as possible was as prominent a teaching in the catechetical literature for laity as it was in the confessional manuals for priests. The religious life to which the most popular late-medieval German lay catechism, Dietrich Coelde's *Mirror of the Christian Man*, exhorted laity was a mirror image of that of the clergy. Every conceivable sinful thought and deed, from oversleeping to

69. Ibid., pp. 180–85.
70. Ibid., pp. 226, 231. I think Tentler actually disproves his own thesis that penance effectively balanced consolation with discipline. For a fuller review of this important work, see my comments in *The Journal of Religion* 58 (1978): 204–06.
71. See *The Reformation in the Cities*, pp. 49–56.
72. Tentler, *Sin and Confession on the Eve of the Reformation*, p. 320.

masturbation, was dealt with as a matter of lay religious concern. When this catechism cited signs of God's favor, they were the preoccupations of cloistered people: a feeling of oppression and sadness about one's sins; eagerness to confess one's sins (free and frequent confession to the abbot was the monastic rule); obedient compliance with what the father-confessor prescribed (obedience was the great monastic virtue, and the father-confessor appears to stand in the same relation to the lay penitent as the abbot to the penitent monk); a resolve never to sin again; eager attendance at sermons; regular and thorough searching of one's conscience (laity are instructed to meditate daily on their "ten or twelve" most committed sins); and, finally, constant sincere prayer for the forgiveness of forgotten sins and preservation from unwitting sins.[73]

Whereas in earlier times the monastic life had inspired the laity, by the eve of the Reformation it had become an object of criticism, even ridicule, by reformers and humanists. This was probably owing as much to changing religious needs as to actual abuses within religious houses and clerical ranks, which critics usually exaggerated. A monastically derived lay piety with prominent clerical ideals of obedience and sexual purity seemed incongruous to an increasingly literate, socially mobile urban laity, who prized simplicity, directness, and respectful treatment in all spheres of their lives.

The perceived inadequacy of traditional religion is manifest in the many reforms and experiments that extended from the Waldensians and Franciscans in the thirteenth century to the Hussites and Modern Devotionalists in the fifteenth. Before the Reformation and Counter Reformation redefined Christendom, a multitude of intellectual and devotional options, heterodox and orthodox, were embraced by venturesome laity and clergy. Although the forms of piety were apparently never before so numerous or varied than at the end of the Middle Ages,[74] almost all were restorational in nature, that is, basically attempts to return to the example of the Apostles and revive the moral and ascetic ideals that had transformed the church in

---

73. Albert Groteken, ed., "Der älteste gedruckte deutsche Katechismus und die niederdeutschen Volksbücher des seligen Dietrich Kolde von Münster," *Franziskanische Studien* 37 (1955): 57–75, 189–217, 388–410. See the discussion in Ozment, *The Reformation in the Cities*, pp. 28–32. Closer to the Reformation is the vernacular mirror of confession, published in 1517: *Ein gar schon tractetlin von der erkantnüsz der sünden/und etlicher tugent/dem menschen vast nutzlich zu seiner Selenheit. Gemacht durch einen vast volgelerten mann zu Ingolstatt/zu lob und eren der selben hohenschul. Der Beycht spiegel* (Strasbourg, 1517). It follows a traditional division according to the Ten Commandments; the Seven Deadly Sins and their subspecies; the circumstances of sin (*quis, quid, ubi, per quos, quotiens, cur, quomodo, quando*); the sins of the five senses; the nine alien sins; the seven sacraments; the seven gifts of the Holy Spirit; the works of mercy; the "rueffenden" sins; the sins against the Holy Ghost; the twelve parts of the Christian faith; and the four angelic virtues.

74. Rapp, *L'église et la vie religieuse*, p. 146.

earlier times.[75] The reform movements that broke with official church piety and on many points anticipated later Protestant reform continued to conceive lay religious life in terms of traditional, ascetic ideals, as if a purer asceticism could resolve the crisis in late medieval piety. The Reformation, while coming in their wake, was not necessarily in their spirit. The Protestant reformers both built on and transcended the religious reforms and experiments of the previous centuries.

Despite Protestant attempts to find precedents for their teaching in the Middle Ages and their glorification of prior opposition to the medieval papacy, Protestants remained at best ambivalent about their medieval "forerunners." They came to identify no more with the teaching of late medieval reformers than they did with the church these reformers criticized. Like late medieval reformers, Protestants endorsed political efforts to make the church and clergy more obedient "citizens," yet once established in power, Protestant clergy also demanded predominance over the moral life of laity.[76] Protestants embraced a conciliar theory of church government and developed their own consistorial (Lutheran), presbyterian (Calvinist), and congregational (sectarian and Puritan) organizations, but they never believed that church councils were inerrant or even peculiarly trustworthy.[77] Protestants shared with late medieval reform movements a concern for simplicity in religious life, but like contemporary humanists, they also rejected the pious contempt for the secular world that characterized groups like the Modern Devotion.[78] Protestants sympathized with efforts to create special communities of devout Christians (*ecclesiolae in ecclesia*), especially in time of persecution, but they scorned the lay religious confraternities of the late Middle Ages as an offense to the egalitarian nature of the priesthood of all believers.[79] Preaching became the Protestant "sacrament," and late medieval preacherships served at times as platforms for Protestant doctrine, yet the reformers spurned most late medieval sermons as moralistic and Pelagian.[80] The Reformation might not have occurred without humanism, yet

75. See Strauss, *Manifestations of Discontent*, pp. xi–xix; Frantisek Graus, "The Crisis of the Middle Ages and the Hussites," in *The Reformation in Medieval Perspective*, pp. 76–103; Scott H. Hendrix, "In Quest of the Vera Ecclesia: The Crises of Late Medieval Ecclesiology," *Viator* 7 (1976): 347–48.

76. Ozment, *The Reformation in the Cities*, pp. 151–55.

77. For Luther's views, see Christa Tecklenburg-Johns, *Luthers Konzilsidee in ihrer historische Bedingtheit und ihren reformatorischen Neuansatz* (Berlin, 1966); H. A. Oberman, introduction to Brian Tierney, *Ockham, the Conciliar Theory, and the Canonists* (Philadelphia, 1971), pp. viii–x.

78. This is the larger thesis of R. R. Post, *The Modern Devotion* (Leiden, 1968).

79. Ozment, *The Reformation in the Cities*, pp. 84–85.

80. Cf. E. J. Dempsey-Douglas, *Justification in Late Medieval Preaching: A Study in John Geiler of Kaysersberg* (Leiden, 1966). See the interesting recent comparision of Luther with

humanists who became Protestants believed they had entered a totally different world.[81] And while Luther could say of the Wittenberg reformers, "We are all Hussites without realizing it," he still faulted Wyclif and Huss for seeking a narrow, moralistic reform.[82]

What the Reformation did have in common with late medieval reform movements was the conviction that traditional church authority and piety no longer served the religious needs of large numbers of people and had become psychologically and financially oppressive. Luther's inability to satisfy his own religious anguish by becoming a self-described "monk's monk" was an experience many laity also knew in their own way, for they too had sought in vain consolation from a piety based on the penitential practices of monks.

Savonarola by Josef Nolte, "Evangelicae doctrinae purum exemplum: Savonarolas Gefännismeditationen im Hinblick auf Luthers theologische Anfänge," in *Kontinuität und Umbruch: Theologie und Frömmigkeit in Flugschriften und Kleinliteratur an der Wende vom 15. zum 16. Jahrhundert,* ed. Josef Nolte et al. (Stuttgart, 1978), pp. 59–92. Demonstrating parallels between Savonarola's meditations on Psalms 50 (51) and 30 (31) and Luther's comments on these same psalms in the *Dictata super Psalterium* (1513–15), Nolte argues as forcefully as one can without explicit proof that Luther must have known these meditations during his first lectures on the Psalms and they provided an "impulse" for the development of his doctrine of justification by faith alone and his understanding of the coincidence of the *iustitia Dei* and *iustitia Christi.*

81. See below, pp. 302–09. Cf. James M. Kittelson, "Humanism and the Reformation in Germany," *Central European History* 9 (1976): 303–22.

82. Letter to Georg Spalatin, *WABr* 2, p. 42 (no. 254). See Scott H. Hendrix, "'We are All Hussites'? Hus and Luther Revisited," *ARG* 65 (1974): 134–61.

CHAPTER 6

The Mental World
of Martin Luther

Young Man Luther

THE religious demands placed on Luther the monk were not unlike those known by earnest laity; both shared a common experience of unresolved religious oppression. Many laity derived no more consolation from the sacrament of confession than Luther from monastic exercises. This shared religious experience formed the basic bond between Luther and the multitude who became Protestant. When Luther articulated his complaints against the medieval church and religion in the famous Reformation pamphlets of 1520, ordinary people knew immediately what he was talking about, because his complaints were also theirs. The "Grievances of the Holy Roman Empire and Especially the Entire German Nation," presented by the German estates to the emperor at the Diet of Worms in March 1521 on the eve of Luther's appearance and representing both aristocratic and ordinary burgher resentment, echoed Luther on point after point as they brought forth complaints of a fiscal, legal, and religious nature against the pope, German high prelates, and the church and clergy in general. Because these grievances derived from a common religious culture, their resolution was also to be primarily religious in nature; it resulted from a new theology that transformed the concept, practice, and institutions of traditional religious life.

One of the most provocative books ever written in the field of Reformation studies, Erik Erikson's *Young Man Luther* (1958), attempted to relate Luther's theology and the Reformation's popular success to the experiences of a common oppressive childhood, not to dissatisfactions stemming from a shared oppressive religious culture. Luther's theological and religious problems are seen to have been more parentally than culturally induced, the product of a universal spiritual odyssey of youth rather than of a timebound religious culture. For Erikson, the Reformation was an unsuccessful attempt to resolve by cultural revolution the universal problems of childhood and adolescence. Hence, it is the transhistorical young man Luther, not Luther the sixteenth-century theologian, who fascinates.

Historians have not taken kindly to Erikson's book, partly because his conclusions do not meet the canons of historical demonstration and partly because historians remain skeptical of the methods of "psychohistory." Such criticism by historians is as predictable as psychologists' preference for the experiences of childhood as explanations for adult behavior. In dealing with the past, historians and psychologists find themselves vocationally at odds with one another. The historian is trained to explain the past in its own terms rather than in those of present experience. He tries to appreciate Luther's actions in light of the historical culture of Luther's time, a time in which the historian too is immersed through his study of primary sources. He sees Luther's actions as based on religious motives that are largely self-explanatory, given good historical knowledge of the period.[1] Historians worry about committing what Lucien Febvre described as "psychological anachronism," the attribution to an earlier age of the emotional make-up of a later one.[2]

The modern psychologist, on the other hand, is convinced that the evidence he derives from his clinical experience says something universal about the nature of man, regardless of the particular historical period or culture in which he is found. Because his findings are seen to be empirical and scientific, they are considered capable of elucidating human behavior wherever and whenever it occurs. To the psychologist, man is a far more constant and predictable creature than he is to the historian. If such faith in the explanatory power of his craft causes the psychologist to seem all too confident to the historian, it also has the advantage for the psychologist to make him impervious to the historian's criticism.

Psychologists can, of course, recognize the role of historical cultures in shaping the actions of individuals and groups, even though they are not

1. Attention has been called to the importance of studying the cultural derivation of Luther's religious problems by George A. Lindbeck, "Erikson's *Young Man Luther:* A Historical and Theological Reappraisal," *Soundings* (1973): 210–27; and Lewis W. Spitz, "Psychohistory and History: The Case of *Young Man Luther,*" in Roger A. Johnson, ed., *Psychohistory and Religion: The Case of Young Man Luther* (Philadelphia, 1977), pp. 84–85. Johnson appends a helpful bibliography of reviews of *Young Man Luther.* See also the bibliographical summary of Jean Delumeau, *Naissance et affirmation de la réforme* (Paris, 1965), pp. 280–300.

2. "History and Psychology," in Lucien Febvre, *A New Kind of History and Other Essays,* ed. Peter Burke (New York, 1973), p. 9. A more up-to-date catalogue of the historian's objections to psychohistory, by one actually sympathetic to social-scientific techniques in historical study, is Lawrence Stone, "The Massacre of the Innocents," *New York Review of Books* 21, no. 18 (14 November 1974), pp. 25–31. An attempt to rebut Stone in defense especially of Erikson's relevance to historical study is Frank L. Halla, "Childhood, Culture, and Society in Psychoanalysis and History," *The Historian* 39 (1977): 423–28.

trained to know thoroughly any culture but their own. And historians can certainly appreciate the way the experiences of childhood and adolescence influence adult behavior, even though their craft does not involve them in the clinical study of youth. The crucial issue for the historian must remain, however, whether the results of such psychological research, when applied to a particular historical epoch, actually illumine this epoch in its particularity or simply reduce the culture in question to supposedly transhistorical truths about humankind. The sociologist Robert Bellah has rightly challenged historians critical of Erikson: "The only real critique of Erikson on Luther that will stand up is . . . a portrait of the cultural development of Luther which is more compelling than the one which [Erikson] has given us."[3]

Young Man Luther is the most important test case to date for the application of modern clinical psychology to past history. Erikson describes his work as a study of a delayed identity crisis in a "young great man." By "identity crisis" Erikson means the major trauma of adolescence, a crisis occurring at that point in a young person's life when he must either fall prey to his confusion over who he is or overcome it by squaring his own self-judgment and expectations with those of authorities and superiors, especially his parents. In Erikson's words, the identity crisis occurs in that period of the life cycle "when each youth must forge for himself some central perspective and direction, some working unity, out of the effective remnants of his childhood and the hopes of his anticipated adulthood."[4] The crisis is considered to be the fifth in a series of eight that Erikson sees beginning in earliest childhood, continuing through adolescence and adulthood, and subjecting the individual repeatedly to opposed feelings and attitudes.[5]

Erikson is guided in his work on Luther by his own clinical studies of gifted young people. Believing childhood experiences to be the key to human behavior, he searches the "spiritual and intellectual milieu" of the young Luther for evidence of real or possible emotional reactions to his parents and the world in which he grew up. Unfortunately, there are not a lot of undisputed facts about Luther's youth with which the psychohistorian can begin to work. We know that Luther was born on November 10, 1483 in Eisleben in Saxony; that he grew up in Mansfeld, attended school at Magdeburg (1497) and Eisenach (1498), and matriculated at the University of

3. Comment on George A. Lindbeck's "*Young Man Luther:* A Historical and Theological Reappraisal," in *Encounter With Erikson: Historical Interpretation and Religious Biography,* ed. Donald Capps et al. (Missoula, Montana, 1977), pp. 29–30.

4. *Young Man Luther* (New York, 1962), p. 14.

5. See *Childhood and Society* (New York, 1963), part 3, ch. 7, esp. pp. 261–62.

Erfurt in May 1501, where he received his bachelor's degree in September 1502 and his master's in January 1505. He was at this time twenty-two years of age and destined to the study of law in compliance with his parents' wishes. However, he abruptly changed these plans after being terrified by a thunderstorm in early July 1505, while returning to Erfurt after a visit with his parents. Fulfilling a vow made during the storm to St. Anne, the patron saint of travelers in distress, Luther entered the Augustinian monastery upon his arrival in Erfurt on July 17. He said his first mass in May 1507, taught Aristotelian philosophy at Wittenberg in 1508, and journeyed to Rome on the business of his order in November 1510. After his return to Erfurt in April 1511, he was permanently transferred to Wittenberg, where he became a doctor of theology in October 1512 at twenty-eight. Between 1513 and 1515 he gave his first lectures, a glossing of the Psalms. Many scholars believe that it was during these years that he experienced clearly for the first time the meaning of justification by faith.[6] Two years later (1517), at age thirty-four, he posted his theses against indulgences and launched his career as a reformer.

With almost no direct evidence for the reconstruction of Luther's early childhood, Erikson argues that "a clinician's training permits and in fact forces him to recognize major trends even where the facts are not all available."[7] Aided by this sense of mission and Luther's recollections of his childhood experiences, Erikson constructs an interesting if ultimately unverifiable portrait of Luther's childhood.

Luther recalls having received three beatings as a child: one from his father, which made him very anxious until they were reconciled; the actual drawing of blood by his mother after he had stolen a nut; and fifteen whacks in school for speaking German rather than Latin.[8] Although Luther gives the impression that the parental beatings were exceptions to the way his parents normally treated him, and the caning in school was nothing unusual for the fifteenth century, Erikson draws the conclusion that Luther grew up a brutalized child, lacking a sense of basic trust from his parents.[9]

6. Other scholars place the conversion experience as late as 1518. See the discussion in *Der Durchbruch der reformatorischen Erkenntnis bei Luther* ed. Bernhardt Lohse (Darmstadt, 1967); Ernst Bizer, *Fides ex Auditu: Eine Untersuchung über die Entdeckung der Gerechtigkeit Gottes durch Martin Luther* (Neukirchen, 1961), pp. 29–31, 51. Heinrich Bornkamm, "Zur Frage der Iustitia Dei beim jungen Luther," *ARG* 52 (1961); *ARG* 53 (1962). Roland H. Bainton provides a helpful chronology of Luther's life in *Here I Stand: A Life of Martin Luther* (New York, 1950), pp. 12–14.
7. *Young Man Luther*, p. 50.
8. Ibid., pp. 64–65, 68, 79. See the discussion of these reports by Spitz in Johnson, *Psychohistory and Religion*, pp. 70–71, 75, and by Roland H. Bainton, "Psychiatry and History: An Examination of Erikson's *Young Man Luther*," *Religion in Life* 40 (1971): 458–61, reprinted in Johnson, *Psychohistory and Religion*, pp. 19–56.
9. *Young Man Luther*, p. 65.

Drawing on studies of second-generation emigrants to America who moved out of rural poverty and into a degree of affluence in industry, Erikson surmises that Luther's father, a second-generation peasant who rose to power and wealth in the mining industry, must have been exceedingly demanding, arbitrary, and paternalistic. Life in such an environment is seen to have weighed Luther down with an "overweening superego" so that he felt all his life "like some sort of criminal" who had continually to be justifying himself.[10] Erikson also sees in Luther's love-hate relationship with his parents the origins of his later preoccupation with the righteousness of God and his attack on the cult of the Virgin.[11]

This is all certainly very suggestive. Was Luther's father guided by love or malice when he punished his son and demanded more of him than he could do? Is God guided by love or malice when, in seemingly arbitrary fashion, he damns some and saves others? One can see how a problem with parental wrath in childhood might directly influence the formation of a theology like Luther's that is preoccupied with the righteousness of God.

Erikson's portrait of Luther's father, however, is demonstrably fabricated, and the weight of reliable historical evidence strongly indicates that Luther's childhood was unhappy neither at home nor in school.[12] Nor was preoccupation with the righteousness of God unprecedented in medieval theology.[13] Luther's overpowering sense of unworthiness, which Erikson skillfully detects, seems clearly to have been culturally rather than parentally derived. In all probability it was popular religious practice, centered on the sacrament of penance and known to Luther from his childhood, and the traditional theology taught at Erfurt, both the dominant Ockhamism and the persisting Thomism, that magnified for him, as it did for so many others, the tension between divine mercy and divine wrath and the individual's responsibility to placate the latter and ensure the former by doing his best with the aid of grace.

Erikson deals at length with the crisis that brought Luther into the monastery. He finds the thunderstorm experience, during which Luther promised St. Anne he would enter the monastery if he came to safety, very revealing of the personal stress Luther was under at this time. Erikson

10. Ibid., pp. 68, 77.
11. Ibid., pp. 58, 67-61.
12. See Spitz in Johnson, *Psychohistory and Religion*, pp. 73, 76-77. Johnson makes a case for viewing Erikson's description of Luther's father as Erikson's own "ideological construct" rather than a portrait resultant from a careful application of psychology to the past (*Psychohistory and Religion*, pp. 136-37).
13. See Harry J. McSorley, *Luther: Right or Wrong: An Ecumenical-Theological Study of Luther's Major Work: The Bondage of the Will* (New York, 1969); English translation of *Luthers Lehre vom unfreien Willen* (Munich, 1967).

suspects that he had argued with his father during his visit home, probably because he had expressed reservations about studying law and a desire to enter a religious vocation. He sees the young Luther as torn between distaste for a career he himself had not chosen and fear of disappointing his parents, whose ambitions for him were not his own. The vow in the thunderstorm gave him the courage to resist his father, who could not countermand the wishes of God, and the monastery provided a much needed "moratorium," time for him to reflect on what he himself wanted his life to be.[14]

These speculations on Luther's motives and mental state could be perfectly true and Luther's entrance into the monastery still be satisfactorily explained in terms of his religious culture. If anything about the young Luther is as clear as his fear of disappointing his parents may have been real, it is his temperamental attraction to religion and theological genius. As Erikson also knows, Luther was almost as "natural" a *homo religiosus* and theologian as he was a son.

Rather than resolving Luther's anxiety, the monastery only aggravated it. Erikson finds two events that occurred during his stay in the monastery particularly revealing. The first is an alleged seizure Luther suffered while singing in choir a short time after he had entered the monastery; the second, the celebration of his first mass in the presence of his father. According to a report, Luther became extremely emotional in choir one day after hearing the story from the gospel of Mark about Jesus's exorcising a dumb spirit from a boy (Mark 9;17) and he began to shout out, "I am not, I am not," apparently meaning, "I [Luther] am not this boy possessed by a dumb spirit." Erikson speculates that Luther was here defending his decision to enter the monastery against his father's strong disapproval and his own subconscious feeling that he was not cut out for the religious life. He compares Luther's well-known scrupulosity as a monk with that of modern teenagers and young adults who, having repudiated a rule imposed on them by others, become fanatically devoted to something they themselves have chosen.[15]

Luther's behavior at the celebration of his first mass in the presence of his parents also suggests to Erikson the intensification of an identity crisis. Once again the young Luther was confronted by paternal disapproval and his own dawning doubts about the decision he had made. His father publicly criticized him during a banquet following the mass. In the days prior to the performance of the mass, Luther tells of waking in the night in cold

14. *Young Man Luther,* pp. 90–97.
15. Ibid., pp. 23–48.

sweats, something that recurred throughout his monastic career. Erikson even finds evidence suggesting that Luther became so tense that he experienced spontaneous ejaculations.[16]

Historians largely discount the story of the fit in the choir because it originated with Johannes Cochlaeus (1497–1552), a contemporary Catholic polemicist, who related the story in support of his own charge that Luther was demon-possessed; the chances of the story's being fabricated are at least as good as those of its being true. But even without this particular episode, a solid case can be made that Luther was extremely anxious and behaved neurotically in the monastery. What remains at issue between the historian and the psychologist is the more likely cause—brooding over paternal disapproval and vocational self-doubt, as Erikson maintains, or, as I would argue, subjection to medieval religious culture in its purest form, the monastic regimen. In a letter to his father, written as a preface to an attack on monastic vows in 1521, Luther apologized for having taken vows without his father's knowledge and consent and admitted to having been "forcibly struck" at the time by his father's criticism of his decision. But what he most regretted about his action in retrospect was that his vows turned out to be a true seduction. By Luther's own confession it was the monastic life, not his parents, which proved to be the tyrant.[17] Luther and his followers constantly depicted the cloistered life as a kind of training in mental illness, driving boys and girls mad by its "unnatural" demands of poverty, chastity, and obedience; in so arguing, they claimed the authority not only of Holy Scripture, but also of their own experience under vows.[18]

The final key event in the life of Erikson's Luther is his conversion experience in the tower room of the Augustinian cloister, when Luther saw clearly for the first time the meaning of justification by faith. Luther described the event in a preface to the 1545 edition of his Latin works:

> Though I lived as a monk without reproach, I felt that I was a sinner before God with an extremely disturbed conscience. I could not believe that he was placated by my satisfaction. I did not love, yes, I hated the righteous God who punishes sinners, and secretly . . . I was angry with God. . . . Nevertheless, I beat importunately upon Paul [in Romans 1:17]. . . . At last, by the mercy of God, meditating day and night, I gave heed to the context of the words, namely, "In [the gospel] the righteousness of God is revealed, as it is written, 'He who through faith is righteous shall live.'" There I began to understand that the righteous-

16. Ibid., pp. 137–60.
17. *WA* 8, pp. 573–76 = *LW* 48, pp. 330–36.
18. See below, ch. 12.

ness of God is that by which the righteous live by a gift of God, namely by faith. And this is the meaning: the righteousness of God is revealed by the gospel, namely, the passive righteousness with which merciful God justifies us by faith. . . . Here I felt that I was altogether born again and had entered paradise itself.[19]

Erikson, who dates this event between 1513 and 1515, finds it significant that Luther was in his early thirties, an important age for people with a delayed identity crisis. Even more significant for Erikson is Luther's confiding at table that the Holy Spirt gave him this new understanding in the tower room "auff diser cloaca," literally, "in the men's room."[20] Believing *cloaca* refers to an actual facility, Erikson, as several before him, connects Luther's religious breakthrough with his lifelong suffering from constipation and urine retention. He believes the religious insight was accompanied by a great physical release, a loosing of long-repressed emotions and physical processes.[21] Erikson sees the experience prepared for by Luther's close contact with Johannes von Staupitz, a grandfatherly senior confidant, who lessened Luther's fears about his unworthiness and helped him relax. Quite perceptively, Erikson describes the relationship with Staupitz as giving Luther a much needed feeling of "benevolent parental presence."[22]

On the meaning of *cloaca,* however, the historians have done their homework better than the psychologists. In the late Middle Ages, the descriptions of oneself as being *in cloaca, in stercore,* or *in latrina* were common religious rhetoric, actually derived from the Bible and connoting a state of utter humility and dependence of God.[23] When Luther described his Reformation insight as occurring "in cloaca," he was saying no more than that he received his understanding of the righteousness of God after a long period of humble meditation in the tower room—actually the library—of the monastery. Once again an understanding of the religious culture of the period proves more illuminating than conjectures based on modern clinical psychology. And could we not also say that any feelings of benevolent parental presence communicated to Luther by Staupitz would be as helpful an aid against an oppressive religious culture as against a supposed oppressive childhood?

There is not a more positive and admiring evaluation of the young

19. *LW* 34, pp. 336–337.
20. *WATr* 3, no. 3232 a, b, c (9 June–12 July 1532), p. 228.
21. *Young Man Luther*, pp. 204–206.
22. Ibid., p. 168.
23. Heiko A. Oberman, "Wir sein Pettler. Hoc est Verum. Bund und Gnade in der Theologie des Mittelalters und der Reformation," *ZKG* 78 (1967): 232–52. Cf. also Spitz in Johnson, *Psychohistory and Religion*, pp. 78–82.

Luther than that of Erikson. Although he believes the old Luther became a manic-depressive who "inadvertently helped increase and refine authoritarianism," he praises the young Luther as one who "tried to free individual conscience from totalitarian dogma" and "give man credal wholeness."[24] I believe this latter conclusion, to which I would also strongly subscribe, is far better understood and more plausibly explained by a grasp of the religious culture and theology of the Middle Ages than by the importation of the findings of clinical psychology into the sixteenth century. So to believe is not to prefer abstractions to reality. Luther's suffering was no less real because a religious culture rather than an oppressive childhood induced it. Nor was its resolution any less real because it proved ultimately to be theological in nature. In the culture of the premodern world, what is religious and theological cannot be distinguished from what is emotional and psychological in terms of the less and the more real. It is an age when reality wears a tonsure. For this reason we must take young theologian Luther as seriously as young man Luther.

Luther and Scholasticism   WE are so accustomed to think of the young Luther as a melancholy monk preoccupied with his own salvation that we sometimes lose sight of the fact that he was the age's most brilliant theologian. He led the revolution against Rome and traditional religion not as a visionary spiritual reformer, but as a skilled doctor of theology. At the base of all the religious changes brought about by the Reformation lay the new theology of justification by faith. If recollections of the ordeals of young man Luther give insight into his life and work, even more suggestive are reports of the thoughts and feelings of young theologian Luther.

Consider one such report. According to Anton Lauterbach, Luther, in a cheerful mood, was conversing one evening with Nicholas von Amsdorf about "the [theological] works of the prior age when the most talented men were preoccupied with vain studies." Luther reminisced:

> Those sophistical pursuits are completely behind us now. The men of our age would look upon them as barbarous. [Duns] Scotus, Bonaventura, Gabriel [Biel], and Thomas [Aquinas], having lived when the papacy was flourishing, were the most idle of men. With so much time on their hands, they naturally gave free rein to their fantasy. Gabriel wrote a book on the canon of the Mass. In my youth I considered it the

24. *Young Man Luther*, pp. 231, 252.

best of books. When I read it, my heart flowered. For me no authority
on the Bible could match Gabriel. In fact, I still have his books, which I
have annotated. Scotus wrote best on Book III of the *Sentences*. And
Ockham, zealous for method, was the most ingenious of all. He was
devoted to expanding and amplifying a topic endlessly. Thomas was
the most loquacious because he had been seduced by metaphysics. But
now God has wondrously led us away from all that. It is now over twenty
years since he snatched me, still knowing, away.[25]

Between 1509–10, when he wrote his commentary on Peter Lombard's
Sentences, and the indulgence controversy of 1517, Luther was an exceedingly active scholar. He read deeply in Aristotle's *Physics, Metaphysics,* and
Ethics. In addition to sermons and letters, he wrote lectures on the Psalms
(1513–15) and on St. Paul's letters to the Romans (1515–16) and to the
Galatians (1516–17). Preparation for these lectures required extensive reading in medieval biblical commentaries. He further annotated works by St.
Augustine (1509–10), the *Psalterium quincuplex* of Jacques Lefèvre d'Etaples
(1513), the sermons of Johannes Tauler (1515–16), and Gabriel Biel's *Exposition of the Canon of the Mass* and *Sentences* commentary (1517). He edited
a portion of an anonymous mystical treatise, which he entitled the *German
Theology* (1516), and later published the full manuscript of this work (1518),
calling it a precedent for the new "Wittenberg theology."

For many years Luther was in daily contact with the written and oral
traditions of his own Order of the Hermits of St. Augustine. In the library
of the order were volumes that protested the inordinate influence of Aristotle on theology, apprised Luther of the anti-Pelagian writings of St. Augustine, and introduced him to the text-critical studies of humanism. Echoes of
the fourteenth-century works of the Augustinians Simon Fidati of Cascia
and Hugolin of Orvieto have been noted in Luther's irreverent remarks on
Aristotle in his maiden theological work, the commentary on Lombard's
Sentences.[26] Luther later praised two members of his order most highly:
Gregory of Rimini and Johannes von Staupitz. He looked on Gregory as the
sole scholastic completely free of Pelagianism. To Staupitz, his immediate
superior and confidant, he even gave credit for the Reformation itself.[27]

25. *Luthers Werke in Auswahl,* vol. 8, *Tischreden,* ed. by Otto Clemen (Berlin, 1950), no.
3722 (1538), pp. 149–50.
26. Adolar Zumkeller, "Die Augustinertheologen Simon Fidati von Cascia und Hugolin
von Orvieto und Martin Luthers Kritik an Aristoteles," *ARG* 54 (1963): 15, 37. Oberman
describes "the schola Augustiniana moderna" as the "*occasio proxima—not causa!—*for the
inception of the *theologia vera* in Wittenberg" ("Headwaters of the Reformation: Initia
Lutheri-Initia Reformationis," in *Luther and the Dawn of the Modern Era: Papers for the Fourth
International Congress for Luther Research,* ed. H. A. Oberman [Leiden, 1974], p. 82).
27. "Ex Erasmo nihil habeo. Ich hab all mein ding von Doctor Staupitz." *WATr* 1, no.

As these facts and comments indicate, the young Luther was closely acquainted with the medieval theological traditions in their various exegetical,
mystical, and scholastic forms. If Melanchthon can be believed, he not only
mastered late medieval theology, but even committed portions of the work
of Pierre d'Ailly and Biel to memory.[28] Luther did not enter the indulgence
controversy of 1517 as an innocent. His last work prior to the ninety-five
theses against indulgences was a broad attack on the whole of late medieval
theology: the *Disputation Against Scholastic Theology* of September 4, 1517.
Here Luther joined the classic medieval debates over the nature of religious
justification and the extent of man's natural knowledge of God. Because of
its proximity to the ninety-five theses, the work provides an important
gauge of his thought on the eve of this famous controversy and a clue to
what he believed to be at stake in the Reformation.

It was a traditional teaching of the medieval church, perhaps best formulated by Thomas Aquinas, that a man who freely performed good works in
a state of grace cooperated in the attainment of his salvation. Religious life
was organized around this premise. Secular living was in this way taken up
into the religious life; good works became the sine qua non of saving faith.
He who did his moral best within a state of grace received salvation as his
just due. In the technical language of the medieval theologian, faith formed
by acts of charity (*fides caritate formata*) received eternal life as full or condign merit (*meritum de condigno*). Entrance into the state of grace was God's
exclusive and special gift, not man's achievement, and it was the indispensable foundation for man's moral cooperation. An *infusio gratiae* preceded
every meritorious act. The steps to salvation were:

1	2	3
Gratuitous infusion of grace	Moral cooperation: doing the best one can with the aid of grace	Reward of eternal life as a just due

Among that group of theologians known as late medieval Ockhamists, or
nominalists, a significant adjustment was made in this traditional scheme.
These men desired to preserve human freedom, even from the salutary
causality of a prevenient infusion of grace. If man loved God simply be-

---

173 (1532), in *Dokumente zu Luthers Entwicklung (bis 1519)*, ed. Otto Scheel (Tübingen, 1929),
p. 86.

28. Preface to volume 2 of the 1546 Wittenberg edition of Luther's Latin writings, in
Martin Luther's 95 Theses with the Pertinent Documents from the History of the Reformation, ed.
Kurt Aland (St. Louis, 1967), p. 43.

cause God moved him to do so by a special internal grace, did he really love God freely? Was not free choice also a measure of a meritorious act? Impressed by man's ethical resources, Ockhamists believed that God's natural gifts of reason and conscience had not been eradicated by the Fall. Were there not historical examples of pagans who loved country and neighbor above self? Ockhamists were further impressed by biblical injunctions that seemed clearly to say that each person had both the ability and the duty to take the initiative for his salvation: "Turn to me and I will turn to you" (Zechariah 1:3); "Draw near to God, and he will draw near to you" (James 4:8); "If you seek me, you will find me" (Luke 11:9).

With such concerns in mind, Ockhamists asked: If God rewards good works done in a state of grace with eternal life as a just due, could he not also be expected to reward good works done in a state of nature with an infusion of grace as an appropriate due? Had God not in fact promised to do precisely that? Ockham and Biel answered these questions in the affirmative: in accordance with God's gracious goodness (*ex liberalitate Dei*), he who does his best in a state of nature receives grace as a fitting reward (*meritum de congruo*).[29] In summary:

1	2	3	4
Moral effort: doing the best one can on the basis of natural moral ability	Infusion of grace as an appropriate reward	Moral cooperation: doing the best one can with the aid of grace	Reward of eternal life as a just due

Ockhamists did not consider this to be Pelagian teaching, but part of the arrangement God had freely willed for man's salvation, God's very covenant. Absolutely considered, it was not human activity, either outside or within a state of grace, that determined man's salvation; it was God's willingness to value human effort so highly. Ockhamist theologians remained convinced, however, that God meant for people to acquire grace as semimerit within a state of nature and to earn salvation as full merit within a state of grace by doing their moral best. All the subtle and important qualifications notwithstanding, this theology taught that people could at least initiate their salvation.[30]

29. See Gabriel Biel, *Canonis missae expositio*, ed. H. A. Oberman and W. J. Courtenay (Mainz, 1965), Lect. LIX P, 2: 443. See above, pp. 37–41.

30. Heiko A. Oberman, *The Harvest of Medieval Theology* (Cambridge, Mass., 1963), p. 175. For a dissenting view, see Wilhelm Ernst, *Gott und Mensch am Vorabend der Reformation: Eine Untersuchung zur Moralphilosophie und Theologie bei Gabriel Biel* (Leipzig, 1972), p. 394.

It was this position that Luther assailed in the *Disputation Against Scholastic Theology,* arguing that man by nature lacks the freedom of will to do the good that Scotus, Ockham, d'Ailly, and Biel attribute to him. Luther was led to this conclusion both by his personal experience in the monastery and his own careful study of the Bible and St. Augustine. On this score, he felt he stood squarely with Augustine against the "new Pelagians."[31]

Luther's arguments in the *Disputation* culminated in a wholesale condemnation of Aristotle's *Ethics:* "The whole of Aristotle's *Ethics* is the worst enemy of grace" (thesis 41). He saw Aristotelian moral philosophy at the root of scholastic error. Specifically, he singled out Aristotle's definition of moral virtue as "acquired" virtue. For Aristotle, moral virtues, unlike natural virtues, must be gained by practice and effort; morally, one becomes virtuous by performing virtuous acts. Natural virtues, by contrast, precede their exercise; people have the power of sight, a natural virtue, before they see. According to Aristotle, people are naturally equipped to attain moral virtue; but they are not actually virtuous until they have learned to be so by habit.[32] Luther spied in this philosophical position the model for the arguments of the new Pelagians.

It has been argued that Luther at this time opposed in principle any theological use of Aristotle, believing the Bible alone sufficient for theologians. Opposition to the new Pelagians was accordingly a consequence of opposition to scholastic theology generally. Hence, it was not so much specific theological errors as Aristotelian philosophy that he resisted, whether employed by Scotists, Ockhamists, or Thomists.[33]

Luther's opposition to Aristotle's influence on theology is indeed striking in 1517, especially in correspondence relating to the reform of the University of Wittenberg.[34] However, the *Disputation* of 1517 did not focus primarily on the inappropriateness of Aristotelian philosophy, but rather on the Pelagianism to which Luther believed its theological application led: scholastic error disturbed Luther more than scholastic method. As the later conflict with Erasmus confirmed for him, criticism of scholasticism did not necessarily ensure release from its errors. In defense of freedom of the will, the prince of the humanists repeated the very Ockhamist position so emphatically condemned by Luther.[35] Luther turned against scholastic theol-

31. See theses 5–8, 17–20, 28–30 of the *Disputation Against Scholastic Theology, WA* 1, pp. 224–26.

32. Aristotle, *Nichomachean Ethics* 1103a–1103b, in *The Basic Works of Aristotle,* ed. Richard McKeon (New York, 1941), p. 952.

33. Leif Grane, "Die Anfänge von Luthers Auseinandersetzung mit dem Thomismus," *Theologische Literaturzeitung* 95 (1970): 242–48.

34. See below, pp. 310–13.

35. See below, p. 295.

ogy because his own study and experience convinced him that its teaching
was false, whether phrased in the categories of Aristotle or in those of the
Bible and the church fathers.

The criticism of Aristotle at this point in the *Disputation* may also offer a
clue to Luther's extension of his arguments to embrace "all scholastics," not
just the four mentioned by name. Did he really mean to attack the traditional
as well as the peculiarly Ockhamist version of the way to salvation? How
could he have considered the former also Pelagian?

One possible explanation is that the Aristotelian model influenced the
thought of all scholastics, Thomists as well as Scotists and Ockhamists. Aristotle's definition of moral virtue was as applicable to the movement from a
state of grace to eternal life as it was to the movement from a state of nature
to a state of grace. In both instances, whether in an initial or in a penultimate stage of the Christian's activity, moral effort remained imperative and
meritorious. By doing one's best in a state of nature one earned grace,
according to Biel. By doing one's best in a state of grace one earned eternal
life, according to all scholastics. The same pattern appeared on two different levels of the religious life. In the final analysis, earning by moral
effort salvation as condign merit was only a higher form of earning by
moral effort saving grace as semimerit. To Luther in 1517, the former
probably appeared to be only a more cautious Pelagianism. For although
good works were now done with the aid of grace, they still remained necessary for salvation.

Having said this, it must be added that Luther did appear to be primarily
concerned with views peculiar to Ockhamists. Still, it is not necessarily to be
inferred from this that he erroneously identified the whole of scholastic
theology with Ockhamism. Till the end of his life he associated "scholastic
theology" with "Pelagianism" and the latter especially with the technical
terms favored by Ockhamists: "doing the best that is in one" (*facere quod in se
est*) and "congruent merit" (*meritum de congruo*).[36] To the extent that his
early writings already distinguish ethical activity and religious justification
in principle—so that good works, whether done within or outside a state of
grace, never contribute to one's salvation—the Thomist position squares as
well with his definition of scholastic theology as does that of the Ockhamists.
From Luther's point of view, they were two sides of the same coin.

Although Ockhamists seem so boldly Pelagian, such was not, as Luther
must also have known, the sum total of their teaching. If they glorified the
will of man, they also exalted the will of God. They left little doubt that,
when all things were considered, salvation hinged not on man's activity but

36. Cf. *WA* 2, p. 401 and Scheel, *Dokumente zu Luthers Entwicklung*, no. 488, p. 162.

on God's willingness to accept and value human effort so highly. It has been argued that Ockhamists inconsistently juxtaposed an Aristotelian concept of man with an Augustinian concept of God.[37] This dual heritage of Ockhamism should be borne in mind when we see Luther force an Augustinian consistency on the issue in the *Disputation*.

The *Disputation Against Scholastic Theology* scored illicit theological speculation as well as Pelagianism. To Luther, the schoolmen understood the relationship between reason and revelation no better than that between man's will and salvation. He opposed in particular the efforts of Pierre d'Ailly and Robert Holcot, O.P., to construct a higher "logic of faith" (thesis 46). D'Ailly and Holcot believed that reason was powerless to penetrate beyond God's revelation, but once given this revelation, reason could set about analyzing it. Among scholastics it was especially the Ockhamists who speculated on the conditions of revelation, surmising what might have been had God in eternity decided, as he was free to do, to pursue alternative systems of salvation. Such speculation was intended to show both the contingency and the appropriateness of the system God finally ordained. Despite the infinite possibilities open to him in eternity, God had chosen to save people through a church, priests, sacraments, infused grace, and good works—all things considered, a fair and sensible arrangement.[38]

It was clear to d'Ailly and Holcot that syllogistic or Aristotelian logic (all men are mortal; Socrates is a man; Socrates is mortal), strictly applied, was no tool for the data of revelation. One could not properly demonstrate in Aristotelian syllogisms that three are one and one is three. D'Ailly and Holcot nonetheless believed that reason could be very helpful in clarifying articles of faith, and Aristotelian logic was for all the model of rationality. One might not be able to demonstrate the truth of the Trinity, but one could make the Trinity an object of systematic rational inquiry and employ logical rules that made sense to faith. In this way, the probable arguments of reason served revelation. It has been argued that by such an approach these Ockhamists actually maintained the *harmony* of reason and faith.[39]

Luther clearly would have none of this: "In vain does one transcend natural logic to construct a logic of faith" (thesis 46). He saw here only an effort to manipulate revelation with reason, to conform the thoughts of

---

37. Leif Grane, *Contra Gabrielem: Luthers Auseinandersetzung mit Gabriel Biel in der Disputatio contra Scholasticam Theologiam 1517* (Gyldendal, 1962), p. 217.

38. See above, pp. 39–40, 59–60.

39. Bengt Hägglund, *Theologie und Philosophie bei Luther und in der occamistischen Tradition* (Lund, 1955), p. 86. Cf. H. A. Oberman, "Facientibus Quod in se est Deus non Denegat Gratiam: Robert Holcot, O.P., and the Beginnings of Luther's Theology," in S. Ozment, ed., *The Reformation in Medieval Perspective* (Chicago, 1971), pp. 128–29.

God to the thoughts of men, just as the new Pelagians had also tried to manipulate God's grace with free will and man's natural moral ability. Here again Aristotle was singled out as at the root of an effort to rationalize faith out of existence; hence, the (in)famous snort, "The whole of Aristotle is to theology as darkness to light" (thesis 50).

In its context, this statement rejected neither reason nor Aristotle per se; it was rather a plea to keep syllogisms, even of a higher order, and inordinate speculation on the conditions of revelation out of the sphere of faith. Where logic applied, Luther argued, one dealt with knowledge and not with faith (thesis 49). As he later put it in his inimitable way: the articles of faith are "not against dialectical truth [Aristotelian logic], but rather outside, under, above, below, around, and beyond it" (*non quidem contra, sed extra, intra, supra, infra, citra, ultra omnem veritatem dialecticam*).[40]

Here Luther may have been more consistently Ockhamist than were d'Ailly and Holcot. The latter appear to be closer to Anselm of Canterbury and Thomas Aquinas on this particular point than to the stricter Ockhamist view of reason's limits.[41] Indeed, the proximity of their arguments to the Thomist definition of theology as a rational science with its own axioms and logic may be another clue to Luther's extension of the *Disputation* to embrace "all scholastics." All scholastics truly desired a theology that was a rational science on the model of Aristotelian philosophy. Ockhamists no more than Thomists were ready to surrender the medieval ideal of faith seeking understanding (*fides quaerens intellectum*) for the "sheer faith" (*sola fides*) of the Reformation. By contrast, Luther's restriction of reason's sphere of competence in theological matters accords with a strict Aristotelian definition of *scientia*.

When Luther later praised Ockham as his master, he did so in terms of his dialectical skills, as a philosopher, not for any theological teaching or eloquence. "Ockham, my teacher, was the greatest of the dialecticians, but he was not skilled in preaching [the gospel]."[42] "Ockham alone understood dialectic, that it involves defining and distinguishing words, but he was no preacher."[43] "Ockham was the most prudent and the most learned [of scholastics], but rhetoric was not among his skills."[44] It was not from Ockham, the "doctor who is more than subtle," or from any of the scholastic doctors, but from the Bible and the church fathers that Luther learned the "divine arts." Still, despite his protests, he may also have learned from

40. Cited by Hägglund, *Theologie und Philosophie bei Luther*, p. 53.
41. See above, pp. 49–50.
42. *WATr* 2, no. 2544a (1532), in Scheel, *Dokumente zu Luthers Entwicklung*, no. 223, p. 87.
43. *WATr* 1, no. 193 (1532), in ibid., no. 220, p. 86.
44. *WATr* 1, no. 338 (1532), in ibid., no. 239, p. 94.

Ockham's example, as well as from St. Paul, that in matters of reason and revelation, good fences make good neighbors. For on this issue, as also on that of grace and free will, the Ockhamist tradition could be its own worst enemy.

Luther and Mysticism

WAS mysticism a more congenial medieval source of Luther's theology than scholasticism? During the important formative years 1516–18, he had only the highest praise for the German mystical tradition. In a letter to his friend Georg Spalatin he described Johannes Tauler's sermons as "pure and solid theology" and professed to know no contemporary work in either Latin or German more beneficial and in closer agreement with the Gospels.[45] When he defended the ninety-five theses in 1518, he confessed to having found more good theology in Tauler than in all the scholastic theologians combined.[46] In that same year he published the full text of the *German Theology*, declaring that only the Bible and St. Augustine had taught him more about God, Christ, man, and all things.[47]

Given such positive statements, it is little wonder that scholars have looked to the German mystical tradition for the medieval roots of Protestant theology and considered Eckhart and Tauler true forerunners of the Reformation.[48] The *Catalogus testium veritatis* (1556) of Flacius Illyricus, which formed the core of the later *Magdeburg Centuries* (1559–74), the first Protestant church history, praised Tauler as an exponent of salvation by faith and trust in God.[49] Modern scholars have argued that German mysticism was the most important source of Luther's attack on medieval penitential practice[50] and his chief ally against the positivistic faith and Pelagianism of the Ockhamists.[51]

There is no question that Luther had a genuine and well-informed interest in both German and Latin mysticism. But those features that most at-

---

45. *Dr. M. Luthers Briefwechsel,* ed. E. L. Enders (Frankfurt a. M., 1884), vol. 1, p. 75.
46. *WA* 1, p. 57.
47. *WA* 1, pp. 153, 378.
48. See Carl Ullmann, *Reformatoren vor der Reformation,* vols. 1–2 (Gotha, 1866); Wilhelm Preger, *Geschichte der deutschen Mystik im Mittelalter,* vols. 1–3 (Leipzig, 1874–93). Cf. also Ingeborg Degenhardt, *Studien zum Wandel des Eckhartbildes* (Leiden, 1967), pp. 144–45, 257.
49. Matthias Flacius Illyricus, *Catalogus testium veritatis* (Strasbourg, 1562), p. 507.
50. A. V. Müller, *Luther und Tauler auf ihrem theologischen Zusammenhang neu untersucht* (Bern, 1918), pp. 25, 168.
51. Bengt Hägglund, "Luther's Doctrine of Justification in Late Medieval Theology," *Lutheran World* 8 (1961): 25–46; Reinhold Seeberg, *Die religiösen Grundgedanken des jungen Luther und ihr Verhältnis zu dem Ockhamismus und der deutschen Mystik* (Berlin, 1931).

tracted him, while prominent in mystical writings, were not distinctively mystical at all, and peculiarly mystical teachings actually elicited his consistent criticism. The nonscholastic method and personal treatment of religion that he found in all mysticism especially appealed to him;[52] themes of passivity, suffering, and self-denial, which had also captivated him during his first reading of the Psalms, were a welcome change from the Ockhamist moralism in which he had been trained.[53] That Tauler's sermons and the *German Theology* were vernacular, not Latin, works also impressed Luther, especially after 1517. He cited both as precedents for his own "German" theology and used them to answer charges of doctrinal innovation. In the preface to the 1518 edition of the *German Theology,* written as he was coming under serious official scrutiny, he twice insisted that the Wittenberg theology, like the *German Theology,* was ancient, not "new" theology.[54]

At the same time, however, Luther also recognized that mysticism lent support to teachings he opposed in the Ockhamists, especially the mystical doctrine of a divine spark or power in the soul. In the same year that he read Tauler's sermons for the first time, he singled out belief in such a spark (*synteresis, scintilla animae*) as leading the theologians into the Pelagian heresy.[55] Indeed, it has even been argued that mysticism led Luther himself to espouse for a time the very error he condemned in the Ockhamists. Mature Lutheran theology considered reliance on interior acts of humility in the quest for grace no less Pelagian than reliance on exterior good works—a point of view from which the mystical way of salvation, with its contemplative exercises and programmatic self-denial, became as vulnerable to criticism as the Ockhamist theology of free will. The proximity of these two teachings may not have been appreciated by Luther until after 1518. Prior to that time he too believed that reliance on exterior good works was Pelagian while accepting interior good works as meritorious of salvation. Here he agreed with the spiritual traditions of the Middle Ages that God gave his grace only to the humble. It is the thesis of Ernst Bizer that before 1518 Luther conceived saving faith to be "faith formed by humility" (*fides humilitate formata*)—not the faith of mature Reformation theology that

---

52. Artur Rühl, *Der Einfluss der Mystik auf Denken und Entwicklung des jungen Luthers* (Oberhessen, 1960), pp. 112–14, 132–33; Bernd Moeller, "Tauler und Luther," in *La mystique Rhénane: Colloque de Strasbourg 16–19 Mai 1961* (Paris, 1963), p. 159.

53. In addition to A. V. Müller, cited above, see H. A. Oberman, "Luther and Mysticism," in Ozment, ed., *The Reformation in Medieval Perspective,* p. 229.

54. *WA* 1, p. 379.

55. "They believe that because the will has that spark it is, although feebly, inclined to what is good, and they dream that this little motion toward doing the good, which man is naturally able to make, is an act of loving God above all things" (*Lectures on Romans* [1515–16], *WA* 56, pp. 275, 1. 17).

came only by hearing God's word (*fides ex auditu*).[56] In this interpretation is correct, mysticism aided Luther against perceived Ockhamist errors in the years prior to 1518 only by leading him into a more subtle form of Pelagianism.

That far more discontinuity than continuity existed between Protestantism and mysticism has been argued repeatedly and persuasively.[57] Despite his high praise for the German mystics, Luther consistently showed no noteworthy interest in either their speculation on man's divine powers or their view of man's union with God as a deification (*Vergöttung*)—the most distinctive features of German mystical teaching. In a striking marginal comment on one of Tauler's sermons, Luther even substituted "faith" for what Tauler had called the "spark of soul or man's highest part," indicating that belief alone, not some special quality of soul, made people spiritual beings.[58] Luther also described faith as the agent of a mystical marriage

56. Bizer comments on Luther's lectures on Romans (1515–16): "Es rechtfertigt also nicht eigentlich der Glaube, sondern das Ergebnis des Glaubens, die Haltung, zu der es führt, die Selbstverleugnung in der humilitas, und der Ausdruck: fides ad iustitiam perducens, ist der gemeinten Sache genau angemessen: der Glaube rechtfertigt nicht als solcher, sondern er *führt* zur Gerechtigkeit" (*Fides ex auditu*, p. 29; see also pp. 42, 51).

57. In a perceptive contrast, Heinrich Bornkamm cited ten fundamental differences between Luther and Eckhart:

1. Less bold and speculative than Eckhart, Luther confined himself to Scripture and biblical terms.
2. He believed that religious *intellectus* was the special insight of faith, not, as Eckhart taught, a latent ability in the ground of man's soul.
3. Luther could find no "still point" in the depths of the soul which served as a medium for divine purity.
4. Luther conceived man as a whole being, not as a composite of contradictory natural and supernatural essences.
5. Luther saw man's union with God to bring a new understanding of his distance from God, while Eckhart believed it removed all sense of distinction.
6. Luther did not believe that union with God came by ascetical exercises, as the final state of contemplation, as Eckhart taught the nuns of Cologne.
7. Critical of external works and religiosity, Eckhart held that the inner work of humility performed in quest of mystical union was meritorious of grace.
8. For Luther, people were as divinely called into worldly vocations as into clerical ranks.
9. Whereas for Luther preaching and the sacraments were the only media of God's spirit and truth, Eckhart considered them external aids to the individual's retreat into the depths of the soul, where the inner word and spark of the soul served as the true media of the Spirit.
10. Luther did not share the mystic's disdain for the world as something unreal and to be surrendered—"the world was more filled with God for Luther than for Eckhart."

Eckhart and Luther (Stuttgart, 1936). For a comparison of Luther with Tauler and the *German Theology* on many of these same points, see my *Homo Spiritualis* (Leiden, 1969) and *Mysticism and Dissent* (New Haven, 1973), ch. 2.

58. *WA* 9, p. 99.

between Christ and the soul.[59] This particular passage deeply shocked traditional theologians, who protested that only a soul purified by *love* could
become so united with God.[60] Here Luther contradicted the most basic of
all medieval religious axioms: the belief that likeness to God was the indispensable condition of both saving knowledge of him and a saving relationship with him.[61] In medieval theology, only like could truly know like. This
was the underlying rationale of monastic practices: through rigorous physical and intellectual exercises to replace one's own false self with a godlike
self. It was the precondition of mystical union: "Our becoming like God
[*similitudo*]," wrote Gerson, "is the cause of our union with him."[62] And it
was the raison d'être of the sacramental system of the church: infused grace
qualitatively conforms human to divine being. The final goal of monk,
mystic, and pilgrim alike was conformity so complete that only God remained an object of consciousness, a point where likeness gave way to
identity. Medieval theology remained devoted to the proposition that God
became man so that men could be godlike.

For the medieval theologian the central religious concept was accordingly
caritas—love—not faith. The way of salvation was *fides caritate formata*, faith
formed by acts of love. Faith alone, by contrast, was only an initial intellectual assent to the data of revelation made by one who was still far more
pure and godly. *Sola fides*, all agreed, was a *fides informis*, even a *fides
mortua*—an unformed, dead faith which even demons could have. Such
faith left man on the fringe of the religious life, very much at a distance
from God. Love, not faith, was the religious glue. Love bound together the
persons of the Trinity, the soul with God, and man with his neighbor. In
medieval theology, the Holy Spirit, the reciprocal love of Father and Son,
was "uncreated love"; sacramental grace was "created love"; and meritorious works were "acts of love." Because it was the principle of likeness, love
was the principle of union.

The same reasoning underlay descriptions of human nature and the

59. *WA* 6, p. 26.
60. See Ozment, "Homo Viator: Luther and Late Medieval Theology," *HThR* 62 (1969):
275–87. Johannes von Walter comments on this famous passage in the *Freedom of a Christian*:
"Das Bild wird des mystischen Sinne vollständig entkleidet und zu einem Gleichnis der
zugerechneten Gerechtigkeit" (*Mystik und Rechtfertigkeit beim jungen Luther* [Gütersloh,
1937], p. 28). Comments Werner Elert on the same passage: "Inniger als durch das Gleichnis
des bräutlichen Verhältnisses kann Luther das Verhältnis zwischen Christus und dem
Glaubenden nicht ausdrücken. Es ist klar dass es ihm nur durch Glauben und imputierte
Gerechtigkeit zustande kommt—das ist der wesentliche und bleibende Unterschied von der
Mystik Bernhards" (*Morphologie des Luthertums*, vol. 1, *Theologie und Weltanschauung des Luthertums hauptsächlich im 16. und 17. Jahrhundert* [Munich, 1931], p. 150).
61. See above, p. 46.
62. *De mystica theologia speculativa*, cons. 41, p. 111. See above, p. 117.

efficacy of the sacraments. Medieval theologians commonly assumed that an inextinguishable spark of goodness existed in man's reason and will (*synteresis rationis et voluntatis*), a natural point at which every person, even if he did not consciously choose to be such, was conformed to God. Each person experienced this residue of prefallen and even precreated purity as pangs of conscience and an irrepressible desire for truth and goodness—a permanent reminder of man's eternal origin and original unity with God. Sacramental grace was described as a *gratia gratum faciens,* a grace that transformed man, purifying the soul and subjecting it to God. Like the *synteresis,* grace "likened" man to God in being and in act. In Thomistic terminology, it was an accidental form of the soul, a habit of godly living, the elevation and perfection of human nature. In medieval theology, opposites did not attract.

The conviction that God and man must be like each other if they were ever to be at one with each other became the theological cornerstone of the oppressive religious culture of the later Middle Ages. As early as his first lectures on the Psalms, Luther distanced himself from this fundamental medieval belief. Impressed by the way the Psalmist relied solely on God's word and promise for salvation, finding no hope whatsoever in himself, Luther drew parallels between the Old Testament faithful and contemporary men of faith; each, he discovered, possessed as much as he believed.[63] He was further struck by the way the righteous man confessed his utter dissimilarity from God. According to the Psalmist, Luther concluded, "it is not he who considers himself the most lowly of men, but he who sees himself as even the most vile, who is most beautiful to God."[64] Recognition and confession of sin actually brought God and man together.[65] In this sense "unlikeness" was the unitive principle in religion: to be conformed with God meant to agree with his judgment that all men are sinful and still believe his promise to save them nonetheless.

For Luther, the key religious problem came to be one of trust and belief—transformation from a state of doubt and uncertainty to confidence in words and promises that lacked immediate verification. The basic question was not whether one was inwardly and outwardly righteous, but whether God was truthful in his judgment of human nature and destiny.

63. See above, pp. 71–72; cf. Reinhard Schwarz, *Fides, Spes und Caritas beim jungen Luther* (Berlin, 1962).

64. Scholia to Psalm 50 (51):6, *WA* 3, pp. 287–92.

65. For a reminder of parallel themes in traditional spirituality, see Jared Wicks, S. J., *Man Yearning for Grace: Luther's Early Spiritual Teaching* (Washington, D.C., 1968). Although, as Wicks insists, we must not too hastily read the mature reformer into the young doctor of Scripture, we must also not overlook, as Wicks tends to do, the novel treatment given traditional themes by Luther.

Could God be depended upon to save those who could not fulfill his law and remained unworthy? The individual question of personal salvation remained secondary to an objective assessment of the nature of man and God.

Where did Luther get such ideas? His own imaginative reflection on the Bible was clearly basic. However, Ockhamist theology may have been equally influential, certainly far more so than any mystical tradition. Luther's Ockhamist training exposed him to a view of the world fundamentally different from that found in medieval mysticism. It was a world in which God and man related to one another by will and by words. Following Duns Scotus, Ockham rejected the view that a saving relationship with God depended in any final sense on qualities within an individual or on metaphysical connections between God, grace, and the soul. The Franciscans Scotus and Ockham here directly opposed the teaching of the Dominicans Aquinus and Eckhart. For Scotus and Ockham, salvation depended upon the trustworthiness of God's word, not on the character of the church, the sacraments, or the souls of believers. As in his philosophy Ockham made terms or verbal conventions the link between the mind and reality in matters of knowledge, so in his theology, words—divine promises—became the essential link between the soul and God in salvation.[66] Eckhart, by contrast, directly opposed Scotist covenant theology, which made infused habits of grace secondary in importance to the divine will, and defended to the point of exaggeration the Thomist view of the primacy of grace as a supernatural power within the soul.[67]

In the teaching of Scotus and Ockham, traditional religious institutions ceased to be the essential link in a great hierarchical chain of being. Their uniqueness lay rather in a contingent divine act; from an infinite number of theoretical possibilities God had chosen them to be the instruments of his will in time. For those who subscribed to such a point of view the things of religion were only as real as one could believe them to be. From Luther to the American Puritans the central religious problem of mainstream Protestantism became the certitude of salvation—not the rationality of faith or the proof of God's existence, but the trustworthiness of God's word and promise. It is not farfetched to see here the legacy of Ockham.

66. See above, pp. 39–40.
67. See Heinrich Ebeling, *Meister Eckharts Mystik: Studien zu den Geisteskämpfen um die Wende des 13. Jahrhunderts* (Aalen, 1966), pp. 146–59, and my "Eckhart and Luther: German Mysticism and Protestantism," *The Thomist*, 42 (1978): 258–80.

CHAPTER 7

Society and Politics
in the German
Reformation

Imperial Politics in the
First Half of the
Sixteenth Century

ON April 17, 1521, Martin Luther, a condemned heretic under the pope's ban, stood before Charles of Hapsburg, king of Spain and newly elected Holy Roman Emperor, at the imperial Diet of Worms. Luther was at this time thirty-eight. In the emperor's presence he refused to recant his alleged errors and made a famous declaration:

> Unless I am convinced by the testimony of Scripture or by clear reason, for I do not trust either in the pope or in councils alone, since it is well known that they have often erred and contradicted themselves, I am bound by the Scriptures I have quoted and my conscience is captive to the Word of God. I cannot and will not retract anything, for it is neither safe nor right to go against conscience. I cannot do otherwise, here I stand, may God help me, Amen.[1]

Attorneys for the church and the empire placed the adamant Luther in the camp of the Arians, Montanists, Photinians, Nestorians, Eutychians, Beghards, Waldensians, Poor Men of Lyons, Wyclifites, and Hussites—the great heresiarchs of past and recent church history.[2] Such association occurred when the point of no return had been reached with an obstinate heretic.[3] Luther departed the diet with a three-week safe-conduct from the emperor, a brief period of grace in which to reconsider before he came under the imperial ban and subject to capital punishment.

---

1. LW 32, pp. 112–113.
2. Ibid., pp. 128–29.
3. During the first Zurich Disputation (1523), Johann Faber associated Zwingli's views with Novatian, Montanist, Sabellian, Ebionite, Marcionite, Beghard, Bohemian Brethren, Wyclifite, and Hussite heresies. See G. R. Potter, *Zwingli* (Cambridge, 1976), p. 103.

Frederick the Wise (1463–1525), the elector of Saxony and Luther's highest immediate political authority, found himself in a difficult position after the Diet of Worms. On the one hand, he was advisor, friend, and subject of the emperor, who was especially beholden to him at this time for the key role he had played in Charles's election in 1519. On the other hand, Luther had brought fame, albeit now notoriety, to the new University of Wittenberg, Frederick's own creation, and of this too Frederick was proud. In addition, Luther had by this time become a national hero. German humanists championed him and many common people looked to him for deliverance from both social and religious bondage. Recalling that John Huss had attended Constance under an imperial safe-conduct and weighing the tumult he knew would result in Saxony should Luther be harmed, Frederick ignored the Edict of Worms and conspired to remove Luther to a safe refuge in Wartburg Castle.[4]

On May 8, 1521 Charles signed the warrant for Luther's arrest. Thereafter it became treason against the emperor as well as blasphemy against the church to give Luther aid and comfort.

Luther seemed to derive a perverse satisfaction from his notoriety. In August 1521, three months into his seclusion, he concluded a letter to his fretful younger associate, Philip Melanchthon, with the exhortation: "Be a sinner, Philip, and sin boldly! Only still more boldly believe and rejoice in Christ."[5] Modern critics have cited this famous statement as proof that justicification by faith leads to antinomianism. Such an interpretation, however, fails to see how accurate a description it was of Luther himself at this time—truly the boldest sinner in Christendom.

How did Luther avoid capture and execution? Why was the imperial ban not enforced? How did the Protestant Reformation, unlike so many other late medieval reform movements, escape being nipped in the bud or rendered harmless in its course? To understand Luther's survival and the success of the inchoate Reformation we must take account of the larger political rivalries and dynastic struggles of the first half of the sixteenth century. For Protestantism owed its triumph to no small extent to the manifold distractions of imperial politics.

Charles V has been described as the last medieval emperor to whom the religious and political unity of Christendom was "both the ideal purpose of

4. On Frederick's relation to Luther and the Reformation, see Paul Kirn, *Friedrich der Weise und die Kirche: Seine Kirchenpolitik vor und nach Luthers Hervortreten im Jahre 1517* (Leipzig/Berlin, 1926); and Karlheinz Blaschke, "Kürfürst Friedrich der Weise von Sachsen und die Luthersache," in *Der Reichstag zu Worms von 1521: Reichspolitik und Luthersache*, ed. Fritz Reuter (Worms, 1971), pp. 316–35.

5. *Luthers Werke in Auswahl*, ed. Hanns Rückert (Berlin, 1955), 6: 56.

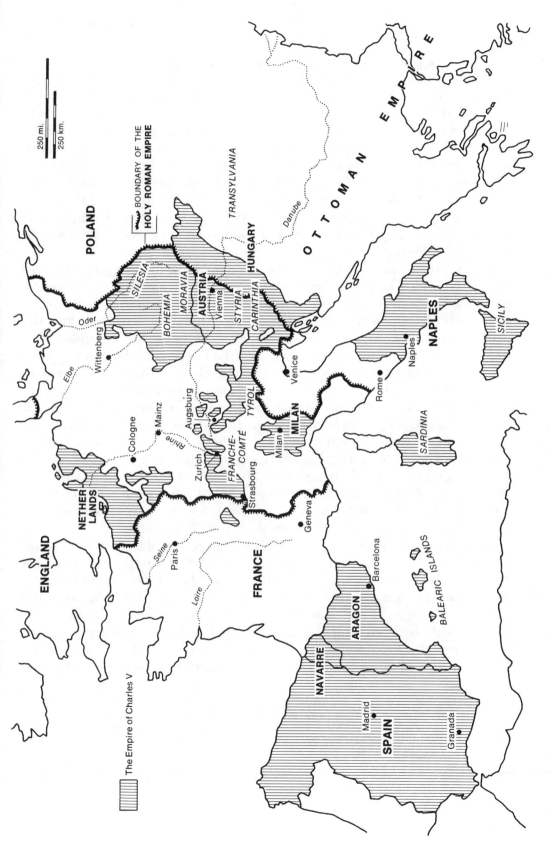

BOUNDARY OF THE
HOLY ROMAN EMPIRE

250 mi.

250 km.

POLAND

SILESIA

BOHEMIA

MORAVIA

AUSTRIA

Vienna

STYRIA

CARINTHIA

HUNGARY

TRANSYLVANIA

Danube

OTTOMAN EMPIRE

Oder

Wittenberg

Elbe

Cologne

Mainz

Rhine

Augsburg

Zurich

TYROL

FRANCHE-
COMTÉ

Strasbourg

MILAN

Milan

Venice

Rome

Naples

NAPLES

SICILY

SARDINIA

ENGLAND

NETHER-
LANDS

Seine

Paris

Loire

Geneva

FRANCE

Barcelona

BALEARIC ISLANDS

NAVARRE

ARAGON

Madrid

SPAIN

Granada

Map 1. The Empire of Charles V

his life *and* a practicable object of policy."[6] The planned accidents of birth
blessed him territorially. His father, Archduke Philip the Fair, was count of
Flanders, Holland, Zealand, Namur, and Hainault, in addition to being
duke of Brabant, Limburg, and Luxemburg. His mother, Joanna of Spain,
was the daughter of Ferdinand and Isabella. Charles profited as none before or after him from the shrewd marriage diplomacy of the House of
Hapsburg. When he came to power in Spain in 1516 he inherited a kingdom that included the Netherlands, Luxemburg, Burgundy, Alsace, Castile, Aragon, Naples, Sicily, Austria, Sardinia, the Balearics, and the newly
acquired American Spanish territories. After the Holy Roman Empire was
added in June 1519, Charles surveyed a kingdom vaster than any since the
days of Charlemagne.

Geography, however, can be a deceptive measure of strength. The very
size of Charles's kingdom became its weakness. Even in time of peace,
of which the sixteenth century knew little, communications and logistics
were difficult at best in such a diverse and sprawling kingdom, and the
distractions were constant. Imperial efforts to unify the Netherlands under
a loyal central administration clashed with the interests of the many provincial governments and the Netherlands Estates-General. Barbary pirates and
African Moors, assisted by Moriscos in Spanish coastal towns, preyed regularly on Charles's southern flanks. In addition, the Ottoman navy began at
this time to challenge Spanish ships for dominance in the Mediterranean.

Linguistic as well as geographical and political barriers handicapped the
emperor, whose native language was French. He never became fluent in
Flemish, and he learned Spanish only after he had become king. He could
speak no German, and his Latin was poor. Nor did he ever master the Slavic
languages of his Danubian possessions, which he progressively turned over
to his brother and eventual imperial successor, Ferdinand.

Charles's possessions covered over twice the geographical area of France
and completely encircled his great rival. His French counterpart, Francis I
(1515–41), was also a young man, having assumed the French throne in 1515
at age twenty. (Charles became emperor at nineteen.) In the sixteenth
century, old men were sent to die in wars created by young men.
Sandwiched between the Spanish and Austrian possessions of the
Hapsburgs, the French quickly discovered a peculiar advantage in being
surrounded: one never wanted for an immediate and unsuspecting place to

---

6. H. G. Koenigsberger, *The Hapsburgs and Europe 1516–1660* (Ithaca, 1971), p. 1. My
sketch is influenced by the works of Karl Brandi, *The Emperor Charles V*, trans. C. V.
Wedgwood (London, 1939); Otto, Archduke of Austria, *Charles V*, trans. Michael Ross
(New York, 1970); and Fernández Alverez, *Charles V: Elected Emperor and Hereditary Ruler*,
trans. J. A. Lalaguna (London, 1975).

strike. This advantage actually proved more psychologically threatening to Spain than strategically important to France; until the late 1530s, Charles and Francis managed to fight their major wars on other peoples' lands.

The French had Charles at another disadvantage: he ruled a kingdom lacking his adversary's clever internal management of royal finances. Charles repeatedly threatened, flattered, and/or made political concessions to the Cortes to obtain funds, and when these efforts failed or the promised revenues fell short, he begged loans from the Fuggers.

Charles's maternal grandfather, the emperor Maximilian I, died on January 11, 1519. His will stipulated that he be buried at the imperial residence of Wiener-Neustadt, his corpse so arranged under an altar that when the priest celebrated Mass in his memory he stood directly above Maximilian's heart, a commentary on the strong traditional piety of the Hapsburgs. For the incipient Reformation in Germany, Maximilian's death could not have been more opportune. It came precisely at the moment when Luther was coming under close official scrutiny. In August 1518, Cardinal Cajetan had summoned him to Augsburg for his first serious interrogation. In the month prior to Maximilian's death, on December 18, 1518, Frederick the Wise had protested to Cajetan that he would permit no action against Luther until the reformer had first received a public hearing. At the very moment when forces were gathering to strike Luther down, Maximilian's death dramatically shifted attention to the more important matter of Maximilian's successor.

Although Hapsburg succession to the imperial throne had become a century-old tradition, both the pope and the king of France opposed Charles's election, fearing any further expansion of an already too powerful Hapsburg kingdom. Strong opposition also existed within Spain itself, especially among Charles's Castilian subjects, who, seeing only increased hardship for themselves in Charles's new imperial office, would greet it with the *comunero* revolt.

Charles and Francis competed fiercely for the imperial crown. Francis attacked Charles as politically naive and the son of a mad woman, a reference to his mother's insanity, while Charles presented Francis as a despot intent on ending traditional German liberties. The papacy initially encouraged Henry VIII and Frederick the Wise to stand as contenders, but neither was a realistic candidate. Frederick, the more credible of the two, lacked both the ambition and wherewithal to administer the empire, and his election would, in time, have had a divisive effect. In the end Rome supported the king of France, while Frederick, who actually won (and refused) a first-ballot vote, became Charles's champion and easily drew the other electors into the Spanish camp. Frederick apparently hoped at this time to marry his

Frederick the Wise Praying to the Blessed Virgin. Lucas Cranach the Elder. Luther's protector, Frederick the Wise, was a model of Catholic piety. As a youth he had gone on a pilgrimage to Jerusalem (1493). He spent a lifetime assembling one of Europe's largest relic collections, holding over 19,000 pieces by 1520, including such treasures as a piece of the burning bush before which Moses stood, soot from the fiery furnace through which Shadrach, Meshach, and Abednego trod, and a complete corpse of an innocent slain by King Herod. Frederick reportedly admired Luther and was attracted to certain of his teachings. His deep belief in providence may also have given him pause before the Reformation. However, he supported Luther primarily for political reasons and out of pride in the University of Wittenberg, which he had founded in 1502, not because of any deep personal commitment to Lutheran doctrine.

nephew, Crown Prince John Frederick, to Charles's youngest sister, Catalina, thereby enhancing Saxon power within the empire. The subsequent success of the Reformation in Saxony caused these ambitious plans to be abandoned, however, and John Frederick, who succeeded his father as Saxon elector in 1532, became instead Luther's most outspoken princely supporter—hardly the role of a proper imperial brother-in-law. The emperor's brother Ferdinand reportedly said that he would prefer his sister drowned than married to the future Protestant elector of Saxony.[7]

The seven imperial electors voted unanimously for Charles on June 28, 1519, and he received his crown in Aachen on October 23, 1520 in a service conducted by the archbishops of Mainz and Trier. One elector who had initially expressed strong reservations about Charles and favored Francis was the archbishop of Mainz, Albrecht of Brandenburg, the object of Luther's attack on indulgences in 1517. Brandenburg and Saxony had long been rival political dynasties. Frederick the Wise had become especially suspicious of his neighbor after Albrecht obtained the archbishopic of Mainz in 1515, his third major ecclesiastical office and the most powerful. The pope, finding Albrecht his strongest ally among the electors, attempted to strengthen him by granting dispensations that enabled Albrecht to hold multiple offices and an archbishopric at the noncanonical age of twenty-one. (Archbishops were supposed to be thirty years of age.) Frederick, however, interpreted Albrecht's success as a political maneuver against Saxony, for Saxony fell within the ecclesiastical jurisdiction of the archbishop of Mainz.

To fund his ecclesiastical offices, Albrecht had borrowed heavily from the House of Fugger, incurring a debt in excess of 26,000 ducats. Through the sale of the St. Peter's indulgence throughout his dioceses, he hoped to repay this great debt. The papacy, the House of Fugger, and Albrecht himself had a large financial stake in the success of the indulgence, which was to be preached for eight years, half of the proceeds going to Rome and half to Albrecht and his creditors. John Tetzel, the immediate object of Luther's protest, was commissioned to preach the indulgence because he was a veteran indulgence salesman in the employ of both the papacy and the Fuggers. Although the motives of Frederick the Wise were strictly political, he supported Luther's opposition to Albrecht's extension of the indulgence into Saxon lands. Already before the new emperor was chosen, these ecclesiopolitical events had created a fateful alliance between Saxon politics and Lutheran religious reform.

Charles paid dearly for his election, both in gold coins and in political

7. Kirn, *Friedrich der Weise und die Kirche,* p. 149.

M D X X III
SIC·OCVLOS·SIC·ILLE·GENAS·SIC·ORA·FEREBAT·
ANNO·ETATIS·SVE·XXXIIII

ALBERTVS·MI·DI·SA·SANC·ROMANAE·ECCLAE·TI·SAN·
CHRYSOGONI·PBR·CARDINA·MAGVN·AC·MAGDE·
ARCHIEPS·ELECTOR·IMPE·PRIMAS·ADMINI·
HALBER·MARCHI·BRANDENBVRGENSIS·

Cardinal Albrecht of Brandenburg. Albrecht Dürer. Albrecht authorized the preaching of the St. Peter's indulgence in the dioceses under his jurisdiction. Proceeds from the sale were to assist the rebuilding of St. Peter's in Rome and the repayment of debts incurred by Albrecht in accumulating bishoprics in Halberstadt, Magdeburg, and Mainz. Luther's protest against this indulgence in October 1517 has come to mark the beginning of the Reformation.

IACOBVS FVGKER CIVIS AVGVSTÆ

Jacob Fugger the Rich of Augsburg. Sebald Beham. Loans from the Fuggers of Augsburg, sixteenth-century Europe's wealthiest banking house, made possible Albrecht of Brandenburg's accumulation of three major church offices and permitted Charles I of Spain to win the imperial election of 1519.

concessions. The electors received 850,000 florins, mostly in bribes; 500,000 of these were borrowed from the banking houses of Fugger and Welser. Among the political concessions were the use of German and Latin as the official languages of the empire; no stationing of Spanish troops on German soil; appointment of only Germans to imperial posts; and consultation with the estates of the empire when political decisions affecting it were made. Charles also restored the lapsed imperial Supreme Court and Council of Regency and granted the Council power to govern in his absence. He further agreed that he would sit in judgment on no German without due cause and a public hearing.

Charles's election revived the medieval idea of a universal emperor, both in Charles's mind and in those of his enemies. In the imperial mythology of the Middle Ages, the emperor represented God's justice on earth; he enforced peace in both the secular and ecclesiastical realm. That had been Frederick II's concept of office, and Marsilius of Padua had praised it in support of Louis IV of Bavaria and Philip the Fair, two rulers who won major contests with Rome. Dante gave it a classic formulation. He argued in his *Monarchia* that a universal political monarchy, reflecting the hierarchical order of the world, was the key to peace and like Marsilius, he opposed papal aspiration to world monarchy.

Charles's associates identified him with this medieval imperial tradition. After his election as emperor, his tutor and closest advisor, Mercurio Gattinara, a student of Dante, assured him:

> Sire, God has been very merciful to you: he has raised you above all the kings and princes of Christendom to a power such as no sovereign has enjoyed since your ancestor Charles the Great. He has set you on the way towards world monarchy, towards the uniting of all Christendom under a single shepherd.[8]

The French and the pope plotted the opposition to Charles. The French had most to fear from the Hapsburgs, but the pope had long been alarmed by the emperor's control of Naples and Milan and resented imperial efforts to arbitrate Europe's religious differences independently. Entanglement in military operations against these European opponents and the Ottoman Turks, who increasingly threatened the eastern Hapsburg lands, prevented Charles from even setting foot within the empire between 1521 and 1530, the formative years of the Reformation. The emperor's total preoccupation with his enemies made Luther's survival possible; it was the major political factor in the Reformation's success.

8. Cited by Frances A. Yates, *Astraea: The Imperial Theme in the Sixteenth Century* (London, 1975), p. 26.

Between 1521 and 1559 the French and the Spanish fought four wars over their respective dynastic claims. The first ended in so thorough an imperial victory at Pavia on February 24, 1525 that Spanish troops took the French king himself captive to Madrid. Charles's ally at the time, King Henry VIII of England, advocating what would become his own favored method of handling political and domestic problems, urged Francis's execution posthaste.[9] Henry had elaborate plans at this time; with the French king out of the way, he hoped to renew English dynastic claims and take much of France for himself. However, the execution of a legitimate monarch was a drastic step in the sixteenth century; it worked against the self-interests of royalty everywhere, as Elizabeth Tudor came later to know far better than her father, when she was forced to execute the exiled Mary, queen of Scots.

Charles, war-weary and broke, was in no position to undertake the reconstruction of Europe desired by Henry. He chose a far less final solution in the Treaty of Madrid (January 14, 1526). This agreement required Francis to renounce all claims to Burgundy, the Netherlands, and French Italian territories; to take Charles's eldest sister, Eleanore, the recently widowed queen of Portugal, to wife; and to surrender his two sons by a previous marriage as hostages to be held in Madrid. Charles further required the French king to restore to power Charles of Bourbon, a recently imprisoned French magnate and longtime political foe whose freedom, it was believed, would so preoccupy Francis at home that he would be unable to make war abroad. Henry VIII never forgave the emperor for turning his back on so golden an opportunity to enhance both Spanish and English power at French expense; thereafter he plotted with Charles's enemies to limit imperial power on the continent.

After the defeat of the French at Pavia, the broad wings of the Hapsburg eagle seemed to overshadow the whole of Europe, giving substance to fears that Charles intended to recreate the old Roman Empire. The French, however, were only down, not yet out. Francis had signed the Treaty of Madrid under obvious duress, and such agreements were neither morally nor legally binding. As soon as he had safely crossed the border into France, he renounced the treaty and began preparations for a new war against the Spanish, this time supported by powerful new allies. To maintain a balance of power, the League of Cognac formed against Charles on May 22,

---

9. See J. J. Scarisbrick, *Henry VIII* (Berkeley, 1968), pp. 137–38. In addition to Thomas More and John Fisher, who opposed the Act of Supremacy, and his shrewdest advisor, Thomas Cromwell, who protected suspected heretics too well and was blamed for the king's brief, unsuccessful political marriage to Anne of Cleves, Henry also executed two of his wives (on apparently justified charges of adultery): Anne Boleyn and Catherine Howard.

1526; it brought together France, Florence, Venice, Milan, the pope, and Charles's former ally, England.

The pope's involvement in the League particularly enraged the emperor, who soon had an unexpected, bittersweet revenge. In May 1527 unpaid imperial troops, many of whom were German mercenaries, mutinied in Rome and sacked the city, killing many civilians, looting churches, raping nuns, and taking the pope himself prisoner. Although he defended the event as a fitting punishment for the treacherous pope, the idealistic Charles was deeply shocked by such an outrage. His biographers cite it as the beginning of the melancholia that plagued him until his abdication in 1555.

As he had done earlier with the captive king of France, Charles permitted the pope's restoration to power. He released Clement VII on condition that he would promise to call a general council of the church to deal with the religious revolt in Germany, which by the late 1520s had become firmly entrenched. This was not a realistic pledge to extract from the pope; no more than Francis I had intended to heed the Treaty of Madrid did Clement intend to convene a general council of the church, if he could avoid it. Sixteenth-century popes still had vivid memories of the fifteenth-century councils of Constance and Basel, which had successfully asserted conciliar supremacy over the papacy. Preservation of the papal monarchy obsessed Renaissance popes, and after the mid-fifteenth century they tolerated councils only as limited instruments of their own will. While pressure for a general church council to deal with the Lutheran revolt began to build as early as 1526, such a council would not actually convene until a full twenty years later.

The second Hapsburg-Valois war ended in the summer of 1529 after an unsuccessful French campaign in Italy. In the Peace of Barcelona (June 1529) Charles forced the pope, who had assisted the French, to recognize imperial claims to Naples and cooperate with the emperor against the Lutherans. To seal the new agreement, Clement crowned Charles emperor in Bologna in 1530, the last such papal coronation of an emperor. Charles made peace with France in the Treaty of Cambrai (August 5, 1529), which rebound Francis to the basic conditions of the Treaty of Madrid, while conceding Burgundy to the French. The cords of Cambrai, however, hobbled the French king no more successfully than those of Madrid had done.

During the 1520s the Turks also began to figure prominently in the political success of the Reformation. By defeating the king of Hungary at the Battle of Mohacs in August 1526, they exposed Austrian Hapsburg lands to attack and threatened the whole of central Europe. This forced Charles to take a firm stand in eastern Europe as well, and at the very time when his representatives were negotiating with Protestants in Germany at the Diet of Speyer. Turkish success at Mohacs made forceful action against the Lutheran princes impossible; Charles needed German troops of whatever religious persuasion to man the new eastern front. His representatives at Speyer gave the Protestants an important concession: the promise of a fair hearing before a general council of the church. This promise effectually suspended the Edict of Worms against Luther and guaranteed Protestants at least their present status until a church council could be convened.

By 1530 the second war with France had been successfully concluded and the Turkish onslaught, which reached the gates of Vienna in 1529, had been checked. Charles at last was in a position to deal directly with his German subjects. The second Diet of Speyer in 1529 had alerted Protestants to the emperor's intention not to keep the promises of the first. Charles chose the imperial Diet of Augsburg in 1530 as the occasion to resolve the great religious dispute personally.

Luther was not permitted to attend this diet. Sequestered in nearby Coburg Castle, he did send instructions and encouragement almost daily to the Protestant representatives, who were led by Melanchthon. To bolster the faint-hearted Melanchthon, who inclined easily to compromise and suffered depressions, Luther once offered the consolation that the worst that could befall the negotiating team would be their execution.[10]

The final pronouncement of the diet rejected both the Lutheran Augsburg Confession, which Melanchthon had written in a mildly compromising spirit, and the Zwinglian *Confessio Tetrapolitana,* which represented the religious beliefs of the cities of Strasbourg, Constance, Lindau, and Memmingen. In a new attempt to enforce the Edict of Worms, Charles ordered all Protestant territories to return to traditional religious practices by April 1531. This was wishful thinking overriding political reality: the Reformation had by this time become too well established to be commanded away. Scores of cities and towns were now totally or predominantly Protestant; hundreds of Protestant clergy had wives and families; monasteries had been dissolved and their endowments devoted to new purposes. Was all of this now to be reversed in the space of a year?

The Protestant response was as uncompromising as the emperor's ultimatum. In February 1531, Protestants organized a new defensive alliance, the Schmalkaldic League, which quickly grew to embrace electoral Brandenburg and Saxony, Prussia, Hesse, Mansfeld, Brunswick, Anhalt, and other territories containing twenty imperial cities. In the late 1520s, princes in Lutheran lands had assumed the legal and administrative power of the

10. *WABr* 5, pp. 399–400.

old Catholic bishops (Luther described such princes as "emergency bishops"),[11] and consistories or governing boards composed of roughly equal numbers of lawyers and pastors chosen by the princes had sprung up to guide church reform and reorganization. Following the lead of Saxon jurists, Lutheran theologians defended the right of the princes to resist the "tyranny" of the pope and the emperor. Whereas Luther had previously admonished his followers to suffer tyranny passively and the German princes to obey the emperor as their superior, after the Diet of Augsburg, he too endorsed active resistance in self-defense and for conscience's sake, that is, both as a secular and as a religious duty.[12]

Although full-scale war between the emperor and the League was imminent in 1531, more distant drums again delayed a showdown. Soon after the Diet of Augsburg adjourned a new Turkish offensive began in eastern Europe. This new danger forced still another interim agreement, the Peace of Nuremberg (July 1532), in which the emperor pledged once again to delay action against Protestants, pending a general church council.

Exceedingly heavy hung the head that wore the imperial crown. In the mid-1530s the king of France, regrouping his forces, broke the Treaty of Cambrai and reasserted French claims to Milan. Once again Charles watched peace with France slip from his hands. Infuriated, he renewed an earlier public challenge to the French king to face him in a duel, an action that reveals the emperor's medieval temper of mind as well as his understandable frustration.

This time Francis determined to have a victory. He checkmated the pope, now Charles's staunch ally, by arranging the marriage of his son, the future Henry II, to Catherine de Medici, the pope's niece. Then, in February 1536, Francis, who bore the title "most Christian king," signed a formal alliance with Suleiman the Magnificent; Christian joined Turk against Christian. This French-Ottoman alliance held through two wars with Charles, both of which saw imperial armies invade France. The first ended in a standoff negotiated by the pope (June 1538), the second, in still another one-sided Hapsburg victory (1544). In the Peace of Crépy (September 19) that concluded the latter, Francis agreed to assist imperial armies against

11. On this development, see Karl Holl, "Luther und das landesherrliche Kirchenregiment," in *Gesammelte Aufsätze zur Kirchengeschichte*, vol. 1, *Luther* (Tübingen, 1923), 326–80; H.-W. Krumwiede, *Zur Entstehung des landesherrlichen Kirchenregiments in Kursachsen und Braunschweig-Wolfenbüttel* (Göttingen, 1967); Irmgard Höss, "The Lutheran Church of the Reformation: Problems of its Formation and Organization in the Middle and North German Territories," in *The Social History of the Reformation*, ed. L. P. Buck and J. W. Zophy (Columbus, 1973), pp. 317–39.

12. *Dr. M. Luther's Warning to His Dear German People* (1531), *LW* 47, pp. 11–55 (= *WA* 30/3, pp. 276–320). See below, pp. 270–71.

Emperor Charles V. Monogrammist M R. An aged and weary Charles V in 1547, the year his armies defeated the Protestant princes of Saxony and Hesse.

the Turks and the Protestants, while Charles magnanimously promised a Hapsburg princess for Francis's second son and a wedding gift of either Milan or the Netherlands. This was a strange concession for so complete a victor and had it come to pass, it is doubtful that it would have brought Charles the peace he so long desired, for easy success did not sate sixteenth-century political appetites. After Francis's death in March 1547, the offer was not extended to his successor and hence was never realized.

France was very much the loser in the long Hapsburg-Valois contest, which finally ended in 1559 with the Treaty of Cateau Cambrésis. Thereafter, civil and religious war left France too internally divided to mount another serious military challenge to Spain. The Spanish turned their attention to the Mediterranean and the Netherlands, and the English became their new adversary in the contest for European hegemony.

In the year of Francis's death, Charles also subdued the Schmalkaldic

League. On April 24, 1547, under the leadership of the duke of Alva, imperial forces crushed the Protestant armies of John Frederick at Mühlberg. Both John Frederick and Philip of Hesse were taken captive, and Protestant territories and cities fell under what appeared to be the sure control of imperial governors.

Even devastating military defeat could not stay the German Reformation at this late date. Before Charles could enjoy his victory over the Protestants a breach opened with his brother Ferdinand on the question of imperial succession. Charles had earlier engineered Ferdinand's election as king of the Romans, which made him the official heir to the imperial throne. By 1551, however, Charles wanted his son, Philip, to succeed him as emperor, a wish to which Ferdinand would not accede. This rift weakened Charles militarily within the empire, and Protestants quickly took advantage of it. Under the leadership of Maurice of Saxony, German princes, finding an ally in Henry II of France, rallied to defeat Charles's army at Innsbruck in 1552. In August of that same year Charles signed the humiliating Peace of Passau, which set the captive Protestant princes free and recognized the right of Lutherans to worship according to the dictates of their consciences without imperial interference. The agreement effectively ended the emperor's decades-long quest to restore the religious unity of Europe.

On September 25, 1555, the Peace of Augsburg made fully legal the religious divisions that had so long existed in fact. Although the precise phrase, "cuius regio, eius religio," was not coined until a later date,[13] this principle now reigned throughout the empire: where the ruler was Lutheran, the religion would remain Lutheran; where Catholic, Catholic. The emperor and the Catholic estates pledged to respect those who governed their religious lives by the Augsburg Confession, and Lutherans in turn agreed to respect those who chose to remain Catholic. Protestants caught in Catholic lands were given the option of emigrating to territories that practiced a congenial religion, and Catholics received the same privilege. A so-called ecclesiastical reservation, attached to the agreement, required all archbishops, bishops, prelates, and priests who abandoned the old faith for the new after 1552 to forfeit their offices or benefices and all income derived therefrom.[14] Protestants largely ignored the reservation, however, and their success in usurping such offices and incomes became a major

13. It was first used in 1582 by the legist Joachim Stephani. See Lewis W. Spitz, "Imperialism, Particularism and Toleration in the Holy Roman Empire," in *The Massacre of St. Bartholomew: Reappraisals and Documents,* ed. Alfred Soman (The Hague, 1974), p. 72.

14. *Church and State Through the Centuries: A Collection of Historic Documents,* trans. and ed. S. Z. Ehler and J. B. Morrall (New York, 1967), pp. 167–70.

factor in the outbreak of the Thirty Years War in the first half of the seventeenth century.

Soundly defeated within the empire and broken in spirit, Charles V abdicated his various offices to Philip and Ferdinand in October and November 1555 and quietly retired to a monastery. Martin Luther, his first great challenge and in a sense also his nemesis within the empire, offered the following evaluation of the emperor in a tabletalk in 1540.

> Charles is a melancholy and passionate man, but he is not heroic. He does not understand our cause, even when someone reads our books to him. Were he a Scipio, an Alexander, or a Pyrrhus, he would break through the papal net and conquer the Germans himself. He begins many things, but completes few. He captured Tunis, then let it go; he conquered France [at Pavia], but then restored her. The same thing happened when he subdued Rome [in 1527]. He does not follow through with anything. He yields easily in negotiations and this is not because he is a generous spirit. But what am I saying? Germany is without a head. Philip [Melanchthon] has said that Germany is a blind Polyphemus. That is the greatest burden a country must bear, to be without a ruler.[15]

Lutheran Social Philosophy

AT the beginning of the twentieth century two prominent German historians, Wilhelm Dilthey (1883–1911) and Ernst Troeltsch (1865–1923), focused a long debate over whether the Reformation was still medieval in outlook or anticipated basic values of the modern world. Dilthey, an intellectual historian and philosopher, perceived the Reformation to be the religious counterpart of the Renaissance, as Jacob Burckhardt had depicted it. Sharing Hegel's glowing praise of Luther's theology as a major step in mankind's progression to full self-consciousness, Dilthey opposed thinkers like Friedrich Nietzsche, who despised the Reformation as a retarding force in the development of secular civilization, a throwback to the "slave mentality" of traditional Christianity. Dilthey drew on Luther's Reformation tracts of 1520—the *Address to the Christian Nobility of the German Nation* and the *Freedom of the Christian*—to argue that the Reformation was "modern" at three points. First, he saw the doctrine of justification by faith as a defense of the "autocracy of the believing person," an anticipation of the modern concept of individual freedom,

15. *Luthers Werke in Auswahl, Tischreden*, ed. Otto Clemen (Berlin, 1950): 8, no. 5042, p. 206.

the ultimate origins of which Dilthey actually located before Luther in Franciscan piety and late medieval mysticism. Second, Dilthey believed that Luther had uniquely enhanced the inner, personal side of religion against its stultifying external and institutional forms. Finally, he praised Luther for decisively overcoming monasticism and giving his blessing to the secular world. For Dilthey, the Reformation first made it possible for Christian values to penetrate German society and politics and transform German culture.[16]

Dilthey's more famous contemporary, the sociologist Max Weber (1864–1920), whose *Protestant Ethic and the Spirit of Capitalism* appeared in 1904/05, made a similar positive evaluation of Protestantism, but in its later Calvinist and Puritan forms and from a strictly socioeconomic point of view. Weber perceived an "elective affinity" between the methodical religious discipline that Calvinists imposed upon their lives (the "Protestant ethic") and the new ability of people to deal rationally with reality that nurtured modern capitalist institutions (the "spirit of Capitalism").[17] Weber considered the early Lutheran and Calvinist movements, roughly the first two generations of Protestantism, to be still within the ascetic mold of medieval Christianity. However, he found in them the seeds of developments he considered modern. This was especially true of Luther's concept of calling *(Beruf)*, which gave secular vocations a new importance, and Calvin's acceptance of the economic realities of the mid-sixteenth century, in particular his willingness to condone interest on loans.[18]

Ernst Troeltsch, historian and sociologist, entered the debate over the Reformation's modernity as Dilthey's major critic and his work continues to dominate the subject. Acknowledging elements of truth in the work of Dilthey and Weber, Troeltsch believed that the Reformation, especially in its Lutheran form, remained by every measure more medieval than modern in outlook. Far from advocating individual freedom and au-

16. Dilthey's views are summarized in his "Auffassung und Analyse des Menschen im 15. und 16. Jahrhundert" (1891/92), excerpted in Heinrich Bornkamm, *Luther im Spiegel der deutschen Geistesgeschichte* (Heidelberg, 1955), pp. 232–37. See also Bornkamm's discussion of Dilthey (ibid., pp. 65–70). English excerpts of Dilthey's famous treatise are in Lewis W. Spitz, *The Reformation: Material or Spiritual* (Boston, 1962), pp. 8–16.

17. Weber's thesis is debated in two collections: *The Protestant Ethic and Modernization: A Comparative View*, ed. S. N. Eisenstadt (New York, 1968); and *Protestantism, Capitalism, and Social Science: The Weber Thesis Controversy*, ed. R. W. Green (Lexington, Mass., 1973).

18. When Calvin pronounced the charging of interest on productively invested capital to be "nonusurious," he actually did no more than acknowledge what had long been the practice in Geneva and also tolerated by Catholic authorities. See Herbert Lüthy, "Once Again: Calvinism and Capitalism," in *The Protestant Ethic and Modernization*, p. 106. R. W. Tawney recognized the grudging character of Calvin's pronouncement. *Religion and the Rise of Capitalism* (Gloucester, Mass., 1962), pp. 94, 108, 113.

tonomy, Luther's Reformation remained a conservative "church type" of religion. It conceived salvation to be something finished, certain, and sure, a pure gift independent of all individual efforts, and needing only to be appropriated by simple, naive faith.[19] In stark contrast to modern people, whom Troeltsch saw as deriving their highest ideals independently of biblical revelation or any other form of external authority, Lutherans and Calvinists at best only "modified" the Church-dominated civilization of the Middle Ages.[20] They replaced the Catholic doctrine of salvation with a more individualistic concept, but they still attempted to regulate the whole of life—politics and society, science and education, law and commerce—by the standards of a supernatural revelation; their ideal society was one based on the Bible, a "Bibliocracy."[21] They also transformed traditional asceticism into an inner attitude of self-denial, a so-called worldly asceticism that replaced the otherworldliness and escapism of monasticism, but a medieval point of view still dominated their thinking.[22] In Troeltsch's estimation, the overall effect of the Reformation was to perpetuate the "medieval spirit" for two more centuries, until Newtonian science and eighteenth-century philosophy began to secure the victory of truly modern ideas and values.[23]

Despite this overall negative judgment, Troeltsch recognized four modern tendencies in classic Protestantism. The first was its rejection of monasticism and the traditional idealization of celibacy and virginity, which Troeltsch believed helped increase the birth rate, bring about new patterns of family life, make marriage a more ethical and personal matter, and secure a mutual right to divorce for the marriage partners. Protestants did not, however, supplant the medieval patriarchical model of the family; indeed, they are seen to have perpetuated traditional patriarchical culture both at home, where the father dominated wife and children, and in politics, where the prince was absolutely supreme.[24]

19. *The Social Teachings of the Christian Churches,* (New York, 1960), 2: 481.

20. *Protestantism and Progress: A Historical Study of the Relation of Protestantism to the Modern World,* trans. W. Montgomery (Boston, 1958; first English trans., 1912), p. 48. See the assessment of Troeltsch's work by F. W. Kantzenbach, "Die Protestantismusthese von Ernst Troeltsch," *Zeitschrift für bayerische Kirchengeschichte* 42 (1973): 242–59.

21. *Protestantism and Progress,* p. 70.

22. Ibid., p. 80.

23. Ibid., pp. 85–86. "All [that Protestantism] has anywhere done is to favour, strengthen, colour, and modify the course of the development [of modernity], while in some cases it maintained and even reinforced the opposing influences drawn from the late medieval view of life. The modern state, its freedom and constitutional form, its officialdom and military system, modern economics and social stratification, modern science and art, are everywhere, to a greater or less extent, already arising before and apart from [the Reformation]. They have their roots in late medieval developments; above all, in the growth of town life and the territorial state and . . . in the formation of new ideas and forces which characterized the fruitful centuries from the fifteenth to the seventeenth" (ibid., p. 172).

24. Ibid., pp. 93–96.

A second modern tendency in classic Protestantism, according to Troeltsch, was its support of Roman and natural law in opposition to traditional church or canon law, a movement that assisted the evolution of the modern state. The impulse to create a godly society also led Protestants, especially Calvinists, to resist tyrants who denied them the freedom to worship as they chose. On the other hand, Troeltsch recognized that Lutheranism became a bulwark of the authoritarian Prussian state and, once in power in Geneva, Calvinists attempted to erect an intolerant theocracy.[25]

Troeltsch agreed with Weber in finding a third failed modern tendency of the Reformation in the area of economic organization. The Protestant belief in the spiritual equality of all vocations helped break down the medieval view of the superiority of the clergy over the laity and of religious good works over ordinary secular labor. Troeltsch also agreed with Weber that this development became more advanced in Calvinism, which, both believed, adjusted more readily to modern economic institutions, than in Lutheranism, which clung to the values of traditional agrarian society.[26]

Troeltsch cited as a final modern tendency the Reformation's embracing of humanist educational reforms, which initially encouraged critical historical scholarship and a degree of independent judgment in Protestant schools. Steps in this direction proved also to be halting, however, and a narrow confessionalism and resurgent interest in Aristotelian philosophy dominated many Protestant universities in the second half of the sixteenth century.[27]

Troeltsch believed that Anabaptists and Spirituals, who represented what he called the "sect type" of religion, progressed far more in both the domestic and political sphere than Lutherans and Calvinists, granting women greater independence in the home and demanding that their churches be free from state control.[28] Like modern Marxist scholars, Troeltsch accused Luther and Calvin of lowering their religious expectations in order to win political acceptance of their reforms and saw Anabaptists and Spirituals as placing fidelity to high spiritual ideals above mere political success. His description of the radicals of the sixteenth century as precocious defenders of the separation of church and state, free will, and pacifism has won Troeltsch a large and admiring audience among modern scholars.

25. Ibid., pp. 102–09.
26. Ibid., pp. 129–30.
27. Ibid., pp. 146–47.
28. Ibid., pp. 95–96, 135, 139, 174. More recent scholarship challenges the argument that Anabaptists gave women greater independence. See Claus-Peter Clasen, *Anabaptism: A Social History, 1525–1618, Switzerland, Austria, Moravia, South and Central Germany* (Ithaca, 1972), pp. 207–09.

At no point were Troeltsch's criticisms of classic Protestantism more effective than when he dealt with Luther's views on religion and society. He portrayed Luther as a very conservative man, who, convinced that he was living in the last days of the world, urged his followers to retreat into religion and remain "aloof from the world."[29] Troeltsch supported this thesis by pointing to Luther's own distinction between the believer's loyalty and behavior as a Christian and his loyalty and behavior as a member of secular society. As a religious person, Luther argued, one was subject to the law of love and the highest spiritual ideals, while as a citizen of the state, one had to obey laws and follow customs that seemed to fall far short of such ideals. In Troeltsch's estimation, Luther hereby bound the believer as much to the state and its unchristian ways as to the religious teaching of the church; he expected Christians to accept secular institutions as expressions of the created order and divine law "just as [they] accept sun and rain, storm and wind." The effect of such a theology, Troeltsch argued, was the inculcation of unquestioning obedience to reigning political authority. R. W. Tawney, who followed Troeltsch on this issue, concluded of Luther: "The logic of his religious premises ... riveted on the social thought of Protestantism a dualism, which, as its implications developed, emptied religion of its social content and society of its soul."[30] A majority of modern scholars have agreed with Troeltsch and Tawney in finding Luther the least socially progressive of the Protestant reformers.[31]

Luther has not been treated with complete fairness on this issue, in large part because the historical context of his social philosophy has been ignored. Caution was the order of the day in the first decade of the Reformation, and had Protestant leaders been less willing to wait and watch, their reforms would quickly have lost essential magisterial support, which, with few exceptions, was always initially very grudgingly given. Better gradual success than sure failure, most reasoned. Zwingli's advice to his co-worker Leo Jud became a common Protestant experience: "Sometimes you must do what you want least in order to attain what you want most."[32] In the name of law and order, Protestants tolerated the continuance of traditional religious practices long after the Reformation had been effectively established and such practices exposed as unbiblical. Protestants in Wittenberg and

29. *The Social Teachings of the Christian Churches* 2: 495–503, 523–44.
30. *Religion and the Rise of Capitalism*, p. 101.
31. The popular textbook of Helmut Koenigsberger and George Mosse describes Luther as setting magistrates not only *in loco parentis*, but even *in loco Dei* (*Europe in the Sixteenth Century*, p. 130). On the other hand, Koenigsberger and Mosse can appreciate the way the Reformation "inaugurated a new stage in the evolution of secular society" (ibid., p. 133).
32. "Faciendum enim interdum, quod minime velis, ut, quod maxime velis, aliquando sequatur" (*Zwingli Werke*, 7: 220; cited by Potter, *Zwingli*, p. 76, n. 3).

Zurich, for example, waited until 1525 before the Mass was officially abolished, although the Reformation had succeeded in Wittenberg in 1522 and in Zurich in 1523. Luther willingly slackened the pace of the Reformation in Wittenberg at the insistence of Elector Frederick the Wise, who demanded that religious reforms proceed with majority support, preferably a consensus, and no hint of tumult.[33] John Calvin learned the lesson of measured religious reform more slowly than the other major reformers; his aggressiveness in conforming Genevans to God's law led to his exile from Geneva for almost five years.[34]

The distinction between the believer's responsibility as a religious person and his duty as a member of secular society was not peculiar to Luther's theology alone. On the one hand, it expressed a common Protestant rejection of the medieval conception of society as a unified body of Christians *(corpus Christianum),* a social vision Protestants believed had blurred the differences between ecclesiastical and secular power during the Middle Ages. In the 1520s and 1530s revolutionary peasants and Anabaptists still clung to this vision and forcibly attempted to conform the two spheres in the name of religion. On the other hand, the dual personality of the believer helped clarify the civic responsibilities of Protestants before magistrates, who needed reassurance that a religion based on faith alone did not bode endless social disruption, especially in light of the radical social and political experiments of the 1520s. Zwingli and Calvin, who have been misleadingly described as "theocrats," were as careful to differentiate temporal and spiritual spheres of authority as Luther. At the outset of the Reformation in Zurich, Zwingli wrote a major tract on the subject, *On Divine and Human Righteousness* (1523), in which he both sharply distinguished and closely interrelated the internal righteousness that came only by faith and the external righteousness instilled by the magistrate's sword.[35] In Geneva close cooperation between the Consistory and the city councils never reached the point of erasing the legal distinctions between secular and ecclesiastical power, not even at the height of Calvin's reign, when men loyal to him dominated both offices.[36]

Luther, however, did make this issue peculiarly his own, and this distinction stands out in every social issue he addressed. Consistent with his theology, which opposed the imposition of monastic perfection upon the laity, he

33. See Ozment, *The Reformation in the Cities* (New Haven, 1975), pp. 138–45.
34. See below, p. 362.
35. In *Zwingli: Hauptschriften,* ed. Fritz Blanke et al., vol. 7, *Zwingli, der Staatsmann,* ed. R. Pfister (Zurich, 1952), pp. 35–104. See the discussion in my *Reformation in the Cities,* pp. 133–34.
36. See below, pp. 366–67, 372.

rejected the subjection of secular society to the standards of ideal Christian behavior. What was ideal for Christians was not necessarily a basis for the organization of society. While agreeing with radicals like Jacob Strauss that true Christians should, according to their ability, loan to needy neighbors without expectation of any return beyond the principal, as the New Testament taught, he denied that all charging and payment of interest on loans was sinful. Condemning the usurious exactions of Rome and ecclesiastical foundations and exposing as usury such widespread secular practices as taking interest under the guise of a delayed sale *(Zinskauf)*, Luther also acknowledged the propriety of charging 4 to 6 percent interest on certain loans and warned against conveying the impression that people were free to ignore usurious contracts into which they had freely entered. Such economic issues were increasingly seen to be matters of individual conscience rather than strict gospel commands.[37]

The same was true of paying tithes for the support of clergy and magistrates. In making such payments, Christians freely submitted to secular, not divine, law. Luther and his followers left no doubt, however, about both the propriety and expectation of such payments—and well before the Peasants' Revolt necessitated such insistence.[38]

Luther also dealt realistically with the poor, refusing to follow Christian tradition in giving to them freely and indiscriminately. Extending their criticism of burdensome mendicants to the masses of alien, wandering poor generally, Luther and his followers restricted poor relief to the qualified *local* poor. They urged each community to assume full responsibility for the needy within their walls and subject them to programs for rehabilitation and vocational training.[39]

37. *LW* 45, 233–43; Benjamin N. Nelson, *The Idea of Usury: From Tribal Brotherhood to Universal Otherhood* (Princeton, 1949), pp. 32–35, 41, 47–49; Jacob Strauss, *Haubtstuck und Artickel Christenlicher leer wider den unchristlichen wucher* (1523) and *Das Wucher zu nemen und geben, unserm Christlichem glauben und bruderlicher lieb . . . entgegen ist, unuberwintlich leer unnd geschrifft* (1524), esp. C 2 a, C 4 a–b.

38. See, for example, Caspar Hedio, *Von dem Zehenden zwu träffliche Predig* (1525); Andreas Keller, *Von dem Zehenden, Was darvon usz der schrifft zu halten sey* (1525). Both stress that Christians freely give tithes when government demands them and that such tithes should be used manifestly "zu fürderung der eer Gottes / und seins worts / zu errettung des rechtes / zur auffenthaltung der armen" (Hedio, C 2 a–b). Or as Keller complains: "Summa summarium / es ist kein schrifft in der gantzen hailigen schrifft damit man erzwingen mög dz man den Zehenden brauchen sol / so ein faulen mutwilligen hauffen damit zu erhalten" (Keller, C 1).

39. See Carter Lindberg, " 'There Should Be No Beggars Among Christians': Karlstadt, Luther, and the Origins of Protestant Poor Relief," *Church History* 46 (1977): 313–34; Wenceslaus Linck, *Von Arbeyt and Betteln wie man solle der faulheyt vorkommen/und jederman zu Arbeyt ziehen* (Zwickau, 1523); and the Nürnberg ordinance for beggars: *New Ordenung der betthler halben / In der Stadt Nurmberg / hoch von notten beschehen* (Leipzig, 1522). I hope soon to publish a study of the social and political attitudes of Protestants as revealed in such pamphlet literature.

Ain Dialogus vnd Argument

der Romanisten/wider das Christlich heüflein/
den Geytz vnd ander offentlich lafter betreffend zc.
Hanns Sachs.

Ephesios 5.

Hürerey vnd vnraynigkait/oder geytz/laßt nit von
euch gefagt werden/wie den hayligen zů feet.

Title page of Hans Sachs's pamphlet *A Dialog on the Argument of the Romanists Against the Christian Community Regarding its Profiteering and Other Public Offenses* (Nuremberg, 1524). The pamphlet reports Catholic attacks on evangelical doctrine in the city of Nuremberg. The scene on the title page portrays Romanus, the Catholic spokesman, and Reichenburger, a rich citizen who represents the Protestants. Romanus criticizes the unreformed moral lives of Nuremberg citizens, especially their persistent greed and profiteering, despite regular Protestant preaching. That a figure such as Reichenburger should speak for the Protestants has been seen as an indication of the Reformation's accommodation to established power and surrender of its original high social ideals in the mid–1520s. A closer reading of the pamphlet, however, suggests that Reichenburger may rather speak for a Christian morality that is realistic about man and society and distances the Reformation not from ideals, but from radical egalitarian sentiments that it never shared.

Luther never intended his theoretical distinction between Christians and citizens to put religion and society asunder, as if they were alien bodies. Nor did he ever believe that a basic conflict existed between the work of the church and that of secular magistrates. He expected religious values to inform secular life and the sword of the magistrate to defend religious truth. The temporal and spiritual spheres were separate and fundamentally different, but they were also interdependent and required the closest cooperation.

At the base of Luther's social teaching lay a conflict far more disturbing to him than any that might have arisen within an individual's perception of his religious and secular responsibilities. He described this conflict as one between the "kingdom of God" and the "kingdom of the devil" for control over *both* spheres of life. Because the devil wanted to be king as well as pope and fill the world as well as the church with unbelief, hatred, and disobedience, Christians must support the divinely sanctioned goals of law, order, and justice in secular society as well as the high religious ideals of the community of the church. Such a vision was hardly conducive to quietistic withdrawal and surrender of the world to politicians to do with as they pleased.[40] The fact that preachers and magistrates played fundamentally different roles and church congregations and political councils remained fundamentally different bodies did not prevent cooperation and mutual support in what to Luther's mind was a common task.[41] In his own words:

> God has ordained two governments: the spiritual, by which the Holy Spirit produces Christians and righteous people . . . and the temporal, which restrains the unchristian and wicked. . . . Both must be permitted to remain—the one to produce righteousness, the other to bring about external peace. Neither is sufficient in the world without the other.[42]

> As it is the function and honor of the office of preaching to make sinners saints, and dead men live, and damned men saved, and the devil's children God's children, so it is the function and honor of

40. Recent efforts to associate Luther with Anabaptist separatism are unconvincing. James Stayer, for example, has characterized Luther as an "apolitical moderate" who waffled between separatist apoliticism, like that of the Anabaptists, and the *Realpolitik* of reformers like Zwingli (*Anabaptists and the Sword* [Lawrence, Kan., 1972], pp. 33–44).

41. This is especially emphasized by Heinrich Bornkamm, *Luthers Lehre von den zwei Reichen im Zusammenhang seiner Theologie* (Gütersloh, 1960), p. 10. As John Headley summarizes: "What Luther wishes to express with the two ideas of *politia* and *religio* are not two mutually exclusive areas of life, but the two-fold activity of God in the world" (*Luther's View of Church History* [New Haven, 1963], p. 4).

42. *Temporal Authority: To What Extent it Should be Obeyed* (1523), LW 45, p. 91 (= *WA* 11, pp. 245–80).

worldly government to make men out of wild beasts and to prevent
men from becoming wild beasts. . . . Theologians and jurists must continue or all the rest will go to ruin. . . . When theologians disappear,
God's word disappears, and there remain nothing but heathen, nay
nothing but devils; when jurists disappear, the law disappears, and
peace with it, and there remain nothing but robbery, murder, crime,
and violence, nay, nothing but wild beasts.[43]

Despite the preacher's preoccupation with men's souls, he also performed
"great and mighty works for the world." According to Luther, he

informs and instructs all classes in how they are to conduct themselves
outwardly in their [stations in life], so that they may do what is right
before God. He comforts and advises those who are troubled, com-
poses difficulties, relieves consciences, helps to maintain peace and
settle differences, and does innumerable works of this kind every day.
A preacher confirms and strengthens . . . government and temporal
peace. . . . He checks the rebellious; teaches obedience, morals, discipline, and honor; instructs fathers, mothers, children, and servants in
their duties; in a word, he is the teacher of all secular offices and
ranks.[44]

Luther had no difficulty urging Christians to become executioners if they
found such services needed to maintain worldly justice and government.[45]
This became a major point of difference with Anabaptists and sectarians,
who counseled strict Christian pacifism and withdrawal from the coercive
responsibilities of secular society. Luther compared such separatists with
medieval monks and nuns, who had also refused to undertake basic civic
responsibilities in the name of a higher than human calling. In a 1526
sermon, Luther answered the question "Whether Soldiers, Too, Can Be
Saved" by arguing that killing and maiming in defense of the life and
property of one's neighbor were also God-pleasing acts of love.[46]

Obedience to temporal authority had clearly defined limits. As early as
1520, Luther instructed his followers to disobey any prince who presumed
to be their shepherd as well as hangman, that is, to extend his authority over
their consciences,[47] a preachment he himself practiced in the presence of

43. *Sermon on Keeping Children in School* (1530), *Works of Martin Luther* (Philadelphia,
1931), 4: 159, 173 (= *WA* 30/2, pp. 517–88).
44. Ibid., p. 148.
45. *On Temporal Authority*, p. 95.
46. *LW* 46, pp. 93–137 (= *WA* 19, pp. 623–62).
47. "If a prince desired to go to war and his cause was manifestly unjust, we should not
follow nor help him at all . . . . Likewise, if he bade us bear false witness, steal, lie, or deceive

the emperor. As pressures within Saxony and the hostile stance of the emperor threatened the Reformation's survival, Luther emphasized anew the traditional limitations on secular authority. In the *Address to the Christian Nobility* in 1520 he had invited German princes and noblemen, as Christian laity responsible for the welfare of the church, to reform the church by force, clearly expecting such reform to approximate his own religious ideals. When, however, rulers like Duke George of Saxony chose instead to persecute Lutherans and defend the traditional faith, Luther found it necessary to amend his earlier invitation. In a treatise on temporal authority in 1523 he elaborated the thesis that "temporal government has laws which extend no further than to life and property and the external affairs of the earth and God will not permit anyone but himself to rule over the soul."[48]

Like all first-generation Protestant reformers, Luther permitted individuals to resist tyranny and persecution only passively; revolution and regicide were unacceptable remedies. The disassociation of the Reformation from such radical tactics was as essential to its survival in Germany in the 1520s as active resistance was to be to its survival in France and the Netherlands in the second half of the century. Luther believed that rebellion only replaced tyranny with anarchy and mob rule ("Herr Omnes"), actually the worst kind of tyranny.[49] In a manual for princely conduct written for Elector John Frederick in 1534, he confessed: "Sometimes it has seemed to me that government . . . too needs a Luther [that is, someone to reform it fundamentally], but I am worried that they might get instead a [Thomas] Müntzer [to Luther, a castastrophic revolutionary]."[50] Two years before the Peasants' Revolt, Luther emphatically denounced insurrection as "an unprofitable method" of redressing grievances, for "it never brings about the desired improvement [and] generally harms the innocent more than the guilty. No insurrection is ever right, no matter how right the cause it seeks to promote."[51]

Having barred rebellion as a legitimate Christian response to tyranny, Luther counseled his followers to pursue reforms by what he called "darning and patching" corrupt political offices. "It is better to punish the abuse and put bandages and ointment on the small pox," he argued, than to kill the body in order to defeat the disease.[52] In 1520 he spoke of protecting

---

and the like. Here we ought rather give up goods, honor, body, and life that God's commandments may stand" (*Treatise on Good Works* [1520], *Works of Martin Luther*, 1: 271 (= *WA* 6, pp. 202–76]).

48. *On Temporal Authority*, p. 105.

49. *A Sincere Admonition to All Christians to Guard Against Insurrection and Rebellion* (1522), *LW* 45, p. 63 (= *WA* 8, pp. 676–87).

50. *Exposition of Psalm 101* (1534), *LW* 13, p. 271 (= *WA* 51, pp. 200–264).

51. *Sincere Admonition*, p. 63.

52. *Exposition of Psalm 101*, p. 217.

God's honor and commandment and preventing injury and injustice to one's neighbor, "the magistrate by the sword, the rest of us by reproof and rebuke."[53] Preachers, he insisted, were duty-bound to "rebuke and judge [unjust rulers] boldly and openly," while at the same time educating ordinary people in the duties of their rulers and the limits of their authority.[54] Superiors were appointed by God to be "common persons [*gemeine Personen*]," existing not for themselves alone, but for all others.[55] They had been commanded to care for their subjects like a pastor for his congregation, not to treat them like swine or dogs.[56]

After the Diet of Augsburg in 1530, Luther, as we have seen, grudgingly endorsed active resistance to the emperor by the German princes. As in other potentially disruptive stands—the marriage of clergy for example[57]—he proved the more cautious of the Saxon reformers, doubtlessly because his position of leadership made him acutely sensitive to the political consequences of any social tumult resulting from his religious reform. Already in the mid-1520s, Saxon jurists had developed both constitutional and juridical arguments in favor of resistance to the higher authority of the emperor. They stressed especially the emperor's responsibility as a constitutionally limited monarch to the lower authorities who elected him. These jurists won the quick support of such Lutheran theologians as Johannes Bugenhagen, Philip Melanchthon, Martin Bucer, and Andreas Osiander, who added biblical justifications to the constitutional arguments. Although Luther came to support this position both late and reluctantly, his teaching about the two kingdoms and the responsibility of rulers to their subjects actually formed much of its basis. Those colleagues of his who acted in advance of him felt they had drawn conclusions fully consistent with their leader's teaching.[58]

Neither Saxon jurists nor Lutheran preachers, however, viewed "the

---

53. *Treatise on Good Works* (1520), p. 274.

54. *Exposition of Psalm 82* (1530); *Works of Martin Luther*, 4: 292 (= *WA* 31/1, pp. 189–218); *Sincere Admonition*, p. 73.

55. *Whether Soldiers, Too, Can Be Saved*, p. 64.

56. *Exposition of Psalm 82*, p. 294.

57. See below, ch. 12.

58. See the discussion by Cynthia G. Shoenberger, "The Development of the Lutheran Theory of Resistance 1523–1530," *Sixteenth Century Journal* 8 (1977): 61–76. See also Shoenberger's more recent article, "Luther on Resistance to Authority," *Journal of the History of Ideas* 40 (1979): 3–20 and W. D. J. Cargill Thompson, "Luther and the Right of Resistance to the Emperor," in *Church, Society, and Politics*, ed. Derek Baker (Oxford, 1975). Documents are collected by Heinz Scheible, *Das Widerstandsrecht als Problem der deutschen Protestanten 1523–1546* (Gütersloh, 1969). Bucer defended the rights of lower magistrates by pointing out that Romans 13 spoke of "the powers that be," not a single power; and Osiander wrote, in almost Lockean fashion: "A king who is elected [as was the emperor] . . . upon specific conditions remains an authority only so long as he keeps to those conditions and the articles of the oath which he has sworn" (Shoenberger, "The Development of the Lutheran Theory of Resistance," pp. 69–70).

people" as standing in the same juridical relationship to lower magistrates as
they believed the latter stood to the higher authority of the emperor. If
there was a contradiction in the argument that princes could actively oppose
an unjust emperor, while ordinary people could not resist their more immediate unjust superiors, few were prepared to call attention to it in the
first half of the sixteenth century. Pamphleteers for the Peasants' Revolt of
1525 defended the right of ordinary people to judge their rulers by biblical
precepts and violently overthrow those who were manifestly tyrannical and
unchristian,[59] but they represented only a revolutionary minority, whose
cause was thoroughly defeated.

The changed political fortunes of nations and religious groups after midcentury made the concept of popular resistance to tyranny more thinkable.
In tracts urging the overthrow of Mary Tudor and Mary of Lorraine in the
1550s, for example, John Knox put forth arguments similar to those of
Thomas Müntzer and the peasant pamphleteers.[60] Even in the more desperate political circumstances of the second half of the sixteenth century,
however, it was still the ephoral doctrine elaborated by the Lutherans in the
1520s, confining "revolutionary" leadership to established lower political
authority, that won the endorsement of both the Magdeburg Lutherans
who resisted the emperor in the early 1550s and the Huguenots who
warred with French kings in the 1560s and 1570s.

The Revolt of the Common Man   ALL the major Protestant reformers compromised with
magistrates and princes on the
timetable of religious change, and Luther's adjustment to the wishes of
Saxon authorities in this regard was hardly more than prudence. His uncompromising condemnation of the almost contemporaneous Peasants' Revolt, however, is another matter. It has occasioned severe criticism of his
social philosophy—or what to some is the lack thereof. Marxist scholars,
who interpret the Reformation as part of an "early bourgeois revolution"
against feudal structures of authority,[61] have perhaps been Luther's

59. See the pamphlet *An die Versammlung Gemeiner Bauernschaft* (before August 1525),
discussed below, p. 281. Thomas Müntzer recommended a cleansing slaughter to the persecuted in Sangerhausen: "Es ist dye zeyt vorhanden, das ein blutvorgyssen uber die vorgyssen
uber die vorstogkte welt sol ergehen umb yres unglaubens willen" (*Thomas Müntzer: Schriften
und Briefe*, ed. Günther Franz [Gütersloh, 1968], p. 414). See further Leif Grane, "Thomas
Müntzer und Martin Luther," in *Bauernkriegs-Studien*, ed. Bernd Moeller (Gütersloh, 1975),
pp. 69–97.

60. See below, pp. 421–22.

61. See Rainer Wohlfeil, ed., *Reformation oder frühbürgerliche Revolution* (Munich, 1972)
and *Der Bauernkrieg 1524–1526: Bauernkrieg und Reformation* (Munich, 1975); Abraham
Friesen, *Reformation and Utopia: The Marxist Interpretation of the Reformation and Its Antecedents*

severest critics in this regard. He is portrayed as having inspired the peasants to rebellion with his gospel of spiritual freedom and equality, only to
turn his back abruptly on them when they claimed a full share of the fruits
of reform. While few would today follow Friedrich Engels in classifying
Luther among history's "great bootlickers of absolute monarchy," historians
of various ideological persuasions believe that his stance against the peasants in 1525 narrowed forevermore the original social promise of the Reformation.[62]

Protestant preaching against traditional spiritual authority was only one
of many factors that gave rise to the great revolt of 1525. Among other
preconditions, one can cite overpopulation and crowding, problems aggravated by aristocratic expropriation of common lands. A new wave of imperial taxation, begun in 1495 by Maximilian I, had passed rapidly over the territorial princes and the imperial cities to pound the villages. Harvests failed
badly in 1523 and 1524. Finally, there was the emperor's prolonged absence
from the empire, which both disquieted and emboldened the peasants.[63]

In February 1525, Swabian peasants, meeting in Memmingen, a city favorable to their cause, summarized their grievances in twelve famous articles, which circulated widely in twenty-five separate editions during the
year, twenty of which appeared in major cities within two months of the first
printing.[64] Disseminated throughout the empire and known in all the regions where peasant uprisings occurred,[65] the Memmingen Articles provide
a representative summary of the crisis in agrarian government at the end of
the Middle Ages.[66]

The articles were aimed at feudal lords and princes, both secular and
ecclesiastical, who, as landowners and judges, disposed of the property and

(Wiesbaden, 1974); and Josef Forschepoth, *Reformation und Bauernkrieg im Geschichtsbild der
DDR* (Berlin, 1976).

62. See Günter Vögler, *Die Gewalt soll gegeben werden dem gemeinen Volk: Der deutsche
Bauernkrieg 1525* (Berlin, 1975).

63. Volker Press, "Der deutsche Bauernkrieg als Systemkrise," *Giessener Univer-
sitätsblätter* 11 (1978): 114-35. Recent research on the Peasants' War is surveyed by H. C. Erik
Midelfort, "The Revolution of 1525? Recent Studies of the Peasants' War," *Central European
History* 11 (1978): 189-206, and Tom Scott, "The Peasants' War: A Historiographical Review: Part 1, "*The Historical Journal* 22 (1979): 693-720.

64. Editions of the articles were published in Augsburg, Zwickau (2), Magdeburg, Forch-
heim, Speyer, Würzburg, Constance (2), Strasbourg (3), Reutlingen, Erfurt (4), Regensburg (2), Breslau, Worms, Nürnberg (2), Zurich, and one with no place of publication.
Helmut Claus, *Der deutsche Bauernkrieg im Druckschaffen der Jahre 1524-1526: Verzeichnis der
Flugschriften und Dichtungen* (Gotha, 1975), pp. 24-29.

65. The Articles and other statements of the common man's grievances are collected in
Flugschriften der Bauernkriegszeit, Adolf Laube and Hans W. Seiffert, eds. (Berlin, 1975), pp.
26-79. See also the collection, in translation, in Gerald Strauss, *Manifestations of Discontent,
in Germany on the Eve of the Reformation* (Bloomington, 1971), pp. 144-69.

66. Peter Blickle, *Die Revolution von 1525* (Munich, 1975), pp. 22-25, 89.

Der Bauwer.

Ich aber bin von art ein Bauwr/
Mein Arbeit wirt mir schwer vnd sauwr
Ich muß Ackern/Seen vnd Egn/
Schneyden/Mehen/ Heuwen dargegn/
Holtzen/vnd einführn Hew vnd Treyd/
Gült vñ Steuwr macht mir viel hertzleid
Trinck Wasser vnd iß grobes Brot/
Wie denn der Herr Adam gebot.

The Peasant. Jost Amman. From *Das Ständebuch.*

I am a peasant.
My work is hard and bitter.
I must plow, seed, and harrow,
Then cut, reap, and beat.
I gather wood and make hay and grain.
Rents and taxes break my heart.
I live on plain bread and water,
As the Lord has commanded Adam.

persons of their serfs in a new authoritarian manner. The grievances expressed were not only those of peasant farmers. Aggrieved burghers, guildsmen, and miners also participated in significant numbers in the revolt. The revolution of 1525 drew the "common man" in the cities as well as on the land, winning adherents wherever oppressive government forced the unprivileged to reassert their modest, traditional political freedoms and economic rights.[67]

The authors of the twelve articles were Sebastian Lotzer, a Memmingen journeyman furrier, and Christoph Schappeler, a Lutheran pastor in Memmingen, men who attest the degree of urban participation in the peasant's movement.[68] Scorning the accusation that disobedience and rebellion were the "fruit of the new gospel" preached by the peasants, they portrayed the common man as godly, bound in conscience to Scripture, and desiring only his legitimate human and divine rights. What were these rights?[69]

1. *The right of each community to choose and depose its own pastor.* Such local autonomy, while often desired, had no precedent in medieval history. Luther may unwittingly have inspired this demand. In 1523 he published a pamphlet urging local congregations to test traditional religious teaching by the Bible. It bore the title "Proof of Holy Scripture that a Christian Congregation or Community Has the Right and Power to Judge All Doctrine and to Call, Install, and Depose Its Teachers."[70]

67. I follow Blickle here, who summarizes: "Der gemeine Mann ist der Bauer, der Bürger der landsässigen Stadt, der von reichsstädtischen Aemtern ausgeschlossene Städter, der Bergknappe; insofern der gemeine Mann das Korrelat zu Herr bildet, mag es berechtigt sein, von einer politischen Revolution zu sprechen. Vom Begriff Bauernkrieg Abschied zu nehmen, ihn wenigstens mit gehöriger Distanz zu gebrauchen, um sich den Zugang zum Phänomen von 1525 nicht zu versperren, empfiehlt sich angesichts der Sozialstrucktur der Revolution" (ibid., p. 179).

68. On urban participation in and leadership of the Peasants' Revolt, see Bernd Moeller, *Deutschland im Zeitalter der Reformation* (Göttingen, 1977), pp. 96–97; and Blickle, *Die Revolution von 1525*, pp. 165–75. Magistrates in imperial cities never took the initiative to support the peasants in the surrounding countryside. Urban support resulted either from the pressure of guilds or groups of poor burghers, who found their persons and properties oppressed by higher authority in much the same way the peasants did, or it came as a prudent response to the military threat area peasants posed to urban communities (ibid., p. 171). The failure of the peasants to win large-scale urban support made their cause quite hopeless.

69. See Günther Franz, ed., *Quellen zur Geschichte des Bauernkrieges* (Darmstadt, 1963), pp. 175–79. English translation in *Works of Martin Luther*, 4: 210–16. See also Blickle, *Die Revolution von 1525*, pp. 21–24.

70. *Das eyn Christliche versamlung odder gemeyne: recht und macht habe: alle lere tzu urteylenn: und lerer zu beruffen, eyn und ab zu setzen. Grund und ursach auss der scrifft* (Zwickau, 1523). Lay-endowed preacherships were a step in this direction, but such preachers were not the creatures of the local community, nor were they independent of the ecclesiastical hierarchy. A congregational principle of church government, more akin to Anabaptism and later Congregationalism, seems to be suggested in the Memmingen Articles. Luther, of course, was seeking to justify the replacement of Catholic priests with Lutheran pastors.

2. *An end to the small tithes* (klain Zehat) *of cattle for lay and ecclesiastical lords.* Rejecting these tithes as unjust, the peasants agreed that the larger tithe of grain was justly given, for it was a tax with a basis in both Testaments.

3. *Release from serfdom.* The authors here argued that since Jesus had ransomed all people by his sacrifice on the cross, no person should be a bondservant to another. This article actually went beyond the redress of a grievance to request an actual forfeiture of power by feudal lords. Lutheran slogans like "the freedom of the Christian" and "the priesthood of all believers" clearly influenced it.

4. *Free access to fish and game.* This widespread grievance resulted from the exclusion of peasants from more and more tracts of land, which lords and princes designated as their private hunting preserves. Because they took their hunting as seriously as war, these nobles were quick to punish peasant poachers as sternly as captured enemy soldiers.

5. *Free access to firewood as needed.* During the late fifteenth and sixteenth centuries, wood came into short supply in many regions and lords and princes restricted access to their lands, both to conserve their own supply of firewood and to maintain their hunting preserves.

6. *An investigation of excessive tenural services.* To maximize incomes from their lands, lords exacted services with a new rigor in the late fifteenth and early sixteenth centuries. This upset the traditional informality of village life and disturbed its security.

7. *Strict observance by the lords of the agreements made with their servants.* Fearful of being seized upon by their lords for uncontracted services, peasants were set on edge. They wanted a definite end to forced additional private services and dues beyond those clearly specified in contracts with their lords.

8. *New rent assessments, based on equity and justice.* The willful raising of rents, that is, the amount of produce required from tenants living on a lord's land, was another way lords increased their income. In the early sixteenth century harsh new demands were imposed on both the property (rents and dues) and person (services) of the common man.

9. *The basing of legal judgments, that is, punishments, on customary law* (bei alter geschribner Straf strafen) *rather than on constantly appearing arbitrary new laws.* Here the peasants protested the long-developing process of judicial centralization, usually with the aid of Roman legal concepts, that was overriding local law and custom in the name of a higher law of the land administered by representatives of the territorial prince.

10. *The return of expropriated common fields.* This was another protest against the usurpation of lands traditionally free to all, but progressively taken over by lords for their private use.

11. *Abolition of the death tax.* The death tax *(Todfall)* required such things as the surrender to the lord of a deceased self's best horse, cow, or garment. Here the peasants accused lords of robbing widows and orphans of their rightful inheritance.

The final Memmingen article was a pledge to retract any of the above should it be found wanting support in Holy Scripture. Lotzer's and Schappeler's recurring insistence that the Bible and "divine law" justified these demands reflected the influence of the religious reform movements of the late Middle Ages on socioeconomic protest, an interrelationship that went back at least as far as the English Peasants' Revolt of 1381. Peasant demands had traditionally centered on hard economic and political issues and were argued on the basis of ancient or customary law and natural human rights. In Germany after 1513 issues of human justice also became matters of "divine justice."[71]

This broadening of the traditional peasant protest resulted from the *Bundschuh* movement, a peasant league that aspired to transform German society by the egalitarian ideals of the Bible. Although Luther never intended them to be essays in social engineering, his writings on Christian freedom and religious equality deepened the strong current of anti-clericalism in the traditional peasant protest, especially against the many monastic landowners. When in 1521 the Catholic pamphleteer Thomas Murner accused the new Lutheran theology of stirring up "Hans Karst"— Hans, the crude peasant, with pitchfork in hand—Lutherans transformed the peasant into the main representative and spokesman for all ranks of Christian laity. In numerous pre-1525 pamphlets "Karsthans" appears as a quick-witted, God-fearing, Bible-savvy defender of the Reformation, able to rebut all critics. Luther personally admired the peasant's life; he praised peasant's work—earning one's living by the sweat of one's brow—as the work most desired of men by God. Also, theologically Luther was attracted to the paradox of God's preference for the humble and saw the peasant's life as a symbol of the religious attitude desired of man by God. Romanticized by Lutheran apologists, many peasants understandably came to believe that the Reformation sought their social and political freedom as well as their religious welfare.[72] Lutheran theology directly influenced the

71. A point especially stressed by Günther Franz, *Der deutsche Bauernkrieg* (Darmstadt, 1952). Excerpts in Kyle C. Sessions, ed., *Reformation and Authority: The Meaning of the Peasant's Revolt* (Boston, 1968), pp. 1–8.

72. See Kurt Uhrig, "Der Bauer in der Publizistik der Reformation bis zum Ausgang des Bauernkrieges" *ARG* 33 (1936), esp. pp. 76, 95–106, 114–16; Paul Böckmann, "Der gemeine Mann in den Flugschriften der Reformation," *Deutsche Vierteljahrsschrift für Literaturwissenschaft und Geistesgeschichte* 22 (1944), esp. pp. 194, 196, 200.

Ein newer Spruch Wie die Geystlicheit vnd etlich Handtwercker vber den Luther clagen.

Der geitzig clagt auß falschem müt,
Seit jm abgeht an Eer vnd Gůt.
Er zürnet, dobet, vnde wůlt,
In durstet nach des grechten plůt.

Die warheit ist Got vnd sein wort,
Das pleibt ewiglich vnzerstort.
Wie ser der Gotloß auch rumort,
Gott bschützt sein diener hie vnd dort.

Der Grecht sagt die Gotlich warheit,
Wie hart man jn veruolgt, verleit.
hofft er in Gott doch alle zeit,
Pleibt bstendig in der grechtigkeit.

Die clag der Gotlosen.

Antwort .D. Martin.

Das Vrteil Christi.

Hans Sachs Schuster.

A New Saying: The Complaint of the Clergy and Certain Professions against Luther. Illustrated by Sebald Beham. In a flood of pamphlets and illustrations, the peasant was depicted as the chief defender of the new Protestant teaching. The reformers sympathized with the plight of common people in both city and countryside and directly sought their support. In this broadsheet Luther, Bible in hand, confronts a Catholic spokesman, each backed by their supporters. In the crowd of ordinary people behind Luther a defiant peasant with a scythe stands out most prominently. The Catholic spokesman is supported by the high clergy and the professions with an obvious self-interest in the continuation of traditional religious beliefs and practices: bellmakers, goldsmiths, candlemakers, woodcarvers, and fishermen. Heroic portrayals of peasants by Protestant artists quickly ceased after the Peasants' Revolt.

authors of the Twelve Articles and, as we have seen, the ex-Lutheran Thomas Müntzer became a theologian of peasant revolt.[73]

Despite the prominence of the "spiritual", however, the peasant grievances of 1524/25 remained predominantly material in nature and quite traditional.[74] The appeal to divine law against the legal sanctions of landholders reflected a desperate need for a higher legitimation. Where the peasants could defend themselves by ancient law and custom, they did so; but where positive law and custom supported the landholders, who readily invoked tradition, peasant spokesmen turned to higher divine law and the court of ethics and equity.[75] While such appeals gave their cause an ideological justification beyond the purely material, it also created completely unrealistic expectations of the degree to which society could be socially and politically transformed.

The utopian strains in the peasant revolt of 1525 do not, however, distract from the common man's legitimate grievances. Changes in the exercise of lordship, not peasant greed and folly, gave birth to the Twelve Articles of Memmingen and other protests in city and countryside.[76] Prior to the fif-

73. On the theology of Lotzer and Schappeler, see Martin Brecht, "Der theologische Hintergrund der Zwölf Artikel der Bauernschaft in Schwaben von 1525: Christoph Schappelers and Sebastian Lotzers Beitrag zum Bauernkrieg," in Heiko A. Oberman, ed., *Deutscher Bauernkrieg 1525, ZKG* 85 (1974): 30–64; and Barbara Bettina Gerber, "Sebastian Lotzer. Ein gelehrter Laie im Streit um das Göttliche Recht," in *Radikale Reformatoren,* ed. by Hans-Jürgen Goertz (Munich, 1978), pp. 60–64. On Müntzer, see S. Ozment, *Mysticism and Dissent* (New Haven, 1973), pp. 79–97; and Abraham Friesen and H. J. Goertz, eds., *Thomas Müntzer* (Darmstadt, 1978).

74. On the material and spiritual sides of peasant grievances, see H. J. Hillerbrand, "The German Reformation and the Peasants' War," in *The Social History of the Reformation,* ed. L. P. Buck and J. W. Zophy (Columbus, 1972), pp. 106–36; H. Boockmann, "Zu den geistigen und religiösen Voraussetzungen des Bauernkrieges," in Moeller, *Bauernkriegs-Studien,* pp. 9–27; Francis Rapp, "Die soziale und wirtschaftliche Vorgeschichte des Bauernkrieges in Unterelsass," in ibid., pp. 29–45; Hubert Kirchner, "Der deutsche Bauernkrieg im Urteil der frühen reformatorischen Geschichtsschreibung," in Oberman, *Deutscher Bauernkrieg 1525,* pp. 95–125; and H. A. Oberman, "Tumultus rusticorum: Vom 'Klosterkrieg' zum Fürstensieg," in ibid., pp. 157–172. Hillerbrand and Oberman represent extremes in interpretation; Hillerbrand reduces peasant grievances to economic motives, while Oberman argues for recognition of the Peasants' War as a true "Glaubensrevolte" that evolved into economic and political revolt.

75. Blickle comments: "Der Legitimationszwang bestand für beide Seiten: die Herren kämpften mit dem 'gemeinen kaiserlichen und geistlichen Recht,' der Bauer verteidigte sich mit der stumpfgewordenen Waffe des Alten Herkommens. Die Kategorie der Rationalität stand gegen die Kategorie der Ethik. Gefesselt an sein eigenes Rechtsverständnis von Herkommen und Billigkeit konnte der Bauer nur fordern, was er rechtlich begründen konnte. Er benötigte ein Aequivalent zum 'gemeinen kaiserlichen und geistlichen Recht'; er sollte es 1525 finden—im 'göttlichen Recht'" (*Die Revolution von 1525* , p. 134).

76. Ibid., p. 71.

teenth century servitude had been far more flexible and the common man
the beneficiary of greater factual if not legal freedom. He could, for example, choose his own patron(s) and marry beyond his immediate community, if he desired. After 1400, lords imposed new restrictions and
controls that reflected the larger drift of the century toward political
and economic centralization. What had been a comparatively informal
and flexible structure of government before 1400—perhaps in large
part because of the rulers' inability to make it otherwise after the social
upheavals of the fourteenth century—became for the common man a petty,
bureaucratized, rule-laden state during the fifteenth century.[77]

The peasants listed Luther as chief among the theologians who could
attest the conformity of their articles to Holy Scripture. Zwingli, Melanchthon, Andreas Osiander, Theobald Billican, and Matthew Zell were also
cited. Luther formally replied to the Twelve Articles in a tract entitled
An Admonition to Peace, which was written in the apparently sincere belief
that full-scale rebellion could be averted if both sides—but especially the
princes and lords—would only cooperate. At the outset he expressed a fear
that persisted on his part throughout the entire affair and clearly influenced
his actions during it.

> This matter is great and perilous, concerning both the kingdom of God
> and the kingdom of the world; if this rebellion . . . gets the upper hand,
> both kingdoms will be destroyed and there will be neither worldly
> government nor Word of God; there will rather result the permanent
> destruction of all Germany; therefore, it is necessary . . . to speak
> boldly.[78]

Boldly Luther did speak—as it turned out, all too boldly. He acknowledged the justice of the peasants' complaints and laid the blame for the
incipient revolt squarely at the feet of the princes and lords.

> We have no one on earth to thank for this mischievous rebellion, except
> you lords and princes, especially you blind bishops and mad priests and
> monks. . . . In your government you do nothing but flay and rob your
> subjects in order that you may lead a life of splendor and pride, until
> the poor common folk can bear it no longer.[79]

77. Ibid., pp. 40–43, 71–75.
78. In *Works of Martin Luther,* 4: 220 (= *WA* 18, pp. 291–334). There were nineteen
editions of this work, including one Dutch. Claus, *Die deutsche Bauernkrieg im Druckschaffen,*
pp. 44–59.
79. *An Admonition to Peace,* p. 220.

Although he doubted their ability to be advised in the matter, Luther urged the princes and lords to "act rationally" in the face of peasant rage and "try kindness" as a small price for peace.[80] While he also recognized the baser motives of the peasants, he never reversed this initial judgment: the princes and lords inspired the revolt of the common man.

To the peasants, Luther insisted that the rightness of their cause did not justify the use of armed force: "The fact that rulers are wicked and unjust does not excuse tumult and rebellion; to punish wickedness does not belong to everybody, but to the worldly rulers who bear the sword," as Romans 13:4 and 1 Peter 2:7 were seen by Luther clearly to teach. Luther here rejected out of hand the subsequent argument of the famous peasant pamphlet *An die Versammlung gemeiner Bauernschaft* (1525) that Christians had a duty to disobey and oppose godless tyrants.[81] Rebellion, he wrote, is "contrary not only to Christian law and the gospel, but also to natural law and all equity"—condemned by both the Bible and conscience.[82] As for the proclaimed "Christian right" of the peasants' demands, Luther emphatically disassociated the gospel as he understood it from all worldly justice and material gain. In doing so he used language that has ever since branded him a social reactionary.

> Suffering, suffering, cross, cross! This and nothing else is the Christian law! God will help you ... and his gospel will rise with power among you, if you first suffer to the end, leave the case to him, and await his vengeance [on those who persecute you]. ... For no matter how right you are, it is not for a Christian to appeal to law, or to fight, but rather to suffer wrong and endure evil; there is no other way. ... Christians fight for themselves not with sword and gun, but with the cross and suffering, just as Christ, our leader, does not bear a sword, but hangs upon the cross.[83]

Luther here subjected the peasants to the kind of Sermon on the Mount idealism he himself later disavowed in writings against Anabaptists, for example, in his 1526 sermon, "Whether Soldiers, Too, Can be Saved." One

---

80. Ibid., p. 223.
81. The tract defended the rebelling peasants against those who had condemned them. Among the latter was not only Luther, but such other Protestant reformers as Urbanus Rhegius, Johannes Brenz, Johann Lachmann, and Johannes Zwick. *An die Versammlung gemeiner Bauernschaft. Eine revolutionäre Flugschrift aus dem deutschen Bauernkrieg* (1525), ed. S. Hoyer and B. Rüdiger (Leipzig, 1975), ch. 4, pp. 94–95; ch. 9, pp. 112–13.
82. *An Admonition to Peace*, p. 227.
83. Ibid., pp. 231–34.

cannot, however, accuse him of manifest contradiction. Rebellion against legitimate government because some find it tyrannical, which was what the peasants did, and the use of arms to defend such a government against foreign aggression, which Luther glorified in 1526, are quite different matters. There could have been no doubt about Luther's reaction to the specter of rebellion for those familiar with his previous pronouncements on the subject. In 1522, for example, he had admonished Saxon Christians to guard against insurrection, bluntly declaring:

> I am and always will be on the side of those against whom insurrection is directed, no matter how unjust their cause; I am opposed to those who rise in insurrection, no matter how just their cause.[84]

It is to be borne in mind that Luther opposed rebellion, not human rights and social justice. He condoned the peasants' cause, if not their revolutionary tactics, so long as they marched under a banner other than that of "Christian."

> Your name and title must be those of a people who fight because they will not, and ought not, endure wrong or evil, according to the teaching of nature [*wie das die natur gibt*]. You should have that name [the name of those who demand human and natural rights], and let the name of Christ alone, for that is the kind of works you are doing. . . . [As for] the . . . articles about freedom of game, birds, fish, wood, forests, services, tithe, imposts, excises, and the death tax—these I leave to the lawyers [for they are] things [that] do not concern a Christian [who] is a martyr on earth. Therefore, the peasants ought rightly let the name of Christian alone and act in some other name, as men who want human and natural rights [*als die gerne menschlich und natürlich recht wollten haben*], not as those who seek Christian rights.[85]

A parallel may be drawn between this argument and that Luther made earlier about the relationship between good works and salvation. In his 1520 treatise *On the Freedom of a Christian* he categorically denied that good works had any significance for salvation, yet he required the faithful to be daily active in good works. When he now criticizes the peasants' characterization of their demands as "Christian," he also denies that human rights have anything to do with Christian rights, yet he admonishes the princes and lords to be humanly just and fair. Luther permitted religion to be identified with neither ethics nor social justice. Religion, he believed, transcended both

84. *A Sincere Admonition*, p. 63.
85. *An Admonition to Peace*, pp. 234, 241.

and resolved problems of conscience and life's meaning that were beyond moral good and evil. In his argument with the peasants, as also in his dispute at this time with Erasmus,[86] he firmly resisted the slightest diminution of the transcendental character of religion.

While the distinction between human and Christian rights was simple and clear to Luther, the consequences of his argument proved very painful for the peasants. In an item-by-item survey of the Memmingen Articles, he concluded that none had any connection with the gospel. All rather dealt with "worldly matters," everything being directed to one purpose, "that your bodies and your properties may be free.[87] The request for release from the payment of small tithes he scorned as "theft and highway robbery"; the petition to be released "in Christ's name" from serfdom he rejected as "making Christian liberty an utterly carnal thing." He chided the dream of an egalitarian society: "A worldly kingdom cannot stand unless there is an inequality of persons, so that some are free, some bound, some lords, some subjects."[88]

The *Admonition to Peace* ended with a warning to both sides: history, experience, and Scripture oppose the princes and lords, for they teach that all tyrants fall sooner or later; and they are against the peasants, for they also teach that revolution always brings only chaos. Casting a plague on both houses, he pled for a peace he believed to be beyond the will of each.

> Since there is nothing Christian on either side and nothing Christian is at issue between you [inasmuch as] both lords and peasants are dealing with worldly right and wrong and with temporal goods; and since, moreover, both parties are acting against God and are under his wrath . . . let yourselves be advised and attack these matters with justice, not with force or strife, and do not start an endless bloodshed in Germany.[89]

Compromise was a viable option for neither side at this late date, and both princes and peasants must have looked on Luther's advice as completely gratuitous. In April massive peasant revolts occurred in Swabia, Franconia, and Thuringia. As the princes prepared to crush them, Luther, in what may most charitably be described as an unnecessary writing, urged them on in the strongest possible terms. The treatise, which shocked his friends and allies, bore the title *Against the Robbing and Murdering Peasants*

86. See below, p. 301.
87. *An Admonition to Peace*, p. 237.
88. Ibid., p. 240.
89. Ibid., pp. 241–42.

and reached no less than twenty-one editions.[90] It was in part a savage
personal attack on his self-appointed rival, Thomas Müntzer, a leader of the
rebellious peasants, whom Luther described in the tract as the "arch-devil of
Mühlhausen." Luther's enduring animosity toward Müntzer may explain in
part the extreme nature of this treatise. Also, on the eve of its composition,
Luther had received news of a vicious peasant attack on the town of
Weinsburg, during which peasants committed atrocities against the
populace. The recent death of his protector, Frederick the Wise, may be
still another factor in his merciless condemnation of the revolutionaries.
Disappointed by the peasants' refusal to heed his earlier advice and enraged
by their still growing threat to German social order, Luther may even have
perceived the revolt to be the end of his successful religious reform.

Luther accused the peasants of committing three "terrible sins against
God and man": perjury, by breaking their oaths of obedience; blasphemy,
by rising up in the name of Christ; and rebellion, by acting contrary to the
biblical teaching of Luke 20:25, Romans 13, and 1 Peter 2:13. Given the
reality of widespread revolt, Luther felt there could be but one response:

> Let everyone who can smite, slay, and stab [the peasants], secretly and
> openly, remembering that nothing can be more poisonous, hurtful, or
> devilish than a rebel. It is just as when one must kill a mad dog; if you
> do not strike him, he will strike you, and a whole land with you.[91]

Luther softened this harsh judgment slightly by suggesting that "if the
ruler is a Christian and tolerates the gospel," he will proceed against the
peasants by first confessing the rebellion a just judgment on his injustice
and pray to God for guidance; then, he will "offer the mad peasants an
opportunity to come to terms, even though they are unworthy of it." Only
then, when this course has failed, will he "swiftly grasp the sword."[92]
"Strange times these," Luther philosophized, "when a prince can win
heaven with bloodshed, better than other men with prayer."[93]

The princes and lords, both Protestant and Catholic, swiftly grasped the
sword and crushed the revolt. It has been estimated that between 70,000
and 100,000 peasants were killed in Germany in 1525. Philip of Hesse,
fresh from a campaign against the Hessian peasantry, joined Duke George
of Saxony and lesser lords in an attack on Thomas Müntzer's followers in the
Saxon town of Frankenhausen. In this particular engagement 9,000 peas-

90. Claus, *Die deutsche Bauernkrieg im Druckschaffen*, pp. 44–59.
91. *Against the Robbing and Murdering Peasants*, in *Works of Martin Luther*, 4: 248–50 (=
WA 18, pp. 357–361).
92. Ibid., p. 251.
93. Ibid., p. 253.

Thomas Müntzer. Christoffel von Sichem the Elder. Müntzer, perhaps Luther's most effective critic, has become the most influential sixteenth-century dissenter from the Reformation, especially in Marxist historiography. After failing to win the Saxon princes to his radical program of reform, he sent a call to arms to his followers in the city of Sangerhausen: "I tell you the time has come for bloodshed to fall upon this impenitent and unbelieving world. . . . Why do you continue to let yourselves be led around by your noses? One knows full well and can prove it with Scripture that lords and princes as they now present themselves are not Christians. Your priests and monks pray to the devil and there are ever fewer true Christians. All your preachers have become hypocrites and worshippers of man. Why do you continue to place your hope in them?" Following his execution for his role in the Peasants' Revolt, Müntzer's rebellious life and teaching became the subject of a didactic tract by Luther, who pointed out the terrible lessons to be learned from "The Horrible History and Judgment of God upon Thomas Müntzer" (Wittenberg, 1525).

ants, armed mainly with farming tools, confronted crack cavalry and artillery units. When the battle ended, an estimated 5,000 peasants lay dead, while the armies of the princes and lords reported only six casualties. Mühlhausen, the peasants' base, was made a ducal fief and required to pay the equivalent of $600,000 over a twenty-four-year period. The leader of the revolt, Müntzer, was tortured and beheaded.[94]

After the suppression of the revolt, Luther came under sharp criticism both for his "hard book" against the peasants and for having been the inspiration of the revolt in the first place. One of the most stinging critiques

94. Eric Gritsch, *Reformer Without a Church: The Life and Thought of Thomas Müntzer 1488 (?)-1525* (Philadelphia, 1967), pp. 149-52.

came from Johannes Findling, a Catholic apologist who had been general commissioner of indulgences when Luther posted his ninety-five theses in 1517. Findling's popular tract bore the title *Luther Speaks with Forked Tongue, or, How Luther, on the One Hand, Led the Peasants Astray, While, on the Other, He Condemned Them.* Findling traced the revolt to Luther's own challenge of higher authority in the Reformation tracts of 1520.[95] He compared Luther's belated condemnation of the peasants to his earlier efforts to disassociate himself from Wittenberg iconoclasm (1521–22), which also derived, in Findling's view, from Luther's own teaching.[96] In both cases Findling found Luther's actions politically motivated. Even the *Admonition to Peace* was seen as encouraging the peasants by its sharp criticism of the lords and princes.[97]

Such criticism forced replies from Luther and his supporters. The Königsberg pastor, Johannes Poliander (Gramann), writing to still the "swift, intolerant cry everywhere against Luther," accused the majority of Luther's critics of being disappointed supporters of the revolution. According to Poliander, Luther, like Moses, had tried to lead the peasants to a better life and called punishment down on them only after they had proven themselves unworthy.[98] Luther himself remained utterly unapologetic; he dismissed his critics, who demanded mercy for the peasants, as bleeding-heart hypocrites.

> Suppose I were to break into a man's house, rape his wife and daughters, break open his coffers, take his money, set a sword to his breast, and say: "If you will not put up with this, I shall run you through, for you are a godless wretch." Then, if a crowd gathered and

95. *Anzaigung zwayer falschen Zungen des Luthers wie er mit der ainen die paurn verfüret/mit der andern si verdammet hat* (1525), p. A 3 a. This work has recently been edited in Laube and Seiffert, *Flugschriften der Bauernkriegszeit,* together with other Catholic critiques of Luther by Jerome Emser and Johannes Cochläus.

96. "Am end des Buchleins / das man die Mess abthun sol / begerstu [Luther] / das zu Wittenberg der dienst gottes auffgehebt werd / glocken / orgeln / alter / Kirchen / gsanck / messlesen / abthan und zerbrochen werden / zu den zeytten was Carolstat ain gelert man / So er aber deine leer an die werck legt / und die altar abprochen hat / und ir zwen feind aynander worden sein / so schreibstu wider inn / und verdamst in / unnd vergissest / das du in solches gelert hast / Also thustu hie auch / Sy haben auss deiner leer gelernt morstifften wider die oberkait" (*Anzaigung zwayer falschen Zungen des Luthers,* p. B 3 b).

97. "Doch so mustu in soliche mass reden das du mel blasest / und auch mel im maul behaltest. Du underweysest die paurn gar treulich / gibst doch darneben sollich stich der oberkait das sie durch soliche mer wider sie geraitzt werden / dann durch dein schrifftlich unterweisung abgewendt" (ibid., p. A 4 a).

98. *Ein Urtayl Joh. Polianders / uber das hart Büchlein D. Martinus Luthers wider die auffrurn der Pawern / hievor aussgangen* (1525), pp. A 1 b, B 1 a. Poliander's tract also appears in Laube and Seiffert, eds., *Flugschriften der Bauernkriegszeit,* pp. 430–40.

were about to kill me for doing this, or if the judge ordered my head off, suppose I were to cry out: "But Christ teaches that you are to be merciful and not kill me." What would people say then? Well, that is exactly what my peasants and their advocates are doing now.[99]

"The kingdom of this world," Luther preached further,

> is nothing else than the servant of God's wrath upon the wicked and it is a real precursor of hell and everlasting death. It should not be merciful, but strict, severe, and wrathful in the fulfilment of its works and duty. Its tool is not a wreath of roses or a flower of love, but a naked sword; and a sword is a symbol of wrath, severity, and punishment.[100]

Despite his "hard book" against rebelling peasants, Luther joined his critics in recommending mercy for captured peasants. He also condemned the princes and lords in the strongest possible terms, describing them as "furious, raving, senseless tyrants, who, even after the battle, cannot get their fill of blood . . . scoundrels and hogs [to whom] it is all one whether they slay the guilty or the innocent, whether it please God or the devil."[101] On the other hand, Luther stuck to his original conviction that to tolerate rebellion only hastened the end of civilized society. He wrote in retrospect on the affair:

> From the start I had two fears. If the peasants became lords, the devil would become abbot; if these tyrants became lords, the devil's dam would become abbess. Therefore, I wanted to do two things: quiet the peasants and instruct the lords. The peasants were unwilling, and now they have their reward. The lords too will not hear, and they shall have their reward also.[102]

When the choice had to be made, Luther clearly preferred the devil's dam to the devil himself, that is, tyranny to anarchy. A tyrant, he seemed to reason, did at least preserve the essential structures of society and government and to that extent made possible eventual reform, that "darning and patching" to which he had long subscribed. In the sixteenth century such was an appropriate response, very much the majority opinion; from a modern point of view, it may seem to have been an all too human response.

Catholic critics were not the only ones who believed that Lutheran

---

99. *An Open Letter Concerning the Hard Book Against the Peasants* (July 1525), in *Works of Martin Luther*, 4: 264 (= WA 18, pp. 384–401).
100. Ibid., p. 266.
101. Ibid., p. 280.
102. Ibid., pp. 280–81.

preachers, wittingly or unwittingly, had played a role in provoking the revolution. In an official instruction to all subjects after the revolt had been crushed, the authorities of Brandenburg traced its cause to "ignorant, unskilled, and revolutionary preachers," who, having long taught that only faith in God and Christ was needed for salvation, had given "coarse and simple people" the impression that good works were unnecessary.[103] Thereafter simple people had forgotten their obligation to attain "temporal righteousness before their rulers" *(iren oberkaiten zeitliche gerechtigkaiten zuthun)*. Brandenburg princes and lords ordered all preachers in the land to make clear "in good German words" that saving faith was "not a pure, feigned, or dead faith," but a "true, living, love-filled faith, always active in good works" and that Christ had freed people from sin and death in their conscience, not from temporal obedience to their rulers.[104]

Lutheran preachers complied with this and similar ordinances elsewhere. The Lutheran pastor of Schwäbisch Hall, Johannes Brenz, who was "forced by recent events" to issue a sermon "On the Obedience of Subjects to Their Rulers," described Christian freedom as "a true form of obedience," ready to suffer the ruler's command even when it seemed unjust.[105]

Although the events of 1525 strengthened rulers, the result of the Peasants' Revolt seems not to have been, as scholars have previously argued, the effectual beginning of the "absolute state" in Germany. The peasants' lot improved in many regions after 1525. Among the recommendations of the Diet of Speyer in 1526 that led to a redressing of peasant grievances were an end to the payment of annates to Rome and the subjection of laity to ecclesiastical courts; an improvement in the quality of local preachers (although no concession of local power of appointment and dismissal); the removal of nontraditional petty tithes and death taxes and labor services

---

103. The title says it all: *Der Durchleüchtigen Hochgebornen Fürsten und Herren Casimirn und Herren Georgen / als der eltesten Regirenden gebrüder / Margraven zu Brandenburg, etc, meiner gnedigen herrn / anzaigen / wie die gewesen / empörung und auffrürer / nit den wenigsten tayl / auss ungeschickten predigen entstanden sindt. Und dz herwiderumb durch frumm geleert / geschickt / Christlich Prediger / vil auffrür für kummen werden mög. Auch ain kurtze Christenliche Underricht / wie hinfüro in jrer Fürstlichen gnaden Fürstenthummern / Landen und gebüten von rechtem warem Christlichem Glauben / und rechter warer Christlicher freyhait des gaists / geprediget werden soll / damit jrer Gnaden underthone nit durch falsch widerwertigpredigt / zu auffrur und verderbung jrer seelen / leyb / lebens / und guts verfürt werden* (1525), pp. A 1 b–A 2 a.

104. "Das also Christliche freyhayt im gaist / und nit ym flaisch / im gewissen innerlich / und nit eusserlich stet / auch ain freyhait guts / und nit böses zuthun sey" (ibid., p. A 2 b).

105. "Wiewol nun ain oberkait unrecht thut / wann sy sich solcher beschwerd [i.e., an unjust command] gegen den underthonen / underzeycht ist doch der underthon schuldig zu leyden / wie unbillich im geschehe / will er Christenlich oder götlich faren" (*Von Gehorsam der Underthon / gegen jrer oberkait* [1525]). Christians do not return evil for evil, Brenz concluded, but go the extra mile.

beyond those actually contracted; the return to common use of streams, forests, meadows, and fields that had been usurped purely for the purpose of preserving the wild (although the lords retained jurisdictional rights in such areas); finally, the right of peasants to fence in their crops and run dogs in their fields to reduce crop damage from wild animals.[106] These were mild reforms, but they also entailed a new recognition of the common man and his basic rights.

106. Blickle, *Die Revolution von 1525*, pp. 217–23, 242.

CHAPTER 8

Humanism and the Reformation

Erasmus and Luther

THE years 1524–25 saw the Reformation lose many of its early supporters, not only among the peasantry but within the ranks of humanists as well. In these years Luther and Erasmus, after almost a decade of cautious sparring, publicly clashed over the issue of man's freedom of will in salvation. Their debate, seemingly narrow and obscure, actually involved the most fundamental discussion of human nature and destiny. Erasmus, the prince of the humanists, believed that people were essentially neutral moral agents, filled as much with a potential for good as for evil, disposed as much to serve their neighbors as to harm them, and as likely to love God as to curse him—all in accordance with a sovereign, free choice. Luther, on the other hand, believed that people were morally creatures of nature and habit, predisposed in advance by their innermost character to act the way they did, whether for good or for ill, for or against their fellowman, in belief or in hatred of God.

Erasmus attacked Luther's theology in a work entitled *A Disquisition on Free Will (De libero arbitrio diatribe)*. Erasmus completed the manuscript in February 1524 and published it the following September. As early as March 1517, before his theses against scholastic theology and indulgences had been published, Luther confided to a friend that he suspected Erasmus to be a potential foe:

I am now reading Erasmus and each day my estimation of him decreases. I am pleased that he exposes and attacks the ignorance of the monks and priests, but I fear that he does not sufficiently promote Christ and the grace of God. . . . Human things carry more weight with him than divine things. Although it is with a heavy heart that I sit in judgment on Erasmus, I must warn you not to accept everything you read [from him] uncritically. These are perilous times in which we live, and I now can see that not everyone is a Christian or truly wise just

Erasmus of Rotterdam. Albrecht Dürer. Although the Christian humanist broke openly with Luther in 1524, his biblical scholarship and satires on the clergy aided the Lutherans. Luther used Erasmus's Greek edition of the New Testament, published in 1516, and accompanied by a new Latin translation that departed in many particulars from the Vulgate. Erasmus's endorsement of a simple biblical piety (what he called the "philosophia Christi"), opposition to superstition and empty ceremony within the medieval church, and support of such reforms as clerical marriage led leaders in both camps to look on him as a covert Protestant. Catholics condemned him for aiding the enemy; Lutherans, for lacking the courage of his convictions. Scholars have also associated his outspoken pacifism and moral approach to religion with the so-called Radical Reformation.

because he can read Greek and Hebrew. St. Jerome had five languages, yet he did not equal Augustine who had only one, although Erasmus has seen the matter differently. But the judgment of one who attributes something to the will of man [in salvation] is one thing, and that of him who confesses nothing but grace another.[1]

Luther later (March 1534) recollected that he had actually doubted Erasmus as early as 1516, when Erasmus's Greek New Testament appeared, because the introduction to the work, which Erasmus published separately under the title *Paraclesis,* seemed to Luther to reduce Jesus to merely a high ethical example rather than a redeeming sacrifice for the sins of mankind. Erasmus apparently first heard about Luther in a report relayed by Georg Spalatin in 1516 of Luther's criticism of the *Paraclesis* and his advice that Erasmus improve his understanding of the Bible by reading St. Augustine.[2]

Erasmus also expressed his pleasure in finding in Luther another who was routing the superstitions of monks and priests, and many considered Erasmus himself to be a "Crypto-Lutheran" in these early years. When pressed to come out either for or against Luther, however, Erasmus always chose the fence. After 1518, however, it became increasingly dangerous even to be suspected of supporting Luther, and Erasmus's stance toward the incipient Reformation became less ambiguous. On the one hand, he urged Frederick the Wise not to turn Luther over to his enemies and engulf the land in revolution, and he expressed the opinion that Luther was not as bad as many he opposed. On the other hand, Erasmus feared that Luther threatened the liberal arts because he "encumbered good learning with an ill will." In response to those who accused him of favoring Luther, he boasted that he was "the first to condemn Luther's books."[3]

By 1521 it was clear to Erasmus that Luther did not intend a gradual reform within the old faith, but a fundamental recasting of traditional doctrines and practices. He now saw the Lutherans as a new breed of scholastics, disobedient to church authority and intent on reviving the dark debates and narrow theological interests of the Middle Ages. In September 1522 he promised friends that he would take a stand against Luther. In January 1523 the Dutch pope Adrian VI personally petitioned him to raise his pen against the Reformation. Henry VIII of England, himself a recent Catholic publicist against Lutheran sacramentology, also urged Erasmus to

1. To Johann Lang, *WABr* 1, p. 90.
2. See *Inquisitio de Fide: A Colloquy by D. Erasmus Roterodamus 1524,* ed. Craig R. Thompson (New Haven, 1950; 2nd ed., Hamden, 1975), pp. 6-8.
3. Letters written between 14 April and 6 December 1520, in *Erasmus and His Age: Selected Letters of Desiderius Erasmus,* ed. H. J. Hillerbrand, trans. M. A. Haworth, S. J. (New York, 1970), pp. 135-36, 148-49, 161.

join the war against the Germans. Henry, who was looked upon by English humanists, quite deludedly it would prove, as an "Erasmian ruler of peace,"[4] was among the select few to receive an advance copy of the *Disquisition on Free Will*.

Having long insisted that only reason and Scripture could stop Luther, Erasmus resolved to deal with Luther as Luther had dealt with Rome: he would conduct a "Disputation Against Lutheran Theology."

After writing and circulating in draft his attack on Luther, but prior to its publication, Erasmus issued in March 1524 an intriguing little work entitled *A Test of Faith (Inquisitio de fide)*. In this dialogue two speakers appear—Aulus, who speaks for Erasmus, and Barbatius, who speaks for Luther—and they debate the nature of the faith. Having been told that Barbatius is a condemned heretic, Aulus examines him item by item, following the Apostles' Creed. After subjecting him to this test, Aulus discovers to his surprise that Barbatius is completely orthodox.

> *Aulus:* Do you believe all these things [contained in the Apostles' Creed] from your very heart?
> *Barbatius:* I believe them so certainly, I tell you, that I am nearly oblivious to all else.
> *Aulus:* When I was in Rome, I did not find all so sound in the faith.[5]

Why, after having written a soon-to-be-published attack on Luther's theology, did Erasmus compose what appears to be a conciliatory, even approving colloquy? Contrary to all appearances, Erasmus was here actually at his most polemical. The Apostles' Creed says absolutely nothing on the issue of the debate—the freedom or bondage of the will in salvation. It deals with what were for Erasmus the really essential points of Christian doctrine: the Trinity, Incarnation, Church, Resurrection, and Last Judgment— general Christian tenets that Luther also held and more firmly than some in Rome.[6] In the *Disquisition on Free Will* Erasmus declared the teaching of the will's bondage to sin to be among "the useless doctrines we can do without." In his view it was a nonessential, even harmful teaching, yet one over which Luther was prepared to perpetuate discord and schism throughout the

4. G. R. Elton, *Reform and Reformation: England, 1509–1558* (Cambridge, Mass., 1977), p. 27. James K. McConica comments: "The *media via* of the Henrician settlement was to many not simply a compromise, but the fulfilment of a positive tradition rooted in the cause of Erasmian reform" (*English Humanists and Reformation Politics Under Henry VIII and Edward VI* [Oxford, 1965], p. 199).

5. *Inquisitio de fide,* p. 73.

6. Georg Cassander (1512–66), a Flemish Catholic humanist, admirer of Erasmus, and friend of Protestants, later proposed a reunion of Catholics and Protestants on the basis of the fundamental teachings of the Apostles' Creed and the church fathers of the first five centuries, what Cassander described as the "consensus universalis antiquitatis."

church. From this perspective the *Inquisitio de fide* actually made a stinging judgment on Luther's character and concept of reform; far from a conciliatory tract, it was a subtle strafing before the bombardment.[7]

Erasmus focused his attack on a statement Luther had made while defending his teaching against the pope. In the bull that condemned Luther (*Exsurge Domine,* June 15, 1520), Pope Leo X had excerpted forty-one articles from Luther's writings, the thirty-sixth of which, taken from the Heidelberg Disputation of 1518, contained the statement "After the Fall free will is something in name only and when it does what is in it [*facit quod in se est*], it sins mortally."[8] In his *Defense and Explanation of All the Articles Unjustly Condemned by the Roman Bull of Leo X* (1520), Luther had returned to this article to reaffirm his position in the most uncompromising way:

> I have expressed it improperly when I said that the will, before obtaining grace, is only an empty name. I should rather have said straightforwardly that free will is really a fiction... with no reality, because it is in no man's power to plan any evil or good. As the article of Wyclif, condemned at Constance, correctly teaches: everything takes place by absolute necessity.[9]

This is the statement on which Erasmus pounced. In its original form, as article thirteen of the Heidelberg Disputation, it had been directed against the Ockhamist teaching that man had the ability to win grace by doing the best that is in him (*facientibus quod in se est, Deus non denegat gratiam*). Erasmus now raised again in 1524 the very issue Luther had disputed against scholastic theologians in 1517. The connection is important and helps explain both Luther's strong personal attack on Erasmus and his extreme doctrinal defense of supralapsarian predestination. Besieged at this time by peasants, lords, and sectarians, Luther must have sensed a final insult and challenge to his Reformation when the prince of the humanists confronted him with theological arguments he had refuted at length in 1517.

Erasmus, "a delicate soul in all his fibres,"[10] was temperamentally latitudinarian in religion, an intellectual *politique,* who placed tranquility among men far above their religious conformity. By his own admission he

7. Cf. *Inquisitio de fide,* pp. 2–3.

8. "Liberum arbitrium post peccatum res est de solo titulo, et dum facit quod in se est peccat mortaliter" (*Luthers Werke im Auswahl,* 5:378).

9. Cited by Erasmus, *A Diatribe or Sermon Concerning Free Will* in *Erasmus-Luther: Discourse on Free Will,* trans. and ed. E. F. Winter (New York, 1961), pp. 44–45. A more recent, full translation of the debate is *Luther and Erasmus: Free Will and Salvation: Erasmus: De Libero Arbitrio,* trans. and ed. E. Gordon Rupp and A. N. Marlow; *Luther: De Servo Arbitrio,* trans, and ed. Philip S. Watson and B. Drewery (Philadelphia, 1969).

10. Johan Huizinga, *Erasmus and the Age of Reformation* (New York, 1957), p. 118.

preferred those who defined religious doctrine too little to those who defined it precisely. He confessed his deep aversion to argument with Luther and to all "assertions" in religion, recalling, no doubt, that Luther's self-defense against the papal bull had borne the title of an "Assertio." "I am quite aware," Erasmus wrote,

> that I am a poor match in such a contest. I am less experienced than other men and I have always had a deep-seated aversion to fighting. Consequently, I have always preferred playing in the freer field of the muses than fighting ironclad in close combat. In addition, so great is my dislike of assertions that I prefer the views of the skeptics wherever the authority of Scripture and the decision of the church permit—a church to which at all times I willingly submit my own views.... I prefer this natural inclination to one I can observe in certain people who are so blindly addicted to one opinion that they cannot tolerate whatever differs from it.[11]

The confrontation with Luther brought about a shift in Erasmus's theology from a traditional Augustinian-Thomist position, which gave God's grace clear priority in salvation, to the semi-Pelagianism of late medieval Ockhamism, which applied free will directly to man's savlation.[12] "By freedom of the will," Erasmus writes, "I understand . . . the power . . . whereby a man can apply himself to or turn away from that which leads unto eternal salvation."[13] Like the Ockhamists, Erasmus defined sin as only an impediment to man's natural freedom to turn to God, by no means its destruction. "Although free will has been wounded through sin, it is not extinct; though it has contracted a paralysis, making us before the reception of grace more readily inclined towards evil than good, free will has not been destroyed."[14] Alluding to the Stoic and Patristic doctrine of an inalienable "spark" of goodness in man *(synteresis)*, Erasmus appealed to "the authority of the Church Fathers who teach that certain concepts of the ethical good are

11. *A Diatribe . . . Concerning Free Will*, in *Erasmus-Luther*, p. 6.
12. See John B. Payne, *Erasmus: His Theology of the Sacraments* (Richmond, 1970), pp. 74–84. While Payne believes the shift occurred in response to Luther's *De servo arbitrio*, I find the Ockhamist position, which Payne describes as "Scotist-nominalist," already in the *Diatribe*, although the *technical scholastic terminology* of the Ockhamists is not prominent until these subsequent writings. Cf. Charles Trinkaus, "Erasmus, Augustine, and the Nominalists," *ARG* 67 (1976): 5–32. Trinkaus recognizes Ockhamist elements in Erasmus *(meritum de congruo, facere quod in se est*, the *synteresis* doctrine), but sympathizes with his efforts to strike a via media between Manichaeism (the consequence of extreme Augustinian teaching) and Pelagianism (the consequence of extreme Ockhamist teaching).
13. *A Diatribe . . . Concerning Free Will*, in *Erasmus-Luther*, p. 20.
14. Ibid., p. 26. Compare Gabriel Biel in Heiko A. Oberman, *The Harvest of Medieval Theology*, (Cambridge, Mass., 1963), pp. 138–31.

within man by his nature, and that he consequently recognizes and follows in some way the ethical good, although coarser inclinations are also present enticing him in the opposite direction."[15] Erasmus declared his agreement with the opinion that "it is within our power to turn . . . towards or away from grace just as it is our pleasure to open or close our eyes against light; for it is incompatible with the infinite love of God . . . that a man's striving with all his might for grace should be frustrated."[16]

Erasmus thought it inconceivable that God could deal with man in an arbitrary or unjust manner; he could not be God if he overrode man's basic moral sensitivities. To Erasmus, the God of Wyclif and Luther was ungodly and encouraged a natural tendency to godlessness.

> Let us assume the truth of what Wyclif has taught and Luther asserted, namely, that everything we do happens not on account of our free will, but out of sheer necessity. What could be more useless than to publish this paradox to the world? . . . Let us assume that it is true . . . that God causes both good and evil in us and that he rewards us for his good works wrought in us and punishes us for the evil deeds done in us. What a loophole the publication of this opinion would open to godlessness. . . . What wicked fellow would henceforth try to better his conduct?[17]

Erasmus discovered support for his position in both the Old and New Testaments.

> Why does one so often hear of reward if there is no merit at all? How would the obedience of those following God's commandments be praised, and disobedience be damned? Why does Holy Scripture so frequently mention judgment, if merit cannot be weighed . . . ? It is disturbing to think of all the many admonitions, commandments, threats, exhortations, and complaints, if we can do nothing.[18]

Perhaps Erasmus's most eloquent comment on the issue came in response to the biblical locus classicus on predestination, Jeremiah 18:6, where man's relationship to God is compared to clay in the hands of a potter: "As clay in the hand of the potter, so are you in my hand." Despite Jeremiah, Erasmus insisted that people were not lumps of clay, but thinking, willing beings, created in the image of God. "What's the good of . . . man," he asked, "if

---

15. *A Diatribe . . . concerning Free Will*, in *Erasmus-Luther*, p. 64; cf. Biel in Oberman, *Harvest of Medieval Theology*, pp. 65–66.
16. *A Diatribe . . . Concerning Free Will*, in *Erasmus-Luther*, p. 29.
17. *A Diatribe . . . Concerning Free Will*, in *Erasmus-Luther*, pp. 11–12.
18. Ibid., p. 81.

God can treat him like the potter his clay, or deal with him like a rock?"[19]

Although he wrote in defense of the freedom of will in salvation, Erasmus believed himself to be the advocate of a middle course between grace and free will, avoiding, on the one hand, the errors of "the Pelagians," as he described the "more recent theologians" or Ockhamists, and, on the other, those of "the Manichaeans," as he describes strict Augustinians like Luther, whom he felt held man in such low esteem that they seemed to despise the creation itself.[20] "I like the sentiments of those who attribute a little to the freedom of the will, the most, however, to grace," Erasmus declared. "One must not avoid the Scylla of arrogance by going into the Charybdis of desperation and indolence."[21] In a charming parable, highly revealing of the Erasmian temper of mind, Erasmus asked the reader to imagine an apple placed before a child who can just barely walk. The child tries with all his might to reach the apple, but is too weak and falls with every effort. His loving father, seeing his predicament, lifts the child and gently guides him to the apple. Aided by his father, the child progresses until he can at last grasp the apple, which he then enjoys as a reward for his assisted efforts. Comments Erasmus in summary of his position:

> The child could not have raised himself without the father's help; he would not have seen the apple without the father's showing; he would not have stepped forward without the father's helping . . .; he would not have reached the apple without the father's placing it into his hand. What can the child claim for himself? Yet, he did do something, although he must not glory in his own strength, since he owes everything to the father . . . . I readily admit that our striving (after salvation) contributes less to the gaining of eternal life than the boy's running at the hand of his father.[22]

In the debate between Erasmus and Luther, style revealed much of the man. Erasmus, who believed the truth to lie in more than one position on an

---

19. Ibid., p. 93. Compare the Dominican friar Robert Holcot, Ockhamist opponent of the strict predestinarian Thomas Bradwardine, on the clay-potter simile: "Although we are like clay in comparison to God one cannot by any means apply the analogy in every respect to man. Nor is the analogy totally correct, because there is no covenant between the potter and the clay; and even assuming that there could be such a convenant, the potter could very well break it without abrogating the Covenant law. But God cannot break his pact with man without the Covenant being destroyed. Nor can the clay [like man] either partially or fully merit anything from the potter" (*Lectures on the Wisdom of Solomon,* in Heiko A. Oberman, *Forerunners of the Reformation,* (New York, 1967), pp. 149.-150).

20. Trinkaus, "Erasmus, Augustine, and the Nominalists," *ARG* (1976): 26–28.

21. *A Diatribe . . . Concerning Free Will,* in *Erasmus-Luther,* pp. 92–93.

22. Ibid., pp. 86–87.

issue, preferred the indirect and gentle discourse of parable and metaphor. Luther, confident in the extreme, exhorted the reader in blunt and uncompromising speech. Explaining his delay in answering Erasmus, he scorned his opponent with the humor of a man all too sure about the truth.

> You see, Erasmus, I lost all desire to answer you, not because I was busy, or because it would have been a difficult task, nor on account of your great eloquence, nor for fear of you, but simply because of disgust, indignation, and contempt, which, if I may say so, expresses my judgment of your *Diatribe*.... If I answer now, it is because faithful brethren press me to it.... And who knows but that God may even condescend to visit you, dearest Erasmus, through me, his poor weak vessel, and that I may (which from my heart I desire ...) come to you in this book in a happy hour and gain a dearest brother. For although you write wrongly concerning free will, I owe you no small thanks, because you have confirmed my own view. Seeing the case for free will argued with such great talent, yet leaving it worse than it was before, is an evident proof that free will is a downright lie! It is like the woman of the gospel; the more the physicians treat her case, the worse it gets [Luke 8:43; Mark 5:26].[23]

Luther accused Erasmus of sacrificing principle to an illusory quest for tranquility.

> Your words amount to this, that it matters little to you what anyone believes anywhere, as long as the peace of the world is undisturbed.... You seem to look upon Christian doctrines as nothing better than the opinions of philosophers and men.... You wish to end *our* fighting as a peacemaker.... Allow *us* to be assertors. You go ahead and favor your skeptics and academics.... The Holy Spirit is no skeptic, and what he has written into our hearts are no doubts or opinions, but assertions more certain and firm than all human experience and life.[24]

For Luther, the points at issue could not have been more serious, nor the need for a decisive stand more imperative.

> Let me tell you, and ... let it sink deep into your mind, that I am concerned with a serious, vital, and eternal verity, yea such a fundamental one that it ought to be maintained and defended at the cost of

---

23. *The Bondage of the Will*, in *Erasmus-Luther*, p. 98.
24. Ibid., pp. 102–03.

life itself, even though the whole world should not only be thrown into turmoil and fighting but shattered in chaos and reduced to nothing.[25]

Luther especially resented Erasmus's readiness to compromise, what he calls "that prudence of yours [which] carries you along [so that] you side with neither party and escape safely through Scylla and Charybdis."[26] This judgment came to be shared by many Catholic critics of Erasmus in the course of the sixteenth century. By midcentury Catholic authorities cited Erasmus's writings as the inspiration of the Reformation, and in 1559, Pope Paul IV banned them all. After the Council of Trent adjourned (1562), some of Erasmus's works continued to circulate, but only in special expurgated editions.[27] Catholic scholars still today present Erasmus as vacillating between the confessions. According to Joseph Lortz, for example, "Erasmus remained in the church . . . but as a half Catholic . . . indecisive, hesitating, suspended in the middle."[28]

What of the issues at stake? What did Luther mean when he said that God saves people by "absolute necessity," without regard to their wills and desires? Luther protested that Erasmus had caricatured his original statement, which taught that a person's salvation so depended upon God's presence and initiative that if God were not actively present and working within him, then nothing a person did could be good or contribute to his salvation. Fallen human nature, apart from God's grace, "naturally" inclined to the opposite of what God required of it. The "necessity" of salvation was thus a "necessity of immutability," a necessity resulting both from the constant character of God's will and the evil character of fallen human nature. Luther offered the following summary:

A man void of the Spirit of God does not do evil against his will, under pressure, as though taken by the neck and forced to do it . . . but he does it spontaneously and willingly. And this willingness and desire to do evil he cannot, by his own strength, eliminate, restrain, or change.

25. Ibid., pp. 107–08.
26. Ibid., p. 105.
27. Marcella and Paul Grendler, "The Survival of Erasmus in Italy," *Erasmus in English* 8 (1976): 2–21.
28. *Die Reformation in Deutschland* (Freiburg, 1962), 1: 131. See also Harry J. McSorley, *Luther: Right or Wrong?* (New York, 1969). Lest there be any doubts about Erasmus's basic commitment to the Roman Church, lukewarm though it may at times have been, see Myron Gilmore's response to Augustin Renaudet's depiction of Erasmus as a leading advocate of a "third church" intermediary between Wittenberg and Rome: "Italian Reactions to Erasmian Humanism," in *Itinerarium Italicum,* ed. H. A. Oberman and Thomas A. Brady, Jr. (Leiden, 1975), pp. 114–15. As Gilmore makes clear, Erasmus's position was one of "resigned acceptance of Rome and repudiation of Luther."

[Try as he may] he still goes on desiring and craving to do evil. If external pressure compels him to act outwardly to the contrary, still his will within remains averse and chafes under such constraint. . . . this is what we mean by the necessity of immutability: that the will cannot change itself, nor give itself another bent . . . which would not be the case if it were free or had a free will.[29]

Erasmus assumed a certain moral neutrality in human nature; man may be naturally inclined to sin, but good and evil remain his own conscious choice. No one is committed in advance of his actions by a disposition of his nature to act necessarily in either a good or an evil way—evil is only as evil *does;* the deed defines the doer. Like Pico della Mirandola, Erasmus believed that each person was free to create his own moral nature—good by doing good, evil by doing evil.[30]

In contrast, Luther saw man as bound to will in accordance with a set, fallen nature: evil does as evil *is;* the doer defines the deed. This position was fully consistent with his earlier criticism of Aristotle and the Ockhamists, both of whom had taught that moral virtue was acquired and that people became righteous only by doing righteous works. Luther believed this Aristotelian dictum to be the philosophical taproot of the Ockhamist teaching that grace could be earned by doing one's best. As early as 1517, he insisted to the contrary that only those who had first been made righteous by grace could call their works good; virtuous deeds presupposed an antecedently virtuous person.[31]

Luther never meant to deny freedom of choice in everyday life *(in inferioribus);* in matters unrelated to his moral and religious nature, he believed man possessed considerable freedom.

If we do not want to drop this term ["free will"] altogether, which would be the safest and most Christian thing to do, we may still use it in good faith to denote free will in respect not of what is above man, but of what is below him. This is to say, man should know in regard to his goods and possessions that he has the right to use them, to do or to leave undone, according to his free will. . . . However, with regard to God and in all things pertaining to salvation or damnation, man has no

29. *The Bondage of the Will,* in *Erasmus-Luther,* p. 111.
30. It was a common humanist conviction that "vertu requires an effort and cannot be considered a natural gift. Every humanist believed that *humanitas* must be won. What must be acquired, and how, were other questions, but for no one was *humanitas* a simple, given fact" (Sem Dresden, "The Reception of the Italian Renaissance in France," in *Itinerarium Italicum,* p. 182).
31. See above, p. 235.

free will, but is a captive, servant, and bondslave, either to the will of God or to the will of the devil.[32]

For Luther, to endow man with complete freedom of will in morality and religion meant to ascribe truly divine powers to him.[33]

Do not the many imperatives in Scripture that command people to do good and avoid evil suggest innate moral ability? The very thought that God could demand of people what he knew in advance they were incapable of doing shocked Erasmus. For Luther, however, this was exactly God's intention. The many imperatives in Scripture "declare no man's ability but his duty"; they are intended "to goad and rouse man so that he may know by sure experience how unable he is to do any of these things" and throw himself on God's mercy and grace.[34]

Luther also defended the clay-potter simile, offering at this point his strongest criticism of Erasmus, as he summarized the crucial difference between them:

> [That man is to God as clay to a potter]—this is what reason cannot . . . bear [to hear]. This is what offended so many men of outstanding ability, men who have won acceptance down through so many ages. At this point they demand that God should act according to man's idea of right, and do what seems proper to themselves—or else that he should cease to be God. "The secrets of his majesty," they say, "shall not profit him; let him render a reason why he is God, or why he wills and does that which has no appearance of justice in it." It is like asking a cobbler or a belt-maker to take the seat of judgment. [Carnal man] does not deign to give God glory to the extent of believing him to be just and good when he speaks and acts above and beyond the definitions of Justinian's *Code* or the fifth book of Aristotle's *Ethics*.[35]

To Luther, Erasmus's God seemed so much like man that he was hardly God at all.

In retrospect, both the *Disquisition on Free Will* and the *Bondage of the Will* may have been prophetic of subsequent developments in Western intellectual and religious history. Erasmus feared that a God who challenged

---

32. *The Bondage of the Will*, in *Erasmus-Luther*, p. 113.
33. "Free will is a term applicable only to the Divine Majesty; for only God can do, and does . . . 'whatever he wills in heaven and on earth' (Ps. 135:6). If free will is ascribed to men, it is ascribed with no more propriety than divinity itself" (*The Bondage of the Will*, in *Martin Luther on the Bondage of the Will*, trans. J. I. Packer and O. R. Johnston [Westwood, N.J., 1957], p. 105).
34. Ibid., pp. 153, 156.
35. Ibid., pp. 232–33.

man's self-esteem would be abandoned by all save the most naive worshipers;[36] Luther perceived that a God subject to man's own ethical sensitivities would prove to be little more than man's alter ego. From the perspective of modern religious fundamentalism and atheism, the debate between Erasmus and Luther may have been as portentous as each believed.

Protestant Reformers:
Biblical Humanists or
New Scholastics?

THE breach that opened between Luther and Erasmus in 1525 did not end collaboration between humanists and Protestant reformers, and this famous confrontation should not be taken as symptomatic of a larger incompatibility, much less divorce, between humanism and Protestantism. Protestant religious reforms continued to go hand in hand with humanist educational reforms in Protestant cities and towns throughout much of the sixteenth century. Protestant reformers continued to share with humanists a belief in the unity of wisdom, eloquence, and action, even though Protestant views on church doctrine and human nature gave their educational programs a content different from those of the humanists.[37] For Protestants everywhere the *studia humanitatis* remained a more appropriate tool for reform than scholastic dialectic; humanist studies taught the new Protestant clergy the languages needed to deal authoritatively with the original text of Scripture and helped them acquire the rhetorical skills required to communicate Protestant doctrine effectively.

A fundamental and lasting kinship existed between humanism and Protestantism. Neither had been able to find in the dominant late medieval scholastic traditions either attractive personal models or an educational

36. Keith Thomas observes that in England the religion that survived the decline of magic was not that of the Reformation, but a "rational religion" (deism). "When the Devil was banished to Hell, God himself was confined to working through natural causes. 'Special providences' and private revelations gave way to the notion of a providence which itself obeyed natural laws accessible to human study" (*Religion and the Decline of Magic: Studies in Popular Beliefs in Sixteenth and Seventeenth Century England* (London, 1971), p. 639).

37. According to Gerald Strauss, "every school ordinance [of the Lutheran Reformation] gave under the heading *Zucht* a formidable list of prescriptions and proscriptions obviously designed to minimize choice, limit freedom of self-expression, and weaken personal judgment, while at the same time cultivating habits of conformity, deference, and assent" ("Reformation and Pedagogy: Educational Thought and Practice in the Lutheran Reformation," in *The Pursuit of Holiness in Late Medieval and Renaissance Religion*, ed. Charles Trinkaus and Heiko A. Oberman (Leiden, 1974), p. 287). See also Strauss's *Luther's House of Learning: Indoctrination of the Young in the German Reformation* (Baltimore, 1978) pp. 136–145. A more balanced judgment of the content of Luther pedagogy is provided by Lewis W. Spitz, "Further Lines of Inquiry for the Study of 'Reformation and Pedagogy,'" in *The Pursuit of Holiness in Late Medieval and Renaissance Religion*, pp. 295–306.

program appropriate to the changed society of the sixteenth century. Finding the chivalric and clerical traditions of the Middle Ages inadequate to both their literary interests and political aspirations, humanists turned instead to classical antiquity, the church fathers, or both; Protestants, finding medieval religion incapable of resolving their religious problems, turned back to the Bible and the church fathers. Ignatius of Loyola recognized this common feature and warned against humanist and Protestant undercutting of church tradition by a direct reading of Scripture and antiquity. In the *Spiritual Exercises* he insisted that the Bible and church fathers be read only under the guidance of the more recent "scholastic doctors [such] as Thomas Aquinas, Bonaventura, and the Master of the Sentences."[38]

Such German humanists as Conrad Celtis (1459–1508), Johannes Trithemius (1462–1516), Willibald Pirckheimer (1470–1528), Conrad Peutinger (1465–1547), Johannes Reuchlin (1455–1522), and Conrad Mutianus Rufus (1471–1526) had long cultivated the liberal arts, opposed gross religious superstition, and championed a German national culture. In Germany, as also in England, humanism can be said to have created a "preparatory change of atmosphere" that favored the Reformation.[39] After Luther posted his ninety-five theses in 1517, German humanists became his first identifiable supporters; they believed his religious reform to be a continuation of their own criticism of scholasticism and return to purer sources. In the end this proved a misperception of the reformer's full intent, but initially it inspired both sides.[40]

German humanists came to Luther fresh from their own battle with scholastic theologians in the so-called Reuchlin affair, a conflict initiated by a converted Jew named Pfefferkorn, who, to advance the Christian cause, launched in 1506 an almost successful campaign to suppress Jewish writings. In the course of the campaign Pfefferkorn viciously attacked Reuchlin, Europe's foremost Christian authority on Hebrew learning and a most credulous devotee of the magical arts of the Cabala. Although anti-Judaism rather than hostility to humanist studies seems to have been a primary motive of the Cologne scholastics who backed Pfefferkorn, a number of

---

38. "The scholastic doctors, being of more recent date, not only have a clearer understanding of Holy Scripture and of the teachings of the positive and holy doctors, but also, being enlightened and inspired by the Divine Power, they are helped by the Councils, Canons, and Constitutions of our Holy Mother Church" (*The Spiritual Exercises,* trans. A. Mottola [Garden City, N.Y., 1964], p. 140). For an earlier version of this argument, cf. Paul L. Nyhus, "Caspar Schatzgeyer and Conrad Pellican: The Triumph of Dissension in the Early Sixteenth Century," *ARG* 61 (1970): 194.

39. A. G. Dickens, *The English Reformation* (London, 1964), p. 63.

40. See the seminal essay by Bernd Moeller, "Die deutschen Humanisten und die Anfänge der Reformation," *ZKG* 70 (1959): 46–61.

German humanists interpreted the attack on Reuchlin as an assault on "academic freedom" and joined Reuchlin in hot reply. Ulrich von Hutten and the Erfurt humanist Crotus Rubeanus published the most memorable piece in the affair, the gross satire on scholastics entitled *Letters of Obscure Men.* When Luther came under attack by the church's theologians after 1517, Reuchlin himself drew a parallel between his own past difficulties and those the young reformer was then experiencing.[41]

The positive association of humanism and Protestantism, especially in the early years of the Reformation, is only one side of the story, however, as contemporary humanists and kindred critics of Protestantism were quick to point out. Erasmus, as we have seen, came to view the Lutherans as a threat to the liberal arts and good learning.[42] Sebastian Franck (ca. 1499–1542) predicted that the "new scholastics," as he called the Lutherans, would outstrip the papacy in the production of theological tomes and commentaries on Scripture.[43] Sebastian Castellio (1515–63) accused Genevan Calvinists of continuing the "sophistries of the Sorbonne," while the Lutheran spiritualist Valentin Weigel (1533–88) dismissed Philip Melanchthon, the mind behind the authoritative Lutheran creeds, as a mediocre "Greek grammarian and Aristotelian philosopher."[44]

In terms of its intellectual history Protestantism can be identified exclusively with neither humanism nor scholasticism.[45] Nor did the reformers begin as biblical humanists only to end up as scholastics. From the start they were a peculiar blending of distinctive traits of both humanism and scholasticism. Although they replaced scholastic dialectic with the rhetorical ideals of humanism when they reformed university curricula, the reformers con-

41. "God be praised that now the monks have found someone else who will give them more to do than I" (cited by Lewis W. Spitz, "The Course of German Humanism," in *Itinerarium Italicum,* p. 409). A recent study argues that scholars have exaggerated humanist association with Reuchlin: James Overfield, "A New Look at the Reuchlin Affair," in *Studies in Medieval and Renaissance Thought* 8, ed. H. L. Adelson (Lincoln, Neb., 1971), pp. 167–207.

42. Letter to Martin Bucer (2 March 1532), in *Erasmus and His Age: Selected Letters of Desiderius Erasmus,* pp. 259–60.

43. Horst Weigelt, *Sebastian Franck und die lutherische Reformation* (Gütersloh, 1972), p. 48.

44. Castellio, *Contra libellum Calvini in quo ostendere conatur Haereticos jure gladij coercendos esse* (n.p. 1562), p. L 1 a; Weigel, *Dialogus de Christianismo,* ed. A. Ehrentreich in *Valentin Weigel: Sämtliche Schriften* (Stuttgart-Bad Cannstatt, 1967), 4: 47.

45. Paul O. Kristeller believes that the term "Christian humanism" can properly be applied to "those scholars with a humanist classical and rhetorical training who explicitly discussed religious or theological problems in all or some of their writings"—a definition that would exclude Luther, yet embrace, in addition to Melanchthon and Calvin, Erasmus, Vives, Budé, More, Hooker, and many Jesuit fathers (*Renaissance Thought: The Classic, Scholastic, and Humanist Strains* [New York, 1961], pp. 86–87).

tinued to share the preoccupation of medieval theologians with the definition and defense of church doctrine. This was more on a homiletical than on a theoretical level, however; preaching doctrine remained more important to Protestants than contemplating it. Protestants made the liberal arts a handmaiden to a continuing medieval theological ideal. They did not take up the educational program of the humanists for its own sake, nor for any latent moral or social possibilities in it, but because they believed its training in languages and oratorical skills was the more effective way to transmit Christian doctrine and inculcate Christian righteousness in the masses.[46]

There are at least four distinct schools of thought on the nature of Renaissance humanism.[47] One builds on the work of Jacob Burckhardt, who saw the Renaissance as the birth of modern consciousness and praised humanists as advocates of individualism, secularism, and moral autonomy against medieval Christian culture. A second follows the reverse thesis of Giuseppe Tofannin, who has presented Italian humanism as an epitome of medieval Christian culture and humanists as true champions of Christian Neoplatonism and Augustinianism against Averroism and Aristotelianism. Still another school of thought follows Paul Oskar Kristeller in more modestly restricting the definition of humanism to educational and cultural programs dedicated to rhetoric, scholarship, good language, and literature, with only a secondary interest in metaphysics and moral philosophy, whether Christian or pagan. A final school of thought is connected with the controversial work of Hans Baron, which portrays Florentine humanists as proponents of republican liberty and civic responsibility, who urged urban elites to study ancient history and literature primarily for its political and moral instruction.[48]

Humanism and scholasticism not only defy simple, solitary definitions, but also resist a prevalent scholarly tendency to depict them as mortal

46. Cf. Alain Dufour, "Humanisme et Reformation: Etat de la question," in *XIIe Congrès Internationale des Sciences Historiques, Vienne, 29 Aout-5 Septembre 1965: Rapports* (Horn/Wien, 1965), 3: 57–74.

47. I have extrapolated this summary from Donald Weinstein, "In whose Image and Likeness? Interpretations of Renaissance Humanism," *JHI* 33 (1972): 165–76; and Helmar Junghans, "Der Einfluss des Humanismus auf Luthers Entwicklung bis 1518," *Luther-Jahrbuch 1970*, ed. Franz Lau (Hamburg, 1970), pp. 45–51.

48. Baron's thesis was set forth in *The Crisis of the Early Italian Renaissance: Civic Humanism and Republican Liberty in an Age of Classicism and Tyranny* (Princeton, 1955). It has received sharp criticism from Jerrold E. Seigel, "'Civic Humanism' or Ciceronian Rhetoric?," *Past and Present* 34 (1966): 3–48, who found more rhetoric than active defense of republican ideals among Italian humanists. Baron's reply: "Leonardo Bruni: 'Professional Rhetorician' or 'Civic Humanist'?" *Past and Present* 36 (1967): 21–37. A more recent criticism of Baron's work is David Robey, "P. P. Vergerio the Elder: Republicanism and Civic Values in the Work of an Early Humanist," *Past and Present* 58 (1973): 3–37.

enemies. The two movements actually originated together in Italy in the thirteenth century and developed side by side throughout and beyond the Renaissance; attacks on Aristotelianism by humanists like Petrarch and Leonardo Bruni have been characterized as only "interludes within a long period of peaceful coexistence."[49] An authority on German humanism also characterizes the relationship between humanist poets and scholastic theologians at the University of Erfurt, the first north German university to introduce humanist studies in the fifteenth century, as one of "peaceful coexistence."[50] At the University of Heidelberg humanists and scholastics shared a common goal of reform; the scholastic theologian Johannes Wenck urged biblical studies and stressed the importance of applied knowledge (nützlich erkentnis") in an effort to broaden the narrow traditional curriculum.[51] It has been suggested that in their intellectual origins and approach to university studies, many fifteenth-century thinkers were actually hybrids of scholasticism and humanism—"'half humanist' and 'half scholastic' in outlook."[52] What Charles Trinkaus has described as "theologia rhetorica," the union of theological theory with practical preaching, was as much an ideal of reform-minded scholastics as of the humanist critics of scholasticism.[53]

Not only were humanist attacks on scholastic obscurity and impracticality not without precedent among scholastics themselves, but humanists seldom let their criticism of scholasticism lead them to question the basic Christian content of scholastic learning. Critical of scholastic form and method, they became docile before the capital points of scholastic doctrine. Lorenzo Valla, for example, one of the most critical humanists, censured Thomas Aquinas for his preoccupation with logic and metaphysics and his barbarous Latin style and described his theology as inferior to that of the Latin and Greek fathers, yet he accepted Aquinas as a saint whose doctrine was sound.[54] Erasmus answered those who accused him of attempting to

49. "Humanism and Scholasticism in the Italian Renaissance," in *Studies in Renaissance Thought and Letters* (Rome, 1956), pp. 576–77'; "Florentine Platonism and Its Relations with Humanism and Scholasticism," *Church History* 8 (1939): 211. Cf. also R. W. Southern, *Medieval Humanism* (New York, 1970), p. 49.

50. Junghans, "Der Einfluss des Humanismus auf Luthers Entwicklung," p. 65.

51. Gerhard Ritter, *Die Heidelberger Universität*, vol. 1, *Das Mittelalter (1386–1508)* (Heidelberg, 1936), pp. 421–31, 450.

52. Spitz, "The Course of German Humanism," pp. 375–76.

53. Charles Trinkaus, *In Our Image and Likeness: Humanity and Divinity in Italian Humanist Thought* (London, 1970), 2. See above, p. 76.

54. Hanna H. Gray, "Valla's *Encomium of St. Thomas Aquinas* and the Humanist Conception of Christian Antiquity," in *Essays in History and Literature Presented by the Fellows of the Newberry Library to Stanley Pargellis*, ed. H. Bluhm (Chicago, 1965), pp. 37–51. Cf. also Lewis W. Spitz, *The Religious Renaissance of the German Humanists* (Cambridge, Mass., 1963), pp. 8, 38, 206, 275; Trinkaus, *In Our Image and Likeness*, 2: 766.

undermine scholastic theology by insisting he was in truth its friend: "It has not been my wish to abolish it, but that it may become more authentic and serious; in this, unless I am mistaken, I am promoting and not hurting it."[55] Those who chose to abolish scholastic doctrine as well as criticize scholastic method became Protestants.

Despite their complexity, both conceptually and historically, humanism and scholasticism do have definable distinguishing characteristics. The most basic is their different view of the proper method and goal of education. Humanists read classical authors (orators, poets, historians, and moral philosophers) directly in their original tongue and urged that such study of primary sources be made the core of the arts curriculum. This approach to education tended to make the text-oriented individual scholar rather than an established tradition of interpretation the authority on a subject.[56] Scholastics, on the other hand, approached their subjects, whether biblical, theological, or philosophical, indirectly, by juxtaposing the views of recognized past authorities. For scholastics, the scholar's basic task was not to sit in judgment on tradition from a superior vantage point of the original source—herein lay the constant threat of purely humanistic studies—but to harmonize divergent opinions on a subject, reconciling authorities rather than exposing and rejecting them. Where humanists engaged in the edition of original sources on the basis of the best manuscripts at hand, scholastics wrote summaries of traditional teaching and concordances of discordant opinions. Even when scholastic theologians edited texts, as the Augustinians did the works of their founder, they continued to be consumed by questions of its doctrinal unity and the continuity of historical interpretation.

A second distinction between humanism and scholasticism lies in the order of priorities to which their different vocations and educational philosophies inclined. Humanists, as orators and rhetoricians, gave right living and good deeds—the active civic life—priority over right thinking and correct confession, while scholastic theologians, as defenders of church doctrine and tradition, observed the reverse order of priorities. Humanists were, of course, not indifferent to the quality of their thought, the truthfulness of their assertions, or the importance of tradition;[57] and

55. Letter to Louis Ber (30 March 1529), in *Erasmus and His Age*, p. 224. See also Christian Dolfen, *Die Stellung des Erasmus von Rotterdam zur scholastischen Methode* (Osnabrück, 1936), pp. 51, 82.

56. On the threat of humanist method to the scholastic tradition in all fields of learning, see Charles G. Nauert, Jr., "The Clash of Humanists and Scholastics: An Approach to Pre-Reformation Controversies," *Sixteenth Century Journal* 4 (1973); 12–13.

57. As Sem Dresden summarizes: "One [humanist] writer might lay emphasis on the *vita contemplativa*, another on 'civic humanism,' but all acknowledged the need for and value of both and endeavored to do justice to both at the same time" ("The Profile of the Reception of the Italian Renaissance in France," in *Itinerarium Italicum*, p. 184).

scholastics were confident that true doctrine would lead to a responsible moral life. But unlike scholastic theologians, humanists judged doctrine and tradition by their larger moral ends. Although many later Renaissance thinkers (post-1527) seem to have become jaded intellectuals, at home with abstraction and hierarchical thinking and viewing man as basically a creature of intellect rather than of will, this was not the character of the early humanist movement, nor the essence of humanism. Early Renaissance thinkers rejected the abstract man of classical and theological anthropology, with his tiered faculties of reason, will, and sensual appetite. They conceived man as a complex unity, driven mainly by passion and will, who found self-fulfilment not in withdrawn contemplation of eternal verities, but in active engagement in society.[58] For them, it was not a question of simply making will supreme over intellect within the traditional hierarchical view of man, as Scotists and Ockhamists had earlier done, but of breaking altogether with the traditional conceptual scheme. German humanists in the late fifteenth century, "action-oriented and people-directed," rejected all abstract and merely antiquarian pursuits.[59] It was characteristic of the early humanist movement generally to scorn scholastics for "abstracting from life." Against such abstraction Petrarch made the famous declaration "It is better to will the good than to know the truth."[60] There was an abiding disinclination among humanists to pursue doctrinal questions beyond a certain point, to make inquiries for what seemed to be the sake of inquiries. This trait stands out especially in Erasmus, who saw the fall of the church from its true mission in the evolution of church doctrine during the disputatious councils of the patristic era.[61] When Erasmus challenged Luther on the issue of free will, it was because he considered Luther's doctrine of the will's bondage to sin detrimental to moral life *even if it were true.*[62] Such was the humanist's order of priorities. The consequences of ideas were as important as the ideas themselves; the effect of a doctrine had also to be considered, because what was truthful was not necessarily useful.

58. William Bouwsma, "Changing Assumptions in Later Renaissance Culture," *Viator* 7 (1976): 431–40.

59. Spitz, "The Course of German Humanism," pp. 390–97.

60. Cited by Hanna H. Gray, "Renaissance Humanism: The Pursuit of Eloquence," in *Renaissance Essays*, ed. P. O. Kristeller and P. Wiener (New York, 1968), p. 203.

61. Letter to John Carondelet (5 January 1522/23), in *Erasmus and His Age*, pp. 168–69.

62. "Fingamus igitur in aliquo sensu verum esse, quod docuit Vuyclevus, Lutherus asseruit, quicquid fit a nobis, non libero arbitrio, sed mera necessitate fieri, quid inutilius, quam hoc paradoxon evulgari mundo?" (*De libero arbitrio* I a 10, in *Erasmus von Rotterdam: Ausgewählte Schriften* (Darmstadt, 1969), 4: 18). On the intimate relationship between doctrine, language, and behavior (piety) in Erasmus's theology, see the recent study of Marjorie O'Rourke Boyle, *Erasmus on Language and Method in Theology* (Toronto, 1977), pp. 43, 68, 73, passim.

As the church's theologians, scholastics had a peculiar stake in tradition and church dogma. Their vocation inclined them to make the abstract pursuit of truth, or correct confession, an overriding preoccupation. In the high Middle Ages scholastic theology became the most disciplined form of the medieval *fides quaerens intellectum*. Whereas humanists, alert to the ethical consequences of theological doctrines, insisted that good deeds must also be a test of creedal truth, scholastics, sensitive to the necessity of an abiding body of truth, insisted that true creeds must be the fount of good deeds. Luther, who received the most intensive scholastic training, considered his doctorate in theology sufficient authority to contest even the pope in matters of doctrine, whereas Erasmus poked fun at his own theological training, calling it a "foolish project," no more than an accommodation to the custom of the day.[63] For Luther, if a doctrine was true, life had to adjust to it, regardless of the difficulty or the cost; the eternal truth of an idea was more important than its short-term temporal consequences.

Protestantism and Humanist Educational Reforms

PROTESTANTS embraced a basic humanist program of studies and set it in place of the scholastic. Luther himself had come under humanist influence in the early 1500s during his training in the arts at the University of Erfurt, the most humanistically progressive German university at the time, thanks to the importation of Italian humanism by Nikolaus Marschalk. Erfurt humanists were also prominent in the Reuchlin affair after 1512. Although Luther's philosophy teachers at Erfurt, Jodocus Trutfetter and Bartholomäus Arnoldi von Usingen, were trained scholastics, they also sympathized with humanist reforms, and one of Luther's closest friends, fellow monk Johannes Lang, an expert Hebraist and Graecist, eventually became prior of the Erfurt Augustinian order. Before he transferred to Wittenberg, Luther had been exposed to a humanism that encouraged the study of ancient languages, especially Greek, and criticized scholastic theology on the basis of the Bible and the writings of the church fathers.[64]

The University of Wittenberg, located according to a contemporary description "in termino civilitatis," had been founded in 1502, the second youngest German university (after the University of Frankfurt an der Oder,

63. Wilhelm Borth, *Die Luthersache (Causa Lutheri) 1517–24: Die Anfänge der Reformation als Frage von Politik und Recht* (Lübeck/Hamburg, 1970), p. 23; Huizinga, *Erasmus and the Age of Reformation*, p. 62.

64. Junghans, "Der Einfluss des Humanismus auf Luthers Entwicklung bis 1518," pp. 64–76.

established in 1506).[65] Since its founding, it had favored the *via antiqua*, listing courses according to the teaching of Duns Scotus *(via Scoti)* and Thomas Aquinas *(via Thomae)*. Luther's Ockhamist philosophy teacher in Erfurt, Trutfetter, however, taught in Wittenberg between 1507 and 1510, giving the *via moderna* a hearing. Although a contingent of academic humanists had existed in the university since its inception, the dominance of scholastic doctors within the arts faculty deemphasized humanistic studies. Still, between 1502 and 1514, a number of humanist reforms occurred. A modern Latin grammar replaced the traditional work of Alexander of Villa Dei; better Latin translations of Aristotle's works appeared; Greek was intermittently taught and Greek texts published; geography and ethnology became part of the curriculum; and mathematics received special emphasis. All these measures anticipated the major reforms introduced by Luther and Melanchthon in 1518.[66]

Even before his famed assault on scholasticism in the *Disputation Against Scholastic Theology* (September 1517), Luther described Aristotle, Porphyry, and scholastic commentaries on Lombard's *Sentences* as "hopeless studies" *(perdita studia)* and "tyrants" within the schools. In May 1517 he boasted that a new theology and St. Augustine reigned in Wittenberg and Aristotle's "final doom" was only a matter of time.[67] On May 9, 1518, Luther wrote a famous letter to Trutfetter in which he defended the new Wittenberg theology and declared his conviction that the church would never be reformed until canons, decretals, and scholastic theology, philosophy, and logic were eradicated and new studies put in their place.[68]

Between 1518 and 1519 Luther made direct efforts to eliminate traditional Aristotelian studies from the university curriculum. He requested that the course on Aristotle's *Ethics* be made elective "so that students could spend more time with Scripture and true theology."[69] Thrice within as

65. G. A. Benrath, "Die deutsche evangelische Universität der Reformationszeit," in H. Rössler and G. Franz, *Universität und Gelehrtenstand 1400–1800* (Limburg/Lahn, 1970), pp. 63–83.

66. Max Steinmetz, "Die Universität Wittenberg und der Humanismus (1502–1521)," in *450 Jahre Martin Luther Universität Halle-Wittenberg* (Halle, 1952), pp. 108–10, 112–16; E. G. Schwiebert, "New Groups and Ideas at the University of Wittenberg," *ARG* 49 (1958): 65, 67; Maria Grossmann, "Wittenberg Printing, Early Sixteenth Century," in *Sixteenth Century Essays and Studies,* ed. Carl S. Meyer (St. Louis, 1970), pp. 53–74. The conservative bent of Wittenberg humanism prior to Melanchthon's arrival is illustrated by Otto Beckmann, a leading humanist, who, despite his dislike of scholasticism, refused to make sweeping changes in the curriculum. He decided against the Reformation in 1519. See Nikolaus Müller, *Die Wittenberger Bewegung* (Leipzig, 1911), p. 236.

67. To Lang (8 February 1517), *WABr* 1, p. 88 (= *LW* 48, p. 37); (18 May 1517), *WABr* 1, p. 99 (= *LW* 48, p. 41).

68. To Jodocus Trutfettter (9 May 1518), *WABr* 1, p. 170.

69. To Spalatin (18 May 1518; 2 September 1518), *WABr* 1, pp. 174, 196 (= *LW* 48, pp. 63, 82). Protestant criticism of Aristotle's *Ethics* is instructive of the differences the reformers

many months he begged permission to drop the traditional scholastic lectures on Aristotle. Writing directly to Elector Frederick the Wise, he asked that the Thomist lecture on Aristotle's *Physics* be replaced by a simple historical study of Aristotle *(lectio textualis)*. Luther also requested that the Thomist lecture on Aristotle's logical writings be replaced by one on Ovid's *Metamorphoses* and expressed the hope that the Scotist lectures on the same body of Aristotle's works would soon be terminated.[70] In March 1519 he protested to Spalatin that lectures on Aristotle's *Physics, Metaphysics,* and *De Anima* were unworthy of Wittenberg students.[71]

Philip Melanchthon, the great-nephew of Reuchlin, who earned the title "Teacher of Germany," developed the new curriculum for the university. Melanchthon came to Wittenberg on August 25, 1518 as professor of Greek and within days of his arrival delivered a stirring inaugural speech, "On Improving the Studies of the Young." In the name of good letters and classical studies he criticized "those in the schools who . . . are truly barbarians practicing barbarous arts," identifying them as the progeny of Thomas Aquinas, Duns Scotus, Durandus, and Bonaventura *((Thomae, Scoti, Durandi, Seraphici, Cherubici, et reliqui proles)*. To these scholastic theologians he traced contempt for the Greek language, the neglect of mathematics and sacred studies, and the corruption of classical rhetoric and dialectic. Melanchthon further associated the fall of piety with the loss of good letters and the broken alliance between the humanities and divinity; curricular reform promised to be the key to a revival of piety. In place of the traditional scholastic authors, he endorsed the study of classical philosophers, rhetoricians, and poets, especially Plato, Homer, Virgil, Horace, and "the true historical Aristotle" (as distinct from the Aristotle of scholastic commentaries).[72]

By 1520 the curriculum was restructured. There were new chairs of Greek and Hebrew and the equivalent of a modern language lab to assist students with classical and biblical language. Commentaries on Lombard's *Sentences* were dropped, and the old scholastic lectures on Aristotle were supplanted by a straightforward historical study based on the most recent

---

had with humanists as well as with scholastics. Whereas criticism of the *Ethics* was part of the formation of Reformation theology, the embracing of the *Ethics* had been a major feature of "civic humanism." See Hans Baron, "Franciscan Poverty and Civic Wealth as Factors in the Rise of Humanistic Thought," *Speculum* 13 (1938): 1–37.

70. To Spalatin (9 December 1518; 7 February 1519), *WABr* 1, pp. 262, 325. To Frederick the Wise (23 February 1519), *WABr* 1, pp. 349–50. See Karl Bauer, *Die Wittenberger Universitätstheologie und die Anfänge der deutschen Reformation* (Tübingen, 1928), pp. 109–10.

71. To Spalatin (13 March 1519), *WABr* 1, p. 359 (= *LW* 48, p. 112).

72. *Corpus Reformatorum,* 11: 15, 17–18. Compare Erasmus's contemporary program for theological education as set forth in his *Ratio seu methodus compendio perveniendi ad veram theologiam* (1518), in Boyle, *Erasmus on Language,* pp. 60–127.

1526
VIVENTIS·POTVIT·DVRERIVS·ORA·PHILIPPI
MENTEM·NON·POTVIT·PINGERE·DOCTA
MANVS
Ð

Philip Melanchthon. Albrecht Dürer. Melanchthon's activity as an educational reformer won him fame as the "Praeceptor Germaniae." Devoted to Luther, Melanchthon became the author of the major Lutheran confessions. He wrote the first systematic summary of the Lutheran faith, the *Loci communes* of 1521, and acted as the chief Protestant negotiator at the Diet of Augsburg in 1530. Although self-proclaimed "genuine Lutherans" accused him of betraying Luther's teaching during the confessional conflicts of the 1540s and 1550s, Melanchthon exemplified better than any other reformer the alliance between sacred and humanistic studies.

translations. New humanistic lectures on Pliny, Quintilian, and Priscian appeared. Candidates for theological degrees defended church doctrine by their own exegesis of the Bible and studied the ecclesiastical laws of Saxony in place of traditional canon law.[73] Although Luther approved the study of Aristotle's *Logic, Rhetoric,* and *Poetics,* he remained hostile to the physical writings (the *Physics, Ethics, Metaphysics,* and *De Anima*), which he believed had provided the theoretical foundations of many scholastic theological errors and unchristian teachings. Melanchthon, who later moderated his views on Aristotle, stressed the danger to theology of such Aristotelian dogmas as the eternality of the world, the immutability of celestial movements, and the mortality of the soul, and agreed with Luther that

73. Steinmetz in *450 Jahre M. Luther Universität,* p. 126; Schwiebert, *ARG* 49 (1958): 71–72; Bauer, *Die Wittenberger Universitätstheologie,* pp. 98–111.

philosophy and Holy Scripture had incompatible views of law, sin, and grace.[74] Melanchthon's greatest fear, however, perhaps prophetic when one looks ahead to the new popularity of Aristotle in Protestant universities during the second half of the sixteenth century, was that theology might again fall prey to the methods and presuppositions of philosophy and, as in the days of Aquinas, Scotus, and Ockham, be led back into "irreligious and idolatrous teaching."[75]

Melanchthon wrote in his middle age one of the most eloquent defenses of the alliance of sacred studies with the humanities. Adopting a device that placed his comments in direct continuity with late medieval debates, he replied in 1542 under the name of Hermolao Barbaro to Pico della Mirandola's famous defense of scholasticism.[76] Melanchthon, perhaps unfairly, interpreted Pico's defense as an attack on eloquence and the liberal arts. The ideal of the ancients was not truth awkwardly stated, as Melanchthon believed Pico to have argued, but wisdom eloquently expressed and carried over into practice. "I call that man a philosopher," Melanchthon writes, "who, having learned many things that are good and useful to the human race, takes his learning [*doctrinam*] out of the shadow of the school and applies it for the public welfare, teaching people what he knows, whether it be about nature, religion, or civil government." He asks, "Of what use to the world are those monstrous verbal pictures and obscure orations [of the scholastic theologians]? Are they intended to teach men? Do they clarify either civic or religious responsibilities? Are they guides in making decisions? Do they have a role to play in the governance of public and private life?"[77] Those who do not fully understand the words they use and have no practical goal for their craft lose all sense of discrimination and end up speaking absurdities, as Melanchthon found attested by the many questions about common natures, quiddities, distinctions, terms of first and second intention, instances, and other "deliramenta," which consumed scholastic commentaries. True insight into the nature of things—that wisdom of the philosophers so highly valued by Pico—went hand in hand with eloquent

74. Protestant fears of Aristotelian teaching are very similar to those of Catholic authorities in the thirteenth century. See above, p. 13.

75. *Corpus Reformatorum*, 1: 303–05, 307–09. Melanchthon describes Thomas Aquinas as the "impiae doctrinae antesignanus" (ibid., p. 307). Luther spoke of Aquinas as "autor . . . regnantis Aristotelis, vastatoris piae doctrinae" (*WA* 8, p. 127).

76. *Corpus Reformatorum*, 9: 689–702. On Pico and Barbaro, see above, pp. 80–81. On dating Melanchthon's letter, see Wilhelm Mauer, *Der junge Melanchthon zwischen Humanismus und Reformation* I (Göttingen, 1967), p. 224, n. 13. Melanchthon's letter has been translated by Quirinus Breen, "Melanchthon's Reply to Pico," *JHI* 13 (1952): 413–26. For analysis, see Breen, "The Subordination of Philosophy to Rhetoric in Melanchthon," *ARG* 43 (1952): 13–27.

77. *Corpus Reformatorum*, 9: 692.

application; in the circles of the true philosophers, Melanchthon found not wise but ineloquent men, but wise men who conversed eloquently about things human and divine.[78]

Other major Protestant educational reformers shared Melanchthon's belief in the close connection between the humanities, sacred studies, and true piety, and this ideal became part of the heritage of the Reformation. In Zurich students learned the three biblical languages (Hebrew, Greek, and Latin), and their theological training centered on public speaking and preaching exercises known as *Prophezei*.[79] The Strasbourg educator Jean Sturm described the goal of study as "piety and religion" and praised classical philosophers and rhetoricians as indispensable aids.[80] The French humanist Claude Baduel, a man strongly influenced by the ideals of Melanchthon and Sturm, said at the founding of the College and University of Nimes in 1540: "Without letters, no good government and no public order; and without them, the churches would neither be able to conserve good doctrine, nor be able to defend themselves against heresies."[81] Theodore Beza embraced the ideal of knowledge leading to righteousness at the opening of the Genevan Academy in 1559, exhorting his audience to be "imbued with the knowledge of true religion and of all good arts, so as to be able to magnify the glory of God, to be an ornament to the fatherland, and also an aid to yourselves."[82]

From such sources one might be tempted to agree with William Bouwsma's provocative thesis that "the deepest assumptions of earlier humanist culture found theological expression in the Protestant Reformation," that the Reformation was even "the theological fulfilment of the [early] Renaissance."[83] Bouwsma believes that Renaissance rhetoric, conceived broadly as

78. Ibid., p. 701.

79. One may compare the bimonthly declamations required of students by Melanchthon. See W. Friedensburg, *Urkundenbuch der Universität Wittenberg* (Magdeburg, 1926), 1: 129. Zwingli's influence on theological training was still not as progressive as one might have suspected from his humanist training. G. R. Potter describes his legacy as "almost illiberal," an "over-specialization in theology" (*Zwingli* [Cambridge, 1976], pp. 219–20, 224).

80. "Optimum igitur ludi genus est, in quo es doctrinae et morum ratio diligens habetur. Nam tametsi studiorum nostrorum finis sit rerum cognitio, tamen si a doctrina et literis vita dissideat, quid . . . utilitatis habet elegans ac liberalis institutio? Pietas igitur atque religio in scholis proposita sit, et ad eam iuvenilis animus cultura literarum erudiatur" (*De literarum ludis recte aperiendis* [1538], in *Die evangelischen Schulordungen des 16. Jahrhunderts*, ed. by R. Vormbaum [Gütersloh, 1860], pp. 655, 673–74). See also Pierre Mesnard, "La pedagogie de Jean Sturm et son inspiration évangelique (1507–89)," *XIIe Congrès Intl. des Sciences Historiques*, pp. 95–100.

81. In Robert M. Kingdon, ed., *Transition and Revolution: Problems and Issues of European Renaissance* and *Reformation History* (Minneapolis, 1974), p. 179.

82. Ibid., p. 181.

83. *Viator* 7 (1976): 439; "Renaissance and Reformation: An Essay in Their Affinities and Connections," in *Luther and the Dawn of the Modern Era: Papers for the Fourth International Congress for Luther Research*, ed. by H. A. Oberman (Leiden, 1974), p. 129.

the union of virtue, wisdom, and the art of persuasion, was the ideal behind Reformation preaching and stress on the Word of God.[84] We can see that ideal applied by Protestants in their educational reforms. But, as with early humanist and Protestant concepts of man, the similarity between humanist and Protestant interest in rhetoric and eloquence may be more structural than material. Both saw man as a complex unity, driven by will and passion, but Protestants remained far more skeptical about his rational, moral, and religious abilities than most humanists.[85] While the reformers set the humanist curriculum in place of the scholastic, doctrine was always the rider and the humanities the horse. The humanities became for Protestant theologians what Aristotelian philosophy had been to late medieval theologians—the favored handmaiden of theology; the rhetorical arts served the more basic task of communicating true doctrine.

A further difference between humanists and Protestants stemming from the persistence of scholasticism within Protestantism is the Protestant disinclination to subject their teaching to moral critique. The reformers did not permit ethics to sit in judgment on the truth of their doctrine. It became the hallmark of the Anabaptist, Spiritualist, and rational critics of the Reformation, almost all of whom were deeply influenced by Erasmus, to make moral results the test of doctrinal truth and to criticize the followers of Luther, Zwingli, and Calvin for failing to improve the moral quality of life.[86] The Protestant reformers looked upon sectarian efforts to make ethical considerations the norm of doctrine in the same way that the Council of Constance had looked on the teaching of Wyclif and Huss—as resurgent Donatist heresy. Whereas Erasmus saw in the maturing Reformation a new threat to the humanities, Luther beheld in the Christian philosophy of Erasmus the decline of true doctrine. He wrote of the primacy and inviolability of doctrine:

> Doctrine and life are to be distinguished. Life is as bad among us as among the papists. Hence, we do not fight and damn them because of their bad lives. Wyclif and Hus, who fought over the moral quality of

---

84. Ibid., p. 148. Bouwsma sees the Protestant concept of God as "a transcendent expression of the Renaissance ideal of the orator" (ibid). Erasmus described Christ as God's speech, divine oratory incarnate (Boyle, *Erasmus on Language*, pp. 26, 46). Dealing with the ways the Reformation aided and abetted humanism, Spitz writes: "Given Luther's emphasis upon the *verbum evangelii vocale* and the response of the believer's *fides ex auditu*, the instrumental importance of rhetoric gained a new dimension of significance during the Reformation era, despite the comeback staged by Aristotelian dialectic" ("The Course of German Humanism," p. 419).

85. Cf. Bengt Hägglund's criticism of Bouwsma by way of a comparison of Renaissance anthropology (via Juan Luis Vives and Pico) with that of the Protestant reformers: "Renaissance and Reformation," in *Luther and the Dawn of the Modern Era*, pp. 150–57. There is an important structural similarity here, however, which Hägglund does not acknowledge.

86. See my *Mysticism and Dissent* (New Haven, 1973).

life, failed to understand this. I do not consider myself to be pious. But when it comes to whether one teaches correctly about the Word of God, there I take my stand and fight. That is my calling. To contest doctrine has never happened until now. Others have fought over life; but to take on doctrine—that is to grab the goose by the neck! Truly the kingdom and office of the papists is evil. Once we have demonstrated that, it is easy to go on and prove that their lives are also bad. But when the word of God remains pure, even if the quality of life fails us, life is placed in a position to become what it ought. That is why everything hinges on the purity of the Word. I have succeeded only if I have taught correctly.[87]

Life must aspire to doctrine: the truth of doctrine is not judged by the moral failing of those who profess it—that became a basic Protestant rule. Luther once declared that even if Rome had observed the traditional religion with the discipline of the hermits, Jerome, Augustine, Gregory, Bernard, Francis, and Dominic, its false doctrine would still have made the Reformation necessary.[88] Sebastian Castellio complained against the Calvinists in the 1550s: "The Calvinists want men to be judged not on the basis of their morals, but according to their beliefs—[*non ex moribus sed ex doctrina*]."[89]

As a theological movement, Protestantism continued the scholastic enterprise of defining true doctrine. It was peculiar in that it streamlined this undertaking with the *studia humanitatis*. The reformers were truly *new* scholastics, both because they approached their task with the tools of humanism and because they rejected so many traditional scholastic doctrines as unbiblical. A unique blending of movements occurred, as both surviving and later resurgent Aristotelianism and the humanities were "confessionalized," that is, integrated into the larger task of formulating the new Protestant doctrine and communicating it to the faithful.[90]

Scholars have argued that without humanism the Reformation could not have succeeded, and it is certainly difficult to imagine the Reformation occurring without the knowledge of languages, the critical handling of sources, the satirical attacks on clerics and scholastics, and the new national feeling that a generation of humanists promoted.[91] On the other hand, the long-term success of the humanist movement also owed something to the

---

87. *Luthers Werke in Auswahl, Tischreden,* ed. Otto Clemen (Berlin, 1950): 8, no. 624, p. 79.
88. From the *Commentary on Galatians* (1545), *WA* 40, p. 687 (= *LW* 26, p. 459).
89. *Contra libellum Calvini,* p. E 8 b.
90. Cf. H. Liebing, "Die Ausgänge des europäischen Humanismus," in *Geist und Geschichte der Reformation: Festgabe Hanns Rückert* (Berlin, 1966), pp. 370–71.
91. Moeller, *ZKG* 70 (1959): 59; Spitz, "The Course of German Humanism," p. 414.

Reformation. In Protestant schools and universities classical culture found a permanent home. The humanist curriculum, with its stress on languages and history, became a lasting model for the arts curriculum. Classical rhetoric also received a new importance in the training of Protestant clergy.[92] Although humanist influence attenuated in the later stages of the Reformation and the Protestant confessions became intellectually narrow as men with little humanist training assumed positions of leadership,[93] the alliance between sacred and humanistic studies has remained part of the heritage of the Reformation.

92. Spitz, "The Course of German Humanism," p. 386; Robert D. Linder, "Calvinism and Humanism: the First Generation," *Church History* 44 (1975): 167–81.

93. Cf. Brian G. Armstrong, *Calvinism and the Amyraut Heresy: Protestant Scholasticism and Humanism in 17th Century France* (Madison, 1969).

CHAPTER 9

The Swiss Reformation

Zwingli and Zurich

ULRICH Zwingli grew up a farm boy in the village of Wildhaus, where his father was the sixteenth-century equivalent of a county sheriff. Having received primary and secondary education in Basel and Bern, he matriculated at the University of Vienna in 1498 and there gained his first close acquaintance with medieval philosophy and theology and the new humanist studies. In 1502, at eighteen, he entered the University of Basel, where he studied the *via antiqua,* reading the works of Thomas Aquinas and writing a commentary on the *Sentences* of Duns Scotus. On September 18, 1504 he received the bachelor's degree and two years later took his master's.

In each place of study Zwingli came within the orbit of an important humanist educator: in Bern, Heinrich Wölfflin; in Vienna, Conrad Celtis, the so-called German archhumanist; and in Basel, Thomas Wyttenbach, whom Zwingli later credited, with Erasmus, with having set him on the path of reform. In Basel, Zwingli frequented a distinguished humanist society, which included among its members Beatus Rhenanus, a leading German humanist; Glarean (Heinrich Loriti), crowned poet laureate after 1512; Conrad Pellican, a noted Hebrew scholar; Conrad Zwick, the later Protestant reformer of Constance; and Caspar Hedio, the future Protestant reformer of Strasbourg.

Prior to his acquaintance with the works of Erasmus, Zwingli's chief mentor was Wyttenbach (1472–1526). When Zwingli studied with him in Basel, Wyttenbach had become an outspoken critic of Ockhamism and he left his mark on Zwingli, who came to share his preference for the *via antiqua.* Whereas Luther had been steeped in Ockham and the *via moderna,* Zwingli's scholastic training came by way of the earlier scholastics and the new critical humanist studies. Also unlike Luther, Zwingli never plumbed the depths of scholastic theology by taking a doctorate in the subject; nor did he know firsthand the trials of monastic spirituality.[1]

After taking his master's degree in 1506, Zwingli received a parish in

1. His most recent biographer describes him as "one of the most progressive and adaptable of the Reformers," growing and changing his views more than Luther and Calvin

OCCVBVIT ANNO ÆTATIS XLVII·
1531

Ulrich Zwingli. Hans Asper (1531).

Glarus, the chief town of the canton of the same name. The influence of his uncle Bartholomew, who was the rural dean at Weesen, helped win this position, a very good one for a beginning priest. In Glarus, Zwingli's routine duties allowed time to study the classics and the church fathers, especially St. Augustine. He also indulged a favorite pastime, girl chasing, a highly successful avocation that would later threaten his career at a crucial juncture.

The critics of Swiss mercenary trade helped shape Zwingli's life at this time. Providing professional soldiers to other countries had long been a lucrative business for the Swiss Confederacy; mercenaries were a key feature of international treaties and the export item that maintained Swiss "balance of payments." In 1513, Zwingli gained direct knowledge of the mercenary's life by serving as chaplain to the Glarus contingent of troops that fought for the pope against the French at Novara, one in a long series of battles between France, Spain, and the pope over Italian territories begun by the French invasion of Italy in 1494.

Zwingli criticized mercenary trade as early as 1510, raising the specter of possible foreign political domination, either by the French, the pope, or the emperor, each of whom drew armies from Switzerland, and lamenting the internal moral and social turmoil that accompanied the return home of Swiss soldiers between engagements. In a versified Latin allegory entitled *The Story of the Ox*, he depicted the French and the pope as pretending friendship with the Swiss, portrayed as a peaceful ox, only to deceive them into doing things both morally and politically harmful.[2] In 1516, again as chaplain, Zwingli witnessed the massive defeat of Swiss soldiers by the French at Marignano, where an estimated ten thousand died. This experience moved Zwingli to write a famous poem on the subject, "The Labyrinth,"[3] a somber description of the entanglement of the Swiss in foreign alliances and international wars that mortally threatened their existence as a people.

Some scholars have seen the pacifism of Erasmus, whose works Zwingli carefully studied during his last years in Glarus (between 1513 and 1516), behind his opposition to mercenary trade. If such influence existed, however, it was very indirect. Zwingli never practiced strict pacifism and in this matter seems to have acted more out of a strong sense of patriotism and

---

(G. H. Potter, *Zwingli* [Cambridge, 1976], p. 86). Most of this growth and change came, however, by the assimilation of the ideas of others. For Zwingli's theological development, there is the admiring biography of Fritz Büsser, *Huldrych Zwingli: Reformation als prophetischer Auftrag* (Zürich, 1973).

2. *H. Zwinglis Sämtiche Werke* ed. Emil Egli, Georg Finsler (Leipzig and Berlin, 1905-), 1: 10-22.

3. In ibid., pp. 53-60. On the problems posed by mercenary soldiers, see V. G. Kiernan, "Foreign Mercenaries and Absolute Monarchy," in *Crisis in Europe 1560-1660*, ed. Trevor Aston (Garden City, N.J., 1967), pp. 124-49.

Swiss self-interest. To the extent that religious or moral tenets played a role, they more likely came from his own Bible study, especially of the Old Testament. The many examples there of providential punishment of those who neglected divine laws deeply impressed Zwingli;[4] killing the foes of another people for profit seemed a clear temptation of providence. In 1521, with Zwingli as its pastor, Zurich unilaterally suspended participation in the Confederacy's mercenary trade, setting itself at odds with the other cantons, which, despite the risks, accepted mercenary service as a fair exchange for grain and other essential imports.

While continuing to maintain a position in Glarus, Zwingli requested and received a transfer to the parish of Einsiedeln, a small town fifteen miles away. The transfer, which occurred in April 1516, resulted from disagreements with the magistrates of Glarus, who found his outspoken criticism of mercenary trade embarrassing. As people's priest (*Leutpriester*) in Einsiedeln, Zwingli's primary duty was the traditional cure of souls. However, he turned increasingly to biblical preaching and study. A reformer in the Erasmian mold, he had become by this time as accomplished a Greek scholar as any man north of the Alps[5] and also a serious student of Hebrew. He made his devotion to church reform clear in 1518 by rebuking a Franciscan indulgence preacher, Bernhard Sanson, whose crude tactics rivaled those of his Dominican counterpart in Brandenburg, John Tetzel. Zwingli here acted on his own impulses and was not imitating Luther. Nor did he act alone; the bishop of Constance, soon to become the chief opponent of the Swiss Reformation, also opposed Sanson, and a Diet of the Confederacy eventually condemned this egregious example of papal poaching on Swiss ecclesiastical revenues.

In 1518 the post of people's priest at the Great Minster in Zurich fell vacant, and Zwingli became one of two finalists for the office. However, an accusation of serious moral lapses threatened his candidacy. Specifically, opponents accused him of having seduced the virgin daughter of a prominent citizen of Einsiedeln. In a famous letter of self-defense, written to the search committee, Zwingli protested that it was actually *he*, not she, who had been seduced. The girl in question, he protested, was "a virgin by day but a woman by night," known to have had sexual relations with many men, including clerical assistants. She was the daughter of a "prominent citizen" only if one considered barbers prominent citizens.[6]

Priestly concubinage was widespread at this time, and Zwingli's was be-

---

4. See Robert Walton, *Zwingli's Theocracy* (Toronto, 1967), p. 36.
5. This is the estimate of Potter, *Zwingli,* p. 43.
6. *Sämtliche Werke,* 7: 110–13; an account in English is given in Hans J. Hillerbrand, *The Reformation: A Narrative History Related by Contemporary Observers and Participants* (New York, 1964), p. 116.

havior hardly scandalous to his contemporaries. The right of clergy to marry legally and live honorably with women and thereby end such illegal fornication and cohabitation became one of the first reforms of the Swiss Reformation.[7] Zwingli's rival for the post, a man named Laurence Mär, who lived openly in concubinage and was the father of six children, seemed far less "moral" than he in such matters. In December 1518, by a vote of seventeen to seven, Zwingli won the post and assumed his new duties the following January. He was thirty-five years of age.

When did Zwingli become an evangelical preacher? According to his own later testimony, as early as 1516.[8] When in 1523 the publication of his *67 Schlussreden* brought charges of Lutheranism, he protested his independence from Luther and insisted that he had at his own initiative preached directly from the Bible in Glarus and Einsiedeln long before he knew anything of Luther.[9] Scholars have been inclined to view this early dating of his evangelical activity as more expressive of his rivalry with Luther than reliable evidence of a decisive break with traditional teaching as early as 1516. Zwingli had serious theological differences with Luther and he stressed them repeatedly in the 1520s, when they competed in many quarters for Protestant leadership. His Swiss Catholic critics also influenced Zwingli's insistence on the independence of his reform. Finding Luther's theology closer to the old faith than Zwingli's, on both key doctrines (especially the Eucharist) and liturgical practice, they believed it held the possibility of significant compromise. This made identification with Luther a serious impediment to the more radical reforms Zwingli promoted throughout the Confederacy. There were political, theological, and personal reasons for Zwingli to disassociate himself emphatically from Luther, even though their reforms proved very similar.

Unless we are to suspect Zwingli of simulating traditional beliefs he did not really hold,[10] he appears to have been an orthodox Catholic priest at least as late as 1518, when Rome designated him a papal chaplain. The move to Einsiedeln may have brought about an important reorientation of his religious thinking, but it seems not to have been actual conversion to

---

7. See below, pp. 387–88.
8. For relevant passages in Zwingli's works, see *Sämtliche Werke*, 1: 256, n. 4. See also the recent study of Wilhelm H. Neuser, *Die reformatorische Wende bei Zwingli* (Neukirchen-Vluyn, 1976).
9. *Usslegen und gründ der schlussreden oder Articklen, Sämtliche Werke*, 2: 144–50. "Aber die Bäpstler baladend mich und ander mit sölichen namen uss alefantz . . .und sprechend: Du must wol luterisch sin; du predgest doch glych wie der Luter schrybt. Antwurt ich inen: Ich predigen doch glych als wol wie Paulus schrybt; warumb nempstu mich nit as mär einen Paulischen? Ja, ich predgen das wort Christi; warumb nempstu mich nit as mär einen Christen?" (ibid, p. 147).
10. See the discussion of Nicodemism below, pp. 356–57.

evangelical teaching. Still, it is true that he identified more with Wyttenbach and Erasmus than with Luther in the years prior to 1520; he seems not even to have read Luther seriously before 1520, even though Luther's works were readily available earlier.[11]

Thus, 1519 is the more credible year in which to date the beginning of genuine evangelical activity on Zwingli's part. He preached directly from the Bible after his arrival in Zurich in January 1519—sermons, according to his biographer, "such as had not been heard before in Zurich"[12] and ignored forevermore the "canned" official sermons and scholastic commentaries he had previously followed. The year 1519 also brought the kind of personal crisis that clarifies goals and steels wills; Zwingli nearly died from a plague that struck in September. His biblical preaching became an example the city council required all Zurich priests to follow in 1520. Believing this to be the best way to prevent friction as Protestant reforms penetrated southward, the council instructed all the city's preachers to avoid "novelties" (*neuerungen*) in their sermons and stick to simple biblical teaching. Because Rome at this time still counted on Zurich for mercenaries, Catholic authorities tolerated this guideline, which was actually more medieval than Protestant in inspiration[13] and would soon become an imperial rule.

As in Saxony so also in Zurich, popular and official respect for the Bible's authority proved the essential religious factor in the Reformation's success.[14] The test of Scripture became Zwingli's basic reform principle. He set it forth clearly in the *Apologeticus Archeteles,* his first major statement of faith, written in August 1522 as a response to episcopal criticism of the Zurich reform party. Here he described his growing reliance on Scripture as a special religious insight reminiscent of Luther's description of his discovery of the meaning of the righteousness of God.

> I came at length to trust in no words so much as in those which pro-
> ceeded [from the Bible]. And when miserable mortals . . . tried to palm

11. See Potter, *Zwingli,* p. 71; J. F. Goeters, "Zwinglis Werdegang als Erasmianer," in *Reformation und Humanismus. Robert Stupperich zu seinem 60. Geburtstag* (Witten, 1969), pp. 255–71; Arthur Rich, *Die Anfänge der Theologie H. Zwinglis* (Zurich, 1949).

12. Potter, *Zwingli,* p. 61.

13. See Bernd Moeller, "Zwinglis Disputationen: Studien zu den Anfängen der Kirchenbildung und des Synodalwesens im Protestantismus," *Zeitschrift der Savigny-Stiftung für Rechtsgeschichte* 56 (1970): 275–324, esp. pp. 290–91.

14. According to Walton: "[From 1520 on] Zwingli had only to show the councillors what changes the Bible required. Then, in keeping with the pattern of government supervision over the affairs of the church, the council could work out, with Zwingli's help, the timing and method of change . . . . The magistracy was Christian and accepted the Bible as the guide for the religious life of the community" (*Zwingli's Theocracy,* p. 49). While the magistrates were indeed readily guided by Scripture, winning their support proved a difficult struggle, not the easy relationship Walton here depicts.

off their own works as God's, I looked to see whether any means could be found by which one could detect whether the works of man or of God were the better, especially as I saw not a few straining every nerve to make the simple-minded accept their own views as divine even though they were at variance with or in direct opposition to the words of God. As I sought, it occurred to me that all things are made clear in that light which says: "I am the light of the world" (John 8:12)... and "Believe not every spirit, but try the spirits, whether they be of God" (I John 4:1). Seeking a touchstone, I found the stone of offense and the rock of scandal [Jesus Christ, 1 Peter 2:7], upon which are broken all who... impede the word of God with their own traditions.... I began to try every doctrine by this touchstone. If I saw that a teaching could bear the test, I accepted it; if not, I rejected it.... I began to discover whether... anything was added to the real doctrine... and then I could not be driven by any force or threats to put in human things... the same trust as in divine.[15]

Zwingli's reform principle was to test the biblical foundation of traditional ceremonies, practices, and teachings and ask whether they promoted the central message of the New Testament, the redemption of the world in Jesus Christ. What to Zwingli's mind obscured this message ceased to be a matter of obedience. Such a test quickly raised questions about a host of traditional teachings and practices; fasting, the veneration of saints, belief in purgatory, the payment of tithes, and the use of images, vestments, and music in churches.[16]

Here the English and Swiss Reformations had something in common. A Scripture principle similar to Zwingli's also inspired William Tyndale more than Luther's doctrine of justification by faith, despite the admittedly great impact on his thought of Luther's biblical translations and commentaries.[17] Financed by wealthy London merchants, Tyndale translated the New Tes-

---

15. In *The Latin Works and the Correspondence of Huldreich Zwingli, 1510–1522,* ed. Samuel M. Jackson (New York, 1912), 1: 204–05 (= *Sämtliche Werke,* 1: 256–327).

16. Zwingli's *67 Schlussreden,* written in preparation for the first Zurich Disputation (January 1523), is an extensive list of such doubtful beliefs and practices. They are translated in *Ulrich Zwingli (1484–1531): Selected Works,* ed. Samuel M. Jackson, introduced Edward Peters (Philadelphia, 1972), pp. 111–17.

17. Tyndale seems also to have stressed increasingly the importance of Christian obedience to the law in place of justification by faith. See William A. Clebsch, *England's Earliest Protestants 1520–1535* (New Haven, 1964). Clebsch argues this thesis also for the English reformer Robert Barnes. Such differences between Luther and Zwingli and early English reformers should not, however, be overstressed; Luther also subscribed to a Scripture principle and subjected the faithful to the demands of the law, and he found neither to contradict justification by faith alone.

tament into English in 1524, convinced that it alone should determine church beliefs, practices, and institutions.[18] Thomas Cromwell, who believed that a people enlightened in religion would also be patriotic in politics, acted decisively through Parliament to make a vernacular Bible available in every English church.[19] The vernacular Bible remained the most prominent feature of English Protestantism, despite successful royal resistance to the extreme doctrinal, liturgical, and ceremonial simplification that Protestants insisted the test of Scripture required.

The inchoate Zurich reform publicly defied tradition in February 1522, when members of the reform party met in the home of the publisher Christopher Froschauer and broke the Lenten fast. Five of those involved were associates of Conrad Grebel, later leader of the Swiss Anabaptist movement. This action, which seems harmless at first glance, was the equivalent for that day and age of burning draft cards or the flag today, and it precipitated the first serious crisis for the reformers. It may be taken as an indirect commentary on the differences between the two reform movements—the more theological Lutheran and the more practical Swiss—that the Reformation in Germany began in earnest with the posting of scholastic theses against indulgences, while in Switzerland it was launched by the eating of sausages during Lent. Although Zwingli was in attendance when the fast was broken, he did not participate directly in the transgression. The action seems in fact to have caught him by surprise, although he could hardly have disapproved of it in principle. Like Luther, Zwingli remained sensitive to his public position of leadership, aware that desired reforms had to be implemented more cautiously than many of his followers wished, if success were to be realized.

Zurich magistrates suspected the sausage incident was a prelude to more serious violations and arrested Froschauer and his accomplices. Fearing the loss of official support for his reforms and wanting to aid his friends, Zwingli addressed the issue from his pulpit in a special sermon, "On the Choice and Freedom of Foods" (March 23, 1522). He cautioned those eager to overturn the fasting laws against forcing upon others what was actually a matter of indifference for Christians, who were free to fast or not, as they chose. On the other hand, he also made it clear that the Bible contained no prohibitions against eating sausages during Lent.[20]

A parallel can be drawn between Zwingli's sermon and eight Luther preached in rapid succession to calm the Wittenberg citizenry and reassure Saxon authorities after his return from Wartburg Castle, also in March

18. A. G. Dickens, *The English Reformation* (London, 1964), p. 71.
19. See above, pp. 201–03.
20. See Walton, *Zwingli's Theocracy*, pp. 76–86.

1522. Although the immediate issue in Saxony was the abolition of the Mass rather than freedom of foods during Lent, the message of the two reformers was the same. Luther too pleaded for patience and moderation, while defending the reform; declaring the Mass "an evil thing that must be abolished," he nonetheless insisted that "we must first win the hearts of the people . . . and constrain no man by force."[21]

Zurich officials came to agree with Zwingli that God's law had not been violated by those who had broken the fast, a decision that vindicated the reform party. The ruling also illustrated how intimately connected religious reform and political authority were to be in the Swiss Reformation.[22] On July 2, 1522, Zwingli, emboldened by success, proceeded to break still another tradition, when he and nine other Swiss preachers requested the bishop's permission to marry.[23]

The reform movement in Zurich now came directly under the eye of Bishop Hugo of Constance. After a formal investigation in the summer of 1522, the bishop issued a sixty-nine-article admonition to the governing board of the Minster. "We have for some time now . . . heard reports," wrote Bishop Hugo,

> that there are, almost throughout Germany, those who cry out day and night that the people of Christ have been wrongfully oppressed . . . with hard and burdensome regulations, observances, and ceremonies. As a consequence such persons are trying . . . to . . . do away with [such] ceremonies. In this "golden age," as they call it . . . they believe the gospel is at last beginning to shed its light upon mankind and they see themselves leading . . . the people back to the freedom of the gospel. But we observe that when they pull up out of the field of the Lord the human ordinances they call tares and cockles, alas, the wheat also is uprooted.[24]

Clearly not adept in the mollifying arts, the bishop attempted to console the zealous reformers with worldly-wise counsel:

> Granted even that the whole body [of the church] was wrong in establishing . . . a ceremonial system which has been thus far maintained and that, as is the portion of human ignorance and frailty, some things have become mixed with the Christian religion which are not altogether in

21. *LW* 51, pp. 75–77 (= *WA* 10/3, pp. 14–20). See the discussion in my *Reformation in the Cities* (New Haven, 1975) pp. 144–45.
22. Cf. Walton, *Zwingli's Theocracy*, pp. 70–73.
23. See below, pp. 387–88.
24. In *The Latin Works . . . of H. Zwingli,* 1: 208.

harmony with the gospel and Holy Scripture, still Christian piety . . . demands that . . . we make some allowance for those who err with good intentions. . . rather than expose everything to manifest uproar and rebellion. It was no doubt in this sense that the dictum was made: "A universal error has the force of right."[25]

Such episcopal censure emboldened the reform party, who knew of the bishop's unpopularity and political weakness in Zurich. Zwingli snapped back in a long, rambling reply: "What harm is going to happen if the whole rubbish heap of ceremonies be cleared away, since God declares that he is worshipped in vain by these things?"[26]

Events culminated in a disputation in Zurich in January 1523, the first of two such conferences in that year which secured and defined the Swiss Reformation. By order of the Zurich government, which hereafter progressively took control of religious reform, six hundred clergy and laymen assembled to debate the religious differences, and in German, not in Latin. Among them sat an unhappy delegation from the bishop's see, led by Johann Faber, the vicar-general of the diocese of Constance—unhappy because the disputation, following earlier magisterial rulings, allowed only the Bible to be used as an authority in argument. In the Leipzig Disputation of 1519, Luther had debated John Eck on the same grounds, refusing even to consider arguments from other sources. Given this decisive ground rule, the Zurich disputation seemed more a charade than a genuine debate; the confinement of arguments to Scripture settled in advance a large number of divisive issues, as Zwingli's *67 Schlussreden,* written as a set of guidelines for the disputation, had already demonstrated. This advantage still did not calm the reform party, however, who saw only birds in the bush throughout the disputation.

The January disputation ended in success for Zwingli.[27] Zurich clergy were again ordered to confine their preaching to Scripture, a ruling by which Zurich in effect publicly declared itself a Protestant city.[28] Protestant historians glorified the day; according to Oswald Myconius, Zwingli's friend

25. Ibid., 1: 215.
26. Ibid., 1: 219.
27. Cf. Heiko A. Oberman, *Werden und Wertung der Reformation. Vom Wegestreit zum Glaubenskampf* (Tübingen, 1977), pp. 241–51. Oberman corrects the impression left by scholars that the first disputation actually "officially" introduced the Reformation into Zurich. His preoccupation with the absence of an "official" proclamation leads him, however, to underestimate the degree to which this disputation actually secured the Zurich Reformation. The gain in subtlety is a loss in understanding. See on the issue Moeller, "Zwinglis Disputationen," pp. 304, 311.
28. John T. McNeill, *The History and Character of Calvinism,* (New York, 1957), p. 38; Potter; *Zwingli,* p. 104.

and biased biographer, Pope Adrian VI (1521–23) was so impressed by Zwingli's performance that he promised to give him "everything except the papal chair" in exchange for Roman allegiance.[29]

The January disputation made clear the Protestant case against Rome. Although Zurich authorities approved Zwingli's Scripture principle, they refused to order an immediate end to many traditional religious practices. This delay created a new crisis for the reform party, whose radical members found it unacceptable to mandate that Scripture be followed in preaching, yet permit practices to continue for which there was no clear scriptural warrant, like the celebration of the Mass and the use of images in churches. Outbreaks of iconoclasm, inspired by the radicals, occasioned a second, larger religious conference in October 1523. This disputation also ended in victory for Zwingli, who had faithfully adhered to the magistrates' policy of only gradually ending traditional religious practices. After the second disputation, the city resolved to remove images and abolish the Mass—but only when the time was right. Eight months later, on June 15, 1524, a disciplined removal of images from Zurich churches officially began. In December 1524 the city confiscated the Dominican and Augustinian monastic houses and forced all monks and friars who had not already voluntarily departed to lodge together in the Franciscan cloister. On April 14, 1525 the Mass too was abolished. In the meantime, however, the reform party in Zurich had been irreparably fractured.

Conrad Grebel and Swiss Anabaptism

AFTER the second Zurich disputation, Conrad Grebel, the reputed founder of Anabaptism, organized radical opposition to Zwingli. While a student at the University of Basel in 1514–15, Grebel had lived in the household of the poet laureate Glarean, with whom Zwingli too had earlier been associated. Grebel also attended the University of Vienna between 1515 and 1518, where he became attached to the poet laureate Vadian, whose sister he later married. In Basel, Grebel was introduced to the Christian humanism of Erasmus, and in Vienna he came to know the secular humanist scholarship of Conrad Celtis. He also fell victim to syphilis in these student days and suffered from its complications for the remainder of his life.[30]

Grebel attended the University of Paris between 1518 and 1520, again

---

29. *The Latin Works . . . of H. Zwingli*, 1: 13.
30. Harold Bender, *Conrad Grebel ca. 1498–1526: The Founder of the Swiss Brethren* (Goshen, Ind., 1950), p. 25. There is a more recent admiring biography of Grebel by John L. Ruth, *Conrad Grebel: Son of Zurich* (Scottsdale, Penn., 1975).

lodging with Glarean, who had moved there. He appears to have undergone a severe personal crisis at this time. In 1519 he was involved in a student brawl in which two Frenchmen were killed. Gaining a reputation for impetuosity, he lost Glarean's friendship and fell out with his parents and Vadian. After returning to Zurich in 1520, he joined Zwingli's circle, a humanist convert to evangelical Christianity. Zwingli had at this time organized a group that met regularly to study Greek and Hebrew, and he welcomed any who shared their devotion to languages and religious reform. That mutual respect and cooperation held between Zwingli and Grebel in these early years is evident from Grebel's contribution of a short poem to Zwingli's *Apologeticus Archeteles*. The poem is a commentary on Grebel's religious zeal.

> Wrath and jealousy burst in bits all bishops
> Who in spite of their name are wolves voracious!
> Now once more, as in days of old, refulgent
> Shines the light of the gospel's truth upon us,
> Notwithstanding the doughty three-tongued Satan
> Sent to quench it; for God remains master.
> Yea (and verily speak I truth as prophet),
> Their authority, all their sway of tyrants,
> Sins of simony, keys and canons human,
> Cruel murderers of the people's conscience,
> Rows on rows of the wares those men call sacred,
> Bulls, anathemas, and dark superstition—
> These, all conquered, the message of the gospel
> Leads, and ever shall lead, in hard-won triumph.
> Those who in spite of their name are wolves voracious,
> Wrath and jealously burst in bits all bishops.[31]

Scholars have argued for decades over the reasons for the break between Grebel and Zwingli. At stake in the modern discussion is the character of the original Swiss reform movement. Scholars partial to Grebel accept his accusation that Zwingli shifted ground and compromised the original aims of the reform party after the second disputation. They cite Zwingli's willingness to tolerate the payment of tithes (a practice he had earlier condemned), the taking of interest, and the continuance of the Mass. According to this interpretation, Zwingli lacked the courage of his convictions, while Grebel remained true to the original principles of the reform party.

Pro-Grebel scholars argue that Zwingli did not suddenly and dramatically

31. In *The Latin Works . . . of H. Zwingli*, 1: 292.

shift his position, but came only gradually to opt for one of "two [original] strands of his theological personality": a theocratic impulse, inclining him towards a church ruled conjointly by magistrates and clergy, and a vision of a limited, voluntary church of true believers, who refuse every compromise with the world.[32] While Grebel and his followers held to the voluntary church, Zwingli, it is argued, came to endorse a state-run church, for a variety of good reasons: he sincerely believed that the church should use state support to achieve its ends; he was impressed by the outward progress of reform in areas where official support had been forthcoming (for example, in the schools, the creation of a marriage court, and the new political power of the Protestant cantons); he was convinced that once the right to preach from Scripture was granted, the Word of God would, in time, win the day; he sincerely feared that any tumult created by hasty action might undermine political support for the reform as a whole; and, finally, his devotion to cultic unity made it impossible for him to accept religious diversity and minority religious viewpoints.[33] Grebel scholars believe that Zwingli's stand led to the suppression of democratic, congregational church government, to state control of the Swiss churches, and to tacit church support of religious persecution.

In rebuttal, Zwingli scholars have stressed his consistency and the internal division of the reform party long before the second disputation. Zwingli, they argue, had been as prepared to ensure the Reformation's success by compromise in 1520 as in 1523. He never shared the Anabaptist vision of a voluntary church of true believers, but held to the traditional corporate religious ideal, which called for uniform religious belief and practice. In his own mind, Zwingli's original goals and the actual achievement of the Zurich Reformation remained quite close.[34]

Zwingli and the radicals of Zurich had many basic differences, but their opposition came to focus especially on the issue of infant baptism, a practice

32. John Yoder, "The Turning Point in the Zwinglian Reformation," *MQR* 32 (1958): 128–40 and "The Evolution of the Zwinglian Reformation," *MQR* 43 (1969): 95–122, the latter written in response to the criticism of Robert Walton, "Was There a Turning Point of the Zwinglian Reformation?" *MQR* 42 (1968): 45–56. Yoder continues the arguments of the American Mennonite scholars John Horsch and Harold S. Bender, Grebel's biographer. See also the essays in *Umstrittenes Taüfertum 1525–1975*, ed. H.-J. Goertz (Göttingen, 1975); and Arthur Rich, "Zwingli als sozialpolitischer Denker," *Zwingliana* 13 (1969): 72–76.

33. Yoder, "The Evolution of the Zwinglian Reformation," pp. 119–22.

34. Walton, "Was There a Turning Point to the Zwinglian Reformation?" elaborated in Walton, *Zwingli's Theocracy*. See also the recent article by Martin Haas, which argues that the Swiss radicals became separatist and sectarian only after failing to displace Zwingli from leadership and transform the Reformation into an anticlerical social movement: "Der Weg der Taüfer in die Absonderung," in Goertz, *Umstrittenes Taüfertum*.

the radicals believed exposed the error and presumption of traditional religion more clearly than any other. Not only did this practice lack a clear biblical foundation, but it also made the beginning of the religious life wholly impersonal and involuntary. The radicals wanted people to be baptized as mature, consenting adults who had freely chosen a life in imitation of Jesus.

While infant baptism was no more the distinctive doctrine of Zwinglianism than predestination the central teaching of Calvinism, both doctrines were highly vulnerable to commonsense criticism. Radicals found in such practices and doctrines the theological Achilles' heel of the reformers, a point at which their entire theology might be discredited as unbiblical and morally offensive.

Infant baptism remained an important religious and civic rite in the sixteenth century. It conveyed responsibility for a new life into the hands of both congregation and citizenry, who together promised to rear the child in love and obedience to the laws of both God and man. The basic Lutheran argument in its favor had been that the community at large *believed for* the infant and in this sense faith was truly present to receive the sacrament. Luther even found a retort to the Anabaptists in the first chapter of Luke, where the unborn foetus of John the Baptist is reported to have leapt in the womb of his mother at the approach of Mary, then pregnant with Jesus— for Luther, biblical proof positive that even unborn infants had faith and could respond to Christ.[35]

Between 1525 and 1527, Zwingli devoted four major tracts to the subject of infant baptism. He defended the traditional rite as the New Testament successor to the circumcision of infants in the Old Testament; as such, it represented the continuity of God's covenant with man. Neither Luther nor Zwingli saw in the infant's utter passivity and dependence an affront to religious freedom, as the Anabaptists contended; the infant's powerlessness rather symbolized the humility that all should have in the presence of God.

The first adult rebaptism apparently occurred on January 21, 1525, when Grebel baptized George Blaurock in Zurich. Viewed by authorities as blasphemous and seditious, the denial of infant baptism and the rebaptism of adults brought harsh penalities. Adult rebaptism became a capital offense in Zurich on March 7, 1525, and four persons died as a result. Families who refused to submit their children for baptism had eight days to reconsider and obey the law or face expulsion from the city. By the time the Second Diet of Speyer met in 1529, opposition to Anabaptism had become so wide-

35. *Von der Wiedertaufe an zwei Pfaffherrn, WA* 26, p. 156.

spread and hysterical that Charles V revived an ancient Justinian law against rebaptism, making it a capital offense, throughout the empire.[36] Scholars estimate that at least 850 and perhaps as many as 5,000 Anabaptists were legally executed between 1525 and 1618 by burning, decapitation, and drowning.[37]

It is reported that Grebel challenged Zwingli to a public disputation on the issue of infant baptism, pledging to go willingly to the stake should Zwingli prove his case, while promising to spare Zwingli, should he win the argument. Zwingli had no need to enter such a contest and became instead Grebel's chief accuser after he and a colleague, Felix Manz, were arrested. The imprisonment of Grebel and the almost contemporaneous execution of his father (October 1526) on controversial charges of treason strengthened Zwingli's authority over the Swiss reform.[38] Grebel and Manz delayed death by successfully escaping from prison. However, Manz was recaptured and drowned in the Limmat in January 1527, while Grebel died in flight.

The Working Out of Zwinglianism

BETWEEN 1525 and 1530, Zwinglian ideas and practices spread rapidly throughout Switzerland and south Germany, winning congregations in Ulm, Strasbourg, Augsburg, Lindau, Memmingen, Frankfurt, and Constance. In several ways, Zwinglian Protestantism broke more radically with medieval religion than Lutheranism, and cities that chose the former were conscious of this. Whereas Lutherans retained much traditional music and ceremony, Zwinglians simplified liturgy and worship to the point of eliminating organs from their churches. Lutherans continued to teach that sacraments physically contained and conveyed grace, while Zwinglians interpreted the sacraments as signs and memorials. Also, Zwinglians inclined more strongly toward iconoclasm than Lutherans.[39]

To counter the spread of Zwinglianism in the Confederacy, Catholic cantons convened a conference on religion in the Catholic stronghold of Baden in May 1526. The conference may be seen as a Catholic version of

---

36. Potter, *Zwingli*, pp. 242–43, Franklin H. Littell, *Origins of Sectarian Protestantism*, (New York, 1952), pp. 13–14, Horst W. Schraepler, *Die rechtliche Behandlung der Täufer in der deutschen Schweiz, Sudwestdeutschland und Hessen 1525–1618* (Tübingen, 1957), pp. 19–21.

37. The lower estimate is that of Claus-Peter Clasen's provocative study, *Anabaptism: A Social History* (Ithaca, 1972), pp. 370–73, 437; the higher is Schraepler's, *Die rechtliche Behandlung der Täufer*, pp. 47, 105.

38. Bender, *Conrad Grebel*, pp. 151–57; Potter, *Zwingli*, p. 243.

39. The different perceptions of Zwinglianism and Lutheranism are discussed by Bernd Moeller in *Reichsstadt und Reformation* (Gütersloh, 1962), pp. 57–59.

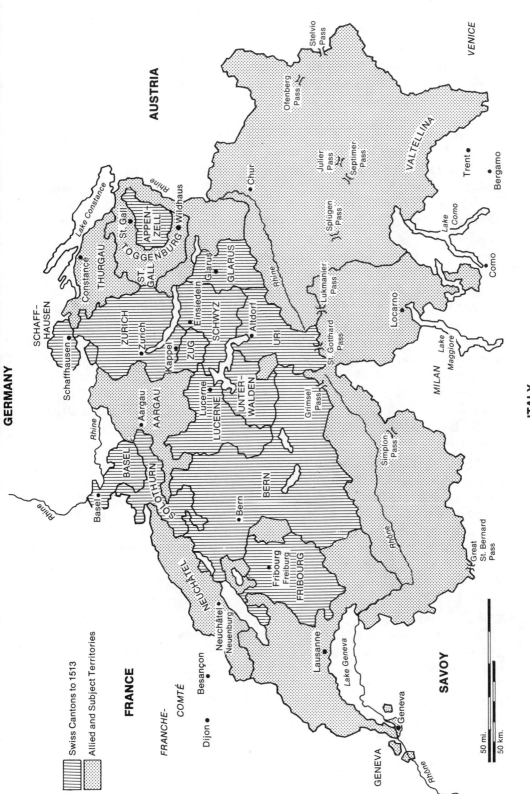

Map 2. The Swiss Confederation in Zwingli's Lifetime

the first Zurich disputation, for it established ground rules in advance that
foreclosed the possibility of a Protestant victory; each meeting, for example,
opened with the celebration of the Mass, while evangelical preaching was
forbidden. Perceiving a charade and apparently fearing for his life, Zwingli
had refused to attend, leaving the task of representing Swiss Protestants at the conference to the Basel reformer Johannes Oecolampadius
(1482–1531). After a debate between Oecolampadius and the Catholic
theologians John Eck, Johann Faber, who had earlier debated Zwingli in
Zurich, and Thomas Murner, a brilliant Franciscan theologian and pamphleteer, the conference, as expected, voted overwhelmingly in favor of
Catholic teaching.

A year and a half later, in January 1528, Protestant cantons responded
with a general conference of their own in the city of Bern. A show of Swiss
and south German Protestant strength, the conference drew many of the
most notable Protestant theologians: Oecolampadius from Basel, Bullinger
from Zurich, Bucer and Capito from Strasbourg, Blarer from Constance,
Pellican from Basel, Hofmeister from Schaffhausen, and Haller from Bern.
No event did more to secure the Swiss Reformation than Bern's turning
Protestant in 1528. A Protestant Bern established Zwinglianism within the
Confederacy and made possible the Genevan political revolt from the
House of Savoy and subsequent development of Genevan Protestantism.[40]

With Bern in the Protestant camp, Philip of Hesse contemplated the
political and military benefits of a confessional alliance between Lutherans
and Zwinglians. Converted to the Reformation in 1524 by Melanchthon,
Philip had by 1528 become an articulate spokesman for the Reformation,
capable of arguing points of doctrine with Luther and Zwingli.[41] Whatever
political motives he may have had, he also understood what it meant
theologically to be a Protestant. More important, he grasped the political
dimension of theological controversy and recognized that German and
Swiss Protestants would not easily unite militarily if Luther and Zwingli
could not agree theologically. To this end he invited the two Protestant
leaders to his castle in Marburg for a special religious colloquy between
October 1 and 4, 1529.

The two Protestant confessions were at this time sharply divided. In June
1529 the Lutherans had published the Schwabach Articles, a proposed
theological basis for a Protestant union, but their anti-Zwinglian view of the

40. Booms Potter: "In some ways the fate of French Huguenots, Dutch and Scots Pres-
byterians, and perhaps 'Free Churches' all over the world was dependent upon the outcome
of a debate held in Berne in January, 1528" (*Zwingli*, p. 257; cf. p. 262). On Bern's role in
Genevan political independence and religious reform, see below, pp. 358–62.
41. René Hauswirth, *Landgraf Philipp von Hessen und Zwingli* (Tübingen, 1968).

Philip of Hesse. Erhard Schoen. Landgrave Philip of Hesse, the political leader of the German Lutherans in the first half of the sixteenth century. Converted to Lutheranism by Melanchthon in 1524, he worked to unify Protestants within the empire politically and theologically. In 1540, however, his actions actually weakened Protestant solidarity. Unable for alleged reasons of conscience to end his unhappy marriage by divorce, as Henry VIII had earlier done, Philip contracted a bigamous second marriage, a step approved by Luther and Melanchthon for questionable political and theological reasons. The illegality of Philip's new situation thereafter so threatened his rule that he was forced into a nonaggression pact with the emperor, a move that weakened the Schmalkaldic League.

Lord's Supper immediately alienated south German and Swiss cities. In addition, Luther's authority had been challenged in recent years by humanists, peasants, and even his own colleagues, and he was ill-disposed to be instructed by Zwingli, whom he considered a spiritualist in the mold of Karlstadt and Müntzer. For his part, Zwingli foresaw political disaster for the Swiss Reformation if he expressed agreement with a view of the Lord's Supper considered basically orthodox by Catholic apologists like John Eck, who shrewdly stressed the Catholic elements in Lutheranism in the hope of encouraging further division between German and Swiss Protestants. Both Zwingli and Luther came to Marburg determined not to compromise.[42]

42. Potter, *Zwingli,* pp. 228, 322.

What of the issues between them? The irreconcilable difference concerned the nature of Christ's presence in the consecrated bread and wine of the Lord's Supper. Zwingli believed that "eating" was interchangeable with "believing" *(edere est credere);* in the sacrament one ate only physical bread and wine with one's mouth, while feeding on the true (spiritual) body and blood of Christ by faith. Zwingli interpreted Christ's words of institution, "This [bread] is my body," to mean "This [bread] *signifies* my body."[43] The actual physical body of Christ, he argued, resided locally in heaven, seated "at the right hand of God the Father," as the Creed stated and, therefore, could not also be truly present in the sacramental elements, as Catholics and Lutherans in their different ways taught. Only within the hearts of believers could a "real presence" of Christ be found.

Luther, by contrast, argued that Christ's body possessed the quality of ubiquity, or omnipresence, by virtue of which it was able to be in more than one place at the same time. Luther arrived at this conclusion by way of his peculiar belief in the *communicatio idiomatum,* the hallmark of Lutheran Christology, which Calvinists still attack today.[44] According to this doctrine, the properties of Christ's divine nature, among them ubiquity, were also characteristic of his human nature; Christ's divine nature could bear his human qualities and his human nature his divine qualities. Hence, Luther argued, wherever Christ was spiritually present, he could also be corporeally present: the partaker of the Eucharist received the one, whole, crucified and risen Christ.

Zwingli, by contrast, believed as firmly as any medieval mystic that tangible things could neither contain nor dispense spiritual reality; the physical could not nourish the spiritual. Neither bread, wine, water, nor the preacher's words contained or conveyed divine grace. Hence, those who received the Eucharist without faith received only bare bread and wine. Zwingli here went beyond others who agreed with his basic position against Luther. Martin Bucer, John Calvin, and Peter Martyr Vermigli also rejected consubstantiation, yet still believed that the "power and effect" of Christ in some essential way came through the sacramental elements.[45]

43. Letter to Matthew Alber (November 1524) in *Sämtliche Werke,* 3: 341, cited by Potter, *Zwingli,* pp. 156–57. The Lutheran formula rejected by Zwingli read: "Wir [the Lutherans] bekennen, das auss vermög diser wort: 'Das ist min lib, das ist mein blut' der lib und das blut Christi warhaftlich (hoc est) substantive et essentialiter, non autem quantitative vel qualitative vel localiter, im nachtmal gegenwertig sey und gegeben wird'" (Potter, *Zwingli,* p. 330).
44. The late Karl Barth traced the anthropological "theology" of Ludwig Feuerbach—and modern atheism—to Luther's attribution of divine characteristics to human nature in his christological teaching. Introduction to Ludwig Feuerbach, *The Essence of Christianity,* trans. George Eliot (New York, 1957), p. xxiii.
45. David C. Steinmetz, *Reformers in the Wings* (Philadelphia, 1971), pp. 158–60. On the

Luther's long developed aversion to "spiritual" religion certainly influenced his position. One of his chief complaints against scholastic theologians had been that they were "theologians of Christ's glory" rather than of his cross, so enamored of the Christ who reigned in eternity that they neglected his incarnation and crucifixion in time. Karlstadt and Müntzer had appealed to the "spiritual Christ" and accused Luther of not being able to see beyond the dead letter of Scripture and history. Zwingli's interpretation of the Eucharist struck Luther as being of one piece with the views of his scholastic and Protestant enemies, and after 1529 he scorned Zwingli as another "fanatic."[46]

Before the two sides departed Marburg, they bowed to pressure from Philip of Hesse and issued the so-called Marburg Articles in which Luther and Zwingli expressed agreement on fourteen articles of faith. On the key issue of the Eucharist, they stated their disagreement in the following conciliatory way:

> Although we have not agreed at this moment whether the true body of Christ be corporeally present in the bread and wine, nonetheless the one side should behave to the other with Christian charity as far as the conscience of each will allow, and both sides will fervently pray to Almighty God that he will confirm in us true understanding by his Spirit.[47]

Little force lay in good intentions, however, and each side soon rallied around its own confessional statement. The Schwabach Articles remained the Lutherans' confessional test until the Augsburg Confession of 1530 became the official Lutheran creed, by which time the Zwinglians had grouped around the Tetrapolitan Confession, a creedal statement by the cities of Strasbourg, Constance, Memmingen, and Lindau, written largely by Martin Bucer.

So it was that in 1530 Lutherans and Zwinglians went their separate ways, both confessionally and politically. Strasbourg later adopted the Augsburg Confession, but only because it needed the military support of the Schmalkaldic League to survive, not because it had made major revisions in its theological viewpoints, which remained unchanged until the ascendancy of conservative Lutheran theologians in the city in the second half of the sixteenth century.

In Switzerland the lines between Catholic and Zwinglian cantons became

---

Marburg Colloquy, see Walter Köhler, *Zwingli und Luther*, vol. 2 (Gütersloh, 1953); Ernst Bizer, *Studien zur Geschichte der Abendmahlstreit im 16. Jahrhundert* (Darmstadt, 1962).

46. Mark Edwards, *Luther and the False Brethren* (Stanford, 1975), pp. 140-42.

47. Original cited by Potter, *Zwingli*, p. 330, n. 2.

firmly drawn after 1529. Basel, Bern, Schaffhausen, Appenzell, and Glarus joined Zurich, while the cantons of Uri, Schwyz, Unterwalden, Zug, Lucerne, and Fribourg remained Catholic, Solothurn managing an accommodation with both confessions. The threat of further Protestant expansion drove the Catholic cantons into an alliance with Archduke Ferdinand in 1529; however, new Turkish attacks in the east so preoccupied the new Swiss ally that the military significance of the pact proved at this time quite small.

Hot war between Protestant and Catholic cantons broke out after Catholics executed a captured Protestant preacher named Jacob Kaiser. The action culminated a long dispute over religious policy in the so-called mandated territories, areas conjointly governed by the Confederacy as a whole and traditionally Catholic. Throughout the 1520s the two sides had respected the rights of each canton to determine its own religious policy, an unwritten version of the later formulated principle of *cuius regio, eius religio*. Protestants wanted to extend such freedom of choice also to mandated territories, while the Catholic cantons recognized such extension as an open door to Protestant proselytizing. It was while preaching Protestant doctrine in a mandated area that Kaiser had been captured by Schwyz authorities and burned as a heretic.

The resulting war between Protestant and Catholic cantons lasted only sixteen days; the mere show of strength by Protestant armies marching from Zurich proved sufficient to force an armistice on June 24, 1529, the First Peace of Kappel. Zwingli and Zurich now dreamed of an all-Protestant Confederacy. More moderate Bern believed such hopes to be unrealistic, however, and insisted that the peace terms recognize the rights of both sides. The Catholic and Protestant cantons agreed to permit each other to worship as they pleased and to force no canton to adopt a faith not of its own choice. They also recognized the parishes of the mandated areas as having such freedom in religion.

The second war between the Protestant and Catholic cantons broke out in 1531, the direct result of a Protestant economic blockade, inspired by Zurich, against Catholic territories that refused to admit Protestant preachers. Catholic cantons retaliated by successfully attacking overconfident and militarily unprepared Zurich. Among the large number of casualities at battle's end lay Zwingli himself. Discovered among the wounded, he was slain, quartered, burned, and his ashes mixed with dung and scattered about so that Protestants would have no relics to inspire and console them.[48] The ensuing Second Peace of Kappel (1531) firmly reestablished the principle of cantonal sovereignty in religion.

48. Ibid., p. 413.

Zwingli, a stubborn and uncompromising man once established in power, managed during his lifetime to be as great an obstacle to internal Swiss Protestant unity as Luther was to internal German Protestant unity. Under his more moderate successor, Heinrich Bullinger (1504–75), however, Zurich and Bern reconciled their differences and Zwinglian and Calvinist Swiss Protestants also found common ground on which to unite. Their union created the Reformed Protestant tradition. The *Consensus Tigurinus* (1549) established theological agreement on disputed doctrines and prepared the way for the more comprehensive and definitive union of the two bodies in the Second Helvetic Confession (1566).

CHAPTER 10

The Sectarian Spectrum: Radical Movements within Protestantism

NOT every "protestant" who was unhappy with Rome rejoiced over the alternatives provided by Luther, Zwingli, and Calvin. Reform movements normally have moderate and extreme wings, those who are satisfied by half a loaf and those who will settle for nothing short of the whole, and the Reformation was no exception. Original colleagues and co-workers became critics and opponents of the major reformers almost immediately and formed their own countermovements. Andreas Bodenstein von Karlstadt and Thomas Müntzer separated from Luther in the early 1520s; Conrad Grebel and the Swiss Brethren broke with Zwingli in Zurich in 1523; and Sebastian Castellio, Calvin's handpicked schoolmaster, became the leader of intellectual opposition to Calvinism after his dismissal from Geneva in 1544.

These Protestant separatists, dissenters within the Protestant movement itself, made up what has traditionally been referred to as the "left wing" of the Reformation. Those who have so characterized them envision a spectrum of religious practice ranging from medieval and reactionary, on the far right, to liberal and modern, on the far left. Such an approach attempts to typify the various religious bodies of the sixteenth century by the degree to which they broke with medieval religion and society. By this measure Catholics were the most medieval and reactionary; Lutherans, conservative to moderate; Calvinists and Zwinglians, moderate to liberal; and the radical reformers—Anabaptists, Spiritualists, and Evangelical Rationalists—liberal and modern.[1] As Roland H. Bainton, a defender of this assessment of the radicals, has summarized:

1. See the introduction to *Der linke Flügel der Reformation,* ed. Heinold Fast (Bremen, 1962); also the bibliographical surveys by George H. Williams, "Studies in the Radical Reformation (1517–1618): A Bibliographical Survey of Research Since 1939," *Church History* 27 (1958): 46–69; 27/2 (1958): 124–60; and James M. Stayer et al., "From Monogenesis to

They anticipated all other religious bodies in the proclamation and exemplification of three principles which, on the North American continent, are among those truths which we hold to be self-evident: the voluntary church, the separation of church and state, and religious liberty.[2]

The modern historian who has most influenced this evaluation is Ernst Troeltsch. Writing in the late ninetenth century, he depicted the Anabaptists and "Spirituals" as far more progressive than the major Protestant reformers, almost on a par with Renaissance humanists. Troeltsch particularly praised the radicals for breaking with the "patriarchialism" of mainstream Protestantism. In opposition to the territorial church state of Lutheranism and the presbyterian system of church government in Calvinism, they established a "modern" church of voluntary believers, independent of all outside control and committed to an egalitarian reconstruction of society in recognition of basic individual rights.[3]

Before the work of Troeltsch, scholarship on radical Protestantism had been dominated by the dark picture drawn in the writings of sixteenth-century Lutherans, Zwinglians, and Calvinists. Luther's influential views on Anabaptists and Spiritualists had resulted from his bitter personal feuds with Karlstadt and Müntzer and never rose above them. A good scholar and authority on St. Augustine, Karlstadt had assumed leadership in Wittenberg after Luther's removal to Wartburg Castle following the Diet of Worms. In Luther's absence he had directed a short-lived suppression of the Mass, setting in place of the traditional rite an informal communion with bread and wine administered in a vernacular service. Karlstadt was also the first major Protestant theologian to take a wife, and he successfully urged other monks and nuns at this time (1521) to leave the cloister and marry. In addition, he condoned the strong-arm tactics and iconoclasm of Wittenberg radicals. Such activities shocked Elector Frederick the Wise, who feared they might occasion widespread tumult. Shortly before Luther's return to Wittenberg in 1522, Frederick dismissed Karlstadt from the city, removing him for attempting to do prematurely in 1521 what Luther himself actually brought about several years later. The Mass officially ended in Wittenberg in 1525, the year Luther married.

Polygenesis: The Historical Discussion of Anabaptist Origins," *MQR* (1975): 83–121, and "The Swiss Brethren: An Exercise in Historical Definition," *Church History* 47 (1978): 174–95.

2. *Studies in the Reformation* (Boston, 1963), 2: 199.

3. *Protestantism and Progress: A Historical Study of the Relation of Protestantism to the Modern World,* trans. W. Montgomery (Boston, 1958), pp. 48, 95–96, 104, 153, 174.

Luther seems never to have forgiven Karlstadt's precocity and rivalry.[4] In 1525 he wrote a special tract against Karlstadt in which he drew parallels between the religious iconoclasm to which Karlstadt's "spiritualism" led[5] and the anarchy of the peasant insurrection in that year. The smashing of external things—in effect, attaching supreme religious importance to what was material—was, in Luther's judgment, the presupposition behind both.[6] Luther added still another condemnation of Karlstadt: despite appearances, he and the pope were reverse sides of the same coin, each equally opposed to the teaching of the Reformation:

> Both are enemies of Christian freedom. The pope destroys it through commandments, Dr. Karlstadt through prohibitions. The pope commands what is to be done, Dr. Karlstadt commands what is not to be done. Through them Christian freedom is destroyed . . . on the one hand, when one commands . . . what is to be done, although it is not so commanded by God [that is, the new traditions of the pope which lack a biblical basis], and, on the other hand, when one forbids . . . doing that which is neither prohibited nor forbidden by God [Karlstadt's rejection of allegedly neutral religious practices].[7]

Luther's animosity toward Müntzer was even more intense. His fiercest critic, Müntzer had attempted to displace him as leader of the Reformation in Saxony. In 1524, having won an audience with the Saxon princes, he preached a sermon in which he depicted himself as a true spirit-guided prophet, like Daniel in the Old Testament, who perceived the present course of history far better than Luther, whom he caricatured as a "fat swine."[8] In a pamphlet celebrating his rival's death, Luther called Müntzer's execution in 1525 a fitting divine judgment upon both his theology and his revolt.

---

4. Luther's extreme sensitivity to the slightest challenge to his authority is discussed with special reference to Karlstadt by Mark Edwards, *Luther and the False Brethren* (Stanford, 1975).

5. For a more equitable assessment of Karlstadt's role in the Reformation, see Ronald J. Sider, *Andreas Bodenstein von Karlstadt: The Development of His Thought, 1517–1525* (Leiden, 1974); and Gordon Rupp, *Patterns of Reformation* (Philadelphia, 1969), pp. 47–153.

6. *Against the Heavenly Prophets in the Matter of Images and Sacraments, LW* 40: 89.

7. Ibid., p. 128. In a later tabletalk comparison of Melanchthon, Erasmus, Karlstadt, and himself, Luther revealed his enduring hatred of Karlstadt: "Philip has substance and eloquence [*res et verba*]; Erasmus eloquence without substance [*verba sine re*]; Luther substance without eloquence [*res sine verbis*]; and Karlstadt neither substance nor eloquence [*nec res nec verba*]" (*WATr* 3, no. 3619 [August, 1537], p. 460).

8. In George H. Williams, ed., *Spiritual and Anabaptist writers: Documents Illustrative of the Radical Reformation* (Philadelphia, 1957), pp. 54, 61.

Such feelings influence historical judgments. The major Protestant reformers of the sixteenth century, from Luther to Heinrich Bullinger, looked on Anabaptists and Spiritualists as dangerous fanatics, utopians, and revolutionaries and urged their suppression for the sake of both religious and political order.[9] This judgment became all the more severe after Anabaptists came to power in the Netherlands town of Münster in 1534 and established in place of the Lutheran government a repressive theocracy, replete with polygamy and charismatic prophets.[10] Thereafter the entire spectrum of radical Protestantism came to be interpreted in the twin terms of rebellious Müntzer and polygamous Münster.

By and large, the nonconformists of the sixteenth century have received a favorable press only when they have written their own history. Following in the steps of Troeltsch, modern Mennonite scholars, who are heirs to the Anabaptist tradition, and Marxist historians, who look back to Müntzer as a precocious leader of an early proletarian revolt,[11] have attempted to rescue the radical reformers from the prejudicial treatment to which Lutheran and Reformed historiography have subjected them. Conrad Grebel's biographer has accused the originators of the stereotype of revolutionary Anabaptism of employing the term "Anabaptist" to describe all whom they considered "the enemies of truth, the opponents of God . . . , the greatest threat to the existing order, the state, and Christendom,"[12] in short, as a scapegoating epithet, sincerely believed by the radicals' persecutors, much like the term "witch" in the sixteenth and seventeenth centuries.[13]

Modern historians have generally tended to disassociate the Anabaptist

9. Traditional interpretations are summarized by Franklin H. Littell, *The Origins of Sectarian Protestantism* (New York, 1964), pp. 143–61. Lutheran historiography is traced by John S. Oyer, *Lutheran Reformers Against Anabaptists: Luther, Melanchthon and Menius and the Anabaptists of Central Germany* (The Hague, 1964).

10. See especially K. H. Kirchhoff, *Die Taüfer in Münster 1534/35: Untersuchungen zum Umfang und zur Sozialstruktur der Bewegung* (Münster i. W., 1973), pp. 86–89. Relevant sources describing the years of Anabaptist rule in Münster and bibliography are assembled in *Das Taüferreich zu Münster 1534–1535: Berichte und Dokumente*, ed. Richard van Dülmen (Munich, 1974).

11. See the works of M. M. Smirin, *Die Volksreformation des Thomas Münzer und der grosse Bauernkrieg* (2nd ed., Berlin, 1956); Manfred Bensing, *Thomas Müntzer und der Thüringer Aufstand 1525* (Berlin, 1966); and Gerhard Zschäbitz, *Zur mitteldeutschen wiedertäuferbewegung nach dem grossen Bauernkrieg* (Berlin, 1958); Max Steinmetz, ed., *Der deutsche Bauernkrieg und Thomas Müntzer* (Berlin, 1976); and Abraham Friesen, "Thomas Müntzer in Marxist Thought," *Church History* 34 (1965): 306–27.

12. Harold S. Bender, "The Zwickau Prophets, Thomas Müntzer and the Anabaptists," *MQR* 27 (1953): 3–16; see also Robert Friedmann, "Thomas Müntzer's Relation to Anabaptism," *MQR* 31 (1957): 75–87'.

13. See H. R. Trevor-Roper, "The European Witch-Craze of the Sixteenth and Seventeenth Centuries," in *The European Witch-Craze . . . and Other Essays* (New York, 1969), pp. 90–192.

movement from Thomas Müntzer, who shared neither its belief in adult baptism nor its pacifism, and to dismiss the later stages of the Münster theocracy as an aberration highly uncharacteristic of mainline Anabaptism. As evidence for the independent origins and pacifistic nature of Anabaptism, historians favorable to the radicals cite Grebel's own letters to Müntzer, written in search of new allies after the break with Zwingli in 1523. Grebel did not hesitate to criticize Müntzer for his indifference to adult baptism, his continuing use of medieval liturgy, the erection in his church of stone tablets bearing the Ten Commandments, and his defense of the right of his followers to bear arms against "the godless."[14]

The twentieth-century scholar who has perhaps done most to rehabilitate the radical movements of the sixteenth century is George H. Williams. Williams has popularized the term "Radical Reformation" as the most fitting description of the entire spectrum of sixteenth-century dissent,[15] rejecting "left wing" as too limited a concept and biased in favor of church-state issues. Like modern Catholic scholars who oppose the characterization of sixteenth-century Catholic reform as a *Counter-Reformation,* basically a reaction to Protestant success, Williams has resisted the description of the radicals as simply an extreme variation upon—"left wing of"—the reforms of Luther, Zwingli, and Calvin. The radicals are rather seen to have formed a positive movement in their own right, independent in origin and fundamentally in disagreement with the basic teachings of the major reformers. For Williams, those who found mainstream Protestantism as uninviting as the traditional church and separated from Wittenberg, Zurich, and Geneva as resolutely as Luther, Zwingli, and Calvin had separated from Rome deserve recognition as an autonomous movement as distinct and historically fateful as Lutheranism, Calvinism, and Anglicanism. Hence their description as a fourth Protestant body: the Radical Reformation.

Expanding on the typology of Troeltsch, who had earlier distinguished between Anabaptists and Spirituals,[16] Williams has classified the radical reformers into three basic groups: the Anabaptists, whose modern heirs are the Mennonites and the Amish; the Spiritualists, who have a modern counterpart in the Schwenckfelder church, named after the Silesian spiritualist Caspar von Schwenckfeld (1489–1561); and those Williams describes as Evangelical Rationalists and Anti-Trinitarians, the ancestors of modern-day Unitarians.

Williams defines Anabaptists in terms of the following distinguishing

14. In *Spiritual and Anabaptist Writers,* pp. 71–85.
15. William's typology is summarized in *Spiritual and Anabaptist Writers,* pp. 19–35 and the introduction to *The Radical Reformation* (London, 1962).
16. *The Social Teachings of the Christian Churches* (New York, 1960), 2: 742–43.

marks: primitivism, or the desire to restore a simple, biblical pattern of life;[17] biblical literalism, or fundamentalism in the interpretation of Scripture; a disciplined communal life; and adult baptism and "free faith" in place of the "state religion" of Lutherans and Catholics. Within this larger definition Williams isolates three basic types of Anabaptists: the revolutionaries of Münster, who briefly established an Old Testament theocratic community under the leadership of charismatic prophets; "contemplative Anabaptists," like Hans Denck (ca. 1500–1525), a leader of south German Anabaptism, who shunned all formal association and taught, in proto-Quaker fashion, religious individualism and quiet mystical illumination by the inner Christ; and the majority "evangelical Anabaptists," who followed the apostolic model of the New Testament by creating pacifistic communities in separation from the world. Within this last group Williams places the Swiss Brethren, the Hutterites, and the Mennonites—the mainstream of Anabaptism.

William's second major group of radicals, the Spiritualists, attached little importance to the authority of written documents and traditional practices and institutions. Unconcerned to restore past ideals and patterns of life, they looked for guidance to present revelations of the spirit. Here three groups are distinguished in parallel to the three types of Anabaptists: "revolutionary Spiritualists," who include the Zwickau prophets, who invaded Wittenberg during Luther's absence, and Karlstadt and Müntzer, who drew inspiration from medieval mystics and sought to sanctify the world by force; "contemplative Spiritualists" like Sebastian Franck, Paracelsus (ca. 1493–1541), and Valentin Weigel, who taught religious individualism, pacifism, latitudinarianism, and universalism; and the majority party of "evangelical Spiritualists," advocates of a mystical piety who believed spiritual perfection attainable in this life. This latter variety of Spiritualism became prominent in later Pietism and Methodism.

Williams's final group, the Evangelical Rationalists, are the advocates of toleration and common sense who formed the intellectual opposition to Calvinism. Champions of a rational Christianity, they fought for a religion shorn of scholastic speculation and such "immoral" doctrines as original sin, the bondage of the will, and predestination. Here Williams finds the forerunners of the Enlightenment and the most "modern" radical reformers, citing such figures as Erasmus, Michael Servetus, Bernardino Ochino

---

17. Littell sees the defining characteristic of Anabaptism in its "restorationist" frame of mind, which he contrasts with the "reformist" frame of mind among the major reformers (*Origins of Sectarian Protestantism*, pp. 47, 79). This is oversimple, however; Luther, Zwingli, and Calvin also considered themselves to be restoring a biblical rule of life when they reformed the medieval church.

(1487–1564), the Capuchin leader who converted to Protestantism, Castellio, and Lelio (1525–62) and Faustus Sozzini (1539–1604), the founders of Socinianism.

Despite the great variety of radical reformers, Williams insists that the movement was basically unified around several common concerns.[18] All the radicals, for example, expressed disappointment with the "moral aspects of territorial Protestantism"; they found no significant moral improvement in society through the work of Luther, Zwingli, and Calvin. All defended free will in religion, whether by the practice of adult baptism, like the Anabaptists, criticism of doctrines of original sin and predestination, like the Evangelical Rationalists, or the advocacy of religious universalism and the direct proximity of every soul to God, like the Spiritualists. Williams finds resistance to the "linking together of church and state" to have been their most common trait. In all these matters he believes that the radicals remained more faithful to the biblical roots of Christianity—"radical" from *radix,* meaning root—than were their Lutheran, Zwinglian, and Calvinist counterparts. Hence, their description as both more "ancient," in the sense of adhering closely to a biblical pattern of life, and more "modern," in the sense of anticipating present religious values, than the other religious movements of the sixteenth century.

In more recent studies, the obsession with origins and typology that characterizes sectarian historiography has persisted.[19] Late-medieval ascetic movements, represented by groups like Franciscan tertiaries and the Brethren of the Common Life, have been presented as the major inspiration of Anabaptism.[20] Such investigations have also revived a long scholarly association of Anabaptism with Erasmus and Christian humanism.[21] Still

18. See the brief summary in *Spiritual and Anabaptist Writers,* pp. 20–21, and the chapter on "Sectarian Ecumenicity," which discusses the "underlying catholicity in the Radical Reformation," in *The Radical Reformation,* p. 815.

19. See part I of *The Origins and Characteristics of Anabaptism/Les Débuts et les caractéristiques de l'Anabaptisme,* ed. Marc Lienhard (The Hague, 1977).

20. Kenneth Davis, *Anabaptism and Asceticism: A Study of Intellectual Origins* (Scottsdale, Pa., 1974), pp. 293–97. See also Werner Packell, "The Origins of Anabaptism: Ascetic and Charismatic Elements Exemplifying Continuity and Discontinuity," in *The Origins and Characteristics of Anabaptism,* pp. 27–41.

21. Davis makes the most extreme argument, finding the distinctive core of Anabaptism in Erasmus's pre-1525 religious writings, a summary, he believes, of the late medieval, lay-oriented ascetic reform that Franciscan tertiaries and the Brethren of the Common Life represented. "Anabaptists can best be understood as . . . a radicalization and Protestantization . . . of the lay-oriented, ascetic reformation of which Erasmus is the principle [sic] mediator" (*Anabaptism and Asceticism,* p. 192). See also Davis's article, "Erasmus as a Progenitor of Anabaptist Theology and Piety," *MQR* 47 (1973): 163–78. Equally positive on the connection between Erasmus and Anabaptism is Robert Kreider, "Anabaptism and Humanism," *MQR* 26 (1952): 123–41. See also on this issue: Delio Cantimori, *Eretici italiani*

another line of recent scholarship has traced the intellectual origins of south German Anabaptism to late medieval mystical, spiritual, and apocalyptic movements and found Karlstadt and Müntzer, who searched such traditions for allies against Luther, to be key intermediaries.[22] While historians still follow Mennonite scholars in setting Müntzer the revolutionary apart from the mainstream of Anabaptism, they now also recognize Müntzer the theologian and ethicist as an important source of Anabaptist thought.

It may be a sign of too much success that the revision of the traditional view of sixteenth-century radicals has itself been subjected to a revision in recent studies. Issue has been taken, for example, with the portrayal of evangelical Anabaptists as uniformly peaceful and "apostolic." One study delineates a variety of Anabaptist viewpoints on political power, finding both "crusaders" and "advocates of *Realpolitik*" among the Anabaptists. Although by century's end the vast majority of Anabaptists had become "apolitical separatists," denying the possibility of any ethical use of force and rejecting all religious coercion as immoral and unchristian, it is now clear that they evolved through other options before reaching this "orthodox" position; the depiction of evangelical Anabaptism as uniformly pacifistic is a stereotype no less historically inaccurate than the Lutheran caricature of all Anabaptists as revolutionary.[23]

Another study has accused modern scholars of gross exaggeration of the importance of sixteenth-century sectarian movements. Led by statistical samples to the conclusion that actual Anabaptists in south and central Germany, Switzerland, and Austria could not have numbered more than 30,000 between 1525 and 1618, Claus-Peter Clasen has characterized the entire Anabaptist movement as a "minor episode in the history of sixteenth-century German society"; from a purely quantitative point of view, he argues, there is no justification for describing Anabaptists and the far less numerous Spiritualists and Evangelical Rationalists as an independent "Radical Reformation."[24] The further discovery that 85 percent of all Anabaptists during the peak growth years 1525–29 came from areas where

---

del Cinquecento (Florence, 1939), pp. 42–49; 196–201; Johan Huizinga, *Erasmus and the Age of Reformation*, (New York, 1957), pp. 177–78; Williams, *The Radical Reformation*, pp. 8–26; and Roland Bainton, *Erasmus of Christendom* (New York, 1969), p. 261.

22. H. J. Goertz, *Innere und Aeussere Ordnung in der Theologie des Thomas Müntzers* (Leiden, 1967); Gottfried Seebass, *Müntzers Erbe: Werk, Leben und Theologie des Hans Hut* (Erlangen, 1972); Werner O. Packull, *Mysticism and the Early South German-Austrian Anabaptist Movement 1525–1531* (Scottsdale, Pa., 1977); and Ozment, *Mysticism and Dissent* (New Haven, 1973).

23. James M. Stayer, *Anabaptism and the Sword* (Lawrence, Kan., 1972), pp. 1–22, 329–37.

24. *Anabaptism: A Social History, 1526–1618* (Ithaca, 1972), pp. 26–27, 29, 428. "In 76% of all towns and villages affected by Anabaptism, fewer than 10 persons accepted the new doctrines in the course of almost a century!" (ibid., p. 28).

Lutherans and/or Zwinglians had first succeeded suggests that Anabaptism may have been more a "left wing" of mainline Protestantism than an independent reform movement in its own right.[25]

Sheer numbers do not, however, automatically measure social impact or importance.[26] Both Anabaptists and their ideas were widespread in the 1520s and 1530s, despite the apparently low number of known Anabaptists, and people feared them far out of proportion to their actual numbers and potential threat to society. Such fear seems to have resulted in large part from the association of German Anabaptist leaders with Thomas Müntzer and the brief success of the Münster theocracy, but the active pacifism of majority Anabaptists also encouraged it. Anabaptist rejection of military obligations and refusal to swear civil oaths struck most people in the sixteenth century as an unrealistic and seditious challenge to the most basic responsibilities of citizenship.[27]

The unrealistic terror with which Anabaptism could be viewed is revealed in a report by Eberhard von der Tann to Philip of Hesse, which describes the activities of the captured leader of central German Anabaptism, Melchior Rinck.

> He began by making government hateful to the hearts of men. Then, when this was done, he urged the common people to obstruct and oppose with force such unchristian and hated government, as he described it, finally to overturn it completely and clear it away so that a Müntzerite mob without any government could be set in its place. But where there is no government, or where government is not honored, there can be no peace, and without peace no farming and harvest; nor is there any protection against crimes, thievery, banditry, bullying, immorality, and other outrages. In such a state so little time can be devoted to teaching children God's word, rearing them in the fear of God, and disciplining them accordingly, that both spiritual and secular government must finally go to ruin and the entire earth succumb to mob rule.[28]

25. Ibid., p. 299.

26. It is difficult to get actual numbers of Anabaptists, and Clasen's accounting is far from conclusive. On the problem of estimating Anabaptists in Strasbourg, where the destruction of records makes an exact count impossible, see Jane Abray, "The Long Reformation: Magistrates, Clergy and People in Strasbourg 1520–1598" (Dissertation, Yale University, 1978), pp. 127–28.

27. See, for example, the confession of Michael Sattler to Catholic authorities in *Spiritual and Anabaptist Writers*, p. 141. On the anarchistic tendencies in Anabaptism, see Clasen, *Anabaptism: A Social History*, pp. 179–83.

28. Written between November 1531 and March 1532. In Paul Wappler, *Die Täuferbewegung in Thüringen von 1526–1584* (Jena, 1913), pp. 334–35.

The major Protestant reformers also share some responsibility for generating such fears of Anabaptists and Spiritualists. Perceiving a threat to their own hard-won political support in successful Anabaptist competition, they too raised the specter of indiscriminate sectarian violence and anarchy.

How are the radicals finally to be assessed? If they were not uniformly fanatical, utopian, and revolutionary, as their contemporary critics maintained, did they form a movement ahead of its time, as their modern supporters have claimed?[29]

The separation of church and state is considered their most distinctive achievement. However, radical leaders in Switzerland, south Germany, and the Netherlands would readily have accepted a magistrate who would have been unequivocally *their* magistrate. Conrad Grebel's partisan biographer leaves no doubt about Grebel's willingness to exchange places with Zwingli.[30] Müntzer, Hans Hut, Balthasar Hubmaier, and Melchior Hoffmann urged their followers to elect magistrates who shared their religious ideals, and Müntzer and militant Melchiorites[31] resorted to force when they found that political power could not be gained and maintained peacefully.

To the extent that Anabaptists and Spiritualists anticipated the modern separation of church and state and religious pluralism and toleration, they did so as the indirect result of their own failure to win political support for their religious programs. It has been pointed out that Anabaptist "apoliticism" was not only a "corollary of the belief in a church that was spiritually separated from the world," but also "the most meaningful response to the forlorn prospects of [their] religious party."[32] Ideology and political reality here truly intersected; what more natural response to oppression could a persecuted minority that had no chance of becoming politically dominant make than nonresistance and separation from the world?

Before they won political support, Lutherans, Zwinglians, and Calvinists too had been dissenting minorities and, as such, had argued eloquently for freedom to preach and practice their religion as conscience dictated. Since the first century, religious minorities had responded to persecution by in-

29. Cf. Ronald J. Sider, *Karlstadt's Battle with Luther: Documents in a Liberal Radical Debate* (Philadelphia, 1978), pp. 139–59.

30. According to Grebel, "Individual members of the church have the right to seek to elect a 'Christian' magistracy or council in order that the government may be influenced to follow the principles of divine righteousness" (Harold S. Bender, *Conrad Grebel ca. 1498–1526: The Founder of the Swiss Brethren* [Goshen, Ind.], p. 205). Still more to the point is J. M. Stayer, "Die Anfänge des schweizerischen Täufertums im reformierten Kongregationalismus" in *Umstrittenes Täufertum 1525–1975*, ed. H.-J. Goertz (Göttingen, 1975).

31. The best discussion of the Melchiorites is Stayer, *Anabaptists and the Sword*, part 4.

32. Ibid., pp. 102, 113.

voking the independence of conscience and demanding toleration of their religious beliefs; in such matters the radicals of the sixteenth century cannot claim novelty. When, in reaction to the execution of Michael Servetus in 1553, Sebastian Castellio composed his famous pseudonymous anthology on toleration, he appealed for support not only to the Bible and common sense, but also to the early writings of Luther and Calvin, Servetus's accuser.[33] Luther declared in his treatise "On Temporal Authority" (1523): "How a man believes or disbelieves is a matter for the conscience of each individual, and since this takes nothing away from the temporal authority, [government] should be content to attend to its own affairs and let men believe this or that as they are able and willing, and constrain no one by force." Luther further appealed to "the common saying, found also in Augustine, 'No one can or ought to be forced to believe.' "[34]

Although the Reformation was not a "representative" movement in the modern sense—many became Protestants because the laws of the land forced it upon them—neither was it "undemocratic" by sixteenth-century standards. If Lutherans, Zwinglians, and Calvinists succeeded with the aid of the magistrate's sword and the legislation of town councils, they did so because enough people had exerted force from below to elicit a positive response from political authority. Sixteenth-century governments, conservative to the point of being reactionary, permitted religious and other social change to occur only gradually, piecemeal, and after the forces favoring them had been stalled as long as possible.[35] Intolerance of religious minorities like Anabaptists also reflected majority sentiment in favor of a uniform religious practice. Such intolerance forced Anabaptism, which had begun in the cities with as broad a following as the Lutheran and Reformed faiths, into rural areas after the late 1520s, when urban and imperial laws against Anabaptism became severe and executions not unusual.[36]

From a modern point of view there is fault in the sixteenth-century presumption that society must be religiously and politically one; confusion of religious and political allegiance breeds intolerance and persecution. On the

33. *On Heretics: Whether They Should be Punished by the Sword of the Magistrate.* Photoreprint of the Basel Latin original, ed. Sape van der Woude (Geneva, 1954); English translation Roland Bainton (New York, 1965).

34. *LW* 45, p. 108.

35. See my *Reformation in the Cities* (New Haven, 1975) ch. 4; Franz Lau, "Der Bauernkrieg und das angebliche Ende der Lutherischen Reformation als spontaner Volksbewegung," *Luther Jahrbuch* 26 (1959): 109-34; Bernd Moeller, *Reichsstadt und Reformation* (Gütersloh, 1962), p. 26; Gottfried Seebass, "The Reformation in Nürnberg," in L. P. Buck and J. W. Zophy, eds., *The Social History of the Reformation*, (Columbus, 1972), pp. 17-40.

36. Paul Peachey, "Social Background and Social Philosophy of the Swiss Anabaptists, 1525-1540," *MQR* 28 (1954): 102-27, esp. pp. 105, 110, 115: Clasen, *Anabaptism: A Social History*, p. 22.

other hand, it may be asked whether the removal of religious values from political power in sectarian and modern versions of the separation of church and state has been an altogether unmixed blessing for society. Does society always profit when religion is a stranger to politics? Without raising the specter of theocracy, it may be asked which is the greater risk: the loss of religious purity, as Anabaptists feared, when religion becomes politically involved or the loss of the ability to judge and transform political institutions by ancient religious wisdom, as mainline Protestants feared, when religion turns politically passive?[37]

A recent assessment has argued that mainstream Anabaptism was motivated, above all, by the problem of the "ethics of coercion."[38] Having taken the position that religious beliefs and practices could not be forced on people, Anabaptists opted for separation from a society that attempted to do so. In so opting, they rejected the pragmatic compromises of the major reformers and became "a minority hermetically separated from the fallen world and the coercion necessary for its preservation."[39]

From another point of view, the Anabaptists and Spiritualists of the sixteenth century may be said to have been "pre-ethical" in outlook. Was the problem with which they wrestled the ethics of coercion or their own inability to accept a world that fell short of the highest Christian ideals? Ethical people labor to implement values and ideals they know to be fragile and beyond full human realization. Who are the ethical people? The eloquent advocates of the New Jerusalem who live on the fringes of society and ignore or attack it in the name of ideals it cannot attain? Or those who attempt to bring such ideals to bear in part on society at the cost of compromise and the risk of defeat? Where the sectarians of the sixteenth century seem to have been most novel is not in their separation of church and state—a version of which had existed since the Investiture Struggle—but in their willingness to put religion and society asunder. Monks and nuns had separated from secular society throughout the Middle Ages—but as part of a church in constant communion with it and devoted to its transformation. Only the sectarians of the sixteenth century maintained in principle that true religion required total separation from the world. The legacy of the radical reformers is to have made more difficult the penetration of society and culture by classical religious values.

37. This question is debated in a dated but still useful essay by the late Lutheran church historian Karl Holl, who severely criticized the sectarian legacy, while praising, somewhat unduly, the Lutheran church-state. "Die Kulturbedeutung der Reformation," in *Gesammelte Aufsätze zur Kirchengeschichte* (Tübingen, 1948), 1: 468–543. The essay first appeared in 1911, well before the rise of National Socialism.

38. Stayer, *Anabaptists and the Sword*, p. 1.

39. Ibid., p. 330.

CHAPTER 11

Calvin and Calvinism

Young Calvin

IN 1523, at age fourteen, John Calvin entered the Collège de la Marche in Paris, where, in accordance with his father's wishes, he began a course of study intended to prepare him for a career in divinity.[1] In his determination to shape the vocational lives of his children, Gerard Calvin, a respected advisor to the bishop of Noyon in Picardy, was fully a match for Luther's father, although ultimately no more successful. He obtained for his son ecclesiastical benefices in the cathedral church of Noyon and the village church of Pont l' Evêque, which paid for the greater part of Calvin's education.

At the college in Paris, Calvin came under the tutelage of Maturin Cordier, a Latin scholar considered one of the founders of modern pedagogy. Cordier introduced Calvin to the scholarly world of humanism and won his lasting loyalty. Later, in 1559, when their roles of authority had become reversed, Cordier joined Calvin in Geneva, where he undertook to do for the city's young scholars what he had done for the young Calvin in Paris.

In these formative years Calvin also became aware of the native French reform movement, which Jacques Lefèvre d'Etaples, a leading evangelical humanist and biblical scholar, inspired and Bishop Briçonnet of Meaux actively led.[2] Briçonnet was spiritual advisor to Marguerite, eldest sister of King Francis I and future queen of Navarre (after 1527) and a generous patron of the French reform party. Marguerite encouraged humanist

---

1. Basic for Calvin's biography is the contemporary and admiring portrait by Theodore Beza, *The Life of John Calvin*, trans. Francis Gibson (Philadelphia, 1836). Among the modern biographers is Alexandre Ganoczy, *Le jeune Calvin: Genèse et évolution de son vocation réformatrice* (Wiesbaden, 1966).

2. Henry Heller describes Lefèvre as "heterodox" by 1525 and "no longer confined within a traditional Catholic mold," although by no means so radical as the Protestants Zwingli, Oecolampadius, and Farel, who strongly influenced him ("The Evangelicism of Lefèvre d'Etaples: 1525," *Studies in the Renaissance* 19 [1972]: 75-76). On the Meaux circle, see R. J. Lovy, *Les origines de la Réforme française: Meaux 1518-1546* (Paris, 1959) and Christine Martineau et al., eds., *Guillaume Briçonnet, Marguerite d'Angouleme, Correspondence (1521-1524)*, vol. 1, *Années 1521-1522* (Geneva, 1975).

A portrait of John Calvin.

studies at court and criticized contemporary religious life on the basis of her own independent study of antiquity. She wrote an introspective book on Christian meditation, *The Mirror of a Sinful Soul,* which the theologians of the Sorbonne banned in 1532 because of its Protestant flavor.

Calvin continued his education in Paris at the Collège de Montaigu, an institution renowned for its strict discipline and Catholic orthodoxy. The school became the butt of ridicule by Erasmus and Rabelais, both of whom believed they had suffered unduly while students there. According to Erasmus, the school served spoiled food, beat students, and forced them to sleep in filthy cubicles, an especially awful ordeal for the neurotically fastidious Erasmus.[3]

In the Collège de Montaigu Calvin received his first dose of traditional scholastic education. He studied philosophy with a Scotsman, John Major, a leading Gallicanist who had joined the faculty in 1525 and sympathized with the Ockhamist tradition. The school proved well suited to Calvin's censorious, no-nonsense frame of mind. It is reported by a classmate, who also confesses to having disliked Calvin, that Calvin was known among his peers as "the accusative case."[4]

Calvin received the master's degree in 1528 at the age of eighteen. Thereafter, he left Paris for law school in Orleans when his father decided that legal studies were the surer road to success for his son. If Calvin was displeased by this turn of events, there is no record of protest. His natural tendency seems always to have been rapid adjustment to the surroundings in which he found himself and mastery over them. The Orleans jurist Pierre de l'Estoile, a man of notable piety and discipline, became a personal model for the young Calvin. Calvin was also befriended in Orleans by a German classical scholar, Melchior Wolmar, a man of Lutheran persuasion, who taught him the rudiments of Greek. Wolmar also tutored Theodore Beza, who would succeed Calvin in Geneva.

In 1532, at twenty-two, Calvin received his doctorate in civil law. In April of the same year he published his first scholarly work, a commentary on Seneca's *De clementia.* A humanistically trained civil lawyer, he aspired at this time to be like Guillaume Budé, the dean of French humanism, not a French Martin Luther.[5] The Seneca commentary, written in the style of reform-minded humanism, reveals his good Latin, belief in moral education, and devotion to antiquity. If Calvin was at this time committed to

3. Johan Huizinga, *Erasmus and the Age of Reformation* (New York, 1957), pp. 22, 117.

4. John T. McNeill, *The History and Character of Calvinism* (New York, 1957), p. 99.

5. Quirinus Breen, *John Calvin: A Study in French Humanism,* 2nd ed. (Grand Rapids, 1968), p. 2.

church reform, it was strictly by way of friendly persuasion, not yet by doctrinal dispute and religious revolt.

Calvin's views changed between the summer of 1532 and the spring of 1534, the period in which he converted to Protestantism. He described the experience in a later commentary on the Psalms (1557):

> At first I remained so obstinately addicted to the superstitions of the papacy that it would have been hard indeed to have pulled me out of so deep a quagmire by a sudden conversion. But God subdued and made teachable a heart which, for my age, was far too hardened in such matters. Having received some foretaste and knowledge of true piety, I was inflamed with such great desire to profit by it that, although I did not give up my other studies, I worked only slackly at them. I was wonderstruck, when, before the year was out, all those who had some desire for true doctrine ranged themselves around me to learn, although I was hardly more than a beginner myself.[6]

The key phrase here is "God's subduing and making teachable a stubborn heart." Later, as the reformer of Geneva, Calvin strongly inclined to view his ministry as a continuous struggle to subdue and make teachable undisciplined and hardened hearts.

Scholars have argued over the precise date of this conversion. Some believe it occurred as early as 1527–28, pointing out that Calvin had by this time become acquainted with Luther's works and had even been tutored in Greek by Wolmar, a convinced Lutheran. Calvin also described himself in these years as moving away from the "darkness of the papacy" under the impact of Luther's writings.[7] Other scholars, however, attach less importance to Calvin's early criticism of the papacy, and expressions of appreciation for Luther. Such criticism, they argue, was commonplace and Luther's works had circulated in Paris since 1521; Luther influenced many reform-minded Frenchmen in the 1520s without turning them into Protestants. The strongest argument against the early dating of Calvin's conversion, however, is his own commentary on Seneca. Written a full four years after the alleged conversion, it contains nothing distinctly Protestant.[8]

The date to which most scholars now assign Calvin's conversion is May

6. Cited by François Wendel, *Calvin: The Origins and Development of His Religious Thought,* trans. P. Mairet (New York, 1963), pp. 37–38.

7. *RGG* 1: 1588; Wendel, *Calvin,* p. 39. Exponents of this early dating tend to be older scholars, among them Emile Doumergue, Karl Holl, and Peter Barth.

8. Cf. McNeill, *History and Character of Calvinism,* p. 110.

1534. At this time he returned to his home in Noyon and surrendered the ecclesiastical benefices he had held since he was twelve—a public action indicating a definite change of heart and mind. This decision had doubtlessly been in preparation throughout the winter of 1533–34. What seems most to have discontented Calvin about the native French reform movement was its failure to implement its ideals and bring about actual reforms.[9] The union of internal belief and external behavior would become the hallmark of Calvinism. Calvinists distinguished themselves, above all, by their fervent belief that religion not only changed inward self-perception, but also transformed public life and manners; beliefs could not sit idly in the mind, but must renew individuals and societies. Nothing stands out more prominently in the history of Calvinism than the enforcement of a high standard of individual and social sanctification.

Throughout his ministry Calvin remained extremely sensitive to two groups, which he labeled and ridiculed as "Libertines" and "Nicodemites." Libertines were people whose lives were loose and faith unsure; believing little they drifted valuelessly, slaves to their affections. As Michael Walzer has pointed out in his study of Puritanism, the one thing Calvinists could never abide was "masterless men."[10] Calvin described Libertines as "the most execrable and pernicious sect the world has ever known."[11] In Geneva he identified them with a powerful aristocratic family, the Favres, who boldly transgressed the blue laws of the Consistory. Calvin once excluded the patriarch of the family, François, from the sacrament because of immoral behavior and censored his wife for dancing lewdly at a wedding.

Nicodemites were people who protested true (evangelical) belief, but could not bring themselves to act on it; to all practical intents and purposes they only simulated true faith. Their name derived from the biblical story of Nicodemus, a Jew who claimed to believe the teaching of Jesus, but was unable to understand what "new birth" meant (John 3:1). Calvin may initially have had the French humanist reformers in mind, men who preached reform with great eloquence, yet remained publicly allied with an unreformed church.[12] It has been argued that the Nicodemites were actually

9. Cf. Breen, *John Calvin*, p. 90.
10. *The Revolution of the Saints: A Study in the Origins of Radical Politics* (New York, 1970), p. 313.
11. *Letters of John Calvin*, trans. Jules Bonnet (Philadelphia, 1858), 1: 455. See Actes du Colloque Intl. de Sommiers, *Aspects du libertinisme au XVIe siècle* (Paris, 1974); R. W. Collins, *Calvin and the Libertines of Geneva* (Toronto, 1968).
12. Beza describes Nicodemites as "certain Persons in France, who, having renounced the Protestant religion at the commencement, through fear of persecution, had begun afterwards so far to flatter themselves as to deny there was any sin in being present with their bodies only at the celebration of the mass, provided they embraced the true religion in their

advanced Protestant intellectuals who, after the Reformation failed to realize its social promise, became devoted to Spiritualism but for survival's sake in the increasingly intolerant sixteenth century found it necessary to simulate orthodox beliefs.[13] It remains a question whether Nicodemites were ever such a self-conscious, organized group.[14] On the other hand, the problem of simulated belief unquestionably vexed Calvin throughout his career as a reformer.

Prior to Calvin's forfeiture of his benefices, two events helped clarify his decision to turn Protestant. One involved a friend from his schooldays at the Collège de Montaigu, Nicholas Cop, the newly elected rector of the University of Paris. In the fall of 1533, Cop sharply attacked the theologians of the Sorbonne in an address on All Saints' Day. He had previously clashed with them over Marguerite of Navarre's *Mirror of a Sinful Soul.* Although Cop's criticism was in line with that of the native humanist reform party, his address advocated reform so forcefully that opponents condemned it as Lutheran propaganda. He cited a sermon of Luther's in the address, but it was actually the reform sentiments of Erasmus, especially those of the *Paraclesis* (which Luther had found objectionable), and Lefèvre that predominated. Calvin's close association with Cop cast suspicion on him as a possible coauthor, and the two became objects of heresy proceedings. Cop fled to Basel, while Calvin made his way in disguise to Noyon.

Sometime in the spring of 1534, shortly before he surrendered his benefices, the fugitive Calvin visited Lefèvre, apparently to seek advice on the best course of action now that persecution of the French reform party and Protestants had begun in earnest. No record of their conversation exists. Calvin's American biographer has surmised that Calvin must have been overwhelmed by the impotence of the native reform movement as he sat with the aged Lefèvre and recognized, perhaps fully for the first time, that continuing obedience to the old church was the true obstacle to reform.[15] Clearly, if Lefèvre attempted to dissuade Calvin from his new

---

hearts" (*Life of Calvin,* p. 39). See Albert Autin, *Une épisode de la vie de Calvin: La crise du Nicodèmisme 1535-45* (Toulon, 1917).

13. Carlo Ginzburg, *Il nicodemismo: Similazione e dissimulazione religiosa nell' Europe del '500* (Turin, 1970). Ginzburg cites as Nicodemites Otto Brunfels, the reputed originator, Wolfgang Capito, Bartholomäus Westheimer, Sebastian Franck, Johannes Brenz, Clement Ziegler, Camilio Renato, and Jacques Lefèvre.

14. See the critique of Ginzburg's work by Carlos M. N. Eire, "Calvin and Nicodemism: A Reappraisal," *Sixteenth Century Journal* 10 (1979) 45-69.: see also Eire's dissertation, "Idolatry and the Reformation: A Study of the Protestant Attack on Catholic Worship in Germany, Switzerland, and France, 1500-1580" (Yale, 1979), ch. 5.

15. McNeill, *The History and Character of Calvinism,* pp. 114-15.

course, he was most unconvincing. Shortly after the visit Calvin forfeited his benefices and entered the Protestant camp.

Political Revolt and
Religious Reform in Geneva

BETWEEN the summer of 1534 and the spring of 1536, Calvin traveled in France and to Italy, where he visited the duchess Renée of Ferrara, daughter of Louis XII. The new turmoil in his life did not impede his scholarly work. His new religious orientation inspired an eloquent apology, the *Institutes of the Christian Religion,* the first edition of which appeared in March 1536 and quickly earned him an international reputation. This work grew through subsequent editions into a *summa* of Reformed Protestantism by the final edition of 1559.

At this time the French king, Francis I, on the verge of a third war with the emperor and needing unity and manpower on the home front, issued a general amnesty for French religious exiles that permitted Calvin to return to France in the summer of 1536. He visited Paris, where he settled some family business, and then departed for what was apparently to be a leisurely scholarly life in Protestant Strasbourg. The war, however, forced him to detour to Geneva, where he arrived in August 1536.

Geneva had undergone a political revolution in the 1520s before undertaking Protestant reforms in the 1530s.[16] Whereas in Lutheran Saxony a religious reform, undertaken at the initiative of theologians, led to a political revolt by princes against the emperor, in Geneva a political revolt against the House of Savoy, led by the city's magistrates, prepared the way for the introduction of Protestant religious reforms.

Geneva had traditionally been ruled by a resident prince-bishop, a reflection of feudal town government that reached back to the tenth century. The prince-bishop held jurisdiction over all civil and criminal cases and regulated the city's religious life. He executed his responsibilities through a special council presided over by a handpicked vicar, who also represented him in the city during his frequent prolonged absences. Despite his theoretical autonomy, the Genevan prince-bishop had long represented the political interests of the House of Savoy, the dominant political and military power south of Lake Geneva. On the northern side of the lake lay Bern, which turned Protestant in 1528, and Catholic Fribourg, powerful Swiss counterweights to Savoy. Both were actively expanding southward in the

16. My reconstruction of these events is based on E. W. Monter, *Calvin's Geneva* (New York, 1967); Henri Naef, *Les origines de la réforme à Genève* (Geneva, 1968); Rudolf Pfister, *Kirchengeschichte der Schweiz* vol. 2 (Zurich, 1974); and John T. McNeill, *The History and Character of Calvinism.*

first quarter of the sixteenth century. Bern especially eyed the Savoyard Pays de Vaud and between 1536 and 1564 progressively took full control of these Genevan hinterlands. Not only did Bern and Fribourg successfully extend their influence over Geneva, but Geneva's merchants, the dominant political force in the city, favored a Swiss alliance. The Swiss and German fairs had become the pillars of the Genevan economy, and Genevan merchants retained close business and personal ties with the north. Assisted by these larger political developments, the Genevans seized the opportunity to challenge their prince-bishop, Pierre de la Baume, in the 1520s.

The Savoyards responded to Swiss expansion by tightening their hold on Geneva, and the city found itself divided into Savoyard and Swiss factions. Outspoken opposition to the prince-bishop and the duke of Savoy surfaced as early as 1517, and in January 1519 a group of eighty-six Genevans, led by the later historian of the city, François Bonivard, moved to Fribourg and became citizens. Although the Savoyards managed to annul a Genevan treaty with Fribourg, its short-lived existence was an ominous straw in the wind.

The showdown came in 1525. In that year Lausanne, which Savoy had dominated in the same way it controlled Geneva, successfully allied with Bern. Suspecting that the Genevans might try a similar arrangement, the Savoyard Duke Charles III ordered the Genevans to resist the Swiss and reaffirm their traditional allegiance to Savoy and their prince-bishop. Under coercion the city agreed, but at the same time Genevan exiles, led by Besançon Hugues—from whom the term "Huguenot" would be derived—began negotiations in Geneva's name with both Fribourg and Bern. In February 1526 a formal alliance was struck, placing Geneva thereafter firmly within the Swiss political camp.

The Eidguenots, as the supporters of the Swiss alliance were called, now easily triumphed over the prince-bishop. A citizen assembly ratified the treaties negotiated with the Swiss by Besancon Hugues. Henceforth, Genevan government fell to two aristocratic councils, which assumed the traditional powers of the prince-bishop, who fled to Fribourg in August 1527: the Council of Two Hundred, the main political body with both legislative and judicial functions, and the Little Council, an executive body of twenty-five, sixteen of whom were appointed by the Council of Two Hundred, and the other nine members, who consisted of the four syndics, the city treasurer, and four holdovers from the previous year's Little Council, elected annually by the citizenry.

Geneva won its independence from Savoy for two basic reasons: it had a militarily superior ally in Bern, and Besançon Hugues and the merchants who headed the Eidguenot movement were superior leaders of men; the prince-bishop and the Savoyards were overmatched militarily and outmaneuvered politically. The city survived an interdict in April 1528 and, thanks to aid from Bern and Fribourg, overcame a Savoyard blockade in 1530.

On the heels of this successful political revolution came the religious reform of Geneva. The Protestant Reformation in Geneva was part of the *consolidation* of the political revolution of the 1520s, not of that revolution itself.[17] Even though Luther's works had circulated in the city as early as 1524, militant Protestant activity did not begin there until the summer of 1532, when pamphlets and placards appeared denouncing the Catholic church. In 1533, Bern despatched a team of Protestant preachers to Geneva—Guillaume Farel, Antoine Saunier, and Pierre Olivetan—with instructions to establish a Protestant mission. The leader, Farel, had earlier directed Protestant reforms as a Bernese agent in Neuchâtel. As Bern had been decisive in Geneva's political revolution, so it now moved to dominate Geneva's religious reform also.

The ascendency of "heresy" in the city distressed Geneva's other Swiss ally, staunchly Catholic Fribourg, especially after a Fribourg citizen named Werli was killed during a religious riot in 1533. Seizing the event as an opportunity to reverse the course of Geneva's religious reform, Fribourg sent the exiled prince-bishop, who was now a Fribourg puppet, back to Geneva to try the culprits. But de la Baume, finding himself ignored and powerless, remained in the city only a fortnight. Genevan officials later apprehended and executed Werli's murderers, but on civil, not episcopal authority, and in the name of law and order, not as a sign of reviving Catholic piety.

Relations between Geneva and Fribourg rapidly distintegrated after these events. In January 1534, Farel and a Dominican named Guy Furbity held a public disputation on the religious issues. In the course of the debate Furbity, with some accuracy, accused the Genevans of being pawns of Bern. The debate ended in a riot. At Bern's insistence, Furbity was later arrested and punished. Suspecting calculated political intrigue on Fribourg's part, the Genevan magistrates broke off relations and Bern became Geneva's only Swiss ally. Although politics played a more important role than religion in this development, Geneva's political and religious destiny were hereafter closely intertwined. In addition to occasioning the new political alliance with Bern, the Furbity affair also led to the formal establishment of a Protestant church in Geneva.

17. Cf., however, Robert M. Kingdon, "Was the Protestant Reformation a Revolution? The Case of Geneva," in Robert M. Kingdon, ed., *Transition and Revolution: Problems and Issues of European Renaissance and Reformation History* (Minneapolis, 1974), pp. 53–76.

A second disputation on religion occurred in June 1535 amid a climate of extreme civic unrest. There had been iconoclastic riots, and a Genevan canon had attempted to poison Farel's co-worker Pierre Viret. Following the disputation, the city councils provisionally suspended the Mass in all city churches—in Geneva, as elsewhere, a sure sign of Protestant success. In December 1535 magistrates laid before the Catholic clergy the option of conversion to the new evangelical faith or exile from the city.

In this same period Savoy besieged Geneva in a last-ditch effort to restore the Catholic status quo ante. Aided again by Bern, Geneva preserved its political independence. As so often in sixteenth-century politics, however, the ally now became the enemy. Having successfully liberated Geneva, the Bernese attempted to impose their political will upon the city and to deal with it to all intents and purposes as a new prince-bishop. Lausanne had earlier capitulated to Bern in a similar situation, and the Bernese apparently expected the Genevans to offer little resistance. Freedom, however, died hard in Geneva, as both Bern and later John Calvin painfully discovered. As the magistrates pointed out to their presumptuous ally:

> We have [not] endured war against both the Duke of Savoy and the Bishop for ... twenty years ... because we intended to make this city subject to [another] power, but because we wished that our poor city, which has warred and suffered so much, should have her liberty.[18]

In August 1536 the Bernese formally recognized Genevan sovereignty. Although Bern remained the dominant military power in the region until the 1560s, it never succeeded in subjugating Geneva to its will.

On May 25, 1536 the Genevan people accepted the Reformation, pledging "to live according to the Law of the Gospel and the Word of God, and to abolish all Papal abuses."[19] Calvin arrived that summer, just as Farel and his co-workers were beginning to implement this new mandate. Learning of Calvin's presence and knowing his reputation, Farel earnestly urged him to join the work of reform. Calvin later recalled having been so "overcome by shame and anxiety" after Farel's petition that his sense of duty forced him to abandon his Strasbourg plans and assist the Genevan reforms.[20]

Almost overnight Calvin assumed leadership of the Genevan Reformation; as Sebastian Castellio later reported, the simple evangelical movement of Farel became "Calvinized."[21] In 1537, Calvin spelled out for the Genevans

18. Cited by Monter, *Calvin's Geneva,* p. 55.
19. Document in Kingdon, *Transition and Revolution,* pp. 96–97.
20. *Corpus Reformatorum* 59, pp. 23–26.
21. "Ipsemet Farellus (heu dolor!) jam calvinizet" (*Contra libellum Calvini* [n.p., 1562], no. 72, p. D 8 b).

what living according to God's law entailed. He presented an ecclesiastical ordinance for the magistrates' approval on January 16, 1537, twenty-
one "Articles on the Organization of Church and Worship," which ex-
pounded his conception of the church's role in Geneva's moral and political
life. He also provided at this time a new catechism, *An Instruction in the Faith,*
which defined the responsibilities of individual Christians.

The proposed ordinance and catechism subjected the Genevans to more
control over their religious lives than they had bargained for in supporting
the Reformation. Calvin wanted to place in the hands of the ministers what
he called "the correction and discipline of excommunication." In his scheme
"persons of good life and witness from among the faithful" would be elected by the councils and given "oversight of the [moral] life and government"
of every quarter of the city. Their findings of misconduct were to be reported to the ministers for corrective action. Calvin further urged the
magistrates themselves to make an exemplary public confession of faith in
preparation for a public religious oath by all citizens.[22] Although such
oath-taking ceremonies actually took place in September and November,
compliance was far from universal, and both magistracy and populace remained divided over the propriety of such a requirement. Obviously concluding that the power of the preachers over the city's life had become too
great, the councils refused to punish nonjurors.

Calvin and Farel had demanded too much from a city only recently liberated from an episcopal overlord. Were the new Protestant ministers themselves aspiring to become prince-bishop? Accused of "mixing themselves in
magistracy," the reformers now encountered serious internal opposition.
Simultaneously came new pressures on Geneva from Bern to maintain a
more moderate Protestant reform. In particular, Bern wanted the Genevans
to restore baptismal fonts, the use of unleavened bread in the Lord's Supper,
and such traditional religious celebrations as Christmas, New Year's, An-
nunciation, and Ascension—all of which Calvin and Farel had eliminated.[23]

Such internal and external criticism proved too much for Calvin and
Farel. In January 1538 the Council of Two Hundred denied them power of
excommunication, something Calvin had considered indispensable to the
success of the reform. The election of members to the Little Council in the
following month brought to power syndics who opposed the reformers. In
an evident act of repudiation, the Council of Two Hundred readopted the
controversial traditional church practices. Resistance to these actions
brought the reformers' dismissal from the city in April 1538.

---

22. *Calvin: Theological Treatises,* trans. J. K. S. Reid (Philadelphia, 1954), pp. 47–55.
23. Pfister chronicles these events in *Kirchengeschichte der Schweiz,* 2: 204–06.

Strasbourg and Martin Bucer

AFTER visits to Zurich and Basel and abortive efforts to win a hearing on his ouster from Geneva before a conference of Swiss churches, Calvin settled in Strasbourg, his original destination before the fateful detour to Geneva. There he became a lecturer in the university and pastor to a French refugee church. The three year sojourn in Strasbourg not only gave him time to lick his considerable wounds, but also to learn at the hand of an accomplished master how to implement religious reform. That master was Martin Bucer, leader of the Strasbourg clergy. So influential did Bucer become in Calvin's maturation as a Protestant reformer that one historian has declared: "The type of church which we call Calvinistic or Reformed is really a gift of Martin Bucer to the world through the work of his strong and brilliant executive, John Calvin."[24]

Unlike the other major reformers, Bucer, the son of a cooper and a midwife, grew up in relative poverty. His parents deposited him at an early age with his grandfather in Schlettstadt, while they labored in Strasbourg. There Bucer attended Latin school and at age fifteen entered the Dominican order (1506). The order transferred him to the convent in Heidelberg in 1516. In Heidelberg he earned a master's degree in the university and learned Greek from Johannes Brenz, a later Lutheran reformer. Bucer was present at the Heidelberg Disputation between Luther and his Catholic opponents in 1518 and reportedly dined with Luther and Staupitz. The Reformation's impact on him became visible by 1521, when he petitioned and received release from his monastic vows. After serving as a chaplain at the court of Franz von Sickingen and taking a renegade nun, Elizabeth Silbereisen, to wife, Bucer settled in Strasbourg in May 1523, where he joined the work of the Protestant reform party.

When Calvin arrived in Strasbourg, the city had long since become a model of ecclesiastical organization, despite exaggerated clerical complaints of insufficient magisterial support for their reforms.[25] Four church offices—those of preacher, lay elder, lay deacon, and doctor—integrated the religious into the civic life. Bucer was at this time active in the ecumenical movements of the period, both that attempting to heal the division between Lutherans and Zwinglians and that seeking reconciliation between Protestants and Catholics. Strasbourg's ability to be a signatory to both the Lutheran Augsburg Confession and the Zwinglian *Confessio Tetrapolitana*

---

24. Wilhelm Pauck, *The Heritage of the Reformation* (Glencoe, 1961), p. 91.
25. See Jane Abray, "The Long Reformation: Magistrates, Clergy, and People in Strasbourg 1520–1598" (Dissertation, Yale University, 1978); and Miriam U. Chrisman, *Strasbourg and the Reform* (New Haven, 1967) p. 161.

reflected Bucer's theological flexibility as well as the magistrates' political agility. Bucer led the Protestant side at the ecumenical discussions with Catholics in Hagenau, Worms, and Regensburg in the early 1540s, the last such efforts before the Council of Trent made permanent the division of Christendom. With his Catholic counterpart, John Gropper, he wrote a compromise formula known as the *Book of Ratisbon* (also called the *Book of Regensburg*), which many hoped would prove a confessional basis for re-union.[26]

Through Bucer Calvin came to play a minor role in these colloquies, and his letters about them are among the best historical sources of these events. In them he criticized Bucer's readiness to compromise Protestant doctrine and accused both Bucer and Melanchthon, the other leading Protestant negotiator, of not sufficiently "dread[ing] that equivocation in matters of conscience than which nothing can possibly be more hurtful."[27] Although Calvin disassociated himself from such "accommodations to the time," he praised Bucer and Melanchthon for their good intentions and gained much personally from the experience.

Bucer was the most ecumenical and "international" of the reformers;[28] a comprehensive history of the Reformation might be written around his life. Converted by Luther, yet also Zwinglian in his theology, he debated the leading Anabaptists, corresponded frequently with Erasmus, played power politics with Strasbourg magistrates and German territorial princes, became Calvin's mentor, served as a chief Protestant negotiator with Catholics in the 1530s and 1540s, and spent the last years of his life (1548–51) in England assisting Thomas Cranmer with the English Reformation. His last work, *De regno Christi,* was dedicated to King Edward VI.

In Strasbourg Calvin also beheld an exemplary educational system fashioned by the humanist Jean Sturm, which, like Bucer's ecclesiastical organization, he later emulated in Geneva. Sturm divided Strasbourg schools into three levels: a kindergarten for those under six, a nine-year gymnasium, and a five-year high school. The curriculum, based on humanist ideals, required knowledge of Greek and Latin, direct reading of the classics, and moral and religious training.[29]

26. See below, p. 405.

27. *Letters of John Calvin*, 2:263.

28. One historian finds his theology to be a composite of humanist, Platonist, Lutheran, Anabaptist, Anglican, and Catholic themes. See Heinrich Bornkamm, *Martin Bucers Bedeutung für die europäische Reformationsgeschichte* (Gütersloh, 1952).

29. Hastings Eells, *Martin Bucer* (New Haven, 1931), p. 228. The bibliography for a needed study of Sturm has been compiled by Jean Rott, "Bibliographie des oeuvres imprimées du recteur Strasbourgeois Jean Sturm (1507–1589)," in *Actes du 95e congrès national des sociétés savantes (Reims, 1970)* (Paris, 1975), 1: 319–404.

During his Strasbourg "exile," Calvin completed the second edition of the *Institutes*, which he expanded in the 1539 edition from the original six to seventeen chapters, and he wrote his first biblical commentary, an exposition of Paul's letter to the Romans. He also composed an important reply to the enterprising Catholic bishop of Carpentras, Jacopo Sadolet (1477–1547), who had tried to take advantage of Calvin's ouster by inviting the Genevans to return to the Roman fold. In a long, forceful letter that both questioned Calvin's personal motives and criticized Protestant religious practices, Sadolet urged the Genevans to ponder carefully whether it was more expedient for their salvation to trust an institution that had existed for fifteen hundred years or to stake everything on the innovations of the last twenty-five.[30] Urged by the Guillermins (after Guillaume Farel), a Protestant faction sympathetic to the reforms of Calvin and Farel, Calvin responded to Sadolet in August 1539 with an eloquent personal defense and one of the clearest statements of the new Protestant faith.[31]

During his stay in Strasbourg Calvin also chose a wife, an undertaking in which he received unsolicited advice from both Farel and Bucer, who seemed to compete in playing Cupid to Calvin. Calvin had his own very clear ideas on the matter, however, which he shared with Farel. "Keep in mind what I seek to find in her," he wrote.

I am none of those insane lovers who embrace also the vices of those they are in love with, when they are smitten at first sight with a fine figure. This only is the beauty which attracts me: if she is chaste, if not too nice or fastidious, if economical, if patient, if there is hope that she will be interested about my health.[32]

In August 1540 Calvin wed Idelette de Bure, the widow of an Anabaptist he himself had apparently been instrumental in converting.

Calvin's Geneva: 1541–64

WHEN Calvin and Farel were exiled in 1538, they had been opposed by newly elected syndics and Geneva's powerful ally Bern. The elections of 1539 brought neutral syndics to power, and by 1540 a strong anti-Bern faction held sway within the councils. The political climate thereafter favored Calvin's return. In September 1540 the councils passed a resolution inviting him to resume

---

30. In *John Calvin and Jacopo Sadoleto: A Reformation Debate*, ed. and trans. John C. Olin (New York, 1966), p. 40.

31. Ibid.

32. *Letters of John Calvin*, 1: 141.

his former post. Learning of this development, Farel wrote from Neuchâtel, where he had happily settled, urging Calvin to return, and Heinrich Bullinger wrote from Zurich to point out the strategic importance of Geneva for the Reformation. Calvin agonized for a year before accepting the invitation; he confided to a friend, "There is no place under heaven of which I have greater dread" and acknowledged his fear that a return might subject him to the same contests and outcome as his first visit.[33] For a man of Calvin's ego, to be twice defeated was to be destroyed.

Calvin arrived in Geneva on September 13, 1541. Within six weeks of his arrival he submitted to the magistrates a new ecclesiastical ordinance, which followed the Strasbourg model. Church discipline remained as important to him in 1541 as it had been in 1537. In a statement to the councils after their revocation of his sentence of exile, he warned:

> If you desire to have me for your pastor, correct the disorder of your lives. If you have with sincerity recalled me from my exile, banish the crimes and debaucheries which prevail among you. I cannot behold without the most painful displeasure ... discipline trodden under foot and crimes committed with impunity. I cannot possibly live in a place so grossly immoral. ... I consider the principal enemies of the Gospel to be, not the pontiff of Rome, nor heretics, nor seducers, nor tyrants, but bad Christians. ... I dread abundantly more those carnal covetousnesses, those debaucheries of the tavern, of the brothel, and of gaming. ... Of what use is a dead faith without good works? Of what importance is even truth itself, where a wicked life belies it and actions make words blush? Either command me to abandon a second time your town and let me go and soften the bitterness of my afflictions in a new exile, or let the severity of the laws reign in the church. Reestablish there pure discipline.[34]

Calvin did not make the same mistakes in 1541 that he had made in 1537-38. The 1537 Articles on the Organization of Church and Worship, which the councils had refused to accept without change, had given the impression that he and Farel wished to "meddle in magistracy." The church ordinance of 1541 scrupulously respected the political sovereignty of the councils and subjected the clergy to an emphatic oath of allegiance before the Lord Syndic and Little Council.[35] The clergy's power within the city now lay within the office of elder, one of four church offices (pastors, elders, deacons, and doctors) adopted following the practice of the Strasbourg

33. Ibid., 1: 231.
34. Cited in Beza, *Life of Calvin*, n. 1, pp. 25-26.
35. "Draft Ecclesiastical Ordinances," in *Calvin: Theological Treatises*, pp. 71-72.

church. The elders were chosen by and from the Genevan councils—two from the Little Council, four from the council of Sixty, and six from the Council of Two Hundred—and given the mandate to "oversee the life of everyone, admonish amicably those whom they see to be erring or living a disordered life, and, where it is required, enjoin fraternal correction."[36] Together the pastors and the elders formed the Consistory, a church-run moral and religious judiciary. Although a powerful body, the Consistory held no actual coercive power. Prior to 1555, when Calvin finally succeeded in winning the Consistory's right of excommunication, only the magistrates could coercively discipline the morally lapsed and ban them from the sacrament.

While religious and moral discipline was new neither in theory nor in statute in Geneva, it came to be more successfully enforced there than elsewhere and largely because of Calvin's devotion to it. Calvin's care in this regard can be seen not only in the new ecclesiastical ordinance, but also in the *Genevan Catechism,* issued in November 1541. Unlike the 1537 *Instruction in Faith,* which had taken the form of a treatise, the new catechism set forth prepared questions and answers. Also unlike its 1537 predecessor, the catechism no longer followed Luther's practice of treating the law, that is, the Ten Commandments, before faith, that is, the Creed and basic doctrine.[37] The placement of faith before the law reflected the Calvinist belief that the commandments were not intended primarily to drive one to self-despair and subsequent faith, as Lutherans inclined to teach, but were to be embraced in a positive way, as a guide to daily living, by all confessed Christians. This was the so-called third use of the Law: in addition to establishing political discipline and terrifying the consciences of the wicked and the prideful, God's commandments provided true believers with a sure guide for their individual and social lives.

Calvin's Geneva was neither the New Jerusalem John Knox proclaimed it to be nor the concentration camp popular literature has made it.[38] The remarkable thoroughness of the moral discipline achieved by Calvin was not matched by severity of punishment, save in a few celebrated cases of doctrinal heresy. Whereas Martin Bucer, allegedly the most tolerant Protes-

---

36. Ibid., pp. 63–64.

37. See Pfister, *Kirchengeschichte der Schweiz,* 2: 212. The later version of this catechism is in *Calvin: Theological Treatises,* pp. 83–139.

38. See the sympathetic treatments of R. M. Kingdon, "The Control of Morals in Calvin's Geneva," in *The Social History of the Reformation,* ed. L. P. Buck and J. W. Zophy (Columbus, 1972), pp. 3–16; and E. W. Monter, "Crime and Punishment in Calvin's Geneva," *ARG* 64 (1973): 281–87. On the importance of the religious refugees in creating the various myths about Geneva, see Alain Dufour, "Le Mythe de Genève au temps de Calvin," in *Histoire politique et psychologie historique suivie de deux essais sur Humanisme et Reformation et Le Mythe de Genève aux temps de Calvin* (Geneva, 1966).

tant reformer in the most tolerant Protestant city of the time, sought, un-successfully, to have adulterers stoned in Strasbourg, public adultery in Geneva brought a maximum penalty of imprisonment for nine days on bread and water.[39] The Genevan Consistory also had the right to summon high officials who had lapsed morally; "executive privilege" did not exist on a modern scale in Geneva. Calvin's readiness to punish prominent citizens as quickly and as thoroughly as ordinary people ensured tension between the ecclesiastical and political governments. Until 1555, when religious ref-ugees devoted to Calvinist reforms came to make up approximately one-third of Geneva's inhabitants and Ami Perrin, the leader of aristocratic opposition to Calvin, fell from power, Calvin struggled to maintain his authority and respect. According to Beza, in these difficult years Genevans even called their dogs "Calvin."[40]

The celebrated confrontations that have earned Calvin's popular reputa-tion as a theocratic tyrant all concerned a challenge to his authority. This was the touchiest point for the first generation of Protestant reformers. The most basic and persistent criticism of their Catholic opponents was that the reformers were unauthorized innovators. On this basis Sadolet had urged the Genevans to return to the traditional faith. Calvin no more than Luther and Zwingli could tolerate the suggestion that he lacked the competence to reform religious practice.[41] He adopted a thoroughly Machiavellian stance on the issue: the success of his reform depended on nothing so much as fear and respect for his leadership and authority.

An early celebrated confrontation involved a playing-card manufacturer named Pierre Ameaux, who had petitioned the Consistory for a divorce from his adulterous wife. Angered by the delay in acting on his request, Ameaux publicly questioned Calvin's sense of fairness and competence as a theologian. Imprisoned for slander, Ameaux was required, at Calvin's insis-tence, to make a public penance; clad in a penitential shirt, he walked about the city, pausing at the public corners and begging God's mercy—actually a proclamation, for all to hear, of Calvin's authority.

Two other famous episodes concerned Jacques Gruet and Jerome Bolsec. Gruet, whom Calvin considered a Libertine, had written letters critical of the Consistory and, more serious, petitioned the Catholic king of France to intervene in the political and religious affairs of Geneva. With Calvin's concurrence he was beheaded for treason. Bolsec publicly challenged Cal-

39. Bucer, *Das ym selbs niemant, sonder andern leben soll*, in *M. Bucers Deutsche Schriften* ed. Robert Stupperich (Gütersloh, 1960), 1: 57; "Ordinances for the Supervision of Churches in the Country" (1547), in *Calvin: Theological Treatises*, p. 82.

40. *Life of Calvin*, p. 44.

41. On this issue, cf. Wendel, *Calvin*, p. 92.

vin's teaching on predestination, a doctrine Bolsec, with many others, found morally repugnant. Banished from the city in 1551, he revenged himself in 1577 by publishing a biography of Calvin that charged him with greed, financial misconduct, and sexual aberration.[42]

No event has more influenced history's judgment of Calvin than the role he played in the capture and execution of the Spanish physician and amateur theologian Michael Servetus in 1553. This event has overshadowed everything else Calvin accomplished and continues to embarrass his modern admirers. In 1903, for example, on the occasion of the three-hundred-and-fiftieth anniversary of Servetus's execution, Emile Doumergue, at the time the dean of Calvin scholars, led a group of Calvinists to the site of Servetus's execution, where they erected an expiatory monument from the "sons of Calvin."[43] The execution of Servetus also provided the spark for what has come to be known as the toleration controversy of the sixteenth century,[44] a prolonged assault on Calvinist theology in the name of common sense and Christian love from which key Calvinist doctrines never recovered. This assault was initially led by Sebastian Castellio, Geneva's schoolmaster between 1541 and 1544, whom Calvin forced to leave the city because of theological differences.[45]

Servetus is credited with being the first Western physician to recognize the significance of the pulmonary circulation of blood, that is, that passage through the lungs oxygenates blood. What the Peasants' Revolt was to Lutheranism, the execution of this early scientist became to Calvinism: a sign of the collapse of the Reformation's social promise. For many, Calvin's role in the death of Servetus attached the same reactionary stigma to Protestantism that the Inquisition's later treatment of Galileo brought to the Catholic Church.

Servetus attained notoriety at the age of twenty, when, after reading the Bible and studying the opinions of theologians, he concluded that the doctrine of the Trinity was nonsensical and so argued in a book published in Strasbourg in 1531 entitled *Seven Books on the Errors of the Trinity*. With a view of church history reminiscent of Erasmus, he looked on the emergence of Trinitarian doctrine at the Council of Nicea (325) as a sign of the

---

42. *Histoire de la vie, moeurs, actes, doctrine, constance et mort de Jean Calvin . . . pub. a Lyon en 1577*, ed. M. Louis-Francois Chastel (Lyon, 1875).

43. McNeill, *The History and Character of Calvinism*, p. 176.

44. See especially Joseph Lecler, *Toleration and the Reformation*, trans. T. L. Westow (New York, 1960, pp. 325–64.

45. They clashed over the canonical status of the Song of Songs, which Castellio considered a lascivious love poem undeserving of a place in Holy Scripture, and over the creedal affirmation that Christ descended into hell, a notion Castellio found unworthy of a Christian creed. See my *Mysticism and Dissent* (New Haven, 1973), p. 170.

church's falling away from its biblical mission and into sophistry.[46] Although Sebastian Franck befriended Servetus and praised his book,[47] the major Protestant theologians joined Catholic authorities in condemning it, their sensitivity all the more increased by the efforts of Catholic pamphleteers to brand it a Protestant work.

Servetus responded to his critics with a second work, *Two Dialogues on the Trinity* (1532), in which he acknowledged his immaturity as a scholar, but also refused to make a retraction. Thereafter he prudently assumed the pseudonym Michel de Villeneuve and retired from public view. In this disguise he worked as a translator and editor in Lyons—among his accomplishments was a Spanish translation of some works of Thomas Aquinas— studied medicine, and became a practicing physician in Vienne in the 1540s. Although he was secure in anonymity and a new profession, Servetus's theological interests remained irrepressible. From Vienne he struck up a pseudonymous correspondence with Calvin, who recognized him as the notorious anti-Trinitarian Servetus and, playing along, responded under a pseudonym of his own, Charles Despeville. Servetus, who may have been toying with the idea of moving to Geneva, sent Calvin a manuscript copy of a new work in progress, *The Restoration of Christianity*. To rescue Servetus from his heresies, Calvin replied with the latest edition of his *Institutes of the Christian Religion*, which Servetus promptly returned with insulting marginal comments. Despite Servetus's pleas, Calvin, who developed an intense dislike of Servetus during their correspondence, refused to return any of the incriminating material. If ever Servetus comes to Geneva, Calvin declared to Farel in a report of their intrigue, "I will not suffer him to get out alive."[48]

The publication of *The Restoration of Christianity* in 1553 made Servetus once again a hunted heretic. This work contained revised versions of his earlier anti-Trinitarian tracts, a treatise on spiritual rebirth, a self-defense against Philip Melanchthon's condemnation of his views on the Trinity, and letters received from Calvin during their pseudonymous correspondence. When copies of the work began to circulate in Geneva among Calvin's opponents, Calvin sent Servetus's correspondence, together with the manuscript sections of *The Restoration of Christianity* and the copy of the *Institutes*

---

46. On Servetus's theology, see Roland H. Bainton, *Hunted Heretic: The Life and Death of Michael Servetus 1511–1553* (Boston, 1960), pp. 46–48; Jerome Friedman, *Michael Servetus: A Case Study in Total Heresy* (Geneva, 1978).

47. See the remarks in Franck's *Letter to John Campanus* in G. H. Williams, ed., *Spiritual and Anabaptist Writers: Documents Illustrative of the Radical Reformation* (Philadelphia, 1957), pp. 158–59.

48. Bainton, *Hunted Heretic*, p. 70.

Servetus had annotated, to a friend in Vienne who had contacts with the Inquisition in Lyons. This material apparently assisted the Inquisition's location and capture of Servetus, who was confronted with it during his interrogation.

On August 13, 1553, Servetus escaped from his Catholic captors and fled south, apparently to find a safe haven in Italy. Curiosity, however, had clearly gotten the better of him, for he turned up in Geneva, where Lyons Calvinists spotted him in attendance at Calvin's worship service. He was immediately arrested. During the subsequent trial, Servetus received the opportunity to comment at length on such delicate theses as the equation of Trinitarians with atheists. Was this what he had come to Geneva seeking, a scholarly confrontation with the famous Calvin, even at the risk of death? He was effective enough in debate; after one exchange Calvin, unnerved, reportedly exclaimed: "[May] little chickens . . . dig out his eyes a hundred thousand times."[49]

Convicted and facing execution, Servetus drew up his own charges against Calvin, whom he described as an evil sorcerer, himself deserving execution. Among Servetus's charges was the question: "Whether Calvin did not well know that it is not the office of a minister of the gospel to make a capital accusation and pursue a man at law to his death?"[50] Although it hardly brightens his role in the affair, Calvin did endeavor to have Servetus beheaded rather than burned at the stake, by sixteenth-century standards a more dignified and humanitarian punishment. The effort was not, however, successful, and on October 27, 1553, Servetus, accompanied to the stake by Farel, who urged him to recant at every step, was burned to death for "blasphemies against the Holy Trinity, the Son of God, the baptism of infants, and the foundations of the Christian religion."[51]

In the controversy that followed the execution, Castellio memorably summarized what to many contemporaries became the simple truth of the episode. "To kill a man," he wrote, "is not to defend a doctrine, but simply to kill a man."[52] Although that assessment has also proved to be history's view of the matter, another century of religious warfare would be required before this principle became firmly established in law.

The influx into Geneva of large numbers of religious refugees from France, England, and Scotland after 1553 combined with the political defeat of Calvin's internal political opponents to increase greatly his influence

---

49. Ibid., p. 195.
50. Ibid., p. 200. The charges against Servetus and his reply are in *Corpus Reformatorum,* 36: 727–35.
51. Bainton, *Hunted Heretic,* p. 208.
52. *Contra libellum Calvini,* no. 77, p. E 2 a.

within the city. The approximately five thousand refugees made Geneva a truly international city and one of Europe's most carefully watched. In 1559, Calvin became a citizen, a step previously resisted by both sides in a symbolic gesture of the mutual independence of ecclesiastical and secular power, despite the fact that other Genevan clergy held citizenship. In the same year was founded the Genevan Academy, perhaps Calvin's most constructive and lasting work. This new school system consisted of a primary school of seven grades, which served the youth of Geneva, and the academy proper, which provided theological training for an international body of preachers. There were chairs in theology, Hebrew, Greek, and philosophy, and Calvin handpicked the teachers, chief among whom was the Greek professor Theodore Beza, who came from Lausanne with other outstanding French scholars from the recently dissolved Bernese Academy there. Beza served as the academy's rector and succeeded Calvin as head of the Genevan church. In 1562 the academy enrolled 162 students, only four of whom were native Genevans.[53] Almost overnight it became the intellectual training ground for Protestant leadership during the period of religious wars that engulfed western Europe in the second half of the sixteenth century.

Were Calvinists Really Protestants?

ALTHOUGH John Calvin was the least original of the major reformers, he gave the Reformation its most eloquent theological statement in the *Institutes of the Christian Religion* and its most disciplined institutional form in the Genevan church. If modern scholars lament his dogmatism and personal vindictiveness, they still consider the movement he inspired more socially and politically progressive than Luther's. Many find Calvinism congenial to new developments in both early modern economics and politics. R. H. Tawney, for example, described Calvinism and its offshoots as "standing on the side of the [economic] activities which were to be most characteristic of the future."[54] Other modern scholars look to Calvin's political thought for the germs of modern theories of resistance to tyrants, especially his recognition of the right of lower magistrates, so-called magistrates of the people (*populares magistratus*), to resist unjust higher authority.[55]

53. Monter, *Calvin's Geneva*, p. 113.
54. R. W. Tawney, *Religion and the Rise of Capitalism*, (Gloucester, Mass., 1962) pp. 108–09.
55. The sixteenth-century origins of this doctrine were actually Lutheran rather than Calvinist. See above, p. 271, and below, pp. 419–20.

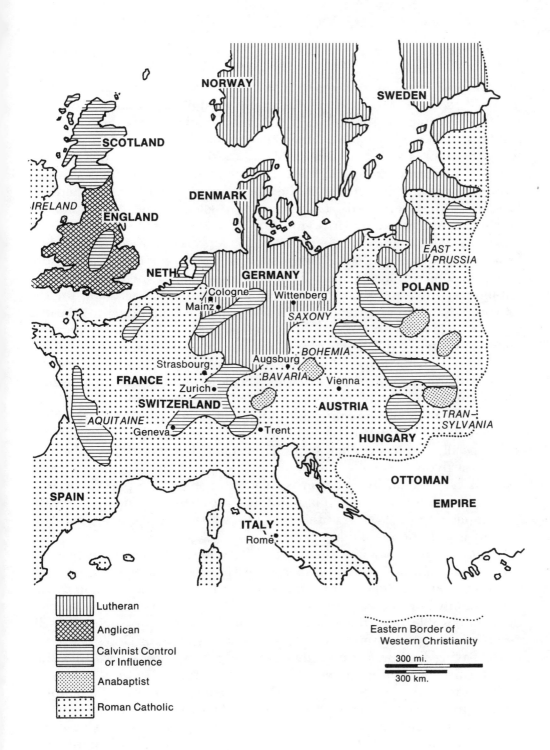

NORWAY

SWEDEN

SCOTLAND

IRELAND

DENMARK

ENGLAND

NETH.

GERMANY

EAST
PRUSSIA

POLAND

Cologne

Wittenberg

Mainz

SAXONY

Strasbourg

Augsburg

BOHEMIA

FRANCE

BAVARIA

Vienna

Zurich

SWITZERLAND

AUSTRIA

TRAN-
SYLVANIA

AQUITAINE

Geneva

Trent

HUNGARY

OTTOMAN

SPAIN

EMPIRE

ITALY

Rome

	Lutheran
	Anglican
	Calvinist Control or Influence
	Anabaptist
	Roman Catholic

Eastern Border of
Western Christianity

300 mi.

300 km.

Map 3. The Division of Christendom by the Reformation (Mid-sixteenth Century)

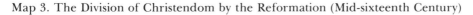

Calvin and his followers did adjust to the new economic and political forces of the sixteenth century, albeit only grudgingly, because they were powerless to impede them. When Calvin recognized Genevan monetary practices, including 5 percent interest on loans, and later Calvinists conceded the right of active political resistance to Christians, it was in large part because historical circumstances left them no alternative. In time Calvinists learned to use the new forces of the age to their own advantage: indeed, socialist Tawney perceived a tragic Christian sellout to the low morality of capitalism among seventeenth-century English Puritans.[56]

A remarkable feature of the later Middle Ages is that theology and religion also had lives of their own independent of larger historical circumstances; people could act apart from and even against their best material self-interest for the sake of theological abstractions. In searching for the sources of Calvinist activism in society and politics it is necessary to take into account such religious motivation as well as the patent political and economic self-interest of enterprising Calvinist nobles and burghers. Behind the ethic of Calvinism lay not only an accommodation to new economic and political forces, but also a reactionary theological adjustment of original Protestant teaching to more traditional religious expectations. This change in the Protestant conception of the Christian life, for which Calvin's theology may be held primarily responsible, did not necessarily make Calvinists more socially responsive than other Protestants, but it did give social and political activism a theological importance within Calvinism that it never attained in Lutheranism. It began as an attempt on Calvin's part to correct a serious, if unintended, inadequacy in Lutheran theology, and it ended as a re-Catholicizing of Protestant theology at its most sensitive point, the doctrine of justification by faith.

For medieval theologians the present life remained an anxious pilgrimage; man lived in unresolved suspense, fearing damnation and hoping for salvation, ever in need of confession and indulgence, discipline and consolation, saintly intercession and the self-help of good works. Nothing seemed more impossible than this-worldly certitude of salvation; such was self-deception and presumption at best, seditious rejection of God's church at worst. Saving faith was constantly developing faith, *fides charitate formata,* faith formed by continuous works of love and charity.

The most distinctive feature of Luther's theology was its bold attempt to resolve the pilgrim status of the medieval Christian. Therein lay its revolutionary character: justification by faith offered individuals personal certitude of salvation, already in this life, provided only that they believe it. To

---

56. Tawney, *Religion and the Rise of Capitalism,* pp. 94, 105.

be saved meant to trust in the righteousness of Christ above and apart from all the actual and conceivable good works a person could do. Nothing in the labor done in one's vocation, or in the good deeds performed for one's neighbors, or in the special religious works done for the church saved anybody; faith only sufficed, but completely.

Liberating at first, even to the point of condoning religious indifference and antinomianism in the minds of some,[57] the doctrine of justification by faith created a totally unexpected religious problem for earnest believers. In the normal course of their secular lives, people measured their worth in terms of efforts expended and deeds done; in the eyes of others, they were what they did. Could people so accustomed to weighing their secular lives by their works realistically be expected to remove from consideration their every achievement when they evaluated their lives religiously? Was the demand to count all human effort as naught when one stood before God an impossible religious ideal, so contrary to people's natural way of thinking and daily experience that it frustrated rather than consoled them? Was salvation by faith alone itself, in other words, ultimately more burdensome to the conscience than the religious introspection and good works it was designed to replace? From the point of view of secular experience, making salvation dependent in part on good works proved less presumptuous of human ability than the complete disassociation of salvation from such works proposed by Luther.

Luther grappled directly with this problem in a sermon preached in 1532, in which he made clear his own unsuccessful efforts to live before God by faith alone. Here is the confession of the new Lutheran "pilgrim":

> Even when [salvation by faith] is taught in the best possible way it is difficult enough to learn it well, especially for us, who have been so habituated and trained in the doctrine of works and pointed only to the law and ourselves. And besides this [there is] our own nature, which is itself inclined in this direction. The doctrine of works is also rooted in and strengthened by habit ... so that we cannot get away from it or think anything except that, if I have lived a holy life and done many great works, God will be gracious to me. Thus, we must contend both with our nature and with strong habit. And it is exceedingly difficult to get into another habit of thinking in which we clearly separate faith and

57. See Luther's response to the visitations of 1528 in his *Sermons on the Catechism* (Nov.–Dec. 1528), *LW*, 51: 135–37 (*WA* 30/1, pp. 57–121), and *Large Catechism* (1529), trans J. L. Lenker (Minneapolis, 1935), pp. 35–39, 49, 56 (*WA* 20/1, pp. 129–333). The Silesian Spiritualist Caspar Schwenckfeld criticized justification by faith as an excuse for immorality (*Corpus Schwenckfeldiorum*, 12: 485–86.)

[works of] love, for . . . even though we are now in faith . . . the heart is always ready to boast of itself before God and say: "After all, I have preached so long and lived so well and done so much, surely he will take this into account." We even want to haggle with God to make him regard our life. . . . But it cannot be done. With men you may boast: I have done the best I could toward everyone, and if anything is lacking I will still try to make recompense. But when you come before God, leave all that boasting at home and remember to appeal from justice to grace. [But] let anybody try this and he will see and experience how exceedingly hard and bitter a thing it is for a man, who all his life has been mired in his work righteousness, to pull himself out of it and with all his heart rise up through faith in the one Mediator. I myself have now been preaching and cultivating it through reading and writing for almost twenty years and still I feel the old clinging dirt of wanting to deal so with God that I may contribute something, so that he will have to give me his grace in exchange for my holiness. Still I cannot get it into my head that I should surrender myself completely to sheer grace; yet [I know that] this is what I should and must do.[58]

For the devout Protestant the threat posed by justification by faith was not religious indifference and antinomianism, but the radical circumscription of his religious life. Although Luther's theology demanded constant good works from the Christian, it also severed every conceivable connection between these works and his salvation. Luther observed that people found it exceedingly unnatural to do good works simply out of thanksgiving to God and love of their neighbor, with no expectation of divine reward.

Because of the narrow limits within which Protestant theology is usually criticized, scholars have not realized how pervasive this problem was. Luther's teaching has traditionally been accused of favoring "justification" over "sanctification." According to this criticism, Luther remained preoccupied with the individual's guilty conscience and his gaining acceptance in the eyes of God (justification); unlike Zwingli, Bucer, and Calvin, he found it difficult to recognize a positive role for God's law and self-discipline within the Christian's life (sanctification).[59] This, however, is an over-

---

58. *Sermon on the Sum of the Christian Life, LW,* 51: 284 (*WA* 36, pp. 352–75).

59. See William A. Clebsch, *England's Earliest Protestants 1520–1535* (New Haven, 1964); Wilhelm Pauck, "Luther and Butzer," in *The Heritage of the Reformation* (Glencoe, Ill., 1961), pp. 73–83; Arthur Rich, "Zwingli als sozial-politischer Denker," *Zwingliana* 13 (1969): 67–89; Wendel, *Calvin,* pp. 196–208, esp. 256–57. Gerald Strauss has recently argued that Lutherans confused ordinary people by teaching, on the one hand, that grace sufficed for salvation and all human effort was of no avail, yet insisting, on the other hand, that they could mend

simplification. *All* Protestant theologians shared the common problem of giving good works a constructive role within the believer's life without at the same time succumbing to the Pelagian covenant theology of the Middle Ages, in opposition to which Protestant theology had been born.[60] On this issue Luther may be said to have been the more cautious; while he too recognized the commandments as a guide to Christian behavior and stressed them as emphatically as any other Protestant leader,[61] he also resisted more firmly than any other the temptation to find either evidence of salvation where good works were present or indications of damnation where they were not. With remarkable consistency he spoke only of faith and unbelief in direct proximity with salvation and damnation.

Other reformers went farther down the road to compromise. Martin Bucer and his Catholic counterpart in the ecumenical Regensburg Colloquy (1541), Johannes Gropper, attempted to merge justification by faith with the ethical motivation of traditional religious practice. Their solution was a doctrine of "double justification" (*justificatio duplex*). According to Gropper's original formulation, salvation involved both a "justification of the impious," or "regeneration," which faith accomplished apart from any preceding works or merits as it transformed the recipient into a faithful son of God, and a "justification of works," or "santification," which built on and consummated this freely given faith and love.[62] Both justifications presupposed the presence of God's grace, the first exclusively, the second as the

---

their ways, if they chose to do so. (*Luther's House of Learning: Indoctrination of the Young in the German Reformation* [Baltimore, 1978], pp. 216, 220–21). I believe the relationship between grace and works was far more manageable than Strauss supposes. The more difficult conflict was that between one's self-evaluation in ordinary human experience, where works defined one's person, and one's self-evaluation in the new theology, where reward had no connection with either personal or earned merit.

60. See above, pp. 231–39.

61. The discussion of the Law in the *Large Catechism* concludes with the statement:

Let all the wise and all the saints stand forth and show us if they can produce any work like these commandments, upon the fulfilment of which God so sternly insists and which he enjoins under threat of his greatest wrath and punishment, though adding glorious promises of an outpouring of all manner of good things, all blessings, if we obey him. They are, therefore, to be taught above all other things, and to be prized and valued as the richest treasure God has given us (*Luther's Large Catechism*, pp. 110–11).

Although he believed no person capable of doing so perfectly, Luther expected all Christians to try and fulfill the commandments both before and after "justification."

62. "Der Originalentwurf zum Regensburger Buch," in *Briefwechsel Langraf Philipps des Grossmuthigen*, ed. Max Lenz (Leipzig, 1891), 3: 42. See also Robert Stupperich, "Der Ursprung des Regensburger Buches und seine Rechtfertigungslehre," *ARG* 36 (1939): 88–116, which cites extensively from Gropper's *Enchiridion* (1538), and Walter Lipgens, *Kardinal Johannes Gropper (1503–1559) und die Anfänge der katholischen Reform in Deutschland* (Münster/Westphal, 1951).

foundation of the believer's own ethical endeavor. The final formulation in the *Book of Regensburg* described "justifying faith" as

> living faith . . . which apprehends God's mercy in Christ, believes that the righteousness of Christ is imputed to it gratis, and simultaneously receives the promise and love of the Holy Spirit. Hence, justifying faith is faith which is effective in [works of] love. We are justified by this faith, however, that is, accepted and reconciled to God, only insofar as it grasps the mercy and righteousness which God imputes to us because of Christ and his merit, not because of the dignity and perfection of the righteousness communicated to us.[63]

Despite the prominence given imputed righteousness in the Regensburg formula, Luther and other Protestant leaders saw little difference between this definition and the majority medieval point of view; and despite the direct integration of charity into justifying faith, papal spokesmen considered the doctrine basically Lutheran.

Regensburg's doctrine of double justification neither reunited Christendom nor, in smaller compass, provided a solution to the dilemma posed by justification by faith. Was it really possible for good works to have a prominent place within religious life and yet not earn salvation? Could Lutheran certitude of faith and the ethical motivation of traditional Catholic piety truly coexist? Where Luther and the ecumenists of Regensburg seem to have failed, John Calvin may have succeeded. Calvin described good works variously as "testimonies of God dwelling and ruling in us . . . fruits of the saints' regeneration . . . proofs of the indwelling of the Holy Spirit and signs of the [saints'] calling by which they realize their election."[64]

> When we rule out reliance on works we mean only this: that the Christian mind may not be turned back to the merit of works as to a help toward salvation, but should rely wholly on the free promise of righteousness. We do not, however, forbid the Christian from undergirding and strengthening this faith by signs of the divine benevolence toward him.[65]

What are these signs of divine benevolence? The believer's own good works. The Calvinist saint is saved by faith undergirded and strengthened by works that attest divine presence and grace. He may not say that he is saved by these works, yet regular good works are clear signs of present

---

63. "Liber Ratisbonesis," in *Corpus reformatorum*, 4: 199–200. See below, p. 405.
64. *Institutes of the Christian Religion*, ed. John T. McNeill, trans. Ford L. Battles (Philadelphia, 1960), 3, ch. 14, sects. 18–20, pp. 785–86.
65. Ibid., 2, ch. 14, sect. 18, p. 785.

divine favor and assure him that he is on the path to glory. Religious confidence is thus "formed" by the fruits of self-discipline as well as by the promises of God; in actual practice, good works are presumptive evidence that one is among the elect.

Luther too expected true believers to be busy with good works, but their presence did not constitute an indirect commentary on one's salvation nor their absence the suggestion of anyone's eternal damnation. For Luther, works might attest a strong faith, but they resolved no man's anxiety over his final destiny; only faith in God's promise did that. Justification by faith was a solution designed specifically for those unable to derive religious peace of mind from good works.[66] Therein lay both its strength and its weakness *and* the distinctiveness of original Protestant teaching.

For Calvin, good works did not have the direct bearing on salvation that medieval theology taught; they attested divine favor and gave presumptive evidence of election, but they did not put one in a position to expect salvation as condign merit. On the other hand, Calvin's teaching, like his conduct of the Genevan church, once again made good works and moral behavior the center of religious life and reintroduced religious anxiety over them. In Calvinism the presence or absence of good works came to be taken as a commentary on one's eternal destiny.

Max Weber argued that worry over predestination was the root of Calvinist activism; methodical discipline and success in one's vocation alleviated the anxiety that resulted from not knowing whether one was among the elect or the reprobate.[67] Calvinism was even more complex. Predestination had another side, one perhaps even more basic to Calvinist activism. If worry over election made the Calvinist saint doubt his individual destiny, the doctrine of predestination also made him supremely confident about the ultimate course of history as a whole. That had been the original purpose of Calvin's teaching on predestination: to assure the disconsolate faith-

---

66. The road from God to faith to works was not a two-way street. "The work never makes the workman like itself, but the workman makes the work like himself . . . . As the man is, whether believer or unbeliever, so also is his work—good if it was done in faith, wicked if it was done in unbelief. But the converse is not true, that the work makes the man either a believer or unbeliever. As works do not make a man a believer, so also they do not make him righteous. But as faith makes a man a believer and righteous, so faith does good works" (Luther, *Freedom of a Christian,* in *Three Treatises: Martin Luther* [Philadelphia, 1960], pp. 297–98).

67. Max Weber, *The Protestant Ethic and the Spirit of Capitalism,* trans. Talcott Parsons (New York, 1958), esp. pp. 104–17. John Bossy points out that the ethical-religious activism Weber associates so exclusively with Calvinism was just as prominent among Jesuits and the Tridentine church. See his comments in H. O. Evennett, *The Spirit of the Counter-Reformation* (Cambridge, 1968), pp. 171–32. Perhaps this was in part because the theologies of both, in their different ways, made good works a commentary on one's salvation. See below.

ful that all life remained in God's sure hand, despite appearances to the contrary.[68] Such conviction also inspired social and political activism. Anxiety over personal fate was matched by confidence in the righteousness and final success of God's cause, in the service of which the Calvinist saint firmly stood, regardless of his individual destiny. Confident, yet insecure, at one with history's larger course, yet possibly destined not to enjoy the fruits of victory personally—such was the state of the new Calvinist pilgrim.[69]

68. Calvin describes the doctrine of predestination as "our only ground for firmness and confidence" (*Institutes*, 3, ch. 21, sec. 1, p. 922), as a doctrine that "rightly understood, brings no shaking of faith but rather its best confirmation" (ibid., 3, ch. 14, sect. 9, pp. 975–76). He lists among the benefits of the doctrine of divine providence—which prior to the 1559 edition of the *Institutes* was always treated together with predestination— "incredible freedom from worry about the future" (ibid., 1, ch. 17, sect. 7, p. 219).

69. Beza documents Calvin's abiding fear, even in his last days when he was very sick and his death imminent, of being found idle. "When admonished and entreated by us to forbear, at least in his sickness, from the labour of dictating, or at least of writing, 'What, then,' he said, 'would you have my Lord find me idle when he cometh?'" (*Life of Calvin*, p. 79; see also p. 71).

CHAPTER 12

Marriage and the
Ministry in the
Protestant Churches

T HE Lord God has wanted three things made right again before the Last Day," Luther declared at table in 1532: "the ministry of the Word, government, and marriage."[1] No institutional change brought about by the Reformation was more visible, responsive to late medieval pleas for reform, and conducive to new social attitudes than the marriage of Protestant clergy. Nor was there another point in the Protestant program where theology and practice corresponded more successfully. The reformers argued theologically and attempted to demonstrate by their own lives the superiority of a married over a celibate clergy. In doing so they extolled as had few before them the virtues of marriage and family life.

All the Wittenberg reformers had married by 1525. As in other areas of Protestant practice, Luther was among the last to break openly with tradition, even though he approved of clerical marriage long before he wed Katherine von Bora on June 13, 1525. It is significant that in terms of its founding (1502) and the ages of its professors, Wittenberg was the second youngest German university. In 1521, Luther, at thirty-eight, was among the older faculty. His co-workers, men in their twenties and early thirties, were immediately touched by the issue of celibacy.[2] Although Protestants

---

1. *Luthers Werke in Auswahl, Tischreden*, ed. Otto Clemen (Berlin, 1950): 8, no. 433, p. 53.

2. August Franzen, *Zölibat und Priesterehe in der Auseinandersetzung der Reformationszeit und der katholischen Reform des 16. Jahrhunderts* (Münster, 1969), p. 30. On the Reformation as a young man's movement, a generational conflict between younger and older humanists, see Bernd Moeller, "Die deutschen Humanisten und die Anfänge der Reformation," *ZKG* 70 (1959): 46-61; and Lewis W. Spitz, "The Third Generation of German Renaissance Humanists," in *Aspects of the Renaissance*, ed. Archibald R. Lewis (Austin, 1967), pp. 105-21.

Wie gar gfarlich sey. So
Ain Priester kain Ee weyb har. Wye Vn
christlich. vnd schedlich aim gmainen
Nutz Die menschen seynd. Welche
hindern die Pfaffen Am Eelichen stand. Durch
Johan Eberlin Von Güntzburg. Anno.

1522.

The title page of Johann Eberlin von Günzburg's pamphlet in defense of clerical marriage:
How Extremely Dangerous It Is for a Priest to be Without a Wife. How Unchristian and Destructive of Public Order are Those Men Who Prevent Priests From Entering the Estate of Marriage (1522). While flute and drum are played, clergy both high and low, regular and secular, are joined in holy matrimony.

continued to recognize and respect those who could live truly celibate lives, they believed their numbers exceedingly low; Luther reckoned no more than one in a thousand religious lived such a life. The reformers concluded that marriage and family life, not celibacy and the monastery, were the divinely intended spheres of Christian perfection. Protestants transferred the accolades previously reserved for the solitary life to the home. Convinced that they had not only the authority of their own experience under vows but also that of Holy Scripture and much tradition on their side, the reformers boldly attacked the traditional monastic ideal. Luther spoke for generations of Protestant apologists when he concluded, with some exaggeration:

> On our side we have Scripture, the church fathers, ancient church laws, and even papal precedent. We will stick to that. On their side [the defenders of celibacy] have the contrary statements of a few church

fathers, recent church canons, and their own mischief, without any support from Scripture and the Word of God. We will let them have that.[3]

In the Reformation treatises of 1520, Luther urged marriage upon that "wretched multitude of priests who now sit in shame and heaviness of conscience" and declared baptism the sole and all-sufficient Christian vow.[4] But it was not Luther who wrote the first incisive Protestant assault on celibacy. That honor belonged to Andreas Karlstadt, whose *De Coelibatu, monachatu et viduitate* appeared in Wittenberg in June 1521. A highly partisan work, it was immediately embraced by Luther's own Augustinian order in Wittenberg and came to shape basic Protestant attitudes on the subject.

To Karlstadt's mind, papal and episcopal desire to increase the wealth of the church and control the clergy lay at the root of celibacy. An alleged seedbed of sexual perversion and crime, the celibate life was seen to encourage homosexuality and that greatest of sexual transgressions, masturbation, the giving of one's seed to Moloch.[5] To Karlstadt, such an ideal could only encourage fornication and guilt, which the church in turn absolved for an appropriate fee.[6]

Karlstadt drew seven conclusions in opposition to the traditional practice. First, the period of probation for the religious should cover the full duration of sexual desire and titillation; only at age sixty might one reasonably be expected to fulfil celibate vows. Until then nuns might better be "living temples" by motherhood. "It is better to make a home and teach the Word of God to one's family than to mutter frigid prayers alone in a sanctuary";

---

3. Preface to Steffan Klingebeyl, *Von Priester Ehe* (Wittenberg, 1528), p. B 1 a (= *WA* 26, p. 533, 1. 26–31).

4. *An Open Letter to the Christian Nobility of the German Nation* in *Three Treatises: Martin Luther* (Philadelphia, 1960), pp. 67–68 (= WA 6, pp. 440–43); *The Babylonian Captivity of the Church*, in ibid., pp. 198–99.(= WA 6, pp. 538). Already in Luther's *Dictata super Psalterium* (1513–1516) and *Lectures on Romans* (1515–1516), faith, not chastity, is described as the antidote to concupiscence, and the ideal of Christian community, embracing laity and clerics, is critically juxtaposed to the "separatism" of the cloistered (Bernhard Lohse, *Mönchtum und Reformation: Luthers Auseinandersetzung mit dem Mönchsideal des Mittelalters* [Göttingen, 1963], esp. pp. 236–41, 269). According to Lohse, the key to the final break with celibate vows was the conviction that baptismal vows were absolutely final for all Christians (ibid., pp. 278, 333, 351–52).

5. P. A 4 b. Karlstadt's views are discussed by Hermann Barge in *Andreas Bodenstein von Karlstadt* (Leipzig, 1905), p. 265. On why masturbation was considered so bad, see above, p. 218.

6. *De Coelibatu, monachatu et viduitate*, p. A 3 a. A schedule of fines and penalties was long established for de facto clerical marriage and its attendant problems. In the diocese of Constance the bishop's fiscal collected around four gulden per year per child in fines for the approximately 1,500 children of priests in the diocese. See Oskar Vasella, *Reform und Reformation in der Schweiz* (Münster, 1965), pp. 28–34; Ozment, *The Reformation in the Cities* (New Haven, 1975), pp. 57–58.

domestic life and labor in the secular world were "honestius."[7] Second, Karlstadt believed that only those who were or had been married should be qualified to take holy orders, a conclusion he extracted from 1 Timothy 3:2.[8] Third, if any in religious orders burned with desire, they could and should be permitted to marry.[9] Fourth, since vows were valid only when the one vowed to reciprocated (Num. 30:12), the vows of celibacy remained invalid and unfulfilled until it was known whether God approved; signs of divine approval were most likely to appear, Karlstadt argued, after age sixty.[10] Fifth, Karlstadt argued that the incontinence of those under vows was a far greater evil than the lust of a husband for his wife, and, judged by their fruits, marriage a far greater good than celibacy. "Marriage produces children, rears them in the faith, makes adults of them, cultivates the earth, and is vigilant in charity, whereas celibacy very often destroys boys and girls and makes deserts upon the earth."[11] Sixth, it was no sin for clergy to break their vows and marry, because such had been based on a false, unbiblical understanding of human nature.[12] Finally, inasmuch as marriage was seen to be the only effective cure for fornication, Karlstadt wanted all bishops to order priests under their jurisdiction to marry their concubines,[13] a proposal enacted into law when Protestants rewrote the marriage ordinances of their regions.

Luther puzzled over some of Karlstadt's scriptural interpretations, but empathized with the "wretched men, boys, and girls vexed with pollutions

7. *De Coelibatu, monachatu et viduitate*, B 3 b; C 2 a–C 4 a. The age limit of sixty is derived from 1 Timothy 5:9.
8. Ibid., C 4 a.
9. Ibid., D 2 a–b.
10. Ibid., D 3 a.
11. Ibid., D 3 b.
12. Ibid., D 4 a. That the vow of chastity contradicted Scripture and human nature was the most common argument against it by early Protestant apologists. See the anonymous *Ain schöne / gaistliche / und der hailigen schrifft gegründte underweysung von wegen der gelübten* (1523); *Ain christenliches lustige gesprech / das besser gotfelliger und des menschen selhaylsamer seye / auss den Klöstern zukommen und Eelich zuwerden / dann darinnen zubleiben und zuverharren / Wöllichs gesprech / nit menschen thandt oder der selbigen yrrigen gesatzen / sondern allain inn der hayligen, göttlichen, Biblischen, und Ewangelischen geschrifft gegründt / gemacht und darauss gezogen ist* (1524); Thomas Stör, *Der Ehelich standt von Got mit gebenedeyung auffgesetzt / soll umb schwärhait wegen der seltzamen gaben der Junckfrawschaft yederman frey sein / und niemant verboten werden* (1524); Bartholomäus Bernhardus, *Das die Priester Eeweiber nemen mügen und sollen. Beschützred / des würdigen herren Bartholomei Bernhardi / Probsts zu Camberg / so von Bischoff von Meydburg gefordertt / antwurt zugeben / das er in priesterlichem standt / ain junckfraw zu der Ee genomen hat.* (1522); and Johann Eberlin von Günzburg, *Wie gar gfarlich sey So ain Priester kain weib hat. Wie unchristlich und schedlich am gmainen nutz Die menschen seynd Welche hindern die pfaffen am Eelichen stand* (1522). There are copies of all these works in the Lutheran tracts (Tractt. Luth.) in Oxford's Bodleian library.
13. *De Coelibatu, monachatu et viduitate*, D 4 b.

Martin Luther and Katharina von Bora. Hans Brosamer.

and burnings."[14] He could not, however, at this time go so far as Karlstadt and equate the freely elected vows of monks and nuns with those imposed on secular priests.[15] Although distrustful of his hesitation ("I don't know what phantom of pomp and human opinion is plaguing me here") and even convinced that chastity should not be vowed by anyone,[16] he still assured Spalatin in August 1521: "Good Lord! Will our people at Wittenberg give wives even to monks? They will not push a wife on me!"[17]

Luther acknowledged the right of regular clergy to marry in his treatises *On Monastic Vows* (late 1521) and *On the Married Life* (1522). The former set forth the magisterial Protestant case against clerical celibacy. It argued that vows lacked scriptural authority and opposed faith, evangelical freedom, the commandment to love one's neighbor, and common sense and reason. In the Bible, Luther maintained, Jesus discouraged rather than counseled celibacy, having dealt with it approvingly only in a passing statement on

14. Letter to Melanchthon (1 August 1521), in *LW*, 48: 279 (= *WABr* 2, p. 371).
15. Ibid., p. 277 (= *WABr* 2, p. 370)
16. Letter to Melanchthon (3 August 1521), in ibid., pp. 285, 287 (= *WABr* 2, pp. 374–75).
17. Letter to Spalatin (6 August 1521), in ibid., p. 290 (= *WABr* 2, p. 377).

eunuchs, and St. Paul discussed it only as an "open matter," not as a direct invitation. "A *vow* of chastity," Luther concluded, "is diametrically opposed to the Gospel."[18]

Celibate vows were also seen to oppose faith because they implied that the "vow" made to God by all Christians in baptism was penultimate. This assumption of the religious superiority of celibate vows led Luther finally to release monks and nuns also from their freely chosen vows. "They teach justification and salvation by works and depart from faith," he complained. "They think that their obedience, poverty, and chastity are certain roads to salvation and their ways more perfect than those of the rest of the faithful."[19]

Luther considered vows to be in opposition to Christian liberty because they infringed upon the "pact of freedom" God made with Christians in baptism. According to this pact, the individual was bound only to what ensured freedom on conscience.[20] Vows transgressed the commandment to love one's neighbor because they encouraged a "narrow and artificial love . . . that prevents service to any but fellow monks"[21] and contradicted common sense and reason because they ignored human nature. Echoing Karlstadt, Luther suggested that celibate vows be confined to sixty years and older for women and seventy or eighty for men.[22] Comparing the breaking of the vow of chastity when one "burned" to stealing when one faced starvation, Luther appealed to the time-honored legal principle of equity; in such emergency situations the spirit overrode the letter of the law.[23]

Luther's writings had a tremendous impact. From the cloister key reformers entered the work of the Reformation and the estate of marriage. From the Augustinians came Wenceslaus Linck (1483–1547), Johann Lang (ca. 1487–1548), and Gabriel Zwilling (ca. 1487–1558); from the Franciscans, Eberlin of Günzburg (ca. 1465–1530), Conrad Pellican (1478–1556), Francis Lambert of Avignon (1486–1530), and Friedrich Myconius (1490–

18. *LW*, 44: 262 (= *WA* 8, p. 584).
19. Ibid., p. 285 (= *WA* 8, p. 589). The flagellants of the fourteenth century also described their self-punishment as a "second baptism," superior to sacramental baptism. See Gordon Leff, *Heresy in the Later Middle Ages* (Manchester, 1967), 2: 489.
20. *LW*, 44: 315 (= *WA* 8, p. 616).
21. Ibid., p. 335 (= *WA* 8, p. 628). The *Confessio Tetrapolitana* of south German and Swiss cities censured monastic vows for suspending man's first social duty: the love and service of his neighbor (Bernd Moeller, *Reichsstadt und Reformation* [Gütersloh, 1962], p. 46, n. 63). Moeller, I believe, makes too much of the contrast between Luther's "theologically" oriented attack on vows and Bucer's "socially" directed attack. The theological and practical sides of the issue were appreciated fully by both reformers.
22. *LW*, 44: 360, 387, 398 (= *WA* 8, pp. 644, 661, 667).
23. Ibid., p. 391 (= *WA* 8, p. 663).

1546); from the Dominicans, Martin Bucer; and from the Benedictines, Ambrosius Blarer (1492–1564). Johann Bugenhagen (1485–1558), Justus Jonas (1493–1555), Georg Spalatin (1484–1545), Nicholas of Amsdorf (1483–1565), Urbanus Rhegius (1489–1541), and Johann Oecolampadius were prominent Protestant clergy who stepped forth from the ranks of the secular clergy.[24]

While Karlstadt and Luther stressed biblical and theological arguments against the vow of celibacy, they also wrote with real-life situations in mind. In their own experience, Protestant clergy had found the celibate life an intolerable personal and vocational burden, a tyrannical ideal, an "impure purity" (*non casta castitas*), as Jonas put it.[25] The personal dimension of the problem was nowhere made clearer than in the petition of July 1522 by eleven prominent Swiss clergy: *Petition of Certain Preachers of Switzerland to the Most Reverend Lord Hugo, Bishop of Constance, That He Will Not Suffer Himself to be Persuaded to Make Any Proclamation to the Injury of the Gospel, Nor Endure Longer the Scandal of Harlotry, but Allow the Priests to Marry Wives or at Least Would Wink at Their Marriages.* The clergy, led by Zwingli, who was at the time cohabiting with a widow, Anna Reinhart, depicted the present situation, with numerous priests maintaining unlawful wives, as a great detriment to the ministry. "How," they asked, "will the simple-minded common man believe in him who even while he preaches the Gospel to them is thought by them to be licentious and a shameless dog?"[26] In addition, these same clergy claimed that efforts to maintain chastity had nearly driven them out of their minds:

> While we willingly yield this glory to those who live chastely, we are grieved that it has been denied unto us.... We have been so on fire from passion—with shame let it be said—that we have done many things unseemly, yet whether this should not be laid upon those to some extent who have forbidden marriage we refrain from saying now,

24. Franzen, *Zölibat und Priesterehe*, p. 29.

25. *Adversus Iohannem Fabrum Constantienem Vicarium, scortationis patronum, pro coniugio sacerdotali, Iusti Ionae defensio* (Wittenberg, 1523), p. B 4 a.

26. *The Latin Works and Correspondence of Huldreich Zwingli, 1510–22*, ed. Samuel M. Jackson (New York, 1912), 1: 155 (= *Sämtliche Werke*, 1: 197–209). A German version of the petition circulated widely throughout the Confederacy. On these complaints, see also Gerald Strauss, *Manifestations of Discontent in Germany on the Eve of the Reformation* (Bloomington, Ind., 1971), p. 61. An anonymous pamphlet from this period complained especially about the contradiction, clear to all laity, of letting priests whom the church considered to be living in sin (adultery, whoring, or sodomy) freely celebrate the sacraments. See *Ein Christliche frage Simonis Reuters vonn Schlaytz / an alle Bischoffe anndere geystliche / auch zum teyl weltliche regenten / warumb sy doch an Priestern und an andern geistlich geferbten leuten / den eelichen standt nicht mügenn leyden* (1523), p. A 2 a.

thinking it enough that the fire of passion alone (and that so frequent and violent as to threaten the mind) is pronounced sufficient reason for marriage.[27]

The Zurich petition concluded with a warning to the bishop that clerical marriage was an idea whose time had come. "There is a report that most of the ecclesiastics have already chosen wives, not only among our Swiss, but among all peoples everywhere, and to put this down will certainly be not only beyond your strength but beyond that of one far more mighty, if you will pardon our saying so."[28]

To a significant extent the end of clerical celibacy in Zurich climaxed rather than introduced clerical marriage; a centuries-old practice of de facto clerical marriage was made legal and respectable. The same might be said of legislation passed in England during the reign of Edward VI; according to one historian, "contemporaries did not look upon it so much in the light of a reform as of a kind of legitimizing of women hitherto in an ambiguous position."[29] Zwingli married publicly in April 1524, shortly before the arrival of a child. The new Zurich marriage ordinance promulgated in May 1525 and enforced on the surrounding villages in June 1526 gave clergy living in concubinage two weeks either to sever the relationship or be publicly married. The marriage court established by the ordinance consisted of six judges—two clerics and four laymen from the city councils—who met twice a week. Compared to pre-Reformation practice, the new Protestant marriage court brought considerable clarity to matrimonial status and conflicts. For example, it expanded and defined grounds for divorce, recognizing, in addition to adultery and impotence, extreme incompatibility, desertion, physical and mental illness, and fraud. With the improvement in domestic life that such clarification brought came also, however, a new degree of governmental intervention.[30]

Clerical marriage was an issue on which Protestants persisted. John Calvin echoed the moral urgency of the Zurich petition in a special reform tract prepared for Charles V in anticipation of the 1544 Diet of Speyer.[31] In

27. *The Latin Works . . . of Huldreich Zwingli,* 1: 160.
28. Ibid., 1: 164.
29. James Gairdner, *Lollardy and the Reformation in England* (1908-13), 3: 57-58, cited by Philip Hughes, *The Reformation in England* (New York, 1963), 2: 115.
30. Oskar Farner, *Zwingli the Reformer: His Life and Work,* trans. D. G. Sear (1968), pp. 88-89; *Huldrych Zwingli: Seine Verkündigung und ihre ersten Früchte, 1520-1525* (Zurich, 1954), pp. 500-501; G. R. Potter, *Zwingli* (London, 1976) pp. 215-16; Walter Köhler, *Züricher Ehegericht und Genfer Konsistorium,* vol. 1 (Leipzig, 1932).
31. In *Calvin: Theological Treatise,* trans. J. K. S. Reid (Philadelphia, 1954), p. 215 (=*Corpus Reformatorum,* 34: 498). Francis Biot traces Calvin's criticism of monasticism in *The Rise of Protestant Monasticism* (Baltimore, 1963), pp. 29-46.

the Anglican community the anonymous *Defence of Priestes Mariages*, written during the Marian persecutions, protested the "pretendying Chastitie" of clerical celibacy, then being forcibly reinstated, as "the verie high waie to unspeakeable whoredomes and filthinesse."[32]

If celibacy was a burden to the ministry, marriage was a boon, according to Protestant apologists. Jeremy Taylor (1613–67) summarized a century of Protestant eulogies to marriage with an eloquent contrast:

> Celibacy, like an insect in the heart of an apple, dwells in solitude: but marriage, like the useful bee, builds a house, gathers sweetness from every flower, labours, forms societies, sends out colonies, feeds the world with delicacies, obeys the sovereign, keeps order, exercises many virtues, promotes the interest of mankind, and is that state of good things to which God hath designed the present constitution of the world.[33]

Apologists repeatedly stressed two practical advantages of marriage: it gave the minister a personal point of contact with his married parishioners, and it stabilized the personal lives of the majority of clerics who were incapable of chastity. Jonas, who had married a Wittenberg girl in February 1522 and wrote in defense of marriage at Luther's request, argued that "no one knows better what men suffer in raising a family and what the holy cross of marriage is than one who daily experiences it in his own home." For the married cleric the home became a "warm-up in love" (*praeexercitamentum charitatis*), which made possible a more skilful exercise of love towards others.[34] Booms the author of the *Defence of Priestes Mariages*:

> When . . . was religion more in honour then when priestes were maried at will without compulsion? though diverse others having the gifte of soole lief [solitary life] continued in their gifte, not despisying others. . . . When kept they their vessels *in honore et sanctificatione* . . . more safely, then when they had the libertis of mariage for the perill of incontinencie? When was hospitalitie and residentie better kept, then when the Pastor had his familie in a place certain to move him homeward? When were their houses kept in better reparations, then when

32. *A Defence of Priestes Mariages, Stablysshed by the Imperial Lawes of the Realme of England, Against a Civilian Naming Himself Thomas Martin, Doctour of the Civile Lawes.* (London, 1567?), p. 2 b.

33. *The Marriage Ring; or, the Mysteriousness and Duties of Marriage* (Birmingham, 1809), p.14.

34. Jonas, *Adversus Iohannem Fabrum*, p. D 2 b.

they were resident? When had the people more relief by them then when they kept houses?[35]

A celibacy too highly praised was seen by William Tyndale to lead to both misogyny and whoring:

Beware that thou get thee not a false fayned chastitie made with the ungodly persuasions of St. Hierome or of Ovid in his filthy booke of the remedy agaynst love; lest, when throughe such imaginations thou hast utterly despised, defied, and abhorred all womankynde, thou come into such case throughe the fierce wrath of God, that thou canst neither lyve chaste nor finde in thy hart to mary.[36]

Protestants viewed the ministry as an ethical service among spiritual equals, not a superior religious state, and considered pastoral authority derived from the immediate community of believers rather than from a sacramentally infused character.[37] Such a point of view made effective contact with the daily life of parishioners very important. In the early years of the Reformation the home was of necessity often the place of worship. Luther spoke for common Protestant experience when in 1523 he wrote to Christians in Bohemia, who had been deprived of an archbishop and ordination since 1421, that the essentials of the Christian faith could be fully maintained in the "homes of laymen."[38]

The second benefit of clerical marriage was more individual and psychological. A truly celibate cleric could concentrate solely on his ministry, and Luther conceded that his was the better way "in a worldly sense," that is, in terms of sheer man-hours on the job.[39] Marriage, however, did for the man who could not "contain" what celibacy did for one who could: it removed the sexual cares and distractions that impeded his work. "It is no slight boon," Luther wrote three years before his own marriage, "that in wedlock fornication and unchastity are checked and eliminated. This in itself . . . should be enough to induce people to marry forthwith."[40] He further observed that marriage made for a "sound body and a good con-

---

35. *Defence of Priestes Mariages,* p. 30.
36. From the *Prologue to Numbers,* cited by C. S. Lewis, *English Literature in the Sixteenth Century Excluding Drama* (Oxford, 1954), p. 191.
37. See Luther's *Concerning the Ministry* (1523), *LW,* 40: 35 (= *WA* 12, p. 190).
38. Ibid., 40: 9–10 (= *WA* 12, p. 171).
39. *The Estate of Marriage, LW,* 45: 47 (= *WA* 10/2, p. 302).
40. Ibid., 45: 43 (= *WA* 10/2, p. 299). Freedom from fornication and masturbation and their attendant guilt are stressed in Jacob Fuch's defense of clerical marriage, *Ain schöner Sendbrieff an Bischof von Wirtzburg Darinn auss hayliger geschrifft Priester Ee beschirmbt und gegrundt wirdt* (1523).

science" and that women with children were "healthier, cleanlier, and happier."[41]

Much Protestant ink was spent against the cruelty of imposing "that which is most foreign to human nature" upon thousands of men and women. "If you are a man," wrote Jonas, "it is no more in your power to live without a woman than it is to change your sex. . . . That inborn desire and innate affection by which men and women desire one another is not in our power to control; it is the way God has created and made us."[42] Joseph Hall (1574–1656), dean of Worcester, reported a hard truth learned during the reign of Mary Tudor:

> John Haywood . . . told Queen Mary, Her Clergie was sawcy; if they had not Wives, they would have Lemans. Where there is not the gift of holy Continency, how could it bee otherwise? Where the water is dammed up, and yet the streame runs full, how can it choose but rise over the banks.[43]

Hall's treatise was written in 1620, the date itself a commentary on the slow acceptance of clerical marriage in the Anglican church. His purpose was to demonstrate to a contemporary critic of clerical marriage "how little a well-ordered marriage is guiltie of deadding our spirits, or slacking our hands." He dismissed as "envy of matrimoniall fruitfulnesse" the stock Catholic criticism that marriage distracted clerics from the work of God.[44]

Some Protestants, however, discovered that marriage, which was designed to end sexual frustration, instead occasioned new heights of lust. In a published sermon, Jacob Strauss scolded those who believed that clerical marriage gave "freedom to the flesh and power to the old Adam"; as God has provided food to satisfy hunger, not to awaken it, so he has ordained marriage to quench the fire of unchastity, not to justify "debauchery" (*wollust*).[45]

---

41. *The Estate of Marriage*, p. 46 (=WA 10² p. 301).

42. Jonas, *Adversus Iohannem Fabrum*, pp. C 1 b, D 1 b.

43. *The Honor of the Married Clergie Maintayned Against the Malicious Challenges of C.E. (Cavillator Egregius) Masse-Priest* (London, 1620), p. 288. The tract was directed against a Catholic priest named E. Coffin, the "C.E." of the title.

44. Ibid., pp. A 3 b–A 4 a, 164.

45. Jacob Strauss, *Eyn Sermon in der deutlich angezeigt und gelert ist die pfaffen Ee / in Evangelischer leer nitt zu den freiheit des fleische / und zu bekrefftigen den allten Adam / wie ettlich fleischlich Pfaffen das Elich (= Ehelich) wesen mit aller pomp / hoffart und ander teuffels werck anheben / gefundiert* (Erfurt, 1923), p. B 4 a. Compare, however, Martin Bucer's insistence that had he desired only to fulfill the lusts of his flesh, he would never have married his wife. Sex with women, he goes on, is simply not so all-consuming a passion; indeed, had he the opportunity to have two or three women every morning and change them every week (like the papists do), he would not be interested: "Und sag, wo ich nit gott geförcht het und hette

While Protestant apologists glorified "honest husbands" by contrasting them with "fornicating friars,"[46] they still considered marriage more than simply an outlet for sexual drives. Marriage created the conditions for a new awareness of human community. "Man has strange thoughts the first year of marriage," wrote Luther. "When sitting at table he thinks, 'Before I was alone; now there are two.' Or in bed, when he wakes up, he sees a pair of pigtails lying beside him which he had not seen there before."[47] "Marriage does not consist only of sleeping with a woman—anybody can do that—but keeping house and bringing up children."[48] "There must be harmony with respect to patterns of life and ways of thinking. The bonds of matrimony alone will not do it."[49] As if to expose an ancient slander, Protestant leaders left touching portraits of their wives as indispensable companions in their ministry. Luther boasted simply: "I would not give up my Katy for France or Venice."[50] The Puritan Richard Mather (1596–1669) a century later found the death of his wife "the more grievous, in that she being a Woman of singular Prudence for the Management of Affairs, had taken off from her Husband all Secular Cares, so that he wholly devoted himself to his Study, and to Sacred Imployments."[51] None was more eloquent than John Calvin, who wrote to a friend at the death of his wife:

> I have been bereaved of the best companion of my life, of one who, had it been so ordered, would not only have been the willing sharer of my indigence, but even of my death. During her life she was the faithful helper of my ministry. From her I never experienced the slightest hindrance.[52]

---

des fleischs lust allein wöllen suchen, so hette ich sye (seine frau) in kein weg genummen. Seind doch die frauwen nit so theür wo mirs alles daran wer gelegen, hette ich doch wol zwo oder drey für ein mögen haben und die all acht tag verändern und doby ein grosser her sein wie ander papisten" (*Verantwortung M. Butzers* in *Martin Bucers Deutsche Schriften,* ed. Robert Stupperich [Gütersloh, 1960–62], 1: 175).

46. Cf. Hall, *The Honor of the Married Clergie,* p. 42.

47. Tabletalk no. 3178a (1532), *LW,* 54: 191.

48. Tabletalk no. 5513 (1542/43), ibid., 54: 441.

49. Tabletalk no. 5524 (1542/43), ibid., 54: 444.

50. Tabletalk no. 49 (1531), ibid., 54: 8.

51. Cited by Edward S. Morgan, *The Puritan Family* (Boston, 1944). Further examples in Roland H. Bainton, "Marriage and Love in Christian History," *Religion in Life* (1948), pp. 9–13.

52. *Letters of John Calvin,* ed. and trans. Jules Bonnet (Philadelphia, 1959), 2: 216 Natalie Davis may have let a modern woman's concept of freedom and equality becloud her judgment when she argues that Calvinists looked on women as "just wives"; "the reformed model of the marriage relation subjected the wife to her husband as surely as did the Catholic" ("City Women and Religious Change in Sixteenth Century France," in *A Sampler of Women's Studies,* ed. Dorothy G. McGuigan [Ann Arbor, 1973], pp. 31, 36).

Despite the rosy assessment of Protestant apologists, marriage brought difficult personal and social changes to the clergy. At first it meant excommunication and even imprisonment, as the first clerics to test the marital waters in Wittenberg and Strasbourg learned.[53] Usually, severe financial hardship ensued, especially for those in the villages. Although sixteenth-century Europe was generally plagued by gradual inflation and intermittent recession, the Reformation tended to make its own financially uncomfortable bed. It rejected as superstition the more popular revenue-gathering devices of the medieval church. In the wake of Protestant polemic against indulgences, pilgrimages, and mendicant orders, many wondered whether it was religiously proper to give clergy any handouts whatsoever. Members of the nobility shied away from Protestant austerity; new pastors came from the ranks of schoolteachers, sextons, clerks, typesetters, printers, and clothmakers—the middle and lower social strata.[54] The young church found itself pushed towards ever greater dependence upon existing political power for its economic survival.[55] When on October 31, 1525 Luther wrote Elector John Frederick of matters requiring immediate attention if social order were to prevail, at the top of his list came the petition:

> Everywhere the pastors are poverty-stricken. No one gives, no one pays. Alms and tithes have fallen away. Incomes are either non-existent, or too little. The common man esteems neither preacher nor pastor. If bold political support of the clergy is not forthcoming from your grace, in a short time there will be no parish houses, schools or students, and God's word and service will vanish.[56]

If the granaries had been full in the monasteries, they were not so in the parish houses of Protestant clergy. Many moonlighted to make ends meet, thankful they had mastered alternative secular trades. In 1531, Luther still could write that "the preachers are poorer than before [the Reformation], and those with wife and children are truly beggars."[57] He seems even to have wondered whether he had opened a Pandora's box by joining the attack on monastic vows, complaining that large numbers of religious had

---

53. Waldemar Kawerau, *Die Reformation und die Ehe* (1892), p. 15; Miriam Chrisman, *Strasbourg and the Reform* (New Haven, 1968), p. 131; Roland H. Bainton, "Katherine Zell," in *Medievalia et Humanistica N.S.* (1970). 1: 3–28.

54. Paul Drews, *Der evangelische Geistliche in der deutschen Vergangenheit* (Jena, 1905), p. 16; Wilhelm Pauck, *The Heritage of the Reformation* (Glencoe, Ill., 1961), p. 139.

55. Alfred Schultze, *Stadtgemeinde und Reformation* (Tübingen, 1918), pp. 50–51.

56. Cited by Drews, *Der evangelische Geistliche*, p. 27.

57. Pauck, *The Heritage of the Reformation*, pp. 140–41; Drews, *Der evangelische Geistliche*, p. 25.

left cloisters to marry "even though this type of person is not in a position to assume the responsibility incident to the married estate."[58] It was not until the 1540s that some upgrading and standardization of the wages of the clergy occurred.[59]

Beyond the financial straits lay still another difficulty for some Protestant clergy, that of breaking a centuries-old custom. Lay tolerance of clerical concubinage as a relationship akin to marriage had grown in the late fifteenth century.[60] Still, the idea of a legally married clergy did not come easily to all clergy and laity. In the early years Luther found married clerics needed continual fortification of conscience.[61] When the monasteries of Saxony and Hesse were dissolved, teams of preachers prepared the way with instruction and consolation. But the psychological battle was not won during Luther's lifetime. In August 1545, for example, he preached the marriage sermon for Sigismund of Lindenau, a cathedral dean who had been secretly married for seven years before he summoned the courage to make it public. Luther dwelt on the importance of realizing that God had created men and women for marriage: when one can know and believe that, then one can be "happy and confident and . . . live in the holy ordinance of marriage with a good conscience and a happy mind." He censured the persistence of the medieval quest for angelic perfection: "If we are going to talk about the purity and chastity which the angels possess, you will not find it anywhere, either in marriage or outside of marriage in the unmarried state; that kind of purity does not exist."[62]

Clerical confusion and anxiety about marriage were reinforced by the indecisive stance of Emperor Charles V. Although the final recess of the Diet of Augsburg (1530) enjoined married priests to abstain from their wives and even to eject them, imperial enforcement was delayed pending a future council of the church.[63] Had the emperor not found France and the Turks more threatening than the ecclesiastical revolt in Germany, and had not the protective umbrella of the Schmalkaldic League formed, it is con-

---

58. Letter to Spalatin, *WABr* III, p. 109, l. 12–15, cited by D. B. Miller, *The Dissolution of the Religious Houses of Hesse During the Reformation* (Dissertation, Yale, 1971), p. 199. Cf. Schultze, *Stadtgemeinde und Reformation*, p. 44.

59. Cf. Drews, *Der evangelische Geistliche*, p. 28; Schultze, *Stadtgemeinde und Reformation*, pp. 45–46.

60. Bernd Moeller speaks of there having been "schon Anfänge einer Legalisierung und damit einer gewissen Versittlichung dieser Verbindungen" ("Frömmigkeit im Deutschland um 1500," *ARG* 56 [1965]: 26).

61. *LW*, 51: 80 (= *WA* 103, p. 23).

62. *LW*, 51: 360, 365; cf. 262 (= *WA* 49, pp. 799–800, 803).

63. Henry C. Lea, *An Historical Sketch of Sacerdotal Celibacy in the Christian Church* (Philadelphia, 1867), p. 429; Franzen, *Zölibat und Priesterehe*, p. 41.

ceivable that imperial power would have forced the same painful decisions upon married clergy on the continent that the reign of Mary Tudor forced upon married clergy in England, when, according to the polemical *Defence of Priestes Mariages,* "twelve of sixtene thousande" were deprived of their offices for refusing to put away their wives.[64] By the time the emperor took decisive action against Protestants, clerical marriage had become a permanent feature and Charles so recognized it in the Augsburg Interim of 1548.

That laity also had difficulty adjusting to a married clergy is especially evident in the English Reformation. Although the archbishop of Canterbury, Thomas Cranmer, was married to the niece of the Lutheran theologian Andreas Osiander, and Thomas Cromwell favorably disposed towards relaxing the rule of celibacy for all clergy, Henry VIII strictly forbade clerical marriage and instituted stiff penalties for those who failed to observe their vows.[65] During the reign of Edward VI, the clergy secured the legal right to marry, yet lay dissatisfaction remained. When Cranmer ordered a visitation in his province, among the points of inquiry was: "Whether any do contemn married priests, and, for that they be married, will not receive the communion or other sacraments at their hands." On February 10, 1552 a bill was passed by Parliament defending the children of married clerics as legal heirs, not bastards, as popular sentiment held.[66] Mary did not drum married clergy out of the ministry without considerable popular sympathy. And although Elizabeth reinstated the right of clerical marriage and even appointed married bishops, she found married clergy as bitter a pill as her father had. It is reported that when she turned to thank the wife of Archbishop Matthew Parker after a visit to the archiepiscopal palace, she could only say to her hostess: "And you—madam I may not call you, mistress I am ashamed to call you, so I know not what to call you—but, howsoever, I thank you."[67] A reformed clergy was one thing, a married clergy quite another for many laity.

One of the long-term consequences of clerical marriage in the Protestant churches may have been the domestication of religion itself. Spurning traditional asceticism and otherworldliness, Protestants everywhere embraced

64. *Defence of Priestes Mariages,* p. 7 a. Lea reduces this estimate to three thousand; it was probably less. *An Historical Sketch of Sacerdotal Celibacy,* p. 495. Many married clerics were summarily dismissed by the queen, with neither a hearing nor the opportunity to choose otherwise.

65. See the *Six Articles* of 1539 in H. Bettenson, ed., *Documents of the Christian Church* (New York, 1961). pp. 330–31; Lea, *An Historical Sketch of Sacerdotal Celibacy,* pp. 477–79, 483–84.

66. Ibid., pp. 489, 491. Cf. Hughes, *The Reformation in England,* 2: 115. On the other hand, the visitations sent out in the 1560s to enforce the reform measures of Trent in Catholic territories on the continent often found genuine lay acceptance of married priests.

67. Cited by Lea, *An Historical Sketch of Sacerdotal Celibacy,* p. 504.

the home and family as the superior context for the service of God and man. Experiences within the home provided analogies for understanding the deepest mysteries of God. Religion was, so to speak, brought down to earth. Luther described mothers and fathers as "apostles, bishops, and priests to their children" and praised parenthood as the one vocation where spiritual and temporal authority came together.[68] Such views were elaborated in a long series of Protestant *Ehespiegel* in the sixteenth century, each glorifying the family as the training camp for both church and state. Justus Menius (1499–1558) extolled marriage and parenthood as the greatest of all God's vocations and compared the *Kinderzucht* of Christian parents to the creation of great cities.[69] Erasmus Alberus (ca. 1500–1553) saw marriage as a school for the elect, ordained to serve the future as well as the present life.[70] Tributes traditionally reserved for the monastic life were transferred to the estate of marriage: "Jerome's unfortunate comment, 'Virginity fills heaven, marriage the earth,' must be corrected," Alberus complained. "Let us rather say, 'Connubium replet coelum, marriage fills heaven.'"[71] Jeremy Taylor praised marriage as "the seminary of the church" and "the proper scene of piety."[72] It was perhaps not accidental that the most home-minded Protestants, the New England Puritans, were also the most covenant-minded, intent on worshiping a fair and reasonable God, "a God who can be counted upon, a God who can be lived with."[73]

68. *LW*, 45: 46(=*WA* 10² p. 301).

69. *An die hochgeborne Fürstin / Fraw Sibilla Hertzogin zu Sachsen / Oeconomia Christiana / d.i. / von Christlicher Haushaltung* (Wittenberg, 1529), B 2 a; cf. A 4 b.

70. *Ein Predigt vom Ehestand* (Wittenberg, 1536), C 1 b.

71. Ibid., C 3 b. Johannes Bugenhagen had earlier attacked Jerome's famous dictum by arguing that faith, not chastity, fills heaven: "Der glawbe fullet das Paradis, nicht die Jungkfrawschaft" (*Von dem ehelichen stande der Bischoffe und Diaken an Herrn Wolffgang Reyssenbusch der Rechte Doctor und Preceptor zu Lichtemberg Sant Anthonius Ordens* [Wittenberg, 1525], D 1 a–D 3 b).

72. Taylor, *The Marriage Ring*, pp. 12–14.

73. Perry Miller, *Errand into the Wilderness* (New York, 1964), p. 63.

CHAPTER 13

Catholic Reform and Counter Reformation

MODERN historians interpret the Counter Reformation of the sixteenth century as less a reaction to the success of Protestantism than the continuation of late medieval efforts to reform the medieval church. They see both the Reformation and the Counter Reformation in close continuity with the religious history of the later Middle Ages. As the late H. O. Evennett observed: "The Reformation on its religious side and the Counter Reformation on its religious side can reasonably be regarded as two different outcomes of the [same] general aspiration toward religious regeneration which pervaded late fifteenth and early sixteenth century Europe."[1] For this reason, Evennett criticized the term "Counter Reformation" as "essentially 'reactionary' and backward-looking," obstructing the view of sixteenth-century Catholic reform as "the evolutionary adaptation of the Catholic religion and of the Catholic church to new forces both in the spiritual and the material order [of the sixteenth century]."[2] While Protestant success can be said to have had a "catalytic effect" on Catholic reform, making it more urgent and earnest than it might otherwise have been, the Counter Reformation was far more complex than simply a response to the Protestant challenge.[3]

Modern scholars also view the Counter Reformation as part of an ongoing effort to heal the breach that opened in the fourteenth century between

---

1. *The Spirit of the Counter Reformation*, The Birkbeck Lectures in Ecclesiastical History, University of Cambridge, May 1951 (Cambridge, 1968), p. 9.

2. Ibid., p. 3. The Counter Reformation was no "frightened response to Protestantism" (Marvin R. O'Connell, *The Counter Reformation 1559–1610* (New York, 1974), p. 29). See also Hubert Jedin, *Katholische Reformation oder Gegenreformation? Ein Versuch zur Klärung der Begriffe* (Lucerne, 1946). The term "Counter Reformation" is actually an eighteenth-century creation; contemporaries preferred to speak of Catholic reform. See A. Elkan, "Entstehung und Entwicklung des Begriffs 'Gegenreformation,'" *Historische Zeitschrift* 112 (1914): 473–93.

3. Evennett, *The Spirit of the Counter Reformation*, pp. 28–29.

lay piety and official church religion. They blame this division on such varied forces as Ockhamism and mysticism, the aloofness of the religious orders, and the remoteness of papal and episcopal authority—all of which are seen to have driven ordinary people to a piety that minimized the differences between clergy and laity and encouraged religious individualism and subjectivity.

Granted continuity between late medieval and sixteenth-century reform movements, both Protestant and Catholic, why did pre-Reformation efforts to reform the medieval church fail so miserably? Why did an effective Catholic lay spirituality have to await the formation of the Society of Jesus and the work of the Council of Trent in the mid-sixteenth century?

The Quest for Catholic Reform:
From Constance to Trent

WHEN the Council of Constance convened in 1414, it had three objectives: to end the schism, which by 1409 had produced three contending popes, each with his own curia and political allies; to harness the raging Hussite heresy, which, because of Bohemian military might, threatened disruption in both western and eastern Europe; and to reform the church in head and members. The council accomplished its first goal by the decree *Sacrosancta,* which declared church councils superior to popes. On this basis, it forced the contending popes from office and elected a new pope in their stead. The council tried to meet its second objective by executing John Huss and Jerome of Prague, a solution that only intensified Bohemian dissent and militancy. Finally, the fathers of Constance took steps to ensure thoroughgoing administrative and moral reforms by mandating regular councils of the church (the decree *Frequens*).[4]

During the decades in which decisive power lay with church councils—from 1414 to about 1440—significant administrative and moral reforms still eluded the church. The Council of Constance sat in judgment on popes and executed heretics, but basic religious reforms remained beyond its grasp. The reason for this failure lay largely in continuing papal opposition to the conciliar movement; the pope, understandably obsessed with regaining his sovereignty within the church, cooperated only grudgingly with church councils and always with an eye to eventually rendering them ineffectual. The latter goal was largely realized by the decree *Execrabilis* in 1460, which reasserted preconciliar arguments for Peter's primacy within the church. The conciliar theory of church government continued to find supporters

4. See above, pp. 155–64, p. 172.

in the fifteenth and sixteenth centuries—Jacques Almain and the "conciliabulum" of Pisa, for example—but it ceased to be a dominant force
within the church after 1460. It lived on as a theory without effect in
a church again controlled by the pope, on whose goodwill reform now
depended.[5]

Church reform at the discretion of the pope had obvious disadvantages.
Advocates of reform had long agreed that the key to renewal within the
church at large lay in the reform of the papacy, cardinalate, and episcopacy.
The agents of reform, however, resisted reform, for it seemed to threaten
the immediate self-interests of the church hierarchy. The cardinals, for
example, who became increasingly Italian in composition during the late
fifteenth and sixteenth centuries, were the strongest supporters of a system
that permitted them to live in Rome and accumulate wealth from benefices
both within and outside Italy. As late as 1560 seventy Italian bishops resided
in Rome rather than in their appointed sees. Such absenteeism, by no
means confined to Italy, weakened the religious and administrative discipline of the church in dioceses and parishes.

Even reform-minded popes discovered that needed administrative and
moral reforms could threaten their prerogative and security, a dilemma
they attributed to the legacy of the conciliar movement. Popes resisted
reforms that required for their success an increase in the power and responsibility of potentially competitive groups; yet significant reform required precisely the urging of a strong independent group within the
church—either a general council, the cardinalate, or the episcopate. After
1460 no such independent, reform-minded body existed.[6]

Between the pontificates of Pius II (1458–64) and Julius II (1503–
13)—from *Execrabilis* to the eve of the Reformation—little reform radiated
from the papal court. Pius II drafted a potentially significant reform bull,
which contained the proposals of the eminent conciliarist turned papal
advocate, Nicholas of Cusa. These proposals provided, among other things,
for regular visitations by committees empowered to enforce discipline even
within the Curia itself and would have given reform teeth.[7] Unfortunately,

5. See Francis Oakley, "Conciliarism in the Sixteenth Century: Jacques Almain Again,"
ARG 68 (1977): 111–32. Oakley seems oblivious to the fact that although the mainstream of
conciliar thought "was still flowing strong on the very eve of the Reformation itself," it was no
longer a dominant current within the church. See Daniel E. Zerfoss, "The Twilight of the
Conciliar Era," in *Defensorium obedientiae apostolicae et alia documenta*, ed. and trans. H. A.
Oberman, D. E. Zerfoss, and W. J. Courtenay [Cambridge, Mass., 1968], pp. 3–59).

6. Hubert Jedin, *A History of the Council of Trent* trans. D. E. Graf (St. Louis, 1957–
62), 1: 118–21; Evennett, *The Spirit of the Counter Reformation*, pp. 108–12.

7. Cf. Erwin Iserloh, *Reform der Kirche bei Nikolaus von Kues* (Wiesbaden, 1965). Cusa's
"Reformatio generalis" is reprinted in the *Historisches Jahrbuch* 32 (1911): 274–307.

Cusa's flattering vision of the church as the unfolding of the power of Peter[8] appealed to restoration popes far more than his reform program; Pius's bull never became church law. Another reform bull, *In apostolicae sedis specula*, was drafted by Pope Alexander VI (1492–1503), but, in the words of Hubert Jedin, "it by-passed precisely those issues which were the heart of the matter, viz., the personal reform of the pope."[9] The overriding preoccupation of high Renaissance popes with their own self-preservation expressed itself in Pope Leo X's bull *Pastor aeternus* (1516), a reassertion of papal supremacy over church councils,[10] apparently intended as a reminder to the members of the Fifth Lateran Council (1512–17). Leo also revived the bull *Unam sanctam* (1301) as an unheeded reminder of Peter's worldly preeminence to the king of France, whose armies had rampaged throughout Italy since the invasions of 1494.

The Fifth Lateran Council represented the last official effort at church reform before the Reformation broke out. Pope Julius II (1503–1513) convened the council in Rome in 1512 in response to a maverick church council assembled in Pisa in September 1511 by King Louis XII of France, with whom the pope was at war. Composed of dissident French and north Italian bishops who espoused a conciliar theory of church government, the Council of Pisa, as designed, embarrassed the pope. Recognized only within areas of French influence, it proved mischievous in nature and abortive in effect, its prime historical achievement the occasioning of Fifth Lateran. In circles favorable to the pope the council came to be known as the "conciliabulum" of Pisa, a term designating a marketplace or a brothel, a comment on the council's illegitimacy.

Among the working papers presented to the pope on the eve of Fifth Lateran was an ambitious reform program drafted by two Venetian monks, Tommaso Giustiniani and Vincenzo Quirini—"the broadest and boldest of all the many reform programs drawn up since the conciliar era."[11] Giustiniani and Quirini called for worldwide missions, especially to the newly discovered Americas, and renewed efforts at reconciliation with the Eastern Orthodox Church. The heart of their program, however, concerned the sad state of the church's internal life, for which they directly blamed the pope's preoccupation with secular politics. High on their list of priorities

8. See above, p. 178.

9. Jedin, *A History of the Council of Trent*, 1: 126–27.

10. "Etiam solum Romanum Pontificem pro tempore existentem tanquam auctoritatem super omnia concilia habentem, conciliorum indicendorum, transferendorum ac dissolvendorum plenum ius et potestatem habere" (*Pastor aeternus*, in Denzinger, no. 1445, p. 355).

11. Jedin, *A History of the Council of Trent*, 1: 128.

stood a thorough revision of the *Corpus juris canonici*, the massive body of church law which authorized papal practice and ensured papal preroga-tive.[12] The Venetian reformers understood the need for fundamental legal and doctrinal reform if meaningful institutional and moral reform were ever to occur. Luther too recognized this, only more violently, when, eight years later, he cast the *Corpus juris* into a bonfire prepared for the papal bull that had excommunicated him. Giustiniani and Quirini further recom-mended a reduction in the number of mendicant orders, which had tra-ditionally acted independently of local church authority and competed loc-ally with secular clergy in the cure of souls. This measure was also designed to correct the state of poor discipline into which many religious houses had fallen. Liturgical uniformity, intended to insure universal observance of basic standards in cultic practice, was another proposed reform. Finally, Giustiniani and Quirini called for frequent meetings of the governing boards of religious orders and of all diocesan and provincial synods. Al-though they did not themselves subscribe to a theory of conciliar supre-macy, they echoed the Council of Constance in recommending that church councils be held every five years and given authority to discipline the whole of church life.[13]

The Fifth Lateran Council weighed action against the Turkish threat in eastern Europe and reaffirmed church teaching on the immortality of the soul against doubts expressed by contemporary humanists like Francesco Pompanazzi. At the conclusion of its ninth session, on May 5, 1514, the council issued a reform bull. Although it included measures for adminis-trative and moral reforms, they fell far short of the proposals of Giustiniani and Quirini and received only mild official endorsement. The results of this last church council before the Reformation confirmed what earnest advo-cates of reform had long known: at official levels the church inclined to talk reform rather than actively to pursue it.[14]

Insight into the hierarchy's frame of mind can be gained from the key-note address to the Fifth Lateran Council by Giles of Viterbo, the superior general of the Hermits of St. Augustine, Martin Luther's own order. Giles placed a very conservative mandate before the council fathers. "It is right," he declared, "that people be changed by religion, not religion by people (*homines per sacra immutari fas est, non sacra per homines*); we should imitate divine things, not make them imitate us" (*imitemur enim divina nos oportet, non a divinis imitandi nos sumus*).[15] Like the popes of the period, Giles too

---

12. It was also a source of the conciliar theory. See above, p. 160.
13. Jedin, *A History of the Council of Trent,* 1: 129–30.
14. Ibid., 1: 132.
15. John O'Malley, *Giles of Viterbo on Church and Reform* (Leiden, 1968), p. 140.

feared all "res novae" in doctrine.[16] In practical terms this meant that reform was strictly a matter of renewal on the basis of accepted teachings, laws, and institutions; the latter were not to be changed but permitted to function according to their original intention.

Within six months of Fifth Lateran's adjournment, Luther both challenged the teaching of the church's theologians and issued theses against indulgences. More in the spirit of Giustiniani and Quirini than in that of Fifth Lateran, Luther concluded that the church's teaching, its doctrines and laws, posed the true obstacle to reform. Unlike Giles and Fifth Lateran, the Protestant reformers acted in the belief that people could not be reformed by religion unless it was manifestly the "right" religion. Their first task was to change traditional religion itself so that it might better change people.

The work of Catholic reformers had been difficult enough before the Reformation broke out; thereafter the Reformation's success made internal Catholic criticism and reform more difficult than ever. To censure even the most flagrant church abuses after 1517 was to be suspected of Lutheran sympathies. How could Catholic reformers decry the abuses of indulgences without appearing Lutheran themselves? Protestant printing presses, ever vigilant to Catholic self-criticism, quickly reprinted it in support of the Reformation. A case in point is the *Consilium . . . de emendanda ecclesia*, the report of a special reform commission appointed by Pope Paul III (1534–49) in 1536. Among its members sat several reputedly progressive cardinals who had received their caps only the year before: Gaspar Contarini (1483–1542), a close friend of Giustiniani and Quirini; Gian Pietro Caraffa, the future Pope Paul IV (1559–65); Reginald Pope (1500–58), the exiled English reformer; and Jacopo Sadolet, who would attempt to win the Genevans back to Roman allegiance after Calvin's ouster from the city in 1538. Their report, presented to the pope in March 1537, bluntly criticized Rome and anticipated administrative reforms later adopted by the Council of Trent, especially the strengthening of the episcopacy. The report condemned papal patronage of church offices and the many dispensations from normal religious practice, at the root of which it saw economic rather than genuine spiritual considerations. It dwelt especially on the benefice system, which permitted unqualified and often nonresident clergy to hold many high church offices. Such criticisms had also been long-standing Prot-

16. "True reform consisted in a resounding reaffirmation . . . of the ancient customs, the ancient laws, the ancient practices, the ancient beliefs, and the ancient traditions" (ibid., pp. 161, 191).

estant complaints, and Luther published the *Consilium* in 1538 with his own mocking commentary.[17]

Such indirect Lutheran applause doubtless helped prevent papal adoption of the *Consilium's* proposals. The failure of this reform program also signaled the demise of the conciliatory wing of the church's hierarchy. Like Erasmus, who, despite manly efforts, never fully succeeded in removing the albatross of Lutheranism from his neck, Contarini and other Catholic reformers who favored some compromise with the Protestants became "crypto-Lutherans" in the eyes of their critics. Substantial Catholic self-criticism and ecumenical initiatives came increasingly to be perceived as aiding and abetting the enemy.

The papal Curia had much to lose by major administrative reforms that would curb its powers of patronage and dispensation. Pretridentine popes remained as wary of a reformed and independent episcopate as they did of autonomous reforming church councils. Another facet of this complex problem was that papal culture was elitist humanist culture, largely isolated from the world of ordinary men and women. The recurring theme in the sermons preached to popes at court was the glory of man;[18] while parishes deteriorated and lay movements organized against the church, popes listened amid splendor to idealistic orations on the dignity of man. When popes did think seriously about reform, they envisioned a return to the decretals of the early Middle Ages—a simplification of the rules by which they governed, not a lessening of their actual power.[19]

Those on whom successful reform most depended were also those most reluctant to pursue it; that is the basic reason why late medieval efforts to reform the church failed so miserably. The absence of papal leadership did not, however, prevent independent initiatives by lesser clergy and laity, often with the support of local secular authorities, who found the political goal of law and order furthered by a disciplined religious life. Before 1517 friars, humanists, popular preachers, and devout laity filled as best they could the void created by the failure of papal and episcopal leadership. An

17. Jedin, *A History of the Council of Trent*, 1: 412–13, 426–31; A. G. Dickens, *The Counter Reformation* (New York, 1970), pp. 97–102.

18. See John O'Malley, "Preaching for the Popes," in *The Pursuit of Holiness in Late Medieval and Renaissance Religion*, ed. Charles Trinkaus and Heiko A. Oberman (Leiden, 1974), pp. 408–43.

19. Jedin summarizes their point of view: "The basic elements of the organization of the Roman curia and its claims were to be preserved and only the obvious abuses removed, that is, those that infringed 'the old laws' as understood by them. They were opposed to the issuance of new laws; it was enough to present and give effect to the old ones, or to adapt them intelligently to present needs" (*A History of the Council of Trent*, 1: 421).

ecumenical group of late medieval spiritual writers anticipated Jesuit
spirituality and inspired the work of Philip Neri (1515–95), Teresa of Avila
(1515–82), John of the Cross (1542–91), and Bishop Charles Borromeo
(1538–84). Among these authors were the Dominicans Johannes Tauler
and Jan van Ruysbroeck (1293–1381), the Franciscan David of Augsburg
(ca. 1200–72), the fifteenth-century Carthusians Denys and Vincent of
Aggsbach, the secular priests Pierre d'Ailly and Jean Gerson, and the
Modern Devotionalists Florence Radewijns (1350–1400), Gerlach Peters,
Gerhard Zerbolt of Zutphen (1367–98), and Jan Mombaer (Mauburnus)
(1460–1501). Others turned humanist scholarship to the service of reform.
Prominent among them was the Spanish Cardinal Ximenes (1436–1517),
founder of the University of Alcalá and editor of the Complutensian Poly-
glot Bible, a monumental scholarly project that made the Bible available in
parallel columns of Greek, Latin, and Hebrew; John Colet (ca. 1469–1519),
Reginald Pole, the martyred Thomas More (1477–1535), and John Fisher
(1459–1535) in England; and Jean Standonck and Jacques Lefèvre
d'Etaples in France. In Germany leading Catholic apologists against
Luther in the 1520s—Eck, Thomas Murner (poet laureate in 1505), Jerome
Emser (1478–1527) (editor of Pico's works), and Johannes Cochlaeus
(1479–1552)—all had humanist training.

Special religious societies known as oratories became still another force
for pre- and post-Reformation Catholic reform. Created at clerical initiative, they came to embrace both clergy and laity, in certain respects serving
from the clerical side a purpose similar to that of the Modern Devotion and
the lay confraternities of the later Middle Ages. By attempting to bring the
highest religious ideals to bear on lay spirituality, the oratories revived the
Franciscan example of regular clergy directly active in the secular world.
They conducted simple religious services and stressed a direct, ethical piety.
The most distinguished of these societies, the Oratory of Divine Love, active
in Rome after 1517, counted among its members the future cardinals Contarini and Giovanni Morone (1509–80). The reform sentiments of the
oratories also inspired the new religious orders of Theatines (fd. 1524),
Capuchins (fd. 1528), Barnabites (fd. 1533), and Ursulines (fd. 1535).

Like internal Catholic criticism, these native efforts at constructive re-
form also aided the Protestant cause.[20] Spiritual writers like Tauler and
Gerson directly influenced Luther, as did the biblical commentaries of
Lefèvre.[21] The controversial vicar-general of the Capuchins, Bernardino

20. Ibid., 1: 152–53, 164–65; and Heiko A. Oberman, *Forerunners of the Reformation: The
Shape of Late Medieval Thought* (New York, 1966), pp. 3–43.

21. Lefèvre's enemies, led by Noel Beda, accused him, quite indefensibly, of Lutheranism
in the 1520s. See Richard M. Cameron, "The Charges of Lutheranism Brought Against
Jacques Lefèvre D'Etaples," *HThR* 63 (1970): 119–49.

Ochino, created a mild scandal when he converted to Protestantism in the early 1540s. The irenic Catholic reformers Contarini, Morone, Girolamo Seripando (1492-1563), Pole, Johannes Gropper (1503-59), and Juan de Valdes (ca. 1490-1541) drew their theologies from the same Augustinian tradition that inspired the major Protestant theologies. In the Jesuit-dominated Tridentine church, Catholic authorities turned progressively against those features of the Augustinian heritage that had served the Protestants.[22]

By the late 1530s both sides looked with genuine horror on the prospect of a permanently divided Christendom. Before the decrees of Trent made this prospect a reality, a final grand attempt was made to reunite Protestants and Catholics. It came in a series of ecumenical discussions initiated by Charles V, who once again required German unity to prosecute a war with France, this time a France allied with the Turks.[23] These discussions also received support from Catholic and Protestant princes within the empire, who saw in the worsening political disunity of religious conflict a threat to their ability to maintain independence from the emperor.

After poorly attended sessions in Hagenau in June 1540, talks began in earnest between John Eck and Philip Melanchthon, the leaders respectively of the Catholic and Protestant sides, in Worms in January 1541. A more fitting locale for such a conference could not have been chosen; in Worms Luther's famous stand had initiated the religious division and conflict. The basis for the talks was to be the Lutheran Augsburg Confession. After four days of preliminary debate, however, this proved not to be a congenial format. The eager emperor, who was willing at the outset to concede the Protestants clerical marriage and communion with bread and cup, ordered the colloquy moved to the city of Regensburg, where an imperial diet was then in session. His chancellor, Nicholas Perrenot de Granvelle, took steps in advance to provide a more promising basis for the discussions. This was the *Book of Regensburg,* a work secretly drafted in Worms by the most irenic spokesmen for the two camps, Johannes Gropper, its main author, and Martin Bucer, who supplied "Protestant" modifications to Gropper's formulations. The resulting work consisted of twenty-three articles on divisive doctrinal issues.

With Gropper, Julius Pflug (1499-1564), and John Eck leading the Catholic side and Bucer, Melanchthon, and Johannes Pistorius (d. 1583) the Protestant, serious discussions began in Regensburg in April 1541. Within the space of a few weeks the conferees concurred on the first five articles of the *Book of Regensburg.* These concerned man's nature before the Fall; the

22. Cf. Dickens, *The Counter Reformation,* pp. 132, 182, 194.
23. See above, p. 257.

loss of free will in Adam and its restoration in Jesus Christ; the volitional nature of sin; the debilitating effects of original sin; and, most important for ecumenical hopes, a compromise formula on the nature of salvation known as "double justification."

According to the doctrine of double justification, man was justified before God *both* by an alien, imputed righteousness, as the Lutherans maintained, and an inherent righteousness partly of his own creation, as the medieval church had traditionally taught.[24] Cardinal Contarini, who wrote a tract celebrating the doctrine in 1541, considered it a major breakthrough, as initially did John Calvin.[25] The final authorities on both sides, however, found the doctrine artificial at best and the "non placets" rang from on high. Although Luther and the pope roundly condemned double justification, the doctrine continued to find advocates, no doubt because it offered a solution to what many, perhaps naively, considered the crucial theological issue of the day. Contarini and Seripando revived it at the Council of Trent, where the Jesuit Diego Lainez (1512–65) skillfully exposed its implications for traditional doctrine and sacramental practice. He argued that a saving righteousness that could in no way be called one's own achievement did not complement, but rather reduced to insignificance, the inherent righteousness the church taught people their daily good works acquired. It seemed further to render the concepts of merit and purgatory useless, eliminate progress and degrees of perfection in the religious life, and place the morally righteous and unrighteous on the same level as far as their salvation was finally concerned.[26]

The failure of the ecumenical movement of the early 1540s was the fault of neither side, although each blamed the other. As Jedin has observed, its collapse was rather owing to "an impersonal factor—the irreconcilable opposition of contradictory doctrines."[27] Trent made the doctrinal incompatibility of Protestantism and Catholicism fully manifest to all who would see it. Conciliators like Contrarini and Seripando had their say, but the council belonged to the pope and the new order of Jesuits. The men who dominated Trent had no romantic illusions about reunion with Protestants and

24. See above, pp. 377–78.

25. Peter Matheson, *Cardinal Contarini at Regensburg* (Oxford, 1972), pp. 105–13. Interpretations of Contarini's theology are Hanns Rückert, *Die theologische Entwicklung Gasparo Contarinis* (Bonn, 1926); and Hubert Jedin, *Kardinal Contarini als Kontroverstheologe* (Münster i W., 1949).

26. See Hanns Rückert, *Die Rechtfertigungslehre auf dem tridentinischen Konzil* (Berlin, 1925), pp. 245–52.

27. Jedin, *A History of the Council of Trent,* 1: 391. See also Jedin's "An welchen Gegensätzen sind die vortridentinischen Religionsgespräche zwischen Katholiken und Protestanten gescheitert?" *Theologie und Glaube* 48 (1958): 50–55.

were not prone to compromise. Their overriding concerns were, first, to establish the machinery for tight control over religious life so that a revolution like that of Luther, Zwingli, and Calvin would never again occur in the church and, then, to find new ways to make traditional religion more appealing to laity, including the many who had succumbed to Protestantism. The council met in three separate sessions over a period of almost twenty years. In contrast to the far more representative fifteenth-century councils of Constance and Basel,[28] Trent confined voting to individual bishops, the generals of the church's religious orders, and key monastic representatives— an arrangement that gave the Italian delegation, and hence the pope, very firm control of the proceedings. The first session ran from March 1545, to the winter of 1547, at which time plague drove a majority of the fathers to Bologna, where deliberations continued until October 1549. The second session began in May 1551, to be dispersed exactly one year later by still another Hapsburg-Valois war. The final session spanned the first of the French religious wars, from April 1561 to December 1563.

Trent rejected the Reformation on every important doctrinal issue. Against justification by faith the council reaffirmed the traditional view that faith formed by works of love saved people, salvation coming to man on the basis of an acquired, inherent righteousness, not an imputed, alien righteousness. The sacrament of penance, which Protestants had attacked as mischievous and burdensome to conscience, continued in its traditional form. Against Protestant belief in the sole authority of the Bible, Trent upheld two sources of church authority: Scripture and tradition, the rulings of popes and councils. The council reaffirmed the seven sacraments against the Protestant reduction to two. It reiterated the traditional belief that the Mass repeated Christ's sacrifice and the consecrated bread and wine of the Eucharist became the very substance of Christ's body and blood. Rejecting the practice of Hussites and Protestants, Trent permitted laymen to receive communion in bread only, a reflection of the traditional division between the laity and the clergy. Whereas the Protestant clergy freely married, Trent strictly forbade clerical marriage and took harsh measures to end the surrogate status of clerical concubinage. The council gave purgatory, indulgences, the worship of saints, and the veneration of relics and sacred images a new endorsement, while calling for an end to manifest abuses. Efforts to supplant the traditional scholastic education of priests with a humanist program of study were beaten back. So closed to new teachings and approaches did the council prove that the disputed doctrinal issues were debated in terms of the options presented by late medieval Thomists,

28. See above, p. 178.

Scotists, and Ockhamists.[29] Despite the brief appearance of a Protestant delegation at the second session of the council, Protestants quickly recognized that their reforms would find no sympathetic ear, much less favor, at Trent. The Protestant reaction to the council became uniformly negative and fearful.[30]

Trent did mandate important administrative reforms that attempted to answer some late medieval and Protestant criticisms. Chief among these was the restoration of the powers of bishops.[31] Papal control of choice benefices and the reservation of the right to absolve numerous sins and crimes had played havoc with diocesan discipline during the later Middle Ages. Such papal powers encouraged episcopal absenteeism and pluralism and weakened the power of resident bishops both within their regions and throughout the church at large. At issue in the rehabilitation of the episcopate was the degree to which bishops could be said to hold their powers directly from God, and therefore to be supreme within their own dioceses, and the degree to which such powers derived from the pope and could be regulated by him. Popes had little inclination to weaken their traditional authority over the episcopate, and from their side the bishops appreciated the existence of a "supreme monarch" to represent the church's interests among the nation-states of Europe. On the other hand, without considerable autonomy within their dioceses, bishops could not effectively police spiritual and moral life. Trent proposed a compromise in which the pope remained the highest court of appeal within the church, yet voluntarily restricted his disruptive interference in the jurisdiction of bishops by ceasing to encourage appeals beyond their decisions. A "special relation" with Rome was no longer to inhibit the disciplinary measures of bishops.[32] Administrative decentralization within the church came in this way to coexist with strong papal control over the church; power was dispersed, but not divided.

Trent passed new rules for bishops to ensure so far as possible the responsible use of the new powers given them. Bishops could not be absent

---

29. See Rückert, *Die Rechtfertigungslehre auf dem tridentinischen Konzil;* Gordon Spykman, *Attrition and Contrition at the Council of Trent* (Kampen, 1955); and Heiko A. Oberman, "Das tridentinische Rechtfertigungsdekret im Lichte spätmittelalterlicher Theologie," *ZThK* 61 (1964): 251–82.

30. See Robert M. Kingdon, "Some French Reactions to the Council of Trent," *Church History* 33 (1964): 149–55; and Theodore Casteel, "Calvin and Trent," *HThR* 63 (1970): 91–117.

31. Evennett describes the restoration of such powers as "the nodal point of every aspect of reform . . . [and] a cornerstone of the Counter Reformation church" (*The Spirit of the Counter Reformation,* p. 97).

32. Pierre Janelle, *The Catholic Reformation* (Milwaukee, 1949), pp. 86–94.

from their dioceses for long periods without special permission. They were expected to preach regularly, conduct annual visitations, hold annual synods, and attend triennial provincial synods. They were encouraged to create new seminaries and ordain only educated, trained, and thoroughly examined priests. They superintended diocesan hospitals and charitable organizations, staffed the offices in their parishes, licensed preaching within their dioceses, oversaw the internal life of convents, redistributed income and benefices as need required, and administered the new reforms and laws that radiated from Rome. Finally, they were held accountable for moral faults and administrative abuses, including concubinage among their clergy, and expected to set an example in every facet of their public life.[33]

The Society of Jesus THANKS in large measure to the dispersal of cardinals and bishops from Rome, the Tridentine church began to reestablish spiritual discipline over its parishes. This had been the major goal of the Council of Trent: the diversion of the many streams of popular religion into a single channel and reimposition of long absent parochial religious conformity.[34] The council also undertook to make traditional religious life *intrinsically* more attractive to laity, to this end encouraging a highly personal and activist spirituality.[35] Its special agent in this undertaking was the newly formed Society of Jesus.[36] What the Council of Trent was to the renewal and discipline of church doctrine and institutions, the Society of Jesus became to the revival and discipline of its spirituality.

33. Evennett, *The Spirit of the Counter Reformation*, p. 99; Hubert Jedin, *L'évêque dans la tradition pastorale du XVIe siècle*, trans. Paul Broutin (Bruges, 1953).

34. John Bossy, "The Counter-Reformation and the People of Catholic Europe," *Past and Present* 47 (1970): 52, 60.

35. Evennett describes it as "a spirituality which . . . reflected the bustle and energy and determination of sixteenth century man, [who felt] at last that he had a power over himself and over things to be applied, in the Counter Reformation, for the greater glory of God and the revival of his church" (*The Spirit of the Counter Reformation*, p. 32).

36. Evennett cites among the basic features of the new Jesuit spirituality:

constant stress on activity of all kinds; active use of the mind and intellect, with all their powers, in prayer, and especially in pictorial meditation, as against contemplative trends; the doctrine of the insufficiency of purely passive resistance to temptation with its corollary of the necessary counterattack, the principle of *agendo contra;* the development of casuistry in a humane and accommodating direction; respect for each individual and his "special case"; reaction against excessive corporal mortifications, either for themselves or penitents; active struggle against self; activity on behalf of others; frequent recourse to the sacraments; prayer found in work and action in the world rather than in eremetical retirement from it (ibid., pp. 43–44).

The methods of the society derived from traditional spirituality as shaped by the remarkable personal experience of its founder, Ignatius of Loyola (1491–1556). The youngest in a family of thirteen children, Ignatius grew up a courtier and caballero, captive to the romantic ideals of medieval chivalry. For ten years, from 1507 to 1517, he lived in the household of Spain's royal treasurer, thereafter entering active military service. In May 1521, during the first of the wars between Francis I and Charles V, the French invaded Navarre, and in the ensuing battle Ignatius suffered severe wounds in both legs. The attending surgeons, whose procedures for dealing with such serious wounds remained primitive, improperly set one of his legs. Determined to be again the dashing young man he had been before the mishap, Ignatius endured not only a resetting of the leg, but also an operation to remove a protruding piece of bone and a stretching rack designed to bring the leg back to its normal length.[37] During his lengthy convalescence in Loyola, he became absorbed in two religious classics: Ludolphus of Saxony's *Life of Christ* and a collection of saints' lives known as *The Golden Legend (Flos sanctorum)*. Later, Thomas à Kempis's *Imitation of Christ* became his favorite book, another indication of the continuity between late medieval and Counter Reformation spirituality. The legendary deeds of St. Dominic and St. Francis gripped Ignatius's mind; he became convinced that they had accomplished far greater feats than any knight on horseback and without benefit of sword and armor. Ignatius confided to his biographer that he personally felt impelled to do whatever he read that Dominic and Francis had done.[38] In this way the soldier of the king gradually evolved into a soldier of Jesus.[39]

Once recuperated, Ignatius made a pilgrimage to Montserrat, the legendary mount of the Holy Grail and home of a shrine to the Virgin. There, in March 1522, in imitation of the knights he had read about as a young man, he dedicated himself to his newly chosen vocation of spiritual knighthood at the altar of Our Lady of Montserrat.[40] Thereafter, he journeyed to Man-

37. *Autobiography of St. Ignatius Loyola*, ed. J. C. Olin, trans. J. F. O'Callahan (New York, 1974), pp. 21–23.

38. Ibid., p. 23.

39. Modern historians have pointed out the compensatory nature of Ignatius's decision to seek a spiritual mission—a predictable reaction by an athletic youth to the prospect of remaining a cripple. A decision to fight for the "heavenly king and queen," however, whether produced by pleasure or by pain, remained a decision to fight for the heavenly king and queen. The modern reader should not let the religious dimension of the decision go unappreciated because it can also be understood psychologically.

40. *Autobiography*, p. 31. According to Rene Fulöp-Miller, the ceremony followed exactly the dedication service of a knight as portrayed in an episode in *Amadis of Gaul*, Ignatius's favorite chivalric romance (*The Jesuits: A History of the Society of Jesus* [New York, 1963], p. 42).

Ignatius of Loyola. After a painting by Peter Paul Rubens (engraving by Schelte a Bolswert).

resa, where in imitation of Christ's forty days in the wilderness he went begging, fasted for periods as long as a week, and spent seven hours a day in prayer. He withheld from himself all his youthful pleasures and systematically consumed his old values and habits by rigorous self-denial. The Manresa period became a time of coerced spiritual transformation, a deliberate remaking of himself. Ignatius designed special exercises to bring about desired feelings and states of mind. The first draft of the *Spiritual Exercises,* the Counter Reformation's manual of self-discipline for clergy and laity, came in this way to be composed in Ignatius's own experience long before it received its first written conceptual form in 1548.[41] Ignatius learned through his struggle with physical pain how to control mental anguish; mastery over basic physical reactions gave him insight into more complex psychological responses. The *Spiritual Exercises* built most perceptively on the interconnectedness of emotion, belief, and behavior. What justification by faith had attempted to accomplish for the anguished Protestant saint, Ignatius's disciplined exercises tried to do for the troubled Catholic saint. The routines it prescribed overcame old habits and prepared individuals for new states of mind and morality by playing directly on their basic emotions of fear and love. Particular sins, for example, were eliminated by attacking each with all five senses and the mind's power of imagination at regular daily intervals.

During the ten months at Manresa, Ignatius received a special enlightenment that made religious issues both vital and clear to him.[42] The retreat brought not only a new self-discipline, but also a mystical inspiration that made it desirable. When Ignatius left Manresa, the secular soldier and devotee of chivalric romances had been replaced by what one biographer calls "the cold master of [religious] affect[ion]s."[43] The contrast with Luther's biography is noteworthy. In the persons of their founders the antithetical character of original Protestant and Counter Reformation piety is strikingly revealed. Whereas Luther had despaired of calculated efforts at self-reform and salvation, concluding that neither sublimation nor repression, no matter how diligently practiced, could ever bring peace of mind, Ignatius carefully examined himself and discovered a self-control like that of the first man, who could sin or not sin at will. Here was a new type of religious self-confidence that ran counter not only to the Reformation, but to much traditional spirituality as well.

In September 1523, Ignatius arrived in Jerusalem on a solitary preaching

---

41. *The Spiritual Exercises of St. Ignatius,* trans. A. Mottola (Garden City, 1964), pp. 59, 62.

42. *Autobiography,* pp. 39–40.

43. Fulöp-Miller, *The Jesuits,* p. 47.

crusade. Denied support by the resident Franciscan colony and suspected by local authorities of being a rabble-rouser, he was at length dismissed. Returning to Spain, he pursued his neglected education, sitting among schoolchildren in Barcelona to acquire the rudiments of Latin before moving to Alcalá and Salamanca. In February 1528, at age thirty-seven, he enrolled in the Collège de Montaigu in Paris, the same year that Calvin departed it. There Ignatius completed his formal education, receiving a master's degree in 1534.

While in Paris, Ignatius gathered his first co-workers, Peter Faber (1506–46) and Francis Xavier (1506–52), his roommates at the Collège de Montaigu. Later Diego Lainez and Alfonso Salmeron (1515–85), men destined to play important roles at the Council of Trent, joined them. By 1534 the group had grown to ten. In August they took private vows of poverty and chastity and pledged, given papal permission, to undertake a preaching mission to the Holy Land. War, however, prevented this project and the group worked instead in and around Rome as preachers, educators, and hospital chaplains. They won an important friend in Contarini, who perceived in them a major force for church reform. Contarini directly assisted their confirmation as a new order of the church in September 1540. According to the original charter, the society was to be limited to sixty members, each of whom vowed, according to the petition drawn up by Ignatius,

> to abandon his own will, to consider ourselves bound by special vow to the present pope and his successors to go, without complaint, to any country whither they may send us, whether to the Turk or other infidels, in India or elsewhere, to any heretics or schismatics, as well as to the faithful, being subject only to the will of the pope and the general of the order.[44]

At the time of Ignatius's death in 1556 the order had grown to over one thousand members and was widely respected for its orphanages, homes for prostitutes, relief agencies, retreats, and progressive secondary-school education.

As a religious order the Jesuits could be "experimental" to the point of appearing revolutionary. They favored an active, outgoing spirituality in place of the traditional religious life in retreat. They abandoned recitation of the canonical hours in choir, a distinctive religious habit, set daily rituals, and compulsory ascetic exercises. They encouraged a more personal and individual piety than had been customary in the older religious com-

---

44. Cited in B. J. Kidd, *The Counter Reformation 1550–1600* (London, 1933), p. 28. Jesuit obedience to the pope has been characterized as the order's "fourth vow."

munities. And while they remained very traditional in educational philosophy, they attached a new importance to education and required for admission into the society the successful completion of a definite program of study.[45]

To such internal flexibility was juxtaposed a still more dominant Jesuit trait: devotion to hierarchical order and authority. Some critics have accused the Jesuits of a narrow military mentality.[46] One of the most sympathetic historians of the order concedes that in the Jesuit environment "something of the attitude of subject to Renaissance monarch, private soldier to generalissimo, could be detected."[47] One should not, however, dwell too long on such comparisons, for they only partially elucidate Jesuit respect for hierarchical order and authority. The Jesuits intended to provide both an effective antidote to Protestantism and the means by which traditional religion could be revived. A new discipline and respect for authority were essential to these goals and became prominent from the start in both Jesuit organization and practice. This reflected less the growing absolutism of the age than the very essence of the society's reform program. Luther's twin sins, after all, had been disobedience and innovation. On the basis of his own subjective experience and interpretation of Scripture, he had defied the authority of the pope, broken openly with the traditions of the church, and to all intents and purposes created his own religion. Such disobedience and innovation became the special targets of Counter Reformation spirituality, especially as the Jesuits shaped it.

Ignatius summarized fully his own views on this subject in a remarkable "Letter on Obedience" sent to the members of the society in Portugal on March 26, 1553. Members of the Portuguese society had become inordinately attached to a popular leader, Simon Rodriguez, one of the original nine members of the society who had taken private vows with Ignatius in Montmartre in August 1534. Upon his retirement, Portuguese Jesuits refused to obey any successor other than one personally approved by him,

---

45. Evennett, *The Spirit of the Counter Reformation,* p. 79. Evennett compares the training of the Jesuit with the life of the founder.

> The first two years of probation, with their initiation into the spirituality of the society, the performance of the *Exercises,* and the six specific trials laid down for novices in the constitutions, reflect the ardent pilgrim of Montserrat, Manresa, and Jerusalem. . . . Then come the long years of study in the Scholasticate, with their definite "let-up," so to speak, in spiritual tension, giving a training in prudence, patience, self-control, toleration of the humdrumness of life, as St. Ignatius had steeled and trained himself in Paris in his long years of study (ibid., p. 77).

46. Evennett believes parallels with the political history of the age (its absolutism) are more revealing (ibid., p. 83).

47. Ibid., p. 82.

with the result that a mutiny seemed possible in the chapter. This was the state of affairs to which Ignatius addressed his letter. He pointed out that absolute obedience should be the hallmark of the Society of Jesus.

> Although I wish all of you perfection in every virtue and spiritual gift, it is . . . in obedience more than in any other virtue that I desire to see you excel. And that because, as St. Gregory says, obedience is the virtue which plants all the other virtues. . . . We may allow ourselves to be surpassed by other religious orders in fasts, watchings, and other austerities . . . but in the purity and perfection of obedience and the true resignation of our wills and abnegation of our own judgment, I am very desirous . . . that . . . this Society be conspicuous, so that by this virtue its true sons may be recognized as men who regard not the person whom they obey, but in him Christ our Lord, for whose sake they obey. For your superior is to be obeyed not because he is prudent, or good, or qualified by any other gift of God, but because he holds the place and the authority of God, as the Truth [Christ] has said: "He who hears you hears me; he that despises you, despises me."[48]

According to Ignatius, the very office of the superior places him in a hierarchical chain of command that makes his word to inferiors effectually God's word. The obedience here demanded, however, went even beyond blind execution of commands assumed to be ultimately divine.

> The first degree of obedience is very low, consisting in the [bare] execution of what is commanded; it does not deserve the name of obedience [nor] attain the worth of this virtue, unless it rises to a second degree. It must make the superior's will one's own in such a way that there is not only effectual execution of the command, but also an interior conformity, an inner wish to do [what has been commanded].[49]

One not only obeys his superior without question; one *wishes* so to obey his superior. "He who wishes to rise to the virtue of obedience must rise to this second degree, which, over and above the execution of a command, makes the superior's will one's own; putting off one's own will, one clothes oneself

---

48. *Letters of St. Ignatius of Loyala*, ed. and trans. William J. Young, S.J. (Chicago, 1959), pp. 287–88. Earlier, in his *Autobiography*, Ignatius had also spoken of superiors as standing in the place of Christ. Recalling when he set out to find a master for his studies at the University of Paris, "he imagined that the master would be Christ, that one of the students would be called St. Peter and another St. John, and so with each one of the apostles. 'When the master commands me, I will think that Christ commands me; when someone else commands me, I will think that St. Peter commands me'" (*Autobiography*, p. 74).

49. *Letters*, p. 289.

with the divine will as interpreted by the superior."[50] For Ignatius, this too remained only a penultimate degree of obedience.

> He who aims at an entire and perfect oblation of himself, in addition to his will, must offer his understanding, which is the highest degree of obedience. He must not only will, but also think the same as the superior, submitting his own judgment to the superior so far as a devout will can bend the understanding.[51]

Such reasoning gave birth to the famous thirteenth rule for "thinking with the church" in the *Spiritual Exercises:* "If we wish to be sure that we are right in all things, we should always be ready to accept this principle: I will believe that the white that I see is black, if the hierarchical church so defines."[52]

Ignatius concluded the letter to the society in Portugal by suggesting three aids to the attainment of perfect obedience: first, that one behold in the person of the superior not a man subject to errors and miseries, but "Christ the highest wisdom, immeasurable goodness, and infinite charity, who cannot be deceived and does not wish to deceive you"; second, that one always seek reasons that defend rather than question the wisdom of a superior's command; and, finally, that one keep in mind the example of Abraham, who, upon hearing God's command to sacrifice Isaac and neither comprehending nor approving it, nonetheless obeyed.[53] Thus it will be, Ignatius envisioned, that just as the heavenly hierarchy is arranged in perfect subordination of lower to higher, so upon earth perfect obedience will reign from the individual to his superior, to rectors, provincials, the general of the order, and, finally, to the pope, God's vicar on earth.[54]

Such was the vision that inspired the Counter Reformation at official levels and made the Jesuits fully a match for Lutherans and Calvinists during the confessional wars that engulfed Europe between 1560 and 1648. With the assistance of determined rulers, an estimated one-third of earlier losses to Protestants within the empire, especially in Hapsburg Austria and Bavaria and major Rhenish episcopacies, was recovered by century's end.

Despite important changes in administration, new educational programs, and the respectability of genuine church reform, the Counter Reformation remained profoundly conservative in religious belief and practice. The Council of Trent held the line against the Protestants on every disputed

50. Ibid., p. 290.
51. Ibid.
52. *The Spiritual Exercises*, pp. 140–41.
53. *Letters*, pp. 293–94. For further correspondence on this subject, see ibid., pp. 159, 164, 225.
54. Ibid., p. 295.

Map 4. The Religious Map of Europe by 1600, Revealing the Success of the Counter Reformation

doctrine, and the new spiritual writers and catechists revived for laity a streamlined version of traditional ascetic spirituality. However, the most important factor in the Counter Reformation's success, at least among the masses of ordinary people, may have been the inertia of human nature itself rather than the labors of reformers and politicians on either side. If the Counter Reformation was aided by rulers determined to maintain the traditional religion and by *politiques* willing to compromise Protestant settlements for the sake of national unity, it was also assisted by widespread popular religious conservatism. Many laity in the parishes responded to Protestant overtures by clinging all the more naively to the faith of their fathers, reformed neither by Protestants nor by the Tridentine church.[55]

55. See A. N. Galpern, *The Religions of the People in Sixteenth Century Champagne* (Cambridge, Mass., 1976), pp. 157–60; Bossy, "The Counter-Reformation and the People of Catholic Europe," pp. 62–63, 68; Werner Zeissner, *Altkirchliche Kräfte in Bamberg unter Bischof Weigand von Redwitz (1522–1556)* (Bamberg, 1975), pp. 219–20; Gerald Strauss, *Luther's World of Learning: Indoctrination of the Young in the German Reformation* (Baltimore, 1978), pp. 266, 276.

CHAPTER 14

Protestant Resistance to Tyranny: The Career of John Knox

DESPITE their different conceptions of the relationship between religion and society and church and state, Protestants in the first half of the sixteenth century—Anabaptists, Lutherans, Zwinglians, and Calvinists alike—had agreed that individuals, as private persons, had no right to rise up against legitimate rulers, no matter how tyrannical or heathenish the latter might become. All saw rulers as divinely established in their offices and tyrants as a just divine judgment on the sins of their subjects. The individual had only one legitimate recourse to tyranny: passive resistance. Aware that the final consequence of such action might be exile or execution, he remained free to disobey those who asked of him what conscience could not bear. The majority of Anabaptists, who expected little from magistrates and came to prize religious suffering and martyrdom, adjusted more easily to such situations than did Lutherans, Zwinglians, and Calvinists, whose political experience had been more successful and encouraged a *Realpolitik* stance toward secular authority. The major Protestant reformers looked to lower magistrates—the princes of Germany, the councils of Zurich and Geneva, the nobility of France as represented in the Estates-General and regional parliaments—to oppose tyrannical higher authority. As part of the legitimate political order, these lower magistrates were seen to share its divine mandate; as agents for justice, they represented the rights of subjects within government.

In the 1520s Lutheran jurists and theologians argued on constitutional, juridical, and theological grounds that princes who elected the emperor also had the right and the duty to oppose the unjust coercion of his subjects' religious beliefs.[1] Such theories helped preserve Lutheranism from political defeat in the first half of the sixteenth century, especially after the emperor's victory over the princes of Saxony and Hesse in

1. See above, p. 271.

1547. In the Magdeburg Confession of 1550–51, Lutheran conservatives led by Matthias Flacius Illyricus (1520–75) defended the right of political resistance by lower magistrates as both a divine and natural right.[2] The Magdeburg Confession influenced the later and more elaborate Huguenot tracts on the subject by François Hotman (1524–90), Theodore Beza (1519–1605), and Philippe du Plessis Mornay (1549–1623). Beza's and Mornay's works came in the wake of the St. Bartholomew's Day Massacre of French Protestants, while Hotman's views had been formulated much earlier.[3] Beza actually printed his *Right of Magistrates* under the guise of an anonymous Lutheran political tract originating in midcentury Magdeburg.

In arguing for the right of people to take action against tyrants through their chosen representatives, Huguenot pamphleteers cited many justifications. They pointed to ancient and present historical practice, especially in France and England, where the Estates-General and Parliament had long shared power with the king.[4] They cited the legal precedents of feudal compacts and the corporation theory in canon law, from which had come the popular dictum: "What concerns all should be approved by all."[5] Biblical and classical examples of lower magistrates who had acted against tyrants were also invoked. Roman consuls, praetors, city prefects, and governors, the leaders of the twelve tribes of Israel, the biblical captains of thousands, hundreds, and fifties, and the elders of the people appeared to Beza to be ancient counterparts to contemporary French dukes, marquises, counts, viscounts, barons, and chatelains—the ranks of the Calvinist nobility.[6] The biblical concept of a covenant binding both king and people to strict observance of God's law made it possible for Mornay to interpret Romans 13:1 to mean: "We [the people] are to obey God before the king; we obey the king because of God and surely not against Him."[7] Beza believed that "equity and natural law" gave those who had created a king the power also to depose him.[8] Then came arguments based on the factual

2. See the summary by O. K. Olson, "Theology of Revolution: Magdeburg, 1550–51," *Sixteenth Century Journal* 3 (1972): 56–79.

3. For the Europe-wide impact of the massacre, see Alfred Soman, ed., *The Massacre of St. Bartholomew: Reappraisals and Documents* (The Hague, 1974). Also helpful is the review article by Gordon Griffiths, "Saint Bartholomew Reappraised," *Journal of Modern History* (1976): 494–505.

4. This is the leitmotif of Hotman's *Francogallia* (1573), in *Constitutionalism and Resistance in the 16th Century: Three Treatises by Hotman, Beza, and Mornay*, ed. and trans. J. H. Franklin (New York, 1969), pp. 93–96. See also Mornay's appeal to the examples of contemporary England, Sweden, Denmark, and France, *Vindiciae contra tyrannos* (1579), in ibid., p. 184.

5. *Francogallia*, in *Constitutionalism and Resistance*, pp. 67, 91.

6. *Right of Magistrates*, in *Constitutionalism and Resistance*, pp. 110–18.

7. *Vindiciae contra tyrannos*, in *Constitutionalism and Resistance* pp. 143–47.

8. *Right of Magistrates*, in *Constitutionalism and Resistance*, p. 124.

priority of peoples to rulers, kingdoms to kings, and sovereignty to sovereigns; lesser magistrates were seen to represent a primal authority; unjust rulers and their sycophants had only derived authority.[9] Such arguments also owed something to the conciliar theory of church government, which held that a church council, allegedly guided by God's spirit, had higher authority than popes and canon lawyers. Both Beza and Mornay appealed directly to the example of the ecumenical councils of the church.[10]

No major Protestant writer, however, made provisions for popular political resistance when leadership from lower magistrates was not forthcoming. That is as true of the Huguenot defenders of the constitutional rights of subjects as it is of Luther, Zwingli, and Calvin. Lower magistrates might overthrow tyrannical higher authority and even take the initiative in doing so individually,[11] but neither collectively nor privately did ordinary people have the right to overthrow tyrannical magistrates, whether higher or lower. Protestant reformers warned vaguely that anarchy was the wages of tyranny and foresaw a time when God would inspire popular revolts against hardened tyrants. But all forbade private citizens from consciously plotting and participating in the overthrow of such rulers. Behind this apparent inconsistency were belief in the nonviolent nature of Christianity and the fear of "Münsterite" anarchy if ordinary people became convinced that they could redress perceived tyranny at will. Historical circumstances may, however, have contributed as much to this point of view as theology and fear of social upheaval. In practically every area of Protestant resistance, lower magistrates could be found who were prepared and even eager to resist higher authority, if not in heartfelt defense of Protestant religious freedom, then simply for their own political gain.

Two major Protestant thinkers stand out as exceptions to the general rule of nonresistance by private individuals: the revolutionary spiritualist Thomas Müntzer and that chief among the Marian exiles, John Knox.[12]

---

9. *Francogallia*, in *Constitutionalism and Resistance*, p. 79; *Right of Magistrates*, in *Constitutionalism and Resistance*, pp. 111–12; *Vindiciae contra tyrannos*, in *Constitutionalism and Resistance*, p. 164.

10. *Right of Magistrates*, in *Constitutionalism and Resistance*, p. 129; *Vindiciae contra tyrannos*, in *Constitutionalism and Resistance*, pp. 150, 193. On the conciliar theory, see above, pp. 156–57.

11. See Franklin's introductory comments in *Constitutionalism and Resistance*, pp. 42–43, and his *Jean Bodin and the Rise of Absolutist Theory* (Cambridge, 1973), pp. 46–47.

12. Knox's views were shared by his fellow English exiles John Ponet, bishop of Wincester after 1551, and Christopher Goodman. Goodman's *How Superior Powers Ought to be Obeyed* was published in Geneva in 1558, a few months in advance of Knox's *First Blast of the Trumpet Against the Monstrous Regiment of Women* (1558), and Goodman joined Knox in Scotland in September 1559. More insistent than Knox on the duty of subjects to overthrow tyrants, Goodman later recanted his views (April 1571) and forcefully confessed his belief that a woman could lawfully govern a realm. See Dan G. Danner, "Christopher Goodman and the English Protestant Tradition of Civil Disobedience," *Sixteenth Century Journal* 8 (1977):

Both believed that government had a primary responsibility to maintain true religion and Christian subjects a primary duty to overthrow rulers who did not. Each sanctioned a specifically *Christian* use of the sword—by lower magistrates where possible, by private individuals where necessary, but ideally by both in concert. And each called for the violent overthrow of legitimate governments—in Müntzer's case, the Lutheran princes of Saxony;[13] in Knox's, the Catholic regimes of Mary Tudor and Mary of Lorraine.

The year of John Knox's birth, 1513, was a key date in Scottish history. In that year English soldiers routed King James IV and an invading army of Scots at the Battle of Flodden in a defeat that ended forever Scotland's pretensions to great-power status in the larger European community. Thereafter Scotland's political and religious history became more closely tied to the fortunes of its powerful neighbor to the south. Because the two countries remained traditional enemies, each despising the other as near barbarians, Henry VIII's break with Rome in the 1530s had the effect of binding Scottish patriotism more tightly than ever with Catholicism and enhancing the Scots' alliance with Catholic France.

Luther's writings and Tyndale's English Bible circulated in Scotland in the 1520s and 1530s. Scottish Protestantism did not take root, however, until after the death of King James V in 1542, when power in Scotland fell to the earl of Arran, regent for the baby Mary Stuart, future queen of Scots (1542–87). Eager to take advantage of every opportunity to minimize French and papal influence in Scotland, Henry VIII made overtures to Arran. A marriage contract was drawn up between Mary and Henry's infant son, Edward, and Protestant preaching made its appearance at the Scottish court. The Protestant sermons of Arran's court chaplain, Thomas Gwilliam, first attracted Knox to Protestantism.

Despite these initiatives, anti-English and anti-Protestant sentiments continued to run high in Scotland in the 1540s. Urged by the Scottish chancellor and accomplished persecutor of Lutherans, Cardinal David Beaton, and the queen dowager, Mary of Lorraine, a member of the French Guise family, Arran abandoned détente with the English. He repudiated the marriage contract between Mary and Edward and permitted a new wave of Protestant persecution to sweep the country. Henry VIII retaliated with a

---

61–73. François Hotman met both Goodman and Ponet in Strasbourg and, according to Hotman's biographer, was "more than likely" influenced by their views on resistance to tyrants (Donald R. Kelley, *François Hotman: A Revolutionary's Ordeal* [Princeton, 1973], p. 93). While Hotman believed the "right of the people" underlay the authority of kings and gave "the people" the power to depose them, he understood "the people" to be a part of the Estates-General, that is, an element of magistracy expressing itself in council, not individuals acting collectively at their own initiative.

13. See above, pp. 272, 342.

A portrait of John Knox. From a woodcut by Vaensoun.

policy of calculated terrorism, sending raiding parties into Scotland, one of which burned much of Edinburgh to the ground. The new English aggression so demoralized the government and distracted it from its campaign against the Protestants that the Scottish Reformation had time to put down deep roots.

Knox associated at this time with a popular Protestant preacher named George Wishart (ca. 1513–46), a man familiar with both Lutheran and Zwinglian theology who had visited Germany and Switzerland. Knox found himself in the Protestant camp by a very circuitous route. He had studied at St. Andrews University in the early 1520s, probably sitting at the feet of John Major, who later taught Calvin scholastic philosophy at the Collège de Montaigu in Paris. In 1535, at the age of twenty-two, Knox received full ordination as a priest. At this time, however, there were too many priests within a defensive and deteriorating traditional church, and Knox found himself without a benefice and jobless, a circumstance that made him susceptible to the anticlerical theology of Wishart. Ever enterprising, Knox landed a job as a minor notary in the area of Haddington, a position that nurtured his political instincts.

The government cracked down on Protestants in the mid-1540s. Wishart was captured and executed in 1546. The following summer Protestants retaliated by stabbing Cardinal Beaton to death and displaying his mutilated body at the end of a rope hung from his own castle walls. Condemned by Parliament for treason, these revolutionary Protestants defiantly occupied the castle of St. Andrews. Knox also resided at this time in St. Andrews, where he worked as a tutor in French and Latin for the children of a Protestant nobleman. Already deeply involved with the Scottish Protestant party, he joined the revolutionaries in the castle of St. Andrews. These "castilians" had expected aid from the English; they received instead a shelling from the French. The 120 who survived—the radical leadership of Scottish Protestantism—were condemned to be galley slaves. Knox spent nineteen months chained to the oar of a French ship. A robust man of thirty-three, his health did not break until the summer of 1548; his captors permitted him to settle in England in the spring of 1549.

The English Reformation had at this time reached a crossroad. After the execution of Thomas Cromwell (ca. 1485–1540), who had been a cautious friend of basic Protestant reforms and largely responsible for the success of the English Bible, Henry VIII, ever an extreme conservative in religious doctrine, chose to persecute English Protestants. This drove many second-generation Protestants to continental refuges in Strasbourg and Zurich. The conservative reaction during the first half of the decade forced recantations and sent several Protestant heretics to the stake. The Act for the Advancement of True Religion (1543) forbade the use of Tyndale's New Testament and limited the right to read authorized vernacular Bibles to the higher classes of nobility, gentry, clergy, and wealthy merchants, pointedly excluding women and the great mass of unprivileged ordinary people. A new religious formulary, the *King's Book* (1543), attempted to enforce the orthodox Catholic doctrine of the Six Articles (1538). Advocates of religious and social reform still remained active, however—men like Nicholas Ridley (ca. 1500–55), Thomas Lever, Hugh Latimer (ca. 1485–1555), and Robert Crowley (1518–88)—and Erasmian reform sentiment, always strong in England, found an eager patron in Queen Catherine Parr, Henry's sixth and final wife, who had survived two previous husbands and would survive Henry to take still a fourth. There was also an active group of "lay students of the body politic," heirs of Cromwell like Sir Thomas Smith, who, beyond the educational reforms of humanists and the religious reforms of Protestants, undertook to cure basic economic and political ills.[14]

14. Elton, *Reform and Reformation: England, 1509–1558* (Cambridge, Mass., 1977), pp. 321–23; J. J. Scarisbrick, *Henry VIII* (Berkeley, 1968) p. 523.

After Henry's death on January 28, 1547, Edward Seymour (ca. 1506–52), the earl of Hartford, taking the title of the duke of Somerset, ruled as regent for the ten-year-old Edward VI. Both Somerset and his successor, John Dudley (1502–53), the earl of Warwick, who reigned as the duke of Northumberland, remained as committed to royal supremacy and lay dominance over religion as Henry VIII and Cromwell had been. But Somerset and Northumberland also sincerely desired a religious reformation of the commonwealth, especially Northumberland, whose religious devotion seems to have matched that of the king in fervor and naiveté.[15] During their regencies major changes occurred. Continental reformers found refuge from persecution in London and Oxford, among them Martin Bucer, John à Lasco (1499–1560), Peter Martyr Vermigli (1500–62) and Bernardino Ochino. Parliament repealed the Six Articles and passed acts requiring Protestant religious uniformity in 1549 and 1551. Two editions of Thomas Cranmer's Book of Common Prayer (1549, 1552) imposed a new Scripture-based service of worship. Clergy freely married. Protestant sermons replaced the traditional Mass as the center of worship in all Sunday services. And outspoken Protestants like Ridley, John Ponet, Miles Coverdale (1488–1568), John Scory (d. 1585), and John Hooper (ca. 1495–1555) became bishops.[16]

Knox took a direct role in shaping the Edwardian church, quickly becoming a "consummate politician."[17] Identified with the radical English Protestants whom John Hooper led, he made a mark for himself by successfully challenging the propriety of kneeling during Holy Communion, an act he and others considered blasphemous and idolatrous. Knox's protestations won the temporary inclusion in the Prayer Book of the so-called Black Rubric, a note explaining that the consecrated elements of the sacrament were not Christ's actual body and blood and the reverent act of kneeling did not imply such.[18] For both political and religious reasons Northumberland, who usurped power in late 1549, cultivated Hooper and Knox, going so far as to offer Knox the bishopric of Rochester. Suspecting an attempt to render him a benign cog in the wheel of state, Knox flatly refused; a reformer

---

15. Elton describes Edward's Protestantism as "an uncompromising bigotry very characteristic of the newly converted adolescent" (*Reform and Reformation*, p. 354).

16. Ibid., p. 343.

17. Jasper Ridley, *John Knox* (New York, 1968), p. 90. I have relied heavily on Ridley for the reconstruction of Knox's biography. Other helpful recent works, especially for Knox's pastoral activity and theology, are W. Stanford Reid, *Trumpeter of God: A Biography of John Knox* (New York, 1974) and *John Knox: A Quartercentenary Reappraisal*, ed. Duncan Shaw (Edinburgh, 1975).

18. Ridley, *John Knox*, p. 109.

who thrived on crisis, he was incapable of diplomacy, much less the role of a lapdog.

Edward VI had never been in good health, and court insiders knew that in the likely event of his premature death his stepsister Mary would gain the throne. They also knew that once in power Mary, who had been reared a Catholic, would attempt to restore at least the state of religion that had existed under her father. Throughout the Edwardian Reformation she had been permitted her private Mass and Catholic advisors, an inconsistency in official policy that Knox publicly challenged. Invited to preach a Lenten sermon at court, he used the occasion to denounce the nobility for not acting to secure the safety of Protestantism.[19]

Edward died on July 6, 1553 after contracting tuberculosis. Before his death, he and Northumberland conspired to exclude Mary from the throne on grounds of her illegitimacy as the daughter of Catherine of Aragon, whose marriage to Henry VIII the Reformation Parliament had declared null and void. In Mary's stead Lady Jane Grey (1537-54), the Protestant grandniece of Henry VIII and, equally pertinent, daughter-in-law of Northumberland, was designated to succeed Edward. However, popular patriotism and an almost mystical belief in hereditary succession to the throne foiled this scheme. Many resented the heavy-handed Northumberland regime and believed that the denial of Mary's orderly succession to the throne tempted providence. Even Elizabeth Tudor, a far more promising candidate to succeed Edward than Jane Grey, refused to become involved in Northumberland's plot for this reason. Later, as queen, Elizabeth would also refuse to deny another Catholic queen, Mary, queen of Scots, her rightful place on the Scottish throne, despite the triumph of Protestantism in Scotland.

During the nine days of Jane Grey's rule, Knox preached in her behalf and warned against popery and Spanish domination of England should Mary reach the throne. However, after London declared for Mary on July 19, 1553, she proved irresistible and came easily to the throne. In August she silenced Protestants by requiring all preachers to obtain a special royal license. By the end of September she had Hooper, Coverdale, Latimer, Cranmer, and Ridley—the leadership of Edwardian Protestantism—in the Tower on charges of treason. Like Thomas More before them, these Protestant leaders embraced martyrdom as the ultimate protest against an unjust ruler. In November, Cardinal Pole arrived from Rome to reconcile England with the papacy. In December, Parliament repealed the Act of Uniformity,

19. Ibid., pp. 120-24.
20. Elton, *Reform and Reformation*, p. 382.

making England once again a Catholic land. By 1555 approximately eight hundred English Protestants had fled to the continent, and English settlements thrived in Frankfurt, Zurich, and Geneva.[20] Others, like Sir William Cecil (1520–98), who, as Lord Burghley, later became Elizabeth's most trusted advisor, chose to accept the Mass rather than suffer the chopping block. Since policy dictated that foreign Protestants be expelled rather than executed, Knox also escaped death. Utterly devoid of romantic illusions about martyrdom, Knox departed England in late January 1554, gladly accepting the chance to flee and fight again another day.

During his exile on the continent Knox developed revolutionary views on the rights of ordinary subjects to overthrow godless rulers. He envisioned a genuine revolution by the people as a whole, both a popular and a magisterial revolt. In defense of such action, however, he ran afoul of the teaching and example of all previous major Protestant reformers. Always an unsubtle thinker, Knox moved resolutely to the point. In a letter to the faithful in English parishes written in December 1553 as he prepared for exile, he declared that obedience to idolaters, "be they kings or queens," was complicity in idolatry and God would reward it as such. Upon his arrival in Geneva in late January 1554, he addressed ominous questions to Calvin:

> Whether a woman was entitled by divine law to rule and govern . . . ?
> Whether it was necessary to obey a magistrate who enforces idolatry and condemns true religion? Whether men of position who have castles and towns are entitled to defend themselves and their followers by armed force against this ungodly violence?[21]

In July 1554 Knox not only pointed out in print how wise it would have been to have sent Mary Tudor to hell during the reign of Edward, but also declared Emperor Charles V a tyrant worse than Nero.[22] Such sentiments later brought his dismissal from Frankfurt, where he had served as a pastor to English refugees.

Calvin firmly rejected Knox's suggestion that subjects had a right to take up arms against idolatrous rulers. Zwingli's successor, Bullinger, however, agreed that such rulers did not deserve obedience.[23] Calvin later refused to sanction French Protestant revolt against Henry II (1547–59). In a letter to Coligny in 1561, disassociating himself from the Amboise conspiracy, a plot by Calvinist nobles to remove the young king Francis II (1559–60) from his Guise advisors, Calvin described armed revolts in the name of religion as no

---

21. Ridley, *John Knox*, pp. 178–79.
22. *Faithful Admonition unto the Professors of God's Truth in England,* discussed by Ridley, *John Knox,* pp. 184–86, 209.
23. Ibid., pp. 179–80.

part of the Reformation.[24] Neither Scottish nor French Huguenot resistance occurred with Calvin's blessing, even though Calvin had laid a basis for the views of both Knox and Beza by acknowledging the right of lower magistrates to correct willfully tyrannical rulers.[25]

While Knox was on the continent, Mary of Lorraine sought the support of powerful Protestant nobles in Scotland for the marriage of her daughter, Mary, future queen of Scots, to the future French king, Francis II, by unofficially tolerating Protestantism. This policy permitted Knox to return to Scotland in September 1555. At the time of his return Protestants had chosen to boycott the parish churches and worship together in private homes. Such meetings had also been part of the transitional phase for continental Protestants, and in Scotland they gave birth to a national political-religious party. In the face of mounting Protestant strength, Scotland's Catholic rulers acted irresolutely. They brought heresy proceedings against Knox in the spring of 1556, but these came to naught. Such indecision emboldened Protestants, who united in a national covenant in the fall of 1557.

Such success brought Knox's political ideas to their revolutionary conclusion. In 1558 he published his infamous *First Blast of the Trumpet Against the Monstrous Regiment of Women,* a work in which he drew on a seemingly inexhaustible fund of near misogynist sentiment in the Bible, ancient philosophy, the pagan classics, and the church fathers to defend the widely held belief that both divine and natural law opposed the rule of women over men. Knox chastised both Englishmen and Scotsmen for bowing at the command of their women rulers.

> I [see that] the Nobilitie both of England and Scotland [are] inferior to brute beastes, for that they do to women which no male amongest the common sorte of beastes can be proved to do to their female, that is, they reverence them, and qwake at their presence; they obey their commandements, and that against God. Wherefore I judge them not only subjects to women, but sclaves of Satan, and servants of iniquitie.[26]

While Knox was no woman-hater—he was respectably married—he did not hesitate to exploit such sentiments against women for political gain. Feelings ran very deep on this matter, especially in England, where the

24. April 16, 1561 in *Ioannis Calvini Opera . . . omnia,* ed. G. Baum et al. (Brunsvigae, 1878), 18: 426–31.

25. *Institutes of the Christian Religion* (McNeill/Battles), IV, ch. xx, sects. 30–32, pp. 1517–21; John T. McNeill, ed., *Calvin: On God and Political Duty* (New York, 1956), pp. xvii–xix.

26. *First Blast of the Trumpet Against the Monstrous Regiment of Women,* in *Works of John Knox,* ed. David Laing (Edinburgh, 1855), 4: 396.

unhappy twelfth-century reign of Queen Matilda (1141–47) remained a vivid memory. Henry VIII's panic over the political consequences of not having a male heir had first opened the breach with Rome and launched his own succession of unhappy marriages. The sixteenth century was peculiar in having highly unpopular women rulers in England, Scotland, and France (Catherine de Medici).[27] This gave Knox's arguments unusual force and relevance among his readers. Misogyny, however, served only as the vehicle, not the message of the *Blast*. The latter was for the sixteenth century a far more serious matter, something that required a popular foundation, or perhaps distraction, for Knox called upon the English and the Scots to overthrow their legitimate rulers by armed force.

Knox held the highly seditious view that neither laws, customs, nor previous oaths of allegiance bound people in loyalty to rulers who were heathen tyrants. His arguments amounted to a kind of political Donatism in which the authority and efficacy of a government were directly tied to the religious belief professed by its sovereign.

> If any thinke, that because the Realme and Estates thereof have geven their consentes to a woman, and have established her and her authoritie, that therefore it is lawfull and acceptable before God, let the same remembre . . . that God cannot approve the doing nor consent of any multitude, concluding anything against his worde and ordinance; and therefore they must have a more assured defense against the wrath of God than the approbation and consent of a blinded multitude, or ellse they shall not be able to stand in the presence of the consuming fire: That is, they must acknowledge that the Regiment of a Woman is a thing most odious in the presence of God; they must refuse to be her officers, because she is a traitoresse and rebell against God; and finallie, they must studie to represse her inordinate pride and tyrannie to the uttermost of their power.[28]

The *Blast* was published in Geneva without name of author, printer, or place of publication and also without the prior knowledge and approval of Calvin. When its publication in Geneva became known, it embarrassed Calvin and the Genevans. Calvin had long been Knox's patron, and the Genevans had recently made Knox a citizen. Like other sixteenth-century men, Calvin shared Knox's belief in the basic inferiority of women and the im-

---

27. Hotman discusses the evils of the rule of women in obvious reference to Catherine de Medici (*Francogallia*, in *Constitutionalism and Resistance*, pp. 87–88).

28. *First Blast of the Trumpet*, p. 415. These views were elaborated further in other works of 1558 addressed to the nobility and commonality of Scotland. See Ridley, *John Knox*, pp. 270–80.

propriety of their rule. Calvin also believed, however, with the great majority, that God sometimes specially called women to rule over men and that such women, as providential exceptions to the divine and natural law of male dominance, were fully legitimate. This Knox was unwilling to concede the Catholic rulers of England and Scotland. Calvin reaffirmed his point of view in an apology to William Cecil for the publication of the *Blast* in Geneva.

> Two years ago John Knox asked of me, in a private conversation, what I thought about the Government of Women. I candidly replied, that as it was a deviation from the original and proper order of nature, it was to be ranked, no less than slavery, among the punishments consequent upon the fall of man; but that there were occasionally women so endowed, that the singular good qualities which shone forth in them made it evident that they were raised up by Divine authority; either that God designed by such examples to condemn the inactivity of men, or for the better setting forth of his own glory. I brought forward [the Old Testament examples of] Huldah and Deborah.... I came ... to this conclusion, that since ... by custom, public consent, and long practice, it has been established that realms and principalities may descend to females by hereditary right, it did not appear to me necessary to move the question, not only because the thing would be invidious, but because in my opinion it would not be lawful to unsettle governments which are ordained by the peculiar providence of God.[29]

In this same vein, the exiled Italian reformer Peter Martyr Vermigli sent Elizabeth the following exhortation on the occasion of her succession to the throne:

> Go forward ... O holie Debora of our times.... We have verie great hope, that you shall bee the same Hester which shall drive Haman unto hanging, which thirsteth for the slaughter and blood of the people of God. Let these holie women be an incouragement unto your Maiestie: and suffer not yourselfe to faint for this cause that you are not born a man but a woman.[30]

Knox's *Blast* proved not only an embarrassment to Calvin, but also a lasting political liability for Knox. No sooner had it been published than

---

29. Cited in *Works of John Knox*, 4: 357.
30. Cited from Martyr's *Common Places* by Marvin W. Anderson in *Peter Martyr: A Reformer in Exile (1542–1562): A Chronology of Biblical Writings in England and Europe* (Nieuwkoop, 1975), pp. 284–85.

Mary died and a woman ruler friendly toward Protestants, Elizabeth (1558–1603), ascended the English throne, henceforth to be the dominant figure in both the English and Scottish Reformations. Elizabeth never forgave Knox for the *Blast* and he remained persona non grata in England during her reign. Fortunately for the Reformation in Scotland, Elizabeth and her chief counsel, Cecil, feared the French and the Spanish far more than they disliked Knox. The Scottish Reformation became for them a way to expel foreign influence from the British Isles and secure Scotland as an English satellite. This was cautiously undertaken, however; Protestants in Scotland were to be aided "first with promises, next with money, and last with arms."[31] Knox, ever enterprising and abrasive, urged Elizabeth to look on English aid to Scottish Protestants as an atonement for the godless reign of her predecessor.[32]

French efforts to win Spanish military support in Scotland failed because of Philip II's growing suspicion of France and his preoccupation with military campaigns in the Netherlands and the Mediterranean. On July 6, 1559 the Treaty of Edinburgh brought about the withdrawal of all French troops from Scotland. The following month the Scottish Parliament passed legislation that abolished Catholicism and made Scotland officially Protestant. Pushed aside by these events as Scottish nobles took political control of the country, Knox still participated in them vicariously by writing his great *History of the Reformation in Scotland,* begun in October 1559.

Knox was not one to watch passively from the wings while a great historical drama unfolded; he soon found the role only he could play. Scottish nobles had hoped that Elizabeth might marry the earl of Arran and rule with him as queen of Scotland. Elizabeth would never have chosen such a course; she had no intention of displacing the rightful heir to the Scottish throne or squandering so important an instrument of diplomacy as her matrimonial hand for the sake of lowly Scotland. Hence, her firm support for the return to Scotland from France of the eighteen-year-old Mary Stuart, who came to rule as Mary, queen of Scots, a charming Catholic queen of a thoroughly Protestant country. The Protestant nobles permitted their queen her private Mass and Catholic advisors, even though Parliament had made the celebration of Mass a capital crime for all other Scots. Knox, however, remained—as Elizabeth and Cecil knew he would—completely impervious to the charms of the Catholic queen and outraged by the performance of even one Mass in Scotland. He scolded the new queen regularly from his pulpit, and their personal confrontations, which reportedly

31. Cited by Ridley, *John Knox,* p. 337.
32. Ibid., p. 341.

left Mary on occasion near hysteria, have become legend. It is a commentary on the success of the Reformation that what began so modestly in 1517 with an obscure university professor posting scholarly theses against indulgences found expression in the 1560s in the spectacle of an internationally famous reformer bringing a queen to tears with the approval of one of the two most powerful nations in the world.

Mary was the great-granddaughter of Henry VIII's sister Margaret, and her supporters in Scotland and England harbored the hope that Elizabeth might die early and childless and Mary succeed to the English throne in a bloodless restoration of Catholicism. These hopes inspired direct plots against Elizabeth after Mary's abdication and flight to England in 1568 following a public scandal. Mary's husband, Lord Darnley, had murdered a court favorite in a fit of jealousy and plotted with Protestants, Knox among them, to replace Mary as Scotland's sovereign. In defense of the queen, James Hepburn, the earl of Bothwell, assassinated Darnley in February 1567. Whether or not he and Mary were actually lovers at the time and plotted together against Darnley, as rumor had it, their subsequent marriage only three months after Darnley's death aroused so much suspicion and moral outrage that Scottish nobles forced the queen to abdicate to her son, James VI of Scotland (1567–1625), the future James I of England (1603–25).

The execution of Mary for treason on February 18, 1587 dashed almost all hope for a Catholic England. Elizabeth's vigilant state secretary, Sir Francis Walsingham, had caught the exiled Scottish queen in a Spanish plot against England's queen, a matter too grave to be forgiven. The execution had no effect on the Scottish Reformation, which had long since been settled, but it did bring the Spanish Armada into the English Channel and end the precarious détente between England and Spain.

With Elizabeth on the throne, English Catholic refugees, led by Robert Parsons (1546–1610) and Cardinal William Allen (1532–94), found themselves in much the same position that Knox had been in during the reign of Mary Tudor. Catholic apologists did not appeal, however, to a higher covenant or to the divine rights of lower magistrates to defend their resistance to a Protestant sovereign.[33] Protestants had turned to such alternative au-

---

33. Allen did, however, urge Philip II to invade England after Mary was imprisoned on charges of treason in 1586. See Arnold Pritchard's lucid and provocative account of England's Catholic community in the reign of Elizabeth, *Catholic Loyalism in Elizabethan England* (Chapel Hill, 1979). See also J. W. Allen, *A History of Political Thought in the Sixteenth Century* (London, 1967), pp. 202–06. On egalitarian political movements among Catholic laity in France in the second half of the sixteenth century, see Robert Harding, "The Mobilization of Confraternities Against the Reformation in France," forthcoming in the *Sixteenth Century Journal*.

thorities in time of political persecution because they no longer had the higher authority of the pope. What the ordinance of God and the duties of lower magistrates had become for Protestant subjects, papal excommunication continued to be for Catholic subjects—a religious ground for breaking oaths of allegiance to "tyrannical" and "heathen" rulers. Pius V's bull *Regnans in excelsis,* which excommunicated Elizabeth on February 25, 1570, declared her subjects "forever released from obedience" to her, deprived her of "her alleged right to the throne," and ordered her subjects "not to obey her commands and laws."[34] This was the Catholic trumpeter's "blast" against the terrible regiment of a Protestant woman.

Protestant and Catholic resistance, even to the point of regicide, made necessary new defenses of the rights of monarchs. The most famous of these in the sixteenth century, Jean Bodin's *République* (1576), came in direct response to the Huguenot tracts of the 1570s. Bodin damned advocates of political resistance as spokesmen for "licentious anarchy, which is worse than the severest tyranny that ever was" and depicted Huguenot apologists as threatening the very foundations of civilization "under the pretext of exemption from burdens and the people's liberty."[35] Bodin believed that a "right" of political resistance by lower magistrates and the people at large fundamentally contradicted political sovereignty. A sovereign, by definition, ruled absolutely; his coronation oath to his subjects placed no limits on him. Whereas Knox had argued that subjects could break their oaths of allegiance to sovereigns who transgressed God's word and ordinance, Bodin insisted that sovereigns remained free to break their word to their subjects, if they deemed such justified by historical circumstance. Instead of being under inescapable obligations to their subjects, as resistance theorists had argued, Bodin's ruler held an absolute right over them. Such arguments reappeared in new forms in James VI of Scotland's *True Law of Free Monarchies* (1598) and Bishop Bossuet's *Politics Drawn from the Very Words of Holy Scripture* (1681), classic defenses of the divine right of kings. They became prominent also in the covenanted absolutism of Thomas Hobbes's *Leviathan* (1651). A century of religious and civil warfare had moved many to fear political anarchy far more than political tyranny.

34. Cited by Marvin O'Connell, *The Counter Reformation 1559–1610* (New York, 1974), p. 167.

35. Cited by Franklin, *Jean Bodin and the Rise of Absolutist Theory,* pp. 51, 54–55.

CHAPTER 15

The Legacy of the Reformation

THE Reformation did not reform the whole church, much less European society, and well before midcentury it needed reform itself. Politicians successfully manipulated it, transforming theological counsel originally intended to advise the political conscience into justifications for independent political actions.[1] Doctrinal quarrels divided it internally, as a new Protestant scholasticism engulfed the second half of the sixteenth century. Even before his death, Martin Luther was looked upon by many of his colleagues as a hopeless reactionary. Bloody civil wars and revolutions under Protestant and Catholic banners blighted Europe in the hundred years after the Diet of Augsburg (1555). Little wonder the Reformation has been proclaimed a "failure."[2]

To assess a movement in terms of its unrealized hopes or aberrations, however, is neither fair nor enlightening. It can be argued that obscure theological debates, patriarchical culture, catechetical indoctrination, social injustice, anti-Semitism, and state-run churches were a prominent side of the Reformation. But they were not the predominant side, nor did they mean to contemporaries what they have come to mean to modern people. What seems to the modern scholar an obscure theological discussion was often an illuminating essay in truth for sixteenth-century laymen. What the modern scholar spurns as oppressive patriarchical culture, clergy and laity of Protestant persuasion understood to be a new experiment in companionship and community. The catechetical instruction in sin and faith that

1. *Gewissenberatung* progressively became *Gewissensentlastung*—"religiöse Sanktionierung und Absicherung der im übrigen autonomen und oft bereits vorweg festgelegten Entscheidung der Politiker" (Eike Wolgast, *Die Wittenberger Theologie und die Politik der evangelischen Stände: Studien zu Luthers Gutachten in politischen Fragen* [Gütersloh, 1977], p. 298).

2. Gerald Strauss, *Luther's House of Learning: Indoctrination of the Young in the German Reformation* (Baltimore, 1978), esp. pp. 299, 307. This judgment is made in assessment of the Reformation's educational goals and achievements, which, for Strauss, embody best the reformers' own understanding of the nature of the Reformation.

causes modern scholars to wince became a defense against burdensome superstitions for many parents who submitted their children to the priest. Where the modern scholar sees only profiteering and brutality in the treatment of the protesting poor, contemporaries, who were themselves not without conscience, sensed a mortal threat to their fragile social order. The old Luther who wanted to exile Jews to a land of their own may justifiably bear the modern scholar's censure of anti-Semitism, but he also deserves understanding as one who had hoped all too much for their conversion. And what the modern scholar disparages as government-controlled religion, contemporaries also appreciated as the layman's self-defense against a reimposition of coercive spiritual judgment and the church's opportunity to invest society's established institutions with moral and religious values.

No historical movement can fairly be blamed for failing to mold future generations by its highest ideals. It must be weighed by its management of what it could control: its immediate history. Specifically, we should look to the changes it brought about in contemporary laws and institutions and the new opportunities such changes made possible for those who could and did grasp them. The Reformation, in a word, should be judged above all by its continuity and discontinuity with the Middle Ages, not with the twentieth century.

Viewed in these terms, the Reformation was an unprecedented revolution in religion at a time when religion penetrated almost the whole of life. The Reformation constituted for the great majority of people, whose social status and economic condition did not change dramatically over a lifetime, an upheaval in the world as they knew it, regardless of whether they were pious Christians or joined the movement. In the first half of the sixteenth century cities and territories passed laws and ordinances that progressively ended or severely limited a host of traditional beliefs, practices, and institutions that touched directly the daily life of large numbers of people: mandatory fasting; auricular confession; the veneration of saints, relics, and images; the buying and selling of indulgences; pilgrimages and shrines; wakes and processions for the dead and dying; endowed masses in memory of the dead; the doctrine of purgatory; Latin Mass and liturgy; traditional ceremonies, festivals, and holidays; monasteries, nunneries, and mendicant orders; the sacramental status of marriage, extreme unction, confirmation, holy orders, and penance; clerical celibacy; clerical immunity from civil taxation and criminal jurisdiction; nonresident benefices; papal excommunication and interdict; canon law; papal and episcopal territorial government; and the traditional scholastic education of clergy.[3] Modern scholars may argue over the degree to which such changes in the official

3. I belabor this point in my *Reformation in the Cities* (New Haven, 1975).

framework of religion connoted actual changes in personal beliefs and habits.[4] Few, however, can doubt that the likelihood of personal change increased with the incorporation of Protestant reforms in the laws and institutions of the sixteenth century. As historians write the social history of the Reformation, I suspect they will discover that such transformations in the religious landscape had a profound, if often indirect, cultural impact.

While the Reformation influenced the balance of political power both locally and internationally, it was not a political revolution in the accepted sense of the term; a major reordering of traditional social and political groups did not result,[5] although traditional enemies often ended up in different religious camps and the higher clergy was displaced as a political elite. The larger social impact of the Reformation lay rather in its effectively displacing so many of the beliefs, practices, and institutions that had organized daily life and given it security and meaning for the greater part of a millennium. Here the reformers continued late medieval efforts to simplify religious, and enhance secular, life. If scholars of popular religion in Reformation England are correct, Protestant success against medieval religion actually brought new and more terrible superstitions to the surface. By destroying the traditional ritual framework for dealing with daily misfortune and worry, the Reformation left those who could not find solace in its message—and there were many—more anxious than before,[6] and especially after its leaders sought by coercion what they discovered could not be gained by persuasion alone. Protestant "disenchantment" of the world in this way encouraged new interest in witchcraft and the occult, as the religious heart and mind, denied an outlet in traditional sacramental magic and pilgrimage piety, compensated for new Protestant sobriety and simplicity by embracing superstitions even more socially disruptive than the religious practices set aside by the Reformation.[7]

Ideas, like energy, are transformed, not destroyed. In assessing the Reformation we should also appreciate the way its original goals survived in

4. See G. R. Elton, *Reform and Reformation: England 1509–1558* (Cambridge, Mass., 1977), pp. 366–69; Strauss, *Luther's House of Learning*, p. 307.

5. Despite both urban and peasant rebellions, the larger process of political centralization begun by kings and princes in the fourteenth century ran apace in the sixteenth, and the customary social tensions between guilds and aristocratic governments—and within guilds between artisans and masters— continued in cities and towns, despite the acquisition of a significant role in urban government by some guilds. And, as the examples of Zurich, Nuremberg, and Strasbourg indicate, Catholic patricians did not fall from power when the Reformation proved irresistible, but continued in their traditional roles as converted or nominal Protestants.

6. A. D. J. MacFarlane, *Witchcraft in Tudor and Stuart England* (New York, 1970), p. 195.

7. Keith Thomas, *Religion and the Decline of Magic* (London, 1971), pp. 69, 76, 493–95, 497–99, 561.

new forms and under the auspices of new authorities. By its original teaching and example, the Reformation, above all, encouraged people to resist religious tyranny; many scholars view it also as a major force for political freedom and social justice, at least before the Peasants' Revolt of 1525 worked to restrict its social promise.[8] The Reformation was born of such resistance, and this has been its basic legacy. Its example of nonconformity has outlived its own narrowing and come to sit in judgment on its own bigotry. If the disciplinary and conformist impulses of Protestantism came to predominate at official levels, its original ideals have remained bright among laymen both within and outside its camp, who, by indifference and direct attack, have continued the Reformation's resistance to the bullying of conscience.

The great shortcoming of the Reformation was its naïve expectation that the majority of people were capable of radical religious enlightenment and moral transformation, whether by persuasion or by coercion. Such expectation directly contradicted some of its fondest convictions and the original teaching of its founder. Having begun in protest against allegedly unnatural and unscriptural proscriptions of the medieval church and urged freedom in the place of coercion, the reformers brought a strange new burden to bear on the consciences of their followers when they instructed them to resolve the awesome problems of sin, death, and the devil by simple faith in the Bible and ethical service to their neighbors. The brave new man of Protestant faith, "subject to none [yet] subject to all" in Luther's famous formulation,[9] was expected to bear his finitude and sinfulness with anxiety resolved, secure in the knowledge of a gratuitous salvation, and fearful of neither man, God, or the devil. But how many were capable of such self-understanding?

In a recent study of witch-hunts in late medieval and early modern Europe, Norman Cohn has speculated that "*unconscious* resentment against Christianity as too strict a religion, against Christ as too stern a taskmaster" motivated the actions of both judges and victims; imagined erotic fantasies with Christ's antagonist, Satan, expressed repressed hostility to a religion that demanded more self-denial and discipline than people were capable of achieving.[10] Whether or not such speculation explains the witch-trials of the period, it does remind us of the *conscious* and *constructive* rebellion against

8. Strauss, *Luther's House of Learning*, p. 7; Benjamin N. Nelson, *The Idea of Usury: From Tribal Brotherhood to Universal Otherhood* (Princeton, 1949), p. 35. For Marxist and other versions of this thesis, see above, pp. 272–73.

9. *De libertate Christiana*, WA 7, p. 49.

10. *Europe's Inner Demons: An Enquiry Inspired by the Great Witch-Hunt* (London, 1975), p. 262.

oppressive Christianity that occurred during the Age of Reform. Late medieval and Protestant reformers attempted to fashion a religion more in accord with human nature as well as with divine decree. That the Reformation adopted its own repressive measures was not the reason it failed. Its failure rather lay in its original attempt to ennoble people beyond their capacities—not, as medieval theologians and Renaissance philosophers had done, by encouraging them to imitate saints and angels, but by demanding that they live simple, sober lives, prey not to presumption, superstition, or indulgence, but merely as human beings. This proved a truly impossible ideal; the Reformation foundered on man's indomitable credulity.

List of Abbreviations

AHR	*American Historical Review* (New York, 1895–)
ARG	*Archiv für Reformationsgeschichte* (Gütersloh, 1903–)
Denzinger	Heinrich Denzinger, ed., *Enchiridion symbolorum definiti-onum et declarationum de rebus fidei et morum,* 34th ed. (Barcelona, 1967)
HThR	*Harvard Theological Review* (Cambridge, Mass., 1908–)
JHI	*Journal of the History of Ideas* (Lancaster, Pa., 1940–)
LW	*Luther's Works,* ed. J. Pelikan and H. Lehman (St. Louis, 1957–)
MQR	*Mennonite Quarterly Review* (Goshen, Ind., 1927–)
PL	*Patrologia Latina,* ed. J. P. Migne (Paris, 1844–90)
RGG	*Die Religion in Geschichte und Gegenwart,* 6 vols. (Tübingen, 1957–67)
WA	*D. Martin Luthers Werke: Kritische Gesamtausgage* (Weimar, 1883–)
WABr	*D. Martin Luthers Werke: Briefwechsel* (Weimar, 1930–48)
WATr	*D. Martin Luthers Werke: Tischreden* (Weimar, 1912–)
ZKG	*Zeitschrift für Kirchengeschichte* (Gotha, 1877–)
ZThK	*Zeitschrift für Theologie und Kirche* (Tübingen, 1891–)

Index